THE BUDDHISM OF TIBET OR LAMAISM

THE EUCHARIST OF BUDDHISM.

THE BUDDHISM OF TIBET OR LAMAISM

WITH ITS MYSTIC CULTS, SYMBOLISM AND MYTHOLOGY,
AND IN ITS RELATION TO INDIAN BUDDHISM.

BY

L. AUSTINE WADDELL, M.B.,

F.L.S., F.R.G.S.,
MEMBER OF THE ROYAL ASIATIC SOCIETY,
ANTHROPOLOGICAL INSTITUTE, ETC.,
SURGEON-MAJOR H.M. BENGAL ARMY

GYAN

Published by

GYAN

Gyan Publishing House
5, Ansari Road
Daryaganj, New Delhi-110002
Phone: 011-47034999, 9811692060
E-mail: books@gyanbooks.com

Distribution Network
gyanbooks.com
India, USA, Canada, UK, Australia, France

ISBN : 978-81-212-3167-1 (PB)
First Published, 1895

2nd Impression 2020

Printed at: Gyan Press, Delhi.

The Buddhism of Tibet or Lamaism
Author: L. Austine Waddell

THE

BUDDHISM OF TIBET

OR

LAMAISM

WITH ITS MYSTIC CULTS, SYMBOLISM AND MYTHOLOGY, AND IN ITS RELATION TO INDIAN BUDDHISM.

BY

L. AUSTINE WADDELL, M.B.,

F.L.S., F.R.G.S.,

MEMBER OF THE ROYAL ASIATIC SOCIETY, ANTHROPOLOGICAL INSTITUTE, ETC.,
SURGEON-MAJOR H.M. BENGAL ARMY.

LONDON:
W. H. ALLEN & CO., LIMITED,
13, WATERLOO PLACE, S.W.
1895.

TO

WILLIAM TENNANT GAIRDNER, M.D., LL.D., F.R.S.,

IN ADMIRATION OF HIS NOBLE CHARACTER,
PHILOSOPHIC TEACHING, WIDE CULTURE, AND
MANY LABOURS DEVOTED WITH EXEMPLARY FIDELITY TO
THE INTERPRETATION OF NATURE AND THE SERVICE OF MAN,

THIS BOOK
IS RESPECTFULLY DEDICATED
BY THE AUTHOR.

PREFACE.

NO apology is needed for the production at the present time of a work on the Buddhism of Tibet, or "Lāmaism" as it has been called, after its priests. Notwithstanding the increased attention which in recent years has been directed to Buddhism by the speculations of Schopenhauer and Hartmann, and the widely felt desire for fuller information as to the conditions and sources of Eastern religion, there exists no European book giving much insight into the jealously guarded religion of Tibet, where Buddhism wreathed in romance has now its chief stronghold.

The only treatise on the subject in English, is Emil Schlagintweit's *Buddhism in Tibet*[1] published over thirty years ago, and now out of print. A work which, however admirable with respect to the time of its appearance, was admittedly fragmentary, as its author had never been in contact with Tibetans. And the only other European book on Lāmaism, excepting Giorgi's curious compilation of last century, is Köppen's *Die Lamaische Hierarchie*

[1] Leipzig and London, 1863. That there is no lack of miscellaneous literature on Tibet and Lāmaism may be seen from the bibliographical list in the appendix ; but it is all of a fragmentary and often conflicting character.

und Kirche[1] published thirty-five years ago, and also a compilation and out of print. Since the publication of these two works much new information has been gained, though scattered through more or less inaccessible Russian German, French, and Asiatic journals. And this, combined with the existing opportunities for a closer study of Tibet and its customs, renders a fuller and more systematic work now possible.

Some reference seems needed to my special facilities for undertaking this task. In addition to having personally studied "*southern* Buddhism" in Burma and Ceylon; and "*northern* Buddhism" in Sikhim, Bhotān and Japan; and exploring Indian Buddhism in its remains in "the Buddhist Holy Land," and the ethnology of Tibet and its border tribes in Sikhim, Asam, and upper Burma; and being one of the few Europeans who have entered the territory of the Grand Lāma, I have spent several years in studying the actualities of Lāmaism as explained by its priests, at points much nearer Lhāsa than any utilized for such a purpose, and where I could feel the pulse of the sacred city itself beating in the large communities of its natives, many of whom had left Lhāsa only ten or twelve days previously.

On commencing my enquiry I found it necessary to learn the language, which is peculiarly difficult, and known to very few Europeans. And afterwards, realizing the rigid secrecy maintained by the Lāmas in regard to their seemingly chaotic rites and symbolism, I felt compelled to purchase a Lāmaist temple with its fittings; and prevailed on the officiating priests to explain to me in full detail the symbolism and the rites as they proceeded. Perceiving how much I was interested, the Lāmas were so oblig-

[1] Berlin, 1859.

ing as to interpret in my favour a prophetic account which exists in their scriptures regarding a Buddhist incarnation in the West. They convinced themselves that I was a reflex of the Western Buddha, Amitābha, and thus they overcame their conscientious scruples, and imparted information freely. With the knowledge thus gained, I visited other temples and monasteries critically, amplifying my information, and engaging a small staff of Lāmas in the work of copying manuscripts, and searching for texts bearing upon my researches. Enjoying in these ways special facilities for penetrating the reserve of Tibetan ritual, and obtaining direct from Lhāsa and Tashi-lhunpo most of the objects and explanatory material needed, I have elicited much information on Lāmaist theory and practice which is altogether new.

The present work, while embodying much original research, brings to a focus most of the information on Lāmaism scattered through former publications. And bearing in mind the increasing number of general readers interested in old world ethics, custom and myth, and in the ceaseless effort of the human heart in its insatiable craving for absolute truth; as well as the more serious students of Lāmaism amongst orientalists, travellers, missionaries and others, I have endeavoured to give a clear insight into the structure, prominent features and cults of this system, and have relegated to smaller type and footnotes the more technical details and references required by specialists.

The special characteristics of the book are its detailed accounts of the external facts and curious symbolism of Buddhism, and its analyses of the internal movements leading to Lāmaism and its sects and cults. It provides material culled from hoary Tibetan tradition and explained to me by Lāmas for elucidating many obscure points in primitive Indian Buddhism and its later symbolism. Thus a clue is supplied to several disputed doctrinal points of fundamental importance, as for example the formula of the Causal Nexus. And it interprets much of the interesting Mahāyāna and Tāntrik developments in the later Indian Buddhism of Magadha.

It attempts to disentangle the early history of Lāmaism from the chaotic growth of fable which has invested it. With this view the nebulous Tibetan "history" so-called of the earlier periods has been somewhat critically examined in the light afforded by some scholarly Lāmas and contemporary history; and all fictitious chronicles, such as the Maṇi-kah-'bum, hitherto treated usually as historical, are rejected as authoritative for events which happened a thousand years before they were written and for a time when writing was admittedly unknown in Tibet. If, after rejecting these manifestly fictitious "histories" and whatever is supernatural, the residue cannot be accepted as altogether trustworthy history, it at least affords a fairly probable historical basis, which seems consistent and in harmony with known facts and unwritten tradition.

It will be seen that I consider the founder of Lāmaism to be Padma-sambhava—a person to whom previous writers are wont to refer in too incidental a manner. Indeed, some careful writers[1] omit all mention of his name, although he is considered by the Lāmas of all sects to be the founder of their order, and by the majority of them to be greater and more deserving of worship than Buddha himself.

Most of the chief internal movements of Lāmaism are now for the first time presented in an intelligible and systematic form. Thus, for example, my account of its

[1] *E.g.* W. R. S. Ralston in his *Tibetan Tales*.

sects may be compared with that given by Schlagintweit,[1] to which nothing practically had been added.[2]

As Lāmaism lives mainly by the senses and spends its strength in sacerdotal functions, it is particularly rich in ritual. Special prominence, therefore, has been given to its ceremonial, all the more so as ritual preserves many interesting vestiges of archaic times. My special facilities for acquiring such information has enabled me to supply details of the principal rites, mystic and other, most of which were previously undescribed. Many of these exhibit in combination ancient Indian and pre-Buddhist Tibetan cults. The higher ritual, as already known, invites comparison with much in the Roman Church; and the fuller details now afforded facilitate this comparison and contrast.

But the bulk of the Lāmaist cults comprise much deep-rooted devil-worship and sorcery, which I describe with some fulness. For Lāmaism is only thinly and imperfectly varnished over with Buddhist symbolism, beneath which the sinister growth of poly-demonist superstition darkly appears.

The religious plays and festivals are also described. And a chapter is added on popular and domestic Lāmaism to show the actual working of the religion in everyday life as a system of ethical belief and practice.

The advantages of the very numerous illustrations—about two hundred in number, mostly from originals brought from Lhāsa, and from photographs by the author—must be obvious.[3] Mr. Rockhill and Mr. Knight have kindly permitted the use of a few of their illustrations.

---

[1] *Op. cit.*, 72. [2] But see note on p. 69.

[3] A few of the drawings are by Mr. A. D. McCormick from photographs, or original objects; and some have been taken from Giorgi, Huc, Pander, and others.

A full index has been provided, also a chronological table and bibliography.

I have to acknowledge the special aid afforded me by the learned Tibetan Lāma, Padma Chhö Phél; by that venerable scholar the Mongolian Lāma She-rab Gya-ts'ô; by the Ñiṅ-ma Lāma, Ur-gyän Gya-ts'ô, head of the Yang-gang monastery of Sikhim and a noted explorer of Tibet; by Tun-yig Wang-dan and Mr. Dor-je Ts'e-ring; by S'ad-*s*gra S'ab-pe, one of the Tibetan governors of Lhāsa, who supplied some useful information, and a few manuscripts; and by Mr. A.W. Paul, C.I.E., when pursuing my researches in Sikhim.

And I am deeply indebted to the kind courtesy of Professor C. Bendall for much special assistance and advice; and also generally to my friend Dr. Islay Muirhead.

Of previous writers to whose books I am specially under obligation, foremost must be mentioned Csoma Körösi, the enthusiastic Hungarian scholar and pioneer of Tibetan studies, who first rendered the Lāmaist stores of information accessible to Europeans.[1] Though to Brian Houghton Hodgson, the father of modern critical study of Buddhist doctrine, belongs the credit of discovering[2] the Indian nature of the bulk of the Lāmaist literature and of procuring the material for the detailed analyses by Csoma and Burnouf. My indebtedness to Köppen and Schlagintweit has already been mentioned.

[1] Alexander Csoma of Körös, in the Transylvanian circle of Hungary, like most of the subsequent writers on Lāmaism, studied that system in Ladāk. After publishing his *Dictionary*, *Grammar*, and *Analysis*, he proceeded to Darjiling in the hope of penetrating thence to Tibet, but died at Darjiling on the 11th April, 1842, a few days after arrival there, where his tomb now bears a suitable monument, erected by the Government of India. For details of his life and labours, see his biography by Dr. Duka.

[2] *Asiatic Researches*, xvi., 1828.

Jaeschke's great dictionary is a mine of information on technical and doctrinal definitions. The works of Giorgi, Vasiliev, Schiefner, Foucaux, Rockhill, Eitel, and Pander, have also proved most helpful. The Narrative of *Travels in Tibet* by Babu Ṣaratcandra Dās, and his translations from the vernacular literature, have afforded some useful details. The Indian Survey reports and Markham's *Tibet* have been of service; and the systematic treatises of Professors Rhys Davids, Oldenberg and Beal have supplied several useful indications.

The vastness of this many-sided subject, far beyond the scope of individual experience, the backward state of our knowledge on many points, the peculiar difficulties that beset the research, and the conditions under which the greater part of the book was written—in the scant leisure of a busy official life—these considerations may, I trust, excuse the frequent crudeness of treatment, as well as any errors which may be present, for I cannot fail to have missed the meaning occasionally, though sparing no pains to ensure accuracy. But, if my book, notwithstanding its shortcomings, proves of real use to those seeking information on the Buddhism of Tibet, as well as on the later Indian developments of Buddhism, and to future workers in these fields, I shall feel amply rewarded for all my labours.

L. AUSTINE WADDELL.

London,
31*st October*, 1894.

CONTENTS.

		PAGE
Preface	... ...	vii
Note on Pronunciation	... ...	xvii
List of Abbreviations ...	... ...	xix
I.	Introductory—Division of Subject	1–4

A. HISTORICAL.

II.	Changes in Primitive Buddhism leading to Lāmaism	5–17
III.	Rise, Development, and Spread of Lāmaism ...	18–53
IV.	The Sects of Lāmaism	54–75

B. DOCTRINAL.

V.	Metaphysical Sources of the Doctrine ...	76–131
VI.	The Doctrine and its Morality	132–154
VII.	Scriptures and Literature	155–168

C. MONASTIC.

VIII.	The Order of Lāmas	169–211
IX.	Daily Life and Routine	212–225
X.	Hierarchy and Re-incarnate Lāmas	226–254

D. BUILDINGS.

XI.	Monasteries	255–286

		PAGE
XII.	TEMPLES AND CATHEDRALS	287–304
XIII.	SHRINES AND RELICS (AND PILGRIMS)	305–323

E. MYTHOLOGY AND GODS.

XIV.	PANTHEON AND IMAGES	324–386
XV.	SACRED SYMBOLS AND CHARMS	387–419

F. RITUAL AND SORCERY.

XVI.	WORSHIP AND RITUAL	420–449
XVII.	ASTROLOGY AND DIVINATION	450–474
XVIII.	SORCERY AND NECROMANCY...	475–500

G. FESTIVALS AND PLAYS.

XIX.	FESTIVALS AND HOLIDAYS	501–514
XX.	SACRED DRAMAS, MYSTIC PLAYS AND MASQUERADES	515–565

H. POPULAR LĀMAISM.

XXI.	DOMESTIC AND POPULAR LĀMAISM...	566–573

APPENDICES.

I.	Chronological Table	575–578
II.	Bibliography	578–583

	INDEX	585–598

PRONUNCIATION.

The general reader should remember as a rough rule that in the oriental names the vowels are pronounced as in German, and the consonants as in English, except *c* which is pronounced as "ch," *ṅ* as "ng" and *ñ* as "ny." In particular, words like *Buddha* are pronounced as if spelt in English "Bŏŏd-dha," *Ṣākya Muni* as "Shā-kya Mŏŏ-nee," and *Karma* as "Kur-ma."

The spelling of Tibetan names is peculiarly uncouth and startling to the English reader. Indeed, many of the names as transcribed from the vernacular seem unpronounceable, and the difficulty is not diminished by the spoken form often differing widely from the written, owing chiefly to consonants having changed their sound or dropped out of speech altogether, the so-called "silent consonants."[1] Thus the Tibetan word for the border-country which we, following the Nepalese, call Sikhim is spelt *'bras-ljoṅs,* and pronounced "Dén-jong," and *bkra-s'is* is "Ta-shi." When, however, I have found it necessary to give the full form of these names, especially the more important words translated from the Sanskrit, in order to recover their original Indian form and meaning, I have referred them as far as possible to footnotes.

The transcription of the Tibetan letters follows the system adopted by Jaeschke in his Dictionary, with the exceptions noted below,[2] and corresponds closely with the analogous system for Sanskritic words given over the page. The Tibetan pronunciation is spelt phonetically in the dialect of Lhāsa.

---

[1] Somewhat analogous to the French *ils parlent.*

[2] The exceptions mainly are those requiring very specialized diacritical marks, the letters which are there (JAESCHKE'S *Dict.*, p. viii.), pronounced *ga* as a prefix, *cha, nya,* the *ha* in several forms as the basis for vowels ; these I have rendered by *g*, *ch'*, *ñ* and ' respectively. In several cases I have spelt words according to Csoma's system, by which the silent consonants are italicized.

For the use of readers who are conversant with the Indian alphabets, and the system popularly known in India as "the Hunterian," the following table, in the order in which the sounds are physiologically produced—an order also followed by the Tibetans—will show the system of spelling Sanskṛitic words, which is here adopted, and which it will be observed, is almost identical with that of the widely used dictionaries of Monier-Williams and Childers. The different forms used in the Tibetan for aspirates and palato-sibilants are placed within brackets:—

(gutturals)	k	kh(k')	g	gh	ṅ
(palatals)	c(c')	ch(ch')	j	jh	ñ
(cerebrals)	ṭ	ṭh	ḍ	ḍh	ṇ
(dentals)	t	th(t')	d	dh	n
(labials)	p	ph(p')	b	bh	m
(palato-sibil.)	(ts)	(ts')	(z & ds)	(z')	
	y	v	r	l	
sibilants)	ṣ	sh(s')	s		
	h				aṃ

ABBREVIATIONS.

B. Ac. Ptsbg. = Bulletin de la Classe Hist. Philol. de l'Academie de St. Petersbourg.

Burn. *I.* = Burnouf's *Introd. au Budd. indien.*

Burn. *II.* = „ *Lotus de bonne Loi.*

cf. = confer, compare.

Csoma *An.* = Csoma Körösi *Analysis* in *Asiatic Researches,* Vol. xx.

Csoma *Gr.* = „ „ *Tibetan Grammar.*

Davids = Rhys Davids' *Buddhism.*

Desg. = Desgodins' *Le Tibet,* etc.

Eitel = Eitel's *Handbook of Chinese Buddhism.*

Jaesch. *D.* = Jaeschke's *Tibetan Dictionary.*

J.A.S.B. = Jour. of the Asiatic Soc. of Bengal.

J.R.A.S. = Journal of the Royal Asiatic Soc., London.

Hodgs. = Hodgson's *Essays on Lang., Lit.,* etc.

Huc = *Travels in Tartary, Tibet,* etc., Hazlitt's trans.

Köppen = Köppen's *Lamaische Hier.*

Markham = Markham's *Tibet.*

Marco P. = Marco Polo, Yule's edition.

O.M. = Original Mitt. Ethnolog. Königl. Museum fur Völkerkunde Berlin.

Pander = Pander's *Das Pantheon,* etc.

pr. = pronounced.

Rock. *L.* = Rockhill's *Land of the Lamas.*

Rock. *B.* = „ *Life of the Buddha,* etc.

Sarat = Ṣaratcandra Dās.

S.B.E. = *Sacred Books of the East.*

Schlag. = E. Schlagintweit's *Buddhism in Tibet.*

Skt. = Sanskṛit.

S.R. = Survey of India Report.

T. = Tibetan.

Tāra. = *Tāranātha's Geschichte,* etc., Schiefner's trans.

Vasil. = Vasiliev's or Wassiljew's *Der Buddhismus.*

BELOW TANG-KAR PASS.

INTRODUCTORY.

TIBET, the mystic Land of the Grand Lāma, joint God and King of many millions, is still the most impenetrable country in the world. Behind its icy barriers, reared round it by Nature herself, and almost unsurmountable, its priests guard its passes jealously against foreigners.

Few Europeans have ever entered Tibet; and none for half a century have reached the sacred city. Of the travellers of later times who have dared to enter this dark land, after scaling its frontiers and piercing

View into S.W. Tibet
(from Tang-kar La Pass, 16,600 ft.).

its passes, and thrusting themselves into its snow-swept deserts, even the most intrepid have failed to penetrate farther than the outskirts of its central province.[1] And the information, thus perilously gained, has, with the exception of Mr. Rockhill's, been

---

[1] The few Europeans who have penetrated Central Tibet have mostly been Roman missionaries. The first European to reach Lhāsa seems to have been Friar Odoric, of Pordenne, about 1330 A.D. on his return from Cathay (Col. Yule's *Cathay and the Road Thither*, i., 149, and C. Markham's *Tibet*, xlvi.). The capital city of Tibet referred to by him with its "*Abassi*" or Pope is believed to have been Lhāsa. In 1661 the Jesuits Albert Dorville and Johann Gruher visited Lhāsa on their way from China to India. In 1706 the Capuchine fathers Josepho de Asculi and Francisco Marie de Toun penetrated to Lhāsa from Bengal. In 1716 the Jesuit Desideri reached it from Kashmīr and Ladāk. In 1741 a Capuchine mission under Horacio de la Penna also succeeded in getting there, and the large amount of information collected by them supplied Father A. Giorgi with the material for his *Alphabetum Tibetanum*, published at Rome in 1762. The friendly reception accorded this party created hopes of Lhāsa becoming a centre for Roman missionaries; and a *Vicar apostolicus* for Lhāsa is still nominated and appears in the "*Annuario pontificio*," though of course he cannot reside within Tibet. In 1811 Lhāsa was reached by Manning, a friend of Charles Lamb, and the only Englishman who seems ever to have got there; for most authorities are agreed that Moorcroft, despite the story told to M. Huc, never reached it. But Manning unfortunately left only a whimsical diary, scarcely even descriptive of his fascinating adventures. The subsequent, and the last, Europeans to reach Lhāsa were the Lazarist missionaries, Huc and Gabet, in 1845. Huc's entertaining account of his journey is well known. He was soon expelled, and since then China has aided Tibet in opposing foreign ingress by strengthening its political and military barriers, as recent explorers: Prejivalsky, Rockhill, Bonvalot, Bower, Miss Taylor, etc., have found to their cost; though some are sanguine that the Sikhim Trade Convention of this year (1894) is probably the thin edge of the wedge to open up the country, and that at no distant date Tibet will be prevailed on to relax its jealous exclusiveness, so that, 'ere 1900, even Cook's tourists may visit the Lāmaist Vatican.

almost entirely geographical, leaving the customs of this forbidden land still a field for fiction and romance.

Thus we are told that, amidst the solitudes of this "Land of the Supernatural" repose the spirits of "The Masters," the *Mahātmas*,

CAPTAIN OF GUARD OF DONG-KYA PASS.
(S.-Western Tibet.)

whose astral bodies slumber in unbroken peace, save when they condescend to work some petty miracle in the world below.

In presenting here the actualities of the cults and customs of Tibet; and lifting higher than before the veil which still hides its mysteries from European eyes, the subject may be viewed under the following sections:—

a. HISTORICAL. The changes in primitive Buddhism leading to Lāmaism, and the origins of Lāmaism and its sects.

b. DOCTRINAL. The metaphysical sources of the doctrine. The doctrine and its morality and literature.

c. MONASTIC. The Lāmaist order. Its curriculum, daily life, dress, etc., discipline, hierarchy and incarnate-deities and re-embodied saints.

d. BUILDINGS. Monasteries, temples, monuments, and shrines.

e. PANTHEON AND MYTHOLOGY, including saints, images, fetishes, and other sacred objects and symbols.

f. RITUAL AND SORCERY, comprising sacerdotal services for the laity, astrology, oracles and divination, charms and necromancy.

g. FESTIVALS AND SACRED PLAYS, with the mystic plays and masquerades.

h. POPULAR AND DOMESTIC LĀMAISM in every-day life, customs, and folk-lore.

Such an exposition will afford us a fairly full and complete survey of one of the most active, and least known, forms of existing Buddhism; and will present incidentally numerous other topics of wide and varied human interest.

For Lāmaism is, indeed, a microcosm of the growth of religion and myth among primitive people; and in large degree an object-lesson of their advance from barbarism towards civilization. And it preserves for us much of the old-world lore and petrified beliefs of our Aryan ancestors.

II.

CHANGES IN PRIMITIVE BUDDHISM LEADING TO LĀMAISM.

"Ah! Constantine, of how much ill was cause,
Not thy conversion, but those rich domains
That the first wealthy Pope received of thee."[1]

TO understand the origin of Lāmaism and its place in the Buddhist system, we must recall the leading features of primitive Buddhism, and glance at its growth, to see the points at which the strange creeds and cults crept in, and the gradual crystallization of these into a religion differing widely from the parent system, and opposed in so many ways to the teaching of Buddha.

ṢĀKYA MUNI.

No one now doubts the historic character of Siddhārta Gautama, or Ṣākya Muni, the founder of Buddhism; though it is clear the canonical accounts regarding him are overlaid with legend, the fabulous addition of after days.[2] Divested of its embellishment, the simple narrative of the Buddha's life is strikingly noble and human.

Some time before the epoch of Alexander the Great, between the fourth and fifth centuries before Christ,[3] Prince Siddhārta appeared in India as an original thinker and teacher, deeply conscious of the degrading thraldom of caste and the

---

1 DANTE, *Paradiso*, XX. (Milton's trans.)

2 See Chapter V. for details of the gradual growth of the legends.

3 See Chronological Table, Appendix i.

priestly tyranny of the Brāhmans,[1] and profoundly impressed with the pathos and struggle of Life, and earnest in the search of some method of escaping from existence which was clearly involved with sorrow.

His touching renunciation of his high estate,[2] of his beloved wife, and child, and home, to become an ascetic, in order to master the secrets of deliverance from sorrow; his unsatisfying search for truth amongst the teachers of his time; his subsequent austerities and severe penance, a much-vaunted means of gaining spiritual insight; his retirement into solitude and self-communion; his last struggle and final triumph—latterly represented as a real material combat, the so-called "Temptation of Buddha":—

TEMPTATION OF SĀKYA MUNI
(from a sixth century Ajanta fresco, after Raj. Mitra).

"Infernal ghosts and hellish furies round
Environ'd thee; some howl'd, some yell'd, some shriek'd,
Some bent at thee their fiery darts, while thou
Sat'st unappall'd in calm and sinless peace"; [3]

[1] The treatises on Vedic ritual, called the Brāhmaṇas, had existed for about three centuries previous to Buddha's epoch, according to Max Müller's Chronology (*Hibbert Lectures*, 1891, p. 58)—the initial dates there given are Ṛig Veda, tenth century B.C.; Brāhmaṇas, eighth century B.C.; Sūtra sixth, and Buddhism fifth century B.C.

[2] The researches of Vasiliev, etc., render it probable that Siddhārta's father was only a petty lord or chief (cf. also OLDENBERG'S *Life*, Appendix), and that Ṣākya's pessimistic view of life may have been forced upon him by the loss of his territories through conquest by a neighbouring king.

[3] MILTON'S *Paradise Regained*, Book iv

his reappearance, confident that he had discovered the secrets of deliverance; his carrying the good tidings of the truth from town to town; his effective protest against the cruel sacrifices of the Brāhmans, and his relief of much of the suffering inflicted upon helpless animals and often human beings, in the name of religion; his death, full of years and honours, and the subsequent

BUDDHA'S DEATH
(from a Tibetau picture, after Grünwedel).

burial of his relics,—all these episodes in Buddha's life are familiar to English readers in the pages of Sir Edwin Arnold's *Light of Asia*, and other works.

His system, which arose as a revolt against the one-sided development of contemporary religion and ethics, the caste-debasement of man and the materializing of God, took the form, as we shall see, of an agnostic idealism, which threw away ritual and sacerdotalism altogether.

Its tolerant creed of universal benevolence, quickened by the bright example of a pure and noble life, appealed to the feelings of the people with irresistible force and directness, and soon gained for the new religion many converts in the Ganges Valley.

And it gradually gathered a brotherhood of monks, which after Buddha's death became subject to a succession of "Patriarchs,"[1] who, however, possessed little or no centralized hierarchal power, nor, had at least the earlier of them, any fixed abode.

About 250 B.C. it was vigorously propagated by the great Emperor Aṣoka, the Constantine of Buddhism, who, adopting it as his State-religion, zealously spread it throughout his own vast empire, and sent many missionaries into the adjoining lands to diffuse the faith. Thus was it transported to Burma,[2] Siam, Ceylon, and other islands on the south, to Nepal[3] and the countries to the north of India, Kashmīr, Bactria, Afghanistan, etc.

In 61 A.D. it spread to China,[4] and through China, to Corea, and,

---

[1] The greatest of all Buddha's disciples, Ṣāriputra and Maudgalyayāna, who from their prominence in the system seem to have contributed materially to its success, having died before their master, the first of the patriarchs was the senior surviving disciple, Mahākāṣyapa. As several of these Patriarchs are intimately associated with the Lāmaist developments, I subjoin a list of their names, taken from the Tibetan canon and Tāranātha's history, supplemented by some dates from modern sources. After Nāgārjuna, the thirteenth (or according to some the fourteenth) patriarch, the succession is uncertain.

LIST OF THE PATRIARCHS.

1. Mahākāṣyapa, Buddha's senior disciple.
2. Ananda, Buddha's cousin and favourite attendant.
3. Ṣaṇāvāsu.
4. Upagupta, the spiritual adviser of Aṣoka, 250 B.C.
5. Dhṛiṭaka.
6. Micchaka or Bibhakala.
7. Buddhananda.
8. Buddhamitra (= ? Vasumitra, referred to as president of Kanishka's Council).
9. Pārṣva, contemporary of Kanishka, *circa* 78 A.D.
10. Suṇaṣata (? or Puṇyayaṣas).
11. Aṣvaghosha, also contemporary of Kanishka, *circa* 100 A.D.
12. Maṣipala (Kapimala).
13. Nāgārjuna, *circa* 150 A.D.
14. Deva or Kānadeva.
15. Rāhulata (?).
16. Saṅghanandi.
17. Saṅkhayaṣeta (?)
18. Kumārada.
19. Jayata.
20. Vasubandhu, *circa* 400 A.D.
21. Manura.
22. Haklenayaṣas.
23. Siṅhalaputra.
24. Vaṣasuta.
25. Puṇyamitra.
26. Prajñātāra.
27. Bodhidharma, who visited China by sea in 526 A.D.

[2] By SONA and UTTARO (*Mahavanso*, p. 71).

[3] BUCHANAN-HAMILTON (*Acct. of Nepal*, p. 190) gives date of introduction as A.D. 33; probably this was its re-introduction.

[4] During the reign of the Emperor Ming Ti. BEAL (*Budd. in China*, p. 53) gives 71 A.D.

in the sixth century A.D., to Japan, taking strong hold on all of the people of these countries, though they were very different from those among whom it arose, and exerting on all the wilder tribes among them a very sensible civilizing influence. It is believed to have established itself at Alexandria.[1] And it penetrated to Europe, where the early Christians had to pay tribute to the Tartar Buddhist Lords of the Golden Horde; and to the present day it still survives in European Russia among the Kalmaks on the Volga, who are professed Buddhists of the Lāmaist order.

Tibet, at the beginning of the seventh century, though now surrounded by Buddhist countries, knew nothing of that religion, and was still buried in barbaric darkness. Not until about the year 640 A.D. did it first receive its Buddhism, and through it some beginnings of civilization among its people.

But here it is necessary to refer to the changes in Form which Buddhism meanwhile had undergone in India.

Buddha, as the central figure of the system, soon became invested with supernatural and legendary attributes. And as the religion extended its range and influence, and enjoyed princely patronage and ease, it became more metaphysical and ritualistic, so that heresies and discords constantly cropped up, tending to schisms, for the suppression of which it was found necessary to hold great councils.

Of these councils the one held at Jalandhar, in Northern India, towards the end of the first century A.D., under the auspices of the Scythian King Kanishka, of Northern India, was epoch-making, for it established a permanent schism into what European writers have termed the "Northern" and "Southern" Schools: the Southern being now represented by Ceylon, Burma, and Siam; and the Northern by Tibet, Sikhim, Bhotan, Nepal, Ladāk, China, Mongolia, Tartary, and Japan. This division, however, it must be remembered, is unknown to the Buddhists themselves, and is only useful to denote in a rough sort of way the relatively primitive as distinguished from the developed or mixed forms of the faith, with especial reference to their present-day distribution.

[1] The *Mahāvanso* (TURNOUR's ed., p. 171) notes that 30,000 Bhikshus, or Buddhist monks, came from "Alasadda," considered to be Alexandria.

The point of divergence of these so-called "Northern" and "Southern" Schools was the theistic *Mahāyāna* doctrine, which substituted for the agnostic idealism and simple morality of Buddha, a speculative theistic system with a mysticism of sophistic nihilism in the background. Primitive Buddhism practically confined its salvation to a select few; but the Mahāyāna extended salvation to the entire universe. Thus, from its large capacity as a "Vehicle" for easy, speedy, and certain attainment of the state of a Bodhisat or potential Buddha, and conveyance across the sea of life (*saṃsāra*) to Nirvāṇa, the haven of the Buddhists, its adherents called it "The Great Vehicle" or *Mahāyāna*;[1] while they contemptuously called the system of the others—the Primitive Buddhists, who did not join this innovation—"The Little, or Imperfect Vehicle," the *Hinayāna*,[2] which could carry so few to Nirvāṇa, and which they alleged was only fit for low intellects.

This doctrinal division into the Mahāyāna and Hinayāna, however, does not quite coincide with the distinction into the so-called Northern and Southern Schools; for the Southern School shows a considerable leavening with Mahāyāna principles,[3] and Indian Buddhism during its most popular period was very largely of the Mahāyāna type.

Who the real author of the Mahāyāna was is not yet known. The doctrine seems to have developed within the Mahā-saṅghika or "Great Congregation"—a heretical sect which arose among the monks of Vaiṣāli, one hundred years after Buddha's death, and at the council named after that place.[4] Aṣvaghosha, who appears to have lived about the latter end of the first century A.D., is credited with the authorship of a work entitled *On raising Faith in the Mahāyāna.*[5] But its chief expounder and developer was Nāgārjuna, who was probably a pupil of Aṣvaghosha, as he

---

[1] The word *Yāna* (Tib., *T'eg-pa ch'en-po*) or "Vehicle" is parallel to the Platonic ὄχημα, as noted by BEAL in *Catena*, p. 124.

[2] Tib., *T'eg-pa dman-pa.*

[3] Cf. HIUEN TSIANG'S *Si-yu-Ki* (BEAL'S), ii., p. 133; EITEL, p. 90; DHARMAPĀLA in *Mahābodhi Jour.*, 1892; Taw Sein Ko, *Ind. Antiquary*, June, 1892.

[4] The orthodox members of this council formed the sect called *Sthaviras* or "elders."

[5] He also wrote a biography of Buddha, entitled *Buddha-Carita Kāvya*, translated by COWELL, in S.B.E. It closely resembles the Lalita Vistara, and a similar epic was brought to China as early as 70 A.D. (BEAL'S *Chinese Buddhism*, p. 90). He is also credited with the authorship of a clever confutation of Brāhmanism, which was latterly entitled *Vajra Sūci* (cf. HODGS., *Ill.*, 127).

followed the successor of the latter in the patriarchate. He could not, however, have taken any active part in Kanishka's Council, as the Lāmas believe. Indeed, it is doubtful even whether he had then been born.[1]

Nāgārjuna claimed and secured orthodoxy for the Mahāyāna doctrine by producing an apocalyptic treatise which he attributed to Ṣākya Muni, entitled the *Prajñā-pāramitā*, or "the means of arriving at the other side of wisdom," a treatise which he alleged the Buddha had himself composed, and had hid away in the custody of the Nāga demigods until men were sufficiently enlightened to comprehend so abstruse a system. And, as his method claims to be a compromise between the extreme views then held on the nature of Nirvāṇa, it was named the *Mādhyamika*, or the system "of the Middle Path."[2]

དཔལ་མགོན་ཀླུ་སྒྲུབ

NĀGĀRJUNA.

This Mahāyāna doctrine was essentially a sophistic nihilism; and under it the goal Nirvāṇa, or rather Pari-Nirvāṇa, while ceasing to be extinction of Life, was considered a mystical state which admitted of no definition. By developing the supernatural side of Buddhism and its objective symbolism, by rendering its

---

[1] Nāgārjuna (T., kLu-grub.) appears to belong to the second century A.D. He was a native of Vidarbha (Berar) and a monk of Nālanda, the headquarters of several of the later patriarchs. He is credited by the Lāmas (*J.A.S.B.*, 1882, 115) with having erected the stone railing round the great Gandhola Temple of "Budh Gāya," though the style of the lithic inscriptions on these rails would place their date earlier. For a biographical note from the Tibetan by H. WENZEL, see *J. Pali Text Soc.*, 1886, p. 1, also by SARAT, *J.A.S.B.*, 51, pp. 1 and 115. The vernacular history of Kashmīr (Rājatārangiṇī) makes him a contemporary and chief monk of Kanishka's successor, King Abhimanyu (cf. also EITEL, p. 103; SCHL., 21, 301-3; KÖPP., ii., 14; O.M., 107, 2; CSOMA, *Gr.*, xii., 182).

[2] It seems to have been a common practice for sectaries to call their own system by this title, implying that it only was the true or reasonable belief. Ṣākya Muni also called his system "the Middle Path" (DAVIDS, p. 47), claiming in his defence of truth to avoid the two extremes of superstition on the one side, and worldliness or infidelity on the other. Comp. the *Via media* of the Anglican Oxford movement.

salvation more accessible and universal, and by substituting good *words* for the good *deeds* of the earlier Buddhists, the Mahāyāna appealed more powerfully to the multitude and secured ready popularity.

About the end of the first century of our era, then, Kanishka's Council affirmed the superiority of the Mahāyāna system, and published in the Sanskrit language inflated versions of the Buddhist Canon, from sources for the most part independent of the Pāli versions of the southern Buddhists, though exhibiting a remarkable agreement with them.[1]

And this new doctrine supported by Kanishka, who almost rivalled Aṣoka in his Buddhist zeal and munificence, became a dominant form of Buddhism throughout the greater part of India; and it was the form which first penetrated, it would seem, to China and Northern Asia.

Its idealization of Buddha and his attributes led to the creation of metaphysical Buddhas and celestial Bodhisats, actively willing and able to save, and to the introduction of innumerable demons and deities as objects of worship, with their attendant idolatry and sacerdotalism, both of which departures Buddha had expressly condemned. The gradual growth of myth and legend, and of the various theistic developments which now set in, are sketched in detail in another chapter.

MAÑJUṢRI
(the Bodhisat-God, holding the Book of Wisdom and wielding the Sword of Knowledge).

As early as about the first century A.D., Buddha is made to be existent from all eternity and without beginning

And one of the earliest forms given to the greatest of these metaphysical Buddhas—Amitābha, the Buddha of Boundless Light

[1] Several of the Chinese and Japanese Scriptures are translated from the Pāli BEAL'S *Budd. in China*, p. 5) and also a few Tibetan (cf. Chap. vii.).

—evidently incorporated a Sun-myth, as was indeed to be expected where the chief patrons of this early Mahāyāna Buddhism, the Scythians and Indo-Persians, were a race of Sun-worshippers.

The worship of Buddha's own image seems to date from this period, the first century of our era, and about four or five centuries after Buddha's death;[1] and it was followed by a variety of polytheistic forms, the creation of which was probably facilitated by the Grecian Art influences then prevalent in Northern India.[2] Different forms of Buddha's image, originally intended to represent different epochs in his life, were afterwards idealized into various Celestial Buddhas, from whom the human Buddhas were held to be derived as material reflexes.

VAJRA-PĀṆI
(the Wielder of the Thunderbolt).

About 500 A.D.[3] arose the next great development in Indian Buddhism with the importation into it of the pantheistic cult of Yoga, or the ecstatic union of the individual with the Universal Spirit, a cult which had been introduced into Hinduism by Patanjali about 150 B.C. Buddha himself had attached much importance to the practice of

---

[1] Cf. statue of Buddha found at Ṣrāvasti, CUNNINGHAM's *Stupa of Barhut*, p. vii. So also in Christianity. Archdeacon Farrar, in his recent lecture on "The Development of Christian Art," states that for three centuries there were no pictures of Christ, but only symbols, such as the fish, the lamb, the dove. The catacombs of St. Callistus contained the first picture of Christ, the date being 313. Not even a cross existed in the early catacombs, and still less a crucifix. The eighth century saw the first picture of the dead Christ. Rabulas in 586 first depicted the crucifixion in a Syriac Gospel.

[2] SMITH's *Græco-Roman infl. on Civilization of Ancient India*, *J.A.S.B.*, 58 *et seq.*, 1889, and GRÜNWEDEL's *Buddh. Kunst.*

[3] The date of the author of this innovation, Asaṅga, the brother of Vasubandhu,

abstract meditation amongst his followers; and such practices under the mystical and later theistic developments of his system, readily led to the adoption of the Brāhmanical cult of Yoga, which was grafted on to the theistic Mahāyāna by Asaṅga, a Buddhist monk of Gandhārā (Peshawar), in Northern India. Those who mastered this system were called *Yogācārya* Buddhists.

The Yogācārya mysticism seems to have leavened the mass of the Mahāyāna followers, and even some also of the Hinayāna; for distinct traces of Yoga are to be found in modern Burmese and Ceylonese Buddhism. And this Yoga parasite, containing within itself the germs of Tantrism, seized strong hold of its host and soon developed its monster outgrowths, which crushed and cankered most of the little life of purely Buddhist stock yet left in the Mahāyāna.

SAMANTA-BHADRA
(a Celestial Bodhisat).

About the end of the sixth century A.D., *Tantrism* or Ṣivaic mysticism, with its worship of female energies, spouses of the Hindū god Ṣiva, began to tinge both Buddhism and Hindūism. Consorts were allotted to the several Celestial Bodhisats and most of the other gods and demons, and most of them were given forms wild and terrible, and often monstrous, according to the supposed moods of each divinity at different times. And as these goddesses and fiendesses

the twentieth patriarch, has not yet been fixed with any precision. It seems to be somewhere between 400 A.D. and 500 A.D.—Cf. VASIL., *B.*, p. 78; SCHIEFNER'S *Tāra.*, p. 126; JULIEN'S *Histoire de la vie de Hiuen Tshang*, 83, 93, 97, 106, 114.

were bestowers of supernatural power, and were especially malignant, they were especially worshipped.

By the middle of the seventh century A.D., India contained many images of Divine Buddhas and Bodhisats with their female energies and other Buddhist gods and demons, as we know from Hiuen Tsiang's narrative and the lithic remains in India;[1] and the growth of myth and ceremony had invested the dominant form of Indian Buddhism with organised litanies and full ritual.

Such was the distorted form of Buddhism introduced into Tibet about 640 A.D.; and during the three or four succeeding centuries Indian Buddhism became still more debased. Its mysticism became a silly mummery of unmeaning jargon and "magic circles," dignified by the title of *Mantrayāna* or "The Spell-Vehicle"; and this so-called "esoteric," but properly "exoteric," cult was given a respectable antiquity by alleging that its real founder was Nāgārjuna, who had received it from the Celestial Buddha Vairocana through the divine Bodhisat Vajrasattva at "the iron tower" in Southern India.

ELEVEN-HEADED AVALOKITA.

In the tenth century A.D.,[2] the Tantrik phase developed in Northern India, Kashmīr, and Nepal, into the monstrous and polydemonist doctrine, the Kālacākra,[3] with its demoniacal Buddhas, which incorporated the Mantrāyāna practices, and called itself the *Vajra-yāna*, or "The Thunderbolt-Vehicle," and its followers were named *Vajrācārya*, or "Followers of the Thunderbolt."

---

1 See my article on Urén, *J.A.S.B.*, 1891, and on Indian Buddhist Cult, etc., in *J.R.A.S.*, 1894, p. 51 *et seq.*

2 About 965 A.D. (CSOMA, *Gr.*, p. 192).

3 Tib., *'Dus-Kyi-'K'or-lo*, or *Circle of Time*, see Chap. vi. It is ascribed to the fabulous country of Sambhala (T., De-jun) to the North of India, a mythical country probably founded upon the Northern land of St. Padma-*sambhavā*, to wit Udyāna.

In these declining days of Indian Buddhism, when its spiritual and regenerating influences were almost dead, the Muhammadan invasion swept over India, in the latter end of the twelfth century A.D., and effectually stamped Buddhism out of the country. The fanatical idol-hating Afghan soldiery[1] especially attacked the Buddhist monasteries, with their teeming idols, and they mas-

གྲུབ་ཆེན་ནཱ་རོ་པ་

NĀRO

(an Indian Buddhist Vajrācārya Monk of the Eleventh Century A.D.).

sacred the monks wholesale;[2] and as the Buddhist religion, unlike the more domestic Brāhmanism, is dependent on its priests and monks for its vitality, it soon disappeared in the absence of these latter. It lingered only for a short time longer in the more remote parts of the peninsula, to which the fiercely fanatical Muhammadans could not readily penetrate.[3]

But it has now been extinct in India for several centuries, leaving, however, all over that country, a legacy of gorgeous architectural remains and monuments of decorative art, and its

---

[1] See article by me in *J.A.S.B.*, lxvi., 1892, p. 20 *et seq.*, illustrating this fanaticism and massacre with reference to Magadha and Asam.

[2] *Tabaqat-i-Nāsirī*, ELLIOT's trans., ii., 306, etc.

[3] Tāranātha says it still existed in Bengal till the middle of the fifteenth century A.D., under the "Chagala" Raja, whose kingdom extended to Delhi and who was converted to Buddhism by his wife. He died in 1448 A.D., and Prof. Bendall finds (*Cat. Buddh. Skt. MSS. intr.* p. iv) that Buddhist MSS. were copied in Bengal up to the middle of the fifteenth century, namely, to 1446. Cf. also his note in *J.R.A.S.*, New Ser., xx., 552, and mine in *J.A.S.B.* (Proc.), February, 1893.

living effect upon its apparent offshoot Jainism, and upon Brāhmanism, which it profoundly influenced for good.

Although the form of Buddhism prevalent in Tibet, and which has been called after its priests "Lāmaism," is mainly that of the mystical type, the Vajra-yāna, curiously incorporated with Tibetan mythology and spirit-worship, still it preserves there, as we shall see, much of the loftier philosophy and ethics of the system taught by Buddha himself. And the Lāmas have the keys to unlock the meaning of much of Buddha's doctrine, which has been almost inacessible to Europeans.

Lāma-Worship.

SOME LĀMA-PRIESTS.[1]

III.

RISE, DEVELOPMENT, AND SPREAD OF LĀMAISM.

TIBET emerges from barbaric darkness only with the dawn of its Buddhism, in the seventh century of our era.

Tibetan history, such as there is—and there is none at all before its Buddhist era, nor little worthy of the name till about the eleventh century A.D.—is fairly clear on the

---

[1] From a photograph by Mr. Hoffmann.

point that previous to King Sroṅ Tsan Gampo's marriage in 638-641 A.D., Buddhism was quite unknown in Tibet.[1] And it is also fairly clear on the point that Lāmaism did not arise till a century later than this epoch.

Up till the seventh century Tibet was inaccessible even to the Chinese. The Tibetans of this prehistoric period are seen, from the few glimpses that we have of them in Chinese history about the end of the sixth century,[2] to have been rapacious savages and reputed cannibals, without a written language,[3] and followers of an animistic and devil-dancing or Shamanist religion, the *Bön*, resembling in many ways the Taoism of China.

Early in the seventh century, when Muhammad ("Mahomet")

---

[1] The historians so-called of Tibet wrote mostly inflated bombast, almost valueless for historical purposes. As the current accounts of the rise of Buddhism in Tibet are so overloaded with legend, and often inconsistent, I have endeavoured to sift out the more positive data from the mass of less trustworthy materials. I have looked into the more disputed historical points in the Tibetan originals, and, assisted by the living traditions of the Lāmas, and the translations provided by Rockhill and Bushell especially, but also by Schlagintweit, Sarat, and others, I feel tolerably confident that as regards the questions of the mode and date of the introduction of Buddhism into Tibet, and the founding of Lāmaism, the opinions now expressed are in the main correct.

The accounts of the alleged Buddhist events in prehistoric Tibet given in the *Maṇi-Kāh-'bum*, *Gyal-rabs*, and other legendary books, are clearly clumsy fictions. Following the example of Burma and other Buddhist nations (cf. Hiuen Tsiang, Julien's trans., i., 179 ; ii., 107, etc.) who claim for their King an ancestry from the Ṣākya stock, we find the Lāmas foisting upon their King a similar descent. A mythical exiled prince, named *gNah-K'ri-bTsan-po*, alleged to be the son of King Prasenjit, Buddha's first royal patron, and a member of the Licchavi branch of the Ṣākya tribe, is made to enter Tibet in the fifth century B.C. as the progenitor of a millennium of Sroṅ Tsan Gampo's ancestors; and an absurd story is invented to account for the etymology of his name, which means "the back chair"; while the Tibetan people are given as progenitors a monkey ("Hilumandju," evidently intended for Hanumānji, the Hindu monkey god, cf. ROCK., *LL.*, 355) sent by Avalokiteṣwara and a *rakshasi* fiendess. Again, in the year 331 A.D., there fell from heaven several sacred objects (conf. ROCK., *B.*, p. 210), including the *Om mani* formula, which in reality was not invented till many hundred (probably a thousand) years later. And similarly the subsequent appearance of five foreigners before a King, said to have been named T'o-t'ori Ñyan-tsan, in order to declare the sacred nature of the above symbols, *without, however, explaining them*, so that the people continued in ignorance of their meaning. And it only tends still further to obscure the points at issue to import into the question, as Lassen does (*Ind. Alt.*, ii., 1072), the alleged erection on Mt. Kailās, in 137 B.C., of a temporary Buddhist monastery, for such a monastery must have belonged to Kashmīr Buddhism, and could have nothing to do with Tibet.

[2] BUSHELL, *loc. cit.*, p. 435.

[3] They used knotched wood and knotted cords (RÉMUSAT'S *Researches*, p. 384).

was founding his religion in Arabia, there arose in Tibet a warlike king, who established his authority over the other wild clans of central Tibet, and latterly his son, Sroṅ Tsan Gampo,[1] harassed the western borders of China; so that the Chinese Emperor T'aitsung, of the T'ang Dynasty, was glad to come to terms with this young prince, known to the Chinese as Ch'itsung-luntsan, and gave him in 641 A.D.[2] the Princess[3] Wench'eng, of the imperial house, in marriage.[4]

Two years previously Sroṅ Tsan Gampo had married Bhṛikuṭi, a daughter of the Nepal King, Aṃṣuvarman;[5] and both of these wives being bigoted Buddhists, they speedily effected the conversion of their young husband, who was then, according

[1] Called also, prior to his accession (says ROCKHILL, *Life*, p. 211) Khri-ldan Sroṅ-btsan (in Chinese, Ki-tsung lun-tsan). His father, g'Nam-ri Sroṅ-tsan, and his ancestors had their headquarters at Yar-luṅ, or "the Upper Valley," below the Yar-lha sam-po, a mountain on the southern confines of Tibet, near the Bhotan frontier. The Yar-luṅ river flows northwards into the Tsang-po, below Lhāsa and near Samye. This Yar-luṅ is to be distinguished from that of the same name in the Kham province, east of Bathang, and a tributary of the Yangtse Kiang. The chronology by Bu-ton (t'am-c'ad K'an-po) is considered the most reliable, and Sum-pa K'an-po accepted it in preference to the Baidyur Kar-po, composed by the Dalai Lāma's orders, by De-Srid Saṅ-gyas Gya-mts'o, in 1686. According to Bu-ton, the date of Sroṅ Tsan Gampo's birth was 617 A.D. (which agrees with that given by the Mongol historian, Sasnang Setzen), and he built the palaee Pho-daṅ-Marpo on the Lhāsa hill when aged nineteen, and the Lhāsa Temple when aged twenty-three. He married the Chinese princess when he was aged nineteen, and he died aged eighty-two. The Chinese records, translated by Bushell, make him die early. Csoma's date of 627 (*Grammar*, p. 183) for his birth appears to be a clerical error for 617. His first mission to China was in 634 (BUSHELL, *J.R.A.S.*, New Ser., xii., p. 440).

[2] According to Chinese annals (BUSHELL, 435), the Tibetan date for the marriage is 639 (C., *G.*, p. 183), that is, two years after his marriage with the Nepalese princess.

[3] Kong-jo = "princess" in Chinese.

[4] The Tibetan tradition has it that there were three other suitors for this princess's hand, namely, the three greatest kings they knew of outside China, the Kings of Magadha, of Persia (*sTag-zig*), and of the Hor (*Turki*) tribes. See also HODGSON'S *Ess.* and ROCKHILL'S *B.*, 213; CSOMA'S *Gr.*, 196; *Bodhimur*, 338.

[5] Aṃṣuvarman, or "Glowing Armour," is mentioned by Hiuen Tsiang (BEAL'S Ed. *Si-yu-ki*, ii., p. 81) as reigning about 637, and he appears as a grantee in FLEET'S *Corpus Inscrn. Ind.* (iii., p. 190) in several inscriptions ranging from 635 to 650 A.D., from which it appears that he was of the Ṭhākurī dynasty and a feudatory of King of Harshavardhana of Kanauj, and on the death of the latter seems to have become independent. The inscriptions show that *devi* was a title of his royal ladies, and his 635 A.D. inscription recording a gift to his nephew, a *srāmin* (an officer), renders it probable that he had then an adult daughter. One of his inscriptions relates to Sivaist *lingas*, but none are expressedly Buddhist. The inscription of 635 was discovered by C. BENDALL, and published in *Ind. Ant.* for 1885, and in his *Journey*, pp. 13 and 73. Cf. also *Ind. Ant.*, ix., 170, and his description of coins in *Zeitchr. der Deutsch.*

to Tibetan annals, only about sixteen years of age,[1] and who, under their advice, sent to India, Nepal, and China for Buddhist books and teachers.[2]

It seems a perversion of the real order of events to state, as is usually done in European books, that Sroṅ Tsan Gampo first adopted Buddhism, and then married two Buddhist wives. Even the vernacular chronicle,[3] which presents the subject in its most flattering form, puts into the mouth of Sroṅ Tsan Gampo, when he sues for the hand of his first wife, the Nepalese princess, the following words: "I, the King of barbarous[4] Tibet, do not practise the ten virtues, but should you be pleased to bestow on me your daughter, and wish me to have the Law,[5] I shall practise the ten virtues with a five-thousand-fold body . . . , though I have not the arts . . . if you so desire . . . I shall build 5,000 temples." Again, the more reliable Chinese history records that the princess said "there is no religion in Tibet"; and the glimpse got of Sroṅ Tsan in Chinese history shows him actively engaged throughout his life in the very un-Buddhist pursuit of bloody wars with neighbouring states.

The messenger sent by this Tibetan king to India, at the instance of his wives, to bring Buddhist books was called Thon-mi Sam-bhota.[6] The exact date of his departure and return are uncertain,[7] and although his Indian visit seems to have been within the period covered by Hiuen Tsiang's account, this history makes no mention even of the country of Tibet. After a stay in India[8] of several years, during which Sam-bhota studied under the

---

1 The *Gyal-rabs Sel-wai Meloṅ* states that S. was aged sixteen on his marriage with the Nepalese princess, who was then aged eighteen, and three years later he built his Pho-daṅ-Marpo Palace on the Red Hill at Lhāsa.

2 The monks who came to Tibet during Sroṅ Tsan Gampo's reign were Kusara (? Kumāra) and Saṅkara Brāhmaṇa, from India; Sila Mañju, from Nepal; Hwa-shang Mahā-ts'e, from China, and (E. SCHLAGT., *Gyal-rabs*, p. 49) Tabuta and Ganuta, from Kashmīr.

3 Mirror of Royal pedigree, *Gyal-rabs Sel-wai Meloṅ*.

4 mT'ah-'k'ob.

5 K'rims.

6 Sambhota is the Sanskrit title for "The good Bhotiya or Tibetan." His proper name is Thon-mi, son of Anu.

7 632 A.D. is sometimes stated as date of departure, and 650 as the return; but on this latter date Sroṅ Tsan Gampo died according to the Chinese accounts, although he should survive for many (48) years longer, according to the conflicting Tibetan records.

8 "*Southern* India" (*Bodhimur*, p. 327).

Brāhman Livikara or Lipidatta[1] and the pandit Devavid Siṅha (or Siṅha Ghosha), he returned to Tibet, bringing several Buddhist books and the so-called "Tibetan" alphabet, by means of which he now reduced the Tibetan language to writing and composed for this purpose a grammar.[2]

This so-called "Tibetan" character, however, was merely a somewhat fantastic reproduction of the north Indian alphabet current in India at the time of Sam-bhota's visit. It exaggerates the flourishing curves of the "*Kuṭila*," which was then coming into vogue in India, and it very slightly modified a few letters to adapt them to the peculiarities of Tibetan phonetics.[3] Thonmi translated into this new character several small Buddhist texts,[4] but he does not appear to have become a monk or to have attempted any religious teaching.

Sroṅ Tsan Gampo, being one of the greatest kings of Tibet and the first patron of learning and civilization in that country, and having with the aid of his wives first planted the germs of Buddhism in Tibetan soil, he is justly the most famous and popular king of the country, and latterly he was canonized as an incarnation of the most popular of the celestial Bodhisats, Avalokita; and in keeping with this legend he is figured with his hair dressed up into a high conical chignon after the fashion of the Indian images of this Buddhist god, "The Looking-down-Lord."

His two wives were canonized as incarnations of Avalokita's consort, Tārā, "the Saviouress," or Goddess of Mercy; and the fact that they bore him no children is pointed to as evidence of their divine nature.[5] The Chinese princess Wench'eng was deified

1 Li-byin = *Li* + "to give."

2 *sGrāhi* bs*tan* b*ch'os sum ch'u-pa*.

3 The cerebrals and aspirates not being needed for Tibetan sounds were rejected. And when afterwards the full expression of Sanskrit names in Tibetan demanded these letters, the five cerebrals were formed by reversing the dentals and the aspirates obtained by suffixing an *h*, while the palato-sibilants *ts*, *tsh*, and *ds* were formed by adding a surmounting crest to the palatals *ch*, *chh*, and *j*. It is customary to say that the cursive style, the "headless" or *U-med* (as distinguished from the full form with the head the *U-ch'en*) was adapted from the so-called "Wartu" form of Devanagri—Hodgson, *As. Res.*, xvi., 420; Schmidt, *Mem. de l'Ac. de Pet.*, i., 41; Csoma, *Gr.*, 204; Sarat, *J.A.S.B.*, 1888, 42.

4 The first book translated seems to have been the *Karanda-vyuha sutra*, a favourite in Nepal; and a few other translations still extant in the Tän-gyur are ascribed to him (Csoma, *A.*, and Rock., *B.*, 212.

5 His issue proceeded from two or four Tibetan wives.

as "The *white* Tāra,"[1] as in the annexed figure; while the Nepalese princess "*Bribsun*," said to be a corruption of Bhṛi-kuṭi, was apotheosised as the *green* Bhṛi-kuṭi Tāra,[2] as figured in the chapter on the pantheon.

༄།།སྒྲོལ་མ་དཀར་པོ་ལ་ན་མོ།།

TĀRÂ, THE WHITE.
The Deified Chinese Princess Wench'eng.[4]

But he was not the saintly person the grateful Lāmas picture, for he is seen from reliable Chinese history to have been engaged all his life in bloody wars, and more at home in the battlefield than the temple. And he certainly did little in the way of Buddhist propaganda, beyond perhaps translating a few tracts into Tibetan, and building a few temples to shrine the images received by him in dower,[3] and others which he constructed. He built no monasteries.

---

[1] E. Schlagintweit (p. 66) transposes the forms of the two princesses, and most subsequent writers repeat his confusion.

[2] She is represented to have been of a fiery temper, and the cause of frequent brawls on account of the precedence given to the Chinese princess.

[3] He received as dower with the Nepalese princess, according to the *Gyal-rabs*, the images of Akshobhya Buddha, Maitreya and a sandal-wood image of Tārā; and from his Chinese wife a figure of Ṣākya Muni as a young prince. To shrine the images of Akshobhya and the Chinese Ṣākya he built respectively the temples of Ramoch'e and another at Rāsa, now occupied by the Jo-wo K'aṅ at Lhāsa (see Chaps. xii. and xiii.). The latter temple was called *Rasa-'p'rul snaṅ gi gtsug-lha-K'aṅ*, and was built in his twenty-third year, and four years after the arrival of the Chinese princess (in 644 A.D., BUSHELL). The name of its site, *Ra-sa*, is said to have suggested the name by which it latterly became more widely known, namely, as Lhā-sa, or "God's place." The one hundred and eight temples accredited to him in the *Mani-Kāh-'bum* are of course legendary, and not even their sites are known to the Lāmas themselves.

[4] After Pander.

After Sroṅ Tsan Gampo's death, about 650 A.D.,[1] Buddhism made little headway against the prevailing Shamanist superstitions, and seems to have been resisted by the people until about a century later in the reign of his powerful descendant Thi-Sroṅ Detsan,[2] who extended his rule over the greater part of Yunnan and Si-Chuen, and even took Changan, the then capital of China.

KING THI-SROṄ DETSAN.

This king was the son of a Chinese princess,[3] and inherited through his mother a strong prejudice in favour of Buddhism.

He succeeded to the throne when only thirteen years old, and a few years later[4] he sent to India for a celebrated Buddhist priest to establish an order in Tibet; and he was advised, it is said, by his family priest, the Indian monk Ṣānta-rakshita, to secure if possible the services of his brother-in-law,[5] Guru Padma-sambhava, a clever member of the then popular Tantrik Yogācārya school, and at that time, it is said, a resident of the great college of Nālanda, the Oxford of Buddhist India.

This Buddhist wizard, Guru Padma-sambhava, promptly responded to the invitation of the Tibetan king, and accompanied the messengers back to Tibet in 747 A.D.[6]

As Guru Padma-sambhava was the founder of Lāmaism, and is now deified and as celebrated in Lāmaism as Buddha himself, than whom, indeed, he receives among several sects more worship, he demands detailed notice.

The founder of Lāmaism, Saint Padma-sambhava or "the Lotus-

[1] He was succeeded in 650 by his grandson Mang Sroṅ Mang tsan under the regency of Sroṅ Tsan's Buddhist minister, Gar (m*k'ar*), known to the Chinese as Chüshih (BUSHELL, *loc. cit.*, 446).

[2] *K'ri-Sroṅ ldeu-btsan.* (Cf. KÖPP., ii., 67-72; SCHLAG., 67; *J.A.S.B.*, 1881, p. 224.) ROCK., *B.*, quotes p. 221 contemporary record in *bsTan-gyur* (xciv., f. 387-391), proving that in Thi-Sroṅ Detsan's reign in the middle of the eighth century, Tibet was hardly recognized as a Buddhist country.

[3] Named Chin cheng (Tib., Kyim Shaṅ), adopted daughter of the Emperor Tchang tsong (BUSHELL, 456).

[4] In 747 (CSOMA, *Gr.*, 183); but the Chinese date would give 755 (BUSHELL).

[5] The legendary life of the Guru states that he married the Princess Mandāravā, a sister of Ṣānta-rakshita.

[6] Another account makes the Guru arrive in Tibet in anticipation of the king's wishes.

THE FOUNDER OF LĀMAISM, ST. PADMA-SAMBHAVA,
in his Eight Forms.

born one,"[1] is usually called by the Tibetans *Guru Rin-po-ch'e*, or "the precious Guru"; or simply *Lô-pön*,[2] the Tibetan equivalent of the Sanskrit "*Guru*" or "teacher." He is also called "Ugyan" or "Urgyan," as he was a native of Udyāna or Urgyan, corresponding to the country about Ghazni[3] to the north-west of Kashmīr.

Udyāna, his native land, was famed for the proficiency of its priests in sorcery, exorcism, and magic. Hiuen Tsiang, writing a century previously, says regarding Udyāna: "The people are in disposition somewhat sly and crafty. They practise the art of using charms. The employment of magical sentences is with them an art and a study."[4] And in regard to the adjoining country of Kashmīr also intimately related to Lāmaism, Marco Polo a few centuries later says: "Keshimur is a province inhabited by people who are idolaters (*i.e.*, Buddhists). . . . They have an astonishing acquaintance with the devilries of enchantment, insomuch as they can make their idols speak. They can also by their sorceries bring on changes of weather, and produce darkness, and do a number of things so extraordinary that no one without seeing them would believe them. Indeed, this country is the very original source from which idolatry has spread abroad."[5]

དམ་ཅན་རྡོ་རྗེ་ལེགས་

DOR-JE LEGS.
A fiend (-priest) subjected by St. Padmasambhava.

The Tibetans, steeped in superstition which beset them on every side by malignant devils, warmly welcomed the Guru as he brought them deliverance from their terrible tormentors. Arriving in Tibet

[1] For legend of his birth from a lotus see p. 380.

[2] sLob-dpon.

[3] The Tibetans state that it is now named Ghazni, but Sir H. Yule, the great geographer, writes (MARCO P., i., 155): "*Udyána* lay to the north of Peshâwar, on the Swat river, but from the extent assigned to it by Hwen Thsang, the name probably covered a large part of the whole hill region south of the Hindu Kush, from Chitral to the Indus, as indeed it is represented in the Map of Vivien de St. Martin (*Pèlerins Bouddhistes*, ii.)." It is regarded by FaHian as the most northerly Province of India, and in his time the food and clothing of the people were similar to those of Gangetic India.

[4] BEAL'S *Si-Yu-Ki*, i., 120.

[5] MARCO P., i., 155.

in 747 A.D., he vanquished all the chief devils of the land, sparing most of them on their consenting to become defenders of his religion, while he on his part guaranteed that in return for such services they would be duly worshipped and fed. Thus, just as the Buddhists in India, in order to secure the support of the semi-aborigines of Bengal admitted into their system the bloody Durga and other aboriginal demons, so on extending their doctrines throughout Asia they paudered to the popular taste by admitting within the pale of Buddhism the pantheon of those new nations they sought to convert. And similarly in Japan, where Buddhism was introduced in the sixth century A.D., it made little progress till the ninth century, when Kobo Daishi incorporated it with the local Shintoism, by alleging that the Shinto deities were embodiments of the Buddhist.

THE TWELVE TAN-MA SHE-DEVILS.
Subjected by St. Padma.

The Guru's most powerful weapons in warring with the demons were the *Vajra* (Tibetan, *dor-je*), symbolic of the thunderbolt of Indra (Jupiter), and spells extracted from the Mahāyāna gospels, by which he shattered his supernatural adversaries.

As the leading events of his march through Tibet and his subjugation of the local devils are of some interest, as indicating the original habitats of several of the pre-Lāmaist demons, I have given a condensed account of these in the chapter on the pantheon at page 382.

Under the zealous patronage of King Thi-Sroṅ Detsan he built at Sam-yäs in 749 A.D. the first Tibetan monastery. The orthodox account of the miraculous creation of that building is referred to in our description of that monastery.

On the building of Sām-yäs,[1] said to be modelled after the Indian Odantapura of Magadha, the Guru, assisted by the Indian monk Ṣānta-rakshita, instituted there the order of the Lāmas. Ṣānta-rakshita was made the first abbot and laboured there for thirteen years. He now is entitled Acārya Bodhisat.[2]

ṢĀNTA-RAKSHITA.
Indian Buddhist monk of the Eighth Century A.D.

Lā-ma[3] is a Tibetan word meaning the "Superior One," and corresponds to the Sanskrit *Uttara*. It was restricted to the head of the monastery, and still is strictly applicable only to abbots and the highest monks; though out of courtesy the title is now given to almost all Lāmaist monks and priests. The Lāmas have no special term for their form of Buddhism. They simply call it "*The* religion" or "Buddha's religion"; and its professors are "Insiders," or "within the fold" (*naṅ-pa*), in contradistinction to the non-Buddhists or "Out-

[1] The title of the temple is Zan-yad Mi-gyur Lhun-gyi dub-pahi tsug-lha-Ksan, or the "Self-sprung immovable shrine," and it is believed to be based on immovable foundations of adamantine laid by the Guru.

[2] And is said to have been of the Svatantra school, following Ṣāriputra, Ananda, Nāgārjuna, Subhaṅkara, Ṣrī Gupta, and Jñāna-garbha (cf. SCHL., 67; KOPP., ii., 68; *J.A.S.B.*, 1881, p. 226; PAND., No. 25.

[3] bLa-ma. The Uighurs (? Hor) call their Lāmas "*tuin*" (YULE'S, *Cathay*, p. 241, *note*).

siders" (*chi-pa* or *pyi-'liṅ*), the so-called "pe-ling" or foreigners of English writers. And the European term "Lāmaism" finds no counterpart in Tibetan.

The first Lāma may be said to be Pal-baṅs, who succeeded the Indian abbot Ṣānta-rakshita; though the first ordained member of this Tibetan order of monks was Bya-Khri-gzigs.[1] The most learned of these young Lāmas was Vairocana, who translated many Sanskrit works into Tibetan, though his usefulness was interrupted for a while by the Tibetan wife of Thi-Sroṅ Detsan; who in her bitter opposition to the King's reforms, and instigated by the Bön-pa priests, secured the banishment of Vairocana to the eastern province of Kham by a scheme similar to that practised by Potiphar's wife. But, on her being forthwith afflicted with leprosy, she relented, and the young "Bairo-tsana" was recalled and effected her cure. She is still, however, handed down to history as the "Red Rahulā she-devil,"[2] while Vairocana is made an incarnation of Buddha's faithful attendant and cousin Ānanda; and on account of his having translated many orthodox scriptures, he is credited with the composition or translation and hiding away of many of the fictitious scriptures of the unreformed Lāmas, which were afterwards "discovered" as revelations.

It is not easy now to ascertain the exact details of the creed—the primitive Lāmaism—taught by the Guru, for all the extant works attributed to him were composed several centuries later by followers of his twenty-five Tibetan disciples. But judging from the intimate association of his name with the essentials of Lāmaist sorceries, and the special creeds of the old unreformed section of the Lāmas—the Ñiṅ-ma-pa—who profess and are acknowledged to be his immediate followers, and whose older scriptures date back to within two centuries of the Guru's time, it is evident that his teaching was of that extremely Tāntrik and magical type of Mahāyāna Buddhism which was then prevalent in his native country of Udyān and Kashmīr. And to this highly impure form of Buddhism, already covered by so many foreign accretions and saturated with so much demonolatry, was added a

[1] The first seven novices (*Sad-mi mi*) who formed the nucleus of the order were d*Bah* d*pal* d*baṅs*, r*tsaṅs*-devendra and Branka Mutik, *'K'o*n Nāgendra, Sagor Vairocana, r*Ma Ācārya rin-ch'en* m*ch'og*, gLaṅ-Ka Tanana, of whom the first three were elderly.

[2] gZa-mar gyal. The legend is given in the T'aṅ-yik Ser-t'eṅ.

portion of the ritual and most of the demons of the indigenous Bön-pa religion, and each of the demons was assigned its proper place in the Lāmaist pantheon.

Primitive Lāmaism may therefore be defined as a priestly mixture of Ṣivaite mysticism, magic, and Indo-Tibetan demonolatry, overlaid by a thin varnish of Mahāyāna Buddhism. And to the present day Lāmaism still retains this character.

A BÖN-PA PRIEST.[2]

In this form, as shaped by the Guru, Buddhism proved more attractive to the people, and soon became popular. Its doctrine of *Karma*, or ethical retribution, appealed to the fatalism which the Tibetans share with most eastern races. And the zealous King, Thi-Sroṅ Detsan, founded other monasteries freely and initiated a period of great literary activity by procuring many talented Indian and Kashmīri scholars for the work of translating the Indian canonical works and commentaries into Tibetan.[1]

The new religion was actively opposed by the priests of the native religion, called Bön,[3] and these were supported by one of the most powerful ministers.[4]

[1] The chief translators employed at this time were the Indian monks, Vimala Mitra, Buddha Guhya, Ṣāntigarbha, Viṣuddhi Siṅha, the Tāntrik Achārya Dharma-kīrti (who translated the *Vajradhātu Yoga* works). The Kashmīri monks, Jina-Mitra, Dāna-Ṣīla and Ananda, assisted by the Tibetan novices, chief of whom was Vairocana. No translations or works ascribed to Padma-sambhava himself occur in the Tibetan Tripiṭaka canon.

[2] After Giorgi.

[3] The word is derived by Gen. Cunningham (MARCO P., i., 287) from *Puṇya*, one of the names of the *Svastikas*, or worshippers of the mystic fly-foot cross, called in Tibetan *gyuṅ druṅ*, though *Puṇya* is simply "a holy man," and seems original of the Burmese title for monk, *Pongyī*. The Bön religion resembles the Taoism of China (see YULE, *loc. cit.;* ROCK., *B.*, p. 206 *et seq.*, and his *L.L.*, p. 217 *n.*, and *J.R. Geog. Soc.*, May, 1894). It is especially associated with the worship of dragons, or *nāgās*, and its reputed founder is gS'*en-rabs Mi-bo.* As now practised, it is deeply impregnated by Buddhism. For a list of some of its deities see SARAT, *Jour. Indian Buddhist Text Soc.*, Vol. i.

[4] Named NamMa-Shanrom-pa-skyes. The ministers who aided the King were Go *Shaṅ-Shi*, and *Da-gyab-ts'an.*

Some of the so-called devils which are traditionally alleged to have been overcome by the Guru were probably such human adversaries. It is also stated that the Bön-pa were now prohibited making human and other bloody sacrifice as was their wont; and hence is said to have arisen the practice of offering images of men and animals made of dough.

Lāmaism was also opposed by some Chinese Buddhists, one of whom, entitled the Mahāyāna Hwa-shang,[1] protested against the kind of Buddhism which Ṣānta-rakshita and Padma-sambhava were teaching.[2] But he is reported to have been defeated in argument and expelled from the country by the Indian monk Kamala-ṣila,[3] who, like Ṣānta-rakshita, is alleged to be of the Sva-tantra Mādhyamika school, and the author of many treatises still extant in the great commentary (Tän-gyur). The excellent Sanskrit-Tibetan dictionaries (*Vyutpatti*) date from this literary epoch.

Padma-sambhava had twenty-five disciples, each of whom is credited with magical power, mostly of a grotesque character.[4]

---

[1] A Chinese term for a Buddhist monk corresponding to Skt. *Upādhyāya* or "master." (See EDKIN's *Dict.* and MAYER's *Hdbk.*)

[2] Two works by *Hwa-shang zab-mo* are found in the Tän-gyur (mDo, xxx., xxxiii. (ROCKHILL's *B.*, p. 220).

[3] Kamala-ṣila was author of an Indian work (*Tarka*) expounding the various philosophic systems of India. (Prof. G. BUEHLER, *J. Buddhist Text Soc. of India*, i., pt. ii., p. x.)

[4] 1. Nam-k'a ñiṅ-po mounted the sunbeams.
2. Saṅ-gyé-ye-ṣe drove iron bolts into rocks.
3. Gyal-wa-ch'og-yan changed his head into a horse s, and neighed thrice.
4. K'ar-ch'en Ch'o-gyal revived the slain.
5. Pal-ki-ye-ṣe overcame three fiendesses.
6. Pal-ki-Seṅ-ge enslaved demons, nymphs, and genii.
7. Vairocana obtained the five heavenly eyes of knowledge.
8. Ṅah-dag-gyalpo attained Samādhi.
9. Yu-drúṅ-Niṅ-po acquired divine knowledge.
10. Jñāna-kumāra worked miracles.
11. Dorje-Duṅ Jem travelled invisibly as the wind.
12. Ye-ṣe-Naṅ visited the fairy world.
13. Sog-pu-Lha-pal (a Mongol) ensnared ferocious beasts.
14. Na-nam-yese soared in the sky.
15. Pal-ki-Waṅ-p'yug killed his enemies by signs.
16. Den-ma-tse-Waṅ had perfect memory.
17. Ka-Wa-pal-tseg perceived the thoughts of others.
18. Shu-bu-pal-seṅ made water run upwards.
19. Khe-hu-c'ug-lo caught flying birds.
20. Gyal-Wai-Lodoi raised ghosts and converted the corpse into gold.
21. Ten-pai-nam-k'a tamed wild yaks of the northern desert.
22. 'Odan-Waṅ-p'yug dived into water like a fish.

And these disciples he instructed in the way of making magic circles for coercing the demons and for exorcism.

The Guru's departure from Tibet was as miraculous in character as his life, and in keeping with the divine attributes with which he has been invested as "Saviour of a suffering world."[1]

23. Ma-t'og rin-ch'en crushed adamant to powder and ate it like meal.
24. Pal-kyi Dor-je passed through rocks and mountains.
25. Lan-dod Kon-ch'og wielded and repelled thunderbolts.

And a twenty-sixth is added: Gyal-wai-Ch'an c'ub sat cross-legged in the air.

[1] After residing in Tibet for about fifty years (say the chronicles, though it is probable he only remained a few years), and founding Lāmaism securely, the Guru, in 802 A.D., much to the grief of the Tibetans, announced his approaching departure for fresh religious triumphs in other lands. Addressing the King, he said: "In Jambudvīp are five Raksha countries with 500 towns apiece. The Central Raksha country is named Sań-do-pal-ri (zańs-mdog-dpal-ri), the king of which is named Langka of the ten necks (? the ten-headed Ravan). To its east lies Lankapuri, to its south dGā-bu-c'an, or "The happy" (Skt., Sukhāvatī or Nandavati), to its west Ko-sha t'ang-dmar-gling, to its north is Byan-lag fort, to its south-east is Bam-ril-t'od-pa-mk'ar, to its north-west is Ma-la-gnam-lchags-rtse, to its north-east is Nal-byih cemetery, and in the south-east is the lake of Phuri. These Raksha countries are crowded with men-eating devils, who if not conquered will depopulate the whole world of Jambudvīp, and except me none other can subdue them. I therefore must go to the stronghold of the Raksha at Sań-do-pal-ri in the country of rÑa-yab-gliń or 'The Yak-tail continent,' which lies to the south-west of Tibet. Thither must I now go."

Then, accompanied by the King and nobles and his two fairy wives (the Tibetan one of which, named Yes'e-ts'o-gyal was to be left behind), he went to the Gung-thang La in Mang-yul on the northern confines of Tibet, and there, after giving farewell advice to the king, priests, and the assembled multitude to keep the doctrine he had taught them, and the revelations he had hidden in caves throughout the land, he was enveloped in a glorious rainbow-halo, within which appeared the four great heroes (dPa-bo) of the world, who assisted him in mounting the celestial horse-car (named "*balaha*" or Chang-sal) in which he was now borne away through the sky in a south-westerly direction, attended by the four heroes and a host of fairies amid heavenly music and showers of flowers. On his departure the assembled multitude were distracted with grief and remained transfixed as if dead. Ultimately they retired below the pass to Srang-*h*dah-sho-*g*tsang-dor and the plain Thang-*d*pal-mo-*d*pal-thang, where they remained for twenty-five days and nights, and were able to see the Guru's celestial party, like a shooting star, sailing away through the sky towards the horizon till lost to sight. After much prayer and worship they sadly departed on King Thi-Sroń Detsan telling them of the Guru's safe arrival at Sań-do-pal-ri, which event he (the king) was able to see through the magical insight he had acquired from the Guru. It appeared that the Guru reached Singala after about two days' journey, and penetrating the iron palace, he entered the body of the Raksha king named "He of the Skull rosary," and preached the doctrine to the thousand daughters of the Raksha and the folk of that country. A few days afterwards he departed for Ña-yab-gliń, and reached the capital Sań-do-pal-ri, where instantly abstracting the life of the demon-king named Yaksha Me-wal, and entering his body, the Guru reigns there supreme over the Rakshas, even up till the present day, and in perpetual youth is preaching there the doctrine of Lāmaism in a paradise which rivals that of Amitābha's western heaven of *Sukhāvatī*.

And notwithstanding his grotesque charlatanism and uncelibate life, he is deified and worshipped as the "second Buddha," and his image under "The eight worshipful Forms"[1] is found in every Tibetan temple of the old sect, as figured at page 25.

Thus established, and lavishly endowed, Lāmaism made steady progress, and was actively patronized by Thi-Sroṅ Detsan's successors for two generations.[2]

The eras of Lāmaism may be divided into (1) primitive or "Augustine" (from King Thi-Sroṅ Detsan's reign to the persecution), (2) mediæval, including the reformation, (3) modern Lāmaism, from the priest-kingship of the Dalai Lāma in the seventeenth century.

An interesting glimpse into the professed religion of the earlier period is given in the bilingual edict pillars "dô-ring," erected at Lhāsa in 822 A.D.,[3] in treaty with the Chinese. In the text of these edicts, which has been translated by Dr. Bushell,[4] occurs the following sentence: "They [? the Fan (Tibetan) and the Han (Chinese)] have looked up to the three precious ones, to all the holy saints, to the sun, moon, stars, and planets, and begged them to be their witnesses."

In the latter half of the ninth century[5] under king Ralpachan, the grandson of Thi-Sroṅ Detsan, the work of the translation of scriptures and the commentaries of Nāgārjuna, Aryadeva, Vasubandhu, etc., was actively prosecuted. Among the Indian translators employed by him were Jina Mitra, Sīlendrabodhi,[6] Surendrabodhi, Prajña-varman, Dāna-ṣila, and Bodhimitra, assisted by the Tibetans Pal-brtsegs, Ye-s'e-sde, Ch'os-kyi-Gyal-ts'an, and at least half of the two collections as we know them is the work

1 Guru ts'an gye. For description of these see p. 379.

2 Thi-Sroṅ Detsan died in 786 (CSOMA, *Gr.*, 183), and was succeeded by his son, Mu-thi tsan-po, who, on being poisoned by his mother soon after his accession, was succeeded by his brother (Sad-na-legs) under the same name (ROCKHILL, *Life*, 222), and he induced Kamalaṣila to return to Tibet and permanently reside in that country. This latter was succeeded by his son Ralpachan.

3 These monoliths are assigned by Tibetan tradition (as translated by SARAT., *J.A.S.B.*, 1881, p. 228) to Thi-Sroṅ Detsan's grandson, Ralpachan.

4 *Op. cit.*, 521.

5 According to Tibetan chronology; but the Chinese make Ralpachan's accession 816 A.D. (ROCKHILL'S *B.*, 223).

6 These two were pupils of Sthiramati (VASILIEV, *Tāranātha*, 320)

of their hands.[1] And he endowed most of the monasteries with state-lands and the right to collect tithes and taxes. He seems to have been the first Tibetan sovereign who started a regular record of the annals of his country, for which purpose he adopted the Chinese system of chronology.

His devotion to Buddhism appears to have led to his murder about 899,[2] at the instigation of his younger brother Laṅ Darma,—the so-called Julian of Lāmaism—who then ascended the throne, and at once commenced to persecute the Lāmas and did his utmost[3] to uproot the religion. He desecrated the temples and several monasteries, burned many of their books, and treated the Lāmas with the grossest indignity, forcing many to become butchers.

But Laṅ Darma's persecution was very mild for a religious one, and very short-lived. He was assassinated in the third year of his reign by a Lāma of Lha-luṅ named Pal-dorje, who has since been canonized by his grateful church, and this murderous incident forms a part of the modern Lāmaist masquerade.[4] This Lāma, to effect his purpose, assumed the guise of a strolling black-hat devil-dancer, and hid in his ample sleeves a bow and arrow. His dancing below the king's palace, which stood near the north end of the present cathedral of Lhāsa,[5] attracted the attention of the king, who summoned the dancer to his presence, where the disguised Lāma seized an opportunity while near the king to shoot him with the arrow, which proved almost immediately fatal. In the re-

BLACK-HAT DEVIL-DANCER.

---

[1] ROCK., *B.*, 225.

[2] The date is variously given, ranging from 838 (BUSHELL, 439 and 522) to 899 A.D. (CSOMA, *Gr.*, 183); 902 (SANANG SETSEN, 49); 914 (KÖPPEN, ii., 72).

[3] Actively aided by his minister, s*Bas-stay-snas*.

[4] See Chap. xx.

[5] And not on the Red Hill latterly named "*Potala.*"

sulting tumult the Lāma sped away on a black horse, which was tethered near at hand, and riding on, plunged through the Kyi river on the outskirts of Lhāsa, whence his horse emerged in its natural white colour, as it had been merely blackened by soot, and he himself turned outside the white lining of his coat, and by this stratagem escaped his pursuers.[1] The dying words of the king were: "Oh, why was I not killed three years ago to save me committing so much sin, or three years hence, that I might have rooted Buddhism out of the land?"

On the assassination of Laṅ Ḍarma the Lāmas were not long in regaining their lost ground.[2] Their party assumed the regency during the minority of Laṅ Darma's sons, and although Tibet now became divided into petty principalities, the persecution seems to have imparted fresh vigour to the movement, for from this time forth the Lāmaist church steadily grew in size and influence until it reached its present vast dimensions, culminating in the priest-kings at Lhāsa.

By the beginning of the eleventh century A.D., numerous Indian and Kashmīri monks were again frequenting Tibet.[3] And in 1038 A.D. arrived Atīṣa, the great reformer of Lāmaism,[4] whose biography is sketched in outline below, as he figures conspicuously in Lāmaism, and especially in its sects.

---

1 He hid in a cave near the monastery of Brag-Yal-pa, about one day's journey east of Lhāsa.

2 Sanang Setsen says (p. 51) that Laṅ Darma's son reigned without the Law.

3 Among whom were Smṛiti, who wrote a Tibetan vocabulary named "The Weapon of Speech"; Dharmapāla, who arrived in 1013 A.D., accompanied by Siddhapāla, Gunapala, and Prajñā-pāla from Eastern India; and Subhūti Ṣrī Ṣānti, who translated some of the Prajñā-pāramitā.

4 His legendary biography, attributed to his pupil Brom-ton, but apparently of later date (and probably written by the Dalai in the sixteenth century, as it credits Brom-ton with being Avalokita's incarnation), has been translated by SARAT in *Jour. Ind. Budd. Text Soc.*, 1893. I have also consulted the original. (Cf. also TĀRA. 241, 243; KÖPP., ii., 78, 79, 117, 127, 295; SCHL., 69, 136; PAND., No. 29.) Atīṣa's proper Indian name is Dīpaṅkara Ṣrī-jñāna, but he is usually called by the Lāmas *Jo-vo-rje-dpal-ldan* Atīṣa, or "The Illustrious Noble Lord Atisha." And he is held to be an incarnation of Mañjuṣrī, the Celestial Bodhisat of Wisdom; though this seems merely a pious way of stating that Atīṣa was *the* Mañjuṣrī of Tibet, or the most learned in scholastic and astrological lore of all the monks who had previously visited Tibet; as India, Nepal, and China already possessed their especial apotheosized wise man as a Mañjuṣrī incarnation. He was born in 980 A.D. (according to his Tibetan chronicles), of the royal family of Gaur at Vikramanipur (?), in Bengal, his father being named Kalyāṇa-ṣrī, and his mother Prabhāvati, and was ordained at

Atīṣa was nearly sixty years of age when he visited Tibet.[1] He at once started a movement which may be called the Lāmaist Reformation, and he wrote many treatises.[2]

ཇོ་བོ་ཆེན་པོ་དཔལ་ལྡན་ཨ་ཏི་ཤ

ATĪSA.

His chief disciple was Ḍom-ton,[3] the first hierarch of the new reformed sect, the Kadam-pa, which, three-and-a-half centuries later, became the Ge-lug-pa, now the dominant sect of Tibet, and the established church of the country.

Atīṣa's reformation resulted not only in the new sect, Kadam-pa, with which he most intimately identified himself, but it also initiated, more or less directly, the semi-reformed sects of Kar-gyu-pa and Sakya-pa, as detailed in the chapter on Sects.

The latter end of the eleventh century saw Lāmaism firmly

---

the Odantapuri Vihara. He underwent training under both Mahāyāna teachers and the Mahā Siddhī (grub-ch'en) or wizard-priests, his most notable masters being Chandrakirti, the Abbot of Suvarnadvīp, or Sudharmanagar, the "Chryse" of the ancients, near "Thaton" in Pegu, Mativitara of the Mahābodhi Vihara, and the Maha-ṣiddhi Nāro, who is especially related to the Kar-gyu-pa Sect. On starting for Tibet, he was a professor of the Vikramasila monastery in Magadha, and a contemporary of Nayapāla, son of King Mahīpāla.

[1] He visited Tibet by way of Ṅari K'or-sum in 1038 A.D. in the company of the Lāma Nag-tsho, and after starting what may be called the Reformed Lāmaism, died in the *s*Ñe-t'aṅ monastery, near Lhāsa, in 1052. It is stated that he came from Vikramasila at the invitation of the Tibetan King, named Lha Lāma Ye-shes-'od, but his route *viâ* Ṅari renders this unlikely, and this Lha Lāma seems to have been a petty chief of N.W. Tibet, who was captured about that time by the Nepalese.

[2] The following works by Atīṣa occur in mDo of bsTan 'gyur: 1, Bodhipatha pradīpa; 2, Caryā sangraha pradīpa; 3, Satya dvayāvatāra; 4, Madhyamopadesa; 5, Sangraha garbha; 6, Hridaya nischita; 7, Bodhisattva manyāvali; 8, Bodhisattva karmādi-margāvatāra; 9, Saranagatādesa; 10, Mahāyānapatha sādhana varna sangraha; 11, Mahāyānapatha sādhana sangraha; 12, Sûtrārtha samuchhayopadesa; 13, Dasakusala karmopadesa; 14, Karma Vibhanga; 15, Samādhi sambhara parivarta; 16, Lokottarasaptaka vidhi; 17, Guru Kriyākrama; 18, Chittotpāda samvara vidhi krama; 19, S'ikshá samucchaya abhi samaya, delivered by Ṣ'rī Dharmapāla, King of Suvarnadvipa to Dīpaṅkara and Kamala; 20, Vimala ratna lekhana, an epistle by Dīpaṅkara to Naya Pāla, King of Magadha by Atīṣa on his departure for Tibet.

[3] *Brom-ston.*

rooted, and its rival sects, favoured by their growing popularity and the isolation of Tibet, were beginning to form at Sakya and elsewhere strong hierarchies, which took much of the power out of the hands of the petty chiefs amongst whom Tibet was now parcelled out, and tended to still further open the country to Chinese and Mongol invasion.

There seems no evidence to support the assertion that this Lāmaist revival was determined by any great influx of Indian monks fleeing from persecution in India, as there is no record of any such influx about the time of the Muhammadan invasion of India.

In the second half of the thirteenth century, Lāmaism received a mighty accession of strength at the hands of the great Chinese emperor, Khubilai Khān. Tibet had been conquered by his ancestor, Jenghiz Khān,[1] about 1206 A.D., and Khubilai was thus brought into contact with Lāmaism. This emperor we know, from the accounts of Marco Polo and others, was a most enlightened ruler; and in searching about for a religion to weld together the more uncivilized portions of his mighty empire he called to his court the most powerful of the Lāmaist hierarchs, namely, the Saskya Grand Lāma, as well as representatives of the Christian and several other faiths, and he ultimately fixed upon Lāmaism, as having more in common with the Shamanist faiths already prevalent in China and Mongolia than had Confucianism, Muhammadanism, or Christianity.

His conversion to Buddhism is made miraculous. He is said to have demanded from the Christian missionaries, who had been sent to him by the pope, the performance of a miracle as a proof to him of the superiority of the Christian religion, while if they failed and the Lāmas succeeded in showing him a miracle, then he would adopt Buddhism. In the presence of the missionaries, who were unable to comply with Khubilai's demands, the Lāmas caused the emperor's wine-cup to rise miraculously to his lips, whereat the emperor adopted Buddhism; and the discomfited missionaries declared that the cup had been lifted by the devil himself, into whose clutches the king now had fallen.

Just as Charlemagne created the first Christian pope, so the

[1] The Tibetan accounts state that he was born in 1182 A.D., and was the son of the Mongol God (? deified ancestor) "The White *Gnam-t'e.*"

emperor Khubilai recognized[1] the Lāma of Saskya, or the Sakya Pandita, as head of the Lāmaist church, and conferred upon him temporary power as the tributary ruler of Tibet, in return for which favour he was required to consecrate or crown the Chinese emperors. And the succession in this hereditary primacy was secured to the Pandit's nephew, Lodoi Gyal-ts'an (or Matidhvaja), a young and able Lāma, who was given the title of Highness or Sublimity (*p'ags-pa*). Khubilai actively promoted Lāmaism and built many monasteries in Mongolia, and a large one at Pekin. Chinese history[2] attributes to him the organisation of civil administration in Tibet, though it would appear that he exerted his authority only by diplomacy through these spiritual potentates without any actual conquest by arms.

The Sakya pope, assisted by a staff of scholars, achieved the great work of translating the bulky Lāmaist canon (Kah-gyur) into Mongolian after its revision and collation with the Chinese texts. Indeed, the Lāmaist accounts claim for the Sakya Pope the invention of the Mongolian character, though it is clearly modelled upon the Syrian; and Syriac and nestorian missionaries are known to have worked in Mongolia long prior to this epoch.

Under the succeeding Mongol emperors, the Sakya primacy seems to have maintained much of its political supremacy, and to have used its power as a church-militant to oppress its rival sects. Thus it burned the great Kar-gyu-pa monastery of Dikung about 1320 A.D. But on the accession of the Ming dynasty in 1368 A.D. the Chinese emperors deemed it politic, while conciliating the Lāmas, as a body, by gifts and titles, to strike at the Sakya power by raising the heads of two other monasteries[3] to equal rank with it, and encouraged strife amongst them.

At the beginning of the fifteenth century a Lāma named Tsoṅ-K'a-pa re-organized Atīṣa's reformed sect, and altered its title to "The virtuous order," or *Ge-lug-pa*. This sect soon eclipsed all the others; and in five generations it obtained the priest-kingship of Tibet, which it still retains to this day. Its first Grand Lāma was Tsoṅ-K'a-pa's nephew, Geden-ḍub, with his succession based on the idea of re-incarnation, a theory

[1] In 1270 A.D.

[2] MARCO P., ii., 38.

[3] The Ka-gyupa, Dikung, and the Ka-dam-pa Ts'al.

which was afterwards, apparently in the reign of the fifth Grand Lāma, developed into the fiction of re-incarnated reflexes of the divine Bodhisat Avalokita, as detailed in the chapter on the Hierarchy.

In 1640, the Ge-lug-pa leapt into temporal power under the fifth Grand Lāma, the crafty Ṅag-waṅ Lô-zang. At the request of this ambitious man, a Mongol prince, Gusri Khan, conquered Tibet, and made a present of it to this Grand Lāma, who in 1650 was confirmed in his sovereignty by the Chinese emperor, and given the Mongol title of *Dalai*, or "(vast as) the Ocean." And on account of this title he and his successors are called by some Europeans "the *Dalai* (or *Tale*) *Lāma*," though this title is almost unknown to Tibetans, who call these Grand Lāmas "the great gem of majesty" (Gyal-wa Rin-po-ch'e).[1]

རྒྱལ་དབང་གྲུབ་ཆེན་པོ

THE FIRST DALAI LĀMA.

Lô-zāṅ Gya-ts'o or Gyal-wa ṅa-pa.[2]

This daring Dalai Lāma, high-handed and resourceful, lost no time in consolidating his rule as priest-king and the extension of his sect by the forcible appropriation of many monasteries of the other sects, and by inventing legends magnifying the powers of the Bodhisat Avalokita and posing himself as the incarnation of this divinity, the presiding Bodhisat of each world of re-birth, whom he also identified with the controller of metempsychosis, the dread Judge of the Dead before whose tribunal all mortals must appear.

Posing in this way as God-incarnate, he built[3] himself the huge palace-temple on the hill near Lhāsa, which he called Potala, after the mythic Indian residence of his divine prototype

---

[1] Cf. CSOMA, *Gr.*, 192 and 198; KÖPP., ii., 168, 235; *J.A.S.B.*, 1882, p. 27.

[2] After Pander.

[3] In 1643, CSOMA, *Gr.*, p. 190

Avalokita, "The Lord who looks down from on high," whose symbols he now invested himself with. He also tampered unscrupu-

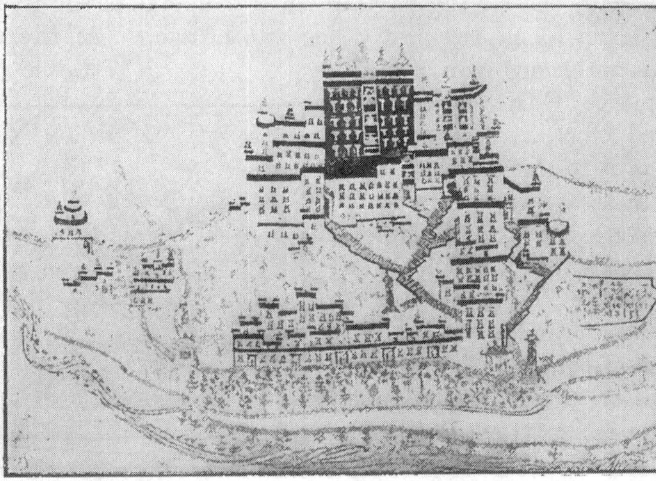

POTALA, THE PALACE OF THE DALAI LĀMA.
(From a native drawing.)

ously with Tibetan history in order to lend colour to his divine pretensions, and he succeeded perfectly. All the other sects of Lāmas acknowledged him and his successors to be of divine descent, the veritable Avalokita-in-the-flesh. And they also adopted the plan of succession by re-incarnate Lāmas and by divine reflexes. As for the credulous populace, they recognized the Dalai Lāma to be the rightful ruler and the existing government as a theocracy, for it flattered their vanity to have a deity incarnate as their king.

The declining years of this great Grand Lāma, Ṅag wañ, were troubled by the cares and obligations of the temporal rule, and his ambitious schemes, and by the intrigues of the Manchus, who sought the temporal sovereignty. On account of these political troubles his death was concealed for twelve years by the minister De-Si,[1] who is believed to have been his natural son. And the succeeding Grand Lāma, the sixth, proving hopelessly dissolute, he was executed at the instigation of the Chinese government,

[1] sDe-srid. CSOMA'S Gram., 191; GIORGI'S Alph.

which then assumed the suzerainty, and which has since continued to control in a general way the temporal affairs, especially its foreign policy,[1] and also to regulate more or less the hierarchal succession,[2] as will be referred to presently.

But the Ge-lug-pa sect, or the established church, going on the lines laid down for it by the fifth Grand Lāma, continued to prosper, and his successors, despite the presence of a few Chinese officials, are now, each in turn, the *de facto* ruler of Tibet, and recognized by the Lāmas of all denominations as the supreme head of the Lāmaist church.

In its spread beyond Tibet, Lāmaism almost everywhere exhibits the same tendency to dominate both king and people and to repress the national life. It seems now to have ceased extending, but shows no sign of losing hold upon its votaries in Tibet.

The present day distribution of Lāmaism extends through states stretching more or less continuously from the European Caucasus to near Kamschatka; and from Buriat Siberia down to Sikhim and Yun-nan. But although the area of its prevalence is so vast, the population is extremely sparse, and so little is known of their numbers over the greater part of the area that no trustworthy figures can be given in regard to the total number of professing Lāmaists.

The population of Tibet itself is probably not more than 4,000,000,[3] but almost all of these may be classed as Lāmaists, for although a considerable proportion of the people in eastern Tibet are adherents of the Bön, many of these are said to patronize the Lāmas as well, and the Bön religion has become assimilated in great part to un-reformed Lāmaism.[4]

---

[1] Thus it procured for Tibet satisfaction from the Gorkhas under Pṛithivī-nārāyan for their invasion of Western Tibet and sack of Tashi-lhunpo in 1768 (KIRKPATRICK's *Acct. of Nepal*, p. 268; BUCHANAN-HAMILTON, *Nepal*, p. 244), and the present seclusion of Tibet against Europeans is mainly due to Chinese policy.

[2] An interesting glimpse into the country of that period is got in the contemporary record of the friar Horace della Penna, translated into English by Markham (*op. cit.*, p. 320 *et seq.*)

[3] ROCKHILL, *L.*, p. 296, estimates it at 3,500,000.

[4] Though it must be remembered that Mr. Rockhill found a large tract of N.E. Tibet exclusively occupied by Bön-pa. In the north-eastern province of Gya-de, with about 50,000 people, between the Dang River and Chamdo, Mr. Rockhill found that the Bön-pa religion reigns supreme, and in order to save these people from persecution at the hands of the Lāmaist Government at Lhāsa, China itself supervises the administration of this province. And "all along the eastern borderland of Tibet from the

The European outpost of the Lāmaist Church, situated amid the Kālmuk Tartars on the banks of the Volga, has been described in some detail by Köppen.[1]

After the flight of the Torgots, about 12,000 cottages of the Kālmuk Tartars still remained in Russian territory, between the Don and the Yaik. Now they number at least 20,000, and contain more than 100,000 souls, of which by far the great majority retain the Lāmaist faith. Of course, since the flight, all intercourse with the priest-god at Lhāsa is strictly forbidden, nor are they allowed to accept from him any orders or patents, nor to send him any ambassadors or presents. Nevertheless, he gives them secret advice by oracle and otherwise, and maintains their religious enthusiasm. Thus, even now, he exercises an important influence on his pious flock on the Volga, so that they can be considered of the Lāmaist church, although the head Lāma (for the Kālmuks still call their head priest "Lāma") is sanctioned at present by the Russian government, and no longer by the Dalai Lāma.

Altogether, evidently for a reason not far to seek, the number of priests has greatly increased since their connection with Lhāsa has been cut off. Formerly the Dalai Lāma had also on the Volga a quite disproportionate number of bondsmen or Schabinären, whose contributions (taxes) went to Lhāsa; but since the flight of the Torgots the money remains there, and the Schabinärs of the remaining Ulusse have been divided amongst the several Churulls. These clergy also would appear to have developed extraordinary zeal, for in the year 1803 it was reported that the Kālmuk priests formed a tenth part of the whole population, that they perpetually enriched themselves at the expense of the people, that they meddled in everything, and received all the young men who were averse to labour at their proper calling, etc., etc.

Since 1838 the Russian government has succeeded, through the head Lāma Jambo Namka, in preventing in some measure these abuses, and severer laws were issued, especially against the

Kokonor to Yun-nan, it (the Bön-pa religion) flourishes side by side with the Lāmaist faith . . . . and in all the southern portions of Tibet, not under the direct rule of Lhāsa, its Lāmaseries may be found. So it seems that this faith obtains in over two-thirds of Tibet, and that it is popular with at least a fifth of the Tibetan-speaking tribes."—*Geographical Jour.*, May, 1894.

[1] *Op. cit.*, ii., 385 *et seq.*

priests interfering in civil affairs; also several hundred worthless priests were expelled.

A more precise census of the Russian empire gives the number of Lāmaist people at 82,000 Kirghis, and 119,162 Kālmuks; while the Buriats in Siberia, near the Baikal lake, are estimated at about 190,000.[1]

Pallas[2] calculated when he visited the Kālmuk country last century that there was one Lāma to every one hundred and fifty or two hundred tents.

In China, except for a few monasteries at Pekin, etc., and these mostly of Mongol monks, the Lāmaist section of Chinese Buddhists seems confined to the extreme western frontier, especially the former Tibetan province of Amdô. Probably the Lāmaists in China number no more than about 1,000,000.

Mongolia may be considered almost wholly Lāmaist, and its population is about 2,000,000. Its Buddhism became extinct on the expulsion of the race from China in 1368; and its reconversion to Lāmaism did not occur till 1577, as detailed in the Mongol history by Sanang Setzen,[3] who was a great grandson of one of the chief agents in this movement. Some details of its history are cited in connection with the Tāranātha Grand Lāma in the chapter on hierarchy. The number of Lāmas are estimated[4] at 10,000 in Urgya in north Mongolia, 2,000 in Tchaitschi in south Mongolia, 2,000 in Altan Züma, and 2,000 in Kukukhotum.

Manchuria is largely Lāmaist, with a population of about 3,000,000.

Ladāk, to which Aṣoka missionaries are believed to have penetrated, is now entirely Lāmaist in its form of Buddhism, and this is the popular religion. Its history is given by Cunningham[5] and Marx.[6] The population was estimated by Cunningham[7] at 158,000 and the Lāmas at 12,000, giving one Lāma to thirty laity.

---

1 KÖPPEN, *Bulletin Hist. Phil. de l'Acad. de St. Petersburg*, ix., p. 335; KEITH JOHNSTON'S *Atlas*, p. 34. Schlagintweit says, *op. cit.*, p. 12, that among the Buriats Buddhism is still extending.

2 *Reisen*, i., 557 (French ed.).

3 *Op. cit.*

4 KÖPPEN, i., p. 381, chiefly based on Huc's data.

5 *Ladāk*, p. 357, *et. seq.*

6 *J.A.S.B.*, *loc. cit.*

7 *Op. cit.*, p. 287.

Recent estimates place the population at about 178,000. Spiti in 1845 had a population of 1,414, and the Lāmas were one hundred and ninety-three, or about one to seven.[1]

The vernacular history of its introduction into eastern Turkestan or Khoten (Tib., *Li-yul*) has been translated by Rockhill.[2]

In Nepal, the number of Buddhists grows every year less under the active proselytizing Hindū influences of the Ghorka Government, which places disabilities upon professing Buddhists. But the majority of the Nepalese Buddhists are now Lāmaist.

Bhotan[3] is wholly Lāmaist, both in its religion and temporal government. Its population has been given at about 40,000 to 50,000 families, or a total of 145,200.[4] But although it is believed to be almost as priest-ridden as Sikhim, the number of its priests is estimated[5] only at about 5,000, distributed in the six districts as follows: In Tassisudon 500, in Punakha also 500, in Paro 300, in Tongso also 300, in Tagna 250, and in Andipur (or Wandipur) 250, in round sum 2,000. Then come 3,000 Lāmas who do not reside in cloisters, but are employed as officers, making a total of 5,000, besides which there are a lot of hermits and nuns.

In regard to Sikhim, where Lāmaism is the state religion, I have elicited from original documents and local Lāmas full details of the mode in which Lāmaism was introduced into that country. Some of these are worth recording as showing in a credible manner the mode in which Lāmaism was propagated there, and it was probably introduced in a similar manner into several of the other areas in which it is now prevalent.

The Lāmas and laity of Sikhim[6] and Tibet implicitly believe that St. Padma-sambhava (Guru Rim-bo-ch'e), the founder of Lāmaism, visited Sikhim during his journeyings in Tibet and its western borderlands; and although he left no converts and erected no buildings, he is said to have hid away in caves many holy books for the use of posterity, and to have personally consecrated every sacred spot in Sikhim.

---

[1] Major Hay, *J.A.S.B.*, xix., 437.

[2] *Life*, etc., p. 230, *et. seq.* See also Dr. Huth's German translation of the *Hor* history.

[3] The word is Sanskritic, and its full form is "*Bhotanta*," or "the end of *Bhot* or Tibet" (cf. Hodgs., *L.*, i., p. 30).

[4] Pemberton's *Mission*, p. 151.

[5] Köppen, ii., p. 363.

[6] The annexed illustration is from a photograph by Mr. Hoffmann.

The authorities for such beliefs are, however, merely the accounts given in the works of the patron saint of Sikhim, Lha-tsün Ch'em-bo, and the fictitious "hidden revelations" of the *Tertöns*, all of which are unreliable. And Lha-tsün rather overdoes it by asserting that the Guru visited Sikhim a hundred times.

Sikhim seems to have been unknown to Tibetans previous to the latter half of the sixteenth century A.D., and Lha-tsün Ch'em-bo's own account of his attempts to enter Sikhim testify to the prevailing ignorance in regard to it, owing to its almost impenetrable

SOME SIKHIM LĀMAS.

Lāma Ugyen Gya-ts'o. Mongol Lāma She-rab. A Kar-gyu Lāma. A Karma Lāma.

mountain and icy barriers. And the *Tan-yik Ser-t'en*, which gives the fullest account of St. Padma's wanderings, and considered the most reliable authority, seems to make no mention of Sikhim. It is extremely improbable that the Guru ever entered Sikhim, especially as, as we have seen, he certainly did not pass through that country either when going to or returning from Tibet.

In keeping, however, with the legendary accounts of his visit, it is alleged by Sikhimite Lāmas that their Lord St. Padma entered the country by the "Lordly pass" *Jo-la* (*Ang.*, Cho-la) and on the east side of the pass is pointed out a rock on which he sat down, called *Z'u-ti*, or throne,[1] and near the pass a spot named *Sinmoi gyip-tsu*,[2] where he surprised a party of female devils preparing to cook their food : here are pointed out two masses of columnar rock alleged to be two of the stones of the tripod used to support the cooking-pot of these demons. And he is said to have returned to Tibet by way of the *Je-lep* pass, resting *en route* on the *Ku-phu* and creating the *Tuko La* by "tearing" up the rock to crush an obnoxious demon.

The introduction of Lāmaism into Sikhim certainly dates from the time of Lha-tsün's arrival there about the middle of the seventeenth century A.D. By this time Lāmaism had become a most powerful hierarchy in Tibet, and was actively extending its creed among the Himalayan and central Asian tribes.

Three generations of Tibetan colonists from the adjoining Chumbi valley had settled on the eastern border of Sikhim, near Gang-tok. And it is highly probable that these Tibetan settlers were privy to the entry of the Lāmas; as it is traditionally reported that the ancestor of that Sikhimite-Tibetan, who was promptly elected king of Sikhim, by Lha-tsün, was a *protége* and kinsman of the Sakya Grand Lāma. And Lha-tsün Ch'em-bo seems to have approached Sikhim *viâ* Sakya, and his incarnations subsequently appeared in the neighbourhood of Sakya, and even now his spirit is believed to be incarnate in the body of the present Sakya Lāma.

Lha-tsün was a native of Kongbu, in the lower valley of the Tsang-po (Brahmaputra), which has a climate and physical appearance very similar to Sikhim, and teems with traces of St. Padmasambhava, "discovered" by celebrated Lāmas, and it had been a happy hunting ground for the Tertöns, or discoverers of the fictitious treatises called "hidden revelations." Arriving, then, in a country so like his own, and having the virgin soil of Sikhim to work upon, Lha-tsün seems to have selected the most romantic spots and clothed them in suitable legendary dress in keeping with his ingenious discovery of St. Padma's previous visits. And to support his statements he also discovered that his own advent as the apostle of Sikhim had been foretold in detail, nine hundred years before, by the Guru himself, in the revelation entitled

[1] bz'ugs khri.

[2] Srin-mohi rgyib gtsug.

"The prophetic mirror of Sikhim."[1] He seems to have been a man of considerable genius, with a lively sense of the picturesque; and he certainly left his mark on his adopted country of Sikhim, where his name is now a household word.

The traditional account of his entry to Sikhim associates with him two other Lāmas, to wit, a Kar-tok-pa and a Ṅa-dak-pa; but they play an inconspicuous part in the work of introducing Lāmaism, and it is extremely doubtful whether any representative of these Ñiṅ-ma sub-sects arrived in Sikhim at so early a period.

As Lha-tsün is so intimately identified with Sikhim Lāmaism, being its *de facto* founder, it is desirable here to give a summary of his life as extracted from the local histories.

LIFE OF ST. LHA-TSÜN, THE PATRON SAINT OF SIKHIM.

Lha-tsün Ch'em-bo[2] is a title meaning "The great Reverend God." His ordinary religious name is *Kun-zaṅ nam-gyé*,[3] or "The entirely victorious Essence of Goodness." He is also known by the title of *Lha-tsün nam-kha Jig-med*,[4] or "The Reverend God who fears not the sky," with reference to his alleged power of flying. And he is sometimes called *Kusho Dsog-ch'en Ch'embo*, or "The great Honourable Dsog-c'en"—*Dsog-ch'en*, literally "The Great End," being the technical name for the system of mystical insight of the Ñiṅ-mapa, and *Kusho* means "the honourable."

He was born in the fire-bird year of the tenth of the sixty-year cycles, corresponding to 1595 A.D., in the district of Kongbu, in south-eastern Tibet. Having spent many years in various monasteries and in travelling throughout Tibet and Sikhim, he ultimately, in the year 1648, arrived in Lhāsa, and obtained such great repute by his learning that he attracted the favourable notice of Ṅag-waṅ, the greatest of the Grand Lāmas, who shortly afterwards became the first Dalai Lāma. Indeed, it is alleged that it was mainly through the special instruction given by Lha-tsün to the Grand Lāma that the latter was so favourably treated by the Chinese emperor and confirmed in the temporal rule of Tibet.

The detailed account of the saint's meeting with the Grand Lāma is worth citing in illustration of the curious mixture of the crude and the marvellous which make up the bulk of these indigenous narratives. In

---

1 *Den-joṅ Lungten Sel-wai Meloṅ.*

2 *Chhem-bo* is the Sikhimite mode of pronouncing "Ch'en-po."

3 *Kun-*bzaṅ-*rnam-rgyal.*

4 *lha-*btsun *nam* mk'*ah 'jigs-med.*

the year previous to that on which the fifth Grand Lāma went to China, which Csoma gives[1] as 1649 A.D., the Grand Lāma, while in his palace at Potala told his attendants, by inspiration, that a sage would that day visit him, and should be admitted to his presence. Lha-tsün, arriving at the site now named Pargo-K'aliṅ, immediately below Potala—the Lāmaist Vatican—blew loudly a *k'āliṅ*, or trumpet of human thigh-bone;[2] but the castle guard, in ignorance of who the

MENDICANT LĀMA BLOWING THIGH-BONE TRUMPET.

man really was, seized him and tied him to the Dô-ring monolith in the neighbourhood, as a punishment for daring to trumpet so close to the castle. The saint, bound in this way, shook the whole hill of Potala, and so his arrival was brought to the notice of the Grand

---

1 *Gr.*, p. 190.

2 The illustration is from a photo by Mr. Hoffmann.

Lāma, who ordered his instant release and admission. On coming into the presence of the Grand Lāma he walked boldly up and struck the latter with his fist and then vomited before him, much to the astonishment of the courtier Lāmas. The Saint then explained: "You are shortly going to China; on the way a great danger besets you, but my striking you has rid you of that danger. In China you will find yourself in great peril some day; then consult this paper I now give you, and you will be relieved. My vomiting in your presence means that you will ultimately be invested with great power and riches through me." The dilemma here prophesied was a query by the Chinese emperor regarding the "essence of the rainbow colour,"[1] which quite confounded the Grand Lāma, till he, remembering the episode with the Saint, consulted the paper and found full information noted therein, and having completely satisfied the emperor, he received great honour and riches. The Grand Lāma, on his return from China, in gratitude for services rendered, offered Lha-tsün much treasure, which the Saint, however, refused.

Previous to his visit to Lhāsa, it is said that the Saint, accompanied by a few disciples, journeyed to the south-west of Tibet, saying: "According to the prophecy of Guru Rim-bo-ch'e, I must go and open the northern gate of the hidden country of the rice-valleys—De-mo-jong,[2] *i.e.*, Sikhim, and I must develop that country religiously." He then proceeded by way of Tashi-lhunpo and Sakya to Zar, a short distance to the north of Tashi-rabkha near the Nepal frontier, where he then, or afterwards, founded a monastery.

He then attempted to enter Sikhim by way of Dsong-ri (Jongri), but could find no path, and remained many days in a cave named *Ñam-gah ts'al*,[3] "the very pleasant grove," near *Kaṅ-la naṅ-ma*. There "the everlasting summit of the five repositories (of snow)," the mountain god, Kaṅ-ch'en dsö-ṅa[4] transformed himself into a wild goose and conversed with the sage; and here, "according to the prophecy of Guru Rim-boch'e," he composed[5] the book named "the complete Book of Worship and offerings for Kaṅ ch'en dsö-ṅa.[6]

At this time another Lāma of the *Kar-tok-pa* sub-sect came by Kangla Nangma searching for a path into Sikhim, and also tried without success the sPreu-gyab-tak (*i.e.*, "Monkey-back rock," with reference to its semblance to a monkey sitting with hands behind back), and Dsong-ri, and the western shoulder of sKam-pa Khab-rag—a ridge of "Kabru," which runs down to the Rāthong river. He then arrived at the cave of "the very pleasant grove," and met the Saint, who told him that as he was not destined to open the northern gate, he should go round and try the western.

Then Lha-tsün, traversing the Kangla Nangma and finding no road beyond the cave of Skam-pa Kha-bruk, flew miraculously to the upper

1 'D*sah ts'on sñiṅ* po.

2 *bras-bmo-ljoṅs*.

3 m*ñam* d*gah-ts'al*.

4 m*dsod*-l*ṅa* r*tag-rtse*.

5 "r*tsom*" is the word used.

6 *gaṅs-ch'en* m*dsod*-l*ṅa* m*ch'od* s*prin* las g*nas-yoṅ dsog*.

part of "Kabru" (24,000 feet), and there blew his kang-ling, and after an absence of two weeks flew down to where his servants were collected and guided them by a road *viâ* Dsongri to Norbu-gang, in Sikhim.

Here soon after arrived two other Ṅiṅ-ma Lāmas. By "the western gate" of Single La came the Kar-tok-pa Lāma above mentioned, named "The Great Soul,"[1] and a Lāma of the Ṅa-dak-pa sub-sect, named The Great Sage,[2] who had opened "the southern gate" by way of Darjiling and Namchi respectively. The place where these three Lāmas met was then called by the Lepchas *Yok-sam*, which means "the three superior ones or noblemen," a literal translation of "the three Lāmas."

The three Lāmas held here a council at which Lha-tsün said: "We three Lāmas are in a new and irreligious country. We must have a 'dispenser of gifts'[3] (*i.e.*, a king) to rule the country on our behalf." Then the Ṅa-dak-pa Lāma said: "I am descended from the celebrated Tertön Ṅa-dak Nan-rél, who was a king; I should therefore be the king." While the Kar-tok-pa Lāma declared: "As I too am of royal lineage I have the right to rule." Then Lha-tsün said: "In the prophecy of Guru Rim-bo-ch'e it is written that four noble brothers shall meet in Sikhim and arrange for its government. We are three of these come from the north, west, and south. Towards the east, it is written, there is at this epoch a man named P'ün-ts'ok, a descendant of brave ancestors of Kham in Eastern Tibet. According, therefore, to the prophecy of the Guru we should invite him." Two messengers were then dispatched to search for this P'ün-ts'ok. Going towards the extreme east near Gangtok they met a man churning milk and asked him his name. He, without replying, invited them to sit down, and gave them milk to drink. After they were refreshed, he said his name was P'ün-ts'ok. He was then conducted to the Lāmas, who coronated him by placing the holy water-vase on his head and anointed him with the water; and exhorting him to rule the country religiously, they gave him Lha-tsün's own surname of Nam-gyé[4] and the title of "religious king." P'ün-ts'ok Nam-gyé was at this time aged thirty-eight years, and he became a Lāma in the same year, which is said to have been 1641 A.D.

Lha-tsün then spent the greater part of the rest of his life in Sikhim, exploring its caves and mountain recesses, composing its Lāmaist legends, and fixing sites for temples and monasteries. He first of all built a hut at Dub-de, which afterwards became the monastery of that name. And he is believed to have built rude shrines at Tashiding, Pemiongchi, and Sang-ṅa-ch'ö-ling; though others assert that Tashiding was first occupied by the original Ṅa-dak-pa Lāma.

In appearance Lha-tsün is usually represented as seated on a leo-

---

[1] *Sems dpah ch'en-po.*
[2] *Rig-'dsin ch'en-po.*
[3] s*byin-dag.*
[4] r*nam-rgyal.*

pard-skin mat with the right leg hanging down and his body almost bare—one of his titles is *He-ru-ka-pa*, which means "unclad." His complexion is of a dark blue hue. Otherwise he is somewhat like his prototype Guru Rim-bo-ch'e. A chaplet of skulls encircles his brow. In his left hand is a skull cup filled with blood, and a trident topped with human heads rests in front of the left shoulder. The right hand is in a teaching attitude.

He is believed to be the incarnation of the great Indian teacher Bhīma Mitra. And he himself is held to have been subsequently incarnated twice as a Sikhim Lāma, the last re-incarnation being *Jik mi Pa-wo*, born at Ok-ja-ling near Sakya, who built the present monastery of Pemiongchi.

I cannot ascertain the place of his death or what became of his body, but he is currently reported to have died in Sikhim of fever contracted during a visit to India. The dark livid hue of his skin is said to refer to his death from malignant fever. His chief object in visiting India was, according to a popular saying, to obtain a rare variety of ruddy leopard-skin (the *sala* leopard) which is highly prized by ascetics as a mat.[1]

All his clothing and personal effects are carefully treasured in Sikhim and worshipped as most sacred relics. They were all stored at Pemiongchi monastery until the Gorkha invasion of last century, when, for greater safety, most of them were taken to the remote Tô-lung monastery. At Pemiongchi are kept one set of his full dress robes after the style of Guru Rim-bo-ch'e, including hat and boots, his hand-drum, bell, and *dorje*, and a miraculous *p'urbu* dagger for stabbing the demons. These objects are only shown at Pemiongchi on special occasions to wealthy worshippers, and they are highly celebrated as a certain cure for barrenness. Couples afflicted in this way, and who can afford the necessary expense, have a preliminary worship conducted in the Pemiongchi chapel, lasting one or two days. Then the box containing the holy relics is brought forth and ceremoniously opened, and each article is placed on the heads of the suppliant pair, the officiating priest repeating meanwhile the charm of his own tutelary deity. Of the marvellous efficacy of this procedure numerous stories are told. And should two sons result, one of them is certainly dedicated to the Church.

Subsequent to Lha-tsün Ch'em-bo's death in the latter end of the seventeenth century, Lāmaism steadily progressed in Sikhim till latterly monks and monasteries filled the country. The list and detailed descripiton of these are given in the next chapter under the heading of Monasteries. What civilization and literature the Sikhimites now possess they owe to Lāmaism, and the Lepcha alphabet too was derived from the Tibetan.

[1] *Sa gya-gar-tu p'yin ba, don-gsah lai pags-pa.*

The religions displaced by Lāmaism were the Pön (Bön), which is usually identified with Taouism, and the earlier animistic and fairy worship of the Lepchas, which can scarcely be called a religion. Numerous traces of both of these primitive faiths are to be found incorporated in Sikhim Lāmaism, which owes any special features that it possesses to the preponderance of these two elements.

Only two sects of Lāmas are established in Sikhim, namely, the Ñiṅ-ma-pa and the Kar-gyu-pa as represented by the Karma-pa. There are no Duk-pa monasteries in Sikhim, nor does there seem ever to have been any.

The Lāmas number nearly one thousand, and are very numerous in proportion to the Buddhist population of the country. In 1840[1] the Lepchas and Bhotiyas of Sikhim were estimated at 3,000 and 2,000 respectively, but Mr. White, in his census of Sikhim in March, 1891, gives the population roughly as :—

Lepchas	5,800
Bhotiyas	4,700
Nepalese, etc.	19,500
	30,000

As the Nepalese, who are of very recent immigration, are all professing Hindūs, the Lāmas are now dependent on the Bhotiyas and Lepchas for support; and we thus get a proportion of one Lāmaist priest to every ten or eleven of the indigenous population. But this does not represent the full priest-force of those two races, as it takes no count of the numerous devil-dancers and Lepcha priests patronized both by Bhotiyas and Lepchas.

In British Sikhim and the Kalim-pong section of British Bhotan, the Lāmaists numbered in the census of 1891 40,520, of which 3,657 were resident in the town of Darjiling.[2]

There is no sign of any decrease of Lāmaism in Sikhim, although large numbers of Hindūized Nepalese have lately been introduced into the country, and the government is no longer in

[1] Dr. CAMPBELL in *The Oriental*, p. 13.

[2] "Census of 1891 Rept.," p. 47. The total Buddhists in Bengal, including a few thousands of Burmese convicts in Bengal jails, numbered 189,122.

the hands of Lāmas. Its Lāmaism is so deeply rooted that, in the absence of any actively anti-Buddhist policy such as has operated in Nepal, it is unlikely to be much affected by the recent political changes, at least for many years to come.

TASHIDING MONASTERY
(in Sikhim).

IV.

THE SECTS OF LĀMAISM.

THE light shed by the lamp of Lāmaism, like that of most other religions, has been broken into variegated fragments by the prisms of later priests.

No sects appear to have existed prior to Laṅ-Darma's persecution, nor till more than a century and a half later. The sectarial movement seems to date from the Reformation started by the Indian Buddhist monk Atīṣa, who, as we have seen, visited Tibet in 1038 A.D.[1]

Atīṣa, while clinging to Yoga and Tāntrism, at once began a reformation on the lines of the purer Mahāyāna system, by enforcing celibacy and high morality, and by deprecating the general practice of the diabolic arts. Perhaps the time was now ripe for the reform, as the Lāmas had become a large and influential body, and possessed a fairly full and scholarly translation of the bulky Mahāyāna Canon and its Commentaries, which taught a doctrine very different from that then practised in Tibet.

A glance at the annexed "Genealogical Tree of Lāmaist Sects" will show that Atīṣa was the only profound reformer of Lāmaism.

The first of the reformed sects and the one with which Atīṣa most intimately identified himself was called the Kah-dam-pa,[2] or "those bound by the orders (commandments)"; and it ultimately, three and a half centuries later, in Tsoṅ K'apa's hands, became less ascetic and more highly ritualistic under the title of "The Virtuous Style," *Ge-lug-pa*, now the dominant sect in Tibet, and the Established Church of Lāmaism.

---

[1] Part of this chapter appeared in the *Asiatic Quarterly* for January, 1894.

[2] *b*Kah-*g*dams-pa.

GENEALOGICAL TREE OF LAMAIST SECTS.

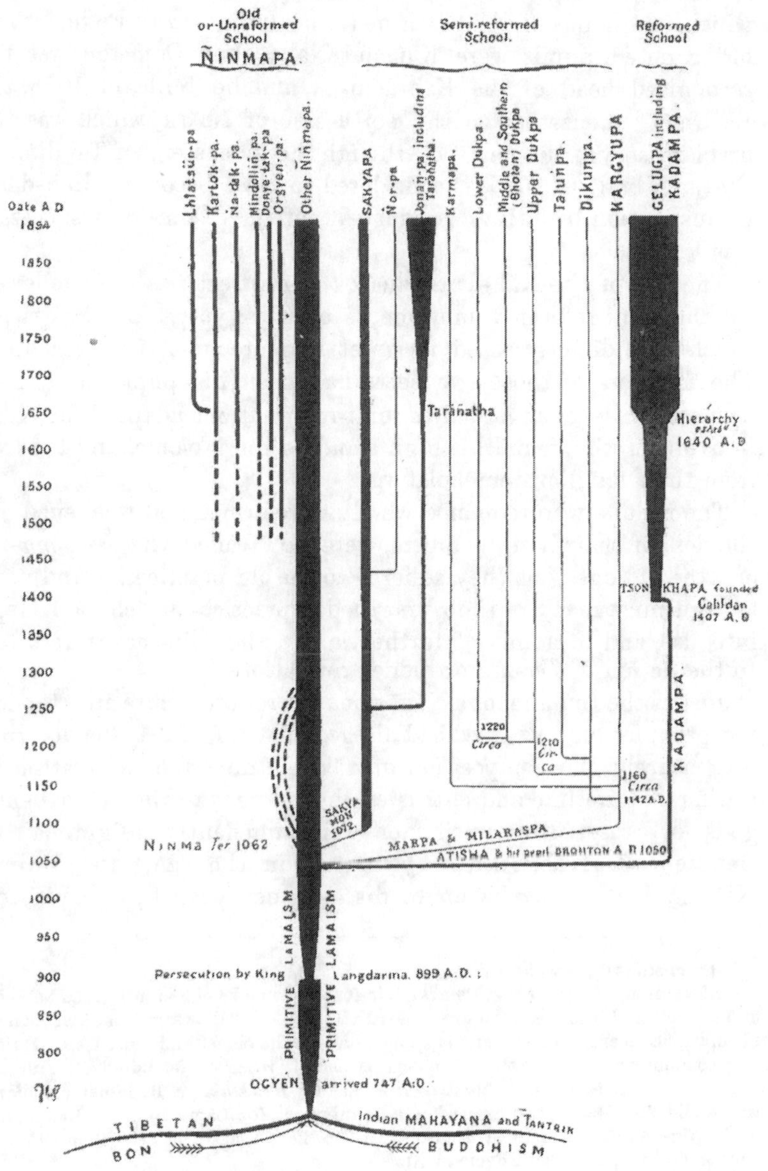

Atīṣa's chief Tibetan disciple was Ḍom-ton,[1] or "Dom Bakshi,"[2] to whom he taught the mystic Mahāyāna and Tāntrik doctrines which he himself had learned in India and Pegu. Two other noted pupils were K'u and Nak; but Ḍom-ton was the recognized head of the Kah-dam-pa, and he built, in 1058, the Ra-Deng[3] monastery to the north-east of Lhāsa, which was the first lāmasery of the new sect, though the monastery of T'ö-diṅ,[4] in Pu-rang, built in 1025, is considered to have become a Kah-dam-pa institution by Atīṣa's residence therein. Ḍom-ton's successor was Poṭova.

The rise of the Kāh-dam-pa (*Ge-lug-pa*) sect was soon followed by the semi-reformed movements of Kar-gyu-pa and Sakya-pa, which were directly based in great measure on Atīṣa's ṭeaching. The founders of those two sects had been his pupils, and their new sects may be regarded as semi-reformations adapted for those individuals who found his high standard too irksome, and too free from their familiar demonolatry.

The residue who remained wholly unreformed and weakened by the loss of their best members, were now called the *Ñiṅ-ma-pa* or "the old ones," as they adhered to the old practices. And now, to legitimize many of their unorthodox practices which had crept into use, and to admit of further laxity, the Ñiṅ-ma-pa resorted to the fiction of *Ter-ma* or hidden revelations.

Just as the Indian monk Nāgārjuna in order to secure an orthodox reception for his new creed had alleged that the Mahāyāna doctrine was entirely the composition of Ṣākya Muni, who had written it during his lifetime and entrusted the volumes to the Nāga demigods for preservation until men were sufficiently enlightened to comprehend so abstruse a system, so in the same way several Niṅ-ma Lāmas now began to discover new gospels, in caves and

[1] 'Brom-ston rGyal-wahi 'Byuṅ-*gnas*.

[2] *Bakshi* is a general term in Central Asia for those monks called in Tibetan Lob-pön, or Teacher; and it is used by Marco Polo (*Yule*, i., 305). Pallas says it is Mongolian for sTon, which means "Guide," and is applied only to the oldest and most learned priest of a community. But the title sTon (-pa) is usually reserved for Buddha. Yule and others believe it to be probably a corruption of "*Bhikhshu*," a Buddhist mendicant monk, and Yule shows it to be used as an equivalent for Lāma by Rashiduddin, and in the Ain-i-Akbāri. Possibly it is also related to the "Abassi" of Friar Odoric (MARKHAM, p. xlvi.). *Conf.* also KÖPPEN, ii., 105.

[3] *Rva-sgren*.

[4] m*T'o-ldiṅ*.

elsewhere, which they alleged were hidden gospels of the Guru, Saint Padma. And these so-called "revealers," but really the *composers* of these *Ter-ma* treatises, also alleged as a reason for their ability to discover these hidden gospels, that each of them had been, in a former birth, one or other of the twenty-five disciples of St. Padma.

Table Showing
DESCENT AND INTER-RELATIONS
OF
THE CREEDS OF THE REFORMED LĀMAIST SECTS.

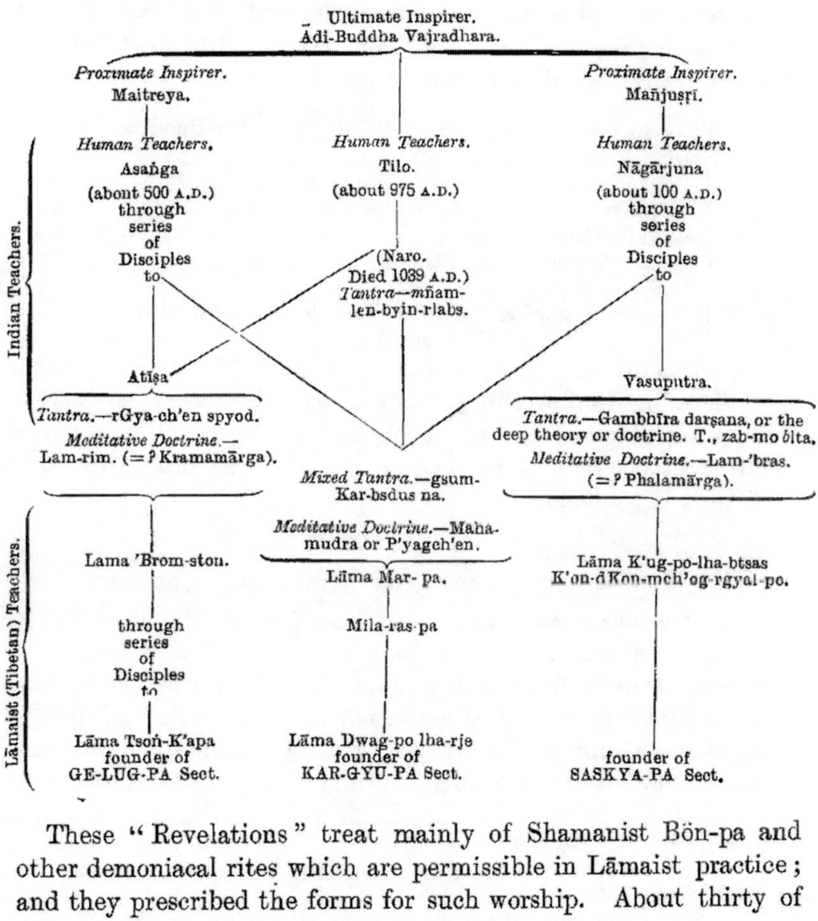

These "Revelations" treat mainly of Shamanist Bön-pa and other demoniacal rites which are permissible in Lāmaist practice; and they prescribed the forms for such worship. About thirty of these revelations have been discovered; but as the number has been oracularly fixed at one hundred and eight, future contingencies are well provided for. These "Revelations," relaxing still further the Lāmaist obligations, were eagerly accepted by most Lāmas, and they play an important part in the schisms which subsequently occurred in both old and reformed sects. Indeed, many of the sub-sects differ from their parent sects merely in having adopted a different *Ter-ma* work as an ordinary code of demoniacal worship.

The sectarian distinctions are of a creedal character, entailing different ritualistic and other practices, and expressed by a difference in dress and symbols. The creedal differences may be categorically classed under the heads of—

1. The personality of the primordial deity or Ādi-Buddha;
2. Special source of divine inspiration;
3. The saintly transmitters of this inspiration;
4. Meditative doctrine or system of mystical insight;[1]
5. Special Tāntra-revelation.
6. Personal Tutelary—a Tāntrik demoniacal Buddha of Sivaist type;
7. Religious "Guardian"-demon, usually of Tibetan type.

In considering the sects individually, let us look first at the sect forming the Established Church—the Ge-lug-pa—as it represents the oldest of the sects, the Kah-dam-pa, and is the purest and most powerful of all, having now the temporal government of Tibet in its hands.

The Ge-lug-pa Sect, or Established Church.

The Ge-lug-pa arose at the beginning of the fifteenth century A.D. as a regeneration of the Kah-dam-pa by Tsoṅ-K'a-pa or Lô-zaṅ-tak-pa[2] or Je-Rim-po-ch'e, though he is better known to Europeans by his territorial title of Tsoṅ-K'a-pa, that is, "Native of the Onion Country," the district of his birth, in the province of Amdo, now within the border of China.[3]

[1] *l*Ta-wa. Skt., *Darṣana.*

[2] b*Lo-bzan tak-po* (Cf. Köppen, ii., 18). O.M., 115; *J.A.S.B.*, 1882, p. 53-57; Pand., No. 41; Howorth, *op. cit.*

[3] He was born in 1355-57 at Kum-bum (see its photograph at page 280).

He was probably, as Huc notes,[1] influenced by the Roman Catholic priests, who seem to have been settled near the place of his birth. Huc's tradition runs that Tsoṅ K'a-pa had intercourse with a stranger from the West with a long nose and piercing eyes, who is believed to have been a Christian missionary. He studied at Zhar-Ch'uṅ, in Amdo, and thereafter at Saskya, DiRung, and Lhāsa. He wrote many books,[2] and most of the extant sacerdotal manuals of the Ge-lug-pa sect are attributed to him. He died (or, as is popularly believed, ascended to Heaven[3]) in 1417, and was canonized as an incarnation of Mañjuṣrī (or, as some say, Amitābha, or Vajrapāṇi). And by the Ge-lug-pa he is considered superior even to St. Padma and Atīṣa, and is given the chief place in most of their temples. His image is placed above, and usually between, those of the dual Grand Lāmas—the Dalai and Pan-ch'en—and, like these, he is given the title of *Gyal-wa*, or The *Jina* or Victor. His image is also worn as a charm in amulet boxes.

TSOṄ-K'A-PA.

rGgyal-ts'ab-rje (disciple). mK'as-grub-rje (disciple).
Vajra-bhairava (tutelary). A votary.

Tsoṅ-K'a-pa received the traditions of the Kah-dam-pa sect from the Lāma Ch'os *skyabs-bzaṅ*-po, the seventy-eighth abbot in succession from Ḍom-ton.

Unlike Atīṣa, Tsoṅ-K'a-pa was an ardent proselytizer, and

1 *Travels in Tartary*, etc., HAZLETT's trans., ii., 48.

2 Chief of which was *The Gradual Way* (*Lām-rim*).

3 His *ascension* is celebrated during the Lāmaist festival of Lamps.

spent most of his strength in organization. He collected the scattered members of the Kah-dam-pa from their retreats, and housed them in monasteries, together with his new followers, under rigid discipline, setting them to keep the two hundred and thirty-five *Vinaya* rules,[1] and hence obtaining for them the title

GE-LUG-PA MONK AND ATTENDANT.

of *Vinaya*-keepers or "*Dul-wa Lāmas.*" He also made them carry a begging-bowl, anardha-chuna,[2] prayer-carpet,[3] and wear patched robes[4] of a yellow colour, after the fashion of the Indian mendicant monks. And he attracted followers by instituting a

[1] Including retirement during Lent for meditation, etc.

[2] The *zla-gam* or crescentic cope or cape.

[3] *g*ding-wa.

[4] dras-drubs. See detailed description at p. 200.

highly ritualistic service, in part apparently borrowed from the Christian missionaries, who undoubtedly were settled at that time in Tsoṅ-K'a, the province of his early boyhood in Western China. He gave the hat named *pän-ssa-sne-riṅ*, or the "Pandit's long-tailed cap"; and as it was of a yellow colour like their dress, and the old Lāmaist body adhered to their red hat, the new sect came to be popularly called the *S'a-ser* or "Yellow-cap," in contradistinction to the *S'a-mar* or "Red-cap" and their more aboriginal Bön-pa co-religionists the *S'a-nak* or "Black-caps."[1]

This seems to be the origin of the sect-titles depending on the colour of the cap. The Kah-dam-pa are said to have worn red caps, and certainly the extant pictures of Atīṣa and other Kah-dam-pa Lāmas give them red caps.

Tsoṅ-K'a-pa named his own monastery, which he built in 1409 about thirty miles east of Lhāsa, *Gah-dan*[2] or Paradise, and it is said that his followers at first went by the name of *Gah*-lug-pa or "Followers of the *Gah-dan* fashion"; but as this name was ill-sounding it was changed to the more euphonic *Ge*-lug-pa or "Followers of the Virtuous order."

།རྡོ་རྗེ་འཆང་ཆེན་པོ།།

VAJRA-DHARA.

The special sectarian distinctions of the Ge-lug-pa, which represent the earlier Kah-dam-pa sect, are that this sect has the mythical Vajra-dhara as its Ādi-Buddha; and derives its divine inspiration from Maitreya—"the coming Buddha," through the Indian Saints ranging from Asaṅga down to Atīṣa, and through the Tibetan Saints from his disciple Brom-ton to Tsoṅ-K'a-pa (Je-Rim-po-ch'e). The Ge-lug-pa mystical insight (*Ta-wa*) is termed the *Lam-rim* or "the Graded Path," and their Tantra is the "Vast Doer" (*r*gya-ch'en spyod).

[1] See page 196 for pictures of the caps.
[2] Skt., "Tushita" or the Happy place.

Its tutelary demoniacal Buddha is Vajra-bhairava (Dorje-'jig-je), supported by Samvara (Dem-ch'og) and Guhya-kālā (Sang-dü). And its Guardian demons are "The Six-armed *Gon-po* or Lord"

THE TUTELARY TAM-ḌIN'S CHARM.

and the Great horse-necked Hayagriva (Tam-ḍin), or the Red Tiger-Devil.

But, through Atīsa, the Ge-lug-pa sect, as is graphically shown in the foregoing table, claims also to have received the essence of Mañjuṣrī's doctrine, which is the leading light of the Sakya-pa sect. For Atīṣa is held to be an incarnation of Mañjuṣrī, the Bodhisat of Wisdom: which is merely a way of stating that he was the greatest embodiment of Buddhist Wisdom that ever visited Tibet. Andin the person of Atīṣa were also united the essentials of the Kar-gyu-pa sect by his pupilage to the Indian sage Nāro.

Thus the Ge-lug-pa sect claims that through Atīṣa it has received the special inspiration of Maitreya, and in addition all that is best in the special systems professed by the other two reformed sects.

The purer morality practised by the Ge-lug monks gained them general respect. So, despite their internecine feuds with the Sakya-pa and other rival sects, its Church grew in size and influence, and became a powerful hierarchy with the succession of its chief abbot based upon the theory of Re-incarnation, namely, that the spirit of the dead chief after his death is re-born in a child, who was forthwith found by oracular presage, and installed in the vacant chair.

Tsoṅ-K'a-pa's nephew, Ge-dun-dub, was installed in 1439 as the first Grand Lāma of the Ge-lug-pa Church, and he built the monastery of Tashi-lhunpo, in 1445, while his fellow workers Je-She-rabSeṅ-age Gyal-Ts'ab-je and Khas-grub-je had built respectively De-p'ung (in 1414), and Se-ra (in 1417), the other great monasteries of this sect.

Under the fourth of these Grand Lāmas, the Ge-lug-pa Church was vigorously struggling for supreme power and was patronized by the Mongol minister of the Chinese Government named Chong-Kar, who, coming to Lhāsa as an ambassador, usurped most of the power of the then king of Tibet, and forced several of the Kar-gyu and Ñiṅ-ma monasteries to join the Ge-lug-pa sect, and to wear the yellow caps.

And, as we have seen in the previous chapter, the Ge-lug-pa sect in 1640, under its fifth Grand Lāma, leapt into temporal power as the dominant sect in Tibet, and has ever since remained the Established Church of the country.

Since then, however, the Ge-lug-pa sect has gradually retrograded in its tenets and practice, till now, with the exception of its distinctive dress and symbols, celibacy and greater abstinence, and a slightly more restricted devil-worship, it differs little from the other Lāmaist sects, which in the pride of political power it so openly despises.

The Kar-gyu-pa Sect.

The Kar-gyu-pa, the next great reformed sect after the Ge-lug-pa, was founded in the latter half of the eleventh century A.D. by

Lāma Marpa[1] of Lha-brag, who had visited India and obtained special instructions from the Indian Pandit Atīṣa and his teacher P'am-thiṅ and Naro, the janitor of Nālanda University, who never visited Tibet. But as Marpa and his successor Mila-ra-pa, while nominally having a monastery at Gro-bu-luṅ and sGrub-p'ug-matog*s*, respectively, led hermit lives, the real organizer of this sect was the Kah-dam-pa Lāma, Dvag-po lha-*r*je,[2] who founded the monastery of Ts'ur-lha about 1150.

MARPA.

The name Kar-gyu-pa[3] means a "follower of the successive orders," expressive of the fact that the sect believes that the rulings of its later sages are inspired. Naro's teacher, the monk Tilo or Telo (about 950 A.D.)[4] is held to have been directly inspired by the metaphysical Buddha Vajra-dhara.

Its distinctive features are its hermit practices, meditation in caves and other retired places, and the following specialities:—

Its inspiration was attributed by their saint Tilo directly to the Ādi-Buddha Vajra-dhara. Its mode of mystic insight (*Ta-wa*) is named *Mahāmudra*[5] or "the Great Attitude," also called *U-mahi Lam* or "the Middle Path," and its Tantra is "Sum-

---

[1] Marpa, according to Sum-pa K'an-po's Ch'os-'byuṅ, was born at Gro-bu-luṅ po *g*sar, as the second son of dbAṅ-p'yug-'od, his mother being sKal-ldan sKyd *g*ñis. His son when riding to Talung monastery to witness a Lāma's dance was thrown down the cliff and fearfully mangled owing to his horse in a rocky defile taking fright at the flight of some rock pigeons. This scene is pictured often in Kar-gyu-pa temples. (Cf. also PAND., No. 32.)

[2] Also called r*Je sGam-po-Va* with title *mñam-med.* He was a native of E. Tibet beyond Kongbu; died 1152. (Cf. PAND., No. 33.)

[3] b*Kah*-br*gyud-pa.*

[4] Cf. TĀRA., 226, PAND., No. 17.

[5] P'yag-rgya-ch'en usually contracted to "*ch'ag-ch'en.*"

ST. MILA-RÄ-PA.

[*To face p.* 64.

kar-*b*suds-sum.[1] Its tutelary demon is Samvara. Its guardian deity "The Lord of the Black Cloak.[2] Its hat is "the meditation hat with the cross-knees," bearing on its front this emblem as a badge like a St. Andrew's cross (X), and a conical centre-piece representing a cave elsewhere. And with these technicalities was associated a stricter observance of the monastic rules and discipline.

The most popular Kar-gyu-pa saint, and one who, while founding no monastery, did more even than Marpa, to establish the sect, was Marpa's pupil, Mila-rä-pa.[3] He never visited India, but led a wandering ascetic life among the mountains of Tibet, and his 100,000 songs[4] containing much Tibetan colouring are popular amongst all the sects of Lāmas, and his name is now a household word throughout Tibet.

He is pictured, as seen in the annexed illustration, as a thinly-clad ascetic almost on the Indian model, enduring great hardships of climate and exposure, and a great magician conquering many demons. His picture is surrounded by scenes illustrative of the leading events of his life.

His biography is sketched here in a footnote,[5] as he is a person of importance in Lāmaism. It is contained in a bulky volume

---

1 Marpa's scripture was based upon the "mñam-len byin rlabs," which he diluted and mixed with more mystic Tantras; hence his Tantra is called "the mixed" (zuṅ-'jug). The so-called esoteric is the "mdo lugs-stong-pa-nyid," and the esoteric "sṅ*ags* lugs *b*de stoṅ dbyer med, which are referred to in the chapter on Doctrine. For some technical details regarding several sects, see transl. by SARAT, *J.A.S.B.*, 1883; also RAMSAY'S *Dict.*

2 *m*Gon-po bar-nag.

3 Mi-la-ras-pa or "the Cotton-clad." (Cf. CSOMA, *Gr.*, 181; TĀRA., 328; PAND., No. 31.)

4 glu-'bum.

5 He was born at Kya-ṅan-tsa in the year 1038 A.D., on the 28th day of the month, under the planet phur-bu, and named Thos-pa-dgal. His father, Mila-shes-rab-rgyal-*m*ts'an, was a wealthy merchant of the K'uṅ-po clan of Uru-chaṅ-ch'og, and his mother was Gyaṅ tsa dkar-rgyan. The father died when Thos-pa-dgal (the young Mila) was only seven years old, leaving his property in his brother's charge till his son reached his majority at fifteen. This uncle, however, appropriated everything to himself, and left young Mila and his mother destitute, and even persecuted them. Young Mila's mother, therefore, sent her son to become a Lāma in order to learn the *mt'u*-art of destroying people by sorcery. So he started off for Lhun-grub grong K'aṅ in Guṅ-t'oṅ-*s*tod, and there joined a party of monks on their way from Upper Ṅari to Ü (or Central Tibet). Passing Yag-sde, and crossing Mar-tsaṅ, he reached T'on-luṅ-raga in Ü, and found at Yar-luṅ skyo-mo-Kruṅ a learned "mt'u" teacher named Yuṅ sTon-p'ro-rgyal, who taught him sorcery for several years, until he obtained the power to destroy his cruel uncle's house and gear. After being instructed in the mode of compelling hailstorms, he went to Magon (or gTsaṅ-roṅ-gi-nar), and then to Ch'os-la sgang, where he became a pupil of Lāma Marpa, who had visited India. Here he was set many tiresome tasks by Marpa, such as building

ascribed to his disciple Räs-ch'uṅ, and dated from the hermitage of the latter.

AFFILIATION OF SUB-SECTS OF THE KAR-GYU-PA.

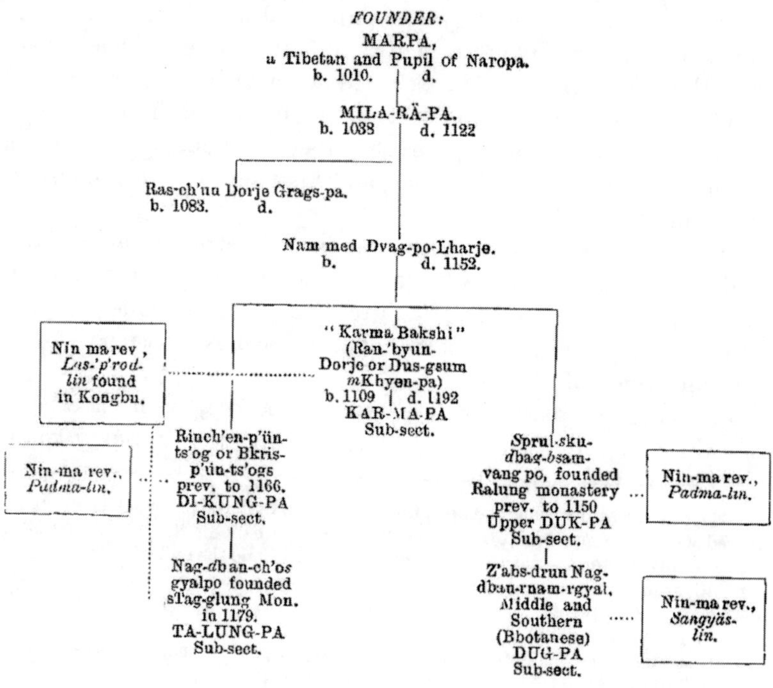

forts and pulling them to pieces again, and the pictures of these tasks are favourite subjects for frescoes in Kar-gyu-pa monasteries. As the tasks seemed endless and Marpa still withheld instruction, the young Mila fled, taking with him the Indian saint Naropa's 'six-bone ornaments and *padma-raga*-rosary, which had been in Marpa's keeping as relics; and which young Mila obtained possession of by the connivance of Marpa's wife, bDag-med-ma. These relics he offered to Lāma rÑog-pa, who in return gave him instruction and the meditation of Groṅ-ldan p'ug-pa. Then Marpa recalled him and initiated him into the mysteries of the magic circles, and gave him the esoteric name of dPal-s'es-pa and the common name of Mila-rdo-rje rgyal mts'an, and set him severe ascetic exercises. Meanwhile Marpa went to India, and met the monk Naropa at the monastery of Bula-hari, and was taught 'p'o-wa-stoṅ-'jug, and returned to Tibet by Ch'os-la gaṅ. When Mila returned home, he found his mother dead, so he dwelt in a cave near by named Kaṅ-mdsod phug. Then his uncle and aunt assaulted him on his begging excursions, but though possessing the power of destroying them, he preferred to flee from them to Brag Kar-rta-so, near Kyi-roṅ, where he remained in meditation for eighteen years, living solely on

Mila-rä-pa's chief pupils were Dvag-po-lha-rje,[1] who continued the succession of the orthodox Kar-gyu-pa doctrine, and Rä-ch'uṅ Dor-je Tag-pa,[2] who did not interest himself in organization.

The hermit-feature of this sect rendered it so unattractive, that several sub-sects soon arose which dispensed with the necessity for hermitage. Thus appeared the sub-sects Kar-ma-pa, Di-kung-pa, Ta-lung-pa, and Duk-pa (the form dominant in Bhotan), which differ from each other merely in having each adopted a different revelation from the Ñiṅ-ma sect as a code of demoniacal worship, and so relaxing the purity of the former Kar-gyu-pa practice.

These differences are shown in the foregoing table.

And the image of the particular founder of the sub-sect shares with that of their Ādi-Buddha, Vajradhara, the chief place in their temples.

The *Kar-ma-pa* sub-sect was founded in the middle of the twelfth century by Kar-ma-pa Raṅ-ch'uṅ Dor-je, also named Dü-sum K'yen-po,[3] a pupil of the aforesaid Dvag-po-lha-rje. His monastery of S'u-Ts'ur Lha-luṅ,[4] built in 1154, at Ts'ur-p'u, about one day's journey to the north of Lhāsa beyond Sera, is still the headquarters of this, the most powerful of all the Kar-gyu-pa sub-sects.[5] This Kar-ma Lāma does not appear to be identical with the famous "Kar-ma-Bakshi,"[6] whose image is the central one in all Kar-ma-pa temples, for his birth is placed by Csoma later.[7] The ninth head Kar-ma-pa Lāma was named dGu-pa-bar Phyug Dor-je, and was alive in 1725 A.D., when the then rāja of Sikhim visited him in Tibet and was prevailed on by him to establish some Kar-ma-pa monasteries in Sikhim.

The so-called monastery, though it is only a temple, in the "Bhotiya-basti" at Darjiling belongs to this sect.

---

vegetables, and performing many miracles. Then he went to Dig-ri plain, where he met Pari, the translator, and his pupils. Thereafter he went to 'Brin-yul, and afterwards to a cave in Lab-ċi-ċu-gar (? Mount Everest), where he died. His favourite god was Kuvera, the King of the Yaksha genii.

1 Also called rJe-Tsun sGam-po. See PANDER, No. 33.

2 Ras-ch'uṅ rdo-rje grags-pa, born 1083, founded Ras-ch'uṅ p'ug monastery.

3 Raṅ-'byuṅ-rdo-rje dus-gsum-mk'yen-po, born 1109, ordained 1124, died 1192.

4 Ts'u-mts'ur.

5 It was zealously patronized by De-si Zaṅ-po, a King of Western Tibet, with his capital at Shigatse.

6 Cf. CSOMA, *Gr.*, 186; *J.A.S.B.*, 51, p. 53; PAND. No. 39.

7 In *Gram.*, 185, Kar-ma-Bakshi's birth is given as 1177 A.D.

It differs from its parent sect in having retrograded towards the Niṅ-ma-pa practices by adopting the Ñiṅ-ma revelation found in Kong-bo and entitled Lé-tö Liṅ-pa,[1] or "the locally revealed merit," and some also have 'Jah-ts'on-pa. Few of the Kar-ma Lāmas are celibate, and Marpa, the founder of the parent sect (Kar-gyu-pa), was married.

The next great sub-sect is the Dug-pa,[2] which also arose with a pupil of Mila-rä-pa's disciple, Dvag-po. Its founder was Pag-Sam-Wang-po,[3] and it originated in the *g*Nam province of Tibet about the middle of the twelfth century, at the Ralung monastery, near Gyan-tse, in Töd or Upper Tibet. To emphasize the change the monastery was called *Ḍug*-Ralung, and a legend of the thunder-dragon or *Dug* is related in connection therewith, and gives the sectarian title. It adopted the same revelation as the Di-kung-pa, but there seems some other distinctive tenet which I have not yet elicited.

Much confusion has been caused in European books by mis-using the name Dug-pa, employing it as a synonym for the "red-hat" sect, which properly is the Ñiṅ-ma.

The *Middle* Dug-pa and the *Lower* Dug-pa arose soon after-wards. The *Middle Dug-pa* adopted the revelation of Saṅ-gyas-liṅ-pa. This is the form of Kar-gyu-pa which now prevails in Bhotan under the name of *Lhô Dug-pa* or "*Southern*" *Dug-pa*. Its chief Lāma is Z'ab-druṅ Ṅag-baṅ-nam-gyal,[4] a pupil of Padma *d*kar-po" or "The omniscient white lotus," who leaving Southern Tibet in the seventeenth century A.D.,[5] settled at "lChags-ri rta mgo" in Bhotan, and soon displaced the Karthok-pa and other forms of Ñiṅ-ma Lāmaism then existing in that country, and which are reputed to have been founded there directly by St. Padma himself, who entered Bhotan *viâ* gZ'as-ma gaṅ and left it by mDuṅ tsaṅ, and at *d*Gon-ts'al p'u are still shown his foot-prints on a rock, and at the *s*Pa-te tak-ts'aṅ or tiger's den.[6]

---

1 Las-'prod-liṅ-pa.

2 'brug-pa. It is Sanskritised in the Chronicle of Ṅag-waṅ Nam-gyal as *Megha Svara* or "Cloud-voice," thunder being regarded as the dragon's roar.

3 *d*Pag-*b*sam *d*baṅ-po, who seems to be identical with, or patronized by, 'Gro-*m*gon *r*tsaṅ-pa *r*gyal ra*s*, "The Victory-clad Patron of Animals" (? born 1160 A.D.).

4 His title is *b*dud-'jom-rdorje, or "the Vajra which Softened the Devils."

5 CSOMA, *J.A.S.B.*, 1832, 126.

6 According to the Thaṅ-yig *s*de-*l*ṅa, some historic notes on the history of Lāmaism in Bhotan are to be found in the book Lho-Ch'o*s* 'byuṅ.

In Bhotan the Dug-pa sect possesses the temporal as well as the spiritual power, and has suppressed all other sects there. Some details of its chief monasteries and hierarchs are given in the special chapters on these two subjects.

The *Dī-kung-pa*,[1] another large sub-sect, also originated with a pupil of Dvag-po. It takes its title from the Dī-kung monastery founded by Rinch'en-p'ün-ts'og and Je-spyan-sṅa-wa, in 1177 A.D.[2] Its revelation is Ñiṅ-ma the Padma-liṅ-pa.

The *Ta-lung-pa*[3] issued from the Dī-kung-pa and takes its title from the Ta-lung monastery founded by Ṅag-*d*baṅ-ch'os-gyalpo in 1178. They differ from their parent Dī-kung-pa in admitting also the revelation work adopted by the Kar-ma-pa, namely, the Lē-tö liṅ-pa.

The Sa-kya-pa Sect.

The last great reformed sect is the Sa-skya-pa[4] or Sakya, taking its name from the yellow colour of the scanty soil at the site of its first monastery in western Tibet, founded in 1071 A.D. It grew into a most powerful hierarchy, and attained for a time the temporal sovereignty over the greater part of Tibet before it was eclipsed by its Ge-lug-pa rival.

Its founder was K'on-dkon-mch'og rgyal-po,[5] a pupil of K'ug-pa lha-btsas, who claimed inspiration from the celestial Bodhisat of wisdom, Mañjuṣrī, through the Indian sages ranging from Nāgārjuna[6] to Vasuputra,[7] and he mixed together the "old" and the "new" Tantras, calling his doctrine the "new-old occult mystery"[8] of "The deep sight."[9] Its mystic insight is called "The fruitful path."[10] Its special gospels are Nāgārjuna's Avataṅsaka, Vasubandhu's Paramārtha. Its tutelary demon is *Vajra*

1 'Bri-guṅ.

2 Csoma, *Gram.*, 185.

3 *s*Tag-luṅ.

4 Sa-skya-pa, from *Sa-skya* = "tawny earth."

5 Born 1033. Details of the sect are found in its records, The Sa-skya *Yig-ts'aṅ.*

6 These are given as Candra-Kirti, Rig-pahi-K'u-p'yug, Buddha "*d*goṅs"-pāla.

7 Yab-sras.—Vasuputra seems a title of the great Indian monk Vasubandhu, the brother of Asaṅga, and the special transmitter of Nāgārjuna's purer Sautrāntika doctrines, inspired by Mañjuṣrī.

8 gsar-ñiṅ.

9 zab-mo-blta—*Gambhira darṣana.*

10 *m*gon-po gur.

phurpa, for whose and other demonist worship it borrowed the Niṅ-ma books, *Dorje phurpach'i ch'oga;* and from the newer school were taken Dem-ch'ok, Dorje-kando, Den-z'i, Mahā-mahā-ma-yab, Saṅgyä t'öpa, and Dorje-dutsi. Its demoniacal Guardians are "the Guardian of the Tent,"[1] and "The Face-Lord."[2] Its Hat is sā-z'u. But now except in a few externals it is practically undistinguishable from the Ñiṅ-ma-pa.

གུར་གྱི་མགོན་པོ་

THE LORD (-FIEND) GUR.

The Sa-kya-pa has two reformed sub-sects, namely, the Ṅor-pa and the Jonaṅ-pa. These differ from one another only in founders.

The Jô-naṅ-po issued from the Sa-kya-pa in the person of Je-Kun-gah-dol-ch'og[3] in the beginning of the fourteenth century. To this sect belonged the illustrious historiographer, Lāma-Tāranātha.

Tāranātha, son of Nam-gyal P'ün-ts'ogs, was born in Tsang on the 8th day of the pig-male-tree year, corresponding to 1573 A.D., and was called Kun-*d*gah sÑyiṅ-po,[4] or "The essence of happiness." He studied in the Jonang monastery, north of Sakya under the religious name of Tāranātha, and in his forty-first year built himself a monastery in the neighbourhood, which he named *r*Tag-*br*ten, and filled it with many images, books, and caityas. He latterly proceeded to Mongolia at the invitation of the people of that country, and founded there several monasteries under the auspices of the Chinese Emperor. He died in Mongolia, and was canonized under the title of "The Reverend Holiness," *Je-tsun dam-pa.*[5] And his "re-incarnate" successors are now installed with great magnificence as Grand Lāmas at Urgya in the Kalkha

1 mGon-po gur.

2 mGon-zhal.

3 Who seems also to be called Dol-bu sher-rgyan. Born 1290, and died 1353.

4 *Skt.*, Ānandagarbha. Another account gives the name as Srī-gcod *r*dorje.

5 *r*Je-*b*tsun dam-pa.

province of Mongolia, to the east of Lob-Nor. Shortly after his death, both Urgya and his old monastery—which was renamed—

A Sa-skya Lāma.

"P'un-ts'o-liṅ," were forcibly converted into Ge-lug-pa institutions, by the aggressive Dalai Lāma on his becoming priest-king.

The *Ṅor-pa*, founded by Kun-gah Zaṅ-po in 1427, issued from the Sa-kya-pa at the time of Tsoṅ-K'āpa. Its founder discarded the Ñiṅ-ma element in its Tāntrik system, retaining only the "new." It has many monasteries in eastern Tibet.

THE ÑIṄ-MA-PA SECTS.

The wholly unreformed section of the Lāmas was, as we have seen, named Ñiṅ-ma-pa, or "the old school. It is more freely than any other tinged with the native Bön or pre-Bnddhist practices; and celibacy and abstinence are rarely practised. This

ÑIṄ-MA LAMAS.

is the real "red-hat" sect of Lāmas, and not the Dug-pa as is stated in European books.

It regards the metaphysical Buddha Samanta-bhadra as its primordial deity or Ādi-Buddha. Its mystic insight is Mahā-utpanna (Dsog-ch'en) or "the great ultimate perfection." Its tutelaries are "The fearful Vajra" (Vajra-"phurba") and Dub-pa-kah-gye.[1] Its guardian demon is "The Lord *Gur*."[2] It worships

[1] sGrub-pa *b*kah-brgyad—the tutelary of the Guru St. Padma.

[2] Gur-gön, a two-handed demon, the highest of the five "Pal-gon."

the Guru Padma-sambhava, the founder of Lāmaism, in a variety of forms, both divine and demoniacal, expressive of his different moods at different times, and also his favourite Kashmīri teacher, Ṣrī Siṅha, and the Indian teacher of the latter, Gah-rab Dorje, who derived his inspiration from the celestial Buddha, Vajra-satwa, who in turn was inspired by the primordial deity, Saman-ta-bhadra Buddha.

Its peculiar red cap is named after the Guru "Urgyen-pān-z'u," and with these characteristics it exhibits a greater laxity in living than any other sect of Lāmas.

But even the Ñiṅ-ma-pa, too, has its sub-sects, based on the adoption of different revelations. Its chief sub-sects are the Dorje-ṭak-pa, Mindol-liṅ, Kar-tok-pa, and Ṅa-dak-pa, named after their respective founders or parent monastery. But their differences are very trifling.

The Dorje-ṭak-pa [1] is named after the greatest of the existent Ñiṅ-ma monasteries, to wit, Dorje-ṭak, near Sam-yäs. It follows the revelation "found" by *r*God-ldem in Zaṅ-Zaṅ Lha brag, and its chief branches seem to be at Hug-pa-gliṅ, Tsa-ṅgi Lhā-ri zim-p'ug, and T'eg-mc'og gliṅ.

An offshoot of it is the Ṅah-dag-pa,[2] taking its name from its founder, Ṅah-dag, "the owner of dominion," and of royal lineage, and represented in several Sikhim monasteries.

Scarcely inferior in extent and repute to the Dorje-ṭak-pa is the Min-dol-liṅ-pa,[3] also named after its chief monastery, Min-dol-liṅ. Its revelation was found by bDag-ling-pa, and its chief branches are at sLe-luṅ, P'uṅ-po ri-wo-ch'e. And in Sikhim it is represented by the large Pemiongchi monastery, which until a few years ago was in the habit of sending to Min-dol-liṅ batches of its young monks for instruction in the higher discipline and ritual.

The Kar-tok-pa,[4] named after Lāma Kar-tok, "The understander of the precepts," adopt the revelation of kLoṅ-ch'en Rab-*h*'byuṅ found in the lake of sGra-mdah. Its chief monasteries are at Byaṅ-ch'ub-gliṅ and sDe-dge ("Der-ge") in the extreme east of Tibet, and the seat of a large printing establishment and township famous for its inlaid metal work.

[1] *r*do-rje-brag-pa. [2] *m*Ṅah-*b*dag-pa. [3] sMin-*g*rol Gliṅ. [4] *b*Kah-*r*tog-pa.

Lho-brag-lha-luṅ-pa follow the revelation of Padma-liṅ-pa like the Dī-kung-pa sub-sect of the Kar-gyu-pa.

The Lha-tsun-pa, named after the founder of Sikhim Lāmaism, adopt the revelation of 'Jah-ts'on-pa, found in Kong-bu, named the Lä-t'ö-liṅ-pa.

The Z'i-jed-pa.

The Z'i-jed-pa ("the mild doer"), or passionless Ascetic, is a homeless mendicant of the *Yogi* class, and belonging to no sect in particular, though having most affinity with the Kar-gyu-pa. They are now almost extinct, and all are regarded as saints, who in their next birth must certainly attain Nirvāṇa. They carry thigh-bone trumpets, skull-drums, etc., and in the preparation of these instruments from human bones, they are required to eat a morsel of the bone or a shred of the corpse's skin. The founder of the order was P'a-dam-pa Saṅs-rgyas (? Jñanaka- or Pita-Buddha), born at Jara Sin(d)ha, in India, his father being named brTson-'grus-go-ch'a and his mother Rasha. He visited Tibet, *viâ* Kashmīr and Ṅa-ri, about the beginning of the twelfth century A.D., his final visit being in 1112 A.D. As this order is highly esteemed in Tibet, I subjoin some details of its chief saints.[1]

Summary of Sects.

It will thus be seen that Lāmaist sects seem to have arisen in Tibet, for the first time, in the latter part of the eleventh century A.D., in what may be called the Lāmaist Reformation, about three centuries after the foundation of Lāmaism itself.

They arose in revolt against the depraved Lāmaism then prevalent, which was little else than a priestly mixture of demonolatry

[1] In Tibet P'a-dam-pa taught his doctrines to *Zhan-zhun-glin-k'awa* and *bön po k'ra-ch'un-'bruk*. Meeting r*Man gra-Serpo*, of *Yar-kluns*, he accompanied him to *Tsang*, where he gave instruction to Lāma *sKyo-bsöd-nam*, who succeeded him.

The second successor was the hermit rMa-sgom, born at Yar-stod-skyer-snar, in 1054 A.D., and forming the *r*Ma order. His pupil was So-ch'un-pa, a dwarf.

The Yogini Ma-gci'g-lab-sgron, born at the southern Ph'a-druk, in 1054 A.D., was the devoted pupil of rMa.

*s*Kam, another great z'i-jed-pa, was a pupil of dge-s'es-gra-pa, and suffering injury from a sa-*g*don demon, he burned its effigy. The demon afflicted him with dropsy and leprosy; but by his zhi-cjed rites he recovered. He died 1119 A.D.

Z'aṅ-dgah-ldan, also a pupil of rMa, was born at Yar-stod-gtsan-z'al, in the tribe of *m*Tshims zaṅ. His pupils were gÑal-ston-dyah ch'uṅ-'bor, sKyog-sgom bsam-tan, K'u-sgom jo-dgah, rGya-dar-sen, and Ch'us-pa-dar brtson.

and witchcraft. Abandoning the grosser charlatanism, the new sects returned to celibacy and many of the purer Mahāyāna rules.

In the four centuries succeeding the Reformation, various sub-sects formed, mostly as relapses towards the old familiar demonolatry.

And since the fifteenth century A.D., the several sects and sub-sects, while rigidly preserving their identity and exclusiveness, have drifted down towards a common level where the sectarian distinctions tend to become almost nominal.

But neither in the essentials of Lāmaism itself, nor in its sectarian aspects do the truly Buddhist doctrines, as taught by Ṣākya Muni, play a leading part.

SASH OF CARVED HUMAN BONES
worn by Lāmas in Necromancy.
(*Reduced* ½, *see also figure, p.* 18.)

V.

THE METAPHYSICAL SOURCES OF THE DOCTRINE.

AS Buddhism is a highly philosophical religion, and Lāmaism, though deeply tinged with non-Buddhist beliefs, still retains much of the loftier philosophy and doctrines of Primitive Buddhism and its earlier developments, we must, in considering the metaphysical basis of the Lāmaist doctrine, glance at the metaphysics of Buddha himself, as well as that of the Mahāyāna and the later "developments." And as Buddha's philosophy is based upon his working theory of the Universe, our subject will fall conveniently under the heads of (*a*) Buddha's Theory of the Universe,[1] (*b*) his Metaphysics, and (*c*) the Metaphysics of the Lāmas.

However inconsistent materialism and theistic theories may appear, with a system avowedly idealistic and practically atheistic, it certainly seems that Buddha, himself a Hindū and a teacher of Hindūs, did adopt the Hindū mythology and cosmic notions current in his day, with slight modifications, which were directed merely towards depriving the gods of their creative functions and rendering them finite and subject to death and the general law of metempsychosis.[2]

His *sūtras*, or sermons, contain numerous references to these divinities, and the earliest of all authentic Buddhist records extant, namely, the Asoka edict pillars of the third century B.C., show a model Buddhist delighting in calling himself "the beloved of the Gods"; and in the Barhut Stupa of the second century B.C.

---

[1] General mythology forms a special chapter (xv.), but it is necessary at this stage to sketch the mythology which bears directly upon the doctrinal developments.

[2] Even in Brāhmanic mythology the hosts of the gods, including Indra, the greatest god in Vedic times, are subject to the universal law of dissolution at the end of a *Kalpa*, or cycle of time, when the Triad god-head A.U.M. becomes simple soul (*Kevalātman*).

the gods and genii are represented with functions identical with those now allotted to them in the latter-day Buddhism of both Burma and Tibet, where, as in the orthodox scriptures of both schools, the gods receive more or less worship on account of the power which they are believed to possess of bestowing temporal blessings. And the coming Buddha is believed by all Buddhists to be even now resident in the Tushita heavens of the gods.

So intimately have these mythological figures been woven into the texture of Buddism, and especially of Lāmaism, which peoples the world with gorgons and hydras and other dire chimeras, that without having gained a general idea of their nature and position, it is impossible to understand the allusions to them which constantly crop out in Buddhist rites and dogma. And, indeed, many of these fantastic beliefs with their deified heroes and Nature-worship are in reality petrified survivals of the archaic beliefs of our Indo-Germanic ancestors.

Buddhist Theory of the Universe.

In sketching the Buddhist world-system, with its "antres vast and deserts idle," existing mostly on the map of the imagination, it is deemed advisable, in order to avoid needless repetition, to give at once the Lāmaist version, even though this is slightly more "developed" than the cosmogony of Buddha's day; although it cannot be very different after all, for the Lāmaist accounts of it are in close keeping with the Barhut lithic remains, and almost identical with the versions found among the Ceylonese and other Buddhists of the south, and the Chinese and Japanese Buddhists.[1]

This, our human, world is only one of a series (the others being fabulous) which together form a universe or chiliocosm,[2] of which there are many.

Each universe, set in unfathomable space, rests upon a warp and woof of "blue air" or wind, liked crossed thunderbolts (*vajra*), hard and imperishable as diamonds (*vajra*), upon which is set "the body of the waters," upon which is a foundation of gold, on which is set the earth, from the axis of which towers up the great

1 Cf. also Giorgi, whose figure is attached; and summary by Burnouf, ii., 599.

2 Skt., Sarva-loka-dhātu.

Olympus—Mt. Meru[1] (Su-meru, Tib., Ri-rab) 84,000 miles[2] high, surmounted by the heavens, and overlying the hills.

In the ocean around this central mountain, the axis of the universe, are set (see figures) the four great continental worlds with their satellites, all with bases of solid gold in the form of a tortoise —as this is a familiar instance to the Hindū mind of a solid floating on the waters. And the continents are separated from Mt. Meru by seven concentric rings of golden mountains, the inmost being 40,000 miles high,[3] and named "The Yoke" (Yugandara),[4] alternating with seven oceans, of fragrant milk,[5] curds, butter, blood or sugar-cane juice, poison or wine, fresh water and salt water. These oceans diminish in width and depth from within outwards from 20,000 to 625 miles, and in the outer ocean lie the so-called continental worlds. And the whole system is girdled externally by a double iron-wall (*Cakravāla*) 312½ miles high and 3,602,625 miles in circumference,—for the oriental mythologist is nothing if not precise. This wall shuts out the light of the sun and moon, whose orbit is the summit of the inmost ring of mountains, along which the sun, composed of "glazed fire" enshrined in a crystal palace, is driven in a chariot with ten (seven) horses; and the moon, of "glazed water," in a silver shrine drawn by seven horses, and between these two hang the jewelled umbrella of royalty and the banner of victory, as shown in the figure. And inhabiting the air, on a level with these, are the eight angelic or fairy mothers. Outside the investing wall of the universe all is void and in perpetual darkness until another universe is reached.

---

[1] Its prototype, as with the Greek Olympus, is terrestrial, namely, Mt. Kailās, 22,000ft., directly north of Lake Manasarovara in the Himalayas (cf. MARKHAM, xxiv.).

[2] The 84,000 is a mathematical figure expressing multitude. The Tibetan measure is a "*d*pag-tshad," which, according to CSOMA (*Dict.*), equals 4,000 fathoms, and hence a geographical mile, but it is used as the equivalent of the Indian unit of measure which is translated in the Ceylonese scriptures as a Yojana, *i.e.*, a unit of about 4 *kos*, about five or six geographical miles.

[3] These mountains are severally named the Ox Yoke-holder, Plough-holder, Sandal-holder, Pleasing Mount, Horse-ear Hill, Demon or Assembly Mount, and Circle or Edge-holder.

[4] The names of the others are Isadara, Karavīka, Sudarsana, Asvakarna, Vināyaka, and Nemiñdhara.

[5] This ocean of milk was churned by the Brāhmanical gods for the recovery of their elixir vitæ and the thirteen precious objects. And the churning produced the beautiful goddess Lakshmi.—Compare with Aphrodite from the froth of the ocean, and the proverbial beauty of the Nāga water nymphs—the Hindū mermaids.

THE UNIVERSE OF THE LĀMAS.

Of the four "continents" all except "Jambudvīpa"[1] are fabulous. They are placed exactly one in each of the four directions, and each has a smaller satellite on either side, thus bringing the total up to twelve. And the shapes given to these continents, namely, crescentic, triangular, round, and square, are evidently symbolic of the four elements.

‖མི་ཏྲི་མཁར་སྤྱོད་ལཾ་ན་མོ‖

A FAIRY.[3]

These continents, shown in the annexed figure, are thus described:—

On the *East* is *Videha*,[2] or "vast body" (P). This is shaped like the crescent moon, and is white in colour. It is 9,000 miles in diameter, and the inhabitants are described as tranquil and mild, and of excellent conduct, and with faces of same shape as this continent, *i.e.*, crescentic like the moon.

On the *South* is *Jamudvīp*[4] (F), or our own world, and its centre is the Bodhi-tree at Budh Gaya. It is shaped like the shoulder-blade of a sheep, this idea being evidently suggested by the shape of the Indian peninsula which was the prototype of Jambudvīpa, as Mt. Kailās in the Himalayas and N.E. of India was that of Mt. Meru. It is blue in colour; and it is the smallest of all, being only 7,000 miles in diameter. Here abound riches and sin as well as virtue. The inhabitants have faces of similar shape to that of their continent, *i.e.*, somewhat triangular.

On the *West* is *Godhanya*,[5] or "wealth of oxen" (I), which in shape is like the sun and red in colour. It is 8,000 miles in diameter. Its inhabitants are extremely powerful, and (as the name literally means, *cow + ox + action*) they are believed to be specially addicted to eating cattle, and their faces are round like the sun.

On the *North* is *Uttara-Kuru*,[6] or "northern *Kuru*"-tribe (M), of square shape and green in colour, and the largest of all the continents,

---

[1] T., Jambu-liṅ.

[2] *Lus-'pags.*

[3] After Pander.

[4] Some Lāmas state that this name is derived from the Jambu tree (*Eugenia Jambolans*), while others believe that the name is onomatopoetic for the sound "Jamb," emitted when the world was thrown by the gods into the outer ocean.

[5] ba-glaṅ spyöd.

[6] sgra-mi-sñan.

being 10,000 miles in diameter. Its inhabitants are extremely fierce and noisy. They have square faces like horses; and live on trees, which supply all their wants. They become tree-spirits on their death; and these trees afterwards emit "bad sounds" (this is evidently, like many of the other legends, due to a puerile and false interpretation of the etymology of the word).

The satellite continents resemble their parent one in shape, and each is half its size. The left satellite of Jambudvīp, namely, "The ox-tail-whisk continent," is the fabulous country of the Rakshas, to which Padma-sambhava is believed to have gone and to be still reigning there. And each of the latter presents towards Mount Meru one of the following divine objects respectively,[1] viz., on the east (? south) the mountain of jewels, named *Amo-likha*, shaped like an elephant's head,[2] and on the south, the wish-granting tree,[3] on the west the wish-granting cow,[4] and on the north the self-sprung crops.[5]

In the very centre of this cosmic system stands "The king of mountains," Mount Meru, towering erect "like the handle of a mill-stone," while half-way up its side is the great wishing tree,[6] the prototype of our "Christmas tree," and the object of contention between the gods and the Titans. Meru has square sides of gold and jewels. Its eastern face is crystal (or silver), the south is sapphire or *lapis lazuli* (vaidūrya) stone, the west is ruby (padmaraga), and the north is gold, and it is clothed with fragrant flowers and shrubs. It has four lower compartments before the heavens are reached. The lowest of these is inhabited by the Yaksha genii—holding wooden plates. Above this is "the region of the wreath-holders" (Skt., *Srag-dharā*), which seems to be a title of the bird-like, or angelic winged Garuḍas. Above this dwell the "eternally exalted ones,"[7] above whom are the Titans.

THE TITANS.

The Titans (*Asura*[8]) or "ungodly spirits."

These are pictured in the "Wheel of Life" (at page 108), in the upper right section. Their leading trait is pride, and this is the world of re-

1 These, according to other accounts, are situate on the flanks of Meru itself.

2 The Yama rocks are on the south.

3 Tib., Yond-'dus-sa-gtol.

4 'dod-'zo-i-ba.

5 ma-smos-pi lo-t'og.

6 The Ri-wo ña-s'in.

7 rtag myos, here the *rta* may represent "horse"—the horse-headed musicians.

8 T., Lha-ma-yin.

birth for those who, during their human career, have boasted of being more pious than their neighbours. The Titans were originally gods; but, through their pride, they were, like Satan, expelled from heaven; hence their name, which means "not a god."[1] And their position at the base of the Mount Meru is intermediate between heaven and earth.

The duration of their life is infinitely greater than the human, and they have great luxury and enjoyment; but in pride they envy the greater bliss of the gods, and die prematurely, fighting vainly against the gods for the fruits of the heavenly tree and the divine nectar.

Their region is represented in the picture, of an almost colourless atmosphere. They live in fortified houses. The ground, both inside and outside the fort, is carpeted with flowers of which the inhabitants, male and female, make the wreaths and garlands which they wear. They are dressed in silk; and when the heroes are not engaged in fighting they spend their time in all sorts of gaiety with their wives. In the right-hand corner is shown their birth from a lotus-flower and their obtaining a wish-granting tree and cow. The rest of the picture is devoted to their misery, which consists in their hopeless struggle and fatal conflict with the gods. The commander of the forces is seen in conclave with his leaders,[2] horses are being saddled and the "heroes" are arming themselves with coats of mail and weapons. Another scene shows the battle raging along the border separating their country from heaven, and the general mounted with his staff as spectators in the background. The warriors of the first line are all killed or horribly mangled by the thunderbolts and adamantine weapons hurled at them by the gods. One of the weapons possessed alike by gods and Titans is a spiked disc.

The ultimate fate of every Titan is to die painfully warring against the gods with whom they are in constant conflict, and they have no access to the ambrosia with which a wounded god obtains instant recovery. Another scene (see picture on page 102) depicts the womenfolk gathered round "The Reflecting Lake of Perfect Clearness" after the departure of their lords to the battle. In this lake are mirrored forth all the doings and ultimate fate of their absent spouses, and there is also shown the region of re-birth of themselves, which is nearly always hell, owing to the passionate life which they lead in the Asura world. And while their lovers die painful and passionate deaths, the misery of the womanfolk of this world is to look into this fascinating lake and experience the horror of such hideous spectacles. In the picture some women are shown peering into the lake, and others on the banks are giving vent to their grief.

---

1 Analogous to this is the common colloquial term *mi-ma-yin* or "not a man" applied to those who lead vicious and dissolute lives.

2 Note that greatness of rank is shown in pictures by enlarged bodily dimensions.

THE HEAVENS AND THE GODS.

Above the region of the Titans, at a distance of 168,000 miles, are the bright realms of the gods. In the lowest compartment

GUARDIAN KING OF THE EAST,
Yul-k'or-sruṅ.

of the heavens are the four "great guardian kings of the quarters" (Tib., rgyal-c̓'en de-z'i; Skt., *Cātur-Mahārāja*), namely:—

1. *Dhṛitarāshṭra* (Yul-k'or-sruṅ [1]), the white guardian of the east, and king of the Gandharvas [2] (see figure over page).

2. *Virūḍhaka* (P'ag-kye-pô [3]), the green [4] guardian of the south, and king of the K'umbhāndas [5] (see figure page 330).

3. *Virūpāksha* (Jä-mi-zaṅ [6]), the red guardian of the west and king of the Nāgās [7] (see figure page 289).

4. *Vaiṣravana* (Nam-t'ö-srä [8]), the yellow guardian of the north and king of the Yakshas.[9] He is an especial favourite, as he is also, in another aspect, the god of Riches (see figure on page 370). Indeed, it would seem that all of the gods, even Indra (Jupiter) himself, were originally considered to be Yaksha genii.

The subjects of these kings are members of the eight great classes of supernatural beings.[10]

These great celestial kings guard the heavens from the attacks of the outer demons; and have to be distinguished from a more extended category of guardian gods, the ten *Lokpals* who guard the world from its ten directions; namely, Indra on the east, Agni (the fire-god) on the south-east, Yama (the death-god) on the south, Rakshas (? Sura) on the south-west, Varuṇa (the water-god) on the west, Vāyu (the wind-god) on the north-west, Yakshas on the north, Soma (the moon) on the north-east, Brāhma, above; Bhūpati, below.

The Buddhists divide every universe into three regions, in imitation, apparently, of the Brāhmanic *Bhavanatraya*, substituting for the *physical* categories (*Bhū* earth, *Bhuva* heaven, and *Svar* space) of the Brāhmans, the *ethical* categories of Desire (*Kāma*), Form *Rūpa* and Formlessness (*Arūpa*), which collectively are known as "The Three Regions" (*Trailokya* [11]), and mostly placed in heaven. They are:—

I. The region of DESIRE, *Kāmadhātu* (Tib., Dod-pahí K'ams), is the lowest of the three, and comprises the six *Devalokas* (Tib., Lha-Yul) or heavens of the gods, as well as the earth.

---

1 yul-'k'or bsruṅ.

2 Dri-za "the Small-eaters."

3 'p'ags skyes-pa.

4 Sometimes the colours of the North and South Guardians are transposed.

5 Grul-bum.

6 spyan mig-bzaṅ.

7 *k*Lu.

8 rnamt 'os sras.

9 *g*Nod-*s*byin or "the injurers."

10 See chapter on Mythology.

11 "K'ams gsum."

II. The region of FORM, *Rūpadhātu* (Tib., *g*Zugs kyi k'ams) is in the purer heavens of Brāhma where form is free from sensuality. It comprises the sixteen Brahmalokas; which are divided into four regions of contemplation (dhyāna).

III. The region of FORMLESSNESS, *Arūpadhātu* (Tib., *g*Zugs med-pahi k'ams) comprises the four highest of the Brāhma heavens and near to Nirvāṇa.

The heavens are thus diagrammatically shown in the form of the funereal monument or caitya; though in other pictures, as in the foregoing chart of the universe, they form an inverted pyramid, increasing in size from below upwards.

The celestial Buddhas therein shown are, it is needless to say, additions of later days.[1]

Diagram of
THE HEAVENS OF THE BUDDHISTS.

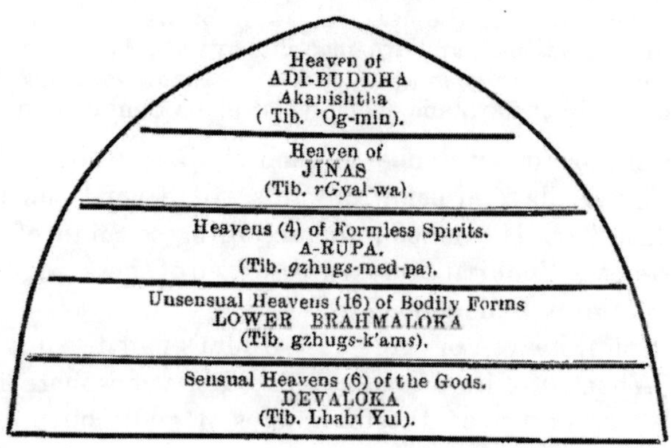

The *Six Devalokas* are in series from below upwards:—

1. *Cātur-mahārājakāyikas.*—The abode of the four guardian kings of the quarters, already mentioned.

2. *Trayastrinsas* (Tib., Sum-cu tsa sum) or "The 33" Vedic gods with Indra or Ṣakra (Jupiter) or the Yaksha spirit Vajrapāṇi as chief.

[1] Compare with Mr. HODGSON'S account (*Lang. and Lit.*, p. 43) of the heavens according to the Nepalese Buddhists.

This heaven is the *svarga* of Brāhmanism, and is shown in the upper compartment of the Wheel of Life.

3. *Yama*, the Hindū Pluto, the king and judge of the dead.

4. *Tushita.* (Tib., *d*Gah *l*dan) or "Joyful place"—the paradise of the Bodhisats prior to their final descent to the human world as Buddhas. Maitreya, the coming Buddha, dwells at present in this heaven.

5. *Nirmānarati* (Tib., 'p'rul *d*gah).

6. *Paranirmita Vasavartin* (Tib., *g*z'an 'p'rul *d*bań byed)—the highest of the heavens of the gods and the abode of Māra.

The *Brahmaloka* worlds are subject to the God Brāhma, and existence ranges from intellectual tranquillity to unconsciousness. These worlds of meditation (*dhyana*) are accounted eighteen in number, and arranged in five groups (3, 3, 3, 2, and 5) corresponding to the five-fold division of Brāhma's world, and are usually named from below upwards as follows: (1) Brāhma parsādyā, (2) Brāhma purohitā, (3) Mahā Brāhmana, (4) Pāritābhā, (5) Apramāna, (6) Abhāsvara, (7) Paritasubhā, (8) Apramānasubha, (9) Subhakrishnā, (10) Utpala, (11) Asañasatya, (12) Avriha or Vrihatpāla, (13) Atapa, (14) Sudasa, (15) Sudasi, (16) Punyaprasava, (17) Anabhraka, (18) Akanishtha (Tib., *Og-min*) or "The Highest"—the abode of the Primordial Buddha-God, the Ādi-Buddha of the Lāmas, viz., Samantabhadra (T., Kuntu-zańpo). This last, together with the next subjacent Brahmaloka, are according to the Lāmaists eternal, and are placed above the Arūpa Brahmalokas.

The *Four Arūpa Brahmalokas* are 1. Akāsānantāyatana, 2. Vijñānāntayatana, 3. Akincañāyatana, 4. Naivāsañjñana Sañjñayatana.

The duration of existence in each of those states is for vastly increasing periods from below upwards, till beyond the sixteenth immortality itself is reached; and according to some of the later Buddhists, each Bodhisat must traverse each of these stages (*Bhum*) before he attains Buddhahood.

The typical heaven of the gods—Indra's paradise—is pictured in the Wheel of Life at page 108. Its atmosphere is yellow, and in it are portrayed the four states of godly birth, bliss, passion and misery and death.

Godly Birth. The god is born at once fully developed within a halo of glory from a lotus-flower,—the oriental symbol of immaterial birth and is provided with the special attributes of a god,—viz., (1) a lotus-footstool, (2) splendid dress and ornaments, (3) goddess-companions,[1] (4) a wish-granting tree, or *pag-sam-shin* (Skt., *Kalpadaru*)[2] which instantly yields any fruit or food wished for, and bends to the hand of the gatherer, its leaves yielding luscious food, its juice nectar, and its

1 Apsaras, celestial nymphs—the "houris" awarded to heroes.

2 The wish-granting tree of Indra's heaven is described in the 45th Section of the *S'ilpa S'ástra.*

fruit jewels, (5) a wish-granting cow (*Kāma-dhenu* or *Surabha*[1]) which yields any drink wished for, (6) self-sprung crops (usually painted as Indian corn or maize), (7) in a golden stall a jewelled horse-of-foreknowledge which Pegasus-like carries his rider wherever wished, throughout the worlds of the past, present, and future, (8) a lake of perfumed nectar or ambrosia (Skt., *Amrita*) which is the *elixir vitæ* and the source of the divine lustre.[2] Shining is a peculiarly divine attribute, and the

HEAVENLY BIRTH.

etymology of the word "*divinity*," is the root *Div*, "to shine," the parent of the Skt. *Deva* and Latin *Deus*.

Godly Bliss. The bliss of the gods is depicted by an assembly of bejewelled gods and goddesses basking in sensuous enjoyment in splendid palaces in the midst of a charming garden enamelled with flowers, of which they make their wreaths. Gay birds warble in the foliage, and noble animals peacefully roam together there. Amongst the quadrupeds are deer, lions, and elephants with jewelled heads. Amongst the birds are the peacock, parrot, cuckoo, and the "*Kala-pinka*," which repeats the mystic 'Om mani padme, Hūṃ!" for the language of the gods is the

1 Images of these are sold in the Indian bazaars as toys for children. Compare this myth of the wishing-cow with the parallels related by Professor Weber in *Sitzungsberichte der Kœnig Preuss., Acad. zu Berlin.*, xxvii., 1890.

2 The cup-bearer is Dhanwantari, the Indian Ganymede.

Deva-nagari or sacred language of India. One of the blissful conditions of godly life especially dwelt upon, is that the most dainty morsels may be eaten without sense of repletion, the last morsel being as much relished as the first.

In the centre of this paradise is the great city of Belle-vue (Sudarṣana), within which is the celestial palace of Vaijayanta (Amarāvati) the residence of Indra (Jupiter), the king of the gods. It is invested by a wall and pierced by four gates, which are guarded by the four divine kings of the quarters. It is a three-storied building; Indra occupying the basement, Brāhma the middle, and the indigenous Tibetan war-god—the *dGra-lha*—as a gross form of Māra, the god of Desire, the uppermost story. This curious perversion of the old Buddhist order of the heavens is typical of the more sordid devil-worship of the Lāmas who, as victory was the chief object of the Tibetans, elevated the war-god to the highest rank in their pantheon, as did the Vikings with Odin where Thor, the thunder-god, had reigned supreme. The passionate war-god of the Tibetans is held to be superior even to the divinely meditative state of the Brāhma.

War with the Titans. The gods wage war with the Titans, who, as we have seen, are constantly trying to seize some of the precious fruit of the great *Yoṅ-du sa-tol* (Skt., *Pārijāta*[1]) tree, or "tree of the concentrated essence of earth's products," whose branches are in heaven, but whose roots are in their country. The climber which encircles this tree is called the *Jambuti* tree, and is the medium by which the quintessence of the most rare delicacies of Jambudvīp are instilled into the larger tree. And the war-god directs the divine army.

To account for the high position thus given to the war-god, it is related that he owes it to the signal assistance rendered by him to the gods in opposing the Asuras.[2]

The misery of the gods. The god enjoys bliss for almost incalculable time; but when his merit is exhausted then his lake of

[1] Identified with the beautiful Indian Coral Tree (*Erythrina Indica*).

[2] It is related that in former times the gods were defeated by the Asuras in fighting for the fruits of the great wishing-tree of Paradise; and the defeated gods under Indra besought *g*Saṅ-bahi-*b*dag-po for council. This divinity advised the gods to call to their aid the war-god *dGra-lha*, and also to obtain from the depths of the central ocean the invisible armour and the nine self-created weapons, viz.:—(1) *rMog-bya khyung-keng-riis*, a helmet of the skeleton bones of the Garuḍa bird; (2) *Khrab-ñi-shar-lto-rgyab*, the coat of mail shining like the sun; (3) *Lba-khebs-rdorje-*

nectar dries up; his wish-granting tree, cow and horse die; his splendid dress and ornaments grow dim and disappear; his palace gets dilapidated; his flowers and garden fade; his body, no longer bathed by nectar, loses its lustre and sweats like mortals, so that his person becomes loathsome to his goddess-companions and the other gods, who shun him, and so the poor god dies miserably.[1] If he has led a virtuous life during his existence as a god then he may be re-born in heaven, otherwise he goes to a lower region and may even be sent to hell. Buddha was born twenty times as the god Ṣakra or Indra (Jupiter) and four times as Brāhma.[2]

THE BUDDHIST HELL.

The antithesis to heaven is hell, which with its awful lessons looms large on the horizon of the Buddhists. For according to their ethical doctrine of retribution, and in the case of the more theistic developments, their conception of God as the supreme type of right-doing, they picture him like a human judge trying and punishing the evil-doers;[3] although, with truly Buddhist idealism, these tortures are believed by the more philosophical Lāmas to be morbid creations of the individual's own ideas, a sort of hellish nightmare. The majority of the Lāmas, however, and

go-c'a, necklet; (4) *Lak-hag-mt'sŏn-c'ā-lam-lok*, a weapon resisting and returning glove; (5) *sÑin-khebs-mdah-mts'ŏn-kun thub*, a breast-plate entirely able to withstand arrows and other weapons; (6) *Püs-khebs-ñes-pa-skyobs-c'ed*, a knee-cap which defends against destruction; (7) *Phubm-sba-dmar-gling-druq*, a six-embossed shield. The nine sorts of weapons are:—(1) a *'K'orlo* or spiked-disc which completely routes the enemy; (2) a *dGra-sta* or an axe which chops the enemy; (3) a *ral-gri* or sword which slices the enemy; (4) a *gZhu* or bow which scatters the brains of the enemy; (5) a "*mDah*" or arrow that pierces the vitals; (6) a *Zhagspa* or noose which ensnares the enemy; (7) a *mDung* or spear which pierces the hearts of the foe; (8) a *Ur-rdo*, a whirring sling-stone that produces the "*ur-r-r*" sound of a thunder-dragon; and (9) a *Dorje* or thunder-bolt which demolishes the enemy. The story seems founded on the Brāhmanical legend of Indra (Jupiter) obtaining from the sea the talismanic banner which conferred victory over his enemies; cf. *Brihat Sañhita*, translated by Dr. KERN, *J.R.A.S.*, vi., p. 44.

The gods having obtained these weapons and armour, invited the war-god, who came enveloped in thunder-clouds and attended by his nine sons, and receiving worship from Indra and the other gods as the price of his assistance, they assailed and utterly routed the Titans.

1 Compare HARDY, *Man*, 143.

2 R.D. *Buddhist Birth Stories* Ci.

3 Cf. MAINE's works on Early Law.

the laity, believe in the real material character of these hells and their torture.

The Buddhist hell (*Naraka*[1]) is a true *inferno* situated in the bowels of the human earth like Hades, and presided over by the Indian Pluto, Yama, the king and judge of the dead, who however is himself finite and periodically tortured. Every day he is forced to swallow molten metal. So, as the shade of Achilles says, "it is better to live on earth as the poorest peasant than to rule as a prince of the dead."[2]

The Great Judgment is determined solely by the person's own deeds, and it is concretely pictured by the ordeal of scales, where the good deeds, as white pebbles, are weighed against the sins, as black counters, in balances, and the judge holds a mirror which reveals the soul in all its nakedness. "Not in the heavens, not in the midst of the sea, not if thou hidest thyself in the clefts of the mountains wilt thou find a place where thou canst escape the force resulting from thy evil actions."[3] "Through the six states of transmigration does the power of our actions lead us. A life in heaven awaits the good. The warders of hell drag the wicked before the king of hell, Yama, who says to them:—

"'Did you not when on earth see the five divine messengers sent to warn you—the child, the old man, the sick, the criminal suffering punishment, and the dead corpse?' And the wicked man answers—'I did see them.'

"'And didst thou not think within thyself: "I also am subject to birth, old age, and death. Let me be careful to do good works"?' And the wicked man answers: 'I did not, sire; I neglected in my folly to think of these things.'

"Then the king, Yama, pronounces his doom: 'These thy evil deeds are not the work of thy mother, father, relatives, friends, advisers. Thou alone hast done them all; thou alone must gather the fruit.' And the warders of hell drag him to the place of torment, rivet him to red-hot iron, plunge him in glowing seas of blood, torture him on burning coals, and he dies not till the last residue of his guilt has been expiated."[4]

Nor is hell a complete expiation of offences, for Buddha is credited with saying, "A harsh word uttered in past times is not lost, but returns again," and the Jātaka tales are full of incidents in illustration.

[1] dmyal-k'ams, or "the region of torment." Compare with Chinese version in BEAL's *Catena*, p. 56, *seq.*

[2] *Odyssey*, xi., 481.

[3] *Dhamma-pada*, 127.

[4] *Deva-dūta-sutta*, transl. by H. OLDENBERG.

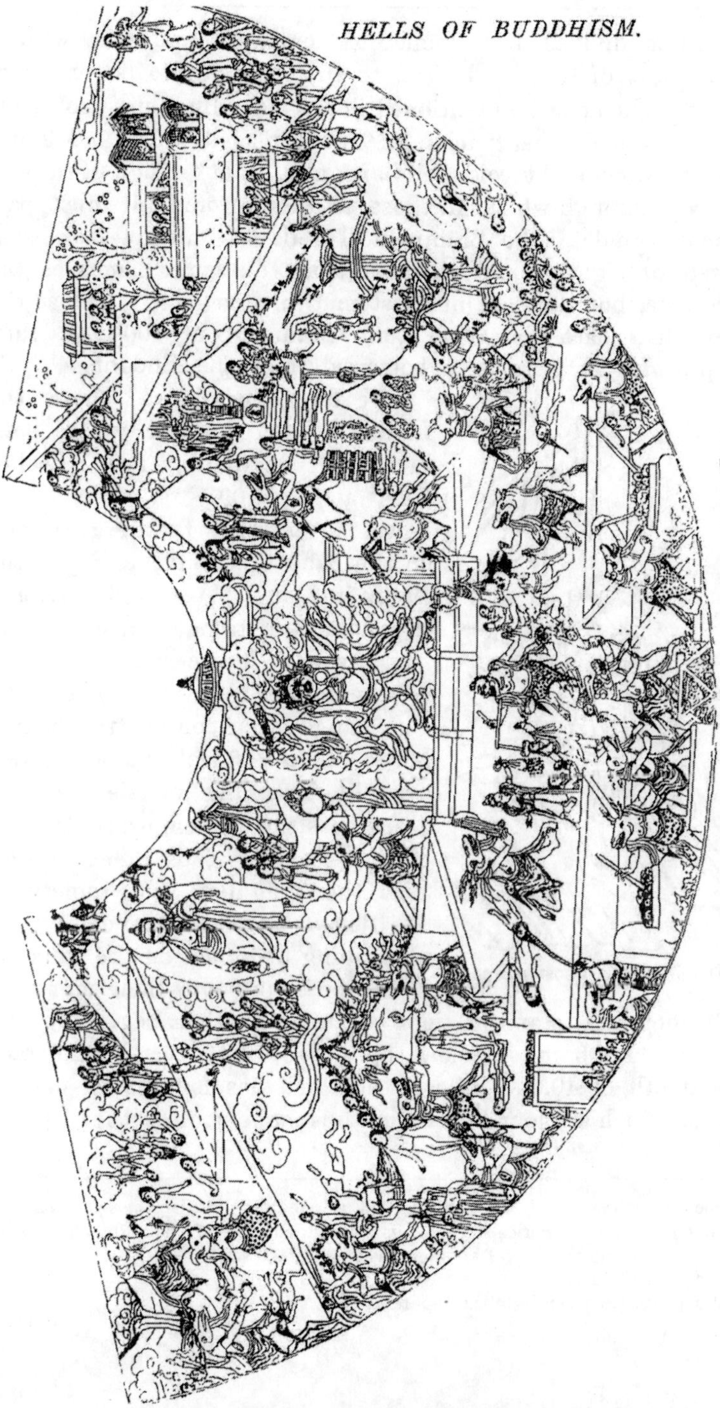

THE GREAT JUDGMENT AND COMPARTMENTS OF THE BUDDHIST HELL.
(From a fresco of a Wheel of Life in Tashiding Temple.)

Hell is divided into numerous compartments, each with a special sort of torture devised to suit the sins to be expiated.

Only eight hells are mentioned in the older Buddhist books, but the Lāmas and other "northern" Buddhists describe and figure eight hot and eight cold hells and also an outer hell (*Pratyeka naraka*), through which all those escaping from hell must pass without a guide. The Brāhmanical hells are multiples of seven instead of eight; some of them bear the same names as the Buddhists, but they are not systematically arranged, and as the extant lists date no earlier than Manu, about 400 A.D., they are probably in great part borrowed from the Buddhists.[1]

THE BUDDHIST PROSPERINE.

The foregoing figure[2] shows the Lāmaist hells, but they are seen in greater detail in "The Wheel of Life," at page 109.

At the entrance to the great hell on the bank of the Hindū Styx—the Baitarāni[3] or "three path" river—sits, according to one version, an old hag, a sort of Prosperine, who strips off the clothes from the new arrivals, and hangs them on a tree behind her.[4] She is 160 feet in stature, with eyes like burning wheels, and she despatches the condemned souls along their respective roads in accordance with the judgment, but sometimes she delays them with endless tasks of heaping up stones on the banks of Styx, and so prolongs their agony.

The hot hells stand in tiers, one upon another, beginning at a depth of 11,900 miles below the surface of the earth, and reach to a depth of 40,000 miles; each hell has four gates, outside each of which are four *ante*-hells, thus making altogether 136 hot hells.

[1] See an article by M. Leon Feer, "L'Enfer indien," in the *Journal Asiatique*, xx. (1892), and i. (New Series 1893), for lists and description of the Brāhmanist hells.

[2] For the tracing of which I am indebted to Mr. J. C. White.

[3] ="The sedent queen."

[4] Her picture is given from the Japanese.

The atmosphere of the hells is of the deepest black:—

> "Light was absent all. Bellowing there groan'd
> A noise, as of a sea in tempest torn
> By warring winds, the stormy blast of hell."
> DANTE, Canto v., 29.

Each hell is enveloped by a wall of fire, and the horrible torments are fit to illustrate Dante's *Inferno*. Indeed, it has been suggested that Dante must have seen a Buddhist picture of these hells before writing his famous classic, so remarkable is the agreement between them. The lictors (*s'in-je*) are savage flame-enveloped monsters with heads of various animals, and all their pincers, and other instruments of torture, are red-hot.

HOT HELL No. 1.

The following are the eight great hot hells.

1. *Sañjīva* [1] = "again revived." Here the wretches are cut and torn to pieces and then re-united and revived only to suffer the same process repeated *ad infinitum* throughout the period spent in this hell.

> "Because our wounds heal ever and anon
> Ere we appear before the fiend again."
> DANTE, Canto xxviii., 36.

This restoration of the body, in order to subject it to fresh torture, is an essential part of the process in all the hells. The body when thoroughly mangled is restored and the racking torture applied afresh, so that the agony never ceases. This is the special hell for suicides, murderers, ignorant physicians who killed their patients, fraudulent trustees, and tyrants.

2. *Kālasūtra* [2] = "black lines." Here the victims are nailed down and eight or sixteen black lines drawn by the lictors along the body, which is then sawn asunder along these lines by a burning hot saw. Another

[1] Yaṅ-sos. [2] t'ig-nag.

punishment here is the especial one of the slanderer, or busy-body, who has his or her tongue enlarged and pegged out and constantly harrowed by spikes ploughing through it. To this hell are assigned those who during life were disrespectful to their parents, or to Buddha, or the priests.

3. *Saṃghāta*,[1] = "concentrated oppression." Here the guilty are

HOT HELL No. 3.

squeezed and crushed between animal-headed mountains, or monster iron books. This last is an especial punishment for monks, laymen and infidels who have disregarded or profaned the scriptures, and also for priests who have taken money for masses which they have not performed. Others here are pounded in iron mortars and beaten on anvils. Here are tortured thieves, those who indulged in hatred, envy, passion, the users of light weights and measures, and those who cast refuse or dead animals on the public roads.

4. *Raurava*,[2] = "weeping and screaming." The torture here is to have molten iron poured down the throat. Those who were prisoners, obstructed watercourses, or grumbled against the weather (? clearly the English hell !), or wasted food, are here tortured.

[1] bsdus 'joms.

[2] ṅu-'bod.

5. *Mahāraurava*,[1] = "greater weeping and screaming." Here they are cooked in seething cauldrons of molten iron. This is the hell for heretics.

6. *Tāpana*,[2] = "heat." The condemned is enclosed in a red-hot fiery chamber. In this hell are punished those who roasted or baked animals for their food.

7. *Pratāpana*,[3] = "highest heat." A three-spiked burning spear is thrust into the wretch's body, which is then rolled up within red-hot iron plates. It is the special torture for apostates and those who reject the truth.

8. *Avīchi*,[4] = "endless torture." This is the most severe and longest of all the infernal torments. The guilty is perpetually kept in flames, though never consumed. This is the hell for those who have reviled Buddha, and others who have harmed or attempted to harm Lāmaism or shed the blood of a Lāma or holy-man.

The Cold Hells, apparently an invention of the northern Buddhists, as cold was an idea rather foreign to the Indian mind, are situated on the edge of the universe below its encircling wall (Cakravala). They are encircled by icy mountains (see plate, page 109), and have attendants of appalling aspect, as in the hot hells. They are thus described :—

1. *Arbuda*,[5] = "blistered or chapped." The torture here is constant immersion of the naked person in ice and glacier water, under which the body becomes covered with chilblains (which torture may be compared with the curse invented by a scribe in the reign of Athelstan for anyone who should break the terms of his charters: "May he be tortured by the bitter blasts of glaciers and the Pennine army of evil spirits."[6])

2. *Nirarbuda*.[7] The chilblains are rudely scarified, producing raw sores.

3. *Atata*,[8] "Ach'u" or "*A-ta-ta*," an exclamation of anguish beyond articulate expression—which resounds through this hell.

4. *Hahava*.[9] A worse degree of cold in which the tongue is paralyzed and the exclamation *Kyi-'ü* or *Ha-ha* alone possible.

5. *Ahaha*.[10] Here both jaws and teeth are spasmodically clenched through cold.

6. *Utpala*.[11] Livid sores which become everted like blue Ut-pal flowers.

---

1 Ṅu-bod Ch'en-po.

2 Ts'a-ba.

3 Rab-tu t'sa-wa.

4 mnar-med.

5 Ch'u-bur ch'en. *Arbu* sounds suspiciously like Mount Abu (B

6 Quoted by Mr. D. W. Freshfield in *J. R. Geog. S.*, 1894.

7 Ch'u-bur-brol-wa.

8 A-ch'u.

9 Kyi-'ud.

10 So-t'am-pa.

11 Ut-pal-ltar gas-pa.

7. *Padma.*[1] The raw sores become like red Lotus-flowers.

8. *Puṇḍarīka.*[2] Raw sores where the flesh falls away from the bones like the petals of the great Lotus; and which are continually pecked and gnawed by birds and insects with iron beaks.

The frontier or anterior hells at the exit from the great hell are called "The near (to re-birth) cycle,"[3] and are divided into four sections.[4] The first bordering hell consists of hot suffocating ashes with foul dead bodies and all kinds of offal. Then is reached a vast quagmire, beyond which is a forest of spears and spikes, which must be traversed like the razor-bridge in Muhammadanism and in Bunyan's *Pilgrim's Progress.* Then succeeds a great river of freezing water; on the further shore of which the ground is thickly set with short squat tree-trunks, each surmounted by three spiked leaves which impale the unwary groping fugitives. Reference to these last two localities occurs in the ordinary litany for the dead, which says "may his *c'hu-wo-rab-med* ocean become a small rivulet, and the *ts'al-ma-ri* tree a divine wish-granting tree."

In addition to the hot and cold hells are eighty-four thousand external hells (Ñe-ts'e-wa, Skt. ? Lokāntarika) situated mostly on the earth, in mountains, deserts, hot springs, and lakes.

Another state of existence, little better than that of hell, is the Preta (Tib., Yi-dag) or *Manes,* a sort of tantalized ghoul or ghost. This world is placed above hell and below the *Sitavan* forest, near Rajgriha, in the modern district of Patna in Bengal.

These wretched starvelings are in constant distress through the pangs of hunger and thirst.[5] This is pictured in the Wheel of

---

[1] Padma-ltar-gas-pa.

[2] Padma ch'en-po-ltar-gas pa.

[3] ñe-'k'or (=? Skt., *Prateyka naraka*) meaning near to re-birth.

[4] Named *Agni-khadā* (me-ma-mur gyi 'obs) or the fiery pit, *Kunapanka* (Ro-myags Kyl 'daṃs) or quagmire of carcases, *Khuradhārāvana* (spu-gri gtams ts'al) or forest of spikes, and *Asidhāravana* (ral-gri loma nays-ts'al) or forest of sword-leaves.

[5] Thirty-six species are described in five groups, namely: (1) *p'yii sgrib-pa chan* or "the foreign or gentile horrid beings," (2) *Nang-gi sgrib-pa chan* or the Buddhist horrid beings, (3) *Zas-skom-gyi sgrib-pa chan* or the eating and drinking horrid beings —these are they who on eating and drinking have the ingested material converted into lacerating weapons, (4) . . . . . and (5) *kha-thor* or free Yi-dags. The latter are not confined in the *Preta*-prison, but are free to roam about in the human world—in graveyards, etc.,—and injure man. These are (BEAL's *Catena*, 67) 1, Flat-bodied; 2, Needle-mouthed; 3, Vomit-eaters; 4, Filth-eaters; 5, Mist-eaters; 6, Water-feeders; 7, Scarcely seen; 8, Spittle-feeders; 9, Hair-eaters; 10, Blood-suckers; 11, Notion-feeders; 12, Flesh-

Life, also in the annexed figure. This is the special torment for those who, in their earthly career, were miserly, covetous, uncharitable, or gluttonous. Jewels, food, and drink are found in plenty, but the Pretas have mouths no bigger than the eye of a needle, and gullets no thicker in diameter than a hair, through which they can never ingest a satisfying amount of

TANTALIZED SPIRITS.

food for their huge bodies. And when any food is taken it becomes burning hot, and changes in the stomach into sharp knives, saws, and other weapons, which lacerate their way out from the bowels to the surface, making large painful wounds. They are constantly crying "water, water, give water!" And the thirst is expressed in the picture by a flame which is seen to issue from their parched mouths, and whenever they attempt to touch

eaters; 13, Incense-feeders; 14, Fever-makers; 15, Secret pryers; 16, Earth lurkers; 17, Spirit-rappers; 18, Flame-burners; 19, Baby-snatchers; 20, Sea-dwellers; 21, ...; 22, King Yama's club-holders; 23, Starvelings; 24, Baby-eaters; 25, Vital-eaters; 26, Rakshas; 27, Smoke-eaters; 28, Marsh-dwellers; 29, Wind-eaters; 30, Ash-feeders; 31, Poison-eaters; 32, Desert-livers; 33, Spark-feeders; 34, Tree-dwellers; 35, Road-dwellers; 36, Body-killers.

H

water it changes to liquid fire. Avalokita is frequently figured in the act of giving water to these Pretas to relieve their misery.[1]

And a famous story of Buddha credits the great Māudgalyāyāna, the right-hand disciple of "the Blessed One," with having descended into the *Preta*-world to relieve his mother. As this story, the Avalambana Sutra, dating to before the third century A.D., gives a very vivid picture of this tantalizing purgatory, and also illustrates the rites for extricating the starveling ghosts,[2] it is here appended.

Māudgalyāyāna's descent into the *Preta* purgatory.

Thus have I heard. Buddha at one time was residing in the country of Srâvasti, in the garden of Jeta, the friend of the orphans. At this time Mugalan, having begun to acquire the six supernatural powers (*irrdhi*), desiring above all things, from a motive of piety, to deliver his father and mother, forthwith called into use his power of supernatural sight, and looking throughout the world he beheld his unhappy mother existing without food or drink in the world of *Pretas* (hungry ghosts), nothing but skin and bone. Mugalan, moved with filial pity, immediately presented to her his alms-bowl filled with rice. His mother then taking the bowl in her left hand, endeavoured with her right to convey the rice to her mouth, but before it came near to her lips, lo! the rice was converted into fiery ashes, so that she could not eat thereof. At the sight of this Mugalan uttered a piteous cry, and wept many tears as he bent his way to the place where Buddha was located. Arrived there, he explained what had happened, and awaited Buddha's instruction. On this the Master opened his mouth, and said, "The sin which binds your mother to this unhappy fate is a very grievous one; from it you can never by your own strength rescue her, no! nor yet all the powers of earth or heaven, men or divine beings: not all these are equal to the task of deliverance. But by assembling the priests of the ten quarters, through their spiritual energy, deliverance may be had. I will now recount to you the method of rescue from this and all similar calamities." Then Buddha continued: "On the 15th day of the seventh month, the priests of the ten quarters being gathered together ought to present an offering for the rescue of ancestors during seven generations past, as well as those of the present generation, every kind of choice food and drink, as well as sleeping materials and beds. These should be offered up by the assembled priesthood as though the ancestors themselves were present, by which they shall obtain deliverance from the pains, and be born at once in a condition of happiness in heaven." And, moreover, the World-honoured One

[1] See my "Indian Cult of Avalokita," *J. R. A. S.*, p. 1, and plates ii. and iii., 1894.

[2] Translated by S. Beal in *The Oriental*, November 6th, 1875. A dramatized version is common in China.—Cf. *Les Fêtes annuellement célébrés à Emoin*, J. J. M. de Groot.

taught his followers certain words to be repeated at the offering of sacrifices, by which the virtue thereof would be certainly secured.

On this Mugalan with joy accepted the instruction, and by means of this institution rescued his mother from her sufferings.

And so for all future time this means of deliverance shall be effectual for the purpose designed, as year by year the offerings are presented according to the form delivered by Buddha.

Having heard these words, Mugalan and the rest departed to their several places, with joyous hearts and glad thoughts.

Related apparently to this story is the Lāmaist account of "The queen of the Pretas with the fiery mouth," whom the Lāmas identify with the celebrated *Yakshini* fiendess Hariti, for whom and her five hundred sons they daily reserve some of their food, relating in support of this practice the following story, evidently borrowed from the story of Hariti in the *Ratnakūṭa Sutra*:—

HARITI, THE CHILD-EATING YAKSHINI, AND "QUEEN OF PRETAS."

Hariti, queen of the hungry ghouls with the burning mouths, had five hundred children, whom she fed on living children. The great Buddha, "Mohugalaputra," coming to her dwelling, hid away Pingala, the youngest and most beloved of her sons, in his begging-bowl, unknown to the gods or demons. The mother, on her return, was drowned in sorrow at the loss of her favourite son, and in her distress appealed to the omniscient Mohugalaputra for aid to recover him. The Buddha then showed her Pingala within his bowl, yet all the efforts of Hariti and her demons failed to release him. So she besought Buddha for aid, who replied, "You, with five hundred children, mercilessly devour the children of men who have only two or three, yet you grieve at the loss of only one!" The *Preta*-queen declared that this one was the most precious of all, and she vowed that were he released she never again would devour human children. The Buddha, consenting, restored her child, and gave her the three Refuges and the five Precepts, and (say the Lāmas) he promised that in future all Buddhist monks would give her a handful of their daily food.[1]

This practice is probably derived from the Hindū offering of food and drink to the manes of departed relatives, the *Sraddha* ceremonial.

Flying visits of mortals to Hades, having their parallels in

[1] The Japanese version of this legend and its pictorial illustration are published by Sir. A. W. Franks, F.R.S., in *Jour. Soc. Antiquaries*, Vol. liii., 1892. Buddha further informed her that "You were the ninth daughter of King Chia-ye at the time of Buddha Kāṣyapa, and performed many great and meritorious actions. But because you did not keep the precepts you received the form of a demon."

Odysseu's and Dante's visits to purgatory, are found in Lāmaism, where they are known as *De-lok*, or "the ghostly returning," and are used for stirring the people to good behaviour.

Buddhist Metaphysics.

Buddha, being a Hindū, accepted the Hindū theory of the universe and its fantastic world-system, with the modifications above indicated, and he started also with the current notions of metempsychosis and *Karma* as part of his mental furniture.

According to the theory of metempsychosis, or more properly palingenesis, which was not unknown to the ancient Hellenic and even Jewish literature, and western fairy-tales,

> "The soul that rises with us, our life's star
> Hath had elsewhere its setting."—Wordsworth.

Death merely alters the form, but does not break the continuity of the life, which proceeds from death to re-birth, and fresh deaths to fresh re-births in constant succession of changing states, dissolving and evolving until the breaking up of the universe after a *kalpa*, or almost an eternity of ages. How Buddha modified this doctrine will be referred to presently.

Karma,[1] or the ethical doctrine of retribution, is accepted as regards its general principle, even by such modern men of science as Huxley.[2] It explains all the acts and events of one's life as

---

[1] Tibetan, las and p'rin-las.

[2] Professor Huxley in his lecture on *Evolution and Ethics* says:—

"Everyday experience familiarizes us with the facts which are grouped under the name of heredity. Every one of us bears upon him obvious marks of his parentage, perhaps of remoter relationships. More particularly the sum of tendencies to act in a certain way, which we call 'character' is often to be traced through a long series of progenitors and collaterals. So we may justly say that this 'character,' this moral and intellectual essence of a man does veritably pass over from one fleshy tabernacle to another and does really transmigrate from generation to generation. In the newborn infant the character of the stock lies latent, and the Ego is little more than a bundle of potentialities, but, very early, these become actualities: from childhood to age they manifest themselves in dulness or brightness, weakness or strength, viciousness or uprightness: and with each feature modified by confluence with another character, if by nothing else, the character passes on to its incarnation in new bodies.

"The Indian philosophers called character, as thus defined, 'Karma.' It is this Karma which passed from life to life and linked them in the chain of transmigrations; and they held that it is modified in each life, not merely by confluence of parentage but by its own acts * * * * * *

"In the theory of evolution, the tendency of a germ to develop according to a

the results of deeds done in previous existences, and it creates a system of rewards and punishments, sinking the wicked through the lower stages of human and animal existence, and even to hell, and lifting the good to the level of mighty kings, and even to the gods.

In this way Buddha explained all the acts and events of his life, his joys and sorrows, his success and failures, his virtues and weaknesses, as results of things done by him in previous states of life, which he recalled to mind as occasion arose for teaching purposes. And thus those anecdotes of the antecedent lives of the Buddha, —the so-called "*Jātaka* tales"—with the moral lessons derived from them, came to be among the most cherished items of Buddhist belief.[1]

The various regions of re-birth or "ways" of life, the so-called *Gati*,[2] are pictorially represented in the accompanying drawing called "The Wheel of Life." They are given as six (or five, as with the primitive Buddhists when the *Titans* were not separately represented), and are thus enumerated in the order of their superiority:—

1st. The Gods (*Sura* or *Deva*, Tibetan, Lha).
2nd. Titans (*Asura*, T., Lha-ma-yin).
3rd. Man (*Nara*, T., Mi).
4th. Beasts (Tiryak, T., Du-dô[3]).
5th. Tantalized Ghosts (*Preta*, T., Yi-dvag).
6th. Hell (Naraka, T., Ñal-k'am).

Bournouf[4] writing from Chinese and Ceylonese sources, classes man above the Titans, but the order now given is that adopted by

certain specific type, *e.g.*, of the kidney-bean seed to grow into a plant having all the characters of *Phaseolus vulgaris*, is its 'Karma.' It is the 'last inheritor and the last result of all the conditions that have effected a line of ancestry which goes back for many millions of years to the time when life first appeared on earth.' As Professor Rhys Davids aptly says, the snowdrop 'is a snowdrop and not an oak, and just that kind of a snowdrop, because it is the outcome of the Karma of an endless series of past existences.'"

1 Buddha's births are usually numbered at 550, of which the latter and more important are called "the Great Births." For list of different forms of existence ascribed to Buddha in his previous births see RHYS DAVIDS' *Jātaka Tales*. Cf. also COWELL'S edition of the Jātakas translated from the Pāli, and RALSTON'S Tales from the Tibetan.

2 "Skt., *Gāti;* Tib., gro-bahi rigs."

3 Literally "the bent goers."

4 *Lotus de la bonne Loi*, p. 377.

the Lāmas.[1] Existence in the first three worlds is considered superior or good, and in the last three inferior or bad. And these

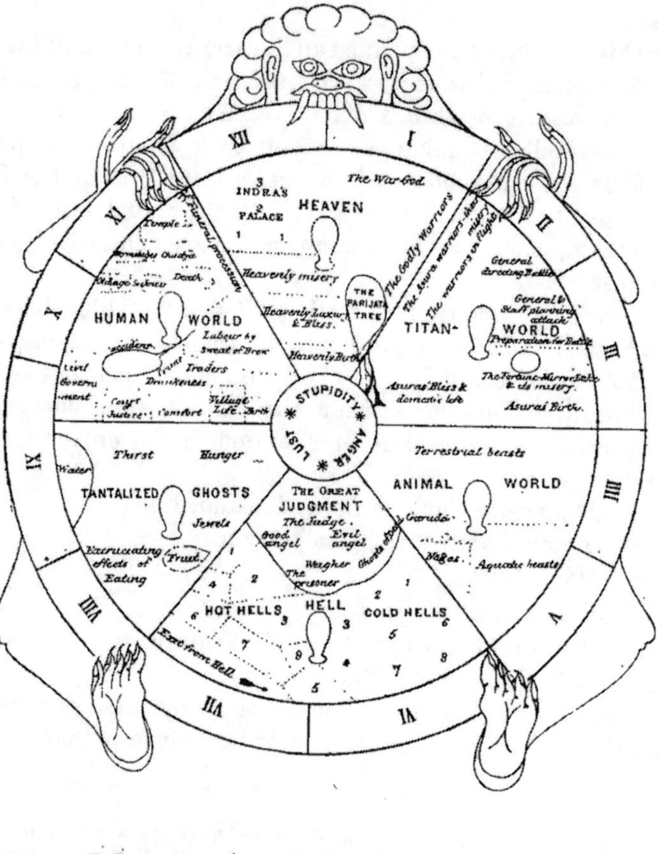

The Roman numerals indicate the Nidānas The interior Compartments are numbered as in the text.

KEY TO WHEEL OF LIFE.
(See p. 109.)

worlds are shown in this relation in the picture, the highest being heaven, and the lowest hell.

The six regions of re-birth are shown in the middle whorl.

[1] Conf., HARDY'S *Man. of Buddhism*, p. 37. The Lāmaist account is contained in the "*m*ṅon-pa-ī *m*dsod," translated by Lotsawa Bande-*d*pal *r*tsegs from the work of the Indian Paṇḍit Vasubandhu, etc.

They are demarcated from each other by rainbow-coloured cordons representing the atmospheric zones that separate the different worlds. No place is allotted to the other phases of existence believed in by the Lāmas, namely, the everlasting existence in the western paradise of *Sukhāvati* and of the celestial Buddhas and demoniacal protectors of Lāmaism, and the expressed absence of such expressions of the current modern beliefs favours the claim of this picture to considerable antiquity.

Of these six states all have already been described except the third and fourth, namely, the state of being a man or a beast, a reference to the Buddhist conception of which is necessary to understand the picture of The Wheel of Life.

The most pessimistic view is of course taken of human life. It is made to be almost unalloyed misery, its striving, it perennially unsatisfied desire, its sensations of heat and cold, thirst and hunger, depression even by surfeiting with food, anxiety of the poor for their daily bread, of the farmer for his crops and cattle, unfulfilled desires, separation from relatives, subjection to temporal laws, infirmities of old age and disease, and accidents are amongst the chief miseries referred to. The miseries of human existence are classed into eight sections, viz.: The miseries of (1) birth; (2) old age; (3) sickness; (4) death; (5) ungratified wishes and struggle for existence; (6) misfortunes and punishments for law-breaking; (7) separation from relatives and cherished objects; (8) offensive objects and sensations.

In the picture the following phases of life are depicted amongst others:—

1st. Birth in a cottage.

2nd. Children at play.

3rd. Manhood, village scenes, people drinking wine under shade of a tree, a man playing a flute, women spinning and weaving, a borrower, two traders, a drunken man.

4th. Labour by sweat of brow, men tilling a field, gathering fuel in a forest, carrying a heavy load.

5th. Accident, a man and horse falling into a river.

6th. Crime, two men fighting, one under trial before the judge, and one undergoing corporal punishment.

7th. Temporal government: the king and his ministers.

8th. Old age—decrepit old people.

9th. Disease, a physician feeling the pulse of a patient.

10th. Death, a corpse with a Lāma feeling whether breath be extinct, and a Lāma at the head doing worship, and a woman and other relatives weeping.

11th. Funeral ceremonies. A corpse being carried off to the funeral pyre on the top of a hill, preceded by a Lāma blowing a thigh-bone trumpet and rattling a hand drum: he also has hold of the end of a white scarf which is affixed to the corpse. The object of this scarf is to guide the soul by the white path to the pyre so that it may be disposed of in the orthodox manner, and have the best chance of a good re-birth, and may not stray and get caught by outside demons. Behind the corpse-bearer is a porter with food and drink offerings, and last of all a mourning relative.

12th. Religion is represented by a temple placed above all other habitations with a Lāma and monk performing worship; and a hermit in his cell with bell, *vajra*-sceptre, and thigh-bone trumpet; and a stupa or caitya (*ch'orten*) circumambulated by a devotee.

The state of the beasts is one of greater misery even than the human. In the picture are shown land and aquatic animals of various kinds devouring one another, the larger preying on the small; and also small ones combining to catch and kill the larger ones. Human hunters also are setting nets for, and others are shooting game. Domestic animals are shown laden with burdens, or ploughing and being goaded; some are being milked and shorn of their wool, others are being branded or castrated or having their nostrils bored, others killed for their flesh or skin, etc. All are suffering great misery through the anxiety and pains of preying or being preyed upon. In the water is shown a *Nāga* or merman's house, with its inmates in grief at being preyed upon by the Garuḍa, a monster bird, like the fabled *roc*, which by the rush of air from its wings cleaves the sea to its depths in its search for *Nāgas*.

We are now in a position to consider Buddha's conception of Human Life—

Buddha's Conception of the Cause of Life and of Misery.[1]

Apart from its importance as an illustration of the earlier intellectual life of humanity, the Buddhist ontology, the most wonderful, perhaps, the world has seen, possesses a paramount interest for all who would arrive at a right understanding of the religion and ethics with which it is associated.

Buddha formulated his view of life into a twelve-linked closed chain called "the Wheel of Life or of 'Becoming'" (*Bhavacakra*), or the Causal Nexus (*Pratītya Samutpāda*); which he is represented, in the Vinaya scripture itself, to have thought out under the Tree of Wisdom.[2] The way in which the narrative is couched, leads, indeed, to the impression that it was precisely the insight into this "Wheel of Life" which constituted his Buddhahood, and distinguished him from the other Arhats. However this may be, he gave it a very leading place in his philosophy, so that the stanza recounting its utterance, *Ye dharmā hetu,*[3] etc., termed by English writers "The Buddhist Creed," is the most frequent of all Buddhist inscriptions, and was certainly in olden days familiar to every lay Buddhist; and it is practically identical with "The four noble Truths," omitting only the initial expression of "suffering."[4]

---

[1] The bulk of this article appeared in the *J.R.A.S.* (1894), pp. 367, etc.

[2] *Vinaya Texts,* Vol. i., pp. 74-84.

[3] "Of all objects which proceed from a Cause
The Tathāgatha has explained the cause,
And he has explained their cessation also;
This is the doctrine of the great Samana."
Vinaya Texts, i., 146.

[4] This famous stanza, says Professor Rhys Davids (*Vinaya Texts,* i., 146), doubtless alludes to the formula of the twelve Nidānas. "The Chain of Causation, or the doctrine of the twelve Nidānas (causes of existence) contains, as has often been observed in a more developed form, an answer to the same problem to which the second and third of the four Noble Truths (Ariya Sacca) also try to give a solution, viz., the problem of the origin and destruction of suffering. The Noble Truths simply reduce the origin of suffering to thirst or desire (Ta*n*hā) in its threefold form, thirst for pleasure, thirst for existence, thirst for prosperity (see i., 6, 20). In the system of the twelve nidānas Thirst also has found its place among the causes of suffering, but it is not considered as the immediate cause. A concatenation of other categories is inserted between ta*n*hā and its ultimate effect; and, on the other hand, the investigation of causes is carried on further beyond ta*n*hā. The question is here asked, what does ta*n*hā come from? and thus the series of causes and effects is led back to *Avigyā* (Ignorance) as its deepest root. We may add that the redactors of the Pitakas who, of course, could not but observe this parallelity between the second and third Ariya Saccas and the

Yet though this chain forms the chief corner-stone of Buddhism, it is remarkable that scarcely any two European scholars are agreed upon the exact nature and signification of some of its chief links, while the sequence of several links is deemed self-contradictory and impossible; and even the alleged continuity of the whole is doubted. The best western authorities who have attempted its interpretation, Childers[1] and Prof. H. Oldenberg, have practically given up the problem in despair; the latter exclaiming, "it is utterly impossible for anyone who seeks to find out its meaning, to trace from beginning to end a connected meaning in this formula."[2]

Such conflict of opinion in regard to this "chain" is mainly due to the circumstance that no commentary on its subtle formula has ever been published; and that the only means hitherto available for its interpretation have been the ambiguous Pāli and Sanskrit terminology for the links themselves. Thus, for one only of these links, namely, *Saṅskāra*, the following are some of the many renderings which have been attempted:—

"Constructing, preparing, perfecting, embellishing, aggregation; matter; *Karma*, the *Skandhas*.—('As a technical term, *Sankāro* has several decided shades of meaning . . . in fact, Sankhāro includes everything of which impermanence may be predicated, or, what is the same thing, everything which springs from a cause'—Childers.)[3] Les Concepts.—(Burnouf)[4]; Composition notion (Csoma); Willen (Schmidt); Discrimination (Hardy); Les idées (Foucaux)[5]; Tendencies, potentialities, confections (Rhys Davids);[6] Gestaltungen: shapes and forms (H. Oldenberg); Conformations (W. Hoey).

This bewildering obscurity of its terminology has somewhat

system of the twelve Nidānas go so far in one instance (Aṅguttara Nikāya, Tika Nipāta, fol. *ke* of the Phayre MS.) as to directly replace in giving the text of the four Ariya Saccas the second and third of these by the twelve Nidānas in direct and reverse order respectively."—*Vinaya Texts*, i., 75.

[1] Colebrooke's *Mis. Essays* 2nd ed., ii., 453 *seq.*

[2] *Buddha*, etc., Eng. trans. by Dr. W. Hoey, p. 226. Recently Mr. H. C. Warren, of Cambridge, Mass. (*Proc. American Oriental Society*, Ap. 6-8, 1893, p. xxvii), has advocated a looser meaning for the word *paccaya*, usually translated "cause," without, however, getting rid of the more serious difficulties which beset the interpretation of the chain.

[3] *Pāli Dict.*, p. 453.

[4] P. 503.

[5] These last four authors are quoted through Köppen, i., 604.

[6] *Buddhism*, p. 91, where the fifty-two divisions are enumerated.

displaced the chain from its due prominence in the European books on the system, notwithstanding the importance claimed for it by Buddhists.

Now I have lately discovered among the frescoes of the ancient Buddhist caves of Ajaṇṭa, in central India, a picture, over thirteen centuries old, which supplies a valuable commentary on this subject. It portrays in concrete form those metaphysical conceptions —the so-called *Nidāna*—which, in their Pāli and Sanskrit terminology, have proved so puzzling to European scholars. And, as this picture, supplemented by its Tibetan versions and its detailed explanation as given me by learned Lāmas, who are thoroughly familiar with it, and possess its traditional interpretation,[1] affords a clue to much that is imperfectly understood, and helps to settle disputed points of fundamental importance, these advantages seem to justify my bringing it to notice, and may also, I hope, justify my attempt, however crude, at exhibiting its continuity as a complete authentic account of human life from the absolute standpoint of the earliest Buddhist philosophy.

One important result of this new interpretation of the ancient formula will be to show that it seems to possess more in common with modern philosophic methods and speculations than is usually suspected. Indeed, it would scarcely be going too far to say that at a period before the epoch of Alexander the Great, in the valley of the Ganges, and at a time when writing was still unknown in India, an Indian anchorite evolved in the main by private study and meditation an ontological system which, while having much in common with the philosophy of Plato and of Kant,[2] and the most profound and celebrated speculations of modern times (such as those of Bishop Berkeley, and Schopenhauer, and Hartmann), yet far surpassed these in elaborateness. And as this bold system formed the basis of Buddhist ethics, its formulas came to be represented for teaching purposes in concrete pictorial form in the vestibules of the Indian monasteries and temples, as they still are in Tibet and China; and although the impermanence of the

[1] As current in mediæval Indian Buddhism.

[2] Buddha seems to have propounded the same truth which Plato and latterly Kant were never tired of repeating, that "this world which appears to the senses has no true Being, but only ceaseless Becoming; it is and it is not, and its comprehension is not so much knowledge as illusion."

materials of the painter's art has unfortunately deprived us of most of its traces in India, where Buddhism has been extinct for centuries, yet I have found it as a relic in the deserted cave-temples of Ajaṇṭa.[1]

Buddha himself may, as the Lāmas relate, have originated the picture of "The Wheel of Life," by drawing it in diagrammatic fashion with grains of rice, from a stalk which he had plucked while teaching his disciples in a rice-field. The introduction of the pictorial details is ascribed to the great Indian monk Nāgārjuna, who lived in the second century A.D., under the patronage of the successors of the Scythian king Kanishka, who we know from Hiuen Tsiang employed artists in great numbers in the decoration of Buddhist buildings. These pictorial details, however, are alleged to be objective representations of the self-same similes used by Buddha himself, who, as is clear from his *Sutras* or sermons, constantly used homely similes and allegories to illustrate his doctrines. And a general account of the construction of the picture occurs in the *Divyāvadāna.*[2]

The particular Indian painting from Ajaṇṭa on which the present article is based, is attributed to the sixth century of our era,[3] while the Tibetan picture which supplements it, is alleged, and with reason, to be a copy of one brought to Tibet by the Indian monk "Bande Yeshe," in the eighth century A.D.[4]

1 See its photograph accompanying my article in *J.R.A.S.*, 1894, p. 370.

2 As noted by Prof. Cowell (MAINE'S *Dissertations on Early Law and Custom*, p. 50), for which reference I am indebted to Mrs. Rhys Davids. In the Divyāvadāna, pp. 299-300, it is related how Buddha, while at the Squirrel's Feeding-ground (Kolandaka) in the Venuvana forest near Rajagriha, instructed Ananda to make a wheel (cakram karayitavyam) for the purpose of illustrating what another disciple, Māudgalyāyāna, saw when he visited other spheres, which it seems he was in the habit of doing. The wheel was to have five spokes (pañcagandakam), between which were to be depicted the hells, animals, pretas, gods, and men. In the middle a dove (pārāvata), a serpent, and a hog were to symbolize lust, hatred, and ignorance. All round the tire was to go the twelve-fold circle of causation in the regular and inverse order. Beings were to be represented "as being born in a supernatural way (anpapādukāh) as by the machinery of a water-wheel falling from one state and being produced in another." Buddha himself is to be outside the wheel. The wheel was made and placed in the "Grand entrance gateway" (dvārakoshthake), and a bhikshu appointed to interpret it.

3 BURGESS, in *Rock Temples*, 309.

4 And now at Sam-yās monastery. For a technical description of it by me see *J.A.S.B.*, lxi., p. 133 *seq.* A confused copy of the picture was figured by GIORGI (*Alphab. Tibet*), and partly reproduced by FOUCAUX, *Annales du Musée Guimet*, Tome sixième, 1884, p. 290, but in neither case with any explanatory description of its details.

THE WHEEL OF LIFE,

Picturing the Buddhist Theory of the Universe.

[To face p. 108.

The Tibetan form of the picture[1] here given should be studied with its Key (p. 102). It is a disc or wheel, symbolizing the endless cycle of Life (*saṃsāra*), of which each re-birth is a revolution. The wheel is held in the clutches of a monster, who represents the hideousness of the Clinging to Life. The broad tire is occupied by the Causal Nexus, and the nave by the three vices or delusions, "The Daughters of Desire," the three vices—*Rāga*, *Dvesa*, *Moha*. Lust, ill-will, stupidity, which lie at the core of re-birth, and are figured here, as in the other Indian picture on page 6, as a dove, serpent, and pig, appropriately coloured red, green, and black; while the body of the wheel, which is considered to be in continuous revolution, is filled with pictorial details of Life in its several forms, or "The Whirling on the Wheel" of Life. And outside the wheel is a figure of Buddha, showing that he has escaped from the cycle, to which he is represented as pointing the way of escape.

The ancient conception of Life under the figure of a wheel of which each re-birth is a revolution is not confined to Buddhism and Brāhmanism. This fancy finds an echo more than once in Hellenic literature.[2]

---

[1] Skt., Bhavacakramudra; T., Srid-pahī 'K'or-lohi p'yag-rgya, or shortly "*Si-pa K'or-lô.*" The Tibetan form of the picture is of two styles, the "old" and "new." The latter is given in the attached plate, and it differs from the "old" only in the introduction of a figure of Avalokita or the God of Mercy, in the form of a *Sage* or *Muni*, into each of the six worlds of re-birth, and in one or two different pictorial symbols for the causes of re-birth.

[2] Cf. note by Prof. C. Bendall on "Platonic Teaching in Ancient India."—*Athenæum*, 10th January, 1891. Mrs. Rhys Davids, commenting on my article (*J R.A.S.*, 1894, p. 388), writes: "In the Orphic theogony we come across the notion of re-birth considered as a weary unending cycle of fate or necessity—*κύκλος τῆς γενέσεως, ὁ τῆς μοίρας τροχός*, etc.—from which the soul longs to escape, and entreats the gods, especially Dionysos (*Διόνυσος λυσιοι θεὸὶ λύσιον*), for release,—*κύκλου τε λῆξαι καὶ ἀναπνεῦσαι κακότητος*. In the verses inscribed on one of three golden funereal tablets dug up near the site of Sybaris the line occurs: 'And thus I escaped from the cycle, the painful, misery-laden' (*Inscr. gr. Sicil. et Ital.* 641). These allusions may be referred to at second-hand in Herr Erwin Rohde's study of Hellenic ideas respecting the soul and immortality, entitled *Psyche* (4to. Hälfte, pp. 416 *et seq.*; 509), recently completed. Pindar, Empedocles, and Plato, as is well known, all entertained the notion of repeated re-birth in this world at intervals ranging from nine to one thousand years, repeated twice, thrice, or an indefinite number of times, and, according to the two latter writers, often including in its phases incarnation as an animal, or even as a vegetable. And throughout there runs the Orphic ideas of each re-birth being a stage in a course of moral evolution and effort after purification. But I do not know whether the actual image of the wheel occurs in other instances besides those I have quoted. Empedocles,

In the pictorial diagram of human life, as conceived by Buddhist philosophy, the causal nexus begins at the left-hand side of the top partition. The twelve links round the rim follow in the usual order and in evolutionary fashion as follows :—

Causal Category.	Sanskrit.	Evolutionary Stage.
I. Unconscious Will	*Avidyā*	Stage of passing from Death to Re-birth.
II. Conformations	*Saṅskara*	Shaping of formless physical and mental materials (in the Gāta).
III. Consciousness	*Vijñāna*	Rise of Conscious Experience.
IV. Self-consciousness	*Nama-rupa*	Rise of Individuality—distinction between self and not-self.
V. Sense - surfaces and Understanding	*Chadāyatana*	Realizes possession of Sense-Surfaces and Understanding with reference to outside world.
VI. Contact	*Sparṣa*	Exercise of Sense-organs on outer world.
VII. Feeling	*Vedanā*	Mental and physical sensations.
VIII. Desire	*Tṛishṇā*	Desire, as experience of pain or delusive pleasure.
IX. Indulgence	*Upādāna*	Grasping greed, as satisfying Desire, inducing clinging to Worldly Wealth and desire of heir to it.
X. Fuller Life	*Bhava*	Life in fuller form, as enriched by satisfying desire of married life and as means of obtaining heir.
XI. Birth (of heir)	*Jāti*	Maturity by birth of heir (which affords re-birth to another spirit).
XII. Decay and Death.	*Jarāmaraṇa*	Maturity leads to Decay and to Death.
I. Unconscious Will.	*Avidyā*	Passing from Death to Re-birth.

The key-note to Buddha's system is that Life in any form must necessarily, and not merely accidentally, be accompanied by suffer-

for instance, sees rather a toilsome *road* or roads of life—ἀργαλέας βιότοιο κελεύθους. With Plato, again, we more readily associate his simile of a re-birth as a fall of the soul from heaven to earth, as it drives its chariot after the procession of the gods, through the steed of Epithumia being dragged down by its craving for carnal things —or, as the Buddhist might say, the steed of Chandarāgo overcome by Upādāna for the skandhas.

"The question of a genetic connection between oriental and Hellenic notions as to re-birth is of the greatest interest. Prof. Leopold von Schrœder's opinion that such a connection exists (*Pythagoras und die Inder*, especially pp. 25-31) seems on the whole to be well founded."

ing as others had taught. *Anityaṃ Duḥkhaṃ Anātmakaṃ!*[1] All is transitory, painful, and unreal!

Buddha, therefore, set himself the task of solving the mystery of Life in order to find the way of escape from continual Becomings, which was clearly involved in misery. Being a Hindū, he adopted the then, as now, current Hindū notion of metempsychosis or palingenesis, the doctrine, namely, that death merely alters the form, but does not break the continuity of life[2] which proceeds from Death to Re-birth, and fresh Deaths to fresh Rebirths in constant succession of changing states dissolving and evolving until the breaking up of the universe after a *Kalpa*, or almost an eternity of countless ages; though it would appear probable that Buddha and the primitive Buddhists denied the real existence of the material and physical world as well as the vital.

In his ontological scheme, while adopting an agnostic attitude towards the Hindū gods and their creative functions, Buddha does not begin by attempting to account for the first life. He accepts the world as a working system on metempsychological lines, and he evades the necessity for a supernatural creator by interpreting the Universe, as Will and Idea, and by placing the *Karma* or ethical doctrine of retribution in the position of the Supernatural Controlling Intelligence or Creator. Perceiving the relativity of knowledge and that nature furnishes presumptive evidence that some evolution has taken place in her methods, he throws his theory of the vital process into a synthetical or developmental form, showing a gradual transition from the simple to the complex, and proceeding from the homogeneous to the heterogeneous by an ever-changing cosmic order in which everything is dominated by causality.

The starting point in Buddha's theory of Life is the connecting link between the old life and the new. Unfortunately, however, even on so elementary a point as this, there exists no consensus of opinion as to what Buddha's view of this link precisely was, for he concerned himself less with the metaphysical aspects of his philosophy than with the practical alleviation and removal of

[1] Pāli, *Aniccam Dukkham Anattam;* in Tibetan, Mi-rtag-pa sdug-bsñal-ba, bdag-med-ba.

[2] But see hereafter.

sorrow. He expressly avoided the use of the term "Soul" (*Ātman*), as this word was already in use in Brāhmanism with the implication of supernatural and theistic creation. Some say that he taught there is no continuity between the old life and the new, that the *Karma* attaches itself to any spirit which may chance to be re-born at the time of the person's death. But if this be so, where is the justice of the *Karma* doctrine? It is said by some that the sole-surviving thing is *Karma*, yet this term is used so elastically as to include products which belong rather to the category of the Will-to-live. Others say that *Vijñāna*, or consciousness alone, survives; and so on.[1]

The view adopted in this paper is based upon that held by one of the Lāmas who explained to me the pictorial *Nidānas;* and it has the advantages of being not only intelligible, but consistent, and seems as reasonable as any ontological theory well can be which postulates a metaphysical absolute.

Our view holds that there is actual continuity of the Individual life (or *Sattva*) between death and re-birth. And this identity of being is supported by the doctrine of *Ekotībhāva*, which word, according to its Tibetan etymology, means "to become one uninterruptedly."[2]

The Surviving Thing, which is carried on into the new career of the individual, would indeed seem to be identical with what is now generally known to occidentals as Hartmann's absolute, "the

[1] See *J.R.A.S.*, 1892, p. 1 *seq.*, for a tabular abstract by Prof. Rhys Davids on the authorities for such conflicting views.

[2] Ekotībhāva is another crux of Buddhism. Childers, in quoting Thero Subhuti's etymology from *eko udeti*, writes: "Ekodibhāvo, the second Jhāna, is said to be *cetaso ekodibhavo*, which Burnouf renders 'Unity of the mind'; but that this is its true meaning is very doubtful, as will be seen from the full extract sent me. . . . In accordance with this gloss I would be inclined to render ekodibhāvo by '*predominance*,' rather than by unity, but I do not feel competent to give a decided opinion as to its meaning."—*Dict.*, p. 134. Dr. Morris (in the *Academy*, 27th March, 1886, p. 222) has a note on the subject, followed by Prof. Max Müller (*Academy*, 3rd April, 1886, p. 241), who would derive it from eka+kodi; and Professor Eggeling has a supplementary note in the *Pali Text Soc. Jour.* (p. 32, 1885), in which it is considered a mental state, and rendered by Prof. Rhys Davids as "exaltation." Prof. Kern (*Introd.* to his translation of the *Saddharma Pundarika*, xvii.) in noting the occurrence of the word *ekotibhāva* in the *Lalita Vistara* (p. 147, 8, and 439, 6), rejects Subhuti's etymology of the word, without assigning any reasons. The Tibetan etymology, however, entirely supports Subhuti. It is translated rGyud-gch'ig-tu-gyur-pa, which means "to become or to be transformed+one+a thread, continuous, uninterrupted"; and my Manuscript Tibeto-Sanskrit Dictionary restores the word to Eka+urthānaṅ+bhāva.

UNCONSCIOUS WILL"; and to this is attached the Karma or retribution of deeds done in former lives.

This, the first link of the Ontological Chain, begins at the instant when the mortal envelope is thrown off or changed, that is at "death," and was termed by Buddha the stage of *Avidyā*, which literally means "*Want of Knowledge*," and usually rendered into English as "Ignorance" or "Nescience." But the word Avidyā is used in different senses. Its ordinary sense is thus defined in the *Vinaya Texts*, i., 76: "Not to know Suffering, not to know the Cause of suffering, not to know the Cessation of suffering, not to know the Path which leads to the cessation of suffering, this is called Ignorance." But *Avidyā*, as the initial link of the Causal Nexus, is, according to our information, what may be termed the *Ignorant* Unconscious-Will-to-Live.

The pictorial representation of this link is a blind she-camel ("Ignorant" Productive Unconscious Will) led by a driver (the Karma).[1]

The camel vividly suggests the long and trying journey of the Unconscious Will across the desert valley of the shadow of death, past death itself to the dawn of the new life beyond. The sex of the camel seems to indicate the potential productiveness of the Unconscious Will. The blindness of the beast represents the darkness of the passage and the blind ignorance of the Unconscious Will, which through spiritual ignorance or stupidity (*Moha*) believes in the reality of external objects. And the ignorant animal is led blindly onwards by its Karma.

In the body of the picture are given the details of the progress across this initial stage to the next link in the chain of casuality. The manner in which the Karma determines the kind of new life is concretely represented as a "judgment scene." Here the sins are figured as black pebbles, and the good deeds as white, which are weighed against each other in scales. And according to whichever preponderates so is the place of re-birth in one or other of the six states. Thus the kind of new life is entirely determined by the individual's own deeds or Karma, which creates a system of

[1] The Tibetan picture usually depicts "a blind old woman" led by a man. This perversion of the Indian picture seems to me to be due to a mistranslation on the part of the Lāmas, who appear to have constructed their picture from a written description in which the little known word *nga-mo*, a she-camel, is interpreted as *ga-mo*, an old woman.

rewards and punishments, sinking the wicked through the lower stages of human and animal existence and even to hell; and lifting the good to the level of mighty kings and sages, and even to the gods. Here it may be noted that hell is an idealistic state, a sort of hellish nightmare, the product of the morbid sinful imagination.

The ignorant Unconscious Will, as a homogeneous aggregate under the influence of the three fires of illusion (*Trividagni*, lust, ill-will, and stupidity), is thus led by its Karma to one or other of the six *gati* or forms of existence with which begins link number II., namely, CONFORMATIONS (*Saṅskāra*).

Here our picture and its Lāmaist tradition have come to our aid, and rendered it certain that out of the manifold renderings of *Saṅskāra* attempted by European scholars, as detailed on a previous page, "*Conformations*" was *the* one intended by the primitive Buddhists; and the Tibetan translation of the Sanskrit word gives "impression" or "formation" + "action." The picture is a potter modelling clay on his wheel, and is identical with the Egyptian image of the creator. It represents the shaping of the crude and formless physical and mental aggregates of the Unconscious Will by the Karma, in accordance with "The Judgment."

> "Our mind is but a lump of clay,
> Which Fate, grim Potter, holds
> On sorrow's wheel that rolls alway
> And, as he pleases, moulds."
>
> C. H. TAWNEY'S trans. *Vairāgya Ṣatakam.*

These so-called aggregates or *Skandha* (Pāli, *Khandha*) require some notice. The Buddhists, in their theory of the nature of sentient beings, pre-suppose the existence of ideal atoms, external and internal, which, by aggregation, constitute man and the rest of the universe. These aggregates or Skandha are grouped into five classes, which are rendered by Professor Rhys Davids as (1) the Material Properties and Attributes (*Rūpa*); (2) the Sensations (*Vedanā*); (3) Abstract Ideas (*Saññā*); (4) Tendencies or Potentialities (*Sankhāra*); and (5) Reason (*Viññāna*).[1] Only the first of these sets, or the *Rūpa Skandha*, appear to be operated on in link number II. or Conformations.

Now the Unconscious Will, no longer amorphous, reaches its

[1] *Buddhism*, p. 90.

next stage of development with the rise of CONSCIOUSNESS, or Conscious Experience (*Vijñāna*), as the third link in the evolutionary process. This is figured by a monkey, which some learned Lāmas explained to me as showing that the rudimentary man is becoming anthropoid, but still is an unreasoning automaton. From this it will be seen that however abstract its basis of metaphysical conceptions, or transcendental the causal machinery by which it is set in motion, Buddha's evolutionary scheme, in its practical aspects, must necessarily depend on a tolerably comprehensive and subtle interpretation of human nature.

The rise of SELF-CONSCIOUSNESS (*Nāma-rupa*, literally "Name" + "Form"), as a result of conscious experience, forms the fourth link or stage, and is represented by a physician feeling the pulse of a sick man. Here the pulse denotes the individuality or distinction between "Self" and "Not Self." And its Sanskrit title of "Name and Form" expresses the commonest features of Individuality, "comes *Nāmarūpa*, local form, and name and bodiment, bringing the man with senses naked to the sensible, a helpless mirror of all shows which pass across his heart."[1] A variant of this picture in some Lāmaist temples is a man in the act of being ferried across an ocean. It is the Individual crossing the Ocean of Life.

As a result of Self-Consciousness, the individual now realises his possession of THE SENSE-SURFACE AND UNDERSTANDING (*Chadāyatana*). And here again the relatively low place given to the understanding is quite in keeping with modern philosophy. The picture represents this link by a mask of a human face, "The empty house of the Senses";[2] and the understanding is indicated by a pair of extra eyes gleaming through the brow of the mask. At this stage seems to be effected the full union of the hitherto passive will with the active co-efficients of a human nature as expressed by "The Three Fires, the Buddhist variant of our Devil, the World and the Flesh" (*Rāga, Dvesa, Moha*), though these have been present concurrently from the initial stage of "Ignorance."[3]

[1] ARNOLD'S *Light of Asia*.

[2] The Tibetan picture represents this literally as "an empty house."

[3] These Three Fires (Skt., *Trividhāgni*) seem to have been substituted by Buddha for the Brāhmanical "Three *Guna*," or moral qualities of animated beings—the "binding qualities of matter" (MON. WILLIAMS'S *Hind.*, p. 88)—namely, *sattva* (Goodness or Virtue), *rajas* (Activity), and *tamas* (Darkness or Stupidity), which in a mystical sense

The exercise of the sense organs and the understanding is CONTACT (*Sparsa*) forming the sixth link or stage, bringing the individual into relation with the outside world. It is pictured by kissing, and in some Tibetan frescoes by a man grasping a plough. It illustrates the exercise of one of the senses.

From Contact comes FEELING (*Vedanā*), both physical and mental, including delusive pleasure, pain, and indifference. It is pictured by an arrow entering a man's eye,[1] evidently a symbolic of "Perception," but explained by the Lāmas in such a way as to render it translatable by "Feeling."

From the operation of Feeling comes DESIRE or thirst (*Tṛishṇā*). This stage, dealing with the origin of Desire, perhaps the most psychologically interesting in Buddhism, is pictured by a man drinking wine, and the same metaphor, namely, thirst, which is the literal meaning of the word for this link, and is adopted by Sir Edwin Arnold in his graceful lines—

> "*Trishnā*, that thirst which makes the living drink
> Deeper and deeper of the false salt waves
> Whereon they float, pleasures, ambitions, wealth,
> Praise, fame, or domination Conquest, love,
> Rich meats and robes and fair abodes and pride
> Of ancient lines, and lust of days, and strife
> To live, and sins that flow from strife, some sweet,
> Some bitter. Thus Life's thirst quenches itself
> With draughts which double thirst."[2]

Thus the conquest of Desire is the greatest step towards Buddhist salvation.

The Satisfying of GREED, or Indulgence of Desire (*Upādāna*) forms the next stage. It is pictured by a man grasping fruit and storing it up in big baskets. It appears to be, and is so explained by the Lāmas, as a clinging or attachment to worldly *objects*, rather than to worldly "*existence*" as Oldenberg has interpreted it.

With the next stage—the tenth link—namely, BECOMING

are interpreted as A, U, M (or OM), the Creator, Preserver, and Destroyer. These three fires which, according to the Buddhists, lie at the core of re-birth, are Lust (T., 'dod-c'ags, cf. JAESCH., p. 281), Anger or Ill-will (T., z'e-sdaṅ), and Stupidity (T., gti-mug or p'rag-sdog, cf. JAESCH., 207; KÖPP., i., 33).

[1] In this particular Tibetan picture the sixth and seventh links have been transposed.

[2] *The Light of Asia*, p. 165.

(*Bhava*), we reach one of the alleged obstacles in the chain, an irreconcilable link which puzzles Oldenberg, and which, together with the next link, is deemed inexplicable and altogether out of place. Up to the preceding link, the ninth, the evolution has clearly been that of the life history of a man. The tenth link is rendered by Oldenberg thus: "From 'Clinging to Existence' comes Re-birth and the Continuance of Being for yet another existence." Very naturally he goes on to say that it is strange to find a man who has long ago "entered on real life" suddenly becoming a child again. And adds, "How can a man be born again when he is old," and before he dies? for death only happens in the twelfth stage.

But here it would seem as if Oldenberg has misled himself by introducing the term "Existence" into the previous link and by interpreting *Bhava* as "Re-birth."

For we find that *Bhava* is pictured by a married woman; and the Lāmas explain the picture by saying that she is the wife of the individual whose life-history is being traced. The word is thus given somewhat the sense of Bhavanaṅ (Childers' *Dict.*: "a house-dwelling"); or, as it might be rendered, "husbandship"; it is the result of the previous link, namely, Greed or Indulgence in Worldliness. It is literally fuller "Becoming" (*Bhava*)—Life as enriched by satisfying the worldly desire of home, and as a means of obtaining an heir to the wealth amassed by Greed.

The eleventh stage or link is another of the alleged stumbling-blocks, which, however, ceased to present any difficulty in the light of the picture and the Lāmas' explanation of it. The picture shows a parent and child. It is the Maturing of the man's life by the BIRTH (*Jāti*) of an heir, and as a result of the married existence of the tenth stage. It must be remembered that according to Buddhist belief there is no propagation of species. Life is held to be indivisible; hence the child is no relation to his parents, as the wandering individual finds its family through its own inherent *Karma*. This dogma so opposed to experience and science carried with it its own refutation; but it forms no essential part of the evolutionary chain.

Maturity of Life then leads to DECAY AND DEATH (*Jarāmaraṇa*), the twelfth and final stage, which in turn leads on to link No. 1—

Re-birth—and so on as before. This stage is pictured as a corpse being carried off to cremation or burial.

Let us now look at the Chain as a whole. Here we are met by the difficulty of finding a suitable expression for the word which connects the several links, the Pāli *paccaya*, usually translated "cause" or "concurrent occasion." Prof. Rhys Davids writes (*Vinaya Texts*, i., 146): "Hetu and *paccaya* (the word so frequently used in the formula of the Nidānas) are nearly synonymous. Colebrooke (*Life and Essays*, Vol. ii., p. 419) says that the Bauddhas distinguish between hetu 'proximate cause,' and *paccaya* (pratyaya) 'concurrent occasion'; but in practical use this slight difference of meaning, if it really existed, has but little weight attached to it."[1] Mr. Warren believes[2] that the term "cause" should be used in a very loose and flexible way, and in different senses, in discussing different members of the series of links. But as Prof. Oldenberg's rendering—"From . . . . . comes . . . . ."—seems sufficient for our purpose, while it preserves uniformity and continuity, it is here adopted. The Chain then runs as follows:

[1] This same difference is observed by Tibetan writers. Pratitya is rendered by rkyen, defined by JAESCHKE (*Dict.*, p. 17) as "a co-operating cause" of an event as distinguished from its proximate (or, rather, primary original) cause rgyu (Skt., *hetu*).

[2] *Loc. cit.* He writes: "Now a great deal of the difficulty experienced by scholars on this subject appears to me to arise from the too strict way in which they use the word 'cause,' and from the idea which they labour under that Time plays an important part here, whereas it would appear to have but a secondary rôle.

"The term 'cause' should be used in a very loose and flexible way, and in different senses, in discussing different members of this series. The native phrase, of which Chain of Causation is supposed to be a translation, is *paticca-samuppāda*. *Paticca* is a gerund, equivalent to the Sanskrit *pratītya*, from the verbal root *i* 'go,' with the prefix *prati*, 'back'; and *samuppāda* stands for the Sanskrit *samutpāda*, meaning a 'springing up.' Therefore the whole phrase means a 'springing up' [into existence] with reference to something else, or, as I would render it, 'origination by dependence.' The word 'chain' is a gratuitous addition, the Buddhist calling it a wheel, and making Ignorance depend on Old Age, etc. Now it is to be noted that if a thing springs up—that is to say, comes into being—with reference to something else, or in dependence on something else, that dependence by no means needs to be a causal one. In the Pāli, each of these members of the so-called Chain of Causation is said to be the *paccaya* of the one next following, and *paccaya* is rendered 'cause.' But Buddhaghosa, in the Visuddhi-Magga, enumerates twenty-four different kinds of *paccaya*, and in discussing each member of the *paticca-samuppāda*, states in which of these senses it is a *paccaya* of the succeeding one.

"The Pāli texts very well express the general relation meant to be conveyed by the word *paccaya* when they say 'If this one [member of the series] is not, then this [next following] one is not.'"

"From the Ignorance (of the Unconscious Will) come Conformations. From Conformations comes Consciousness. From Consciousness comes Self-Consciousness. From Self-Consciousness come The Senses and Understanding. From the Senses and Understanding comes Contact. From Contact comes Feeling. From Feeling comes Desire. From Desire comes Indulgence, Greed, or Clinging (to Worldly Objects). From Clinging (to Worldly Objects) comes (Married or Domestic) Life. From (married) Life comes Birth (of an heir and Maturity of Life). From Birth (of an heir and Maturity of Life) come Decay and Death. From Decay and Death comes Re-birth with its attendant Sufferings. Thus all existence and suffering spring from the Ignorance (of the Unconscious Will)."

The varying nature and relationship of these formulæ is noteworthy, some are resultants and some merely sequences; characteristic of Eastern thought, its mingling of science and poetry; its predominance of imagination and feeling over intellect; its curiously easy and naïve transition from Infinite to Finite, from absolute to relative point of view.

But it would almost seem as if Buddha personally observed much of the order of this chain in his ethical habit of cutting the links which bound him to existence. Thus, starting from the link short of Decay and Death, he cut off his son (link 11), he cut off his wife (link 10), he cut off his worldly wealth and kingdom (link 9), then he cut off all Desire (link 8), with its "three fires." On this he attained Buddhahood, the *Bodhi* or "Perfect Knowledge" dispelling the Ignorance (Avidyā), which lay at the root of Desire and its Existence. *Nirvāṇa*, or "going out,"[1] thus seems to be the "going out" of the three Fires of Desire, which are still figured above him even at so late a stage as his "great temptation";[2] and this sinless calm, as believed by Professor Rhys Davids,[3] is reachable in this life. On the extinction of these three fires there result the sinless perfect peace of Purity, Goodwill, and Wisdom, as the antitypes to the Three Fires, Lust, Illwill, and Stupidity; while *Parinirvāṇa* or Extinction of Life

[1] In Tibetan it is translated "The Sorrowless State" (mya-ñan-med). Cf. also BURNOUF, i., 19; BEAL'S *Catena*, 174, 183, etc.

[2] See Ajanṭa picture, p. 6.

[3] *Buddhism*, p. 14; also O. FRANKFÜRTER, Ph.D. (in *J.R.A.S.*, 1880, p. 549), who shows that the three "fires" are also called the three "obstacles" (*Kiñcana*).

(or Becoming) was reached only with the severing of the last fetter or physical "Death," and is the "going out" of every particle of the elements of "becoming."[1]

Amongst the many curious perversions of the latter Buddhism of India was the belief that by mystical means, the *Sattva* or personal entity may, short of death, and whilst yet retaining a body, be liberated from the influence of *Avidyā*, and thus form the operation of the causal nexus, and so secure immortality. Upagupta and many other noted Buddhist sages are believed to be yet living through this happy exemption.[2]

Buddha's metaphysics appears in the light afforded by the chain, to borrow—like so many other world principles professing to solve the problem of existence—from the distinctions of psychology, and to be based on Will. Schopenhauer indeed admits the affinity of his theory with Buddhism. He writes: "If I were to take the results of my philosophy as the standard of truth I would be obliged to concede to Buddhism the pre-eminence over the rest. In any case it must be a satisfaction to me to see my teaching in such close agreement with a religion which the majority of men upon the earth hold as their own."[3] Hartmann's absolute or his

[1] These are the so-called Skandhas.

[2] Although it is a common belief amongst the Burmese that Upagupta still survives in this way, and, in consequence, is an object with them almost of worship, the monks cannot point to any ancient scripture in support of this popular belief.

[3] *The World as Will and Idea*, by A. SCHOPENHAUER, Eng. trans. by Haldane and Kemp, 1883, ii., p. 371. Schopenhauer indeed claims to have arrived at such agreement independently of Buddha's teaching. He writes: "This agreement, however, must be the more satisfactory to me because, in my philosophising, I have certainly not been under its influence; for up till 1818, when my work appeared, there were very few exceedingly incomplete and scanty accounts of Buddhism to be found in Europe, which were almost entirely limited to a few essays in the earlier volumes of 'Asiatic Researches,' and were principally concerned with the Buddhism of the Burmese" (*loc. cit.*, 371). It is, however, probable that Schopenhauer, such an omnivorous reader, and withal so egotistic, minimizes his indebtedness to Buddha. For the Vedānta philosophy, to which Schopenhauer admits his indebtedness, is very deeply tinged by Buddhist beliefs, and Schopenhauer in his system generally follows the lines of Buddhism; and in his later writings he frequently uses Buddhist works to illustrate his speculations. Thus: "We find the doctrine of metempsychosis . . . . in its most subtle form, however, and coming *nearest to the truth* . . . . in Buddhism" (*loc. cit.*, iii., 302). And illustrating his theme "of Denial of the Will to Live," he refers (*loc. cit.*, iii., 445) to FAUSBÖLL'S *Dhammapadam* and BURNOUF'S *Introduction;* and (p. 303) SPENCE HARDY'S *Manual*, OBRY'S *Du Nirvana Indien* (p. 308); Colebrooke, Sangermano, Transactions St. Petersburg Academy of Science; and frequently to the Asiatic Researches.

Unconscious includes Unconscious intelligence as well as Unconscious Will. In Buddhism intelligence is not denied to Will and accorded a secondary and derivate place as in German pessimism, and we may even infer, from what is set forth as to the directing function of the Karma, as well as from its pictorial representation, that Buddhism in some sense felt the necessity of attributing an intelligent quality to the unconscious principle in order that it might pass from the state of migratory abstractiveness to that of determinate being. But, on the other hand, there is not here as an essential feature of the system a deliberate ascription of intelligence to the unconscious as with Hartmann. The Unconscious Will-to-live maintains the changes of phenomena. "The world is the World's process." All "is becoming," nothing "is." It is indeed, as has been suggested to me, the Flux of Heraclitus, who also used the same simile of Fire and Burning. "The constant new-births (palingenesis) constitute," as Schopenhauer, a Neo-Buddhist says, "the succession of the life-dreams of a will, which in itself is indestructible until instructed and improved, by so much and such various successive knowledge in a constantly new form, it abolishes or abrogates itself."[1]

As a philosophy, Buddhism thus seems to be an Idealistic Nihilism; an Idealism which, like that of Berkeley, holds that "the fruitful source of all error was the unfounded belief in the reality and existence of the external world"; and that man can perceive nothing but his feelings, and is the cause to himself of these. That all known or knowable objects are relative to a conscious subject, and merely a product of the *ego*, existing through the *ego*, for the *ego*, and in the *ego*,—though it must be remembered that Buddha, by a swinging kind of positive and negative mysticism, at times denies a place to the *ego* altogether. But, unlike Berkeley's Idealism, this recognition of the relativity and limitations of knowledge, and the consequent disappearance of the world as a reality, led directly to Nihilism, by seeming to exclude the knowledge, and by implication the existence, not only of a Creator, but of an absolute being.

As a Religion, Buddhism is often alleged to be theistic. But although Buddha gives no place to a First Cause in his system,

[1] SCHOPENHAUER'S *Will and Idea*, Eng. trans., iii., 300.

yet, as is well known, he nowhere expressly denies an infinite first cause or an unconditioned Being beyond the finite; and he is even represented as refusing to answer such questions on the ground that their discussion was unprofitable. In view of this apparent hesitancy and indecision he may be called an agnostic.

In the later developments, the agnostic idealism of primitive Buddhism swung round into a materialistic theism which verges on pantheism, and where the second link of the Causal Chain, namely, *Sañskāra*, comes closely to resemble the *modi* of Spinoza;[1] and Nirvāṇa, or rather Pari-Nirvāṇa, is not different practically from the Vedāntic goal: assimilation with the great universal soul:

> "The dew-drop slips into the shining sea."

And the latter developments generally have been directed towards minimizing the inveterate pessimism of Buddha's ethics which tends to bring the world to a standstill, by disparaging that optimistic bias which is commonly supposed to be an essential element in the due direction of all life-processes.

Lāmaist Metaphysics.

After Buddha's death his personality soon became invested with supernatural attributes; and as his church grew in power and wealth his simple system underwent academic development, at the hands of votaries now enjoying luxurious leisure, and who thickly overlaid it with rules and subtle metaphysical refinements and speculations.

Buddha ceases even to be the founder of Buddhism, and is made to appear as only one of a series of (four or seven) equally perfect Buddhas who had "similarly gone" before, and hence called *Tathāgata*,[2] and implying the necessity for another "coming Buddha," who was called *Maitreya*, or "The Loving One."

[1] "All Sentient beings exist in the essence (*garbha*) of the Tathāgata."—*Angulimaliya Sūtra* (Kah-gyur; Dô, xvi. f. 208, transl. by Rock., *B.*, p. 196).

[2] This theory of multiple Buddhas and the introduction of the name *Tathāgata* seems to have been introduced by the Sautrāntika School (Wass., *B.*, 314). This doctrine is held by the southern Buddhists. Rhys Davids (*B.*, p. 179) writes: "It is not so necessarily implied in or closely connected with the most important parts of his scheme as to exclude the possibility of its having arisen after his death" (cf. also Davids, p. 13, *Buddhist Birth Stories*; Senart's *La Légende du Buddha*).

Then these (four or seven) Buddhas or Tathāgatas are extended into series of 24, 35 and 1,000; in addition to which there are also *Pratyeka* or solitary non-teaching Buddhas.

In the second century after the Nirvāṇa[1] arose the Mahāsānghika sect (latterly grouped under Vaibhāshika) which asserted that the Buddhas are illusory and metaphysical; that the traditions respecting the Buddha having been born into the world as men are incorrect, that the law is Tathāgata,[2] that the "Buddhas have passed beyond all worlds (=*Lokottaravadina*);[3] that "Tathāgata is infinitely extended immeasurably glorious, eternal in duration, that to his power of recollection (*ni-smṛiti*), his power of faith (srādhabala), his experience of joy, and his life there is no end; he sleeps not, he speaks, asks, reflects not, they say that his existence is ever one, and uniform (one heart), that all things born may obtain deliverance by having his instruction."[4]

This theistic phase of Buddhism seems foreshadowed even in orthodox Hinayāna scriptures. Thus in the Mahāvagga (i., 6, 8) Ṣākya Muni is made to say of himself, "I am the all-subduer; the all-wise; I have no stains, through myself I possess knowledge; I have no rival; I am the Chief Arhat—the highest teacher, I alone am the absolutely wise, I am the Conqueror (Jina)." And the Mahāsanghika sect of the Hinayāna discussed the eternity and omnipotence of the Buddha. While the Sautrāntika section asserted the plurality of the Buddhas.

Indeed, even in southern Buddhism, the expressed deification of Buddha can scarcely be said to be altogether absent. For Ceylon monks, following an ancient ritual, chant:—

> "I worship continually
> The Buddhas of the ages that are past,
> I worship the Buddhas, the all-pitiful,
> I worship with bowed head.
>
> * * * * * *
>
> "I bow my head to the ground and worship

---

1 *Mahāwanso*, 20-21. 116 years after Nirvāṇa, BEAL in *Ind. Antiq.*, p. 301. The Tibetan gives the date 110 years and also (ROCKHILL, *B.*, p. 182) 160, which is probably a mistake for the 116 of the Chinese.

2 BEAL, *loc. cit.*

3 ROCKHILL, *B.*, 183, where is given a detailed translation of the features of the eighteen Hinayāna sects.

4 BEAL, *loc. cit.*

The sacred dust of his holy feet,
If in aught I have sinned against Buddha,
May Buddha forgive me my sin."[1]

Here Buddha seems prayed to as an existing and active divinity.[2] About four centuries after Buddha's death the Mahāyāna doctrine had evolved specialized celestial Buddhas and Bodhisatvas residing in worlds as fabulous as themselves; and the human Buddhas are made mere manifestations, and reflexes from celestial counterparts.

The Mahāyāna development seems an offshoot of the Mahāsanghika sect of primitive Buddhism. It assumed a concrete form about the end of the first century A.D. under Aṣvaghosha, who wrote the *Mahāyāna Sraddhotanda Sastra;* but its chief expounder was, as we have already seen, Nāgārjuna.

Buddha, it will be remembered, appears to have denied existence altogether. In the metaphysical developments after his death, however, schools soon arose asserting that everything exists (Sarvāstivada[3]), that nothing exists, or that nothing exists *except* the One great reality, a universally diffused essence of a pantheistic nature. The denial of the existence of the "Ego" thus forced the confession of the necessary existence of the *Non-ego.* And the author of the southern Pāli text, the Milinda Pañha, writing about 150 A.D., puts into the mouth of the sage Nāgasena the following words in reply to the King of Sagala's query, "Does the all-wise (Buddha) *exist?*"[4] "He who is the most meritorious does exist," and again "Great King! Nirwana *is.*"[5]

Thus, previous to Nāgārjuna's school, Buddhist doctors were divided into two extremes: into a belief in a real existence and in an illusory existence; a perpetual duration of the Sattva and total annihilation. Nāgārjuna chose a "middle way" (*Madhyāmika*). He denied the possibility of our knowing that

---

[1] *Pāṭimokkha*, DICKSON, p. 5.

[2] Though some hold this to be merely a chant for luck and not real prayer.

[3] In the middle of the third century after the Nirvāṇa (BEAL, *loc. cit.*) arose the realistic Sarvāstivāda as a branch of the Sthaviras, "those who say all exists, the past, future and the present," and are called in consequence "they who say that all exists," or *Sarvāstivādina* (ROCKHILL, *B.*, 184).

[4] *Eastern Mon.*, p. 300, and RHYS DAVIDS' *Questions of Milinda.*

[5] *East. Mon.*, p. 295.

anything either exists or did not exist. By a sophistic nihilism he "dissolved every problem into thesis and antithesis and denied both." There is nothing either existent or non-existent, and the state of Being admits of no definition or formula.

The *Prajñā pāramitā*[1] on which Nāgārjuna based his teaching consist of mythical discourses attributed to Buddha and addressed mostly to supernatural hearers on the Vulture Peak, etc. It recognizes several grades of metaphysical Buddhas and numerous divine Bodhisats, who must be worshipped and to whom prayers should be addressed. And it consists of extravagant speculations and metaphysical subtleties, with a profusion of abstract terminology.

His chief apocalyptic treatises[2] are the Buddhāvatāṇsaka, Samādhiraja and Ratnakūṭa Sutras. The gist of the Avataṅsaka Sutra may be summarized[3] as "The one true essence is like a bright mirror, which is the basis of all phenomena, the basis itself is permanent and true, the phenomena are evanescent and unreal; as the mirror, however, is capable of reflecting images, so the true essence embraces all phenomena and all things exist in and by it."

An essential theory of the Mahāyāna is the Voidness or Nothingness of things, *Sūnyatā*,[4] evidently an enlargement of the last term of the *Trividyā* formula, *Anātma*. Ṣākya Muni is said to have declared that "no existing object has a nature,[5] whence it follows that there is neither beginning nor end—that from time immemorial all has been perfect quietude[6] and is entirely immersed in Nirvāṇa." But Sūnyatā, or, as it is usually translated, "nothingness" cannot be absolute nihilism. for there are, as Mr. Hodgson tells us, "a Sūnyatā and a Mahā-Sūnyatā. We are dead. You are a little Nothing; but I am a big Nothing. Also there are eighteen degrees of Sūnyatā.[7] You are annihilated,

---

1 *Prajñā* begins with chaos. She produced all the Tathāgatas, and is the mother of all Bodhisattvas Pratyeka-Buddhas and Disciples (Conf. COWELL and EGGELING'S *Catal*, Skt. MS., *J.R.A.S.*, N.S. viii., 3).

2 For some details of these see CSOMA'S *An.*, p. 400.

3 BEAL'S *Catena*, 125.

4 Tib., Tong-pa ñid.

5 Ño-vo-ñid.

6 Zod-manas Zi-ba—"nothing has manifested itself in any form" (SCHL., 343).

7 HODGSON'S *Essays*, etc., 59.

but I am eighteen times as much annihilated as you."[1] And the Lāmas extended the degrees of "Nothingness" to seventy.

This nihilistic doctrine is demonstrated by The Three Marks and the Two Truths and has been summarized by Schlagintweit. The Three Marks are:

1. *Parikalpita* (Tib., Kun-tag) the supposition or error; unfounded belief in the reality of existence; two-fold error in believing a thing to exist which does not exist, and asserting real existence when it is only ideal.
2. *Paratantra* (T., Z'ạn-vaṅ) or whatever exists by a *dependent* or causal connexion, viz., the soul, sense, comprehension, and imperfect philosophical meditation.
3. *Parinishpanna* (T., Yoṅ-grub) "completely perfect" is the unchangeable and unassignable true existence which is also the scope of the path, the *summum bonum*, the absolute.

The two Truths are *Samvritisatya* (T., Kun-dsa-bch'i-den-pa) The relative truth; the efficiency of a name or characteristic sign. And Paramārthasatya (Don-dam-pahi den-pa) the absolute truth obtained by the self-consciousness of the saint in self-meditations.

The world (or Saṃsāra), therefore, is to be renounced not for its sorrow and pain as the Hinayāna say, but on account of its unsatisfying unreality.

The idealization of Buddha's personality led, as we have just seen, to his deification as an omniscient and everlasting god; and traces of this development are to be found even in southern Buddhism. And he soon came to be regarded as the omnipotent primordial god, and Universal Essence of a pantheistic nature.

About the first century A.D. Buddha is made to be existent from all eternity (*Anada*). Professor Kern, in his translation of *The Lotus of the True Law*, which dates from this time,[2] points out that although the theistic term Ādi-Buddha or Primordial Buddha does not occur in that work, Ṣākya Muni is identified with Ādi-Buddha in the words, "From the very beginning (*ādita eva*) have I roused, brought to maturity, fully developed them (the innumerable Bodhisats) to be fit for their Bodhisattva position."[3]

And with respect to the modes of manifestations of the universal essence, "As there is no limit to the immensity of reason and measurement to the universe, so all the Buddhas are possessed of

[1] A. LILLIE, *J.R.A.S.*, xiv., 9.
[2] *Saddharma Puṇḍarīka*, xxii.
[3] *Loc. cit.*, xxv.

infinite wisdom and infinite mercy. There is no place throughout the universe where the essential body of Vairocana (or other supreme Buddha, varying with different sects) is not present. Far and wide through the fields of space he is present, and perpetually manifested.[1]

The modes in which this universal essence manifests itself are the three bodies (Tri-kāya), namely—(1) *Dharma-kāya*[2] or Law-body, Essential Bodhi,[3] formless and self-existent, the Dhyāni Buddha, usually named Vairocana Buddha or the "Perfect Justification," or Ādi-Buddha. (2) *Sambhoga-kāya*[4] or Compensation-body, Reflected Bodhi, the Dhyāni Bodhisats, usually named Lochana or "glorious"[5]; and (3) *Nirmāṇa-kāya*[6] or Transformed-body, Practical Bodhi, the human Buddhas, as Ṣākya Muni.[7]

Now these three bodies of the Buddhas, human and superhuman, are all included in one substantial essence. The three are the same as one—not one, yet not different. When regarded as one the three persons are spoken of as Tathāgata. But there is no real difference, these manifestations are only different views of the same unchanging substance.[8]

One of the earliest of these celestial Buddhas was given the title of "The Infinite Light" (*Amitābha*), and his personality soon crystallized into a concrete theistic Buddha of that name, residing in a glorious paradise (Sukhavati) in the West, where the daily suns hasten and disappear in all their glory, and hence supposed by some to include a sun myth or to be related to sun-worship, probably due to Persian influence; for the chief patrons of the early Mahāyāna, about the time of the invention of this myth, were Indo-Scyths, a race of sun-worshippers.

After Nāgārjuna, the chief expounder of the Mahāyāna philosophy

---

1 BEAL's *Catena*, 123.

2 T., ch'os-sku.

3 EIT., p. 180.

4 long-*s*ku.

5 It is singular to find these Buddhist speculations bearing so close a resemblance to the later Greek theories on the same subject, especially in the plain resemblance of the σῶμα αὐγοειδὲς or luciform body, to the Lochana (Rajana) or "Glorious Body" of the Buddhists. *Vide* the whole subject of these "bodies" treated by CUDWORTH, *Intellec. System*, ii., 788; BEAL's *Cat.*, 123.

6 sprul-*s*ku.

7 On these bodies see also VASILIEV, *B.* (French ed.), p. 127, and EITEL, 179 *seq.*

8 BEAL's *Catena*, 123.

was Vasubandhu, who was less wildly speculative than many of his predecessors and composed many commentaries.[1] Previous to his day, the nihilism of the Mahāyāna had become almost mystic in its sophistry.

This intense mysticism of the Mahāyāna led about the fifth century to the importation into Buddhism of the pantheistic idea of the soul (ātman) and *Yoga*, or the ecstatic union of the individual with the Universal Spirit, a doctrine which had been introduced into Hindūism about 150 B.C. by Patanjāli. This innovation originated with Asaṅga,[2] a monk of Gāndhāra (Peshawar), whose system is known as the Yogācārya, or "contemplative" Mahāyāna. Asaṅga is credited with having been inspired directly by the celestial Bodhisat Maitreya, the coming Buddha, and it is believed that he was miraculously transferred to the Tushita heavens and there received from Maitreya's hands the gospels called "The Five Books of Maitreya," the leading scripture of this party.

His school, the Yogācārya, and especially its later development (into which magic circles with *mantras* or spells were introduced about 700 A.D.), was entitled "*Mantrayāna*" or "the *mantra*-vehicle." And Yoga seems indeed to have influenced also the Ceylonese and other forms of southern Buddhism, among whom flying through the air and other supernatural powers (*Irdhi*) are obtainable by ecstatic meditation (though not expressedly pantheistic), and the recitation of *dhāraṇis*[3]; and the ten "*iddhis*" or miraculous supernatural powers, are indeed regarded as the attribute of every perfected saint or Arhat.[4] "Rahāts (Arhats) flying" is a frequent expression in the southern scriptures, and is illustrated by numerous paintings in the early caves of Ajaṇṭa, in central India.

It is with this essentially un-Buddhistic school of pantheistic mysticism—which, with its charlatanism, contributed to the decline of Buddhism in India—that the Theosophists claim kinship. Its

1 Amitayus sūtropedesa, Buddhagotra Sāstra, on the Saddharma Puṇḍarīka, Vajra Ch'edikā, Dasabhūmika, etc.; and also "the Treasury of Metaphysics" (Abidharma Koṣ-ṣa sāstra), containing many Sautrāntika principles.

2 For his date conf. VASIL., 225, 230 and previous note. The works of his younger brother Vasubandhu, were translated into Chinese 557 A.D.

3 Conf. HARDY'S *E.M.*, p., 252, and GRIMBLOT, *Sept. Suttas pali*, p. 323.

4 CHILDERS' *Pāli Dict.*

so-called "esoteric Buddhism" would better be termed *exoteric*, as Professor C. Bendall has suggested to me, for it is foreign to the principles of Buddha. Nor do the Lāmas know anything about those spiritual mediums—the Mahātmas ("*Koot Hoomi*") —which the Theosophists place in Tibet, and give an important place in Lamāist mysticism. As we shall presently see, the mysticism of the Lāmas is a charlatanism of a mean necromantic order, and does not even comprise clever jugglery or such an interesting psychic phenomenon as mesmerism, and certainly nothing worthy of being dignified by the name of "natural secrets and forces."

But with its adoption of Tāntrism,[1] so-called, Buddhism entered on its most degenerate phase. Here the idolatrous cult of female energies was grafted upon the theistic Mahāyāna and the pantheistic mysticism of Yoga. And this parasite seized strong hold of its host and soon developed its monstrous growths, which crushed and strangled most of the little life yet remaining of purely Buddhist stock.

Tāntrism, which began about the seventh century A.D. to tinge Buddhism, is based on the worship of the Active Producing Principle (*Prakṛiti*) as manifested in the goddess Kāli or Durga, the female energy (*Ṣakti*) of the primordial male (Purusha or Ṣiva), who is a gross presentation of The Supreme Soul of the universe. In this cult the various forces of nature —physical, physiological, moral and intellectual—were deified under separate personalities, and these presiding deities were grouped into *Mātri* (divine mothers), *Ḍākkinī* and *Yogini* (goddesses with magical powers), etc. And all were made to be merely different manifestations of the one great central goddess, Kāli, Ṣiva's spouse. Wives were thus allotted to the several celestial Bodhisats, as well as to most of the other gods and demons; and most of them were given a variety of forms, mild and terrible, according to the supposed moods of each divinity at different times. And as goddesses and

[1] Vasiliev designates this stage as "*Mysticism*"; but surely the developed Mahāyāna and Yogācārya doctrines were already mystic in a high degree; while the name *Tāntrik* exprcsses the kind of mysticism and also conveys a sense of Sivaist idolatry, although the word "*Tāntra*," according to its Tibetan etymology (*r*gyud), literally means "a treatise," it is restricted both in Buddhism and Hindūism to the necromantic books on Ṣākta mysticism.

she-devils were the bestowers of natural and supernatural powers and were especially malignant, they were especially worshipped.

About this time the theory of Ădi-Buddha,[1] which, it has been seen, existed about the first century A.D., underwent more concrete theistic development. He becomes the primordial god and creator, and evolves, by meditation, five celestial *Jinas* or Buddhas of Meditation (*Dhyāni* Buddhas), almost impassive, each of whom, through meditation, evolves an active celestial *Bodhisat*-son, who possesses creative functions,[2] and each human Buddha, though especially related to a particular one of the five celestial Buddhas of Meditation, is produced by a union of reflexes from each of these latter. For pictures of these deities, see the chapter on the pantheon, where also I give a table presenting the inter-relations of these various celestial Buddhas, Bodhisats, and human Buddhas, and also incorporate their mystic symbolism, although this was probably added in the later Mantrayāna stage.

It will be seen that the five celestial Jinas are so distributed as to allot one to each of the four directions,[3] and the fifth is placed in the centre. And the central position thus given him, namely, Vairocana, is doubtless associated with his promotion to the Ādi-Buddhaship amongst certain northern Buddhists; though the reformed and unreformed sects of Lāmas, differ as regards the specific name which they give the Ādi-Buddha, the former calling him Vajradhara, doubtless selected as bearing the title

1 Tib., mCh'og-hi daṅ-pohi Saṅs-rgyas.

2 "According to this system," says Mr. HODGSON, *J.A.S.B.*, xii., 400, "from an eternal, infinite and immaterial Ādi-Buddha proceeded divinely, and not generatively, five lesser Buddhas, who are considered the immediate sources (Ādi-Buddha being the ultimate source) of the five elements of matter, and of the five organs and five faculties of sensation. The moulding of these materials into the shape of an actual world is not, however, the business of the five Buddhas, but it is devolved by them upon lesser emanations from themselves denominated Bodhisattvas, who are thus the tertiary and active agents of the creation and government of the world, by virtue of powers derived immediately from the five Buddhas, ultimately from the one supreme Buddha. This system of five Buddhas provides for the origin of the material world and for that of immaterial existences. A sixth Buddha is declared to have emanated divinely from Adi-Buddha, and this sixth Buddha, Vajrasattva by name, is assigned the immediate organization of mind and its powers of thought and feeling."

3 The five "wisdoms" which the human Buddha embodies are: Ch'o-ki byiṅ ki ye-s'es, Meloṅ ta-bahi, Nambar-ṅed-ki, Sosor tog-pahi, Gya-wa du-pahi ye-s'es.

of "Vajra" so dear to Tāntrik Buddhists, while the unreformed sects consider him to be Samantabhadra, that is, the celestial son of Vairocana. And the Ādi-Buddha is not considered wholly inactive or impassive, for he is frequently addressed in prayers and hymns.

Ṣākya Muni is the fourth of the Mānushi or human Buddhas of this age, and his Dhyāni Buddha is Amitābha, and his corresponding celestial Bodhisat is Avalokiteṣvara, the patron-god of Lāmaism, who is held to be incarnate in the Grand Lāma.

The extreme development of the Tāntrik phase was reached with the Kāla-cakra, which, although unworthy of being considered a philosophy, must be referred to here as a doctrinal basis. It is merely a coarse Tāntrik development of the Ādi-Buddha theory combined with the puerile mysticisms of the Mantrayāna, and it attempts to explain creation and the secret powers of nature, by the union of the terrible Kāli, not only with the Dhyāni Buddhas, but even with Ādi-Buddha himself. In this way Ādi-Buddha, by meditation, evolves a procreative energy by which the awful Samvharā and other dreadful Dākkinī-fiendesses, all of the Kāli-type, obtain spouses as fearful as themselves, yet spouses who are regarded as reflexes of Ādi-Buddha and the Dhyāni Buddhas. And these demoniacal "Buddhas," under the names of Kāla-cakra, Heruka, Achala, Vajra-vairabha,[1] etc., are credited with powers not inferior to those of the celestial Buddhas themselves, and withal, ferocious and bloodthirsty; and only to be conciliated by constant worship of themselves and their female energies, with offerings and sacrifices, magic-circles, special *mantra*-charms, etc.

These hideous creations of Tāntrism were eagerly accepted by the Lāmas in the tenth century, and since then have formed a most essential part of Lāmaism; and their terrible images fill the country and figure prominently in the sectarian divisions.

Afterwards was added the fiction of re-incarnate Lāmas to ensure the political stability of the hierarchy.

Yet, while such silly and debased beliefs, common to the Lāmas of all sects, determine the character of the Tibetan form of the doctrine, the superior Lāmas, on the other hand, retain much of the higher philosophy of the purer Buddhism.

---

[1] Compare with the *Pancha Rakshā*, and see chapter on pantheon, pp. 353 and 363.

LĀMAS SENDING PAPER-HORSES TO TRAVELLERS.[1]

VI.

THE DOCTRINE AND ITS ETHICS.

THE simple creed and rule of conduct which won its way over myriads of Buddha's hearers is still to be found in Lāmaism, though often obscured by the mystic and polydemonist accretions of later days. All the Lāmas and most of the laity are familiar with the doctrinal elements taught by Ṣākya Muni and give them a high place in their religious and ethical code.

A keen sense of human misery forms the starting-point of Buddha's Law or *Dharma*,[2] the leading dogma of which is propounded in "The Four noble Truths,"[3] which may be thus summarized :—

1. Existence in any form involves *Suffering or Sorrow*.[4]

---

[1] After Huc.

[2] *Dharma* is best rendered, says RHYS DAVIDS (*Buddh.*, p. 45), by "truth" or righteousness, and not by "Law," which suggests ceremonial observances and outward rules, which it was precisely the object of Buddha's teaching to do away with.

[3] *Arya Satyāni*. T., 'p'ags-pa bden-pa bz'i.

[4] The word for MISERY (Skt., *Āṣrava;* T. 'zag-pa) means "drops," so-called because it oozes or drops (zag) from out the different regions of the six āyatanas (or sense-sur-

2. *The Cause of Suffering* is Desire and Lust of Life.

3. *The Cessation of Suffering* is effected by the complete conquest over and destruction of Desire and Lust of Life.

4. *The Path leading to the Cessation of Suffering* is "The noble Eight-fold Path," the parts[1] of which are:—

1. Right Belief		5. Right	Means of Livelihood
2. „	Aims	6. „	Endeavour
3. „	Speech	7. „	Mindfulness
4. „	Actions	8. „	Meditation.

Thus Ignorance (of the illusive idealism of Life) is made the source of all misery, and the *right* Knowledge of the nature of Life is the only true path to emancipation from re-birth or Arhatship; and practically the same dogma is formulated in the well-known stanza called by Europeans "the Buddhist Creed."[2] And

faces) as drops water through holes (ROCKHILL'S *Udânavarga*, 10). It seems to convey the idea of tears as expressive of misery.

[1] *Anga.*

[2] "The Buddhist Creed," found so frequently on votive images, is:—

Ye dharmā hetuprabhavā
Hetun teshān tathāgatô
Hyavadata teshāṅ ca yo nirodha
Evaṃvâdī mahāsramaṇah.

It has been translated by Rhys Davids (*Vin. Texts.*, i., p. 146) as follows:—

Of all objects which proceed from a Cause
The Tathāgata has explained the cause,
And he has explained their Cessation also;
This is the doctrine of the great Samana.

The Second Stanza, also found frequently on Buddhist votive images in India (see BURNOUF'S *Lotus*, p. 523, and CUNNINGHAM'S *Arch. Surv. Rep. Ind.*, i., pl. xxxiv., fig. 1, First Stanza), is according to its Tibetan form:—

Sarvapāpasyā karaṇaṃ
Kuṣalusyopasapradâm
Svacittaṃ paridamanu
Etad Buddhānuṣâsanam.

Which has been translated by Csoma thus:—

"No vice is to be committed;
Every virtue must be perfectly practised;
The mind must be brought under entire subjection.
This is the commandment of Buddha."

In Tibetan the first stanza of "the Creed" is widely known, and is:—

Ch'os-nam t'am-c'ad rgyu-las byuṅ
De-rgyu de-z'in-gs'egs-pas gsuṅs
rGyu-la 'gog-pa gaṅ-yin-pa
'Di-skad gsuṅ-ba dge-spyoṅ-ch'i.

the bulk of the Buddhist scriptures is devoted to the proofs and illustrations of the above dogma.

The Moral Code, as expressed in its most elementary form of rules for the external conduct, forms the well-known decalogue (*dasa-sīla*) which enunciates its precepts in a negative and prohibitive form, namely :—

1. Kill not.
2. Steal not.
3. Commit not Adultery.
4. Lie not.
5. Drink not Strong Drink.
6. Eat no Food except at the stated times.
7. Use no Wreaths, Ornaments or Perfumes.
8. Use no High Mats or Thrones.
9. Abstain from Dancing, Singing, Music, and Worldly Spectacles.
10. Own no Gold or Silver and accept none.

BUDDHA PREACHING THE LAW
(in the Deer-park [Mriga-dawa] at Benares).

The first five (the *pañca-sīla*) are binding upon the laity; the whole ten are binding only on the monks; but the layman on certain fast-days, in accordance with a pious vow, observes also one or more of the next four (Nos. 6 to 9). The more austere rules for monastic discipline are indicated in the chapter on the monkhood.

Ṣākya Muni's sermons, as presented in the earlier and more authentic scriptures, have all the simple directness and force which belong to sayings of "the inspired." As an illustration of his moral teaching, his popular sermon on "What is the Greatest Blessing?" (the Maṅgala Sūtra)[1] is here appended :—

BUDDHA'S SERMON ON WHAT IS THE GREATEST BLESSING?

Praise be to the Blessed One, the Holy One, the Author of all Truth!

1. Thus I have heard. On a certain day dwelt the Blessed One[2] at Srivasta, at the Jetavana monastery, in the Garden of Anathapindaka. And when the night was far advanced, a certain radiant celestial being, illuminating the whole of Jetavana, approached the Blessed One and saluted him, and stood aside, and standing aside addressed him with this verse:—

Many gods and men yearning after good have held divers things to be blessings; say thou what is the greatest blessing?

1. To serve wise men and not serve fools, to give honour to whom honour is due, this is the greatest blessing.

2. To dwell in a pleasant land, to have done good deeds in a former existence, to have a soul filled with right desires, this is the greatest blessing.

3. Much knowledge and much science, the discipline of a well-trained mind, and a word well spoken, this is the greatest blessing.

4. To succour father and mother, to cherish wife and child, to follow a peaceful calling, this is the greatest blessing.

5. To give alms, to live religiously, to give help to relatives, to do blameless deeds, this is the greatest blessing.

6. To cease and abstain from sin, to eschew strong drink, to be diligent in good deeds, this is the greatest blessing.

7. Reverence and lowliness and contentment and gratitude, to receive religious teaching at due seasons, this is the greatest blessing.

8. To be long-suffering and meek, to associate with the priests of Buddha, to hold religious discourse at due seasons, this is the greatest blessing.

9. Temperance and chastity, discernment of the four great truths, the prospect of Nirvāṇa, this is the greatest blessing.

10. The soul of one unshaken by the changes of this life, a soul inaccessible to sorrow, passionless, secure, this is the greatest blessing.

11. They that do these things are invincible on every side, on every side they walk in safety, yea, theirs is the greatest blessing.

Indeed, Buddha's teaching is not nearly so pessimistic as it is

[1] From Professor Childers' translation. [2] Bhagavā.

usually made to appear by its hostile critics. His sermon on Love (*Mitra Sutra*) shows that Buddhism has its glad tidings of great joy, and had it been wholly devoid of these, it could never have become popular amongst bright, joyous people like the Burmese and Japanese.

The stages towards Arhatship[1] or emancipation from re-birth are graduated into a consecutive series of four (*cattaro-margā*) paths, a fourfold arrangement of "the eightfold paths" above mentioned; and these depend upon the doctrinal comprehension of the devotee, and his renunciation or not of the world, for the higher stages were only reachable by celibate monks (*śramaṇa*) or nuns (*sramaṇerā*), and not by the ordinary laity or hearers (*sravaka*). Those who have not yet entered any of these stages or paths are "the ignorant and unwise ones." And Meditation (*dhyāna*) is the chief means of entry. The first and lowest stage or step towards Arhatship is the *Srottāpatti*, or the entering the stream—the state of the new convert to Buddhism. He is called Sotāpanno, "One who has entered the stream," *inevitably* carrying him onward—though not necessarily in the same body—to the calm ocean of Nirvāṇa.[2] He, now, can only be re-born[3] as a god or man, and not in any lower births, though his metempsychoses may yet last countless ages.[4]

In the second stage the graduate is called Sakrid-āgāmin, or "he who receives birth once more" on earth. He has freed himself from the first five fetters.

In the third stage he is called An-āgāmi, or "one who will not come back" to earth. Such a person can only be re-born in a Brāhma heaven, whence he reaches Nirvāṇa.

The fourth and highest stage is the attainment of Arhatship in this life. Such a graduate will at death experience no rebirth.

After Buddha's death seems to have arisen the division of

---

[1] Arhant (*Pāli*, Arahā, Rahan, Rahat) as its Tibetan equivalent, dgra-bčom-pa, shows, is derived from *Ari*, an enemy, and *han*, to extirpate, *i.e.*, "he who has extirpated his passions." It seems to have been applied in primitive Buddhism to those who comprehended the four Truths, and including Buddha himself, but lately it was restricted to the perfected Buddhist saint (LAIDLAY'S *FaHian Ki*, 94; BURN., i., 295; ii., 297; KÖPP., i., 400; JAESCH., 88).

[2] HARDY'S *Eastn. Mon.*, Chap. xxii.

[3] Only seven more births yet remain for him.

[4] According to northern Buddhism for 80,000 kalpas, or cycles of time.

Arhats into the three grades of Simple Arhat, Pratyeka-Buddha, and Supreme Buddha, which is now part of the creed of the southern school.

Firstly, "the Simple Arhat who has attained perfection through his own efforts and the doctrine and example of a Supreme Buddha, but is not himself such a Buddha and cannot teach others how to attain Arhatship.

"Secondly, and second in rank, but far above the Simple Arhat, the Pratyeka-Buddha or Solitary Saint, who has attained perfection himself and by himself alone and not . . . through the teaching of any Supreme Buddha.

"Thirdly, the Supreme Buddha, or Buddha *par excellence* (once a Bodhisattva), who, having by his own self-enlightening insight attained perfect knowledge (sambodhi) . . . has yet delayed this consummation (parinirvāṇa) that he may become the saviour of a suffering world . . . by teaching men how to save themselves.[1]

The leading religious feature of the Mahāyāna doctrine was its more universal spirit. Its ideal was less monastic than the Hinayāna, which confined its advantages practically to its cœobitical monks. The Mahāyāna endeavoured to save all beings by rendering Bodhisatship accessible to all, and thus saving all beings in the ages to come. It also called itself the "Vehicle of Bodisats," thus constituting three vehicles (Triyāna) which it described as—(1) Of the hearers or disciples (Ṣrāvaka), whose vehicle was likened to a sheep crossing the surface of a river; (2) of the Pratyeka-Buddhas, or solitary non-teaching Buddhas, whose vehicle was likened to a deer crossing a river; and (3) of the Bodhisats, whose vehicle is likened to a mighty elephant which in crossing a river grandly fathoms it to the bottom. These vehicles "are, in plain language, piety, philosophy, or rather Yogism, and striving for the enlightenment and weal of our fellow-creatures. . . . Higher than piety is true and self-acquired knowledge of eternal laws; higher than knowledge is devoting oneself to the spiritual weal of others."[2] It thus gave itself the highest place.

Its theory of Bodhisatship is, to use the words of Professor

[1] Summary by MON. WILLIAMS's *Buddhism*, p. 134. [2] KERN, *op. cit.*, p. xxxiv.

Rhys Davids, "the keynote of the later school just as Arhatship is the keynote of early Buddhism.[1] The Arhats being dead cannot be active, the Bodhisattvas as living beings can: "the Bodhisattvas represent the ideal of spiritual activity; the Arhats of inactivity."

But, as Professor Kern shows, one of the earliest of the Mahāyāna scriptures, the *Saddharma puṇḍarīka*, dating at least about the second century A.D., goes further than this. It teaches that everyone should try to become a Buddha. "It admits that from a practical point of view one may distinguish three means, so-called Vehicles (*yānas*), to attain *summum bonum*, Nirvāṇa, although in a higher sense there is only one Vehicle—the Buddha Vehicle."[2]

To obtain the intelligence (Bodhi) of a Buddha, and as a Bodhisat to assist in the salvation of all living beings, the six *Pāramitā* or transcendental virtues must be assiduously practised. These cardinal virtues are :—

1. Charity (Skt., *dāna*[3])
2. Morality (*sīla*[4])
3. Patience (*kshānti*[5])
4. Industry (*vīrya*[6])
5. Meditation (*dhyāna*[7])
6. Wisdom (*prajñā*[8])

To which four others sometimes are added, to wit :—

7. Method (*upāya*[9])
8. Prayer (*pranidhāna*[10])
9. Fortitude (*bala*[11])
10. Foreknowledge (? *dhyāna*[12])

Ṣākya Muni, in his last earthly life but one, is held to have satisfied the *Pāramitā* of Giving (No. 1 of the list) as prince Visvantara ("Vessantara") as detailed in the Jātaka of the same name. Aṣoka, in his gift of Jambudvīpa; and Ṣīlāditya, in his gifts at Prayāg (Allahabad), as described by Hiuen Tsiang, are cited as illustrations of this *Pāramitā*.

Meditation, the fifth Pāramitā, was early given an important place in the doctrine, and it is insisted upon in the Vinaya.[13] Through it one arrives at perfect tranquillity (*samādhi*), which is believed to be the highest condition of mind. And in the later

[1] *Origin*, p. 254.
[2] *Sacr. Bks. East*, xxi., p. xxxiv.
[3] sbyin-pa, CSOMA, *Analy.*, 399; BURNOUF, *Lotus*, p. 544.
[4] ts'ul-k'rims.
[5] bzod-pa.
[6] botson-'grus.
[7] bsam-gtan.
[8] s'es-rab.
[9] t'abs.
[10] smon-lam.
[11] stobs.
[12] ye-s'es.
[13] For stages of meditation see BIGANDET's *Legends*, etc., 446. Bodhidharma in the fifth century A.D. exalted meditation as the means of self-reformation.

days of mysticism this led to the ecstatic meditation of Yoga, by which the individual becomes united with and rapt in the deity.

The ten stages through which a Bodhisat must pass in order to attain perfection. These stages are called "The Ten[1] Heavens" (*dasa bhūmīṣvara*[2]), and are objectively represented by the ten "umbrellas" surmounting the spire of a *caitya*, and one of the treatises of the "nine canons" is devoted to their description.[3]

In the natural craving after something real and positive, "When the theory of a universal void became the leading feature of the Buddhist scholastic development, the question pressed upon the mind was this: If all things around us are unreal and unsubstantial, is there anything in the universe real or any true existence? The answer to this question was that "on the other shore," that is, in that condition which admits of no birth or death, no change or suffering, there is absolute and imperishable existence."[4]

The chief of these regions is the western paradise of Amitābha, named Sukhāvatī, or "the Happy Land,"[5] a figure of which is here given, as it is the goal sought by the great body of the Buddhists of Tibet, as well as those of China and Japan. Its invention dates at least to 100 A.D.,[6] and an entry to it is gained by worshipping Amitābha's son, Avalokita, which is a chief reason for the spell of the latter, the *Om maṇi padme Hūṃ*, being so popular.

In the seventh century A.D., under Buddha-palita, and in the eighth or ninth, under Candrakirti, a popular development arose named the Prasanga Madhyamika (Tib., T'al gyur-va[7]), which by a hair-splitting speculation deduces the absurdity and erroneousness of every esoteric opinion, and maintained that Buddha's doctrines establish two paths, one leading to the highest heaven of the universe, *Sukhāvatī*, where man enjoys perfect happiness, but con-

1 They are sometimes accounted thirteen in Nepal (HODGSON, *Lang.*, 16) and also by the Ñiṅ-ma Lāmas.

2 See also LAIDLAY'S *FaHian*, p. 93; *J.R.A.S.*, xi., 1, 21. Sometimes they are extended to thirteen.

3 HODGS., *supra cit.*

4 BEAL'S *Catena*, 275.

5 For its description see BEAL'S *Catena*, p. 117 *seq.*; MAX MÜLLER'S *trans. of Sukhāvatī-vyūha*, *S.B.E.*, xlix.; and SARAT, *J.A.S.B.*, 1891.

6 MAX MÜLLER, *op. cit.*, *supra* ii., xxiii. Avalokita's name also occurs here.

7 VASILIEV, *B.*, 327, 357; CSOMA, *J.A.S.B.*, vii., 144.

THE WESTERN PARADISE OF AMITĀBHA, THE BUDDHA OF BOUNDLESS LIGHT.
(Sukhāvatī.)

nected with personal existence, the other conducting to entire emancipation from the world, namely, Nirvāṇa.[1]

The *Yoga* doctrine of ecstatic union of the individual with the Universal Spirit had been introduced into Hindūism about 150 B.C. by Patanjali, and is not unknown to western systems.[2] It taught spiritual advancement by means of a self-hypnotizing to be learned by rules. By moral consecration of the individual to Iṣvara or the Supreme Soul, and mental concentration upon one point with a view to annihilate thought, there resulted the eight great *Siddhi* or magical powers, namely (1) "the ability to make one's body lighter, or (2) heavier, or (3) smaller, (4) or larger than anything in the world, and (5) to reach any place, or (6) to assume any shape, and (7) control all natural laws, to

> 'Hang like Mahomet in the air,
> Or St. Ignatius at his prayer,'[3]

and (8) to make everything depend upon oneself, all at pleasure of will—*Iddhi* or *Riddi*." On this basis Asaṅga, importing Patanjali's doctrine into Buddhism and abusing it, taught[4] that by means of mystic formulas—*dhāraṇis* (extracts from Mahāyāna *sutras* and other scriptures) and *mantra* (short prayers to deities)—as spells, "the reciting of which should be accompanied by music and certain distortion of the fingers (*mudrā*), a state of mental fixity (*samādhi*) might be reached characterized by neither thought nor annihilation of thoughts, and consisting of sixfold

MYSTIC ATTITUDES OF FINGERS.

---

[1] SCHLAGT., 41-42.

[2] Compare the remark of Beal, "the end to which Plotinus directed his thoughts was to unite himself to the Great God; he attained it by the *unitive* method of the Quietists." —*Critical Dict.*, art. Plotinus, quoted through BEAL's *Catena*, 150.

[3] HUDIBRAS, *Gesta Roman*, 326.

[4] His doctrine is contained in the treatise entitled *Yogicarya-bhūmi Sāstra.*

bodily and mental happiness (*Yogi*), whence would result endowment with supernatural miracle-working power." These miraculous powers were alleged to be far more efficacious than mere moral virtue, and may be used for exorcism and sorcery, and for purely secular and selfish objects. Those who mastered these practices were called Yogācārya.

But even in early Buddhism *mantras* seem to have been used as charms,[1] and southern Buddhism still so uses them in *Paritta* service for the sick,[2] and also resorts to mechanical contrivances for attaining *Samadhi*, somewhat similar to those of the Yogācārya.[3] And many mystic spells for the supernatural power of exorcism are given in that first or second century A.D. work, *Saddharma Puṇḍarīka*.[4]

In the mystic nihilist sense, as the name of a thing was as real as the thing itself, the *written* spell was equally potent with the *spoken*, and for sacerdotal purposes even more so on account of the sacred character of letters, as expressing speech and so exciting the intense veneration of barbarians. No Tibetan will wantonly destroy any paper or other object bearing written characters.

The general use of the mystic OM, symbolic of the Hindū Triad AUM, The Creator, Preserver, and Destroyer, probably dates from this era; though in the Amaravati tope is figured a pillar of glory surmounted by OM proceeding from the throne supposed to be occupied by Buddha.[5] It is doubtful whether its occurrence in some copies of the *Lalita Vistara* and other early Mahāyāna works, as the first syllable of the Opening Salutation, may not have been an after addition of later scribes. The monogram figured on page 386 is entitled "The All-powerful ten,"[6] and is in a form of the Indian character called *Ranja* or "Lantsa."

The Tāntrik cults[7] brought with them organized worship, litanies, and pompous ritual, offerings and sacrifice to the bizarre

1 *Kullavagga*, v., 6.

2 *East. Mon.* RHYS DAVIDS' *Milinda*, 213.

3 HARDY'S *E.M.*, chap. "Ascetic Rites." See also the *mandala* diagrams, p. 252; and "The Contemplation Stone," *J.R.A.S.*, 1894, p. 564.

4 See also BEAL'S *Catena*, p. 284, etc.

5 FERGUSSON'S *Tree and Serp. Worship*, pl. lxxi., figs. 1 and 2.

6 Nam-bc'u-dbaṅ-ldan; cf. also Chinese name for the *Svastika*. The letters are O, U, H, K, S, M, L, V, R, Y.

7 Cf. my *Indian-Buddhist Cult of Avalokita*, etc., *J.R.A.S.*, 1894; BURNOUF'S *Intro.*, 465.

or terrible gods and goddesses for favours, temporal and spiritual. A supreme primordial Buddha-god and superhuman Buddhas and Bodhisats, together with their female energies, mostly demoniacal,

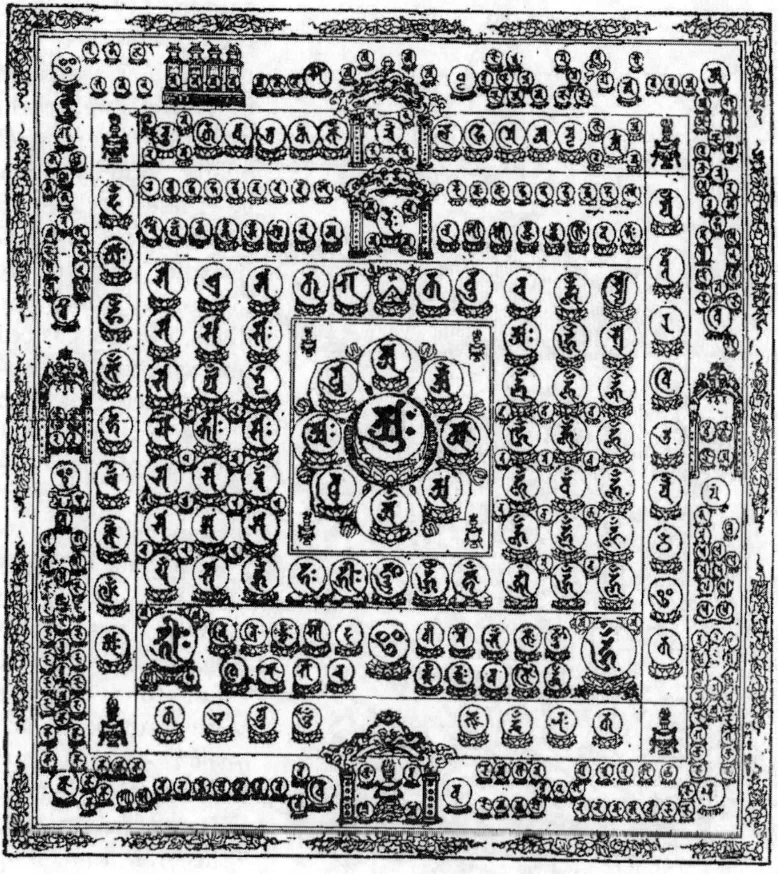

MAGIC "CIRCLE."[1]

demand propitiation by frequent worship and sacrificial offerings. This Tāntrik ritual is illustrated in the chapters on worship.

The excessive use of these mystic Mantras, consisting mostly of unmeaning gibberish, resulted in a new vehicle named the *Mantra-yāna*, which is a Tāntrik development of the Yoga phase

[1] From Japan.

of Buddhism. Charmed sentences (*dhāraṇī*) supposed to have been composed by these several divinities themselves, are used as incantations for procuring their assistance in peril as well as in ordinary temporal affairs. And by means of these spells and mummery the so-called "magic circles" are formed by which the divinities are coerced into assisting the votary to reach "the other shore." And the authors of this so-called "esoteric" system gave it a respectable antiquity by alleging that its founder was really Nāgārjuna, who had received it in two sections of *vajra* and *garbha-dhatu* from the celestial Buddha Vajra-sattva, within "the iron tower" in southern India. Its authorship is, as even Tāranātha himself admits, most obscure.[1]

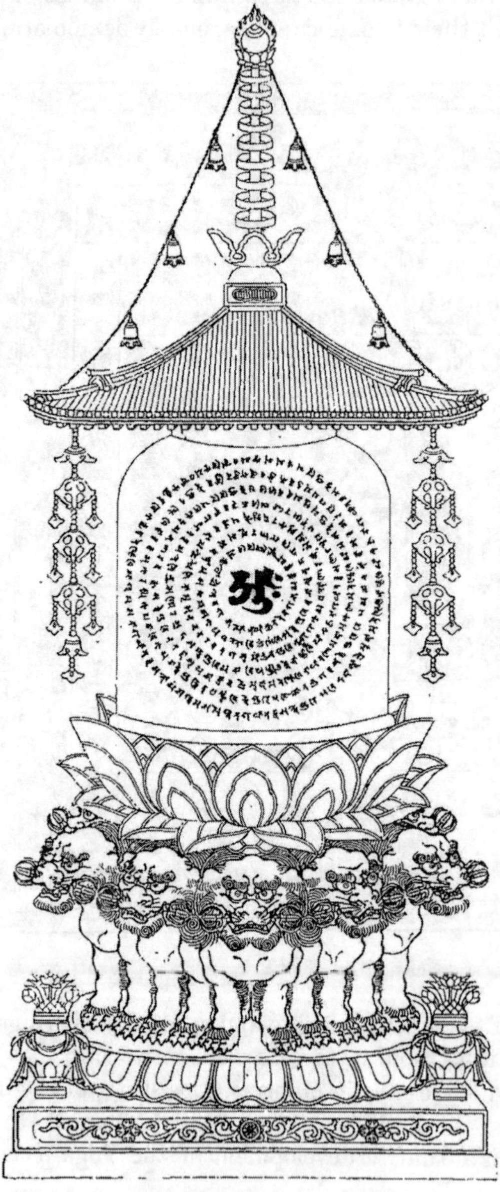

YANTRA OF MAÑJUŚRĪ.
(From Japanese.)

The *Mantra-yāna* asserts that the state of the "Great en-

[1] TĀRAN., 113.

MAGIC-CIRCLE OF AVALOKITA.

lighted or perfected"[1] that is, Buddhaship, may be attained in the present body (composed of the six elements) by following the three great secret laws regarding the body, speech, and thought,[2] as revealed by the fictitious Buddha, Vajrasattva.

Its silly secrets so-called, comprise the spells of the several divinities, and the mode of making the magic-circles (*maṇḍala*) of the two sorts—the outer and inner (*vajradhātu* and *garbha-dhātu*); though something very like, or analogous to, magic-circles are also used in southern Buddhism.[3]

Some idea of its contemptible mummery and posturing and other physical means for spiritual advancement is to be gained from the following three exercises which every Lāma should daily perform:—

The "meditative posture of the seven attitudes" is daily assumed by the Lāma with his associates, in order to subjugate the five senses. These attitudes are—(1) sitting with legs flexed in the well-known attitude of Buddha; (2) the hands resting one above the other in the lap; (3) head slightly bent forward; (4) eyes fixed on the tip of the nose; (5) shoulders "expanded like the wings of a vulture;" (6) spine erect and "straight like an arrow"; (7) tongue arching up to the palate like the curving petals of the eight-leaved lotus. While in this posture he must think that he is alone in a wilderness. And he now, by physical means, gets rid of Rāga, Moha, Dvesa—the three "original sins" of the body—and these are got rid of according to the humoral physiology of the ancients in the three series of *d*buma, roma, and *r*kyaṅ-ma. After taking a deep inspiration, the air of the *roma* veins is expelled three times, and thus "the white wind" is let out from the right nostril three times in short and forcible expiratory gusts. This expels all anger. Then from the left nostril is thrice expelled in a similar way "the red air" which rids from lust. The colourless central air is thrice expelled, which frees from ignorance. On concluding these processes, the monk must mentally conceive that all

[1] Mahā-utpanna or "Atiyoga, Tib., *dsog-ch'en.*

[2] sKu, Suṅ, T'ug. This doctrine seems almost identical with that of the Shingon-shu sect of Japan described by B. NANJIO in his *Jap. Buddh. Sects*, p. 78. Tāranātha also mentions Nāgārjuna's name in connection with its origin, which he admits is most obscure. It probably arose at the end of the seventh century A.D., as in 720 A.D. Vajrabodhi brought it with its magic-circles to China.

[3] These elaborate circles of coloured clay, etc., are described in detail by HARDY, *E. M.*, 252, etc., and I have seen diagrams of an apparently similar character in Burmese Buddhism. Compare also with the mechanical contrivance "the Octagon" (Tib., *Dab-c'ad*) used in the rite *sGrub-byed*, to concentrate the thoughts and coerce the she-devils (*Ḍākkinī*) who confer miraculous powers described. SCHLAG., p. 247. Cf. also "Meditation-stone."

ignorance, lust and anger—the three original sins—have "disappeared like frost before a scorching sun."

He then says the "a-lia-ki," keeping his tongue curved like a lotus petal. This is followed by his chanting "the Yoga of the Lāma," during which he must mentally couceive his Lāma-guide as sitting overhead upon a lotus-flower.

The mere recital of mystic words and sentences (*mantra* or

MYSTIC ATTITUDES.
(Lāmas of Established Church.)

dhāraṇī [T., Z'uṅ]), and their essential syllable (the germs or seed, so-called *vīja*) is held to be equivalent to the practice of the Pāramitās, and subdues and coerces the gods and genii, and procures long life and other temporal blessings, and obtains the assistance of the Buddhas and Bodhisats. Although these

Dhāraṇīs[1] were likely introduced to supply the need for incantations their use is alleged to be based upon the doctrine of unreality of things. As existence is ideal, the name of a thing is equivalent to the thing itself, and of a like efficacy are the attitudes (*mudra*) of the fingers, symbolic of the attributes of the gods. Thus OM is an acceptable offering to the Buddhas, HRI dispels sorrow, and by uttering Ho, *samādhi* is entered. Of such an ideal nature also were the paper horses of Huc's amusing story, which the Lāmas with easy charity bestowed on belated and helpless travellers, as figured at the top of this chapter.

These postures and parrot-like exercises, as practised by the unreformed and semi-reformed sects, according to the book entitled *The complete esoteric Tāntra*[2] and the reputed work of Padma-sambhava, are as follows. The corresponding Ge-lug-pa rites are not very much different :—

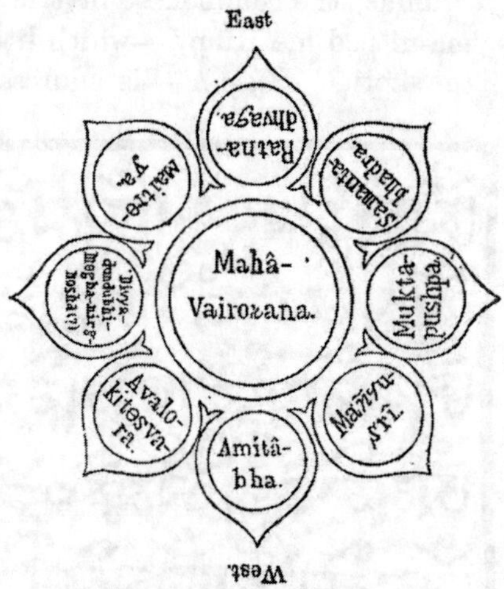

LOTUS-PETALS OF HEART.
On meditating upon Celestial Buddhas.
(A Stage in the Magic-Circle.—After Nanjio.)

1*st.*—The mode of placing the three mystic words, body, speech and thought (*ku, suṅ* and *t'uk*).
2*nd.*—The nectar-commanding rosary.
3*rd.*—The jewelled rosary-guide for ascending.
4*th.*—Secret counsels of the four Yogas.
5*th.*—The great root of the heart.
6*th.*—The lamp of the three dwellings.
7*th.*—The bright loosener of the illusion.
8*th.*—The water-drawing "dorje."
9*th.*—The secret guide to the fierce Ḍākkinī.
10*th.*—The drawing of the essence of the stony nectar.
11*th.*—Counsel on the Ḍākkinī's habits.
12*th.*—Fathoming the mystery of the Ḍākkinīs
13*th.*—Counsel for the Ḍākkinī's heart-root.
14*th.*—The four words for the path of Pardo (limbo).
15*th.*—The Pardo of the angry demons.

[1] Conf. BURNOUF, i., 522-74 ; VASILIEV, 153, 193.

[2] *gsaṅ-sṅags lpyi rgyud*

16*th.*—To recognize the Gyalwa Rig-na or the five celestial Buddhas. Then "Happiness" is reached—this goal is the sensuous happiness of the Jina's Paradise or of Sukhāvati, that of Amitābha, the Buddha of Infinite Light.

The transcendental efficacy attributed to these spells fully accounts for their frequent repetition on rosaries and by mechanical means in the "prayer-wheel," flags, etc.

Thus, the commonest mystic formula in Lāmaism, the "Om-ma-ṇi pad-me Hūṃ,"—which literally means "*Om!* The Jewel in the Lotus! *Hūṃ!*"—is addressed to the Bodhisat Padmapāṇi

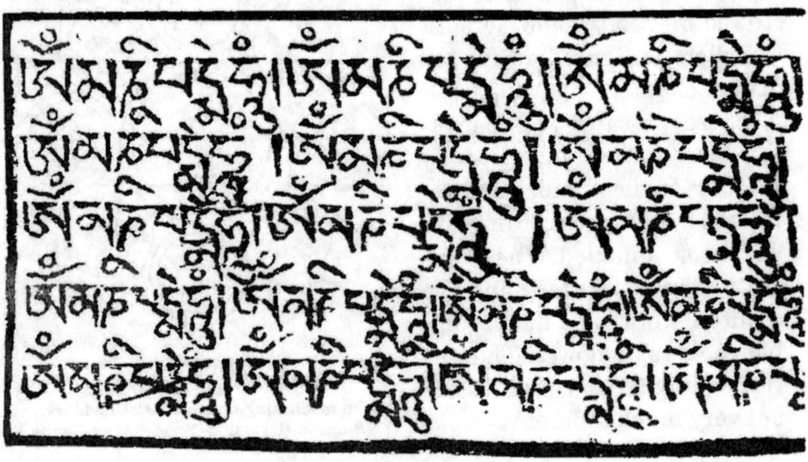

THE PRAYER-WHEEL FORMULA.
Om-ma-ṇi pad-me Huṃ.

who is represented like Buddha as seated or standing within a lotus-flower. He is the patron-god of Tibet and the controller of metempsychosis. And no wonder this formula is so popular and constantly repeated by both Lāmas and laity, for its mere utterance is believed to stop the cycle of re-births and to convey the reciter directly to paradise. Thus it is stated in the Māṇi-kah-bum with extravagant rhapsody that this formula "is the essence of all happiness, prosperity, and knowledge, and the great means of deliverance"; for the *Om* closes re-birth amongst the gods, *ma*, among the Titans *ṇi*, as a man, *pad* as a beast, *me* as a Tantalus, and *Hūṃ* as an inhabitant of hell. And in keeping with this view each of these six syllables is given the distinctive colour of these six states of rebirth, namely *Om*, the godly *white; ma,* the Titanic *blue; ni*, the human *yellow; pad*, the animal *green; me*, the "Tantalic" *red;* and *Hūṃ*, the hellish *black.*

THE *OM MAṆI* FORMULA (in Indian "*Ranja*" characters of about the seventh century).

But the actual articulation is not even needed. The mere inspection of this formula is equally effective, and so also is the passing of this inscription before the individual. And to be effective it does not require to be actually visible, it is therefore printed thousands and millions[1] of times on long ribbons and coiled into cylinders and inserted into the "prayer-wheels" so-called, which are revolved everywhere in Tibet, in the hand (see pages 45, 218, etc.), and as great barrels turned by hand or water or wind,[2] and also printed on stones and on cloth-flags which flutter from every house, so as to ensure the cessation of metempsychosis by re-birth in the western paradise.

The origin of this formula is obscure. The earliest date for it yet found is the thirteenth century A.D.[3]

What seems to be a more expanded version of this spell is known to a few Lāmas and is met with in Japanese Buddhism, namely, "*OM! Amogha Vairocana Mahāmudra MAṆI PADMA Jvala-pravarthtaya HŪṂ!*" But this is addressed to the first of the Dhyāni[4] Buddhas, namely, Vairocana, to whom also the Japanese Mantrayāna sect ascribe their esoteric doctrine, but the ordinary Lāmaist formula is unknown in Japan, where its place is taken by "*Nāmo O-mi-to Fo,*" or "Hail to Amitābha, the Buddha of Boundless Light."

---

[1] In some of the larger prayer-wheels it is printed 100,000,000 times (Baron Schilling, cf. SCHLAG., 121.

[2] For wind-prayer vanes, cf. ROCK., *L.*, p. 147 cf.; also GIORGI, 508.

[3] ROCKHILL, in *The Land of the Lāmas*, London, 1891, page 326, notes that Wilhelm de Rubruk, writing in the second half of the thirteenth century A.D. (*Soc. de Geog. de Paris*, iv., page 283) states regarding the Buddhist monks of Karakorum: "Habent etiam quocumque vadunt semper in manibus quandam testem centum vel ducentorum nucleorum sicut nos portamus paternoster et dicunt semper hec verba *on man baccam*, hoc est *Deus, tu nosti*, secundum quod quidam corum interpretatus est michi, et totiens exspectat, remunerationem a Deo quotiens hoc dicendo memoratur." Mr. Rockhill also, I find, independently arrives at a similar conclusion to myself as regards the relatively modern composition of the Mani-*b*kāh-sbum. Cf. also HUC, ii.; KÖPP., ii., 59-61.

[4] W. ANDERSON, *Catal. Jap. Paintings Brit. Mus.*

From its mystic nature the *Om Maṇi* formula is interpreted in a great variety of ways, including amongst others the phallic,[1] though this latter sense is seldom accorded it. The heterodox Bön-pa followers repeat it in reverse fashion, thus making it mere gibberish.[2]

THE MYSTIC FORMULAS FOR THE ROSARIES.

The repetition of the mystic formulas for the beads follows the prayer, properly so-called, and is believed to contain the essence of a formal prayer, as well as to act as a powerful spell. The formulas are of a Sanskritic nature, usually containing the name of the deity addressed, but are more or less wholly unintelligible to the worshipper.

Different mantras are needed for different deities; but the one most frequently used by the individual Lāma is that of his own tutelary deity, which varies according to the sect to which the Lāma belongs.

The formulas most frequently used are shown in the following table:—

NAME OF DEITY.	THE SPELL.	SPECIAL KIND OF ROSARY USED.
1. Dor-je jik-je.[3] Skt., *Vajra-bhairava*	Om! Ya-măn-ta-taka hūṃ phăt!	Human skull or "stomach-stone."
2. Chā-na dorje.[4] Skt., *Vajrapāṇi.*	Om! Vajrapāṇi hūṃ phăt!	Raksha.
	Om! Vajra dsan-da mahā ro-khana hūṃ!	Ditto.
. Tam-din.[5] Skt., *Hayagriva.*	Om! păd-ma ta krid hūṃ phăt!	Red sandal or coral.
4. Chă-ră-si or T'ug-je-ch'enbo.[6] Skt., *Avalokita.*	Om! maṇi păd-me hūṃ!	Conch-shell or crystal.
5. Döl-ma jaṅ-k'u.[7] Skt., *Tārā.*	Om! Tā-re tut-tā-re ture svā-hā!	Bo-dhi-tse or turquoise.
6. Dö-kar.[8] Skt., *Sitātārā.*	Om! Tā-re tut-tā-re mama ā-yur punye-dsanyana pusph-pi-ta ku-ru svā-hā!	Bodhitse.
7. Dor-je p'ag-mo.[9] Skt., *Vajra-varahi.*	Om! sar-ba Bud-dha dakkin-nī hūṃ phăt!	Ditto.
8. 'O-zer-căn-ma.[10] Skt., *Marīcī.*	Om! Ma-rī-cye mam svā-hā!	Ditto.

[1] As noted by Hodgson.

[2] The characteristic Bön-pa mantra is however: "Ma-tri-mu-tri sa-la dzu." Cf. JAESCH., *D.*, 408; DESGODINS, 242.

[3] rdo-rje-'jigs-byed.

[4] p'yag-na rdo-rje.

[5] rta-mgrin.

[6] T'ugs-rje-c'en-po.

[7] sgrol-ma jaṅ-k'u.

[8] sgrol-dkar.

[9] do-rje p'ag-mo.

[10] 'od-zer-c'an-ma.

Name of Deity.	The Spell.	Special kinds of Rosary used.
9. Gön-po nag-po.[1] Skt., *Kālanātha.*	Om ! Sri Ma-hā-kā-la hūṃ phät svā-hā !	Raksha.
10. Nam-sé.[2] Skt., *Kuvera.*	Om ! Vaī-srā-va-na ye svā-hā !	Nanga-pāni.
11. Dsam-b'a-la.[3] Skt., *Jambhala.*	Om ! Jam-bha-la dsalen-dra ye svā-hā !	Ditto.
12. Sen-ge-da.[4] Skt., *Siṅhanāda.*	Om ! ā-hrīh Siṅ-ha-nāda hūm phät !	Conch-shell or crystal.
13. Jam-yang.[5] Skt., *Mañjughosha.*	Om ! a-ra-pa-ca-na-ḍhi !	Yellow rosary.
14. Dem-ch'ok.[6] Skt., *Samvara.*	Om ! hrih ha-ha hūṃ hūṃ phät !	Bodhitse.
15. Päd-ma juṅ-nä.[7] Skt., *Padma-sambhava.*	Om ! Väjra Gu-ru Pädma sīd-dhī hūṃ !	Coral or bodhitse.

The concluding word *phät* which follows the mystic *hūṃ* in many of these spells is cognate with the current Hindūstani word *phat*, and means " may the enemy be *destroyed utterly !* "

The laity through want of knowledge seldom use with their rosaries any other than the well-known " Jewel-Lotus " formula.

Such mechanical means of spiritual advancement by promising immediate temporal benefits, have secured universal popularity; and possess stronger attractions for gross and ignorant intellects over the moral methods of early Buddhism. The Chinese *literati* ridicule the repetition of these *mantras* by saying,[8] " Suppose that you had committed some violation of the law, and that you were being led into the judgment-hall to receive sentence; if you were to take to crying out with all your might ' Your Worship ' some thousands of times, do you imagine that the magistrate would let you off for that ? "

On the evolution, in the tenth century, of the demoniacal Buddhas of the Kālacakra, the " *Mantra* "-vehicle was developed into " The Thunderbolt-vehicle " or *Vajrayāna*, the proficient in which is called *Vajrācārya*. According to this, the most depraved form of Buddhist doctrine, the devotee endeavours with the aid of the demoniacal Buddhas and of fiendesses (*Ḍākkinī*) and their

1 mgon-po nag-po. 2 rnam-sras. 3 dsam b'a-la.
4 seṅ-ge-sgra. 5 'jam-dbyangs. 6 bde-mch'og.
7 pad-ma byuṅ-gnas.

8 Rémusat, *As. Misc.* Most conspicuous amongst the authors of diatribes against Buddhist worship was Han Yü in the eighth or ninth centuries A.D. Cf. Mayers.

magic-circles to obtain the spiritual powers of *Siddhi*[1] or "The accomplishment of perfection or of one's wishes." Although the attainment of Siddhi is below the stage of Arhatship, the Lāmas value it more highly than the latter on account of its power of witchcraft. Its mystic insight is classed as the external (*Ch'ir-dub*), internal (*Nan-dub*), and esoteric or hidden (*San-dub*), and correspond to the body, speech, and thought. Its followers are called Vajrācarya and its rules are detailed by Tson K'hapa. Its recognized divisions[2] are:—

VAJRAYĀNA.

Lower Tantra		Upper Tantra	
Kriyā Tantra	Cārya Tantra	Yoga Tantra	Anuttara Tantra
bya-rgyud	*spyod*	*rnal-byor*	*bla-na med-pahi-gyud*

In only the last, or Anuttara Tantra, have the tutelary demons spouses.[3]

The rampant demonolatry of the Tibetans seems to have developed the doctrine of tutelary deities far beyond what is found even in the latest phase of Indian Buddhism, although I find at many of the mediæval Buddhist sites in Māgadha, images of several of the devils which are so well-known in Tibet as tutelaries.

Each Lāmaist sect has its own special tutelary fiend, which may or may not be the personal tutelary of all the individual Lāmas of that particular sect; for each Lāma has a tutelary of his own selection, somewhat after the manner of the *ishṭā devatā* of the Hindūs, who accompanies him wherever he goes and guards his footsteps from the minor fiends. Even the purest of all the Lāmaist sects—the Ge-lug-pa—are thorough-paced devil-worshippers, and value Buddhism chiefly because it gives them the whip-hand over the devils which everywhere vex humanity with disease and disaster, and whose ferocity weighs heavily upon all. The purest Ge-lug-pa Lāma on awaking every morning,

[1] *Siddhi*, which seems (according to Sir MON. WILLIAMS, *Budd.*, 536), to correspond to the stage below Arhatship. Eighty Siddhas (saints) are sometimes mentioned. And amongst their supernatural Irdhi powers they obtain "the Rainbow Body" ('jah-lus), which vanishes like the rainbow, leaving no trace behind.

[2] Cf. JAESCH., *D.*, 112.

[3] The directions for these cults are found chiefly in the Ñin-ma "revelations" or *terma* books.

and before venturing outside his room, fortifies himself against assault by the demons by first of all assuming the spiritual guise of his fearful tutelary, the king of the demons, named Vajrabhairava or Samvara, as figured in the chapter on the pantheon. The Lāma, by uttering certain *mantras* culled from the legendary sayings of Buddha in the Mahāyāna Tantras, coerces this demon-king into investing the Lāma's person with his own awful aspect.[1] Thus when the Lāma emerges from his room in the morning, and wherever he travels during the day, he presents spiritually the appearance of the demon-king, and the smaller malignant demons, his would-be assailants, ever on the outlook to harm humanity, being deluded into the belief that the Lāma is indeed their own vindictive king, they flee from his presence, leaving the Lāma unharmed.

A notable feature of Lāmaism throughout all its sects, and decidedly un-Buddhistic, is that the Lāma is a priest rather than a monk. He assigns himself an indispensable place in the religion and has coined the current saying "Without a Lāma in front there is no (approach to) God." He performs sacerdotal functions on every possible occasion; and a large proportion of the order is almost entirely engaged in this work. And such services are in much demand; for the people are in hopeless bondage to the demons, and not altogether unwilling slaves to their exacting worship.

The Chinese contempt for such rites is thus expressed in a sacred edict of the emperor Yung-Ching.[2] "If you neglect to burn paper in honour of Buddha, or to lay offerings on his altars, he will be displeased with you, and will let his judgments fall upon your heads. Your god Buddha, then, is a mean fellow. Take for a pattern the magistrate of your district. Even if you never go near him to compliment him or pay court to him, so long as you

---

1 This process, called lha-sgrub-pa, implies (says JAESCHKE, *D.*, 52) not so much the making a deity propititious to man (CSOMA's definition in his *Dict.*) as rendering a god subject to human power, forcing him to perform the will of man. This coercion of the god is affected by saints continuing their profound meditation (sgom-pa) for months and years until the deity, finally, overcome, stands before them visible and tangible; nay, until they have been personally united with and, as it were, incorporated into the invoked and subjected god. The method of effecting this coercion, of obliging a god to make his appearance, is also called sgrub-tābs.

2 RÉMUSAT, *As. Miscell.*

are honest folk and attentive to your duty, he will be none the less ready to attend to you; but if you transgress the law, if you commit violence, or trespass on the rights of others, it would be useless for you to try a thousand ways of flattering him; you will always be subject to his displeasure."

Thus had these various influences warped the Buddhist doctrine in India, ere it reached Tibet, and there the deep-rooted demon-worship made Lāmaism what it is: a priestly mixture of Shamanist cults and poly-demonist superstitions, overlaid by quasi-Buddhist symbolism, relieved by universal charity and other truly Buddhist principles, and touched here and there by the brighter lights of the teaching of Buddha.

But notwithstanding its glaring defects, Lāmaism has exerted a considerable civilizing influence over the Tibetans. The people are profoundly affected by its benign ethics, and its maxim, "as a man sows he shall reap," has undoubtedly enforced the personal duty of mastery over self in spite of the easier physical aids to piety which are prevalent.

And it is somewhat satisfactory to find that many of the superior Lāmas breathe much of the spirit of the original system. They admit the essentially un-Buddhist nature of much of the prevalent demonolatry, and the impropriety of its being fostered by the church. They regard this unholy alliance with the devils as a pandering to popular prejudice. Indeed, there are many Lāmas who, following the teaching of the earlier Buddhism, are inclined to contemn sacerdotalism altogether, although forced by custom to take part in it.

NOVICE-LĀMA READING SCRIPTURES.

VII.

THE SCRIPTURES AND LITERATURE.

THE sacred books embodying the "Word" of Buddha are regarded by the Lāmas, in common with all other Buddhists, as forming the second member of the Trinity—"The Three precious Ones"—in whom the pious Buddhist daily takes his "refuge."

The books themselves receive divine honours. They are held

materially sacred, placed in high places, and worshipped with incense, lamps, etc.;[1] and even fragments of books or manuscripts bearing holy words are treasured with the utmost reverence. It is deemed the grossest profanity for anyone to throw even a fragment of holy writ upon the ground or to tread upon it, and in this way the Tibetans, like the Chinese, not infrequently express their contempt for Christianity by utilizing, as soles for their shoes, the bundles of tracts which our missionaries supply to them.

But Buddha, like "the Light of the World," and unlike Moses and Muhammad, wrote nothing himself; nor does it appear that his words were even reduced to writing until about 400 years or more after his death,[2] so it is unlikely that most of his sayings have preserved their original form, wholly unaltered, in the process of handing them down orally during several centuries.

The Lāmaist scriptures are faithful translations[3] from the Sanskrit texts,[4] and a few also from the Chinese, made mostly in the eighth and ninth, and the eleventh to the thirteenth centuries

[1] The scriptures are actively worshipped even by southern Buddhists. "The books are usually wrapped in cloth, and when their names are mentioned an honorific is added equivalent to reverend or illustrious. Upon some occasions they are placed upon a kind of rude altar near the roadside, as I have seen the images of saints in Roman Catholic countries, that those who pass by may put money upon it in order to obtain merit" (HARDY'S *East Mon.*, 192). Compare also with Hindus paying respect to their *Şastras* with garlands and perfumes and grains of rice, and the Sikhs to their *Granth*.

[2] The words were at first transmitted down orally; their recital (bhāna = to speak) is one of the duties of a monk even now. The southern (Pāli) scriptures are stated to have been first reduced to writing in Ceylon in 88-76 B.C., in the reign of King Vartagāmani (TURNOUR, *Mahavanso*, 207), and the northern by king Kanishka in the second half of the first century A.D. But as writing was certainly in use in Aṣoka's day—250 B.C.—it is probable that some scriptures were committed to writing at an earlier period than here assigned to the complete collect. Cf. OLDENBERG, *Vinaya Trip.* xxxviii.

[3] The verbal accuracy of these translations has been testified by Max Müller, Rhys Davids, Cowell, Foucaux, Feer, Vasiliev, Rockhill, etc.

[4] Indian, Kashmīri and Nepalese scriptures. A few of the Tibetan translations were made from the Pāli, *e.g.*, vol. 30 of Sutras (ROCKHILL'S *Udvanavarga*, x). Some very old Indian MSS. still exist in Tibet. His Excellency Shad-sgra Shab-pe, one of the Tibetan governors (bKāh-blon) of Lhāsa, while at Darjiling about a year ago, on political business, informed me that many ancient Buddhist manuscripts, which had been brought from India by mediæval Indian and Tibetan monks, are still preserved in Tibet, especially at the old monasteries of Sām-yās, Sakya, Nar-thāng and Phün-tsholing. These manuscripts, however, being worshipped as precious relics, and written in a character more or less unknown to the Lāmas, are kept sealed up and rarely seen by the Lāmas themselves.

A.D.; and a very few small volumes, those first translated into Tibetan, date to the epoch of Thon-mi Sambhota, about 645 A.D.

None of these Tibetan translations, however, seem to have been printed until comparatively recent times, though the exact date of the introduction of printing into Tibet is as yet unknown.

The Tibetan so-called "books" are, strictly speaking, only *xylographs*, being printed from rudely carved wooden blocks. Movable type is unknown, and a large proportion of the books are still written in manuscript. The great canon, the Kāh-gyur, was, it seems, only printed for the first time, at least in its collected form, about two hundred years ago.

The paper, which is remarkably tough, is made from the inner bark of a shrub,[1] and comes mostly from Nepal and other parts of the sub-Himalayas, and the Chinese border-lands. The smaller abstracts from the scriptures, used by the more wealthy devotees, are sometimes written on ornate cardboard, consisting of several sheets of paper pasted together, and varnished over with a black pigment, upon which the letters are written in silver or gold; and occasionally they are illuminated like missals.

Books now abound in Tibet, and nearly all are religious. The literature, however, is for the most part a dreary wilderness of words and antiquated rubbish, but the Lāmas conceitedly believe that all knowledge is locked up in their musty classics, outside which nothing is worthy of serious notice.

The Lāmaist scriptures consist of two great collections, the canon and the commentaries, commonly called the "Kāng-gyur, or properly the Kah-gyur,[2] and Tän-gyur."[3]

The great code, the Kāh-gyur, or "The Translated Commandment," is so called on account of its text having been translated from the ancient Indian language,[4] and in a few cases from the Chinese. The translators were learned Indian and Kashīmri Pandits and a few Chinese monks, assisted by Tibetan scholars.[5]

The code extends to one hundred or one hundred and eight volumes of about one thousand pages each, comprising one thou-

1 The *Daphne Cannabina*. See HODGSON in *J.A.S.B.*, 1832, i., p. 8, for an account of its manufacture.

2 bkah-'gyur.

3 bstañ-'gyur.

4 rgya-gar-skad, or "Indian language," and usually employed as synonymous with "Sanskrit."

5 Lô-tsa-wa.

sand and eighty-three distinct works. The bulk of this colossal bible may be imagined from the fact that each of its hundred or more volumes weighs about ten pounds, and forms a package measuring about twenty-six inches long by eight inches broad and about eight inches deep. Thus the code requires about a dozen yaks for its transport; and the carved wooden blocks from which this bible is printed require, for their storage, rows of houses like a good-sized village.

The Kāh-gyur is printed, I am informed, only at two places in Tibet: the older edition at Narthang,[1] about six miles from Tashi-lhunpo, the capital of western Tibet and headquarters of the Grand Panch'en-Lāma. It fills one hundred volumes of about one thousand pages each. The later edition is printed at Der-ge[2] in eastern Tibet (Kham) and contains the same matter distributed in volumes to reach the mystic number of one hundred and eight. In Bhotān an edition is printed at Punakha;[3] and I have heard of a Kumbum (Mongolian) edition, and of one printed at Pekin. The ordinary price at Narthang is about eight rupees per volume without the wooden boards. Most of the large monasteries even in Sikhim possess a full set of this code. The Pekin edition published by command of the emperor Khian-Lung, says Köppen, sold for £600; and a copy was bartered for 7,000 oxen by the Buriats, and the same tribe paid 1,200 silver roubles for a complete copy of this bible and its commentaries.[4] The Kāh-gyur was translated into Mongolian about 1310 A.D. by Saskya Lāma Ch'os-Kyi 'Od-zer under the Saskyā Paṇḍita, who, assisted by a staff of twenty-nine learned Tibetan, Ugrian, Chinese and Sanskrit scholars, had previously revised the Tibetan canon by collating it with Chinese and Sanskrit texts, under the patronage of the emperor Kublai Khan.

The contents of the Kāh-gyur and Tāṅ-gyur were briefly analyzed by Csoma,[5] whose valuable summary, translated and

---

1 sN'ar-taṅ. 2 sDe-dge.

3 So I have been told.

4 And a copy also of this edition seems to be in the St. Petersburg Academy of Sciences, obtained about 1830 by Baron Schilling de Canstadt, together with about 2,000 Mongolian and Tibetan treatises.—*Bulletin Historico-philologique del' Académie de St. Péterbourg*, tom. iv., 1848, pp. 321-329.

5 Vol. xx., *As. Researches.*

indexed by Feer,[1] and supplemented in part by Schiefner and Rockhill, forms the basis of the following sketch. Hodgson's copy of the Kāh-gyur, on which Csoma worked at Calcutta, contained one hundred volumes, and appears to have been printed from the wooden types prepared in 1731, and which seem to be still in use at Narthang.

The Kāh-gyur is divisible into three[2] great sections, the *Tripitaka*,[3] or three vessels or repositories, corresponding generally to the less inflated Pāli version of the Tripitaka of the southern Buddhists, which has, however, no counterpart of the mystical Sivaist treatises, the Tantras. The three sections are :—

I. The *Dul-va* (Skt., *Vinaya*), or Discipline, the compilation of which is attributed to Upali,[4] in thirteen volumes.

II. The *Dô* (Skt., *Sūtra*), or Sermons (of the Buddhas), compiled by Ānanda[5] in sixty-six volumes inclusive of Tantras. As these discourses profess to be the narrative of the disciple Ānanda,[6] who is believed to have been present at the originals as uttered by Buddha, most of these Sūtras commence with the formula: *Evam mayā srutam*, "Thus was it heard by me ;" but this formula now is almost regarded by many European scholars as indicating a fictitious sūtra, so frequently is it prefixed to spurious sūtras, *e.g.*, the Amitābha, which could not have been spoken by Buddha or recited by Ānanda. The Lāmas, like the southern Buddhists, naïvely believe that when Buddha spoke, each individual of the assembled hosts of gods, demons, and men, as well as the various kinds of lower animals,[7] heard himself addressed in his own vernacular.

III. The *Ch'os-non-pa* (Skt. *Abidharma*), or Metaphysics,

---

1 M. Léon Feer published in 1881 a translation of Csoma's *Analysis* under the title *Analyse du Kandjour et du Tandjour* in the second volume of the "Annales du Musée Guimet," and appended a vocabulary giving all the names which occur in Csoma's *Analysis*, with an Index and *Table Alphabétique de Ouvrages dus Kandjour*. And he gave further extracts in Vol. v. of the same serial.

2 Another classification of the canonical scriptures, especially amongst the Nepalese, is given by Hodgson (*Lang.* 13, 49) as "The nine scriptures (Dharmas)," namely: 1. Prajñā pāramitā. 2. Gandha-vyuha. 3. Daṣa-bhūmīṣvara. 4. Samādhi-rāja. 5. Laṅkāvatāra. 6. Saddharma Puṇḍarīka. 7. Tathāgatha guhyaka (containing the secret Tāntrik doctrines). 8. Lalita Vistara. 9. Suvarna-prabhasa.

3 sde-snod *g*sum.

4 Ñye-var-'K'or.

5 'Kun-dgah-wo.

6 At the first great council when Buddha's word was collated

7 Cf. also Beal's *Romantic Legend*, 244-254, *Gya Tscher Rol-pa*, ch. 26.

including Transcendental Wisdom (*S'er-p'yin*, Skt., *Prajñā Pāramitā*), attributed to Mahā Kāsyapa, in twenty-one volumes.

These three sections are mystically considered to be the antidotes for the three original sins; thus the discipline cleanses from lust (*Rāga*), the sermons from ill-will (*Dvesa*), and the wisdom from stupidity (*Moha*).

By subdividing the Dô or *Sūtra* section into five portions, the following sevenfold division of the canon results:—

"I. Discipline or *Dul-va* (Skt., *Vinaya*), in thirteen volumes, deals with the religious discipline and education of those adopting the religious life, and also contains *Jātakas*, avadanas, vyakaranas, sutras, and ridānas." (It is the *Vinaya* of the Sarvastivadains, and its greater portion has been abstracted by Rockhill.[1]) It is sub-divided into seven parts:

1. "The Basis of Discipline or Education (dul-va-gz'i, Skt., *Vinaya Vastu*), in four volumes (K, K', G, and Ṅ), translated from the Sanskrit in the ninth century by the Pandits Sarvajñyādeva and Dharmakara of Kashmīr and Vidyakara-prabha of India, assisted by the Tibetan Bandes dPal-gyi lhunpo and dPal-brtsegs. (The chief Jātaka and other tales interspersed through these volumes form the bulk of Schiefner's collection of Tibetan tales, translated into English by Ralston.)

2. "Sūtra on Emancipation (So-vor-t'ar-paī-mdo, Skt., *Pratimoksha Sūtra*),[2] in 30 leaves.

3. "Explanation of Education (Dul-va nam-par-'byed-pa, Skt., *Vinaya vibhāga*) in four volumes. Enumerates the several rules (K'rims) of conduct, 253 in number, with examples of the particular transgression which led to the formation of these laws. Directions for dress and etiquette.

4. "Emancipation for Nuns (*dGe-sloṅ mahi so-sor thar pai mod*, Skt., *Bhikshuni pratimoksha Sūtra*), 36 leaves in the ninth volume (T).

5. "Explanation of the Discipline of the Nuns (Skt., *Bhik. Vinaya vibhāga*) in preceding volume (T).

6. "Miscellaneous Minutiæ concerning Religious Discipline (Dul-va p'ran-ts'egs-kyi gz'i, Skt., *Vinaya Kshudraka Vastu*), in two volumes.

7. "The highest text book on Education" (Dul-va gzuṅ bla-ma *Vinaya Uttara Grantha*), in two volumes (N and P), and when spoken of as "the four classes of precepts" (liṅ-de-zhi) the division comprises 1, 2 and 3, 6 and 7.

II. Transcendental Wisdom ("*Ses-rab kyi p'a-rol-tu p'yin-pa*," or curtly, "*Ser-ch'in*" (Skt., *Prajñā-pāramitā*), in twenty-one volumes.

---

[1] *The Life of the Buddha*, etc. Also in part, but not directly for the Dulva, by Schiefner in his *Tibetische Liebenbescriebung Sakra, impl.*, St. Petersburg, 1849.

[2] Cf. translation from the Tibetan by Rockhill, and from the Pāli by Rhys Davids and Oldenberg, *Vinaya Texts*.

They contain, in addition to the metaphysical terminology, those extravagantly speculative doctrines entitled *Prajña-pāramitā*, which the Mahāyāna school attributes to Buddha's latest revelations in his mythical discourses mostly to supernatural hearers at the Vultures' Peak at Rājgriha.[1] There is no historical matter, all is speculation, and a profusion of abstraction.

The first twelve volumes, called *'Bum* (Skt., *Ṣata Sahasrikā*) or "the 100,000 (slokas of Transcendental Wisdom)," treat fully of the Prajñā-pāramitā at large, and the remaining volumes are merely various abridgments of these twelve. Thus the three volumes called *Ñi-k'ri* (pron. *Nyi-ṭhi*) or "the 20,000 (slokas)" is intended for those monasteries or individuals who cannot purchase or peruse the full text; while the single volume, entitled the brgyad-stoṅ-pan (ashta sahasrika) or 8,000 (slokas), contains in one volume the gist of the Prajña-pāramitā, and is intended for the average and junior monks. This is the volume which is figured on the lotus which Mañjuṣrī, the Bodhisat of wisdom, holds in his left hand. And for the use of the schoolboys and the laity there is a recension of three or four leaves, entitled "Transcendental Wisdom in a few letters" or Yige-ñuṅ-du (Skt., *Alpa akshara*).[2] And mystically the whole is further condensed into "the letter A, which is considered "the mother of all wisdom," and therefore of all men of genius; all Bodhisatvas and Buddhas are said to have been produced by "A" since this is the first element for forming syllables, words, sentences, and a whole discourse.

One of the most favourite Sūtras and a common booklet in the hands of the laity, is "the Diamond-cutter" (rDo-rje gc'od-pa, Skt., *Vajrach'edikā*). In it Bhagavāti (Ṣākya) instructs Subhūti, one of his disciples, in the true meaning of the Prajñā-pāramitā.[3]

The full text ('Bum) was translated from the Sanskrit in the ninth century by the Indian pandits Jina Mitra and Surendra Bodhi, and the Tibetan interpreter Ye-s'es-sde.

III. "Association of Buddhas" (P'al-c'ar, Skt., *Buddhāvataṅsaka*), in six volumes. Description of several Tathagatas or Buddhas, their provinces, etc. Enumeration of several Bodhisats, the several degrees of their perfections, etc.

This great Vaipulya (or developed Sūtra) is alleged to have been preached by Buddha in the second week of his Buddhahood and before he turned the "Wheel of the Law" at Benares. And it is asserted to have been delivered in nine assemblies at seven different places, and is thus given pre-eminence over the first historic discourse at Sārnāth.

IV. "The Jewel-peak" (dkon-brtsegs, Skt., *Ratna-kūta*). Enu-

[1] They are alleged to have been delivered in sixteen assemblies at the following sites: Gridhrakūta, Ṣrāvaṣtī, Veṇuvana, and the abode of the Paranirmita-vasavartins. cf. BUN. NANJIO's *Jāp. Budd. Sects*, p. xvii.

[2] This probably corresponds to the Mahāprajña pāramitā hridaya Sūtra, translated by BEAL (*Catena*, 282), and perhaps the original of the more expanded treatises.

[3] It has been translated from the Sanskrit by COWELL, *Mahāyāna Texts*, ii., xii.

meration of several qualities and perfections of Buddha and his doctrine.

V. The Aphorisms (Tib., mDo or mDo-*s*de *Sūtra* or *Sūtrānta*). The amplified or developed *Sūtras* are called *Vaipulya.* In a general sense, when the whole Khā-gyur is divided into two parts, mDo and rGyud, all the other divisions except the rGyud are comprehended in the mDo class. But in a particular sense there are some treatises which have been arranged under this title. They amount to about 270, and are contained in thirty volumes. The subject of the works is various. The greatest part of them consist of moral and metaphysical doctrine of the Buddhistic system, the legendary accounts of several individuals, with allusions to the sixty or sixty-four arts, to medicine, astronomy, and astrology. There are many stories to exemplify the consequences of actions in former transmigrations, descriptions of orthodox and heterodox theories, mural and civil laws, the six kinds of animal beings, the places of their habitations, and the causes of their being born there, cosmogony and cosmography according to Buddhistic notions, the provinces of several Buddhas, exemplary conduct of life of any *Bodhisat* or saint, and in general all the twelve kinds of Buddhistic Scriptures [1] are to be found here.

The second volume (K') contains the romantic biography of Buddha—the *Lalita Vistara*, translated by M. Foucaux.[2] The seventh volume (J) contains the *Saddharma Puṇḍarīka*,[3] or *White Lotus of the Holy Law*, translated from the Sanskrit into French by Burnouf, and into English by Prof. H. Kern,[4] and the most popular treatise with Japanese Buddhists. The eighth volume (N) contains "the Great Decease" (*Mahāparinirvāna*). The ninth volume has, amongst others, the *Suraṅgama Samādhi Sūtra* referred to by FaHian. The twenty-sixth volume (L), folios 329–400, or chapters of "joyous utterance" (Udānas), contains the *Udānavarga*,[5] which Schiefner showed to be the Tibetan version of the *Dhammapada ;* and which has been translated into

[1] This twelve-fold division (*g*suṅ rab yan lay bc'u-gñi*s*) I here extract from the Vyutpatti in the Tāṅ-gyur: 1. *Sutran* (*m*do-*s*dehi-*s*de) discourses. 2. *geyam* (*d*byaṅs kyi*s* *b*sñad), mixed prose and verse. 3. *Vyakaraṅaṅ* (luṅ du-*b*stan), exposition. 4. *Gāthā* (Tshig*s*-su-bc'ad), verse. 5. *Udānan* (C'ed-du-*b*rjod). 6. *Nidānaṅ* (gliṅ-gzhi). 7. *Avadānan* (rtogs-pa-brjod). 8. *Itivrittakan* (de-lta bw byuṅ). 9. *Jātaka* (skyes-pa-rabs). 10. *Vaipulyan* (shin-tu-rgya*s*), very expanded. 11. *Atbhūtdharmmah* (rmad-du byuṅ), mysteries. 12. *Upadesah* (gtun-la-dbab). This division, says BURNOUF (*Introd.*, p. 45-60), writing of Nepalese Buddhism, is made up of the older nine *angas* mentioned by Buddhagosha, A.D. 450, to which were added at a later period Nidana, Avadana, and Upadesa. Conf. also CHILDERS' *Dict.*, BURNOUF's *Lotus*, 355, 356; HARDY's *Man.*; HODGSON's *Ess.*, 15; RHYS DAVIDS' *Budd.*, 214.

[2] Also summarised by CSOMA (*Anal.*, 413) and VASIL., *B.*, 3, 4, 176; FEER's Intro., p. 72. Also abstracted by ROCKHILL, *B.*, ii.; and in part from the Sanskrit by Raj. Mitra.

[3] Dam-pahi ch'os padma dkar-po.

[4] Vol. xxi., *Sacred Books of the East*.

[5] Ch'ed-du brjod pai ts'oms; see also CSOMA's *An.*, p. 477. Its commentary by Prajñāvarman (a native of Bengal who lived in Kashmīr in the ninth century—*Tāranātha*, p. 204, ROCKHILL, xii.) is in Vol. lxxi. of *Tan-gyur*.

English with copious notes by Mr. Rockhill. It contains three hundred verses, which "are nearly identical with verses of the *Dhammapada;* one hundred and fifty more resemble verses of that work." The variations show that the northern translation was made from a different version than the Pāli,[1] and from, as Mr. Rockhill believes,[2] a "Sanskrit version in the dialect prevalent in Kashmīr in the first century B.C., at which period and in which place the compiler, Dharmatrāta,[3] probably lived."

From this (Dô) division of the Kah-gyur are culled out the Indian mystic formulas, mostly in unintelligible gibberish, which are deemed most potent as charms, and these form the volume named *m*Do-maṅ *g*zuṅ[4] *bs*dus, or curtly, *Dô-maṅ* or "assorted aphorisms"—literally "many *Sūtras*." These formulas are not used in the worship of the Buddhas and superior gods, but only as priestly incantations in the treatment of disease and ill-fortune. And as these spells enter into the worship of which the laity have most experience, small pocket editions of one or other of these mystic *Sūtras* are to be found in the possession of all literate laymen, as the mere act of reading these charms suffices to ward off the demon-bred disease and misfortune.

The remaining divisions of the canons are:—

VI. *Nirvāna* (Mya-naṅ-las-'das-pa), in two volumes. An extended version, part of the eighth volume of the mDo on "The Great Decease, or Entire deliverance from Pain." "Great lamentation of all sorts of animal beings on the approaching death of Shākya; their offerings or sacrifices presented to him; his lessons, especially with regard to the soul. His last moments; his funeral; how his relics were divided and where deposited."[5]

VII. *Tantra* (*r*gyud), in twenty-two volumes. "These volumes in general contain mystical theology. There are descriptions of several gods and goddesses. Instruction for preparing *mandalas* or circles for the reception of those divinities. Offerings or sacrifices presented to them for obtaining their favour. Prayers, hymns, charms, etc., addressed to them. There are also some works on astronomy, astrology, chronology, medicine, and natural philosophy."[6]

In the first volume (K) are found the Kālacakra doctrine[7] and *Sambara*. In the third the history of the divine mothers *Vārāhi*, etc.

---

1 ROCKHILL'S *Udānavarga*, ix.

2 *Loc cit.*, x.

3 *Tāranātha*, p. 54, lig. 8.

4 gz'uṅs = Skt. *dharani*, which is a mystic spell like the Hindū *Mantra*.

5 CSOMA, *An.*, p. 487.

6 CSOMA, *An.*, p. 487.

7 CSOMA, *Gram.*, p. 172; *Dict.*, 488.

In the seventeenth volume (M) the expelling of devils and Nāgā-worship. The *Tathāgata-guhyaka* contains a summàry of the Sivaic esoteric doctrine.

The word "*Tantra*," according to its Tibetan etymology, literally means[1] "treatise or dissertation," but in Buddhism as in Hindūism, it is restricted to the necromantic books of the later Sivaic or Sākti mysticism.

The Tantras are arranged into "The four classes" (gyud sde bzhi):

1. *Kriyā* Tantra (bya-bai-rgyud).
2. *Cāryā* T. (spyod-pai rgyud).
3. *Yoga* T. (rual-'byor rgyud).
4. *Anuttara Yoga* T. (rnal-'byor bla-na med-pai rgyud) or "The peerless Yoga."

The first two form together the lower division ('og-ma), and the latter two the higher division (gon-ma). It is only in the Anuttara Yogatantras, including the Atiyoga (Ds og-ch'en), that the tutelary fiends and their *Jinas* have female energies or Mātris.

Those translated from the eighth to the eleventh centuries A.D. are called "the Old," while the latter are "the New." Amongst those *composed in Tibet* are the Hayagriva, Vajraphurba and sKu-gsuṅ-t'ugs yon-tan 'p'rin las.

THE COMMENTARIES (*TÄṄ-GYUR*).

The Buddhist commentators, like those of the Talmud, overlay a line or two with an enormous excrescence of exegesis.

The Tibetan commentary or *Täṅ-gyur* is a great cyclopedic compilation of all sorts of literary works, written mostly by ancient Indian scholars and some learned Tibetans in the first few centuries after the introduction of Buddhism into Tibet, commencing with the seventh century of our era. The whole makes two hundred and twenty-five volumes. It is divided into the classes—the r*Gyud* and m*Do* (*Tantra* and *Sūtra* classes in Sanskrit). The r*Gyud*, mostly on *tantrika* rituals and ceremonies, make eighty-seven volumes. The m*Do* on science and literature one hundred and thirty-six volumes. One separate volume contains hymns or praises on several deities and saints. And one volume is the index for the whole.[2] The first sixteen volumes of the m*Do* class are all commentaries on the *Prajñā-pāramitā*. Afterwards follow several volumes explanatory of the Madhyamikā philosophy (of Nāgārjuna) which is founded on the Prajñā-pāramitā.[3]

---

[1] JAESCHKE, p. 112. [2] CSOMA, *An.*, 553.

[3] A few of the individual treatises have been translated, either in full or *abstract*, by Schiefner, Rockhill, etc. Nāgārjuna's Friendly Epistle (bches-pahi p'rin yig), by WENZEL in *J. Pāli Text Soc.*, 1886

One volume contains the Tibeto-Sanskrit dictionary of Buddhist terminology, the "bye-brag-tu rtogs byad (pron. *je-tak-tu tog-je*) —the Mahāvyutpati.[1] Under this heading would also come the later commentaries, such as the Bodhi-patha (in Mongolian—Bodhi Mur). Its contents include rhetoric, grammar, prosody, mediæval mechanics, and alchemy. But its contents have not yet been fully examined.[2]

THE INDIGENOUS TIBETAN LITERATURE.

The indigenous works composed in Tibet are for the most part devoted to sacred subjects. The secular books exist, as a rule, in manuscript, as the printing is in the hands of the monks.[3]

The sacred books may be divided into (*a*) apocryphal and (*b*) authentic or quasi-authentic.

The apocryphal works are the most numerous and most popular. Chief amongst these are the fictitious "revelations" or *Terma* books, already referred to in describing the part which they played in the origin of the sects of Lāmaism. These *Terma* books may be recognized by their style of caligraphy. For instead of the opening sentences and chapters commencing with the hook-like symbol for *Om*, duplicated or triplicated, as on the cover of this book, and the punctuation periods being vertical lines, as in ordinary orthodox books, the *Terma* books commence with the ordinary *anusvāra* (AṂ), or a vertical stroke enshrined in a trefoil-like curve, and their periods are marked by two small circles one over the other, like the Devanagari *visarga*, but with a curved line with its concavity upwards, intervening. These "revelations," it will be remembered, pretend to be the composition of St. Padma, the founder of Lāmaism.[4]

---

[1] The Sanskrit text of which has been published by Maiyaneff; and much of it is abstracted in the *Buddhistische Triglotte*, printed by Schiefner, St. Petersburg, 1859.

[2] The 2nd vol. of the *Annales du Musée Guimet* contains some additional notes on the Tāṅ-gyur by M. Léon Feer.

[3] Most of the printing-monastic establishments issue lists of the books which they sell.

[4] Amongst the better known are: The Golden Rosary of Displayed Letters (T'ug-yig gser-'p'reṅ), found by Sang-gya*s* gling-pa; The Displayed Lotus Orders (Padma bkāh-t'an), found by O-rgyan gling-pa; Kā-t'ang Zang-gling ma; The Lamp Enlightener of Prophecy (Lung-brtan gsal-baï sgron-me). Also of this nature are: The Directions for the Departed Soul to find its way to bliss (Pa-cha-to's-sgrol).

To this revelation class belong also the fictitious works attributed to King Sroṅ Tsan Gampo.[1]

Of the other most common apocryphal works found in Sikhim are the *Nä-yik*, or "Story of the Sacred Sites of Sikhim," and Lhatsun's inspired manual of worship for the great mountain god Kaṅch'en-dsö-ṅa (English, *Kinchinjunga*). Each monastery possesses in manuscript a more or less legendary account of its own history (*deb-t'er*), although this is kept out of sight. In the Lepcha monasteries and in the possession of a few Lepcha laymen are found the following, mostly translations from the Tibetan: (1) *Tāshi Suṅ*, a fabulous history of St. Padma-sambhava; (2) *Guru Ch'ö Waṅ;* (3) *Sākun de-lok*, the narrative of a visit to Hades by a resuscitated man named Sākun;[2] (4) *Ek-doshi man-lom*—forms of worship.

The large work on the Nāga demigods—the Lu-'bum dkar-po—is regarded as a heterodox Bön-po book.[3]

As authentic works may be instanced, the religious chronologies (Ch'os-'byuṅ) and records (Deb-t'er) by Bu-ton, and Padma-karpo; the histories (Suṅ-'bum) of Zhvā-lu Lô-tsa, and Tāranātha's well-known history of Buddhism in India, and a useful cyclopedia by an Amdô Lāma entitled T'ub-dbaṅ bstan-pāhi Ñima; and as quasi-authentic the fifth Grand Lāma's "royal pedigree."[4] All begin with pious dedicatory sentences and usually end with the Buddhist wish that the writer may acquire merit through his literary work.

But most of the autobiographies so-called (rNam-t'ar) and records (Yig-tsaṅ or deb-t'er) are legendary, especially of the earlier Lāmas and Indian monks are transparently fictitious, not only on account of their prophetic tone, though always "discovered" after the occurrence of the events prophesied, but their almost total absence of any personal or historic details. Some of the later ones

[1] (1) Mani bKāh-bum (already referred to), the legendary history of Avalokita and a maze of silly fables. (2) S'alch'em or Sroṅ Tsan Gampo's *Honourable Will* or Testament, and (3) an exoteric volume entitled "The Sealed Commands," bkā-rgga-ma, which is kept carefully secreted in some of the larger monasteries. It belongs to the silly esoteric class of books called *Saṅ-ṅak*.

[2] Cf. also the play of Naṅsa, The Brilliant Light, Chap. xx.

[3] A German translation by Schiefner of the smaller version has been published by the St. Petersburg Acad. (*Das Weisse Nāga Hunderh tausend.*) Cf. also ROCKHILL, *L.*, p. 217, *n.*

[4] gyal-rabs [Skt., Rājvansa].

dealing with modern personages are of a somewhat more historical character, but are so overloaded by legends as to repel even enthusiastic enquirers.

The leading ritualistic manuals of the various sects are of a more or less authentic character, and small pocket editions of these prayer books (smon-lam) and hymns (bstod-tsogs) are very numerous.[1] Individual Lāmas possess special books according to their private means and inclinations, such as the 100,000 songs[2] of the famous mendicant sage *Mila-rä-pa* on the worship of Tārā and other favourite or tutelary deities, and the mode of making their magic-circles. Mongol Lāmas have the Dsang-lun. The specialist in medicine has one or more fantastic medical works, such as Mannag-rgyud, S'ad-gyud; and the *Tsi-pa* or astrologer has the *Baidyur karpo* and other books on astrological calculations and sorcery, many of which are translated from the Chinese.

Some further details of ritualistic books are found in the chapters on the monkhood and on ritual, where several abstracts are given.

The secular works, through most of which runs a more or less Buddhistic current, are mainly annals or chronicles (lô-rgyu).

Good and clever sayings and reflections (*r*togs-brjod), as "The precious rosary" (rin-ch'en-p'reṅ-wa), a collection of proverbs, and drinking songs.

Tales more or less fabulous (sgruṅs). The best known of these is that of Ge-sar (=? Czar or Cesar), who is described as a mighty war-like king of northern Asia, and who is made to figure as a suitor for the hand of the Chinese princess before her marriage with Sroṅ Tsan Gampo, although it is evident the legendary accounts of him must be more ancient. Baber[3] refers to the story-book named Djriung-yi[4] songs.[5]

---

1 The Ge-lug-pa monk's manual is "The Bhikshu's Timely Memoranda (dGe-sloṅ-gi-du-dran), and his other special books are the two volumes by Tsoṅ K'apa entitled: *The Gradual Path* (*Lam rim c'en-bo*), a doctrinal commentary based on Atīṣa's version of the *Bodi Patha Pradip*, and *The Gradual Path of Vajradhara* (*r*Dor-c'aṅ Lam-rim), a highly Tāntrik book. (Cf. CSOMA, *Gr.*, 197.) For *Bodhi-mur* (Bodhi-patha), see SCHMIDT'S *Ssanang Ssetsen*.

2 gLu-b'um.

3 *Op. cit.*, p. 88.

4 ROCK., *B.*, p. 288, suggests this may be rGyus-yi-dpe.

5 Amongst indigenous geographical works is "A Geography of the World" (*Dsam-liṅ gye-she*). The references to countries outside Tibet are mainly confined to India, and are even then very inexact. Its most useful section is that descriptive of Tibet, translated by SARAT, *J.A.S.B.*, 1887, pp. 1 *et seq.* See also *Wei-tshang thu shi*, abstracted by Klaproth from the Chinese. Cf. also CSOMA's enumeration of Tibetan works, *J.A.S.B.*, vii., 147; ix., 905.

THE LĀMAIST LIBRARY.

The Lāmaist library is usually situated within the temple. The large books are deposited in an open pigeon-holed rackwork. The sheets forming the volume are wrapped in a napkin; and the bundle is then placed between two heavy wooden blocks, as covers, which bear on their front end the name of the book in letters graved in relief and gilt. The whole parcel is firmly bound by a broad tape and buckle tied across its middle. These ponderous tomes are most unwieldy and not easy of reference. When the book is read away from tables as is usually the case, it is held across the knees, and the upper board and the leaves as they are read are lifted towards the reader and repiled in order in his lap. Before opening its fastenings, and also on retying the parcel, the monk places the book reverently on his head, saying, "May I obtain the blessing of thy holy word."

Copyists of manuscript, as well as composers and translators, usually conclude their work with a short stanza expressing their pious hope that "this work here finished may benefit the (unsaved) animals."

An enormous mass of Lāmaist literature is now available in Europe in the collections at St. Petersburg, mainly obtained from Pekin, Siberia, and Mongolia; at Paris, and at the India Office, and Royal Asiatic Society[1] in London, and at Oxford, mostly gifted by Mr. Hodgson.[2]

The St. Petersburg collection is the largest, and extends to over 2,000 volumes.[3]

---

[1] Catalogue of these, by Dr. H. Wenzel, in *J.R.A.S.*, 1891.

[2] The India Office copy of the canon was presented to Mr. Hodgson by the Dalai Lāma.

[3] Notices of these occur in various volumes of the *Melang. Asiat. de St. Petersb.*

A Lāmaist Procession.[1]

VIII.

THE LĀMAIST ORDER AND PRIESTHOOD.

"Without the Lāma in front,
God is not (approachable)."—*Tibetan Proverb.*

As in primitive Buddhism, the monastic order or congregation of the Virtuous Ones[2] forms the third member of the Trinity, "The Three most Precious Ones" of Lāmaism. But owing to the rampant sacerdotalism of Tibet, the order is in a much higher position there than it ever attained in Indian Mahāyāna Buddhism, according to the current Tibetan saying above cited.

The order is composed of Bodhisats both human and celestial. The latter occupy, of course, the highest rank, while the so-called incarnate Lāmas,[3] who are believed to be incarnated reflexes from

---

1 After Giorgi. 2 Skt., *Saṅgha ;* Tib., d*Ge-dun*. 3 sprul-sku, or ku-s'o.

a superhuman Buddha or Bodhisat or a reborn saint, are given an intermediate position, as is detailed in the chapter on the hierarchy.

The Lāmas are "the Bodhisats who have renounced the world,"[1] and thus are held to correspond to the *Saṅgha* of primitive Buddhism consisting of the *Bhikshus* (mendicants), *Śrāmaneras* (ascetic) and *Arhats*. The nuns, excepting the so-called incarnations of celestial Bodhisats (*e.g.*, Dorje-p'agmo), are given an inferior position scarcely higher than lay devotees.

While the laity, corresponding to "the pious householders and hearers"[2] of the primitive Buddhists, who under the Mahāyāna system should be "the Bodhisats who reside in their houses," are practically excluded from the title to Bodhisatship or early Buddhahood like the Lāmas, and are contemptuously called the "Owners of Alms,"[3] those "bound by fear,"[4] and the "benighted people;"[5] although the lay devotees are allowed the title of *Upāsaka* and *Upāsikā*[6] if keeping the five precepts, and those who are uncelibate are called "the pure doer";[7] while the *Ñen-t'o* or *Ñen-nä*[8] keep four of the precepts.

The supreme position which the Lāmas occupy in Tibetan society, both as temporal and spiritual rulers, and the privileges which they enjoy, as well as the deep religious habit of the people, all combine to attract to the priestly ranks enormous numbers of recruits. At the same time it would appear that compulsion is also exercised by the despotic priestly government in the shape of a recognized tax of children to be made Lāmas, named *bTsun-gral* Every family thus affords at least one of its sons to the church. The first-born or favourite son is usually so dedicated in Tibet.[9] The other son marries in order to continue the family name and inheritance and to be the bread-winner; and many families contribute more than one, as the youths are eager to join it.

[1] *Pravrajya.*

[2] HODGS., *Illus.*, p. 98; HARDY, *E.M.*, p. 12.

[3] *sbyin-bdags*

[4] *'jigs-rten*-pa.

[5] *mi-nag-pa.*

[6] d*Ge*-bs*ñen*. This title is also applied to a novice, probationer, or candidate. Cf. KÖPP., ii., 252; SCHLAG., 162; JAESCHK., *D.*, 85.

[7] *mts'an-spyod.*

[8] gs*ñen-gnas*.

[9] Conf. also Pandit, A. K. In Sikhim it is the second son; and also in Ladāk (MARX, *loc. cit.*).

Thus in Tibet, where children are relatively few, it is believed that one out of every six or eight of the population is a priest. In Sikhim the proportion is one to ten.[1] In Ladāk one-sixth.[2] In Bhotān one to about ten.

GRADES.

In every monachism there are naturally three hierarchical seniorities or ranks, namely: the scholars or novices, the ordained, and the reverend fathers or the priests, just as in the common guilds or arts are the grades of the apprentice, the journeyman, and the master. Indian Buddhism had its grades of the Sramaṇera (or the novice), of the expert Sramaṇa or Bhikshu (the moderate one or beggar), and of the Sthavira or *Upāyāhya* (master or teacher).

Lāmaism has naturally these necessary degrees of clerical maturity and subordination, and by dividing the noviciate into two sections it counts four, thus :—

1. The clerical apprentice or scholar. The customary title of this first beginner in holy orders is *Gē-ñen*, which means "to live upon virtue," and is a translation of the Sanskrit word *Upāsaka* or lay-brother. This word has a double meaning; it shows firstly the simple lay believer, who has promised to avoid the five great sins; and secondly the monastic devotee or scholar, who keeps the ten precepts and is preparing for the holy orders to which he partly belongs through the clothes he wears and the official acknowledgment which he has received. He is also called Rab-byuṅ or "excellent born." The Mongols call these "*Schabi*," and *Bandi*, *Banda*, or "*Bante*,"[3] which latter word seems to be of Indian origin. The Kalmaks call them Manji.[4]

2. The *Ge-ts'ul*, the commencing, but not quite fully ordained monk, an under priest, or deacon, who keeps the thirty-six rules.

3. *Ge-long* or "virtuous or clerical beggar," the real monk, the priest, over twenty-five years of age, and who has been fully ordained, and keeps the two hundred and fifty-three rules.

---

[1] See my *Lāmaism in Sikhim.*

[2] Knight, *op. cit.*, p. 130.

[3] Cf. Jaeschke, *D.*, 364.

[4] The Santāls of Bengal, who are believed to be of the so-called Turanian descent, call their chiefs *Manji.*

4. The *K'an-po*, which means the master or Abbot (Skt., *Upādhyāya*). He is the end, the true extremity of the Lāmaist

A TIBETAN DOCTOR OF DIVINITY.
AN ABBOT.

monachism, because he has under him all the scholars, novices, and common monks. And although the regenerated or re-incarnated monks, the Chutuktus, and sovereign priest-gods are above him,[1] their originals were essentially nothing else than abbots. He it is, who in the early time was probably the only one to be honoured by the title Lāma (*Guru* or master), and to whom is given this title even to the present time; although he may be called a Grand Lāma to distinguish him from the other cloister inhabitants. Only the larger cloisters have a K'an-po, who has the right to supervise several smaller Lāmaseries and temples, and whose position seems to be such that he is compared as a rule with the catholic bishop.[2]

THE CURRICULUM.

In sketching the details of the curriculum of the Lāma, I give the outlines of the course followed in the greatest of the monastic colleges of the established church of Tibet—the Ge-lug-pa—as related to me by Lāma-graduates of these institutions, namely, of De-pung, Sera, Gāh-ldan, and Tashi-lhunpo, as these set the high standard which other monasteries of all sects try to follow, and marked departures from this standard are indicated in a subsequent note.

The child who is the Lāma-elect (btsan-ch'uṅ) stays at home till about his eighth year (from six to twelve), wearing the red or yellow cap when he is sent to a monastery, and educated as in a sort of boarding-school or resident college, passing through the stages of pupil-probationer (ḍā-pa), novice (ge-ts'ul), to fully-ordained monk (ge-loṅ), and, it may be, taking one or other of the degrees in divinity, or a special qualification in some particular academic department.

As, however, the applicants for admission into these monastic colleges have usually passed the elementary stage and have already reached, or nearly reached, the stage of noviciate at some smaller monastery, I preface the account of the course in great monastic colleges by the preliminary stage as seen at the leading monastery in Sikhim, the Pemiongchi, which is modelled on that of the great Ñiṅ-ma monastery of Mindolling.

Preliminary Examination—Physical.—When the boy-candi-

[1] Those K'an-pos who have gone through the Tantra or *r*gyud-pa course have a higher repute than the others.

[2] KÖPPEN, ii., 254.

date for admission is brought to the monastery his parentage is enquired into, as many monasteries admit only the more respectable and wealthier class.[1] The boy is then physically examined to ascertain that he is free from deformity or defect in his limbs and faculties. If he stammers, or is a cripple in any way, or bent in body, he is rejected. When he has passed this physical examination he is made over by his father or guardian to any senior relative he may have amongst the monks. Should he have no relative in the monastery, then, by consulting his horoscope, one of the elder monks is fixed upon as a tutor, who receives from the lad's father a present of money,[2] tea, eatables, and beer.[3] The tutor or elder (Ger-gän)[4] then takes the boy inside the great hall where the monks are assembled, and publicly stating the parentage of the boy and the other details, and offering presents of beer, he asks the permission of the elder monks (*db*U-ch'os) to take the boy as a pupil. On this being accorded the boy becomes a probationer.

As a probationer he is little more than a private schoolboy under the care of his tutor, and doing various menial services. His hair is cropped without any ceremony, and he may even wear his ordinary lay dress. He is taught by his tutor the alphabet (the "Ka, K'a, Ga," as it is called),[5] and afterwards to read and recite by heart the smaller of the sacred books,[6] such as :—

Leū bdun ma, or "The Seven Chapters"—A prayer-book of St. Padma.

Bar-c'a*d* lam gsel or "Charms to clear the way from Danger and Injury"—A prayer to St. Padma in twelve stanzas.

Sher-phyin—An abstract of transcendental wisdom in six leaves.

sKu-rim—A sacrificial service for averting a calamity.

Mon-lam—Prayers for general welfare.

sDig sags, or "The Confession of Sins."[1] The mere act of reading

---

1 At Pemiongchi only those candidates who are of relatively pure Tibetan descent by the father's side are ordinarily admitted.

2 In Sikhim definite fees are payable at the different ceremonies for admission to the order, as detailed in my *Lāmaism in Sikhim*, amounting to about 150 Rs., in the case of the highest monastery—Pemiongchi. In Bhotan it is stated (PEMBERTON'S *Report*, p. 118; TURNER'S *Embassy*, 170) that the fee is 100 Bhotanese rupees.

3 This, of course, would not be offered in a Ge-lug-pa monastery.

4 dge-rgan, or "the Virtuous Elder." 5 See p. xviii.

6 Such small manuals are about eight or ten inches long by two to three inches broad, and usually have the leaves stitched together.

this holy booklet even as a school exercise cleanses from sin. Most of the monasteries possess their own blocks for printing this pamphlet. Both the text and its translation are given by Schlagintweit.[2]

rDor gchod—A *Sūtra* from the book of transcendental wisdom.

P'yogs-bc'ui-p'yogs-dral, or description of the ten directions	6	pages.
Namo Guru—"Salutation to the Guru"	5	,,
mC'od-'bul—To give offerings	6	,,
gTorma—Sacred cake	8	,,
bSaṅs bsur—Incense and butter-incense	5	,,
lTo-mc'od—Rice offering	4	,,
Rig-'dsin snön-'gro—The first essay of the sage	4	,,
Drag-dmar snön-'gro—The primer of red fierce deity ...	4	,,
bKā brgyed—"The eight commands" or precepts ...	4	,,
bDe gs'egs kun 'dus—The collection of the Tathāgatas ...	4	,,
Yes'es sku mc'og—The best foreknowledge	5	,,
rTsa-gdun bs'ag-gsal—The root-pillar of clear confession	4	,,

The young probationer is also instructed in certain golden maxims of a moral kind, of which the following are examples:—

Buddhist Proverbs:—

Whatever is unpleasing to yourself do not to another.

Whatever happiness is in the world has all arisen from a wish for the welfare of others. Whatever misery there is has arisen from indulging selfishness.

There is no eye like the understanding, no blindness like ignorance, no enemy like sickness, nothing so dreaded as death.

A king is honoured in his own dominions, but a talented man everywhere.

"*The four Precipices in Speech.*—If speech be too long, it is tedious; if too short, its meaning is not appreciated; if rough, it ruffles the temper of the hearers; if soft, it is unsatisfying.

"*The Requirements of Speech.*—Speech should be vigorous or it will not interest; it must be bright or it will not enlighten; it must be suitably ended, otherwise its effect is lost.

"*The Qualities of Speech.*—Speech must be bold as a lion, gentle and soft as a hare, impressive as a serpent, pointed as an arrow, and evenly balanced as a *dorje* held by its middle (literally "*waist*").

"*The Four Relations of Speech.*—The question should first be stated. The arguments should be duly connected, the later with the earlier. Essential points should be repeated. The meanings should be illustrated by examples.

---

1 The word for *sin* is "scorpion," thus conveying the idea of a vile, venomous, clawing, acrid thing.

2 *Op. cit.*, pages 122 to 142.

"The religious king Sroṅ-Tsan Gampo has said (in the Maṇi-kah-'bum): "Speech should float freely forth like a bird into the sky, and be clothed in charming dress like a goddess. At the outset the object of the speech should be made clear like an unclouded sky. The speech should proceed like the excavation of treasure. The arguments should shoot forth nimbly like a deer chased by fresh hounds, without hesitation or pause."

"*Assemblies.*—People assemble for three purposes, namely, for, (*a*) happiness, (*b*) sorrow, and (*c*) worldly gossip. The assemblies for happiness are three, namely, (1) for virtuous acts, (2) for worship in the temples, and (3) for erecting houses and for feasts. The assemblies for virtuous acts are four, viz., the gathering of the monks, the gathering of the laity for worship, writing and copying holy books, and giving away wealth in charity. There are six kinds of assemblies for worship, namely, the gathering of the rich, the gathering in a separate place of the common men, the gathering for thanksgiving of those who have escaped from their enemy's grasp, traders returned safely and successfully, sick men who have escaped from the devouring jaws of death, and youths on gaining a victory.

"*The eight acts of Low-born persons.*—Using coarse language, impoliteness, talking with pride, want of foresight, harsh manners, staring, immoral conduct, and stealing.

The ten Faults.—Unbelief in books, disrespect for teachers, rendering one's self unpleasant, covetousness, speaking too much, ridiculing another's misfortune, using abusive language, being angry with old men or with women, borrowing what cannot be repaid, and stealing.

Invoking "The Blessing of Eloquence" (ṅag-byin-rlabs). This is a Mantrayāna rite instituted by the "great saint" K'yuṅ-po (Skt., Garuḍa or Puna, or Brika.)[1]

"I go for refuge to the Three Holy Ones! May I attain perfection and benefit the animal beings. The one who brought me to the light is at the tip of my tongue and the white Om made up of the words is above the moon: the white *Ali* (vowels) go by the right circle, the red *Ka-li* (consonants) go by the left and the blue *Ktan-sñiṅ* by the right." I repeat them secretly after deep contemplation:

"Om! a, a, i, i, u, u, ri, ri, li, li, e, ai, o, ou, angah! swaha! (This is to be repeated thrice.) Om! Ka, Kha, Ga, Gha, Ṅa (and here follow all the letters of the alphabet). (Three times). Om! ye dhôrma (here follows 'The Buddhist Creed' thrice.) Through the rays of the seed of the mantra-rosary and the power of the blessings of speech, I summon the accomplishments of the seven precious *rgyal-srid* and 'The eight glorious signs.'" By repeating the above one attains accomplishment in speech.

During this training the boy's relatives call about once a month

[1] Cf. also the "Garuḍa Charm," figured at p. 387.

to enquire after his progress and health, and to pay the tutor his fees for the lad's board and education.

After two or three years of such rudimentary teaching, when the boy has committed to memory the necessary texts (amounting to about one hundred and twenty-five leaves), his tutor sends in an application for his admission as a novice.

The mode of admission to the noviciateship in the great Depung monastery is as follows :—

THE NOVICIATE.

The tutor-Lāma of the applicant for the noviciateship addresses the head monk (spyi-rgan) of his section for permission to admit the applicant, and at the same time offers a ceremonial scarf[1] and the fee of ten rupees. Then, if the applicant be found free from bodily defects and otherwise eligible, a written agreement is made out in the presence of the head monk and sealed by the thumb.

To get his name registered in the books of that particular school of the monastery to which he is to be attached, the pupil and his tutor go to the abbot[2] or principal of that school and proffer their request through the butler or cup-bearer,[3] who conducts them to the abbot, before whom they offer a scarf and a silver coin (preferably an Indian rupee), and bowing thrice before him, pray for admission.

Amongst the questions now put are: Does this boy come of his free will? Is he a slave, debtor, or soldier? Does anyone oppose his entry? Is he free from deformity, contagious disease, or fits? Has he neglected the first three commandments? Has he committed theft, or thrown poison into water, or stones from a hillside so as to destroy animal life, etc.? What is his family? and what their occupation? and where their residence? On giving satisfactory replies, he is then required to recite by heart the texts he has learned; and if approved, then the names of the pupil and his tutor are written down and duly sealed by the thumbs, and a scarf is thrown around their necks, and the boy, who has been dressed in princely finery, has his dress exchanged for the yellow or red robe in imitation of Ṣākya Muni's renunciation of the world; while, if he is rejected, he is ejected from the monastery,

[1] *lha-rdsas.* [2] *mk'an-po.* [3] *gsol.*

and his tutor receives a few strokes from a cane, and is fined several pounds of butter for the temple lamps.

The approved pupil and his tutor then proceed to the head Lāma (z'al-ṅo) of the great cathedral (common to the colleges of the university), and, offering a scarf and a rupee, repeat their requests to him, and the names of the pupil and tutor and his sectional college or residentiary club are registered, so that should the pupil misconduct himself in the cathedral, his teachers, as well as himself, shall be fined.

The neophyte is now a registered student (*ḍa-pa*),[1] and on returning to his club, he is, if rich, expected to entertain all the residents of the club to three cups of tea. If he has no relatives to cook for him, he is supplied from the club stores; and any allowance[2] he gets from his people is divided into three parts, one-third being appropriated by his club for messing expenses. Then he gets the following monkish robes and utensils, viz., a sTod-'gag, bs'am-t'abs, gzan, zla-gam, z'wa-ser, sgro-lugs, a cup, a bag for wheaten flour, and a rosary.

Until his formal initiation as an ascetic, "the going forth from home" (*pravrajyā-vrata*), by which he becomes a novice (Ge-ts'ul, Skt., Ṣramaṇa), the candidate is not allowed to join in the religious services in the monastery. So he now addresses a request to the presiding Grand Lāma[3] to become a novice, accompanying his request with a scarf and as much money as he can offer.

The ceremony of initiation is generally similar to that of the southern Buddhists.[4]

On the appointed day—usually on one of the fast days (Upo satha), the candidate has his head shaven all but a small tuft on the crown [5]; and he is conducted by his spiritual tutor (upadhyāya) before a chapter in the assembly hall, clad in the mendicant's robes, on putting on which he has muttered a formula to the effect that he wears them only for modesty and as a protection

1 grva-pa.

2 'gyed.

3 dGe-lden-K'ri-rin-po-c'he, or s'Kyabs-mgon-rin-poch'e.

4 Cf. Mahāvanso, i., 12. *UpaSampudā-Kammavāka*, translated by F. Spiegel, *op. cit.* Rhys Davids, *B.*, p. 159.

5 My friend, Mr. A. von Rosthorn, informs me that the Lāmas of eastern Tibet usually pass through an ordeal of initiation in which six marks are seared in their crown with an iron lamp, and called *Dipaṃkara*, or "the burning lamp."

against heat, cold, etc. The officiating head Lāma, sometimes the Grand Lāma, addressing the student by his secular name, asks, "Do you subject yourself to the tonsure cheerfully?" On receiving a reply in the affirmative, the presiding Lāma cuts off the remaining top tuft of hair from the head of the novice, who is like Chaucer's monk,

"His hed was balled, and shone like any glas."

The Lāma also gives the kneeling novice a religious name, by which he is henceforth known,[1] and exhorting him to keep the thirty-six precepts and the thirty-six rules, and to look upon the Grand Lāma as a living Buddha, he administers the vows to the novice, who repeats clearly three times the formula, "I take refuge in Buddha, in the Law, and in the Assembly."

The ceremony concludes with the presentation of a scarf and ten silver coins.[2]

At the next mass, the boy is brought into the great assembly hall, carrying a bundle of incense sticks; and is chaperoned by a monk named the "bride-companion" (ba-grags), as this ceremony is regarded as a marriage with the church. He sits down on an appointed seat by the side of the "bride-companion," who instructs him in the rules and etiquette (sGris) of the monkish manner of sitting, walking, etc.

The initiation into the Tāntrik Buddhist priesthood of the Vajrācāryas is detailed below in a foot-note.[3]

---

1 Extra titles are also bestowed, says Sarat, on the descendants of the old nobility. Thus, Ṅag-tshang families are given title of Shab-dung; the sons of high officials and landowners Je-duṅ; and the gentry and Sha-ngo family Choi-je.

2 *Tankas.*

3 The following account of the initiation of the Vajrācārya priests, as given by Mr. Hodgson for Nepal (*Ill.*, p. 139):—

"Early in the morning the following things, viz., the image of a Chaitya, those of the Tri Ratna or Triad, the Prajná Páramitá scripture, and other sacred scriptures, a *kalas*, or water-pot, filled with a few sacred articles, a platter of curds, four other water-pots filled with water only, a *chivara*, mendicants' upper and lower garments, a *Pinda pátra* (alms-bowl) and a religious staff, a pair of wooden sandals, a small mixed metal plate spread over with pounded sandal-wood, in which the image of the moon is inscribed, a golden razor and a silver one, and lastly, a plate of dressed rice, are collected, and the aspirant is seated in the *svastikásana* and made to perform worship to the *Guru Mandala*, and the Chaitya, and the Tri Ratna and the Prajná Páramitá Sástra. Then the aspirant, kneeling with one knee on the ground with joined hands, entreats the Guru to make him a Bandya, and to teach him whatsoever it is needful for him to know. The Guru answers, O! disciple, if you desire to perform the Pravrajya Vrata, first of all devote yourself to the worship of the Chaitya and of the Tri

The novice is now admitted to most of the privileges of a monk, and after a period of three years he passes out of the preliminary stage (rig-ch'uṅ), and is then entitled to have a small chamber or cell to himself, though he is still called a student (ḍa-pa), and, in-

Ratna: you must observe the five precepts or Pancha Siksha, the fastings and the vows prescribed; nor speak or think evilly; nor touch any intoxicating liquors or drugs; nor be proud of heart in consequence of your observance of your religious and moral duties."

"Then the aspirant pledges himself thrice to observe the whole of the above precepts; upon which the Guru tells him, 'If while you live you will keep the above rules, then will I make you a Bandya.' He assents, when the Guru, having again given the three *Rakshás* above-mentioned to the *Chela*, delivers a cloth for the loins to him to put on. Then the Guru brings the aspirant out into the court-yard, and having seated him, touches his hair with rice and oil, and gives those articles to a barber. The Guru next puts on the ground a little pulse and desires a *Chela* to apply it to his own feet. Then the Guru gives the *Chela* a cloth of four fingers' breadth and one cubit in length, woven with threads of five colours, and which is especially manufactured for this purpose, to bind round his head. Then he causes the aspirant to perform his ablutions, after which he makes *pújá* to the hands of the barber in the name of Visvakarma, and then causes the barber to shave all the hair, save the forelock, off the aspirant's head. Then the paternal or maternal aunt of the aspirant takes the vessel of mixed metal above noted and collects the hair into it. The aspirant is now bathed again and his nails pared, when the above party puts the parings into the pot with the hair. Another ablution of the aspirant follows, after which the aspirant is taken again within, and seated. Then the Guru causes him to eat, and also sprinkles upon him the Pancha Garbha, and says to him, 'Heretofore you have lived a householder, have you a real desire to abandon that state and assume the state of a monk?' The aspirant answers in the affirmative, when the Guru, or maternal uncle, cuts off with his own hand the aspirant's forelock. Then the Guru puts a tiara adorned with the images of the five BUDDHAS on his own head, and taking the *kalas* or water-pot, sprinkles the aspirant with holy water, repeating prayers at the same time over him.

"The neophyte is then again brought below, when four Náyakas or superiors of proximate Viháras and the aspirant's Guru perform the Pancha Abhisheka, *i.e.*, the Guru takes water from the *kalsa* and pours it into a conch; and then ringing a bell and repeating prayers, sprinkles the water from the conch on the aspirant's head; whilst the four Náyakas taking water from the other four water-pots named above, severally baptize the aspirant. The musicians present then strike up, when the Náyakas and Guru invoke the following blessing on the neophyte: 'May you be happy as he who dwells in the hearts of all, who is the universal Atman, the lord of all, the Buddha called Ratnasambhava.' The aspirant is next led by the Náyakas and Guru above stairs, and seated as before. He is then made to perform *pújá* to the Guru Mandal and to sprinkle rice on the images of the deities. The Guru next gives him the Chivara and Nivasa and golden earrings, when the aspirant thrice says to the Guru, 'O Guru, I, who am such an one, have abandoned the state of a householder for this whole birth, and have become a monk.' Upon which the aspirant's former name is relinquished and a new one given him, such as Ananda, Shari, Putra, Kāṣyapa, Dharma, Srī Mitra, Paramita Sagar. Then the Guru causes him to perform *pújá* to the Tri Ratna, after having given him a golden tiara, and repeated some prayers over him. The Guru then repeats the following praises of the Tri Ratna: 'I salute that

deed, all the monks, from the novice to the more senior (par-pa), and even the full monk (ge-loṅ) retain the same title in the chief monasteries of Tibet—the term "Lāma" being reserved to the heads of the monastery.

The novice now undergoes a severe course of instruction, during which corporal punishment is still, as heretofore, freely inflicted. The instruction is mainly in ritual and dogma, but crafts and some arts, such as painting, are also taught to those showing special aptitude. The spiritual adviser of the young monk is called "the radical Lāma,"[1] and as he initiates the novice into the

Buddha who is the lord of the three worlds, whom gods and men alike worship, who is apart from the world, long-suffering, profound as the ocean, the quintessence of all good, the Dharma Raja and Munindra, the destroyer of desire and affection, and vice and darkness; who is void of avarice and lust, who is the icon of wisdom. I ever invoke him, placing my head on his feet.

"'I salute that Dharma, who is the Prajná Páramitá, pointing out the way of perfect tranquillity to mortals, leading them into the paths of perfect wisdom; who, by the testimony of all the sages, produced or created all things; who is the mother of all Bodhisatwas and Sravakas. I salute that Sangha, who is Avalokitesvara and Maitreya, and Gagan Ganja, and Samanta Bhadra, and Vajra Pani, and Manju Ghosha, and Sarvanivarana Vishkambhin, and Kshiti Garbha and Kha Garbha.' The aspirant then says to the Guru, 'I will devote my whole life to the Tri Ratna, nor ever desert them.' Then the Guru gives him the Dasa S'ikshá or ten precepts observed by all the Buddhas and Bhikshukas, and commands his observance of them. They are: 1. Thou shalt not destroy life. 2. Thou shalt not steal. 3. Thou shalt not follow strange faiths. 4. Thou shalt not lie. 5. Thou shalt not touch intoxicating liquors or drugs. 6. Thou shalt not be proud of heart. 7. Thou shalt avoid music, dancing, and all such idle toys. 8. Thou shalt not dress in fine clothes nor use perfumes or ornaments. 9. Thou shalt sit and sleep in lowly places. 10. Thou shalt not eat out of the prescribed hours.

"The Guru then says, 'All these things the BUDDHAS avoided. You are now become a Bhikshu and you must avoid them too;' which said, the Guru obliterates the Tri Ratna Mandala. Next, the aspirant asks from the Guru the Chivara and Nivasa, the Pinda Pátra and Khikshari and Gandhar, equipments of a BUDDHA, a short staff surmounted by a Chaitya and a water-pot. Add thereto an umbrella and sandals to complete it. The aspirant proceeds to make a Mandal, and places in it five flowers and five Drubakund, and some Khil, and some rice; and assuming the Utkutak Asan, and joining his hands, he repeats the praises of the Tri Ratna above cited, and then again requests his Guru to give him suits of the Chivara and the like number of the Nivasa, one for occasions of ceremony as attending the palace, another for wearing at meals, and the third for ordinary wear. He also requests from his Guru the like number of Gandhár or drinking cups of Pinda Pátra, and of Khikshari. One entire suit of these the aspirant then assumes, receiving them from the hands of the Guru, who, previously to giving them, consecrates them by prayers. The aspirant then says, 'Now I have received the Pravrajya Vrata, I will religiously observe the Sītla-Skandha and Samádhi-Skandha, the Prajña-Skandha and the Vimukti-Skandha.'"

[1] rT*sa wai* b*lama.* This is not, as Schlagintweit states (*op. cit.*, 139), in any way restricted to particular "priests who originated a specific system of Buddhism."

mysterious rites he is held by the latter in especial reverence all through life.

Frequent examinations are held and also wrangling or public disputations.

In every cloister is a teacher of the law, who, as a rule, takes the highest rank after the chief. But in the larger ones are regular schools or universities, in which the holy books are systematically explained, and theology, etc., is taught. The most celebrated ones of these are of course those near Lhāsa and Tashi-lhunpo, which are visited by students from all provinces of the Lāmaist church. In the countries of southern Buddhism the cloister schools are divided after the three branches of the codes, into three sections, the Sūtras, Vinayas and Abhidharmas. In Tibet the division practically is the same, though sometimes is added a medical one, and also a mystic faculty for magic and conjuration, which, however, seems to be united as a rule with the section for philosophy and metaphysics (Abhidharma), for which in some Lāmaseries special schools are established.

Every Lāma belongs to one or other of these faculties, and the position which he occupies inside the brotherhood depends on the number and class of holy books which he has gone through and understands thoroughly.

As soon as the bell sounds he has to go to his respective room or class, to start with his lection, to receive new ones, to listen to the explanations of the professor, etc., etc., and to prepare for examinations and disputations.

Examinations.—Within a year after his admission to the order he must attempt to pass the first professional examination, and in the following year or two the second examination for promotion. And until he passes these examinations he must perform for the first three years the menial offices of serving out tea, etc., to the elder monks in the assembly hall.

The examinations are conducted in the presence of the heads of the monastery and the assembled monks, who observe a solemn silence, and the test is for the candidate to stand up in the assembly and recite by heart all the prescribed books.[1] The ordeal is a

[1] An idea of the nature of this is got from the following list of text books for the first examination at Pemiongchi, which comprise the worship necessary for three "magic-circles," viz.: The *first* is the magic-circle of dKon-c'og spyi 'dus Rig-'dsin

very trying one, so that the candidate is given a companion to prompt and encourage him. The first examination lasts for three days; and nine intervals are allowed daily during the examination,

---

'dsah ms'an ñing-poī c'os 'k'or (or "Banquet to the whole assembly of the Gods and Demons"). This book contains about sixty pages, and its recitation takes nearly one whole day. It comprises the chapters:—

(1) Ts'e-sgrub or The obtaining of long life.
(2) Z'i-k'ro—The mild and angry deities.
(3) Guru-drag—The fierce form of Padma-sambhava.
(4) Seṅ-gdoṅma—The lion-faced demoness.
(5) Ch'osskyoṅ Mahākāla Yes'es mgonpo.
(6) T'aṅ-lha (Mt. Thang-lha with its spirit "Kiting" is a northern guardian of Sikhim), mDsöd-lṅa, Lha-ch'en and sMan-bstün—Local and mountain deities.
(7) bsKaṅ bs'ag*s*, ts'ogs and 'Tas'i-smon-lam.

The *second* comprises the magic-circle of the collection of the Tathāgathas and "the powerful great pitying one" (Avalokita)—bDe-gs'eg*s*-kün 'dus-gar-dbaṅ, T'ugs-rje chen-po, of about 40 pages.

Then follow the magic circles of the fierce and demoniacal deities Guru-drag-dmar, K'rowo-rol waī gtor-zlog and Drag poī las Guruī-gsol-'deb*s* len-bdun-ma, K'a 'don ch'os spyod.

The books for the second examination, requiring to be recited by heart, are the following:—

(1) The worship of "The lake-born *Vajra*" (mTs'o-skye*s*-rdorje)—*i.e.*, St. Padma-sambhava—and "the sage Guru who has obtained understanding" (Rig 'dsin rtog sgrub-guru).
(2) The three roots of sagedom (Rig 'dsin rtsa-gsum)—
   (*a*) Rig 'dsin lhamaī-las.
   (*b*) Ts'e-sgrub k'og dbug*s*.
   (*c*) gSang sgrub doṅyi sñiṅ-po.
(3) The deeds of Dorje P'āgmo (rDorje p'ag-moī-las), the great happiness of zag-med (zag-med *b*de-ch'en), and the four classes of the fierce guardians—c'os sruṅ drag-po sde *b*zhi. The names of these demons are—on the east, kLu-bdud Munpa nagpo; on the south, Srinpo Lanka-mgrim-bchu; on the west, Mamo S'a-za p'ra-gral nag-po; on the north, gS'enpa sPu-gri-dmarpo.
(4) The subjugation of the host of demons—The offering to the Dhyāni Buddhas bdud dpuṅ zil non, Kun-bzaṅ, mc'od-sprin.
(5) The sacrificial ceremony bskang bshāgs, viz., Rig 'dsin b*s*kang-bshags, Phagmaī b*s*kang bshags.
(6) The prayer of the glorious "Tāshi"—the Lepcha name for Padma-sambhava —Tāshi *s*mon-lam.

   The above books reach to about fifty-five pages.

(7) The circle of the eight commanders of the collected Buddhas. bKāh-bgyad *b*de gsegs 'duspaī dkyil-'khor kyī las and Khrowo-rol waī gtor-zlog gyi skorī bkah brgyad. This has about forty pages. [The names of the eight commanders, bKah-bgyads, are—(1) C'e-mch'og, (2) Yaṅ-dag, (3) gS'in-rje, (4) rTa-mgrin, (5) Phurpa, (6) Mamo, (7) 'Gad *s*toṅ, (8) Rig-'dsin.]

When the young monk recites by heart all these books satisfactorily, and so passes this examination, he is not subject to any further ordeal of examination: this being the final one.

and these intervals are utilized by the candidates in revising the next exercise, in company with their teacher.

Those who disgracefully fail to pass this examination are taken outside and chastized by the provost.[1] And repeated failure up to a limit of three years necessitates the rejection of the candidate from the order. Should, however, the boy be rich and wish re-entry, he may be re-admitted on paying presents and money on a higher scale than formerly, without which no re-admission is possible. If the rejected candidate be poor and he wishes to continue a religious life, he can only do so as a lay-devotee, doing drudgery about the monastery buildings. Or he may set up in some village as an unorthodox Lāma-priest.

The majority fail to pass at the first attempt. And failure on the part of the candidate attaches a stigma to his teacher, while in the event of the boy chanting the exercises correctly and with pleasing voice in the orthodox oratorical manner, his teacher is highly complimented.

PUBLIC DISPUTATIONS.

The public disputations are much more attractive and favourite exercises for the students than the examinations. Indeed, the academic feature of the monastic universities of Tibet is perhaps seen at its best in the prominence given to dialectics and disputations, thus following the speculative traditions of the earlier Indian Buddhists. In the great monastic universities of De-pung, Tashi-lhunpo, Serra and Gāh-ldan, each with a teeming population of monks, ranging from about 4,000 to 8,000, public disputations are regularly held, and form a recognized institution, in which every divinity student or embryo Lāma must take part. This exercise is called expressing "the true and innermost essence (of the doctrine)" (*mTs'an-ñid*), in which an endeavour is made to ascertain both the literal sense and the spirit of the doctrine,[2] and it is held within a barred court. Some details of the manner in which these disputations are held are given below.[3]

---

1 Ch'os-k'rims-pa.

2 Conf. also JAESCHKE, *Dict.*, p. 454, who is inclined to identify this "school" with the Vaiṣeshkas (or Atomists) KÖPP, i., 691.

3 Within the court-ch'os-ra where the disputations are held are seven grades (*'dsin-ra*), namely: (1), *Kha-dog-dkar-dmar*; (2), *Tchedma*; (3), *P'ar-p'yin*; (4), *mDsŏd*; (5), *'Dulwa*; (6), *dbUma*; (7), *bsLab-btub*.

At these disputations there are tree-trunks, called the Sal-tree trunk (Shugs-sdoṅ),

ORDINATION AND DEGREES.

After a course of such training for twelve years, each student is eligible for full ordination, the minimum age for which is twenty, and the ceremony is generally similar to that of the initiation. Those who prove their high capabilities by passing with exceptional distinction through the disputations and examinations conducted by the assembled Lāmaist *literati* and the heads of one or more cloisters, receive academic and theological degrees

---

lchañ-ma-sdoñpo, and yubu; and bounded by a wall, and inside the court is covered by pebbles (rdehu). In the middle there is a great high stone seat for the lord protector (sKyabs-mgön), and a smaller seat for the abbot (mk'anpo) of the school, and one still smaller for the chief celebrant.

On reaching the enclosure, the auditors take their respective seats in the seven grades, in each of which discussions are held. One of the most learned candidates volunteers for examination, or as it is called, to be vow-keeper (*Dam-bchah*). He takes his seat in the middle, and the others sit round him. Then the students stand up one by one, and dispute with him.

The scholar who stands up wears the yellow hat, and, clapping his hands together says, *Ka-ye!* and then puts his questions to the vow-keeper, who is questioned by every student who so desires; and if he succeeds in answering all without exception, then he is promoted to a higher grade. In any case, one is transferred to another grade after every three years.

After twenty-one years of age the rank of *dGe-'ses* is obtained, though some clever students may get it even at eleven. The abbot of the college comes into the enclosure seven days every month, and supervises the disputations of the seven grades. When a candidate has reached the bslab-btub grade, he is certain soon to become a dGe-s'es.

The great disputation, however, is held four times a year, in spring, in summer, in autumn, and in winter, in a great paved courtyard, and lasts five or seven days. On these occasions, all the scholars and abbots of the four schools of the colleges of De-pung congregate there. And all the learned students of the four schools who belong to the grade of bslab-btub volunteer for examination, and each is questioned by the students who ply their questions, says my Lāma, "just like flies on meat." When the voluntary examinee has successfully replied to all the questions he goes to the abbot of his own school, and, presenting a silver coin and a scarf, he requests permission to be examined on the Lhāsa mass day. If the abbot receives the coin and scarf, then the application is approved, and if not, the student is referred to his studies. In the great Lhāsa mass all the monks of Serra, De-pung, and Gāh-ldan congregate, and examinations are held every seventh day, and the dGe-s'es of the three monasteries of Serra, De-pung, and Gāh-ldan act as examiners. If the volunteer can answer them all, then the Lord Protector throws a scarf round his neck, and he thus receives the title of *dGe-s'es*—somewhat equivalent to our Bachelor of Divinity.

The newly-fledged dGe-s'es is now known as a *sKya-ser-med-pa-dGe-bs'es* or "The yellowless-pale Ge-s'e" (pale + yellow = "laymen and priests," says JAESCHKE, *D.*, p. 25). Then he must give soup (called dGe-bs'es T'ugpa) to all the students of his school and club, each student getting a cupful. The soup is made of rice, mixed with meat and butter, and different kinds of fruits. Then the abbot of the school and the Spyi-so of his club, and all his friends and relatives, each gives him a Khadāg scarf and a money present.

and honours, by which they become eligible for the highest and most privileged appointments.

The chief degrees are *Ge-s'e*, corresponding to our Bachelor of Divinity; and *Rab-jam-pa*, or Doctor of Divinity.

The degree of *Ge-s'e*,[1] or "the learned virtuosi," may be called B.D. It is obtained, in the manner above detailed, by giving proof in open meeting of the Lāmas[2] of his ability to translate and interpret perfectly at least ten of the chief books of his religion. The Ge-s'e is eligible to go in for the higher special departments, to which a non-graduate, even though he may be a ge-long, and as such senior to the young Ge-s'e, is not admitted.[3] Many of them become the head Lāmas or lord protectors (skyabs-mgon) of the government monasteries of the established church, not only in Tibet, but in Mongolia, Amdô, and China. Others return to their own fatherland, while some pursue their studies in the higher Tantras, to qualify for the much coveted post of the Khri-pa of Gāh-ldan.

The degree of *Rab-jam-pa*,[4] "verbally overflowing, endlessly," a *doctor universalis*, corresponds with our Doctor of Theology, or D.D., and is, it seems, the highest academical title of honour which can be earned in the Lāmaist universities, and after a disputation over the whole doctrine of the church and faith. The diploma which he receives entitles him to teach the law publicly, and authorizes him to the highest church offices not specially reserved for the incarnate Lāmas. And he is given a distinctive hat, as seen in the foregoing figure, at the head of this chapter. It is said that in Tibet there are only twelve cloisters who have the right to bestow this degree, and it is even more honourable than the titles bestowed by the Dalai Lāma himself. But this is, as a matter of course, a very expensive affair.

The titles of *Ch'o-je*[5] or "noble of the law," and *Paṇḍita* or

---

[1] dGe-s'es. It seems to be the same as the Tung-ram-pa of Tashi-lhunpo and the Kabs-bchu, KÖPPEN, ii.; it also seems to be "p'al-ch'en-pa."

[2] Apparently a joint board of representatives of the three great monasteries aforesaid, De-pung, etc. Conf. also PANDIT *A. K. on* "*Gisi.*"

[3] The Ge-s'e of the three great Ge-lug-pa monasteries may be admitted to one or other of the four Lings or royal monasteries: Tse-nam-gyal, sTan-gyal-ling, Kun-de-ling, and Gyud-sTod-smad, and he may become a *r*Tse-drung of the Grand Dalai Lāma's royal monastery at Potala.

[4] Rabs-'byams-pa, and seems to be the same as the *Kah-c'an* of Tashi-lhunpo.

[5] Ch'os-rje.

"learned," are bestowed by the sovereign Grand Lāmas on those doctors who have distinguished themselves through blameless holiness and excellent wisdom. And between these two seems to lie the title of *Lô-tsa-wa* or "translator." The relative ranks of Rab-jam-pa and Ch'o-je may be seen from the fact that after the second installation of Buddhism in Mongolia, the former were put by law on the same footing as the Tai-jis or barons or counts; and the latter as Chungtaijis or marquesses or dukes. Did the dignity of the *Paṇḍita* allow a more exalted rank, the consequence would be that only the holy princes from K'an-po upwards, that is to say, the K'an-po, the Chubilghan, and the Chutukten, only could have it; but of this nothing certain is known.

Thus the K'an-po, the Ch'o-je, and the Rab-jam-pa form the three principal classes of the higher non-incarnate clergy, and they follow each other in the order described. The K'an-pos take amongst them the first place, and are, as a rule, elected out of the two other classes. As the K'an-po has been compared with a bishop, so could the C'ho-je perhaps be called "vicar-general" or "coadjutor." And often in the same cloister by the side of, or rather under, the K'an-po, are found a Ch'o-je as vice-abbot (a mitred abbot). In the smaller cloisters the chief Lāma as a rule has only the grade of Ch'o-je or Rab-jam-pa.

Special schools, expressly for the study of magic, are erected in the cloisters of Ramo-ch'e and Mo-ru. Those who receive here the doctor's diploma, and thereby acquire the right to carry on the mystery of science practically, especially conjuring, weather prophecy, sympathetical pharmacy, etc., etc., are called Ṅag-ram-pa, which means "master of conjuration." Their uniform is Sivaite, and they probably spring from the red religion, but their science follows strictly the prescribed formulas in the Kah-gyur, and is therefore quite orthodox.[1] Their practices as augurs are detailed under the head of sorcery, along with those of the ordinary illiterate Ṅag-pa fortune-teller.

OFFICIALS AND DISCIPLINE.

The huge cloisters, with several hundreds and occasionally several thousands of monks, necessarily possess an organized body

[1] KÖPPEN, ii., 290.

of officials for the administration of affairs clerical and temporal, and for the enforcement of discipline.

At the head of a monastery stands either a re-generated or re-incarnate Lāma (*Ku-s'o*, *T'ul-ku*, or in Mongolian "*Khubilighan*") or an installed abbot (*K'an-po*, Skt., *Upadhdhaya*), the latter being as a rule elected from the capital, and sanctioned by the Dalai Lāma or the provincial head of the re-incarnate Lāmas; and he holds office only for seven years.

He has under him the following administrative and executive officers, all of whom except the first are usually not ordained, and they are elected by and from among the brotherhood for a longer or shorter term of office:—

1. The professor or master (Lob-pon [1]), who proclaims the law and conducts the lessons of the brethren.
2. The treasurer and cashier (C'ag-dso [2]).
3. The steward (Ñer-pa [3] or Spyi-ñer).
4. Provost marshal (Ge-Ko [4]), usually two who maintain order like police, hence also called vergers or censors, and they are assisted by two orderlies (hag-ñer).
5. The chief celebrant or leader of the choir or precentor (Um-dse).
6. Sacristan (Ku-ñer).
7. Water-giver (Ch'ab-dren).
8. Tea waiters (Ja-ma).

To these are to be added the secretaries,[5] cooks,[6] chamberlain,[7] warden or entertainer of guests,[8] accountant,[9] bearer of benedictory emblem,[10] tax-collectors, medical monks, painters, merchant monks, exorcist, etc.

The general rules of conduct and discipline are best illustrated at the great monastic universities.

The De-pung monastery, with its 7,700 monks, is divided into four great colleges (grwa-ts'an), namely: (1) bLo-gsal-gliṅ; (2) sGo-man; (3) bDe-yaṅs; and (4) sÑags-pa, and each of these schools of the

---

[1] *s*Lob-dpon. [2] p'yag mdsod*s*. [3] gñer-pa.

[4] dge-bsko*s*, also called Ch'o-k'rims-pa or "religious judge," and the provost of the cathedral seems to be called Zhal-ṅo.

[5] spyi-k'yab. [6] gsol-dpon. [7] gźim-dpon.

[8] mgron-gñer ch'en. [9] Tsi-dpon. [10] p'yag-ts'ang or sku-b'c'ar-mkhan-po.

monastery has its own abbot. The monks are accommodated according to their different nationalities and provinces, each having separate resident and messing sections, named K'ams ts'an or provincial messing clubs. The cathedral or great hall of the congregation, named T'sogs-ch'en lha-k'aṅ, is common to the whole monastery.

Sera monastery, with its 5,500 monks, divided into three collegiate schools named: (1) Bye-wa, (2) sÑags-pa, and (3) sMad-pa, and each has its sectional club.

Gāh-ldan with its 3,300 monks is divided into two schools, namely, (1) Byaṅ-rtse, and (2) S'ar-tse, each with its club.

Tashi-lhunpo has three collegiate schools.[1]

Each club has at least two Lāma-officers, the elder of whom takes charge of the temple attached to the club, and teaches his pupils the mode of making offerings in the temple. The younger officer is a steward in charge of the storehouse (gÑer-ts'ang), and the tea presented by the public (Maṅ-ja), or "tea-general," and the kitchen (Ruṅ-k'aṅ). These two Lāmas are responsible for the conduct of the monks of their section, and in case their pupils do wrong, they—the masters—are fined. These two officers are changed every year.

Entry of Pupil.—The applicant for admission goes to the great paved court (the rdo-chal) of the monastic club, the masters are called and ask him whence he has come, and whether he has any relatives or

---

[1] The grand monastery of Tashi-lhunpo is divided, says SARAT (*Jour. Bud. Text Socy. Ind.*, iv., 1893, p. 14), into forty *Kham-tshan* or wards, which are placed under the jurisdiction of the three great *Ta-tshang* or theological colleges, viz.:—(*a*) Thoisamling college exercises control over the following *Kham-tshan*:—

1. Gya *Kham-tshan*.
2. Tíso " "
3. Hamdong *Kham-tshan*.
4. Chawa " "
5. Tanag " "
6. Tang-moc'he *Kham-tshan*.
7. Tinke " "
8. Chûnee " "
9. Lhûm-bu-tse " "
10. Ser-ling *Kham-tshan*.
11. Je-pa, also called *Sha-pa Ta-shang*.
12. Chang-pa *Kham-tshan*.
13. Leg-thúg " "
14. Norpugandan, the first house built when the monastery was established.
15. *S*repa (Hrepa) *Kham-tshan*.
16. Pa-so *Kham-tshan*.
17. Dong-tse *Kham-tshan*

(*b*) The following belong to Shar-tse *Ta-tshang*:—

1. Thon-pa *Kham-tshan*.
2. Gyal-tse-tse *Kham-tshan*
3. Shiné " "
4. Lhopa " "
5. Latoi (Ladak) " "
6. Chang-pa " "
7. Potog-pa *Kham-tshan*.
8. Néñiṅ " "
9. Tom-khaling
10. Déyang-pa.
11. Samlo *Kham-tshan*.
12. Néñiṅnag-po Shara.

(*c*) The following are under Kyi*l*-khang:—

1. Khogyé *Kham-tshan*.
2. Taṅgmo " "
3. Rog-tsho " "
4. Lakha " "
5. Dodan " "
6. Piling *Kham-tshan*.
7. Kha*l*ka " "
8. Darpa " "
9. Lhundub-tse *Kham-tshan*.
10. Tsa-oo *Kham-tshan*, also called Tsa-oo para.

acquaintances in the monastery. If any such there be he is called, and takes the applicant to his own private chamber. But if the applicant has no friend or relative there, tea and wheaten flour are given to him, and he is kept in the Ruṅ-khaṅ for three days. After which period, should no one have come to claim him or search for him, one or other of the two masters of the section take him under their charge, the head master having the preference, and the proper application for his admission is then duly made.

For the general assembly hall or cathedral there is a special staff of officials. The great celebrant (*Tsogs-ch'en dbu-mdsad*) who leads the chant; the two *Z'al-ṅo* are the provosts; the two Naṅ-ma are subordinate orderlies who look after the conduct of the students; the two *Ch'ab-rils* go round the benches giving water to the monks to rinse out their mouths after reciting the mantras (as in Hindū rites of ceremonial purity), and at other times they help the orderlies to look after the pupils. The Lāma dMig-rtse-ma[1] fixes the time for congregation and the "tea-general" of the same. The two orderlies must watch whether the pupils throw away tea or flour, and they also take general care of the temples.

Early in the morning, about four o'clock, a junior pupil chants chhös-*s*had from the top of the temple of the cathedral. Then each of the clubs beat their stone bells (*r*do-*r*ting) to awake the occupants, who arise and wash and dress. They put on the cope (zla-gam), and carry the yellow hat over their shoulders, and take a cup and a bag for wheaten flour. Some bow down in the court, others circumambulate the temple, and others the temple of Mañjusrī, which is behind the cathedral, repeating his *mantra* (*Omah-ra-pa-tcä-na-ḍhi*).

About one o'clock the *Mig-rtse-ma* Lāma chants the "dmig-rtse-ma" in a loud voice, and at once the pupils assemble near the two doors, and having put on their yellow hats, join in the chant. Then after an interval the *ch'abril* opens the door, and all enter in proper order and take their seats according to their rank in their club.[2] The yellow

---

1 Or "The highest idea or imagining" (Skt., *Avalambana*).

2 At Tashi-lhunpo, says SARAT (*Jour. Budd. Text Socy. Ind.*, iv.), the monks sit in nine rows one facing another.

Thoisamling ...	1st row is called Lobûg or Lob-zang bûg *tal*.	
	2nd Champa *tal*	(the row opposite the gigantic image of Maitreya).
	3. Goikû *tal*	(the row opposite the satin tapestry).
	4. Shûthi *tal*	(the row opposite the huge lamp of the hall).
Is common to all	5. Dong *tal*	(the front row opposite the sacerdotal throne of the Grand Lāma).
Kyil-khang ...	6. Ne-chû *tal*	(the row opposite the painted images of the sixteen Sthaviras (sages) on the wall).
	7. Ne-ñing *tal*	(the row opposite the old images of the sixteen Sthaviras).
Shar-tse ...	8. Do*l*-ma *tal*	(the row opposite the image of the goddess Do*l*ma, Tārā).
	9. Go-gyab *tal*	(the row opposite the door of the hall).

Oppósite Dong *tal* is the chapel or *Tsang-khang* containing the image of Buddha,

hat is thrown over the left shoulder, and the cup and the bag are placed under the knees, and all sit facing to their front.

After the repetition of the refuge formula, headed by the chief celebrant, the younger provost arises and dons his yellow hat, "*sGro-rtsem-ma*," and with an iron rod strikes a pillar with it once, on which all the students will go into the refectory, where tea is distributed to each in series, each getting three cupfuls. On drinking it they return and resume their respective seats, and continue the celebration.

When drinking the tea presented by the populace (*mang-ja*) all the pupils sit silent, and the two c'ab-rils spread a carpet and make a seat in the middle for the elder provost, who then steps forward and sits down, and, after having thrice bowed down, then he repeats the *skyabs-'jug*, in which the name of the *Dispenser of the gifts*, who has offered the tea, is called out, and blessings prayed for to extend the doctrines of Buddha, to secure long life to the two Grand Lāmas, and absence of strife amongst the members of the monkhood, and that the rains may descend in due season, and the crops and cattle prosper, and disease, human and of animals, decrease, and that life be long with good luck.

After this service in the cathedral, a lecture is given called Ts'ogs-gtam, in which the rules of etiquette for pupils are laid down, and the manner of walking and conduct at meetings explained, after which should there be any pupil who has infringed the rules of discipline, he is dealt with in an exemplary way, as will be described presently.

The Refectory, or rather tea-kitchen, attached to the cathedrals and temples, has five regular officials: Two tea-masters (Ja-dpon), who look after the distribution of the government tea, and the other after the tea ordered by the provost of the cathedral; also two menial Ja-ma, and the superintendent T'ab-gyog-gi dpon-po, who has twenty-five subordinates on fatigue duty.

The service of general-tea (Maṅ-ja) is given three times daily from the stock supplied by the Chinese emperor as a subsidy amounting to about half-a-million bricks. On the 15th, 25th, and the last day of the month, general-tea is given three times and soup once by the governor of Gāh-ldan palace. There are many dispensers of gifts who offer tea and a donation ('gyed) amounting to three, fifteen, seventeen silver srangs pieces; and it is the custom that if one *Tam-ga* (about $\frac{6}{16}$ of a rupee) be offered to the cathedral, then two Tam-gas must be offered to the college-school, and four to the club. Offerings may be made

---

which has accommodation for eighty monks. It is in charge of the Kyil-khang *Ta-tshang*.

The chapel of Maitreya (Chamkhang) which is three storeys high, and is spacious enough to contain eighty monks. It is under the charge of Thoisamling College.

Opposite to Dolma *tal* is Dolma Lhakhang (the chapel of the goddess Tārā). It can hold forty monks, and is in the charge of Shar-tse *Ta-tshang*.

Opposite Lobûg is the chapel of Paldan Lhamo. It is said that the image of Paldan Lhamo contained in it stands in space, *i.e.*, without any support on any side.

solely to the school without the cathedral, and may be made to the club independently of either. In any case, when offerings are made to the cathedral, then something must be offered both to the school and to the club. This custom has existed at De-pung at least from the time of the great Dalai Lāma Ṅag-waṅ.

The size of the tea-boilers of the larger monastery and at the Lhāsa temple is said to be enormous, as can be well imagined when it is remembered that several thousands have to be catered for. The cauldron at the great Lhāsa cathedral is said to hold about 1,200 gallons.

A very vigorous discipline is enforced. It is incumbent on every member of the monastery to report misdemeanours which come under his notice, and these are punished according to the Pratimoksha rules. Minor offences are met at first by simple remonstrance, but if persisted in are severely punished with sentences up to actual banishment.

If anyone infringes the rules of discipline short of murder, or oath, or wine-drinking, or theft, within the club, the two club-masters punish him; but if within the college or debating-hall, then he is amenable to the provost of the college.

A member of De-pung who commits any of the ten kinds of "indulgence" cannot be tried except in the cathedral. The elder provost calls on the breaker of the rules to stand up in the presence of the assembled students, and the transgressor rises with bent head and is censured by the younger provost and sentenced to a particular number of strokes. Then the two water-men bring in the dGe-rgan of the club and the tutor of the offending student. The dGe-rgan rises up to receive his censure, and so also the tutors. Then the offending pupil is seized by the head and feet, and soundly beaten by the lictors (T'ab-gyog).

The punishment by cane or rod is fifty strokes for a small offence, one hundred for a middling, and one hundred and fifty for a grave offence. In the cathedral no more than one hundred and fifty strokes can be given, and no further punishment follows.

For breach of etiquette in sitting, walking, eating, or drinking, the penalty is to bow down and apologize, or suffer ten strokes.

The most severe punishment, called "Good or Bad Luck" (sKyid-sdug), so called it is said from its chance of proving fatal according to the luck of the sufferer, is inflicted in cases of murder and in expulsion from the order for persistent intemperance, or theft. After the congregation is over the teacher and club-master of the accused are called to the court, and the provost of the cathedral censures them. Then the accused is taken outside the temple and his feet are fastened by ropes, and two men, standing on his right and left, beat him to the number of about a thousand times, after which he is drawn, by a rope, outside the boundary wall (*l*chags-ri) and there abandoned; while his teacher and club-master are each fined one scarf and three silver *Srangs*.

The rule which is most broken is celibacy. The established church alone adheres strictly to this rule; so that, on this account, many of its monks leave the order, as they are always free to do, though suffering social disgrace, as they are called *ban-lok*, or "turncoats." In the other sects many celibate monks are also found, especially in the larger monasteries of Tibet; but the great majority of the members of the unreformed sects, for instance, the Ñiṅ-ma-pa, also the Sa-kya-pa, Duk-pa, etc., are married openly or clandestinely.

The Lāmas also extend their exercise of discipline outside the walls of the monastery. Mr. Rockhill witnessed at Kumbum the following fracas: "Suddenly the crowd scattered to right and left, the Lāmas running for places of hiding, with cries of *Gékor Lāma, Gékor Lāma!* and we saw, striding towards us, six or eight Lāmas, with a black stripe painted across their foreheads, and another around their right arms—black Lāmas (hei-ho-sang) the people call them—armed with heavy whips, with which they belaboured anyone who came within their reach. Behind them walked a stately Lāma in robes of finest cloth, with head clean-shaved. He was a Gékor, a Lāma-censor, or provost, whose duty it is to see that the rules of the Lāmasery are strictly obeyed, and who, in conjunction with two colleagues, appointed like him by the abbot for a term of three years, tries all Lāmas for whatever breach of the rules or crime they may have committed. This one had heard of the peep-shows, Punch and Judy shows, gambling tables, and other prohibited amusements on the fair-grounds, and was on his way with his lictors to put an end to the scandal. I followed in his wake, and saw the peep-show knocked down, Punch and Judy laid mangled beside it, the owners whipped and put to flight, and the majesty of ecclesiastical law and morality duly vindicated."[1]

As the Lāma is comfortably clothed and housed, and fed on the best of food, he cannot be called a mendicant monk like the Buddhist monks of old, nor is the vow of poverty strictly interpreted; yet this character is not quite absent. For the order, as a body, is entirely dependent on the lay population for its support; and the enormous proportion which the Lāmas bear to the laity ren-

[1] Rockhill, *L.*, 65.

ders the tax for the support of the clergy a heavy burden on the people.

Most of the monasteries, even those of the sects other than the dominant Ge-lug-pa, are richly endowed with landed property and villages, from which they derive much revenue. All, however, rely mainly on the voluntary contributions of the worshippers amongst villagers and pilgrims. And to secure ample aid, large numbers of Lāmas are deputed at the harvest-time to beg and collect grain and other donations for their monasteries. Most of the contributions, even for sacerdotal services, are in kind,—grain, bricks of tea, butter, salt, meat, and live stock,—for money is not much used in Tibet. Other sources of revenue are the charms, pictures, images, which the Lāmas manufacture, and which are in great demand; as well as the numerous horoscopes, supplied by the Lāmas for births, marriages, sickness, death, accident, etc., and in which most extensive devil-worship is prescribed, entailing the employment of many Lāmas. Of the less intellectually gifted Lāmas, some are employed in menial duties, and others are engaged in mercantile traffic for the general benefit of their mother monastery. Most of the monasteries of the established church grow rich by trading and usury. Indeed, Lāmas are the chief traders and capitalists of the country.

DRESS.

The original dress of Buddha's order was adapted for the warm Indian climate. Later, when his religion extended to colder climes, he himself is said to have permitted warmer clothing, stockings, shoes, etc. The avowed object of the monk's dress was to cover the body decently and protect from cold, mosquitoes,[1] and other sources of mental disturbance.

The dress of a Tibetan monk[2] consists of a hat covering his closely-shaven crown, a gown and girdle, inner vest, cloak, plaid, trousers, and boots, rosary, and other minor equipments.

LĀMAIST HATS AND COWLS.

No hat is mentioned in the Buddhist scriptures as part of the outfit of a monk, nor does it seem to have been introduced into

[1] HARDY, *East. Mon.*, 122.

[2] See figures on pages 45, 60, 172, etc.

Indian Buddhism even in the later period, judging from its apparent absence in the Ajaṇṭa cave paintings. It is, however, a necessity for tonsured heads in a cold climate,[1] and it is usually made in Tibet of thick felt, flannel, or blanket.

The conspicuousness of the cap lent itself readily to its hat being converted into a sectarial badge. We have seen how the *colour* of the cap afforded a rough distinction into yellow, red, and black hats. But the *shape* is also an important element in differentiating hats, both for sectarian and ceremonial purposes.

The majority of the hats are of an Indian type, a few only being Chinese or Mongolian.

The two most typical hats are believed by the Lāmas to have been brought from India by St. Padma-sambhava, the founder of Lāmaism, and his coadjutor, Ṣanta-rakshita, in the eighth century. And both of these hats are essentially Indian in pattern.

To begin with, the hat, numbered *j* in the figure, named "The red hat, of the great Pandits" (pan-ch'en-z'wa-dmar). It is alleged to have been brought from India on the foundation of Lāmaism by the abbot Ṣanta-rakshita, and it is common to all sects in Tibet except the Ge-lug-pa. Its shape is essentially that of the ordinary cap used in the colder parts of India during the winter (see fig. *n*), with lappets coming over the ears and the nape of the neck, which lappets are folded up as an outer brim to the cap in the hotter part of the day. Such a cap is often worn by Indian ascetics when travelling in India in the winter time; and it is quite probable that Atīṣa, as the Lāmas allege, did arrive in Tibet in such a hat, and possibly of a red colour. The chief difference in the Lāmaist form is that the crown has been raised into a peak, which gives it a more distinguished look, and the lappets have been lengthened.

Tsoṅ-K'apa altered the colour of this hat from red to yellow, and hence arose the title of "Yellow-hat" (S'a-ser), a synonym for his new sect, "the Ge-lug-pa," in contradistinction to the "Red-hat" (S'a-mar) of the Unreformed Lāmas. He raised its peak still higher (*see* figures *b* and *c* in annexed illustration),

[1] In India the only need for a head-covering is as an occasional protection against the sun, but the Indian monk defends his shaven crown from the scorching sun by his palm-leaf fan.

and lengthened its lappets in proportion to the rank of the wearer. Thus he gave himself the longest lappets, forming tails

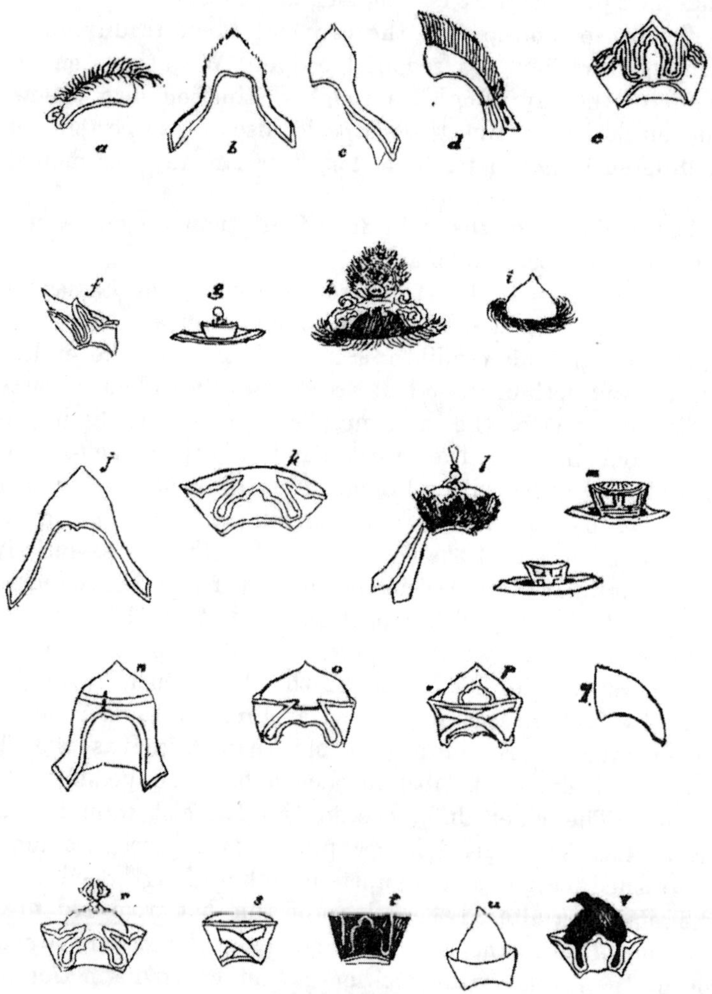

LĀMAS' HATS.

a. rTse-z'va sgro
b. Pan-ch'en sne-riṅ.
c. Ditto, in profile.
d. rTse-z'va sgro-rtse.
e. dGon-'dus dbu.
f. Ditto, in profile.
g. T'aṅ-z'va, for abbots and re-incarnations.
h. sÑags z'va-nag.
i. rTa z'va, for nTse-drung.
j. Pan-ch'en z'va-dmar.
k. Dag z'va-ri-'gra.
l. dGun-z'va.
m. Z'va-dkar skyed k'ra.
n. Jo-z'va gliṅ gsum.
o. Jo-z'va rgyun.
p. Saks-z'u of Sakya.
q. Gra-z'a of Tāranātha (red).
r. Sakya k'ri z'va.
s. sGom-z'va dbUus 'gyud.
t. mKah-'grohi dbu-skra.
u. Kar-ma sṅags z'va.
v. sKar-ma zs-z'va.

down to the waist. The abbots were given shorter tails, and the ordinary monk shorter still, while the novices were deprived altogether of the tails. It can be used when walking and riding.

Padma-sambhava's mitre-like hat is the "U-gyan-Pandit," the typical hat of the unreformed Ñiṅ-ma sect. It is on the same Indian model, with the lappets turned up, and divided so as to suggest the idea of a red lotus, with reference to the etymology of St. Padma-sambhava's name, to wit, "The Lotus-born," and his legendary birth from a red lotus-flower. His native country was Udyāna, between Afghanistan and Kashmīr; and the tall conical crown is still a feature of the caps of those regions. It is also called the Sahor (Lahore ?) Pandit's cap. It is worn by the Ñiṅ-ma sect in empowering (abisheka), and in offering oblations, and in sacred dances. The largest form of this hat, surmounted by a golden *vajra*, is called the "Devil subduer" (dreg-pa zil-non gyi cha lugs), and is figured in the foregoing picture of St. Padma. It is only worn by the head Lāmas when giving the king holy water, and at the highest festivals.

Many of the hats are full of symbolism, as, for example, Figs. *a* and *d*, as described in the footnote.[1]

---

[1] rTse-źwa sgro-lug*s* (Fig. *a*). This helmet-like hat is common to all Ge-lug-pa Lāmas. It was invented by *g*Z'i-bdag ne-ser, and adopted by the first Grand Lāma GedenDub. It is used along with the cope (zla-gam) when going to mass, and is taken off on entering the temple and thrown over the left shoulder, with the tails hanging down in front; on emerging from the temple it is worn or not according to the monk's own wishes. Its long tails are stitched to imitate the beaded covers of a book, so that when the monk grasps the tails, he is to conceive that he has a grasp of the scriptures; and again that he is drawing to salvation thousands of animals represented by the pile on the cap. The three lateral stitches in the tails typify the three classes of scriptures—the *Tripitaka*, as well as the three original sins or "fires" and the sin of body, speech and mind, for which the Tripitaka are the antidotes. The *long* tails also have to suggest to him that the doctrines may be extended and long remain. The marginal stitches represent "the twelve best commands." The inside is often white to suggest that the monk should keep his heart clean and pure. The crest represents the doctrinal insight (*l*ta-wa, Skt., *darṣana*) of the wearer. As he rises by taking a degree in divinity his crest is elevated by an extra stitch.

rTse-źwa sked-bts'em differs from the foregoing in having an extra stitch in its crest (see p. 172). It is confined to the re-embodied m*t*s'an-ñid Lāmas and those who have taken the degree of d*g*e-s'e, or *B.D.*

Nuns wear a skull-cap of woollen cloth or fur, coloured yellow or red, according to their sect.

---

rTse-źwa sgro rts'e has the highest crest. It is confined to the dGe-*bs*kul of De-pung monastic university and the degree of *D.D.*

rTse-źwa sgro-rtse-ma (Fig. *d*) is confined to the Dalai Lāma's chapel-royal of *r*Tse-*r*Nam-gyal, and to the four Lings. It is worn during the *g*tor-*r*gyab sacrifices and dances at these temples only.

dGongs 'du*s* źwa zur-źur (Figs. *e* and *f*). Designed by Pan-ch'en *b*Lo-*b*zaṅ ch'o*s*-kyi *r*gyal *m*ts'an after the shape of *d*Ben-*d*gon hill. It is worn by the Grand Pan-ch'en Lāma and the four abbots of Tashi-lhunpo on going to preside at the wrangling disputations.

Pän-źwa sne-rid' ser-po (Figs. *b* and *c*). This is a yellow variety of the red one of the same name, with the tails much lengthened by Tsoṅ K'apa. It is only worn with these long tails by the Dalai Lāma, the Pan-ch'en (Tashi) Lāma, the Gah-ldan Khri-rinpo-ch'e, and the Tibetan Lāma-king or regent, during the assembly (ñal-k'u) mass and empowering. It is worn with the go*s*-ber robes.

sNe-rin zur źwa is worn by the abbots of the colleges and the head Lāmas of smaller monasteries.

T'aṅ-źwa *db*yar-źwa (Fig. *g*) is the summer hat when riding on horseback, and is confined to the Dalai and Pan-ch'en Grand Lāmas, the regent, or king, and the re-embodied Lāmas, and those abbots who, having obtained highest honours in divinity, have received from the Grand Lāma the diploma of bdag-rkyen.

rTa-źwa zur ltas dgun-źwa. This is the winter riding hat, and is confined to the above privileged persons.

Se-teb-rgyun źwa (Fig. *o*). The summer riding hat for the Tse-drung grade of Lāmas, who are selected on account of their learning and good looks as personal attendants of the Grand Lāma (sKyab*s*-mgon ch'en).

rTa zwa rgyun-źwa (Fig. *i*). The winter riding hat of the Tse-drung.

rTse-drung sga-p'ug is used only by the skyabs-*m*you ch'en-mo in ascending and descending (? Potala hill).

Zwa-dkar skyid-ka (Fig. *m*). Worn by the Tse-drung attendants in summer when accompanying the Grand Lāma wearing preceding hat.

Jo-źwa-gliṅ-gsum (Fig. *n*), "the lord's hat of the three continents." It is formed after the fashion of the Asura cave, and was worn by the Indian *Jo-wo* (Atīsa), the reformer of Lāmaism, while on his way to Tibet, at the Nepalese shrine Svayambhunāth (T., Rang-'byuṅ) Chaitya; afterwards it was the hat of his sect, the Kah-dam-pa. In hot weather its flaps are folded up, and in the cold let down. It was originally red, but changed to yellow by the Ge-lug-pa. Now it is worn only by the hermits (ri-k'rod-pa) of the Ge-lug-pa or established church, and is never worn within the monastery or in quarters.

Sa-skya K'ri-źwa (Fig. *r*). This hat of the Sa-kya sect is of later introduction. Originally all the Sa-kya Lāmas wore the Urgyen-pen-źwa of the unreformed party. When they attained the temporal lordship over

In the outer rainy districts of the Himalayas, in Bhotān and Sikhim, many Lāmas wear straw hats during the summer, or go bare-headed.

---

the thirteen provinces of Tibet, the Chinese king "Se-ch'en" presented this hat to the chief of the sect, his highness 'Phag-pa Rin-po-ch'e, and its central *vajra* upon the "unchangeable" crown is after the Chinese style. It is restricted to those of noble descent (*g*dung-pa), and is only worn when the *g*duṅ-*br*gyud Lāma ascends the throne, or in empowering devotees, or in the *g*Tor *r*gyab sacrificial offering. Cf. also p. 57.

Sa-źu mt'oṅ grol (Fig. *p*). This is a hat of the Sa-kya-pa. It is believed to confer spiritual insight, and to have been invented by the God of Wisdom (Mañjuṣṛi). It is used when empowering the Khri-pa, and for mass.

Sa-skya grwa-źwa (Fig. *q*.) This is the hat of the Jonaṅ-pa sub-sect, to which Tāranātha belonged. It is worn by the junior Sa-kya monks during certain masses, at the beginning and the end, also in religious dances and in the Tor-gya sacrifice.

Karma-paī źwa nag (Fig. *t*). "The black (fairy) hat of the Kar-ma-pa." This hat was conferred upon the reverend Rang-'byuṅ *r*Dorje (Vajra Svayambhu) by the five classes of witches (Ḍākkinī) when he coerced them into granting him the *Siddhi*—power of flying in the air. Each of the Ḍākkinīs contributed a hair from their tresses, and plaited these to form this hat. Whoever wears it can fly through the air. It is kept as a relic at Sa-kya monastery, and only worn in state, or when a wealthy votary comes to the shrine. On such occasions a monk on either side holds the hat to prevent it from carrying off the wearer.

Karma sṅags-źwa (Fig. *u*). "The enchanter's hat" of the K-arma-pa sect. It is shaped after the cake-offering for the angry demons, and is worn during the dances and the *g*tor-*r*gyab sacrifice.

Dwag-źwa ri-'gra (Fig. *k*). A hat of the Kar-gyu-pa sect, worn when empowering or preaching. It is shaped after the hill of Dwag-lha sgam-pa, and was invented by mÑam-med-diwag-po lha *r*jes-ts'eriṅ-ma.

sÑag*s* paī źwa nag (Fig. *h*). The black necromancer's hat. Worn by the sLob-*d*pan Lāma of the unreformed sect in their *g*Tor-rgyab sacrifice, and in the mystic play in all the sects.

gZah-źwa (Fig. *v*). "The planet hat." This raven-crowned hat was designed by Lāma Gyun-ston-k'ro-rgyal on seeing the planet Mercury. It is worn by the Di-kung-pa, Kar-ma-pa, and Niṅ-ma-pa sects during the ceremony of "circling the planets" (*gzaī-bskor*) and the striking and injuring one's enemy (m*t'u*).

The hat of the Grand Lāma of Bhotan (head of the southern Dug-pa church), and figured at page 226, is called *pad-ma-mt'ong* or "the lotus-vision." It has a *vajra*-spikelet which cannot be worn by any but the supreme Lāma. And the hat is finely embroidered with the cross-thunderbolts, lotus-flower, and thunder dragons (*Dug*).

The Tibetans follow the Chinese in the practice of saluting by taking off their hat, so in their temples no hats are worn except during certain ceremonies, and then only a special kind.

THE ROBES.

The robes, which the monks of the established church and the more celibate monks of the other sects wear during certain celebrations, are the three vestments of the shape prescribed in the primitive code of ritual, the *Vinaya*, with the addition of a brocaded collared under-vest[1] and trousers, as seen in the figures. The material of these robes is usually woollen cloth; but silk, though against the precepts,[2] is sometimes worn by those who can afford the expense.

The colour of these robes is yellow or red, according to the sect. Yellow or saffron[3] colour in Tibet is sacred to the clergy of the established church, the Ge-lug-pa; and its use by others is penal. The only instance in which it is permitted is when a layman is bringing a present to the Ge-lug-pa priests. He then is permitted to wear during his visit a flat yellow hat like a Tam-o'-Shanter bonnet.

These three orthodox Buddhist raiments are:—

1. The Lower patched robe, named "*?z'ān*"[4] (= *Sanghāṭi*). The cloth is in several lârgish patches (about twenty-three) and sewn into seven divisions, and fastened by a girdle at the waist.[5]

---

[1] stod 'jag.

[2] In common with most ascetics, Buddha decreed the monastic dress of his order to be of as mean a material and cost as possible, and the colour selected was sad saffron, which, while affording a useful wearable colour not readily soiled, gave uniformity to the wearer and afforded no scope for worldly vanity in fine dress. Yet nothing can be more dignified and becoming than the thin loose robe of the Buddhist monk, falling in graceful drapery, endlessly altering its elegant folds with every movement of the figure. And the ease with which it lends itself to artistic arrangement is seen not only in the Grecian and Indian sculptures of Buddha in a standing posture, but is even retained somewhat in the thicker and relatively unelegant robes of the Lāmaist monk, seen in the several figures.

[3] Literally ṅur-smrig or "Brāhmani goose" (coloured). This sad-coloured bird, the ruddy shell-drake, has from its solitary habits and conjugal fidelity been long in India symbolic of recluseship and devotion, and figures in such capacity on the capitals of the Aṣoka pillars.

[4] gz'an or ? dras-drubs.

[5] The patched robe, which gives the idea of the tattered garments of poverty, is stated to have originated with Ananda dividing into thirty pieces the rich robe given to Buddha by the wealthy physician Jīvaka, and that robe was sewn by Ananda into five divisions like this one.

2. The Outer patched robe, named *Nam-jar* (*P.*, ? *Antarvāsaka*). The cloth is cut into very numerous pieces, about one hundred and twenty-five, which are sewn together in twenty-five divisions.

3. The Upper shawl, named *bLd-gös* (*Uttarāsanghāṭi*). Long and narrow, ten to twenty feet long and two to three feet broad. It is thrown over the left shoulder and passed under right arm, leaving the right shoulder bare, as in the Indian style, but the shoulders and chest are covered by an inner vest. It is adjusted all round the body, covering both shoulders, on entering the houses of laymen. And over all is thrown a plaited cloak or cope, crescentic in shape.[1]

But the ordinary lower robe of Lāmas of all sects is an ample plaited petticoat, named "S'am t'abs,"[2] of a deep garnet-red colour, which encircles the figure from the waist to the ankles, and is fastened at the waist by a girdle, and with this is worn an unsleeved vest, open in front like a deacon's dalmatia. On less ceremonial occasions a sleeved waistcoat is used; and when travelling or visiting, is worn the ordinary Tibetan wide-sleeved red gown, gathered at the waist by a girdle; and always trousers. The sleeves of this mantle are broad and long, and in hot weather, or on other occasions where greater freedom is wanted or the priest has to administer with bare arms, the arms are withdrawn from the sleeves, which latter then hang loose.

WATER-BOTTLE WALLET.

A sash is also usually worn, several yards long and about three inches broad, thrown over the left shoulder, across breast, and tied in a bow over the right hip, and the remainder swung round the body.[3]

Thus it will be seen that Lāmas of every sect, the established church included, ordinarily wear *red* robes, and it is the colour of the girdles (sKe-rag) and the shape and colour of the hats which are the chief distinctive badges of the

[1] zla-gam. [2] or mt'an-gos. [3] KÖPPEN, ii., 268.

sect. The holy-water bottle (Ch'ab-lug), figured on page 201, which hangs from the left side of the girdle, is also fringed by a flap of cloth coloured red or yellow according to the sect.

The boots are of stiff red and particoloured felt, with soles of hide or Yak-hair.

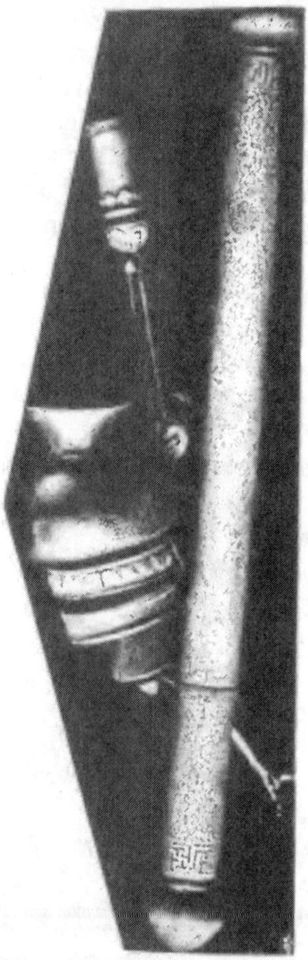

Pen-case, Ink-bottle and Seal. (The pen-case is silver-inlaid iron from Der-ge.)

From the girdle hangs, in addition to the holy-water bottle, a pen-case, purse, with condiments, dice, etc., sometimes the rosary, when it is not in use or worn on the neck or wrist, and the amulet box. And in the upper flap of the coat, forming a breast pocket, are thrust his prayer-wheel, drinking-cup, booklets, charms, etc.

The dress of the nuns generally resembles that of the monks. The head is shaved, and no ornaments are worn.[1]

THE ROSARIES.

The rosary is an essential part of a Lāma's dress; and taking, as it does, such a prominent part in the Lāmaist ritual, it is remarkable that the Tibetan rosary does not appear to have attracted particular notice.

As a Buddhist article the rosary appears only in the latest ritualistic stage when a belief had arisen in the potency of muttering mystic spells and other strange formulas. In the very complicated rosaries of Japan[2] it has attained its highest development.

Amongst southern Buddhists[3] the rosary is not very conspicu-

[1] Cf. Boyle, *Mark.*, p. 109.

[2] "Note on Buddhist Rosaries in Japan." By J. M. James, *Trans. Jap. As. Soc.*, p. 173, 1881.

[3] I have described Burmese Buddhist rosaries, as well as some of the Lāmaist, in *J.A.S.B.*, 1891.

ous, but amongst Tibetans it is everywhere visible. It is also held in the hand of the image of the patron god of Tibet—Chä-rä-si (Skt., *Avalokiteṣvara*). And its use is not confined to the Lāmas. Nearly every lay man and woman is possessed of a rosary, on which at every opportunity they zealously store up merit; and they also use it for secular purposes,[1] like the sliding balls of the Chinese to assist in ordinary calculations: the beads to the right of the centre-bead being called *ta-thaṅ* and registering units, while those to the left are called *c'u-dô* and record tens, which numbers suffice for their ordinary wants.

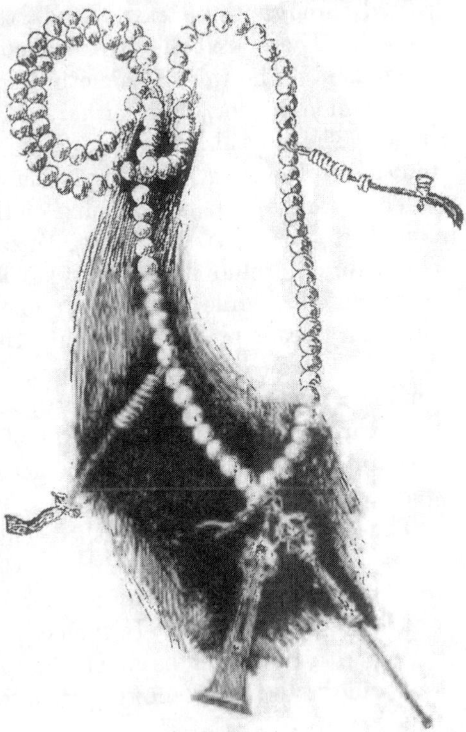

A ROSARY.

The Tibetan name for the rosary is "*'pren-ba*," pronounced *t'eṅ-wa*, or vulgarly *t'eṅ-ṅa*, and literally means "a string of beads."

The rosary contains 108 beads of uniform size. The reason for this special number is alleged to be merely a provision to ensure the repetition of the sacred spell a full hundred times, and the extra beads are added to make up for any omission of beads through absent-mindedness during the telling process or for actual loss of beads by breakage. Ché-ré-si and Dö-ma have each 108

[1] The rosary has proved a useful instrument in the hands of our Lāma surveying spies. Thus we find it reported with reference to Gyantse town, that a stone wall nearly two-and-a-half miles goes round the town, and the Lāma estimated its length by means of his rosary at 4,500 paces. At each pace he dropped a bead and uttered the mystic "Om mam padm hm," while the good people who accompanied him in his *Liṅ-k'or* or religious perambulations little suspected the nature of the work he was really doing.

names, but it is not usual to tell these on the rosary. And in the later Kham editions of the Lāmaic scriptures—the "bkā-'gyur,"—the volumes have been extended from 100 to 108. And the Burmese foot-prints of Buddha sometimes contain 108 sub-divisions. This number is perhaps borrowed, like so many other Lāmaist fashions, from the Hindūs, of whom the Vaishnabs possess a rosary with 108 beads.

The two ends of the string of beads, before being knotted, are passed through three extra beads, the centre one of which is the largest. These are collectively called "retaining or seizing beads," *r*dog-'dsin. The word is sometimes spelt *m*do-'dsin, which means "the union holder." In either case the meaning is much the same. These beads keep the proper rosary beads in position and indicate to the teller the completion of a cycle of beads.

This triad of beads symbolizes "the Three Holy Ones" of the Buddhist trinity, viz., Buddha, Dharma (the Word), and Sangha (the church, excluding the laity). The large central bead represents Buddha, while the smaller one intervening between it and the rosary beads proper represents the church and is called "Our radical Lāma" (or spiritual adviser),[1] the personal Lāma-guide and confessor of the Tibetan Buddhist; and his symbolic presence on the rosary immediately at the end of the bead-cycle is to ensure becoming gravity and care in the act of telling the beads, as if he were actually present.

The Gelug-pa, or established church, usually has only two beads as *dok-dsin*, in which case the terminal one is of much smaller size, and the pair are considered emblematic of a vase from which the beads spring. In such cases the extra bead is sometimes strung with the other beads of the rosary, which latter then contains 109 beads; thus showing that the beads really number 111.

Counters.

Attached to the rosary is a pair of strings of ten small pendant metallic rings as counters. One of these strings is terminated by a miniature *dorje* (the thunderbolt of Indra) and the other by a small bell—in Tantric Buddhist figures the *dorje* is ususlly associated with a bell. The counters on the *dorje*-string register units

[1] *tsa-waī bla-ma.*

of bead-cycles, while those on the bell-string mark tens of cycles. The counters and the ornaments of the strings are usually of silver, and inlaid with turquoise. These two strings of counters, called "count-keepers,"[1] may be attached at any part of the rosary string, but are usually attached at the eighth and twenty-first bead on either side of the central bead.

They are used in the following manner: When about to tell the beads, the counters on each string are slid up the string. On completing a circle of the beads, the lowest counter on the *dorje*-string is slid down into contact with the *dorje*. And on each further cycle of beads being told, a further counter is slid down. When the ten have been exhausted, they are then slid up again, and one counter is slipped down from the bell-string. The counters thus serve to register the utterance of 108 × 10 × 10 = 10,800 prayers or mystic formulas. The number of these formulas daily repeated in this way is enormous. The average daily number of repetitions may, in the earlier stages of a Lāma's career, amount to 5,000, but it depends somewhat on the zeal and leisure of the individual. A layman may repeat daily about five to twenty bead-cycles, but usually less. Old women are especially pious in this way, many telling over twenty bead-cycles daily. A middle-aged Lāma friend of mine has repeated the spell of his tutelary deity alone over 2,000,000 times. It is not uncommon to find rosaries so worn away by the friction of so much handling that originally globular beads have become cylindrical.

Affixed to the rosary are small odds and ends, such as a metal toothpick, tweezer, small keys, etc.

Material of the Beads.

The materials of which the Lāmaist rosaries are composed may to a certain extent vary in costliness according to the wealth of the wearer. The abbot of a large and wealthy monastery may have rosaries of pearl and other precious stones, and even of gold. Turner relates[2] that the Grand Tāshi Lāma possessed rosaries of pearls, emeralds, rubies, sapphires, coral, amber, crystal and lapis-lazuli.

[1] grang-'dsin, but vulgarly they are known as *chub-shé* (c'u-bs'ad) or "the ten makers."

[2] *Embassy to Tibet*, p. 261, 1800.

But the material of the rosary can only vary within rather narrow limits, its nature being determined by the particular sect to which the Lāma belongs and the particular deity to whom worship is to be paid.

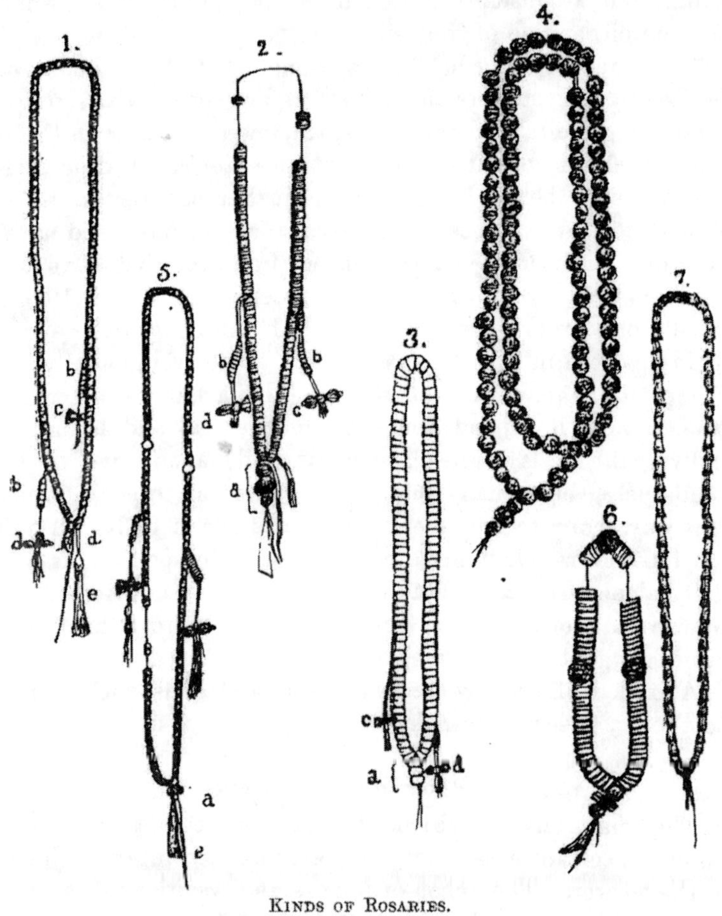

KINDS OF ROSARIES.

Fig. 1. The yellow wooden rosary of Ge-lug-pa sect.
,, 2. The red sandal-wood rosary for Tam-din's worship.
,, 3. The white conch shell rosary for Cha-rasi's worship.
,, 4. The *Raksha* rosary for the furies' worship.
,, 5. A layman's rosary (beads of unequal size).
,, 6. The human skull (discs) rosary.
,, 7. The snake-spine rosary.

a=*dō-dsin*. *d*=*dorge*-pendant.
b=counters. *e*=a tweezer and tooth-pick.
c=bell-pendant.

Kinds of Rosaries.

The yellow rosary or *Ser-t'eṅ*, Fig. 1, is the special rosary of the Ge-lug-pa or "reformed school," also called "the yellow hat sect" (*S'ā-ser*). The beads are formed from the ochrey yellow wood of the *C'aṅ-ch'ub* tree, literally "the Bodhi tree" or tree of supreme wisdom, which is said to grow in central China. The wood is so deeply yellow that it is doubtful whether it be really that of the Pīpal (*Ficus religiosa*), of which was the Bodhi tree under which Gautama attained his Buddhahood. These beads are manufactured wholesale by machinery at the temple called by Tibetans *Ri-wo tse-ṅa* and by the Chinese *U-tha Shan*, or "The Five Peaks," about 200 miles south-west of Pekin. Huc gives a sketch[1] of this romantic place, but makes no mention of its rosaries. This rosary is of two kinds, viz., the usual form of spherical beads about the size of a pea, and a less common form of lozenge-shaped perforated discs about the size of a sixpence. This rosary may be used for all kinds of worship, including that of the furies.

The *Bo-dhi-tse* rosary is the one chiefly in use among the Ñiṅ-ma-pa, or "old (*i.e.*, unreformed) school" of Lāmas, also called the *S'a-mar* or "red-hat sect." It is remarkable that its name also seeks to associate it with the Bodhi tree, but its beads are certainly not derived from the *Ficus* family. Its beads are the rough brown seeds of a tree which grows in the outer Himalayas. This rosary can be used for all kinds of worship, and may also be used by the Ge-luk-pa in the worship of the fiercer deities.

The white conch-shell rosary *Tuṅ-t'eṅ*,[2] Fig. 3, consists of cylindrical perforated discs of the conch shell, and is specially used in the worship of Avalokita—the usual form of whose image holds a white rosary in the upper right hand. This is the special rosary of nuns.

The rosary of plain crystal or uncoloured glass beads is also peculiar to Avalokita.

The red sandal-wood rosary *Tsän-dän-mar*, Fig. 2, consists of perforated discs of red sandal-wood (*Adenanthera pavonina*) or

[1] *Travels in Tartary, Tibet, and China.* By M. Huc (Hazlitt's trans.), i., p. 79, and figured under Shrines.

[2] *Druṅ-p'reṅ.*

other wood of a similar appearance. It is used only in the worship of the fierce deity Tam-din (Skt., *Hayagrīva*), a special protector of Lāmaism.

The coral rosary—*Ch'i-ru-t'eṅ*—is also used for the tutelary fiend, Tam-din, and by the unreformed sects for their wizard-saint Padma-sambhava. Coral being so expensive, red beads of glass or composition are in general use instead. With this rosary it is usual to have the counters of turquoise or blue beads.

The rosary formed of discs of the human skull—the *t'öd-t'eṇ*, Fig. 6—is especially used for the worship of the fearful tutelary fiend *Vajra-bhairava* as the slayer of the king of the Dead. It is usually inserted within the *Bo-dhi-tse* or other ordinary rosary; and it frequently has its discs symmetrically divided by four large *Raksha* beads into four series, one of these beads forming the central bead. There is no rosary formed of finger-bones, as has been sometimes stated.

The "elephant-stone" rosary—*Laṅ-ch'en-grod-pa*—is prepared from a porous bony-like concretion, which is sometimes found in the stomach (or brain) of the elephant. As it is suggestive of bone, it is used in worship of Yama. The real material being extremely scarce and expensive, a substitute is usually found in beads made from the fibrous root of the bow-bambu (*Z'u-shin*), which shows on section a structure very like the stomach-stone, and its name also means "stomach or digestion" as well as "bow."

The *Raksha* rosary, Fig. 4, formed of the large brown warty seeds of the *Elæocarpus Janitrus*, is specially used by the Ñiṅ-ma Lāmas in the worship of the fierce deities and demons. The seeds of this tree are normally five-lobed and ridged, and it is interesting from a botanical point of view to find how relatively frequent is the occurrence of six lobes. Such abnormal seeds are highly prized by the Tibetans, who believe them to be the offspring of some seeds of Padma-sambhava's rosary, which, the legend states, broke at his Halashi hermitage in Nepal, and several of the detached beads remaining unpicked up, these were the parents of the six-lobed seeds. The demand for such uncommon seeds being great, it is astonishing how many of them are forthcoming to diligent search. This rosary is also commonly used by the indigenous Bön-po priests, and it is identical with the rosary of the Hindūs—the *rudrāksha* (Rudra's or the fierce god Ṣiva's eyes, with reference to their red colour), from which the Tibetan name of *Raksha* is apparently derived.

The *Naṅ-ga pā-ni* rosary is used only for the worship of Namsrä, or Vaiṣravana, the god of wealth ; and by the wizards in their mystical incantations. It consists of glossy jet-black nuts about the size of a hazel, but of the shape of small horse chestnuts. These are the seeds of the *Luṅ-t'aṅ* tree which grows in the sub-tropical forests of the S.E. Himalayas. They are emblematic of the eyes of the Garuḍa bird, a henchman of Vajra-pāṇi (a form of Jupiter) and the great enemy of snakes, and hence is supposed to be derived the Sanskritic name of the beads, from *nāga*, a serpent. Its use in the worship of the god of wealth is interesting in associating snakes, as the mythological guardians of treasure, with the idea of wealth.[1]

The rosary of *snake-spines* (vertebræ), Fig. 7, is only used by the sorcerers in necromancy and divination. The string contains about fifty vertebræ.

The complexion of the god or goddess to be worshipped also determines sometimes the colour of the rosary-beads. Thus a turquoise rosary is occasionally used in the worship of the popular goddess Tārā, who is of a bluish-green complexion. A red rosary with red Tam-din, a yellow with yellow Mañjuṣri ; and Vaiṣravan, who is of a golden-yellow colour, is worshipped with an amber-rosary.

The rosaries of the laity are composed of any sort of bead according to the taste and wealth of the owner. They are mostly glass beads of various colours, and the same rosary contains beads of a variety of sizes and colours interspersed with coral, amber, turquoise, etc. The number of beads is the same as with the Lāmas, but each of the counter-strings is usually terminated by a *vajra:* both strings record only units of cycles, which suffice for the smaller amount of bead-telling done by the laity.

Mode of telling the Beads.

When not in use the rosary is wound round the right wrist like a bracelet, as in figure on page 172, or worn around the neck with the knotted end uppermost.

---

[1] See p. 368.

The act of telling the beads is called *taṅ-c'e,* which literally means "to purr" like a cat, and the muttering of the prayers is rather suggestive of this sound.

In telling the beads the right hand is passed through the rosary, which is allowed to hang freely down with the knotted end upwards. The hand, with the thumb upwards, is then usually carried to the breast and held there stationary during the recital. On pronouncing the initial word "*Om*" the first bead resting on the knuckle is grasped by raising the thumb and quickly depressing its tip to seize the bead against the outer part of the second joint of the index finger. During the rest of the sentence the bead, still grasped between the thumb and index finger, is gently revolved to the right, and on conclusion of the sentence is dropped down the palm-side of the string. Then with another "Om" the next bead is seized and treated in like manner, and so on throughout the circle.

On concluding each cycle of the beads, it is usual to finger each of the three "keeper-beads," saying respectively, "Om!" "Ah!" "Hūṃ!"

The mystic formulas for the beads have already been illustrated. They follow the prayer, properly so-called, and are believed to contain the essence of the formal prayer, and to act as powerful spells. They are of a Sanskritic nature, usually containing the name of the deity addressed, and even when not gibberish, as they generally are, they are more or less unintelligible to the worshipper.

The formula used at any particular time varies according to the particular deity being worshipped. But the one most frequently used by the individual Lāma is that of his own tutelary deity, which varies according to the sect to which the Lāma belongs.

The other articles of equipment comprise, amongst other things, a prayer-wheel, *vajra*-sceptre and bell, skull-drum and smaller tambour, amulet, booklets. Some even of the higher Lāmas wear ornaments and jewellery.[1]

[1] The Grand Lāma of Tashi-lhunpo wore a jewelled necklace, which he presented to Mr. Bogle (MARKH., cxl.)

A few possess a begging-bowl and the mendicant's staff,[1] but these are mostly for ritualistic displays, as the Lāma is no longer a mendicant monk living on alms like the Indian Bhikshu of old.

[1] *Khar-sil;* Skt., the onomatopoetic *hi-ki-le* or *kha-kha-rean*, the alarm-staff with jingling rings carried by the mendicant monk to drown out by its jingling worldly sounds from the ears of the monk and to warn off small animals lest they be trod upon and killed. Its use is explained in Kāh-gyur Dô, Vol. xxvi., Csoma, *An.*, p. 479. The Tibetan form is usually tipped by a trident in place of the leaf-like loop.

Alarm-Staff
of a mendicant monk.

IX.

DAILY LIFE AND ROUTINE.

"He who eats Lāmas' food
Wants iron jaws."—*Tibetan Proverb.*[1]

ALTHOUGH the Lāmas are enslaved in the bonds of ritual they are not all gloomy ascetics, wrapped up in contemplation, but most can be as blithe as their lay brothers. Their heavy round of observances, however, often lies wearily upon them, as may be seen from the frequent interruptions in the ordinary Lāma's saintly flow of rhetoric to yawn, or take part in some passing conversation on mundane matters.

The daily routine of a Lāma differs somewhat according to whether he is living in a monastery, or as a village priest apart from his cloister, or as a hermit. As with occidental friars, a considerable proportion of Lāmas have trades and handicrafts, labouring diligently in the field, farm, and in the lower valleys in the forest. But scarcely ever is he a mendicant monk, like his prototype the Indian Bhikshu of old.

MENDICANT LĀMA.[2]

The routine in the convents of the established church is seen at its best in the Grand Lāma's private monastery or chapel-royal of Nam-gyal, on mount Potala, near Lhāsa, and I am indebted to one of the monks

[1] dkor zas sa-la lchag-gi gram-pa dgos.

[2] After Giorgi.

of that monastery for the following detailed account of the practice followed there.

Routine in a Monastery of the Established Church.

Immediately on waking, the monk[1] must rise from his couch, even though it be midnight, and bow thrice before the altar in his cell, saying, with full and distinct enunciation: "O Guide of great pity! hear me! O merciful Guide! Enable me to keep the two hundred and fifty-three rules, including abstinence from singing, dancing, and music, and thoughts of worldly wealth, eating luxuriously, or taking that which has not been given," etc., etc.

Then follows this prayer[2]: "O Buddhas and Bodhisats of the ten directions, hear my humble prayer. I am a pure-minded monk, and my earnest desire is to devote myself towards benefiting the animals; and having consecrated my body and wealth to virtue, I vow that my chief aim will be to benefit all living things."

Then is repeated seven times the following *mantra* from the Sūtra on "the wheel-blessing for the animal universe"[3]: "*Om! Sambhara, Sammahā jaba hūṃ!*" Followed also seven times by this extract from *bharabi manaskar mahā jaba hūṃ! Om! Smara Smarabi manaskara* Norbu-*r*gyas-pahi-gzhal-med-k'aṅ: "*Om! ruci ramini pravartya hūṃ!*"

This is followed by "*Om! Khrecara gaṇaya hri hri svaha!*"—a spell which if the monk thrice repeats and spits on the sole of his foot, all the animals which die under his feet during that day will be born as gods in the paradise of Indra (Jupiter).

Having done this worship, the monk may retire again to sleep if the night is not far advanced. If, however, the dawn is near he must not sleep but employ the interval in repeating several *mantras* or forms of prayer (*s*mon-lam) until the bell rings for the first assembly.

The first assembly, or matin, called "the early gathering" (*s*na-tsog*s*), is held before sunrise. The great bell goes and awakens everyone hitherto slumbering, and it is soon followed by the great conch-shell trumpet-call, on which signal the monks adjust their

---

[1] I have translated by "monk" the word *d*ge-sloṅ, which is literally "the virtuous beggar," corresponding to the Indian Buddhist word Bhikshu, or mendicant.

[2] Composed by *m*'as-grub-ṅag-*d*baṅ-*r*dorje.

[3] 'gro-wa-yongs-su-bsngo-wai-'khor-loi-*m*do.

dress and go outside their cell or dormitory to the lavatory stone-flag or pavement (*r*do-*b*chal) for ablution.

Standing on these stones, and before washing, each monk chants the following *mantra*, and mentally conceives that all his sins, as well as the impurities of his body, are being washed away: "*Om! arghaṃ tsarghaṃ bimanase! utsusma mahā krodh hūmphat!*"

Then with water brought in copper vessels, and with a pinch of saline earth as soap,[1] they perform ablutions usually of a very partial kind.

After ablution each monk repeats, rosary in hand, the *mantra* of his favourite deity (usually Mañjuṣrī or Tārā), or his tutelary fiend, as many times as possible.

On the second blast of the conch-shell, about fifteen minutes after the first, all the fully-ordained monks bow down before the door of the temple, while the novices bow upon the outer paved court. All then enter the temple and take their places according to their grade, the most junior being nearest the door; and during the ingress the provost-marshal stands rod in hand beside the door.

The monks seat themselves in rows, each on his own mat, cross-legged in Buddha-fashion, and taking care not to allow his feet to project, or his upper vestments to touch the mat. They sit in solemn silence, facing straight to the front. The slightest breach of these rules is promptly punished by the rod of the provost-marshal, or in the case of the novices by the clerical sacristan.

At the third blast of the conch-trumpet the following services are chanted:—

Invoking the blessing of eloquence; the refuge-formula; Tsoṅ-K'apa's ritual of lha-brgya-ma.

After which tea is served, but before it is drunk the presiding Lāma says a grace in which all join.

LĀMAIST GRACES BEFORE MEAT.

The Lāmas always say grace before food or drink. Most of these graces are curiously blended with demonolatry, though they always are pervaded by universal charity and other truly Buddhist principles.

---

[1] This earth is called *sug-pa*, but the higher Lāmas use soap: "The Lāma minister of the Grand Lāma," says Sarat's narrative, "formerly used to wash his holiness's head with water and *sug-pa* powder, but now he uses a cake of P——'s transparent soap."

And they throw some light on the later Mahāyāna ritual of Indian Buddhism, from which they are alleged to have been borrowed.

Before drinking, the Lāmas, like the Romans, pour out some of the beverage as a libation to their Lares, and other gods. A common

TEA SERVICE.

grace before drinking tea (which is served out eight or ten times daily at the temples and cathedrals—the service being interrupted for this temporal refreshment) is :—

"We humbly beseech thee! that we and our relatives throughout all our life-cycles, may never be separated from the three holy ones! May the blessing of the trinity enter into this drink!" [Then, here sprinkling a few drops on the ground with the tips of the fore and middle fingers, the grace is continued :—]

"To all the dread locality, demons of this country, we offer this good Chinese tea! Let us obtain our wishes! And may the doctrines of Buddha be extended!"

The grace before food of the established church, the purest of all the Lāmaist sects, is as follows:—

"This luscious food[1] of a hundred tempting tastes, is here reverently offered by us—the animal beings—to the Jinas (the Dhyāni Buddhas) and their princely sons (celestial Bodhisattvas). May rich blessings overspread this food! *Om-Ah Hūṃ!*

"It is offered to the Lāma—*Om Guru vajra naividya-ah Hūṃ!*

"It is offered to all the Buddhas and Bodhisattvas—*Om sarva Buddha Bodhisattva vajra naividya-ah Hūṃ!*

"It is offered to the tutelaries, witches, and *defensores fidei*[2]—*Om Deva Dakini Sri dharmapāla saparivāra vajra naividya-ah Hūm!*

"One piece (is offered) to the powerful demon-lord (*d*baṅ-bahi-'byuṅ-po; Skt., *Bhūtesvara*)—*Om-Agra-Pinda-ashi bhya svahā!*

"One piece to *h*prog-ma—*Om-Harite*[3]*-svahā!*

"One piece to 'the five hundred brothers or sisters'[4]—*Om Harite maha-vajra-yakshini hara-hara sarva papi-mokshi svahā!*

"This food, of little virtue, is offered compassionately and without anger or pride, or as a return for past favours; but solely in the hope that we—all the animal beings—may become holy and attain the rank of the most perfect Buddhahood."

When any flesh-meat is in the diet, then the following grace is repeated seven times in order to cleanse from the sin of slaughter and of eating flesh: "*Om abira khe-ca-ra Hūṃ!*" And by the efficacy of this spell, the animal, whose flesh is eaten, will be reborn in heaven.

The following grace is for the special benefit of the donors of provisions, tea, etc., to the monastery, and it is repeated before the monks partake of food so gifted:—

"Salutation to the all-victorious Tathagata Arhat. The most perfect Buddha. The fiery and most illuminating king of precious light! *Namo! Samanta-prabhā-rāgāya Tathāgatāya Arhate-samayak-Buddhāya Namo Mañjusri-ye. Kumāra-Bhūtāya Bodhisattvaya maha-sattvaya! Tadyathā! Om*

---

[1] *Z*'al-*z*as.

[2] Yidam *m*K'ah-gro ch'os-*s*kyoṅ.

[3] This is the celebrated man-eating *Yakshini* fiendess, with the 500 children, whose youngest and most beloved son, Pingala, was hid away by Buddha (or, as some Lāmas say, by his chief disciple, Maudgalyayana) in his begging-bowl until she promised to cease cannibalism, and accept the Buddhist doctrine as detailed in the *Ratnakūta Sūtra*. See also the Japanese version of this legend, footnote p. 99. The Lāmas assert that Buddha also promised Hariti that the monks of his order would hereafter feed both herself and her sons: hence their introduction into this grace; and each Lāma daily leaves on his plate a handful of his food expressly for these demons, and these leavings are ceremoniously gathered and thrown down outside the monastery gate to these *pretas* and other starveling demons.

[4] The children of the above Hariti.

ralambhe-nira-bhase jaye-jayelabdhe mahā-materakshinamme parisodhāyā svahā. (The efficacy of reciting this *mantra* is thus described, says the Ge-lug-pa manual of daily worship, in the *Vinaya-Sūtra*: "When this is repeated once all sins will be cleansed, and the dispensers of the gifts will have their desires fulfilled." Then here follow with :—)

"May I attain bliss by virtue of this gift!

"May I attain bliss by deep meditation, the ceremonial rites, reverence and the offerings!

"May I attain perfect bliss and the supreme perfection of the real end (*Nirvāna*)!

"May I obtain the food of meditation of the hundred tastes, power, and brightness of countenance by virtue of this food-offering!

"May I obtain rebirths of wisdom, void of thirst, hunger, and disease, by virtue of this repentance-offering!

"May I obtain unalloyed happiness, free from worldly birth, old age, disease, and death!

"May the dispenser of these gifts attain perfection by virtue of these, his liberal gifts!

"May the human beings and all the other animals, obtain deliverance by virtue of this vast offering!

"May all the Buddhists, Nanda, Upananda, etc., the gods of the natural dwelling, the king, this dispenser of gifts, and the populace generally, obtain everlasting happiness, long life, and freedom from disease.

"May all the human beings, by virtue of this (gift), obtain luck in body and fore-knowledge.

"May the hopes of animals be realized as by the wish-granting gem (*Cintāmaṇi*) and the wish-granting tree (*Kalpataru*), and may glory come on all! *maṅgalam!*"

After the tea-refreshment, the following services are performed: The Great Compassionators liturgy, the praise of the disciples or *Sthaviras*, the offering of the magic-circle or *maṅḍala*, though the great circle is not offered every day, *Yön-ten-zhi-gyurma*, and the worship of the awful Bhairava, or other tutelary, such as Saṅdus, Dem-ch'og, or Tārā. But as these latter liturgies are very long, they are interrupted for further tea-refreshment. And at this stage, that is, in the interval between the first and second portions of the tutelary's worship, is done any sacerdotal service needed on account of the laity, such as masses for the sick, or for the soul of a deceased person. In the latter case it is publicly announced that a person, named so-and-so, died on such a date, and his relatives have given tea and such-and-such present, in kind or money, to the Lāmas for masses. Then the Lāmas do the service for sending the soul to the western paradise.[1] Or, if the service is for a sick person, they will do the Ku-rim[2] ceremony.

The tutelary's service is then resumed, and on its conclusion tea and soup are served. Then is chanted the S'es-rab s̄nin-

[1] See chapter on worship.

[2] Not phonetic for "cure him."

po, after which the assembly closes, and the monks file out singly, first from the extreme right bench, then from the extreme left, the youngest going first, and the most senior of the re-incarnated saintly Lāmas last of all.

The monks now retire to their cells, where they do their private devotions, and offer food to their tutelary deities; often marking the time to be occupied by particular devotional exercises by twirling with the finger and thumb their table-prayer-wheel, and while it spins, the exercise lasts.

PRAYER-CYLINDER FOR TABLE.

The orisons are chanted to the clamour of noisy instruments whenever the sun's disc is first seen in the morning. Then the hat is doffed, and the monk, facing the sun, and uplifting his right hand to a saluting posture, chants "It has arisen! It has arisen! The glorious one has arisen! The sun of happiness has arisen! The goddess Marīcī has arisen! Om-Marīcīnām svāhā!" On repeating this mantra of Marīcī seven times, he continues with: "Whenever I recall your name I am protected from all fear. I pray for the attainment of the great stainless bliss. I salute you, O goddess Marīcī! Bless me, and fulfil my desires. Protect me, O Goddess, from all the eight fears of foes, robbers, wild beasts, snakes, and poisons, weapons, firewater, and high precipices."

The second assembly, called "the After-heat" (t'sa-gtiṅ) is held about[1] 9 a.m., when the sun's heat is felt. On the first blast of the conch all retire to the latrine. At the second blast all gather on the pavement, or, if raining, retire to a covered court to read, etc. At the third blast—about fifteen minutes after the

[1] Time is only known approximately, as it is usually, as the name for hour (ch'u-ts'al) implies, kept by water-clocks (See "C'u-ts'al," RAMSAY'S *Dict.*, p. 63), and also by the burning of tapers.

second—all re-assemble in the temple and perform the service of "Inviting the religious guardian (-fiend)." During this worship tea is thrice served, and on its conclusion the monks all leave the temple. The younger monks now pore over their lessons, and receive instructions from their teachers.

The third assembly, called "Noon-tide," is held at noon. On the first blast of the conch all prepare for the sitting. At the second they assemble on the pavement, and at the third they enter the temple and perform the worship of "bS'ags-pa" and "bSkaṅ-wa," during which tea is served thrice, and the meeting dissolves.

Each monk now retires to his cell or room, and discarding his boots, offers sacrifice to his favourite deities, arranging the first part of the rice-offering with scrupulous cleanliness, impressing it with the four marks, and surrounding it with four pieces bearing the impress of the four fingers. After this he recites the "Praise of the three holy ones." [1]

Then lay servants bring to the cells a meal consisting of tea, meat, and *pāk* (a cake of wheat or tsam-pa). Of this food, some must be left as a gift to the hungry *manes*, Hariti and her sons. The fragments for this purpose are carefully collected by the servants and thrown outside the temple buildings, where they are consumed by dogs and birds. The monks are now free to perform any personal business which they have to do.

The fourth assembly, called "First (after-) noon tea" (*d*guṅ-ja-daṅ-po) is held about 3 p.m. The monks, summoned by three blasts of the conch as before, perform a service somewhat similar to that at the third assembly, and offer cakes and praise to the gods and divine defenders, during which tea is thrice served, and the assembly dissolves.

Then the junior monks revise their lessons, and the *pār-pa* or middle-grade monks are instructed in rhetoric and in sounding the cymbals and horns. And occasionally public wranglings as already described are held on set themes to stimulate theological proficiency.

The fifth assembly or vesper, called "The Second (after-) noon tea" is held about 7 p.m. The conch, as formerly, calls thrice to

[1] See chapter on worship.

the temple, where is chanted the worship of Tań-rak and the prayers of glory (*b*kra-shi*s*), during which tea is given thrice, and the assembly dissolves. After this the monks return to their rooms till the second night bell sounds, when the junior monks repeat from memory before their teachers certain scriptures and other texts; and at the third bell all retire to their cells to sleep.

ROUTINE IN AN UNREFORMED MONASTERY.

The routine in the monasteries of the unreformed or Ñiṅ-ma sects departs considerably from the high standard above described, and introduces more demonolatry and the worship of the deified wizard Guru Padma-sambhava.

The practice followed at Pemiongchi monastry is here described :—

In the morning, after offering the sacred food, incense, and butter-incense, a conch-shell is blown, on which all the monks must come out of their chambers. On the second blast all collect in the great assembly hall, and during this entry into the hall the provost-marshal stands beside the door with his rod in hand. All the monks seat themselves in Buddha-fashion, as before described.

The slightest breach of the rules of etiquette and discipline is promptly punished by the rod of the provost-marshal, or, in the case of the younger novices, by the sacristan.

When all have been properly seated, then two or three of the most inferior novices who have not passed their examination, and who occupy back seats, rise up and serve out tea to the assembly, as already described, each monk producing from his breast pocket his own cup, and having it filled up by these novices.

The service of tea is succeeded by soup, named gSol-jam t'ugpa, and served by a new set of the novice underlings. When the cups are filled, the precentor, joined by all the monks, chants "the Sacrificial Offering of the Soup." Three or four cups of soup are supplied to each monk. The hall is then swept by junior monks.

The precentor then inspects the magic circle[1] to see that it is correct, and, this ascertained, he commences the celebration, con-

[1] No layman is allowed to serve out the monks' food in the temple. The lay servants bring it to the outside door of the building, and there deposit it.

sisting of the *sNön-'gro* and the refuge-formula, and *Las-sbyaṅ*, on the conclusion of which the assembly disperses.

About 8 A.M. the conch-shell blast again summons the monks to the assembly hall, where, after partaking of refreshments of tea and parched grain in the manner already described, a full celebration is done. And on its conclusion the monks disperse.

About 10 A.M. a Chinese drum is beaten to muster the monks in the assembly hall. At this meeting rice and meat and vegetables are served out as before, and with this is also served beer called *gSos-rgyab*, the "food-sacrifice" (*lTo-mch'od*) being done as formerly. A full celebration is then performed, and the meeting dissolves.

In the afternoon a conch-shell is blown for tea, and a Chinese gong calls for beer, the monks assembling as before, and doing a full celebration of the worship of the lord (demon) Mahākālā and the guardians of religion respectively.

When sacerdotal celebrations on behalf of laymen have to be done, such are introduced within the latter celebration, which is interrupted for this purpose. And after each of these extra celebrations the monks remain outside the assembly hall for a very short time and then re-assemble. On finishing the extra services, the worship of the religious guardians is then resumed and concluded.

In the evening another assembly, preceded by tea as refreshment, conducts the celebration of *sKaṅ-shags* with one hundred and eight lamps.

Another and final assembly for the day is made by beat of drum, and rice and flesh-meat is served out.

The refreshments and meals usually number nine daily.

LIFE AS A VILLAGE PRIEST.

The monk, immediately on waking, must rise from his couch, even though it be midnight, and commence to chant the *Mi-rtak-rgyud-bskul*, taking care to pronounce all the words fully and distinctly. This contains the instructions of his special Lāma-preceptor, and in its recital the monk must recall vividly to mind his spiritual guide. This is followed by a prayer consisting of numerous requests for benefits of a temporal nature desired by the petitioner.

Then he assumes the meditative posture of the seven attitudes,[1] and gets rid by physical means of the "three original sins."

Then, coercing his tutelary demon into conferring on him his fiendish guise, he chants "the four preliminary services":—

The s*Non-gro* bzi-'*byor*. These are the refuge formula, which cleanses the darkness of the body; the hundred letters, which cleanse all obscurity in speech, and the magic-circle of rice, the *Maṇḍala*, which cleanses the mind; and the prayer enumerating the Lāmas up to the most perfect one, which confers perfection on the monk himself.

This is followed by the chanting of b*La-grub*, "the obtaining of the Lāma," and "the obtaining of the ornaments, s*Ñen-grub*."

The mild deity in this worship is called "The Placid One,"[2] and the demon "The Repulsive."[3] The demoniacal form must be recited the full number of times which the Lāma bound himself to do by vow before his spiritual tutor, namely, one hundred, one thousand, or ten thousand times daily. Those not bound in this way by vows repeat the charm as many times as they conveniently can.

Having done this, he may retire again to sleep, if the night be not very far advanced. But if the dawn is near, he must not go to sleep, but should employ the interval in several sorts of prayer.

As soon as day dawns, he must wash his face and rinse his mouth and do the worship above noted, should he not have already done so; also the following rites:—

1st. Prepare sacred food for the six sorts of beings (*Rigs-strug-gi-gtorma*) and send it to tantalized ghosts.

2nd. Offer incense, butter-incense, and wine-oblation (gS*er*-sK*yem*). The incense is offered to the good spirits—firstly, to the chief god and the Lāma; secondly, to the class of "king" gods; and thirdly to the mountain god "Kanchinjinga." Then offerings are made to the spirits of caves (who guarded and still guard the hidden revelations therein deposited), the "enemy-god of battle," the country gods, the local demigods, and "the eight classes of deities." The butter-incense is only given to the most malignant class of the demons and evil spirits.

Some breakfast is now taken, consisting of weak soup, followed by tea with parched grain. Any especial work which has to be done will now be attended to, failing which some tantrik or other

[1] See p. 145. [2] mt'un. [3] *bzle-pa.*

service will be chanted. And if any temple or Caitya be at hand, these will be circumambulated with "prayer-wheel" revolving in hand, and chanting *mantras.* Then is done any priestly service required by the villagers.

About two o'clock in the afternoon a meal of rice is taken followed by beer by those who like it, or by tea for non-beer drinkers.

About six o'clock P.M. is done the gtor-bsṅös service, in which, after assuming his tutelary dignity, he chants the sṅon-gro and refuge formula. Then is done a sacrificial worship[1] with bell and small drum, followed by an invocation to the hosts of Lāmas, tutelaries, and the supernatural *defensores fidei.*

About 9 or 10 P.M. he retires to sleep.

IN HERMITAGE.

Buddhism in common with most religions had its hermits who retired like John the Baptist into the wilderness. And such

HERMIT-LĀMA.[2]

periodical retirement for a time, corresponding to the Buddhist Lent (the rainy season of India, or *Varsha*, colloq. "barsat"), when travelling was difficult and unhealthy, was an essential part of the routine of the Indian Buddhist. Tsoṅ K'apa enforced the obser-

[1] mCh'oga. [2] After Huc.

vance of this practice, but it has now fallen much into abeyance. Probably the booths which are erected for the head Lāmas in Sikhim during their visits to villages in the autumn, are vestiges of this ancient practice of retirement to the forest.

Theoretically it is part of the training of every young Lāma to spend in hermitage a period of three years, three months, and three days, in order to accustom himself to ascetic rites. But this practice is very rarely observed for any period, and when it is observed, a period of three months and three days is considered sufficient. During this seclusion he repeats the spell of his tutelary deity an incredible number of times. The *Mūla-yoga sṅgon-gro*, complete in all its four sections, must be repeated 100,000 times. In chanting the refuge-formula portion, he must prostrate himself to the ground 100,000 times. The repetition of the *Yige-brgya-pa* itself takes about two months; and in addition must be chanted the following voluminous services: P'yi-'grub, naṅ-'grub, gsaṅ-'grub, bla-'grub, sñen-grub, 'prin-las, and bzi-'grub.

Those who permanently adopt the hermit life are called "the packed-up ones"[1] and those of the highest rank are "the great recluses."[2] They are engaged in ascetic exercises and are usually followers of the Vajrāyāna system, seeking *Siddhi* and its wizard powers by the aid of the Ḍākkinī she-devils and the king-devils who are their tutelaries.

TRADES AND OCCUPATIONS.

Like western friars, the Lāmas have a considerable proportion of their number engaged in trades and handicrafts. The monks are practically divided into what may be called the spiritual and the temporal. The more intelligent are relieved of the drudgery of worldly work and devote themselves to ritual and meditation. The less intellectual labour diligently in field or farm and in trading for the benefit of their monastery; or they collect the rents and travel from village to village begging for their parent monastery, or as tailors, cobblers, printers, etc. Others again of the more intellectual members are engaged as astrologers in casting horoscopes, as painters or in image-making, and in other pursuits contributing to the general funds and comfort of the monastery.

[1] m*ts'am-s-pa*. [2] s*gom-ch'en*.

THE DIET.

The diet of the Lāmas is the ordinary rather Spartan fare of the country [1] consisting mainly of wheat, barley, or buck-wheat and occasionally rice, milk and butter, soup, tea and meat. The only flesh-meat allowed is sheep, goat, and yak; fish and fowl are prohibited. The fully-ordained monks, the Ge-longs, are supposed to eat abstemiously and abstain totally from meat; though even the Grand Lāma of Tashi-lhunpo appears to eat flesh-food.[2]

Neither the monks of the established church nor the holier Lāmas of the other sects may drink any spirituous liquor. Yet they offer it as libations to the devils.

[1] For food of Tibetans, see TURNER's *Embassy*, 24-48, etc.; PEMBERTON, 156; MOORCROFT, i., 182, etc.; HUC, ii., 258; CUNNINGHAM's *Ladak*, 305; ROCK., *L.*, *passim.*

[2] Bogle in MARKHAM, p. 100.

LIBATION-JUG AND CHALICE-CUP
(of silver).

A GRAND LĀMA OF BHOTĀN.

X.

THE HIERARCHY AND RE-INCARNATE LĀMAS.

"*Le roi est mort, vive le roi!*"

"Adam . . . his soul passed by transmigration into David . . . his soul transmigrated into the Messiah."—*The Talmud.*[1]

EARLY Buddhism had neither church nor ecclesiastical organization. It was merely a brotherhood of monks. Even after Buddha's death, as the order grew in size and affluence under the rich endowments from Aṣoka and other kingly patrons, it still remained free from anything like

[1] HERSHON'S *Treasures of the Talmud*, p. 242.

centralized government. The so-called patriarchs had only very nominal power and no generally recognized position or functions. And even the later Indian monasteries had each its own separate administration, and its own chief, independent of the others; a similar state of affairs seems to have prevailed in Tibet until the thirteenth century.

The hierarchical system of Tibet seems to date from the thirteenth century A.D., when the Lāma of the Sas-kya monastery was created a pope by the Great Mongol emperor of China, Kubilai Khan. This Sas-kya Lāma, receiving also a certain amount of temporal power, soon formed a hierarchy, and some generations later we find the other sects forming rival hierarchies, which tended to take the power out of the hands of the petty chiefs who now parcelled out Tibet. In 1417, doctor Tsoṅ K'apa founded the Ge-lug-pa sect, which under his powerful organization soon developed into the strongest of all the hierarchies, and five generations later it leapt into the temporal government of Tibet, which it still retains, so that now its church is the established one of the country.

Priest-kingship, a recognized stage in the earlier life of social institutions, still extends into later civilization, as in the case of the emperors of China and Japan, who fill the post of high-priest. It was the same in Burma, and many eastern princes who no longer enjoy "the divine right of kings," still bear the title of "god," and their wives of "goddess."

The Grand Lāma who thus became the priest-king of Tibet was a most ambitious and crafty prelate. He was named Ṅag-waṅ Lô-zaṅ, and was head of the De-pung monastery. At his instigation a Mongol prince from Koko Nor, named Gusri Khan, conquered Tibet in 1640, and then made a present of it to this Grand Lāma, together with the title of Dalai or "the vast" (literally "ocean") Lāma,[1] and he was confirmed in this title and kingly possession in 1650 by the Chinese emperor. On account of this Mongol title, and these priest-kings being first made familiar to Europeans through the Mongols,[2] he and his

1 The Tibetan for this Mongol word is r*Gya-mts'o*, and in the list of Grand Lāmas some of his predecessors and successors bear this title as part of their personal name. And the Mongolian for rin-po-ch'e is "*Ertenni.*"

2 Through the works of Giorgi, Pallas, and Klaproth.

successors are called by some Europeans "*Dalai* (or *Tale*) Lāma," though the first Dalai Lāma was really the fifth Grand Lāma of the established church; but this title is practically unknown to Tibetans, who call the Lhāsa Grand Lāmas, Gyal-wa Rin-po-ch'e, or "The gem of majesty or victory."

In order to consolidate his new-found rule, and that of his church in the priest-kingship, this prelate, as we have seen, posed as the deity Avalokita-in-the-flesh, and he invented legends magnifying the powers and attributes of that deity, and trans-

FOUR-HANDED AVALOKITA.
(Incarnate in the Dalai Lāma.)

ferred his own residence from De-pung monastery to a palace which he built for himself on "the red hill" near Lhāsa, the name of which hill he now altered to Mount Potala, after the mythic Indian residence of his divine prototype. He further forcibly seized many of the monasteries of the other sects and converted them into his own Ge-lug-pa institutions [1]; and he developed the

[1] Amongst others he seized the monastery of the great Tāranātha, and demolished many of that Lāma's buildings and books, for such an honest historian was not at all to his taste.

fiction of succession by re-incarnate Lāmas, and by divine reflexes.

The other sects accepted the situation, as they were indeed forced to do; and all now, while still retaining each its own separate hierarchical system, acknowledge the Grand Lāma of Lhāsa to be

POTALA. THE PALACE OF THE DALAI LĀMA.
(From Kircher's *China Illustrata.*)

the head of the Lāmaist church, in that he is the incarnation of the powerful Buddhist deity Avalokita. And they too adopted the attractive theory of the re-incarnate succession and divine reflexes.

It is not easy to get at the real facts regarding the origin and development of the theory of re-incarnate Lāmas, as the whole question has been purposely obscured, so as to give it the appearance of antiquity.

It seems to me that it arose no earlier than the fifteenth century, and that at first it was simply a scheme to secure stability for the succession to the headship of the sect against electioneering intrigues of crafty Lāmas, and was, at first, a simple re-incarnation theory; which, however, must not be confused with the orthodox Buddhist theory of re-birth as a result of Karma, for the latter is never confined in one channel. On the contrary, it holds that the spirit of the deceased head Lāma is always reborn in a child, who has to be found by oracular signs, and duly installed in the vacant chair; and he on his death is similarly reborn, and so on *ad infinitum*, thus securing, on quasi-Buddhistic principles, continuous succession by the same individual through successive re-embodiments.

The first authentic instance of re-incarnate Lāmas which I can find is the first of the Grand Lāmas of the Ge-lug-pa, namely, Ge-den-ḍub. Had this theory been invented prior to Tsoṅ K'apa's death in 1417 A.D., it is practically certain that the succession to Tsoṅ K'apa would have begun with an infant re-incarnation. But we find the infant re-incarnationship only beginning with the death of Tsoṅ K'apa's successor, namely, his nephew and pupil, Ge-den-ḍub aforesaid; and from this epoch the succession to the Ge-lug-pa Grand Lāmaship has gone on according to this theory. As the practice worked well, it was soon adopted by the Lāmas of other sects, and it has so extended that now nearly every great monastery has its own re-incarnate Lāma as its chief, and some have several of these amongst their higher officials.

The more developed or expanded theory, however, of celestial Lāma-reflexes, which ascribes the spirit of the original Lāma to an emanation (*Nirmāna kāya*, or, changeable body)[1] from a particular celestial Buddha or divine Bodhisat, who thus becomes incarnate in the church, seems to me to have been of much later origin, and most probably the invention of the crafty Dalai Lāma Ṅag-waṅ, or Gyal-wa Ṅa-pa,[2] about 150 years later. For, previous to the time when this latter Grand Lāma began to consolidate his newly-acquired temporal rule over Tibet, no authentic records seem to exist of any such celestial origin of any Lāmas, and the theory seems unknown to Indian Buddhism.[3] And this Dalai Lāma is known to have taken the greatest liberties with the traditions and legends of Tibet, twisting them to fit in with his divine pretensions, and to have shaped the Lāmaist hierarchy on the lines on which it now exists.

This Dalai Lāma, Gyal-wa Ṅa-pa, is the first of these celestial incarnate Lāmas which I can find. He was made, or, as I consider, made himself, to be the incarnation of the most popular Buddhist divinity possible, namely, Avalokita, and to the same rank were promoted the four Grand Lāmas who preceded him, and who,

[1] Cf. *ante.*

[2] Literally "The fifth Jina." Cf. also PAND., *H.*, No. 46.

[3] None of the so-called biographies of Atīṣa and earlier Indian monks containing any such references can certainly be placed earlier than this period.

together with himself, were identified with the most famous king of Tibet, to wit, Sroṅ Tsan Gampo, thus securing the loyalty of the people to his rule, and justifying his exercise of the divine right of kings; and to ensure prophetic sanction for this scheme he wrote, or caused to be written, the mythical so-called history, Mani kah-'bum. It was then an easy task to adjust to this theory, with retrospective effect, the bygone and present saints who were now affiliated to one or other of the celestial Buddhas or Bodhisats, as best suited their position and the church. Thus, Tsoṅ K'apa, having been a contemporary of the first Grand Lāma, could not be Avalokitesvara, so he was made to be an incarnation of Mañjuṣrī, or "the god of wisdom," on whom, also, Atīṣa was affiliated as the wisest and most learned of the Indian monks who had visited Tibet; and so also King Thi Sroṅ Detsan, for his aid in founding the order of the Lāmas.

It also seems to me that Ṅa-pa was the author of the re-incarnate Lāma theory as regards Tashi-lhunpo monastery and the so-called double-hierarchy; for an examination of the positive data on this subject shows that the first re-incarnate Lāma of Tashi-lhunpo dates only from the reign of this Ṅa-pa, and seven years after his accession to the kingship of Tibet.

Tashi-lhunpo monastery was founded in 1445 by Geden-dub, the first Grand Ge-lug-pa Lāma, who seems, however, to have mostly lived and to have died at De-pung.

It will be noticed from the list of Tāshi Grand Lāmas[1] that Geden-dub, the founder of Tashi-lhunpo, contrary to the current opinion of European writers, does not appear as a Tāshi Lāma at all. This official list of Tashi-lhunpo, read in the light of the biographies of these Lāmas,[2] clearly shows that previous to the Lāma who is number two of the list, and who was born during the latter end of Dalai Lāma Ṅa-pa's reign as aforesaid, none of the Tashi-lhunpo Lāmas were regarded as re-incarnations at all. The first on this list, namely, Lo-zaṅ Ch'o-kyi Gyal-ts'an, began as a private monk, and travelled about seeking instruction in the ordinary way, and not until his thirty-first year was he promoted to the abbotship, and then only by election and on

1 Presently to be given.
2 Some of which have been translated by SARAT (*J.A.S.B.*, 1882, 26 *seq.*).

account of distinguished ability. It is also interesting to note that on the death, in 1614, of the fourth Grand Lāma of the Ge-lug-pa (named Yön-tan), whom he had ordained, he was installed in the abbotship at Gāh-ldan monastery, and in 1622, at the age of 53, he initiated, as fifth Grand Lāma, the infant Ṅa-pa, who was then seven years old, and who afterwards became the great Dalai Lāma.

And he continued to be the spiritual father and close friend and adviser of Ṅa-pa, and seems to have begun those political negotiations which culminated in the cession of Tibet to his *protégé*. When he died, in 1662, his spiritual son Ṅa-pa, who was 47 years old, and had been 22 years in the kingship, promptly re-incarnated him, and also made him out to be his own spiritual father, even as regards the divine emanation theory. Thus the new-born babe was alleged to be an incarnation of Avalokita's spiritual father, Amitābha, the Buddha of Boundless Light; and he was given a considerable share in the management of the established church. This, however, merely perpetuated the relations which had actually existed between these two Grand Lāmas as father and son, and which had worked so well, and had such obvious political advantages in providing against interregnums.

In the hierarchical scheme of succession by re-incarnate Lāmas, the Lhāsa Grand Lāma, who wields the sovereign power, thus gave himself the highest place, but allotted the Tashi-lhunpo Grand Lāma a position second only to his own. Below these come the other re-incarnate Lāmas, ranking according to whether they are regarded to be re-embodiments of Indian or of Tibetan saints. The former class are called "the higher incarnations" or Tul-Ku,[1] and by the Mongols *Khutuktu*. They occupy the position of cardinals and archbishops. The lowest re-incarnate Lāmas are regarded as re-embodiments of Tibetan saints, and are named ordinary *Tul-ku* or "*Ku-s'o*,"[2] or by the Mongols Khublighan or Hoblighan; these mostly fill the post of abbots, and rank one degree higher than an ordinary non-re-incarnate abbot, or *K'an-po*, who has been selected on account of his proved abilities. Most of

[1] sP*rul-sku*.

[2] *sKu-s'og*s. The use of the term for a re-incarnate Lāma seems restricted to Ladāk. In Tibet proper this title is applied to any superior Lāma, and is even used in polite society to laymen of position.

these so-called re-incarnate Lāmas are by a polite fiction credited with knowing all the past life and deeds of individuals, not only in the present life, but also in former births.

In the unreformed sects, where the priests are not celibate, the children succeed to the headship. The ordinary hierarchical distinctions of grades and ranks have already been noted in describing the organization of the order.

The greatest of the Lāma hierarchs, after the Grand Lāmas of Lhāsa and Tashi-lhunpo, are the great Mongolian Lāma at Urgya, the Sas-kya Lāma, and the Dharma Rāja of Bhotān, this last being practically independent of Lhāsa, and the temporal ruler of Bhotān. Here also may be mentioned the female incarnate goddess, "The diamond sow" of Yam-dok Lake monastery.

The following list of Tibetan popes, the Grand Lāmas of Lhāsa, is taken from the printed list.[1] The birth-dates are given upon the authority of a reliable, trustworthy Lāmaist calculator.[2]

LIST OF GRAND (DALAI) LĀMAS OR POPES.

No.	Name.	Birth.	Death.	Remarks.
		A.D.	A.D.	
1	dGe-'dun grub-pa	1391	1475	
2	dGe-'dun rGya-mts'o.........	1475	1543	
3	bSod-nams ,, ...	1543	1589	
4	Yon-tan ,, ...	1589[3]	1617	
5	Ñag-dbaṅ blo-bsaṅ rGya-mts'o	1617	1682	First "Dalai."
6	Ts'aṅs-dbyans rGya-mts'o	1683[4]	1706	Deposed & murdered.
7	sKal-bzan ,,	1708	1758	
8	'Jam-dpal ,,	1758	1805[5]	
9	Luṅ-rtogs ,,	1805[6]	1816	Seen by Manning.
10	Ts'ul-K'rims ,,	1819[7]	1837	
11	mK'as-grub ,,	1837	1855	
12	'P'rin-las ,,	1856	1874	
13	T'ub-bstan ,,	1876		Present pope.

The first Grand Lāma, Ge-'dun-ḍub, was born near Sas-kya, and

1 The modern list precedes the historical names by a series of fifty more or less mythic personages, headed by Avalokita himself.

2 Lāma S'e-rab Gya-ts'o, of the Ge-lug-pa monastery, Darjiling.

3 DESGODINS (*La Miss.*, etc., p. 218) gives 1588.

4 DESG. gives 1682.

5 Other accounts give 1798, 1803, 1808; cf. also KÖPPEN'S *List*, i., 235.

6 DESG., and this corresponds with Manning's account (MARKH., 265).

7 DESG. gives 1815.

not far from the site whereon he afterwards founded Tashi-lhunpo. His successors, up to and inclusive of the fifth, have already been referred to in some detail.

On the deposition and death of the sixth Grand Lāma for licentious living, the Tartar king, Gingkir Khan, appointed to Potala the Lāma of C'ag-poh-ri, named Nagwaṅ Yeshé Gya-mts'o, into whom the sorcerers alleged that, not the soul but the breath of the former Grand Lāma had passed. It was soon announced, however, that the sixth Grand Lāma was re-born in the town of Lithang as Kal-zaṅ, the son of a quondam monk of De-pung monastery. This child was imprisoned by the Chinese emperor, who had confirmed the nominee of the Tartar king, until the war of 1720, when he invested him with spiritual rule at Lhāsa; but again, in 1728, deposed him, as he was privy to the murder of the king of Tibet. So he set in his place the Lāma "Kiesri" Rimpoch'e, of the Chotin monastery, four days' journey from Lhāsa.[1] He seems latterly to have returned to power, and during his reign in 1749, the Chinese put his temporal vice-regent to death, when the people flew to arms and massacred the Chinese.[2]

The ninth is the only Grand Lāma of Lhāsa ever seen by an Englishman. He was seen by Manning in 1811, while still a child of six years old. Manning relates that: "The Lāma's beautiful and interesting face and manner engrossed almost all my attention. He was at that time about seven years old; had the simple and unaffected manners of a well-educated princely child. His face was, I thought, poetically and affectingly beautiful. He was of a gay and cheerful disposition, his beautiful mouth perpetually unbending into a graceful smile, which illuminated his whole countenance. Sometimes, particularly when he looked at me, his smile almost approached to a gentle laugh. No doubt my grim beard and spectacles somewhat excited his risibility. . . . He enquired whether I had not met with molestations and difficulties on the road," etc.[3] This child died a few years afterwards, assassinated, it is believed, by the regent, named Si-Fan.

The tenth Grand Lāma also dying during his minority, and

---

1 This latter Lāma was in power at Potala in 1730 on the arrival of Horace Dellapenna, from whose account (MARKH., p. 321) most of the latter details have been taken.

2 *Ibid.*, lxv.

3 *Ibid.*, p. 266.

suspicions being aroused of foul play on the part of the regent, the latter was deposed and banished by the Chinese in 1844, at the instance of the Grand Lāma of Tashi-lhunpo, and a rising of his confederates of the Sera monastery was suppressed.[1]

The eleventh also died prematurely before attaining his majority, and is believed to have been poisoned by the regent, the Lāma of Ten-gye-ling. A young Lāma of De-pung, named Ra-deng,[2] was appointed regent, and he banished his predecessor "Pe-chi," who had befriended Huc; but proving unpopular, he had eventually to retire to Pekin, where he died.[3] Pe-chi died about 1869, and was succeeded by the abbot of Gāh-ldan.

The twelfth Grand Lāma was seen in 1866 by one of our Indian secret surveyors, who styles him a child of about thirteen, and describes him as a fair and handsome boy, who, at the reception, was seated on a throne six feet high, attended on either side by two high rank officials, each swaying over the child's head bundles of peacock feathers. The Grand Lāma himself put three questions to the spy and to each of the other devotees, namely: "Is your king well?" "Does your country prosper?" "Are you yourself in good health?" He died in 1874, and his death is ascribed to poison administered by the regent, the Tengye-ling head Lāma.

The thirteenth is still (1894) alive. He was seen in 1882 by Sarat Candra Dās, whose account of him is given elsewhere.

The Tashi-lhunpo Grand Lāmas are considered to be, if possible, holier even than those of Lhāsa, as they are less contaminated with temporal government and worldly politics, and more famous for their learning, hence they are entitled "The precious great doctor, or Great gẹm of learning" (*Pan-ch'en Rin-po-ch'e*),[4] or *Gyal-gön*[5] *Rin-po-ch'e*, or "The precious lordly victor." The Sa-kya Grand Lāmas had been called "Pan-ch'en," or the "Great doctor" from the twelfth century, but have ceased to hold the

[1] Huc, ii., p. 166. This account is disbelieved by Mr. Mayers, *J.R.A.S.*, iv., 305.

[2] *rva-sgren*, the "*gyal-po Riting*" of the Pandit, p. xxiv.

[3] Markh., xcvii.

[4] *Pan* is a contraction for the Indian "*Paṇḍit*," or learned scholar, and *rin-po-ch'e* = *ratna* or gem, or precious, or in Mongolian *Irtini* or *Erdeni*, hence he is called by Mongolians "Pan-ch'en Irtini."

[5] Vulgarly "*gyaṅ-gön*."

title since the era of the Dalai Lāmas, when the established church appropriated it to itself.

The following list of "Tashi" Lāmas is taken from that printed at the monastery itself.[1]

LIST OF "TASHI" GRAND LĀMAS.

No.	Name.	Birth.	Death.	Remarks.
		A.D.	A.D.	
1	bLo-bzaṅ ch'os-kyi rgyal-mts'an	1569	1662	
2	bLo-bzaṅ ye-she dpal bzaṅ-po	1663	1737	
3	bLo-bzaṅ dpal-ldan ye-s'es	1738[2]	1780	Bogle's friend, installed 1743.
4	rJe-bstan paḥi ñima	1781	1854	Seen by Turner.
5	rJe-dpal-ldan ch'os-kyi grags-pa bstan-paḥi dbaṅ p'yug	1854	1882	Died in August.
6	... ...	1883		Installed last week of February, 1888.

The third Tashi Lāma was the friend of Mr. Bogle, who seems to be the only European who had the advantage of close and friendly intercourse with one of the Grand Lāmas. Mr. Bogle gives us a delightful glimpse into the amiable character of this holy man.[3]

"The Lāma was upon his throne, formed of wood carved and gilt, with some cushions about it, upon which he sat cross-legged. He was dressed in a mitre-shaped cap of yellow broad-cloth with long bars lined with red satin; a yellow cloth jacket, without sleeves; and a satin mantle of the same colour thrown over his shoulders.

[1] The official list is entitled pan-*sku-p'ren rim-pa* ltar *byon-pa-ni*, and gives no dates. It ends with No. 3 of my list as above, and extends the list backwards to ten additional names, beginning with the somewhat mythical disciple of Buddha, Su-bhuti; and including legendary Indian personages as re-incarnations, as well as the following six Tibetans, the fourth of which is usually held to be the first of the Tashi-lhunpo Grand Lāmas. As, however, Tashi-lhunpo was only built in 1445, only the latter two of this list could be contemporary with it, and as is noted in the text, their biographies show that they were ordinary monks who held no high post, if any at all, at Tāshilhunpo.

SUPPLMENTARY LIST OF SO-CALLED PAN-CH'EN GRAND LĀMAS.

1. *K'ug-pa lhas*-btsas, of rTa-nag monastery.
2. *Sa-skya Pandita* (1182-1252).
3. g*Yun-ston rdo-rje dpal* (1284-1376).
4. mK'as-sgrub d*Ge-legs-dpal* zang-po (1385-1439).
5. pan-ch'en-b*Sod-nams p'yogs kyi-glaṅ*-po (1439-1505)
6. dben-sa-pa blo-bzaṅ *Don-grub* (1505-1570).

[2] At "Tashi-tzay," N.E. of Tashi-lhunpo (M., p. 92).

[3] *Loc. cit.*, p. 83.

On one side of him stood his physician with a bundle of perfumed sandal-wood rods burning in his hand; on the other stood his *So-pon Chumbo*[1] or cup-bearer. I laid the governor's presents before him, delivering the letter and pearl necklace into his own hands, together with a white Pelong handkerchief on my own part, according to the custom of the country. He received me in the most engaging manner. I was seated on a high stool covered with a carpet. Plates of boiled mutton, boiled rice, dried fruits, sweetmeats, sugar, bundles of tea, sheeps' carcasses dried, etc., were set before me and my companion, Mr. Hamilton. The Lāma drank two or three dishes of tea along with us, asked us once or twice to eat, and threw white Pelong handkerchiefs on our necks at retiring.

"After two or three visits, the Lāma used (except on holidays) to receive me without any ceremony, his head uncovered, dressed only in the large red petticoat which is worn by all the gylongs, red Bulgar hide boots, a yellow cloth vest with his arms bare, and a piece of yellow cloth thrown around his shoulder. He sat sometimes in a chair, sometimes on a bench covered with tiger skins, and nobody but *So-pon Chumbo* present. Sometimes he would walk with me about the room, explain to me the pictures, make remarks on the colour of my eyes, etc. For, although venerated as God's vicegerent through all the eastern countries of Asia, endowed with a portion of omniscience, and with many other divine attributes, he throws aside in conversation all the awful part of his character, accommodates himself to the weakness of mortals, endeavours to make himself loved rather than feared, and behaves with the greatest affability to everybody, especially to strangers.

"Teshu Lāma is about forty years of age, of low stature, and though not corpulent, rather inclining to be fat. His complexion is fairer than that of most of the Tibetans, and his arms are as white as those of a European; his hair, which is jet black, is cut very short; his beard and whiskers never above a month long; his eyes are small and black. The expression of his countenance is smiling and good-humoured. His father was a Tibetan, his

[1] He held, according to Turner (p. 246), the second rank in the court of the Tashi Lāma, and was by birth a Manchu Tartar. He was then only about twenty-two years of age.

mother a near relation of the Rājas of Ladak. From her he learned the Hindūstani language, of which he has a moderate knowledge, and is fond of speaking it. His disposition is open, candid, and generous. He is extremely merry and entertaining in conversation, and tells a pleasant story with a great deal of humour and action. I endeavoured to find out in his character those defects which are inseparable from humanity, but he is so universally beloved that I had no success, and not a man could find in his heart to speak ill of him. . . . .

"Among the other good qualities which Teshu Lāma possesses is that of charity, and he has plenty of opportunities of exercising it. The country swarms with beggars, and the Lāma entertains besides a number of fakirs (religious mendicants), who resort hither from India. As he speaks their language tolerably well he every day converses with them from his windows, and picks up by this means a knowledge of the different countries and governments of Hindūstan. . . . He gives them a monthly allowance of tea, butter, and flour, besides money, and often bestows something considerable upon them at their departure. The Gosains who are thus supported at the Lāma's expense may be in number about one hundred and fifty, besides about thirty Musulman fakirs. For although the genius of the religion of Muhamad is hostile to that of the Lāma, yet he is possessed of much Christian charity, and is free from those narrow prejudices which, next to ambition and avarice, have opened the most copious source of human misery." And observing the universal esteem in which the Grand Lāma is held by the monks and people, the looks of veneration mixed with joy with which he is always regarded, Mr. Bogle adds "one catches affection by sympathy, and I could not help, in some measure, feeling the same emotions with the Lāma's votaries,[1] and I will confess I never knew a man whose manners pleased me so much, or for whom, upon so short an acquaintance, I had half the heart's liking."[2]

This Grand Lāma, soon after Bogle's departure, died of smallpox. He had, in response to the invitation of the Chinese emperor, set out for Pekin, attended by 1,500 troops and followers, and sumptuous provision was made for his comfort during the whole

[1] *Op. cit.*, p. 95. [2] p. 133.

of the long journey in Chinese territory. The emperor met him at Sining, several weeks' march from Pekin, and advanced about forty paces from his throne to receive him, and seated him on the topmost cushion with himself and at his right hand. To the great grief of the empress and the Chinese the Lāma was seized with small-pox, and died on November 12th, 1780. His body, placed in a golden coffin, was conveyed to the mausoleum at Tashi-lhunpo.[1]

His successor, while still an infant of about eighteen months, was seen by Captain Turner as the envoy of the British government. This remarkable interview took place at the monastery of Terpa-ling.[2] He found the princely child, then aged eighteen months, seated on a throne of silk cushions and hangings about four feet high, with his father and mother standing on the left hand. Having been informed that although unable to speak he could understand, Captain Turner said "that the governor-general on receiving the news of his decease in China, was overwhelmed with grief and sorrow, and continued to lament his absence from the world until the cloud that had overcast the happiness of this nation was dispelled by his re-appearance. . . . The governor anxiously wished that he might long continue to illumine the world by his presence, and was hopeful that the friendship which had formerly subsisted between them would not be diminished. . . . ." The infant looked steadfastly at the British envoy, with the appearance of much attention, and nodded with repeated but slow motions of the head, as though he understood every word. He was silent and sedate, his whole attention was directed to the envoy, and he conducted himself with astonishing dignity and decorum. He was one of the handsomest children Captain Turner had ever seen, and he grew up to be an able and devout ruler, delighting the Tibetans with his presence for many years, and dying at a good old age.[3] He is described by Huc[4] as of fine majestic frame, and astonishing vigour for his advanced age, which was then about sixty.

---

[1] *Oriental Repertory*, ii., p. 145; and Markham, p. 208.

[2] On the 4th December, 1783.

[3] Turner's *Embassy*, etc. The new Tashi Lāma was installed in October, 1784, in the presence of the Dalai Lāma, the Chinese Minister or Amban, the Gesub Rimboc'e, and the heads of all the monastery in Tibet, as described by Purangir Gosain, the native agent of the Warren Hastings, M., lxxv.

[4] ii., 157.

The Mongolian hierarch at Urgya-Kuren, in the Khalka country, is called "His holy reverence," or *Je-tsun Dam-pa,*"[1] and is regarded as an incarnation of the celebrated historian Lāma, Tāranātha, who, it will be remembered, was of the Sa-kya sect, which had identified itself with Mongolian Lāmaism, having introduced the religion there and given the translations of the gospels. Urgya monastery was doubtless founded by the Sa-kya-pa. However this may be, on the development of the reincarnate Lāma theory, the Khalka[2] Mongols fixed upon Tāranātha as the source of the re-incarnations for their chief hierarch. And the Dalai Lāma, Ṅag-pa, who had climbed into power on the shoulders of the Mongols, had to accept the high position thus accorded to Tāranātha, whom he detested, but he, or one of his early successors, converted the monastery into a Ge-lug-pa institution.

The hierarch, Je-tsun Dam-pa, was the most powerful person in the whole of Mongolia[3] during the reign of the emperor Kang-hi (1662-1723), and had his headquarters at Koukou-Khoton, or "Blue town," beyond the bend of the Yellow river, when the Khalkas quarrelled with the Kalmuks or Sleuths and escaped into territory under Chinese protection. The Kalmuks demanded the delivery of Je-tsun Dam-pa and his brother, the prince Tuschetu-Khan, which of course the emperor refused, and sought the mediation of the Dalai Lāma. But the latter, or, rather, his regent (Tis-ri), for he had been defunct for seven years, to the emperor's surprise, advised the delivering up of these two princes, and such a decision was, perhaps, the first sign to him of the great fraud which was being enacted as Lhāsa. To make matters worse, when the emperor was warring with the Kalmuks "he paid a visit to Je-tsun Dam-pa, and owing to some fancied want of respect on the part of the holy man, one of the emperor's officers drew his sword and killed him. This violence caused a tumult, and soon afterwards it was announced that Je-tsun Dam-pa had reappeared among the Khalkas, who threatened to avenge his former death. The emperor engaged the diplomatic interposition of the Dalai

[1] rJe-btsun-gdam-pa.

[2] The Khalkas, so called after the Khalka river, are the representatives of the Mongol or Yuen dynasty of China, founded by Jingis and Kubilai Khan, and driven from the throne in 1368.—MARKH., p. xlix.

[3] KÖPPEN, ii., 178.

Lāma, who succeeded in pacifying the Khalkas. But it was arranged that the future births of the Je-tsun Dam-pa should be found in Tibet, so that the Khalkas might not again have a sympathizing fellow-countryman as their high-priest."[1]

His "re-incarnation" is now always found in central or western Tibet. The present one is said to have been born in the bazaar (S'ol) of Lhāsa city, and to be the eighth of the series. He is educated at the De-pung monastery as a Ge-lug-pa Lāma; but the present one was carried off, when four or five years of age, to Urga, accompanied by a Lāma of De-pung as tutor. A complete list of these hierarchs and fuller historical information in regard to them is much needed.[2]

The Sa-kya hierarchs, as we have seen, were once extremely powerful and almost *de facto* kings of Tibet. Although the Sa-kya hierarch is now eclipsed by the established church, he still retains the sympathy of the numerous adherents of the unreformed sects, and is now regarded by the Ñiṅ-ma-pa as their head and an incarnation of the Guru himself, and as such scarcely inferior to the Grand Lāma of Lhāsa. Sa-kya was founded, as we saw, by Kungah Ñiṅ-po, born in 1090 A.D., and became famous under Sa-kya Paṇḍita, born 1180, and his nephew was the first of the great hierarchs.

The list of the earlier Sa-kya hierarchs, whose most prosperous era was from 1270 to 1340, is as follows[3]:—

LIST OF SA-KYA HIERARCHS.

1. Sas-kya bsaṅ-po.
2. S'aṅ-btsun.
3. Ban-dKar-po.
4. Chyaṅ-rin bsKyos-pa.
5. Kun-gs'aṅ.
6. gB'aṅ-dbaṅ.
7. Chaṅ-rdor.
8. Aṅ-len.
9. Legs-pa-dpal.
10. Seṅ-ge-dpal.
11. 'Od-zer-dpal.
12. 'Od-ser-seṅ-ge.
13. Kun-rin.
14. Don-yod dpal.
15. Yon-btsun.
16. 'Od-ser Seṅ-ge II.
17. rGyal-va Saṅ-po.
18. Dbaṅ-p'yng-dpal.
19. bSod-Nam-dpal.
20. rGyab-va-Tsan-po II.
21. dBaṅ-btsun.

Its head Lāma is still called by the unreformed Lāmas "Sa-kya

[1] MARKHAM'S *Tibet*, xlix.

[2] For an account of the journey of the present hierarch from Lhāsa to Urga, see *Peking Gazette* for 1874, pp. 68, 74 and 124 (Shanghai abstract 1875). The new incarnation met by the Abbé Huc in 1844, journeying from Urga to Lhāsa appears to have been the seventh.

[3] Cf. also list by SANANG SETSEN, p. 121; CSOMA, *Gr.*, 186; KÖPPEN, ii., 105; SARAT, *J.A.S.B.*, 1881, p. 240.

Pan-ch'en."[1] The succession is hereditary; but between father and son intervenes the brother of the reigning Lāma and uncle of the successor, so as to secure an adult as holder of the headship.

The Bhotān hierarchy is still a strong one and combines the temporal rule of the country. It ousted all rival sects from the land, so that now it has its own sect, namely, the southern Duk-pa form of the Kar-gyu-pa. According to Mr. (Sir Ashley) Eden, the Bhotānese only overran the country about three centuries ago, displacing the then natives, who are said to have come originally from Koch Bihar. The invaders were Tibetan soldiers, over whom a Lāma named "Dupgani Sheptun" acquired paramount influence as Dharma Rāja. On his death the spirit of the Sheptun became incarnate in a child at Lhāsa, who was conveyed to Bhotān. When this child grew up he appointed a regent for temporal concerns, called Deb Rāja,[2] but this latter office seems to have lapsed long ago, and the temporal power is in the hands of the lay governors (Pen-lo) of the country.

The head Lāma is held to be re-incarnate, and is named Lāma Rin-po-ch'e, also "The religious king" or Dharma Rāja. His hat, as seen in the illustration at the head of this chapter,[3] bears the badge of cross thunderbolts, and is surmounted by a spiked thunderbolt, typical not only of his mystical creed, but also of the thunder dragon (Ḍug), which gives its name to his sect—the Dug-pa. His title, as engraved on his seal figured by Hooker,[4] describes him as "Chief of the Realm, Defender of the Faith, Equal to Sarasvati in learning, Chief of all the Buddhas, Head Expounder of the Sastras, Caster out of Devils, Most Learned in the Holy Laws, An Avatar of God, Absolver of Sins, and Head of the Best of all Religions."

LIST OF THE BHOTĀN HIERARCHS.

1. Ṅag-dbaṅ rnam rgyal bdud 'jom-rdorje.	7. Ṅag-dbaṅ ch'os kyi dbaṅ p'ug.
2. " " 'jig-med rtags-pa.	8. " " 'jig-med rtags-pa (second re-incarnation).
3. " " ch'os-kyi rgyal mtshan.	9. " " 'jig-med rtags norbu.
4. " " 'jig med dbaṅ po.	10. " " " " ch'os-rgyal—the present Great Bhotān Lama in 1892.
5. " " Shakya seṅ ge.	
6. " " 'jam dbyaṅs rgyal mts'an.	

[1] He is entitled by Turner (*op. cit.*, p. 315) "Gongoso Rimbochhe."

[2] Rept. cf. MARKH., p. lv.

[3] The figure is from a photo of a Bhotān Lāma, and the hat is that of the present (1893) Grand Lāma of Bhotān.

[4] *Himal. Jours*, i.

Each of these Grand Lāmas has a separate biography (or *nam-t'ar*). The first, who was a contemporary of the Grand Lāma Sonam Gya-tshô, seems to have been married; the rest are celibate. A celebrated Lāma of this Dug-pa sect was named Mi-pam ch'os-Kyi gyal-po.

The Dharma Rāja resides, at least in summer, at the fort of Ta-shi-ch'o. The palace is a large stone building, with the chief house seven storeys high, described and figured by Turner and others. Here live over five hundred monks.

Bogle describes the Lāma of his day as "a thin, sickly-looking man of about thirty-five years of age."[1]

He exercises, I am informed, some jurisdiction over Lāmas in Nepal, where his authority is officially recognized by the Gorkha government.

The number of the lesser spiritual chiefs held to be re-embodied Lāma saints is stated[2] to be one hundred and sixty, of which thirty are in Tibet (twelve being "Shaburuṅ"), nineteen in north Mongolia, fifty-seven in south Mongolia, thirty-five in Kokonor, five in Chiamdo and the Tibetan portion of Sze-ch'wan, and fourteen at Pekin. But this much under-estimates the number in Tibet.

Amongst the re-embodied Lāmas in western Tibet or Tsang are Seṅ-c'en-Rin-po-ch'e,[3] Yaṅzin Lho-pa, Billuṅ, Lô-ch'en, Kyī-zar, Tiṅki, De-ch'an Alig, Kaṅla, Koṅ (at Phagri). In Kham, Tu, Ch'amdo, Derge, etc.

The Lāmaist metropolitan at Pekin is called by the Tibetans "lC'aṅ-skya," and is considered an incarnation of Rol-pahī Dorje. His portrait is given in the annexed figure. He dates his spiritual descent from a dignitary who was called to Pekin during the reign

1 MARKH., p. 27.

2 In the Sheng Wu Ki, and registered by the Colonial Board at Pekin. (MAYER) *J.R.A.S.*, vi., p. 307.

3 The last re-incarnate Lāma bearing this title, and the tutor of the Tashi Grand Lāma, was beheaded about 1886 for harbouring surreptitiously Sarat C. Das, who is regarded as an English spy; and although the bodies of his predecessors were considered divine and are preserved in golden domes at Tashi-lhunpo, his headless trunk was thrown ignominiously into a river to the S.W. of Lhāsa, near the fort where he had been imprisoned. On account of his violent death, and under such circumstances, this re-incarnation is said to have ceased. From the glimpse got of him in Sarat's narrative and in his great popularity, he seems to have been a most amiable man.

of K'ang Hi, probably about 1690-1700 A.D., and entrusted with the emperor's confidence as his religious vicegerent for inner Mongolia.[1]

In Ladāk only four monasteries have resident re-incarnate Lāmas or *Ku-s'o*. Although they are of the red sect, these head Lāmas are said to be educated at Lhāsa. The present (1893) re-incarnate Lāma of Spitak, the seventeenth of the series, is thus described by Captain Ramsay.[2] "A youth, 26 years of age, who lately returned from Lhāsa, where he had been for 14 years. He was handsomely dressed in a robe made of a particular kind of dark golden-coloured and yellow embroidered China silk, which none but great personages are allowed to wear, and he had on Chinese long boots, which he did not remove when he entered the house. His head and face were closely shaved, and one arm was bare. On entering the room he bowed, and then presented the customary 'scarf of salutation,' which I accepted. He impressed me very favourably; his manner and general appearance was superior to anything I had seen among other Lāmas or people of Ladāk."

HEAD LĀMA OF PEKIN.[3]

In Sikhim, where few Lāmas are celibate and where the La-brang Lāma is the nominal head of the fraternity with the title of "Lord protector" (*s*Kyab *m*Gon), the fiction of re-incarnation was only practised in regard to the Pemiongchi and La-brang

[1] *Z.E.* 21, PAND., No. 53. [2] *Op. cit.*, p. 69. [3] After Grünwedel.

monasteries, but has ceased for several generations. In Sikhim, too, the same tendency to priest-kingship cropped out. Several of the Sikhim kings were also Lāmas; and when the king was not a monk, the Lāmas retained most of the temporal power in their hands; and the first king of Sikhim was nominated by the pioneer Lāmas; and the ancestor of the present dynasty, a descendant of the religious king, Thi-Sroṅ Detsan, one of the founders of Lāmaism, was canonized as an incarnation of the Buddhist god, Mañjuṣrī.

The female re-incarnation, the abbess of the monastery of the Yamdok lake, who is considered an embodiment of the goddess *Vajra varāhī*, or "The diamond sow," is thus described by Mr. Bogle[1]: "The mother went with me into the apartment of Durjay Paumo, who was attired in a gylong's dress, her arms bare from the shoulders, and sitting cross-legged upon a low cushion. She is also the daughter of the Lāma's (Tashi) brother, but by a different wife. She is about seven and twenty, with small Chinese features, delicate, though not regular fine eyes and teeth; her complexion fair, but wan and sickly; and an expression of languor and melancholy in her countenance, which I believe is occasioned by the joyless life that she leads. She wears her hair, a privilege granted to no other vestal I have seen; it is combed back without any ornament, and falls in tresses upon her shoulders. Her *Cha-wa* (touch), like the Lāmas', is supposed to convey a blessing, and I did not fail to receive it. Durjay Paumo spoke little. Dr. Hamilton, who cured her of a complaint she had long been subject to, used to be there almost every day."

Let us now look at the manner in which the new re-embodiments or re-births of the hierarchs are discovered. On the death of a re-incarnate Lāma his spirit is believed to flit into the soul of some unknown infant who is born a few days after the death of the Lāma. The mode of determining the child who has been so favoured is based upon the practice followed in regard to the Grand Lāma of Lhāsa, which we will now describe.

Sometimes the pontiff, before he dies, indicates the particular place and even the family in which he will be re-born, but the usual practice is to ascertain the names of all the likely male

[1] MARKH., p. 109.

infants who have been born under miraculous portents just after the death of the deceased Lāma, and with prayer and worship to ballot a selected list of names, which are written by a committee of Lāmas on slips of paper and put into a golden jug, and then amid constant prayer, usually by 117 selected pure Lāmas, to draw by lot in relays, and extending over 31 to 71 days, one of these, which is the name of the new incarnation. As, however, the Pekin

TESTING A CLAIMANT TO THE GRAND LĀMASHIP. [1]

court is believed to influence the selection under such circumstances, the state oracle of Nä-ch'uṅ has latterly superseded the old practice, and the present Grand Lāma was selected by this oracle. Lāma Ugyen Gya-tshô relates[2] that the present Nä-ch'uṅ oracle prophesied disaster in the shape of a monster appearing as the Dalai Lāma, if the old practice were continued. On the other hand he foretold that the present Dalai would be found by a pious monk in person, and that his discovery would be accompanied with "horse neighings." The "pious monk" proved to be the head Lāma of Gāh-ldan monastery, who was sent by the oracle to Chukor-

[1] After Huc.

[2] *Loc. cit.*, para. 59; cf. also Huc, ii., 197.

gye, where he dreamed that he was to look in the lake called Lha-moi-lamtsho for the future Dalai. He looked, and it is said that, pictured in the bosom of the lake, he saw the infant Dalai Lāma and his parents, with the house where he was born, and that at that instant his horse neighed. Then the monk went in search of the real child, and found him in Kongtoi, in the house of poor but respectable people, and recognized him as the child seen in the lake. After the boy (then a year old) had passed the usual ordeal required of infants to test their power to recognize the property of the previous Dalai Lāma, he was elected as spiritual head of Tibet.

These infant candidates, who, on account of their remarkable intelligence, or certain miraculous signs,[1] have been selected from among the many applicants put forward by parents for this, the highest position in the land, may be born anywhere in Tibet.[2] They are subjected to a solemn test by a court composed of the chief Tibetan re-incarnate Lāmas, the great lay officers of state, and the Chinese minister or Amban. The infants are confronted with a duplicate collection of rosaries, dorjes, etc., and that one particular child who recognizes the properties of the deceased Lāma is believed to be the real re-embodiment.

To ensure accuracy the names are written as aforesaid, and each slip encased in a roll of paste and put in a vase, and, after prayer, they are formally drawn by lot in front of the image of the emperor of China,[3] and the Chinese minister, the Amban, unrolls the paste and reads out the name of the elect, who is then hailed, as the great God Avalokita incarnate, hence to rule over Tibet. An intimation of the event is sent to the emperor, and it is duly acknowledged by him with much formality, and the enthronement and ordination are all duly recorded in like manner.

Interesting details of the ceremonies as well as of the prominent part played by China in regulating the pontifical succession, have

[1] Circumstantial stories are told of such applicants to the effect, that when only a few months old the infants have obtained the power of speech for a few moments and informed their parents that the Lāmas have left Potala to come and claim them.

[2] The distant villages of Gada, south-west of Darchhendo (Ta-chhien Lu) and Lithang, have each produced a Dalai Lāma.

[3] The emperor Pure Kien Lung, who died 1796, since his final subjugation of Tibet, has continued to receive homage even posthumously as sovereign of the country. (MARCO P., *loc. cit., L.*, p. 290.)

been supplied by Mr. Mayers[1] from the original Chinese document of Meng Pao, the senior Amban at Lhāsa, and from which the following historic extract is made by way of illustration :—

I. Memorial drawn up on the 9th day of the 12th month of the 20th year of Tao Kwang (January 30th, 1841), reporting that, on instituting an investigation among young children for the embodiment of Dalai Lāma, miraculous signs, of undoubted authenticity, have been verified, which is laid in a respectful memorial before the Sacred Glance.

In the matter of the appearance of the embodiment of the Dalai Lāma, it has already been reported to your majesty that a communication had been received from Kè-lê-tan-si-leu-t'u-sa-ma-ti Bakhshi reporting the dispatch of natives in positions of dignity to inquire into the circumstances with reference to four young children born of Tibetan parents, respectively at Sang-ang-k'iüh-tsung in Tibet, the tribalty of K'ung-sa within the jurisdiction of Ta-tsien-lu in Sze-ch'wan, and [two] other places. The chancellor has now made a further report, stating that in the case of each of the four children miraculous signs have been shown, and that bonds of attestation have been drawn up in due form on the part of members of both the priesthood and laity of the Tibetans. He annexes a detailed statement in relation to this matter; and on receipt of this communication your Majesty's servants have to observe that on the previous occasion, when the embodiment of the tenth Dalai Lāma entered the world, three children were discovered [whose names] were placed in the urn for decision by lot. As the chancellor now writes that each of the four children discovered by the *Khan-pu* on this occasion has been attended by auspicious and encouraging omens, we do not presume to arrogate to ourselves the choice of any one of their number, but, as regards the whole four, have on the one hand communicated in a Tibetan dispatch with the chancellor respecting the two children born within the territory of Tibet, and as regards the two children born within the jurisdiction of the province of Sze-ch'wan, have addressed a communication to the viceroy of that province calling upon them respectively to require the parents and tutors of the children in question to bring the latter to Anterior Tibet. On this being done, your majesty's servants, in accordance with the existing rules, will institute a careful examination in person, conjointly with the Panshen Erdeni and the chancellor, and will call upon the children to recognize articles heretofore in use by the Dalai Lāma; after which your servants will proceed with scrupulous care to take measures for inscribing their names on slips to be placed in the urn, and for the celebration of mass and drawing the lots in public. So soon as the individual shall have been ascertained by lot, your servants will forward a further report for your majesty's information and commands. They now present for imperial perusal a translation of the detailed state-

[1] W. F. Mayer, *Illustrations of the Lāmaist System in Tibet*, drawn from Chinese Sources, *J.R.A.S.*, vi. (1872), p. 284 *seq.*

ment of the miraculous signs attending the children that were discovered on inquiry.

[Enclosure.]

Detailed statement of the miraculous signs attending upon four children, drawn up for his majesty's perusal from the despatch of the chancellor reporting the same:—

1. A-chu-cho-ma, the wife of the Tibetan named Kung-pu-tan-tsêng, living at the Pan-jê-chung post-station in Sang-ang-k'iüh-tsung, gave birth to a son on the 13th day of the 11th month of the year *Ki-hai* (19th December, 1839), upon a report concerning which having been received from the local headmen, the chancellor despatched Tsze-fêng-choni-'rh and others to make inquiry. It was thereupon ascertained that on the night before the said female gave birth to her child, a brilliant radiance of many colours was manifested in the air, subsequently to which the spring-water in the well of the temple court-yard changed to a milk-white colour. Seven days afterwards, there suddenly appeared upon the rock, behind the post-station, the light of a flame, which shone for a length of time. Crowds of people hastened to witness it, when, however, no single trace of fire remained, but upon the rock there was manifested an image of Kwan Yin (Avalokita) and the characters of Na-mo O-mi-to-Fo (Amitabha), together with the imprint of footsteps. On the night when the child was born, the sound of music was heard, and milk dropped upon the pillars of the house. When the commissioners instituted their inquiry, they found the child sitting cross-legged in a dignified attitude, seeming able to recognize them, and showing not the slightest timidity. They placed a rosary in the child's hands, whereupon he appeared as though reciting sentences from the Sūtra of Amita Buddha. In addressing his mother he pronounced the word *A-mā* with perfect distinctness. His features were comely and well-formed, and his expression bright and intellectual, in a degree superior to that of ordinary children.

In addition to the foregoing report, certificates by the local headmen and members of the priesthood and laity, solemnly attesting personal knowledge of the facts therein set forth, were appended, and were transmitted after authentication by the chancellor to ourselves, etc., etc.

. . . .

II. Memorial drawn up on the 8th day of the 6th month of the 21st year of Tao Kwang (25th July, 1841), reporting the verification of the child in whom the re-embodiment of the Dalai Lāma has appeared, the drawing of lots in accordance with the existing rule, and the fact that the entire population of Tibet, both clergy and laity, are penetrated with feelings of gratitude and satisfaction: upon the memorial bringing which to the imperial knowledge the Sacred Glance is reverently besought.

Your servants have already memorialized reporting that the embodiment of the Dalai Lāma having made its appearance, a day had been fixed for the drawing of lots; and they have now to state that they subsequently received a letter from the chancellor to the effect that the children had successively arrived and had all been lodged in the Sangha monastery at Tê K'ing, to the eastward of Lassa, whereupon he had appointed the 21st day of the 5th month for proceeding to put them to the proof. On that day, accordingly, your servants proceeded to the Sangha monastery in company with the Panshen Erdeni, the chancellor, and all the *hut'ukht'u, khan-pu, ko-pu-lun,* etc., when it was ascertained by a careful inquiry into each individual case that the two children born respectively at Sang-ang-k'üh-tsung and at La-kia-jih-wa in Tibet are both aged three years, and the two children born respectively in the tribalty of K'ung-sa in the district of Ta-tsien-lu and at the Tai Ning monastery are both aged four years—that their personal appearance is uniformly symmetrical and proper, and that all alike display an elevated demeanour. Hereupon the Panshen Erdeni and his associates laid before them for recognition the image of Buddha worshipped by the late Dalai Lāma, together with the bell-clapper, swinging drum, and other like articles used by him, all in duplicate, the genuine objects being accompanied by imitations. The children showed themselves capable of recognizing each individual article, without hesitation, in presence of the assembled clergy and people, who, as they crowded around to behold the sight, gave vent aloud to their admiration of the prodigy.

A despatch was subsequently received from the chancellor to the effect that the supernatural intelligence of the four children having been tested by joint investigation, and having been authenticated in the hearing and before the eyes of all, he would request that the names be placed in the urn and the lot be drawn on the 25th day of the 5th month; in addition to which, he forwarded a list of the names bestowed in infancy on the four children and of the names of their fathers. Your servants having in reply assented to the proposed arrangement, masses were performed during seven days preceding the date in question by the *hut'ukht'u* and Lāmas, of mount Pótala and the various monasteries; and, on the appointed day, the Panshen Erdeni, the chancellor, and their associates, followed by the entire body of Lāmas, chanted a mass before the sacred effigy of your majesty's exalted ancestor, the emperor Pure, offering up prayers subsequently in devout silence. On the 25th day of the 5th month your servants reverently proceeded to mount Pótala, and placed the golden vase with due devotion upon a yellow altar before the sacred effigy. After offering incense and performing homage with nine prostrations, they inscribed upon the slips, in Chinese and Tibetan characters, the infant-names of the children and the names of their fathers, which they exhibited for the inspection of the respective relatives and tutors, and of the assembled Lāmas. This having been done, your servant, Haip'u, recited a chapter from the scriptures in unison with the Panshen Erdeni and the other [ecclesiastics], in presence of the multitude, and, reverently sealing up the inscribed slips, deposited them within the vase. The slips being small and the urn deep, nothing was wanting to secure perfect inviolability. After the further recital of a chapter by the Panshen Erdeni and his associates, your servant, Mêng Pao, inserting his hand within the urn upon the altar, turned the slips over and over, several times, and reverently proceeded to draw forth one of their number, which he inspected in concert with the children's relatives and tutors and the assembled Lāmas. The inscription upon the slip was as follows: "The son of Tsê-wang-têng-chu, Tibetan, from the Tai Ning monastery. Infant-name, Na-mu-kio-mu-to-urh-tsi. Present age, four years." The remaining slips having been drawn out and inspected publicly, the Penshen Erdeni, the chancellor, with the greater and lesser *hut'ukht'u* and all the attendant Lāmas, exclaimed unanimously with unfeigned delight and gladsomeness that "by the favour of his imperial majesty, who has given advancement to the cause of the Yellow Church, the established rule has now been complied with for ascertaining by lot the embodiment of the Dalai Lāma, and the lot having now fallen upon this child—who, the son of a poor Tibetan fuel-seller, has manifested prodigies of intelligence, abundantly satisfying the aspirations of the multitude—it is placed beyond a doubt that the actual and genuine re-embodiment of the Dalai Lāma has appeared in the world, and the Yellow Church has a ruler for its governance. The minds of the people are gladdened and at rest, and the reverential gratitude that inspires us humble priests is inexhaustible." After this they performed with the utmost devotion the homage of nine prostrations in the direction of your majesty's abode, expressing their reverential acknowledgments of the celestial favour. Your servants observed with careful attention that the gratitude not alone of the Panshen Erdeni and his attendant ecclesiastics proceeded from the most sincere feelings, but also that the entire population of Lessa, both clergy and laity, united in the demonstration by raising their hands to their foreheads in a universal feeling of profound satisfaction.

The infant is taken to Lhāsa at such an early age that his mother, who may belong to the poorest peasant class,[1] necessarily accompanies him in order to suckle him, but being debarred from the sacred precincts of Potala on account of her sex, she is lodged in the lay town in the vicinity, and her son temporarily at the monastic palace of Ri-gyal Phodaṅ,[2] where she is permitted to visit her son only between the hours of 9 a.m. and 4 p.m. She, together with her husband, is given an official residence for life in a palace about a mile to the west of Potala and on the way to Depung, and the father usually receives the rank of *Kung*, said to be the highest of the five ranks of Chinese nobility.

1 As, for example, in the case of the eleventh Grand Lāma, whose father was a poor fuel-seller.

2 Another account (MAYER, *loc. cit.*, p. 295) states that he is kept at the "Jih-kia" monastery to the east of Lhāsa, or "Chih-ta-wang-pu."

At the age of four the child assumes the monkish garb and tonsure, and receives a religious name, and is duly enthroned at Potala in great state and under Chinese auspices, as shown from the annexed state paper:—

"Memorial dated the 18th day of the 4th month of the 22nd year of Tao Kwang (27th May, 1842), reporting the conclusion of the ceremony of enthronement of the embodiment of the Dalai Lāma. . . . . .

"In obedience to these commands, Your servants proceeded on the 13th day of the 4th month in company with the *Chang-Chia Hut'ukht'u* (the Pekin metropolitan) and the chancellor, followed by their subordinate fuuctionaries, the *hut'ukht'u*, *Lāmas*, and Tibetan officials, to the monastery on mount Jih-kia, for the purpose of escorting the Dalai Lāma's embodiment down the mountain to the town of Chih-ta-hwang-pu, on the east of Lassa, where his abode was temporarily established. Your servants, in respectful conformity with the rules for attendance upon the Dalai Lāma, appointed detachments of the Chinese garrison troops to form an encampment, and to discharge the duty of body-guards during the two days he remained there. On the 15th, your servants escorted the embodiment to the monastery at mount Pótala, where reverent prostrations were performed, and the ceremonial observances were fulfilled before the sacred effigy of your majesty's elevated ancestor, the emperor Pure. On the 16th, your servants reverently took the golden scroll containing the mandate bestowed by your majesty upon the Dalai Lāma's embodiment, together with the sable cape, the coral court rosary, etc., and the sum of ten thousand taels in silver, being your majesty's donations, which they caused to be conveyed upon yellow platforms to the monastery at mount Pótala, and deposited with devout care in due order in the hall called Ta Tu Kang. The couch and pillows were then arranged upon the divan; and on the arrival of the Dalai Lāma's embodiment in the hall, your servants and the secretary of the *Chang-chia Hut'ukht'u*, reverently read out the golden scroll, embodying your majesty's mandate, to the perusal of which the embodiment listened in a kneeling posture, facing toward the east. After the reading was concluded, he received with veneration the imperial gifts, and performed the ceremonial of three genuflections and nine prostrations in the direction of the imperial abode, thus testifying his respectful gratitude for the celestial favours. Having been invested with the garments conferred by your majesty, the embodiment was supported to his seat upon the throne; whereupon the chancellor, at the head of the Tibetan priesthood, intoned a chant of Dhāraṇī formulas, invoking auspicious fortune. All the *hut'ukht'u* and Lāmas having performed obeisances, a great banquet was opened, and the ceremonial of enthronement was thus brought to a close. The day was attended by the utmost fine weather, and everything passed off auspiciously and well, to the universal delight of the entire body of clergy and laity of Lassa. This we accordingly bring to your majesty's knowledge; and in addition we have to state, that as the embodiment of the Dalai Lāma has now been enthroned, it is proper, in conformity with the existing rules, to cease henceforth from using the word 'embodiment.' This we accordingly append, and respectfully bring before your majesty's notice."[1]

He is now admitted as a novice to the Nam-gyal monastery of Potala, and his education is entrusted to a special preceptor and assistants learned in the scriptures and of unblemished character.[2]

At the age of eight he is ordained a full monk and abbot of the Nam-gyal convent and head of the Lāmaist church.

The Dalai Lāma is, as regards temporal rule, a minor till he reaches the age of eighteen, and during his minority a regent carries on the duties of temporal government. And the frequency with which the Dalai Lāma has died before attaining his majority gives some support to the belief that the regents are privy to his premature death; and the Chinese government are usually credited with supporting such proceedings for political purposes.

On the death of a re-incarnate Lāma, his body is preserved. The tombs of the Dalai and Pan-ch'en Lāmas form conspicuous gilt monuments, sometimes as many as seven storeys high, named Ku-tuṅ,[3] at Potala and Tashi-lhunpo. The holiness of such a Lāma is estimated in proportion to the shrinkage of his body after death.

The temporal rule of Tibet is vested in a Lāma who has the title of "king." For when Ṅag-waṅ acquired the temporal power he retained this title for one of his agents, also called "The regent,"[4] and "Protector of the earth,"[5] and "Governor,"[6] and by the Mongols *Nomen-Khan*.

A regent is necessary to conduct the temporal government, especially under the system of papal succession by re-births, where the new Dalai Lāma does not reach his majority and nominal succession to temporal rule till his eighteenth year. In order to avoid plotting against the hierarchs, Ṅag-waṅ ruled that the regent must be a Lāma, and he restricted this office to the head Lāmas of the monastic palaces or *Ling* of Lhāsa, named Tan-gye-ling,[7] Kun-de-ling,[8] Ts'e-ch'og-ling,[9] and Ts'amo-ling,[10] whom, he alleged, by a

[1] MAYER, *loc. cit.*, p. 296.

[2] The preceptor of the tenth and eleventh Grand Lāmas was "Kia-mu-pa-le-i-hi-tan-peï-gyam-tsô." MAYER, *loc cit.*

[3] sku *m*dun. [4] Gyal-tshab. [5] Sa-Kyoṅ. [6] de-sid.

[7] bsTan-rgyas-gliṅ. [8] Kun-'dus gliṅ [9] Tše-mch'og gliṅ.

[10] Ts'a-mo-gliṅ. A Lāma of this monastic palace and a member of Sera, became the celebrated regent Tsha-tur numa-hang (?"Nomen Khan").

polite fiction, to be re-embodiments of the spirits of the four most celebrated ministers of the monarchical period. Thus the spirit of king Sroṅ Tsan Gampo's minister Lon-po Gar is believed to be incarnate in the Lāma of Tan-gye-ling. The office when falling vacant through death (or deposition) passes *cæteris paribus* to the surviving senior of those Lings. The present regent (1893) is the Kun-de-ling Lāma. The regent is assisted in the government[1] by four ministers called *Kā-lon*,[2] who were formerly all laymen, but now some of them are being replaced by Lāmas; also secretaries (*Kā-duṅ*) and district magistrates (Joṅ-pön). And the two Chinese political residents, or Ambans,[3] have administrative as well as consulting functions.

With such large bodies of monks comprising so many fanatical elements, and not at all subject to the civil authorities, who, indeed, possess almost no police, it is not surprising that *fracas* are frequent, and bloody feuds between rival monasteries occasionally happen. Every monastery has an armoury, and in the minor quarrels the lusty young monks wield their heavy iron pencases with serious and even fatal effect.

Since the temporal power passed into the hands of the Lāmas, the Tibetans who, in Sroṅ Tsan Gampo's day, were a vigorous and aggressive nation, have steadily lost ground, and have been ousted from Yunnan and their vast possessions in eastern Tibet, Amdô, etc., and are now hemmed in by the Chinese into the more inhospitable tracts.

1 "De-ba zhuṅ."

2 bKah-blon.

3 "*Amban*" is not Chinese. It is probably Manchu or Mongolian, cf. Rock., *L.*, 51. The resident imperial minister of Tibet is colloquially called Chu-tsaṅ ṭu-chön, and he is always a Manchu, that is, of the ruling race.

MONASTERY OF CHOGORTAN.[1]

XI.

MONASTERIES.

ISOLATION from the world has always been a desideratum of Buddhist monks; not as penance, but merely to escape temptations, and favour meditation. The monastery is named in Tibetan *Gön-pa*,[2] vulgarly *Göm-pa*, or "a solitary place" or hermitage; and most monasteries are situated, if not actually in solitary places, at least some distance off from villages, while around others which were originally hermitages villages have grown up later.

The extreme isolation of some of the Tibetan cloisters has its

[1] After Huc.

[2] *d*gon-pa. The title C'og-sde, or *Choi-de*, a "religious place," is especially applied to temple-monasteries within a village or town. "Liṅ," or "continent," is applied to the four greatest monasteries of the established church especially associated with the temporal government, and is evidently suggested by the four great fabulous continents of the world. gT'sug-lag-k'aṅ' is an academy, though it is used for temples frequently.

counterpart in Europe in the alpine monasteries amid the everlasting snows. Some of them are for the greater part of the year quite cut off from the outer world, and at favourable times only reachable by dangerous paths, so that their solitude is seldom broken by visitors. The monastery of Kye-lang in Little Tibet stands on an isolated spur about 12,000 feet above the sea, and is approached over glaciers, so that sometimes its votaries are buried under avalanches. And the site is usually commanding and picturesque. Shergol in Ladāk, like so many monasteries in central Tibet, is set on the face of a cliff. It is "carved out of a honeycombed cliff, forming, with some other cliffs of the same description, a giant flight of stairs on the slope of a bleak mountain of loose stones. The *Gömpa* itself is painted white, with bands of bright colour on the projecting wooden gallery, so that it stands out distinctly against the darker rocks. There is not a sign of vegetation near—all rouud is a dreary waste of stone.[1]

Such remote and almost inaccessible sites for many of the convents renders mendicancy impossible; but begging-with-the-bowl never seems to have been a feature of Lāmaism, even when the monastery adjoined a town or village.

Several monasteries, especially of the Kar-gyu sect, are called "caves" (hermitages) (or *tak-p'u*), although any caves which may exist accommodate only a very small proportion of the residents of the cloister so named. Yet many gömpas, it is reported, passed through the state of cave-residence as a stage in their career. Firstly a solitary site with caves was selected, and when the monks by extra zeal and piety had acquired sufficient funds and influence, then they built a monastery in the neighbourhood. While, if the venture were not financially successful, the hermitage remained in the cave. One of these struggling cave-hermitages exists at Ri-kyi-sum near Pedong, in British Bhotān. Such caves, as a rule, are natural caverns, wholly unadorned by art, and are specially tenanted by the wandering ascetics named Yogācārya and *Zi-jépa.*[2]

---

[1] Mr. KNIGHT, *loc. cit.*, p. 127, where a picture of the monastery also is given.

[2] Under this heading come the four great caves of Sikhim hallowed as the traditional abodes of St. Padma and Lhatsün Ch'embo, and now the objects of pilgrimage even to Lāmas from Tibet. These four caves are distinguished according to the four cardinal points, viz.:—

The NORTH *Lha-ri ñiṅ p'u*, or "the old cave of God's hill." It is situated about

The site occupied by the monastery is usually commanding and often picturesque. It should have a free outlook to the east to catch the first rays of the rising sun; and it should be built in the long axis of the hill; and it is desirable to have a lake in front, even though it be several miles distant. These latter two conditions are expressed in the couplet :—

> "Back to the hill-rock,
> And front to the tarn."[1]

The door of the assembly room and temple is *cæteris paribus* built to face eastwards. The next best direction is south-east, and then south. If a stream directly drains the site or is visible a short way below, then the site is considered bad, as the virtue of the place escapes by the stream. In such a case the chief entrance is made in another direction. A waterfall, however, is of very good omen, and if one is visible in the neighbourhood, the entrance is made in that direction, should it not be too far removed from the east.

The name of the monastery is usually of a religious nature, ideal or mystic, or, like De-pung, borrowed from the name of a celebrated Indian monastery; but others are merely place-names which are often descriptive of the site,[2] thus :—

TASHI-LHUN-PO, "The mass of glory."
SA-SKYA, the tawny soil.
MIN-DOL-LIṄ, "The place of perfect emancipation."
The "HĪMIS," monastery in Ladāk is called "The support of the meaning of Buddha's precepts."[3]

three days' journey to the north of Tashiding, along a most difficult path. This is the most holy of the series.

The SOUTH *Kah-do saṅ p'u*, or "cave of the occult fairies." Here it is said is a hot spring, and on the rock are many footprints ascribed to the fairies.

The EAST s*Bäs p'u*, or "secret cave." It lies between the Tendong and Mainom mountains, about five miles from Yangang. It is a vast cavern reputed to extend by a bifurcation to both Tendong and Mainom. People go in with torches about a quater of a mile. Its height varies from five feet to one hundred or two hundred feet.

The WEST b*De-ch'en p'u*, or "cave of Great Happiness." It is in the snow near Jongri, and only reachable in the autumn.

1 rgyab ri brag daṅ mdun ri mts'o.

2 See my "Place, River and Mountain Names of Sikhim," *etc.*, *J.A.S.B.*, 1891.

3 SCHLAG., 179.

SAṄ-ṄA-CHÖ-LIṄ (*Ang.*, Sangachiling) gsan, secret or occult, + snags, spell or magic + *c'*os religion + glin, a place. "The place of the occult mystic religion." A catholic Buddhist monastery open to all classes, including deformed persons, nuns, Lepchas and Limbus.

PADMA-YAṄ-TSE (*Ang.*, Pemiongchi) = *padma* (*pr.* "päma") a lotus + *yaṅ*, perfect or pure + r*tse*, the highest "the monastery of the sublime perfect lotus (-born one, *i.e.*, *Padma-sambhava*)." A monastery professing, we believe, only well-born, celibate, and undeformed monks, and especially associated with St. Padma, who is worshipped here.

TA-KA TASHI-DIṄ (*Ang.*, Tashiding) = *brag* (= tag,) a rock + d*kar*, white + bkra-sis (*pr.* tá shi) glory + l*ding*, a soaring up or elevation. The original name is likely to have been 'bring, pronounced "ding," and meaning the middle, with reference to its romantically elevated site between two great rivers at their junction. "The gömpa of the elevated glorious white rock." The site, a bold high promontory at the junction of and between the Great Rangīt and Ratong rivers, is believed to have been miraculously raised up by St. Padma, and amongst other traces a broad longitudinal white streak in the rock is pointed out as being the shadow of that saint.

PHO-DAṄ (*Ang.*, Fadung) = *p'o-*l*daṅ*, a sloping ridge ; such is the site of this gömpa and the usual spelling of the name. As, however, this is the "chapel royal" of the rāja, it seems possible that the name may be *p'o-bran* (*pr.* p'o-dan) = palace, "the gömpa of the palace."

LA-BRAṄ = b*la*, a contraction of Lāma or high-priest + *braṅ*, a dwelling. Here resides the hierarch or chief Lāma.

[*N.B.*—This is one of the very few words in which *br* is literally pronounced as spelt.]

DORJE-LIṄ (*Ang.*, Darjeeling) = r*dô-rje* "the precious stone" or ecclesiastical sceptre, emblematic of the thunder-bolt of Sakra (Indra or Jupiter) + *gliṅ*, a place. The monastery from which Darjīling takes its name, and the ruins of which are still visible on observatory-hill, was a branch of the Dorjeling, usually curtailed into Dô-ling (*Ang.*, Dalling) monastery in native Sikhim; and to distinguish it from its parent monastery, it was termed *Ank-dü* Dorje-ling (db*ang*, power + b*dus*, accumulated or concentrated) on account of its excellent situation, and powerful possibilities.

DE-T'AṄ = *De*, a kind of tree (*Daphne papyraceae*, Wall.), from the bark of which ropes and paper are made + *t'aṅ*, a meadow = "the gömpa of the *De* meadow." Here these trees are abundant.

RI-GÖN (*Ang.*, Ringim = (*ri* + d*gon*, a hermitage = "the hermitage hill." It is situated near the top of the hill.

TÔ-LUṄ = r*do*, a stone + *luṅ*, a valley. This valley is remarkably rocky, and avalanches of stones are frequent.

EN-CE = dben (*pr.* en), a solitary place + lc'e, a tongue. A monastery on a tongue-shaped spur.

DUB-DE = sg*rub* (*pr.* "dub"), a hermit's cell + s*de*, a place. "The place of the hermit's cell"—the oldest monastery in Sikhim, founded by the pioneer missionary Lha-tsün Ch en-bo.

P'EN-ZAṄ = *p'an* bliss or profit + bz*aṅ*, excellent. The monastery of "excellent bliss."

KA-CÔ-PAL-RI (*Ang.* Ketsuperi) = m*k'ā*, heaven + s*pyo*d (*pr.* chö) to accomplish or reach + d*pal*, noble + *ri* = the mona·tery of "the noble mountain of the Garuḍa (a messenger of the gods)" or "of reaching heaven."

MA-ṆI = mā-nī, a tablet inscribed with "Om máni, etc.," a Mendoṅ. "The gömpa of the Mendoṅ"; here the gömpa was erected near an old mendong.

SE-NÖN = *Se*, a sloping ridge + *nön*, depressed. It is situated on a depressed sloping ridge; and is also spelt g*zi*gs (*pr.* zī), a see-er or beholder, + m*nön*, to suppress; and in this regard it is alleged that here St. Padma-sambhava beheld the local demons underneath and kept them under.

YAṄ-GAṄ = *yaṅ*, perfect, also lucky + s*gaṅ*, a ridge. "The monastery of the lucky ridge."

LHUN-TSE = l*hun*, lofty + r*tse*, summit. "The monastery of the lofty summit."

NAM-TSE = r*nam*, a division or district + r*tse*. "Lofty division" one of the subdivisions of native Sikhim, on the flank of Tendong. It is probable that this is a Lepcha name from *tsü* = "Seat of government," as the site is a very old Lepcha one.

TSUN-T'AṄ (*Ang.*, Cheungtham) = b*tsun*, a queen; also "respected one," *i.e.*, a Lāma or monk; also marriage + *thaṅ*, a meadow. This gömpa is situated overlooking a meadow at the junction of the Lachhen and Lachhung rivers. It may mean "the meadow of marriage (of the two rivers)," or "the meadow of the Lāmas," or "the meadow of Our Lady"—its full name as found in manuscript being "b*tsun-mo rin-chen t'aṅ*," implies that the Lāmas derive its name from "the precious Lady (Dorje-p'ag-mo)" whose image is prominently displayed within the gömpa.

RAB-LIṄ (*Ang.*, Rawling) = *rab*, excellent or high + g*liṅ*, a place. This monastery is situated on a high cliffy ridge.

NUB-LIṄ (*Ang.*, Nobling) = *nub*, the west + g*liṅ* = "The gömpa of the western place or country." It lies on the western border of Sikhim.

DE-KYI-LIṄ (*Ang*, Dikiling) = b*de-skyi*d, happiness + g*liṅ* = "The place of Happiness." It is a rich arable site with the beer-millet (*murwa*) cultivation.

The site chosen for a monastery must be consecrated before any building is begun. A chapter of Lāmas is held, and the tutelary deity is invoked to protect the proposed building against all injury of men and demons. At the ceremony of laying the first stone prayers are recited, and charms, together with certain forms of benediction (Tashi-tsig jod), together with relics, are deposited in a hollow stone.[1] And other rites are done. And in repairing a sacred building somewhat similar services are performed.

The size of the Tibetan monasteries is sometimes immense, several containing from 3,000 to 10,000 monks, in this the most priest-ridden country in the world. The larger monasteries are like small towns, as seen in the original drawing of Tashi-lhunpo here given, with long streets of cells, two or three storeys high, and usually surrounding small courtyards which generally contain a shrine in the centre. The chief building is "The assembly hall," which, however, is practically a temple, and is considered under that head.

There are always small halls for teaching purposes, as the monasteries serve also as colleges. But these colleges are for the clergy alone, as Lāmas, unlike Burmese monks, are not the schoolmasters of the people. They teach only those who enter the order. And the lay populace have to be content with the poor tuition obtainable in a few schools (Lob-ta) conducted by laymen.

The architecture seems to have preserved much of the mediæval Indian style. Mr. Fergusson shows[2] that Nepal, in its architecture as well as ethnologically, presents us with a microcosm of India as it was in the seventh century, when Hiuen Tsiang visited it; and that the Sikhim monasteries show a perseverance in the employment of sloping jambs (as in the Tashiding doorway),[3] as used two thousand years ago in the Behar and early western caves; and the porch of the temple at Pemiongchi shows the form of roof which we are familiar with in the rock examples of India.

The architecture of the monastery resembles that of the houses of the wealthy Tibetans, and is often ostentatious. It has been described in some detail by Schlagintweit, Huc, Rockhill,[4] etc., as regards Tibet, and by General Cunningham and Mr. Conway as regards the large monasteries of Ladāk. The monasteries in Sikhim are mean and almost devoid of any artistic interest.

---

[1] Schlag., 178, who there translates the historical document on the founding of Himis; Csoma's *An.*, p. 503; Cunningham's *Ladāk*, 309.

[2] *Hist. Ind. and Eastn. Arch.*, p. 299, *et seq.*

[3] Figured by Hooker, *Him. Jour.*

[4] See also detailed description of the houses of the Lāmas of Kumbum in *Land of the Lāmas*, p. 65.

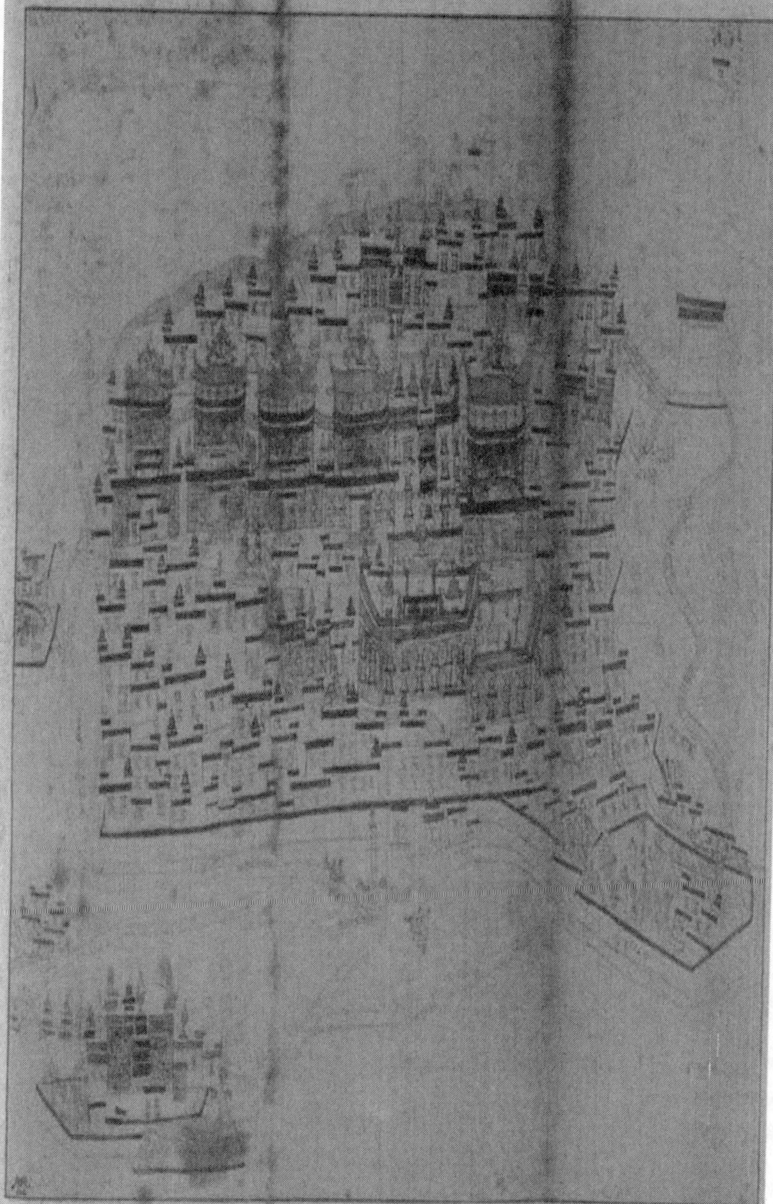

TASHI-LHUNPO MONASTERY.
(From a native drawing.)

[To face p. 260]

As wood is scarce in Tibet most of the monasteries are built of stone or sun-dried bricks. Most have flat roofs, some are in the Chinese style, and most are surmounted by the cylinders of yak-hair cloth crossed by a few white ribbons at right angles to each other, and topped by a crescent and spear, as in figures, and a curtain of yak-hair cloth bearing similar stripes in the form of a Latin cross closes the windows. In the outer Himalayas the cells and dormitories and other buildings cluster round the temple. And in the temple-monasteries, the ground floor is without windows and is generally used as a storehouse, and the upper storeys are reached by a staircase or an inclined beam on which notches are cut for steps; and the scanty furniture is of the plainest.

The well-known Indian name of a Buddhist monastery, namely, Ārāma, or Saṅghārāma ("the resting-place of the clergy"), more strictly applied to the grove in which the monastery was situated, is applied in Tibet, which is almost destitute of groves, to the *auditory* or *library* of the monastery.[1]

CH'ORTEN AND MENDOṄ IN LADĀK.[2]

Lining the approaches to the monastery are rows of tall

[1] Cf., JAESCH., *D.*, 4.

[2] After Mr. Knight.

"prayer"-flags, and several large funereal monuments—*Ch'orten* and long wall-like *Mendoṅ* monuments.

The *Ch'ortens*,[1] literally "receptacle for offerings,"[2] are usually solid conical masonry structures, corresponding to the Caityas and Stūpas or "Topes" of Indian Buddhism, and originally intended as relic-holders; they are now mostly erected as cenotaphs in memory of Buddha or of canonized saints; and they present a suggestively funereal appearance. Some commemorate the visits of Lāmaist saints; and miniature ones of metal, wood, or clay often adorn the altar, and sometimes contain relics.

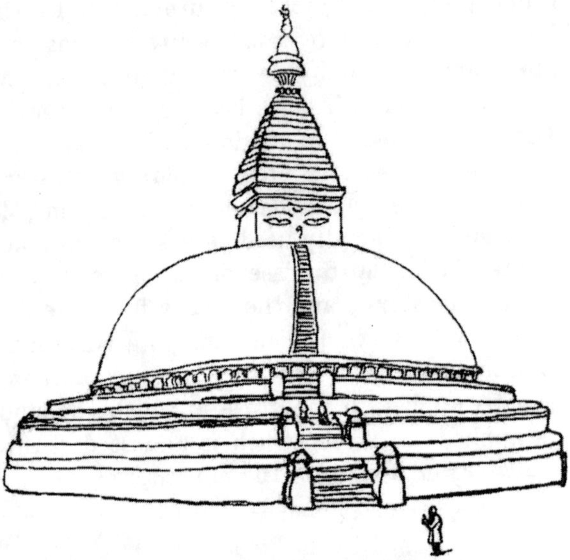

FUNEREAL BUDDHIST MONUMENT
(A Ch'orten *Stūpa* or "Tope").

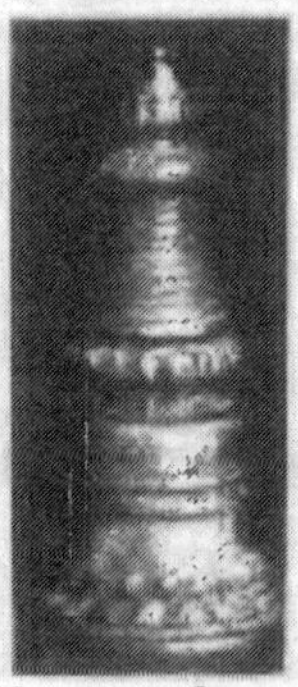

MEDIÆVAL INDIAN BRAZEN CAITYA.
(from Tibet.)

The original form of the Caitya, or Stūpa,[3] was a simple and massive hemisphere or solid dome (*garbha*, literally "womb" enclosing the relic) of masonry, with its convexity upwards and crowned by a square capital (*toran*) surmounted by one or more umbrellas, symbols of royalty. Latterly they became more complex in form, with numerous plinths, and much elongated, especially in regard to their capitals, as seen in the small photograph here given.[4]

[1] mCh'od-r-ten.

[2] Skt., *Da-garbha*.

[3] Cf. HODGS., *Il.*, 30, *et seq.*, for descriptions; also his views about the respective meanings of "Caitya" and "Stūpa."

[4] In Mr. Hodgson's collection are nearly one hundred drawings of Caityas in Nepal; FERGUSSON'S *Hist. Ind. and East. Arch.*, 303; FERG. AND BURGESS' *Cave-Temples;* also CUNNINGHAM'S *Bhilsa Topes*, p. 12.

The Lāmaist Caityas, or Ch'ortens, are mainly of the two forms here shown. They generally adhere to the Indian type; but differ most conspicuously in that the dome in the commonest form is inverted. Both have more or less elaborate plinths, and on the sides of the capital are often figured a pair of eyes, like the sacred eyes met with in ancient Egyptian, Greek, and Roman vases, etc., and believed to be connected with sun-worship. Above the *toran* is a bluntly conical or pyramidal spire, *Cūḍāmani*, of thirteen step-like segments, typical of the thirteen Bodhisat heavens of the Buddhists. This is surmounted by a bell-shaped symbol (usually copper-gilt) called the *kalsa*, the handle of which forms a tapering pinnacle sometimes modelled after a small Caitya, but often moulded in the form of one or two or all of the following objects: a lotus-flower, a crescent moon, a globular sun, a triple canopy, which are finally surmounted by a tongue-shaped spike, representing the *jyoti* or sacred light of Buddha. And sometimes round the base of the *kalsa* is a gilt canopy or umbrella (*catra*).[1]

TIBETAN CH'ORTEN, COMMON FORM.

Many of the Lāmaist Caityas are, like those of the Japanese, symbolic of the five elements into which a body is resolved upon death; thus, as in the annexed figure, the lowest section, a solid rectangular block, typifies the solidity of the *earth*; above it *water* is represented by a globe; *fire* by a triangular tongue; *air* by a

[1] CUNNINGHAM'S *Bhilsa Topes*, 12.

crescent—the inverted vault of the sky, and *ether* by an acuminated circle, the tapering into space.

A miniature *Ch'orten*, containing an enormous number of small images of Lāmaist deities, in niches and in several inner compartments within folding doors, is called "the glorious (*Ch'orten*) of many doors."[1] It is carried about from village to village by itinerant Lāmas for exhibition to the laity.

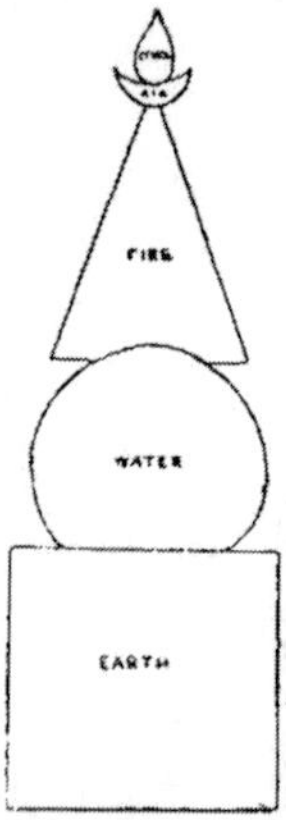

ELEMENTAL-*Ch'orten.*

In the wealthier monasteries the Ch'ortens are regularly white-washed.

The *Mendoṅs*, as figured on page 261, are long wall-like erections sometimes over a mile in length, which divide the road into two lateral halves to allow of the respectful mode of passing it, namely, with the right hand to the wall. They are faced with blocks bearing in rudely cut characters the six-syllabled mystic sentence "*Oṃ maṇi pädme hūṃ*"—the same which is revolved in the "prayer-wheels," and usually called *Maṇi;* and its name is said to be derived from these, namely, *Maṇi-doṅ*, or "The *Maṇi*-faced." It usually has a *ch'orten* terminating it at either end; and occasionally it contains niches to burn incense or to deposit the small clay funereal Caityas,[2] and also bears coarsely outlined figures of the three especial protecting divinities of Lāmaism.[3] As it is a pious act to add to these "*Maṇi*" slabs, a mason is kept at the larger temples and places of special pilgrimage, who carves the necessary number of stones according to the order and at the expense of the donating pilgrim.

The small cairns, surmounted by a few sticks, to which rags are attached by passers by as offerings to the *genius loci*, like the "rag-bushes" of India, are called Lab-ch'a, and figured at page 286.

As with all sacred objects, these monuments must always be passed on the right hand,[4] according to the ancient custom of showing respect. And thus, too, it is that the prayer-cylinders must always be turned in this direction.

In addition to the foregoing objects, there is frequently found in

[1] *Ta-shi-gô-maṅ.* [2] *dharma-ṣarīra.* [3] The *Rig-sum gon-po.* [4] *pradakshina.*

the vicinity of the monastery a stone seat called a "throne" for the head Lāma, when he gives *al-fresco* instruction to his pupils. One of the reputed thrones of the founder of Sikhim Lāmaism exists at the Pemiongchi Ch'orten, where the camp of visitors is usually pitched.

There is no regular asylum for animals rescued from the butchers, to save some person from pending death; but occasionally such ransomed cattle are to be found in the neighbourhood of monasteries where their pension-expenses have been covered by a donation from the party cured. The animals have their ears bored for a tuft of coloured rags as a distinctive and saving mark.

In Sikhim not far from most monasteries are fertile fields of *murwa* (*Eleusine corocana*), from which is made the country beer, a beverage which the Sikhim and Bhotānese monks do not deny themselves.

Over 3,000 monasteries are said to be in Tibet. But before giving a short descriptive list of some of the chief monasteries of Lāmadom it seems desirable to indicate the chief provinces into which Tibet is divided.[1]

Tibet is divided into three sections, namely:—

1. Pöd or "Tibet" proper, or the provinces of U and Tsang, hence the name "*Weitsang*" applied to Tibet by the Chinese.

2. High (or Little) Tibet, or the northern provinces of Töd, Ṅari, and Khor-sum.

3. Eastern Tibet, or the provinces of Kham, Dô, and Gang.

In Tibet proper the central province of U and the western one of Tsang have their capitals at Lhāsa and Tashil-hunpo respectively. U contains the districts of Gyama (and Kongbu, including Pema-Koi), Di-gung, Tsal-pa, Tsang-po, Che'-va, Phag-du, Yah-sang, and Yaru-dag, including the great Yamdok lake. Tsang comprises the districts of north and south Lô-stod, Gurmo, Ch'umig, S'ang, and S'alu.

Little Tibet is divided into the three circles of sTag-mo Ladvags ("Ladāk"), Mang-yul S'ang Shuṁ, Guge Burang ("Purang"),

[1] The best vernacular account of the geography of Tibet is contained in the Dsam-ling Gye-she of Lāma, Tsan-po Noman Khan of Amdo, and translated by SARAT, *J.A.S.B.*, 1887, p. 1, *seq.;* CSOMA, *J.A.S.B.*, 1832, p. 123. For scientific geography, see MARKHAM'S *Tibet*, Indian Survey Reports, Prejvalsky, Rockhill, etc. D'ANVILLE'S map of 1793, compiled on data supplied by Lāmas, is still our chief authority for a large portion of Tibet.

comprising the districts of Purang, Mang-yul Sangs-dKar, hCh'i-va, bLas'a, sBal-te, Shang-shung, upper and lower Khrig-se. East Ṅari includes Dok-t'al and lake Manasarovar. The Ladāk and Balti districts of west Ṅari were conquered by Kashmīr in 1840 and are now British dependencies. Ka-che, sometimes used synonymously with Kashmīr, includes the lofty northern steppes and the gold fields of Thog-Jalung.

Eastern Tibet is the most populous section of the country. The greater part of the low-lying Dô province (Amdô) seems to have been detached from Tibet by the Chinese about 1720. The south-eastern province of Kham borders on Assam and upper Burma, and includes the districts of Po, Lhari-go. The Gang province consists mostly of high bleak ridges, Pömbor, Tsawa, and 'Tsa-Ch'u. The northern Tsai-dam, comprising many marshes between Nan-shan and Altentagh mountains, is peopled by Tanguts and Mongols.

The chief monasteries of central Tibet are :—

Sam-yäs, which as the first monastery founded in Tibet, deserves first mention.

Its full title is "bSam-yas Mi-'gyur Lhun-gyis grub-paī Tsug-lug-K'aṅ" or "The academy for obtaining the heap of unchanging Meditation."

The explorer Nain Singh resided in this monastery in 1874 and has given a good account of it. It is situated (N. lat. 29° 20′, E. long. 91° 26, altitude about 11,430ft.) about thirty miles to the S.E. of Lhāsa, near the north bank of the Tsang-po river amidst hillocks of deep sand, clothed with scanty herbage. It was built about 74 by Thi-Sroṅ Detsan with the aid of the Indian monks, Padma-sambhava and Ṣanta-rakshita, after the model of the Udandapur,[1] temple-monastery of Bihar. But the building is believed to have been altogether miraculous, and an abstract of the legend is given underneath.[2]

[1] For some details see Sarat, in *J. Budd. Texts. Ind.*, i., p. 4, *seq.*

[2] To consecrate the ground and procure supernatural workers St. Padma made the magic-circle of rDo-r je-P'ur-pa with coloured stone-dust, and having the K'ro-wo of the five kinds, and all the necessary offerings arranged in his presence, he worshipped for seven days. Then the five Jinas (Dhyani Buddhas, Gyal-wa-rigs-lṅa) appeared to him, and the king, being empowered, also saw the faces of these five. Then the Guru created several incarnations of himself, some of whom entered the Maṇḍala, while some flew up into the sky. These incarnations caused the Tibetan devils to bring stones and wood from the hills and rivers, and thus the foundation of bSam-yas academy was begun. Human beings built it by day, while the devils worked at it by night, and so the great work rapidly progressed.

When the king saw the great piles of gathered wood he was surprised and was

Part of the original building yet remains. The monastery, which contains a large temple, four large colleges, and several other buildings, is enclosed by a lofty circular wall about a mile and a half in circumference, with gates facing the cardinal points, and along the top of the wall are many votive brick chaityas, of which the explorer, Nain Singh, counted 1,030, and they seemed to be covered with inscriptions in ancient Indian characters. In the centre of the enclosure stands the assembly hall, with radiating cloisters leading to four chapels, facing at equal distances the four sides of the larger temple. This explorer notes that " the idols and images contained in these temples are of pure gold, richly ornamented with valuable cloths and jewels. The candlesticks and vessels are nearly all made of gold and silver." And on the temple walls are many large inscriptions in Chinese and ancient Indian characters. In the vestibule of the chief temple, to the left of the door, is a colossal copy of the pictorial Wheel of Life.

The large image of "Buddha," over ten feet high, seems to be called " the Sam-yäs Jing " (Samyas Gyal-po).

The library contains many Indian manuscripts, but a great number of these were destroyed at the great fire about 1810 A.D.

In a temple close by among the sand is a celebrated chamber of horrors, built of large boulders, and containing gigantic figures of the twenty-five *Gon-po* demons. The images are made of incense, and are about twenty feet high, of the fiercest expression, and represented as dancing upon mangled human corpses, which they are also devouring. And great stains of blood are pointed out by the attendants as

---

awestruck, and asked the Guru to explain. The Guru thereon made the *Maṇḍala* of the " Five," and worshipping for seven days, the Five transformed themselves into five kinds of Garuḍa birds, which were visible to the king. And at that very time the Guru himself became invisible, and the king saw in his stead a great garuḍa holding a snake in his clutches and beak; but not seeing the Guru, the king cried out in fear. Then the garuḍa vanished and the Guru reappeared beside him. The country to the south of Samye was then, it is said, inhabited by the savage "kLa-klo" tribes, which the Tibetans, through their Indian paṇdits, termed Nāgās (cognate with those of the Brahmaputra valley). The next day, a Nāgā, having transformed himself into a white man on a white horse, came into the presence of the king and said, "O king! How much wood do you need for building Sam-yäs? as I will supply you with all you want." On being informed of the requirements, the Nāgā collected wood to an enormous extent.

The building of the Sam-ye academy (gtsug-lag-k'aṅ) swallowed up the wealth of the king. So the Guru, accompanied by the king and his ministers, went to the bank of Mal-gro lake, and keeping the ministers concealed in a small valley, the Guru began to make a *Maṇḍala* of the "Five" and worshipped for seven days, after which Avalokita sinhada, with Amitābha on his head, stood at each of the four directions, where dwell the four gods of the Five. On this the Nāgās of the depths became powerless, and the Guru, addressing them, said, "The wealth of my king being exhausted, I have come to ask wealth." Next day the banks were found lined with glittering gold, which the Guru caused the ministers to carry off to the palace. On this account all the images of gods at Sam-yäs are made of solid gold, and of a quality unequalled in any part of our world of Jambudvīp.

the fresh stains of bodies which the demons have dragged to the place during the previous night.

We have already referred to the miraculous account of the building of this monastery, which is said to rest upon Raksha fiends. On account of the peculiar safety imparted to the locality by the spells of the wizard priest, Padma-sambhava, the Tibetan government use the place as a bank for their reserved bullion and treasure, of which fabulous sums are said to be stored there.

Although it is now presided over by a Sa-kya Lāma, the majority of its members are Ñiṅ-ma.

Gāh-ldan, the monastery founded by Tsoṅ-K'a-pa, is one of the four great Ge-lug-pa or established church monasteries, the others being De-pung, Sera and Tāshi-lhunpo.

Its full name is dGah-ldan rÑam-par Gyal-wahi glin, or the Continent of completely victorious happiness.

This monastery stands enthroned on the db*Aṅ-K'or* hill, about twenty-five miles E. N.E. of Lhāsa. Its founder, Tsoṅ-K'a-pa, raised it to a high pitch of fame and filled it with costly images. The chief object of veneration is the grand tomb of Tson-K'a-pa, which is placed in the Tsug-la-k'aṅ. It is a lofty mausoleum-like structure of marble and malachite, with a gilded roof. Inside this outer shell is to be seen a beautiful Ch'orten, consisting of cube pyramid and surmounting cone, all said to be of solid gold. Within this golden casket, wrapped in fine cloths, inscribed with sacred Dharani syllables, are the embalmed remains of the great reformer, disposed in sitting attitude. Other notable objects here are a magnificent representation of Cham-pa, the Buddha to come, seated, European fashion, on a throne. Beside him stands a life-sized image of Tsoṅ-K'a-pa, in his character of Jam-pal Nin-po, which is supposed to be his name in the Galdan heavens. A rock-hewn cell, with impressions of hands and feet, is also shown as Tson-K'a-pa's. A very old statue of S'inje, the lord of Death, is much reverenced here; every visitor presenting gifts and doing it infinite obeisance. The floor of the large central chamber appears to be covered with brilliant enamelled tiles, whilst another shrine holds an effigy of Tson-K'a-pa, with images of his five disciples (Shes-rab Sen-ge, K'a-grub Ch'os-rje, etc.) standing round him. The library contains manuscript copies of the saint's works in his own handwriting.[1]

Unlike the other large Ge-lug-pa monasteries, the headship of Gāh-ldan is not based on hereditary incarnation, and is not, therefore, a child when appointed. He is chosen by a conclave from among the most scholarly of the monks of Sera, De-pung, and this monastery. The late abbot became ultimately regent of all Tibet. The number of inmates here is reckoned at about 3,300.

De-pung ('bras-spuṅs), the most powerful and populous of all the monasteries in Tibet, founded in and named after the great Indian-Tantrik monastery of "The rice-heap" (Ṣrī-Dhanya Kataka) in

[1] Abstract from *Survey Reports*, etc., by Rev. G. Sandberg.

Kaliṅga and identified with the Kālācākra doctrine. It is situated about three miles west of Lhāsa, and it contains nominally 7,000[1] monks. It is divided into four sections clustering round the great cathedral, the resplendent golden roof of which is seen from afar. It contains a small palace for the Dalai Lāma at his annual visit. Many Mongolians study here. In front stands a stūpa, said to contain the body of the fourth Grand Lāma, Yön-tenn, who was of Mongolian nationality.

Its local genii are the Five nymphs of long Life (Ts'erin-ma), whose images, accompanied by that of Hayagriva, guard the entrance. And effigies of the sixteen Sthavira are placed outside the temple door. In its neighbourhood is the monastery of Nä-Ch'uṅ, the residence of the state sorcerer, with a conspicuous gilt dome.

SER-RA, or "The Merciful Hail."[2] It is said to have been so named out of rivalry to its neighbour, "The rice-heap" (De-pung), as hail is destructive of rice, and the two monasteries have frequent feuds. In connection with this legend there is also exhibited here a miraculous "Phurbu," or thunderbolt sceptre of Jupiter Pluvius.

It is romantically situated about a mile and a half to the north of Lhāsa, on the lower slopes of a range of barren hills named Ta-ti-pu, famous for silver ore, and which surround the monastery like an amphitheatre.

Its monks number nominally 5,500, and have frequently engaged in bloody feuds against their more powerful rivals of De-pung. The Indian surveyor reported only on the idols of the temple. He says: "They differ in size and hideousness, some having horns, but the lower parts of the figures are generally those of men." Huc gives a fuller description: "The temples and houses of Sera stand on a slope of the mountain-spur, planted with hollies and cypresses. At a distance these buildings, ranged in the form of an amphitheatre, one above the other, and standing out upon the green base of the hill, present an attractive and picturesque sight. Here and there, in the breaks of the mountain above this religious city, you see a great number of cells inhabited by contemplative Lāmas, which you can reach only with difficulty. The monastery of Sera is remarkable for three large temples of several storeys in height, all the rooms of which are gilded throughout. Thence the name from ser, the Tibetan for 'gold.' In the chief of these three temples is preserved the famous *tortchê*, which, having flown through the air from India, is the model from which all others, large and portable, are copied. The *tortchê* of Sera is the object of great veneration, and is sometimes carried in procession to Lhāsa to receive the adoration of the people." This "*dorje*," or rather "phurbu," is what is called a *Tam-din-phurbu*, and is said to have originally belonged to an Indian sage named Grub-thob *m*dah-'phyar. It was found on the hill in the neighbourhood named P'urba-Ch'og, having flown from India. In the 12th month of every year (about the 27th

---

1 LĀMA U.G., *loc. cit.*, p. 34, says 10,000.

2 This word is usually spelt *ser*, and seems never to be spelt gSer, or "gold."

day) it is taken out of its casket and carried in state to Potala, where the Dalai Lāma puts it to his head. It is thereafter carried by a high official of Sera monastery to the Chinese Amban, the governors (Shape) and the regent, all of whom touch their heads with it. Afterwards thousands throng to Sera to receive its holy touch on their heads as a defence against all evil and spells.

In the great assembly hall is a huge image of Avalokita with eleven heads.

TASHI-LHUNPO (bkra-s'is Lhun-po), or the "Heap of Glory," the headquarters of the Pan-ch'en Grand Lāma, who to some extent shares with the Lhāsa Grand Lāma the headship of the church. Its general appearance will be seen from the foregoing plate on page 260, from a native drawing. The monastery forms quite a small town, and not even Lāmas other than established church can stay there over-night. It is well known through the descriptions of Bogle, Turner, etc. It is situated near the south bank of the Tsang-po, at the junction of the Nying river, in 89° 7′ E. long., 29° 4′ 20″ N. lat., and altitude, 11,800 feet (MARKH., xxvii.). This celebrated establishment has been long known to European geographers as "Teeshoo Loombo."

Mr. Bogle describes it [1] as being built on the lower slope of a steep hill (Dolmai Ri, or hill of the goddess Tārā). The houses rise one over another; four churches with gilt ornaments are mixed with them, and altogether it presents a princely appearance. Many of the courts are flagged with stone, and with galleries running round them. The alleys, which are likewise paved, are narrow. The palace is large, built of dark-coloured bricks, with a copper-gilt roof. It is appropriated to the Lāma and his officers, to temples, granaries, warehouses, etc. The rest of the town is entirely inhabited by priests, who are in number about four thousand. Mr. Bogle also describes the interior of several of the state rooms and temples. On the top of mount Dolmai Ri is a stone cairn, where banners are always fluttering, and where, on high festivals, huge bonfires are set ablaze. The lay capital of the province, Shigatse, lies on the upper ridges to the N.E. of this hill, hardly a mile from this, the ecclesiastical capital.

The lofty walls enclosing the monastic town are pierced by five gateways. Over the eastern gate has been placed, in large carved letters, a prohibition against smoking within the monastic precincts. The western gateway seems to be regarded as the main entrance. So, entering the monastic premises there, you find yourself in a sort of town, with lanes lined by lofty houses, open squares, and temples.

In the centre of the place is the grand cathedral or assembly hall. Its entrance faces the east. Its roof is supported by one hundred pillars, and the building accommodates two to three thousand monks seated in nine rows on rugs placed side by side on the floor. The four central pillars, called the *Ka-ring*, are higher than the rest, and support a detached roof to form the side skylights through which those seated in the upper gallery can witness the service. The rows of seats arranged

[1] MARK., p. 96.

to the right side of the entrance are occupied by the senior monks, such as belong to the order of Rigch'en, Pharch'enpha, Torampa, Kāh-c'an, etc. The seats to the left side are taken up by the junior monks, such as *Ge-ts'ul* and apprentice monks, etc., of the classes called Dûra and Rigding.

The court around it is used by the monks for religious dances and other outdoor ceremonies. Round the space are reared the halls of the college, four storeys in height, provided with upper-floor balconies. North of these buildings are set up in a line the huge tombs of deceased Pan-ch'en Lāmas. The body of each is embalmed and placed within a gold-plated pyramid raised on a tall marble table, and this structure stands within a stone mausoleum, high and decorated with gilt *kanjira* and small cylinder-shaped finials made of black felt. One of these tombs is much bigger than the rest. It is that of Pan-ch'en Erteni, who died in 1779.

Tomb of Tashi Lāma.[1]

There are four conventual colleges attached to Tashi-lhunpo, all of which receive students from every part of Tibet, who are instructed in Tantrik ritual, and learn large portions of that division of the scriptures. The names of these colleges are Shar-tse Tā-ts'an, Nag-pa Ta-ts'an, Toi-sam Liṅ, and Kyil-k'aṅ Ta-ts'aṅ. Each of these institutions has an abbot, who is the *tul-wa*, or avatār of some bygone saint; and the four abbots have much to do with the discovery of the infant successor to a deceased Pan-ch'en, or head of the monastery. From these abbots, also, one

[1] After Turner.

is selected to act as the prime minister, or chief ecclesiastical adviser in the government of Tsang. The most imposing building of the monastery is the temple and hall of the Ṅag-pa Ta-ts'aṅ, known as the "Ṅagk'aṅ," which is the chief college for mystic ritual in Tibet. Another college, the Toi-san-liṅ, stands at the extreme northern apex of the walls, some way up the slope of the Dolmai-Ri hill.

Hard by the last-named premises, is to be observed a lofty building of rubble-stone, reared to the amazing height of nine storeys. This edifice, which forms a very remarkable object on the hill-side, was sketched by Turner, who visited Tashi-lhunpo one hundred years ago, and his drawing of it is here annexed on opposite page. It is called Gö-Ku-pea, or "The Stored Silken Pictures," as it is used to exhibit at certain festivals the gigantic pictures of Maitreya and other Buddhist deities, which are brought out and hung high up as great sheets outside the walls of the tall building. By the vulgar it is styled Kiku Tamsa. It is used as a storehouse for the dried carcases of sheep, goats, and yak, which are kept in stock for feeding the inmates of the monastery. A wide-walled yard fronts the Kiku Tamsa, and this space is thronged by a motley crowd when (as is the custom in June and November) the pictures are exhibited.

The number of monks generally in residence at Tashi-lhunpo is said to be 3,800. The division into wards and clubs has already been referred to.

The head of the whole monastic establishment resides in the building called *b*La-brang, or "The Lāma's palace."

Nam-gyal Ch'oi-de is the monastery-royal of the Grand Lāma on the red hill of Potala, where the Dalai Lāma holds his court and takes part in the service as a Bhikshu, or common monk.

Ramo-ch'e and Karmakya monasteries, within Lhāsa, are, as already noted, schools of sorcery, and the latter has a printing house.

"Desherip-gay" (elevation 12,220 feet), a monastery two miles from the fort of Chamnam-ring in northern Tsang, is subordinate to Tashi-lhunpo, where the Grand Tashi Lāma was resident at Bogle's visit on account of the smallpox plague at his headquarters. Bogle describes it as "situated in a narrow valley, and at the foot of an abrupt and rocky hill . . . two storeys high, and is surrounded on three sides by rows of small apartments with a wooden gallery running round them, which altogether form a small court flagged with stone. All the stairs are broad ladders. The roofs are adorned with copper-gilt ornaments, and on the front of the house are three round brass plates, emblems of *Om*, *Han* (? Ah), *Hoong*. The Lāma's apartment is at the top. It is small, and hung round with different coloured silks, views of Potala, Teshu Lumbo, etc." [1]

Jan-lache, a large monastery on the upper Tsang-po, in long. 87° 38′ E.; elevation 13,580 feet. It is eighty-five miles above Tashi-lhunpo.[2]

[1] Markham, *op. cit.*, p. 82.

[2] Markham's *Tib.*, p. xxvii.

THE "GÖ-KU-PEA" OR "KIKU-TAMSA" TOWER AT TASHI-LHUNPO.[1]

[1] After Turner.

CHAMNAMRIN (Nam-lin), in the valley of the Shing river, a northern affluent of the Tsang-po, 12,220 feet, seen and visited by Mr. Bogle.

DORKYA LUGU-DOṄ, on the bank of the great Tengri-nor lake.

RA-DENG (Ra-sgreṅ), north-east of Lhāsa, a Ka-dam-pa monastery, founded in 1055 by Brom-ton, Atīsa's pupil.

SA-KYA (Sa-skya) "Tawny-soil," is about 50 miles north of Mount Everest, 48 miles east from Shigatse, and 30 miles from Jang-lache; E. long. 87° 54′, lat. 28° 53′. This monastery gives its name to the Sākya sect, which has played an important part in the history of Tibet. A considerable town nestles at the foot of the monastery. The foundation of the monastery and its future fame are related to have been foretold by the Indian sage, Atīsa, when on his way to central Tibet, he passed a rock, on the present site of the monastery, on which he saw the mystic *Om* inscribed in "self-sprung," characters. Afterwards this establishment became famous as a seat of learning and for a time of the priest-king. It is said to contain the largest single building in Tibet,—though the cathedral at Lhāsa is said to be larger. It is seven[1] storeys in height, and has a spacious assembly hall known as "the White Hall of Worship." It is still famous for its magnificent library, containing numerous unique treasures of Sanskrit and Tibetan literature, unobtainable elsewhere. Some of these have enormous pages embossed throughout in letters of gold and silver. The monastery, though visited in 1872 by our exploring Pandit No. 9, and in 1882 by Babu Sarat Candra Dās, remains undescribed at present. The Sakya Lāma is held to be an incarnation of the Bodhisat Mañjuṣrī, and also to carry Karma, derivable from Sakya Paṇḍita and St. Padma.

The hall of the great temple, called 'P'rul-pahī Lha-k'aṅ, has four enormous wooden pillars, *Ka-wa-miṅ ches zhi*, of which the first pillar is *white*, and called Kar-po-zum-lags, and is alleged to have come from Kongbu; the second *yellow*, Ser-po zum-lags, from Mochu valley; the third *red*, Marpo Tag dzag, from Nanam on Nepal frontier; and the fourth pillar *black*, Nak-po K'un-shes, from Ladāk. These pillars are said to have been erected by K'yed-'bum bsags, the ancestor of the Sikhim king.

TING-GE is a very large Ge-lug-pa monastery to the north of Sakya and west of Tashi-lhunpo.

PHUNTSHOLING (p'un-ts'ogs-gliṅ) monastery, formerly named *r*Tag-*b*rten by Tāranātha, who built it in his forty-first year, was forcibly made a Ge-lug-pa institution by the fifth grand Lāma, Ṅag-waṅ.

It is situated on the Tsangpo, about a day's journey west of Tashi-lhunpo, and one mile to the south-west of it is Jonang, which has a very large temple said to be like Budh Gaya, and, like it, of several storeys and covered by images; but both it and Phuntsholing are said to have been deserted by monks and now are occupied by nuns.

SAM-DING (bsam-ldiṅ ch'oinde). It lies in N. lat. 28° 57′ 15″, and E.

[1] De-pung and the larger monasteries in Tibet have several much smaller buildings distributed so as to form a town.

long., 90° 28′. Altitude, 14,512 feet. An important establishment, noteworthy as a monastery of monks as well as nuns, presided over by a female abbot—the so-called re-incarnate goddess already referred to.[1] This august woman is known throughout Tibet as *Dorje-P'ag-mo*, or "the diamond sow"; the abbesses of Samding being held to be successive appearances in mortal form of the Indian goddess, Vajravarahī. The present incarnation of this goddess is thirty-three years old (in 1889); and is described as being a clever and capable woman, with some claim to good looks, and of noble birth. She bears the name of Ṅag-*d*baṅ Rin-ch'en Kun-*b*zaṅ-mo *d*bAṅ-mo, signifying "The most precious power of speech, the female energy of all good"). Under this lady the reputation which Samding has long enjoyed for the good morals of both monks and nuns has been well maintained. Among other rules, the inmates are forbidden to lend out money or other valuables on interest to the rural folk, usurious dealings being commonly resorted to by the monastic orders. It is said to be of the Ñiṅ-ma sect. The monastery was founded by one Je-tsun T'inle Ts'oma, a flower of the philosophy of Po-doṅ P'yog Legs Nam-gyal, whose writings, to the amazing extent of one hundred and eighteen volumes, are treasured up in the monastic library.

Yamdok lake is remarkable for its scorpionoid shape, the grotesque shaped semi-island anchored to the main shore by two necks of land. Samding is itself placed on the main shore at the juncture of the northern neck. Being built on a conical hill, it appears to be guarding the sacred island from intrusion. The monastery stands like a fortress on the summit of the barren hill some 300 feet above the level of the surrounding country. Huge flags of stone are piled in ascending steps up this hill, and a long low wall mounts beside them like a balustrade. At the top of the steps, a narrow pathway conducts to the foot of the monastery, which is circled by a high wall. Samding is finely placed. To the N.E. it fronts the dark and precipitous mountain spurs which radiate from the lofty central peak of the islands. To the S.E. it looks over the land towards the illimitable waters of the weird and mighty Yamdok herself. To the S. it frowns down on the Dumo Ts'o, the inner lake betwixt the connecting necks of land abovementioned, into which are cast the bodies of the defunct nuns and monks, as food for fishes.

On entering the gates of the monastery, you find yourself in an extensive courtyard, flanked on three sides by the conventual buildings. Part of the fourth side of the parallelogram is occupied by a kind of grand-stand supported on pilasters of wood. Ladders with broad steps, cased in brass, give admission to the first floor of the main building. Here, in a long room, are ranged the tombs of celebrities connected in past times with Samding, including that of the founder, T'inle Ts'omo. The latter tomb is a richly ornamented piece of workmanship, plated with gold and studded with jewels. At the base, on a stone slab is marked the reputed footprint of the saint. In a private, strongly-

[1] See page 245.

barred chamber, hard by to which no one may be admitted, are laid the dried mortal remains of all the former incarnations of Dorje P'ag-mo. Here, in this melancholy apartment, will be one day placed the body of the present lady abbess, after undergoing some embalming process. To the grim charnel-house, it is considered the imperative duty of each incarnate abbess to repair once, while living, to gaze her fill on her predecessors, and to make formal obeisance to their mouldering forms. She *must* enter once, but only once, during her lifetime.

Another hall in this monastery is the *dus-k'aṅ*, the walls of which are frescoes illustrative of the career of the original Dorje P'ag-mo. There, also, have been put up inscriptions recording how the goddess miraculously defended Samding, when, in the year 1716, it was beset by a Mongol warrior, one Yung Gar. When the Mongol arrived in the vicinity of Yamdok, hearing that the lady abbess had a pig's head as an excrescence behind her ear, he mocked at her in public, sending word to her to come to him, that he might see the pig's head for himself. Dorje P'ag-mo returned no angry reply, only beseeching him to abandon his designs on the monastery. Burning with wrath, the warrior invaded the place and destroyed the walls; but, entering, he found the interior utterly deserted. He only observed eighty pigs and eighty sows grunting in the du-khang under the lead of a bigger sow. He was startled by this singular frustration of his project; for he could hardly plunder a place guarded only by hogs. When it was evident that the Mongol was bent no longer on rapine, the pigs and sows were suddenly transformed into venerable-looking monks and nuns, headed by the most reverend Dorje P'ag-mo; as a consequence, Yung Gar, instead of plundering, enriched the place with costly presents.

A certain amount of association is permitted between the male and female inmates of this convent, who together number less than 200. Dorje P'ag-mo retains one side of the monastic premises as her private residence. It is asserted by the inmates that the good woman never suffers herself to sleep in a reclining attitude. During the day she may doze in a chair, during the night she must sit, hour after hour, wrapt in profound meditation. Occasionally this lady makes a royal progress to Lhāsa, where she is received with the deepest veneration. Up in northern Tibet is another sanctuary dedicated to Dorje P'ag-mo. This convent also stands on an islet situated off the west shore of the great lake, 70 miles N.W. of Lhāsa, the Nam Ts'o Ch'yidmo, and is much akin to Samding, comprising a few monks and nuns under an abbess. At Markula, in Lahul, is a third shrine of the goddess.[1]

Di-kung ('bri-guṅ) about one hundred miles N.E. of Lhāsa, is one of the largest Kar-gyu-pa monasteries. It is said to receive its name, the "she-Yak," from the ridge on which it is situated, which is shaped like the back of a yak. It was founded in 1166, by the son of the Sakya Lāma, Koncho Yal-po.

[1] Abstract of Sarat's *Report*, by Rev. G. Sandberg.

MINDOLLING (smin grol-gliṅ), close to the S. of Samye, a great Ñiṅ-ma monastery, sharing with Dorje Dag, not far off, the honour of being the supreme monastery of that sect. It lies across the Tsangpo from Sam-yäs in the valley of the Mindolling river, the water of which turns numerous large prayer-wheels. Its chief temple is nine storeys high, with twenty minor temples with many "beautiful images" and books. A massive stone stairway forms the approach to the monastery.

Its chief Lāma is a direct descendant of the revelation-finder Dag-liṅ. The succession is by descent and not by re-incarnation. One of his sons is made a Lāma and vowed to celibacy, another son marries and continues the descent, and in like manner the succession proceeds, and has not yet been interrupted since its institution seventeen generations ago; but should the lay-brother die without issue the Lāma is expected to marry the widow. The married one is called *g*Dun-pa or "the lineage." The body of the deceased Lāma is salted and preserved. The discipline of this monastery is said to be strict, and its monks are celibate. A large branch of this monastery is Na-s'i,[1] not far distant from its parent.

DORJE-DAG, between Sam-yäs and Lhāsa, is a headquarters of the Unreformed Lāmas. It has had a chequered history, having been destroyed several times by the Mongols, etc., and periodically restored.

PAL-RI (dpal-ri), a Ñiṅ-ma monastery between Shigatse and Gyangtse, where lives the pretended incarnation of the Indian wizard, Lô-pön Hūṅkāra.

SHALU monastery, a few miles E. of Tashi-lhunpo. Here instruction is given in magical incantations, and devotees are immured for years in its cave-hermitages. Amongst the supernatural powers believed to be so acquired is the alleged ability to sit on a heap of barley without displacing a grain; but no credible evidence is extant of anyone displaying such feats.

GURU CH'O-WAṄ, in Lhobrak, or southern Tibet, bordering on Bhotān. This monastery is said by Lāma U. G.[2] to have been built after the model of the famous monastery of Nālanda in Magadha. The shrine is surrounded by groves of poplars, and contains some important relics, amongst others a stuffed horse of great sanctity (belonging to the great Guru) which is called Jamliṅ-nin-k'or, or "the horse that can go round the world in one day."[3] Observing that the horse was bereft of his "left leg," U. G. enquired the cause, and was told how the leg had been stolen by a Khamba pilgrim with a view of "enchanting" the ponies of Kham. The thief became insane, and his friends took him to the high priest of the sanctuary for advice, who instantly divined that he had stolen some sacred thing. This so frightened the thief that the leg was secretly restored, and the thief and his friends vanished from the place and never were seen again.

---

[1] U. G., *loc. cit.*, p. 26.

[2] *Loc. cit.*, p. 23.

[3] Compare with the sacred horse of Shintoism, etc.

The upper Lhobrak is well cultivated; barley, pea, mustard, wheat, and crops of rape were noticed by U. G., surrounding the monastery of Lha Lung. With some difficulty he obtained permission to see the sacred objects of the monastery, whose saintly founder, Lha Lung, has three incarnations in Tibet. One of them is the present abbot of the monastery, who was born in Bhotān, and is a nephew of the Paro Penlo. The monastery is well endowed by the Tibetan government, and rituals are encouraged in it for the suppression of evil spirits and demons.

Sang-kar Gu-t'ok, also in the Lhobrak valley, has one hundred monks, and is a small printing establishment.[1]

Kar-ch'u, also in the Lhobrak valley, said[2] to be one of the richest monasteries in Tibet, and to contain many bronzes brought from Magadha in the Middle Ages. Pilgrims carry off from here the holy water which percolates into a sacred cave.

Gyan-tse, on the Painom river, east of Tashi-lhunpo. Its monastery is named Palk'or Ch'oide. Its hall is reported by Lāma Ugyän Gya-ts'o to be lit by 1,000 lamps. In lofty niches on the three sides, N., E., and W. (implying evidently that the entrance is on the S.), are placed "three huge images of Buddha—Jam-yang, Chanrassig, and Maitreya," copper-gilt. Here also he notes "stone images like those at Buddha Gaya. In the lobby is a collection of stuffed animals, including tigers."

The foregoing are all in the U and Tsang provinces. In Kham, in eastern Tibet, are many large monasteries, the largest of which are perhaps Derge and Ch'ab-mdô (Chiamô), with about 2,000 monks and large printing press.

Derge (sDe-sge), at the town of that name, and capital of one of the richest and most populous of Tibetan provinces, containing "many Lāmaserais of 200 or 300 monks, some indeed of 2,000 or 3,000. Each family devotes a son to the priesthood. The king resides in a Lāmaserai of 300 monks."[3]

Other large monasteries of eastern Tibet are Karthok and (?) Riwochce on the Ṅul river, under the joint government of two incarnate abbots.

In southern Tibet in the district of Pema Köd (map-name Pemakoi) are the monasteries of Dorje-yu (founded by Terton Dorje-thokmi), Mar-puṅ Lek-puṅ (built by Ugyen Dich'en-liṅ-pa), Mendeldem, Phu-pa-ron, Kon-dem, Bho-lun, C'am-nak, Kyon-sa, Narton, Rinc'hensun (built by Ugyen Doduliṅ-pa, the father of Dich'en-liṅ-pa), Tsenc'uk, Gya-pun, Gilin, and Demu, which are all Ñiṅ-ma, except Chamnak and Demu, which are Ge-lug-pa, and all except the last are on the west or right bank of the Tsangpo river, and the number of monks in each is from ten to thirty. Amongst the chief shrines are Horasharki Ch'orten, Mendeldem's shrine, and "Buddu Tsip'ak."

---

[1] Explorer R.N.'s account (*S.R.*, 1889, p. 50). [2] Lāma Ugyen Gya-ts'o, *loc. cit.*, 25.
[3] Baber, *Suppl. Papers, R. Geog. Socy.*; see also Rockhill, *L.*, 184, etc., 96.

IN CHINA.

In China proper there seem to be no truly Lāmaist monasteries of any size except at Pekin and near the western frontier. The Pekin monastery is called "everlasting peace" (Yun-ho Kung), and is maintained at the imperial expense.[1] Its monks, over 1,000 in number, are almost entirely Mongolian, but the head Lāma, a re-incarnate abbot, and his two chief assistants, are usually Tibetans of the De-pung, Sera, and Gāh-ldan monasteries, and appointed from Lhāsa. The abbot, who is considered an incarnation of Rol-pa-dorje, already figured, lives within the yellow wall of the city, and near by is the great printing-house, called "Sum-ju Si," where Lāmaist books are printed in Tibetan, Chinese, and Mongolian. In the chief temple "the

MONASTERY OF U-TAI-SHAN.[2]

great wooden image of Buddha, seventy feet high, richly ornamented and clothed, holding an enormous lotus in each hand, and with the traditional jewel on his breast. In each section of his huge gold crown sat a small Buddha, as perfect and as much ornamented as the great one. His toe measured twenty-one inches. On each side of him hung a huge scroll seventy-five feet long, bearing Chinese characters and a series of galleries, reached by several flights of stairs, surrounded him. The expression of his great bronze face was singularly lofty. Near by were two magnificent bronze lions and a wonderful bronze urn; many temples filled with strange idols hung with thousands of silk hangings, and laid with Tibetan carpets; all sorts of bronze and

[1] EDKIN'S *Relig. in China*, 65. [2] After Huc.

enamel altar utensils, presented by different emperors, among them two elephants in *cloisonne* ware, said to be the best specimens of such work in China, and the great hall, with its prayer-benches for all the monks, where they worship every afternoon at five."[1]

Another celebrated monastery is the Wu-tai or U-tai-shan, "The five towers" in the north Chinese province of Shan-si, and a celebrated shrine.

The great monastery of Kubum (Kumbum), in Sifau, lies near the western frontiers of China. It is the birth-place of St. Tsoṅ-K'a-pa, and has been visited and described by Huc, Rockhill, etc. Its photo-

Kumbum (T'a-erh-ssu).[2]

graph by Mr. Rockhill is here by his kind permission given. Its Mongolian name is *T'a-erh-ssu.*[3]

Here is the celebrated tree, the so-called "white sandal" (*Syringa Villosa*, Vahl), which the legend alleges to have sprung up miraculously from the placental blood shed at Tsoṅ-K'a-pa's birth. Its leaves are said to bear 100,000 images, hence the etymology of the name of the place (s*Ku-'bum*). The image markings on the leaves are said to represent "the Tathāgata of the Lion's Voice" (Sen-ge Na-ro), but Huc describes the markings as sacred letters.[4]

---

1 Newspaper Acct., 1890.

2 After Rockhill.

3 Rockhill, *I.*, 57 said to mean "the Great Tent (Tabernacle)"

4 Cf. also *ibid.*, 58, etc.

Huc's account of it is as follows : " At the foot of the mountain on which the Lāmaserai stands, and not far from the principal Buddhist temple, is a great square enclosure, formed by brick walls. Upon entering this we were able to examine at leisure the marvellous tree, some of the branches of which had already manifested themselves above the wall. Our eyes were first directed with earnest curiosity to the leaves, and we were filled with absolute consternation of astonishment at finding that, in point of fact, there were upon each of the leaves well-formed Tibetan characters, all of a green colour, some darker, some lighter, than the leaf itself. Our first impression was suspicion of fraud on the part of the Lāmas; but, after a minute examination of every detail, we could not discover the least deception, the characters all appeared to us portions of the leaf itself, equally with its veins and nerves, the position was not the same in all; in one leaf they would be at the top of the leaf; in another, in the middle; in a third, at the base, or at the side; the younger leaves represented the characters only in a partial state of formation. The bark of the tree and its branches, which resemble those of the plane-tree, are also covered with these characters. When you remove a piece of old bark, the young bark under it exhibits the indistinct outlines of characters in a germinating state, and, what is very singular, these new characters are not unfrequently different from those which they replace. We examined everything with the closest attention, in order to detect some trace of trickery, but we could discern nothing of the sort, and the perspiration absolutely trickled down our faces under the influence of the sensations which this most amazing spectacle created.

" More profound intellects than ours may, perhaps, be able to supply a satisfactory explanation of the mysteries of this singular tree; but, as to us, we altogether give it up. Our readers possibly may smile at our ignorance; but we care not so that the sincerity and truth of our statement be not suspected."[1]

The large temple (Jo-wo-k'aṅ) is described by Rockhill.[2]

IN MONGOLIA.

In Mongolia the chief monastery is at Urgya-Kuren, on the Tula river in the country of the Ḳhalkas, about forty days' journey west of Pekin, and the seat of a Russian consul and two Chinese ambassadors. It is the seat of the Grand Lāma, who is believed to be the incarnate historian, Lāma Tāranātha, and he is called Je-tsun Tamba, as detailed in the chapter on the hierarchy, and its monks are said to number over 14,000, and during the great new year festival over 20,000 are present. It contains twenty-eight colleges (sGgra-ts'aṅ).

The monastery is named Kurun or Kuren, and is described by Huc. The plain at the foot of the mountain is covered with tents for the use of the pilgrims. Viewed from a distance, the white cells of the Lāmas,

[1] Huc, ii., p. 53. [2] Rockhill, *L.*, 66.

built on the declivity in horizontal lines one above the other, resemble the steps of an enormous altar, of which the temple of Tāranātha Lāma appears to constitute "the tabernacle." Huc says it contains 30,000 monks!

Kuku Khotun, or "blue city," near the northern bend of the Yellow river, is said by Huc to have formerly been the seat of Jetsun-Dam-pa. It contains five monasteries with about 20,000 Lāmas.

IN SIBERIA.

In south Siberia, amongst the Buriats, near the Baikal lake, a large monastery is on a lake thirty versts to the north-west of Selinginsk, and the presiding monk is called the K'an-po Paṇḍita, and claims to be a re-incarnate Lama.[1]

IN EUROPE.

The Kālmak Tartars on the Volga have only temporary, nomadic cloisters and temples, that is to say tents, in which they put up their holy pictures and images, and celebrate divine service. Such temporary cloisters are called "Churull," and consist of two different sorts of tents or *Jurten* (Oergö), the assembly hall of the clergy (Churullün-Oergö) and of the gods and image hall (*Schitäni* or *Burchanün-Oergö*). Some of these *Churulls* contain a hundred priests.

IN LADĀK AND LITTLE TIBET.

He-mi (or "Himis" of survey map). This fine old monastery is situated about 11,000 feet above the sea-level, in a lateral ravine that joins the Indus, a day's journey (eighteen miles SSE.) above Leh, on the left bank of that river. From its secluded position this was one of the few monasteries which escaped destruction on the invasion of the country by the Dogras under Wazir Gerawar, who ruthlessly destroyed much Lāmaist property, so that more interesting and curious objects, books, dresses, masks, etc., are found at Himis than in any other monastery in Ladāk. It was built by sTag-stan-ras-ch'en, and its proper title is *Ch'aṅ-ch'ub sam-liṅ*.

The "Himis-fair," with its mask plays, as held on St. Padma-sambhava's day in summer, is the chief attraction to sight-seers in Ladāk. This Lāmasery is at present still the greatest landowner in Ladāk, and its steward one of the most influential persons in the country. The Lāmas seem to be of the Ñiṅ-ma sect (according to Marx[2] they are Dug-pa, but he appears to use Dug-pa as synonymous with *Red cap* sect). To the same sect also belongs Ts'en-re and sTag-na. A fine photograph of this monastery is given by Mr. Knight,[3] and one of its courts is shown in his illustration of the mystic play reproduced at p. 528

"The principal entrance to the monastery is through a massive door, from which runs a gently sloping and paved covered way leading into a

[1] Köppen, *op. cit.*

[2] *Loc. cit.*, 133.

[3] *Where Three Empires Meet.*

courtyard about 30×40 yards square, having on the left hand a narrow verandah, in the centre of which stands the large prayer-cylinder above mentioned. The larger picturesque doorway, the entrance of one of the principal idol rooms, is in the extreme right hand corner, massive brass rings affixed to large *bosses* of brass are affixed on either door, the posts of which are of carved and coloured woodwork. The walls of the main building, with its bay windows of lattice work, enclose the courtyard along the right hand side, the roof is adorned with curious cylindrical pendant devices made of cloth called "Thook"; each surmounted with the Trisool or trident, painted black and red. On the side facing the main entrance the courtyard is open, leading away to the doorways of other idol rooms. In the centre space stand two high poles "Turpoche," from which hang yaks' tails and white cotton streamers printed in the Tibetan character. Innumerable small prayer-wheels are fitted into a hitch that runs round the sides of the courtyard. A few large trees throw their shade on the building, and above them tower the rugged cliffs of the little valley, topped here and there by *Lhatos,* small square-built altars, surmounted by bundles of brushwood and wild sheep horns, the thin sticks of the brushwood being covered with offerings of coloured flags printed with some *mantra* or other.[1]

LAMA-YUR-RU, elevation about 11,000 feet.[2] Said to be of the Di-kung sect, as also the monasteries of *s*Gaṅ-noṅ and Shaṅ.

The name Yur-ru is said to be a corruption of Yuṅ-druṅ—the Svastika or mystic fly-foot cross.

THO-LING or Tho'lding (mt'o-gliṅ), on the upper Sutlej (in map of Turkistan it is Totlingmat, "mat" = "the lower," *i.e.* lower part of the city). It has a celebrated temple in three storeys, said by some to be modelled after that of Budha Gaya, and the *Sham-bha-la Lam-yig* contains a reference to this temple: "It had been built (A.D. 954, Schl.) by the Lo-tsa-wa Rin-zaṅ-po. The Hor (Turks?) burnt it down, but at some later date it was rebuilt, and now, in its lowest compartment, it contains the 'cycle of the collection of secrets.'" Adolph von Schlagintweit visited it.[3]

THEG-CH'OG is a sister-Lāmasery to He-mi, north of the Indus, in a valley which opens out opposite He-mi. Che-de, vulg. Chem-re (survey map: Chim-ray) is the name of the village to which the Lāmasery belongs.

KOR-DZOGS in Ladāk, 16,000 feet above the sea (*J.D.*, 11). Tik-za (Thik-se) is said (Marx) to be a Ge-*l*dan (?Ge-lug-pa) monastery, as also those of Saṅ-kar (a suburb of Leh), Likir and Ri-dzoṅ. It is pictured by Mr. Knight.[3]

WAM-LE (or "Han-le") in Rukshu, a fine Lāmasery figured by Cunningham. It is about 14,000 feet above sea-level. Its proper name is De-ch'en, and it was built by the founder of the one at *Hemi.*

MASHO is affiliated to Sa-*s*kya.

1 GODWIN-AUSTEN, *loc. cit.*, p. 72. 2 MARX, *loc. cit.*; CUNNINGHAM, *et. al.*

3 See Results of Scientific Mission.

SPI-T'UG, PE-TUB, or "Pittuk" (sPe-t'ub), a Lāmasery and village on the river Indus, five miles south-west of Leh. The Lāmas belong to the "Ge-ldan-pa" order of Lāmas. The Lāmasery has an incarnated Lāma.

SHER-GAL, figured by Knight, *loc. cit.*, p. 127.

KILANG (Kye-laṅ) in British Lahūl, romantically situated near glaciers, at an elevation of about 12,000 feet.

GU-GE, where several translations were made over 800 years ago, and still of repute for printing and for its elegant manuscripts.

KANUM, in Kunaor or Kanawar, where Csoma studied. Also Dub-liṅ, Poyi, and Paṅgi.

IN NEPAL.

In Nepal there appear to be no Lāmaist monasteries of any size, at least in the lower valleys. At the principal Buddhist shrines in that country a few resident Lāmas are to be found.

IN BHOTĀN

In Bhotān the largest monasteries are Tāshi-ch'o-dsong and Pun-t'aṅ or ? "Punakha" (spun-t'aṅ bde-ch'en), each, it is usually said, with over 1,000 monks, though according to other accounts, under 500.

TASHI-CH'O-DSOṄ (bKra-shis ch'os rdsoṅ), or "The fortress of the glorious religion," forms the capital of Bhotān and the residence, at least in summer, of the Grand Lāma of Bhotān—the Dharma Rāja and Deb Rāja. It has been visited and described by Manning, Bogle, Turner,[1] Pemberton,[2] etc.

The other chief monasteries in Bhotān, all of the Duk-pa sect, the established church of the country, are: dbU-rgyan rtso, Ba-kro (Pāto or Pāro) 'Bah, rTa-mch'og rgan, Kra-ha-li, Sam-'jin, K'a Ch'ags-rgan-K'a, Ch'al-p'ug. Of these the first three were formerly Kart'og-pa. In British Bhotān there are a few small monasteries, at Kalimpong, Pedong, etc.

IN SIKHIM.

In regard to Sikhim, as my information is complete, I give it in detail in tabular form on opposite page.

In addition to the monasteries in this list are several religious buildings called by the people *gömpas*, but by the Lāmas only "temples" (*Lha-k'aṅ*), such as Dé-thaṅ, Ke-dum, etc.

The oldest monastery in Sikhim is Dub-de, founded by the pioneer Lāma, Lhatsün Ch'embo. Soon afterwards shrines seem to have been erected at Tashiding, Pemiongchi, and Sang-ṅa-ch'ö-ling over spots consecrated to the Guru, and these ultimately became the nuclei of monas-

[1] Bogle and Turner in 1774 and 1783. MARKHAM, *op. cit.*

[2] In 1837-38. *Op. cit.*

teries. As the last-named one is open to members of all classes of Sikhimites, Bhotiyas, Lepchas, Limbus, and also females and even deformed persons, it is said that the monastery of Pemiongchi was

List of Monasteries in Sikhim.

Serial No.	Map Name.	Vernacular Name.	Meaning of the Name.	Date of Building.	Number of Monks.
1	Sanga Chelling	gsaṅ ṅags ch'os gliṅ	The place of secret spells ...	1697	25
2	Dubdi ...	sgrub-sde ...	The hermit's cell ...	1701	30
3	Pemiongchi ...	pad-ma yaṅtse	The sublime perfect lotus...	1705	108
4	Gantok ...	btsan-mk'ar ...	The Tsén's house ...	1716	3
5	Tashiding ...	bkra-s'is-ld ṅ	The elevated central glory	1716	20
6	Senan ...	gzil-*g*non	The suppressor of intense fear ...	1716	8
7	Rinchinpong ...	rin-ch'en spuṅs	The precious knoll ...	1730	8
8	Ralong ...	ra-blaṅ ...	....	1730	80
9	Mali ...	mad-lis ...	....	1740	15
10	Ram thek ...	Ram-tek ...	A Lepcha village name ...	1740	80
11	Fadung ...	p'o-braṅ ...	The chapel royal ...	1740	100
12	Cheungtong ...	btsun-t'aṅ ...	The meadow of marriage (of the two rivers)... ...	1788	8
13	Ketsuperri ...	mk'ā spyod dpal ri	The noble heaven-reaching mountain ...	...	11
14	Lachung ...	t'aṅ-mô-ch'en...	The large plain ...	1788	5
15	Talung ...	rdo-luṅ ...	The stony valley ...	1789	90
16	Entchi ...	rab-brten-gliṅ	The high strong place ...	1840	15
17	Phensung ...	p'an-bzaṅ ...	The excellent banner, or good bliss ...	1840	100
18	Kartok ...	bKah-rtog ...	The Kartok (founder of a schism) ...	1840	20
19	Dalling ...	rdo-gliṅ ...	"The stony site," or the place of the "Dorjeling" revelation-finder ...	1840	8
20	Yangong ...	gyaṅ sgaṅ ...	"The cliffy ridge," or "the lucky ridge" ...	1841	10
21	Labrong ...	bla-braṅ ...	The Lama's dwelling ...	1844	30
22	Laohung ...	pon-po sgaṅ ...	The Bön's ridge ...	1850	8
23	Lintse ...	lhun-rtse ...	The lofty summit ...	1850	15
24	Sinik ...	zi-mig ...	....	1850	30
25	Ringim ...	ri-dgon ...	Hermitage hill ...	1852	30
26	Lingthem ...	liṅ-t'am ...	A Lepcha village name ...	1855	20
27	Changhe ...	rtsag-nes ...	....	...	...
28	Lachen ...	La-ch'en ...	The big pass ...	1858	8
29	Giatong ...	zi-'dur ...	....	1860	8
30	Lingqui ...	lin-bkod ...	The uplifted limb ...	1860	20
31	Fadung ...	'p'ags rgyal ...	The sublime victor ...	1862	8
32	Nobling ..	nub-gliṅ ...	The western place ...	1875	5
33	Namchi ...	rnam-rtse ...	The sky-top ...	1836	6
34	Pabia ...	spa-'bi-'og ...	....	1875	20
35	Singtam ...	siṅ-ltam ...	A Lepcha village name ...	1884	6

designed, if not actually built, by Lha-tsün as a high-class monastery for orthodox celibate monks of relatively pure Tibetan race. Pemiongchi still retains this reputation for the professedly celibate character and good family of its monks; and its monks alone in Sikhim enjoy the title of *ta-saṅ* or "pure monk," and to its Lāma is reserved the honour of anointing with holy water the reigning sovereign.

The great majority of the monasteries in Sikhim belong to the Lha-tsün-pa sub-sect of the Ñiṅ-ma, only Namchi, Tashiding, Sinön, and T'aṅ-moch'e belong to the Ṅa-dak-pa sub-sect, and Kar-tok and Dôling to the Kar-tok-pa sub-sect of the same. All the Ñiṅ-ma monasteries are practically subordinate to that of Pemiongchi, which also exercises supervision over the Lepcha convents of Ling-t'am, Zimik, and P'ag-gye. Lepchas are admissible to Rigön as well as Sang-ṅa-ch'öling.

Nuns are admitted to a few monasteries in Sikhim, but their number is extremely small, and individually they are illiterate.

The names of the monasteries, as will be seen from the translations given in the second column of the table, are mostly Tibetan, and of an ideal or mystic nature; but some are physically descriptive of the site, and a few are Lepcha place-names, which are also of a descriptive character.

A Lāmaist Cairn.
Lab-ch'a, afterHuc.

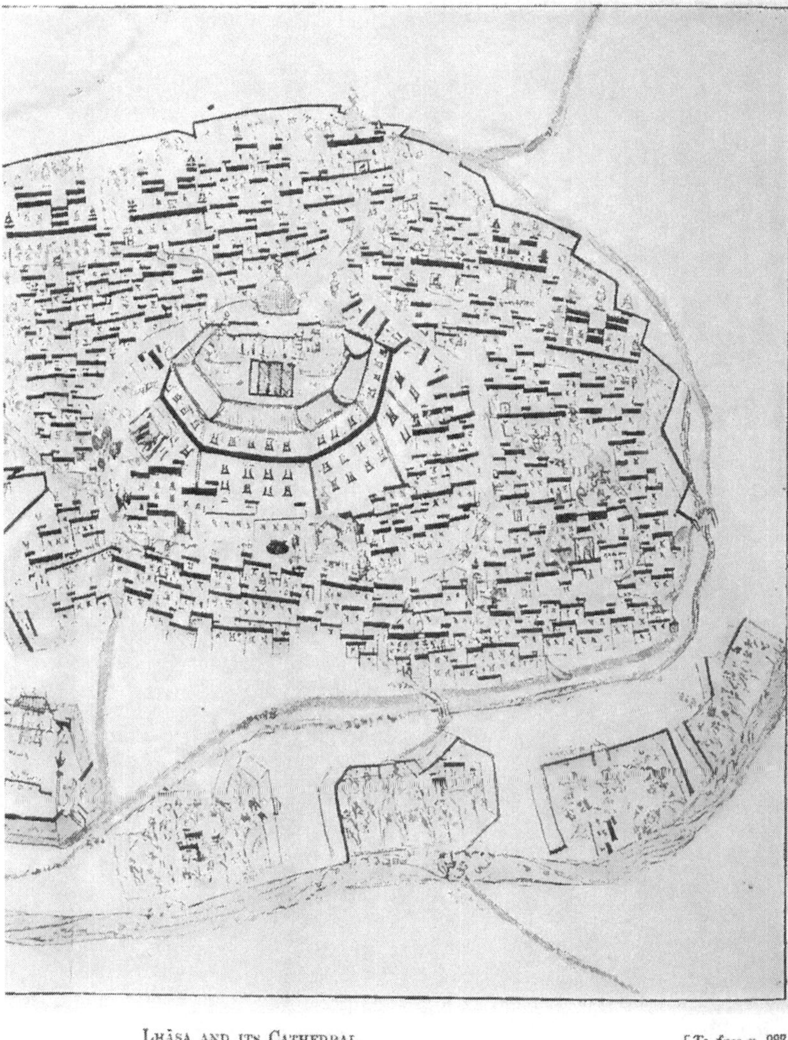

LHĀSA AND ITS CATHEDRAL.
(From a native drawing.)

[*To face p.* 287.

XII.

TEMPLES AND CATHEDRALS.

IN primitive Buddhism the temple had, of course, no place. It is the outcome of the theistic development with its relic-worship and idolatry, and dates from the later and impurer stage of Buddhism. The Lāmaist temple is called "God's house" (*Lha-k'an*).

It is usually the central and most conspicuous building in the monastery, and isolated from the other buildings, as seen in the foregoing illustrations. The roof is surmounted by one or two small bell-shaped domes of gilt copper[1]; if a pair, they are placed one on either end of the ridge, and called *jira*[2]; if a solitary one in the middle of the ridge, it is called "the banner."[3] They are emblematic of the royal umbrella and banner of victory. At the corners of the roof are erected cloth cylinders called *gebi*.[4] The building is often two storeys in height, with an outside stair on one flank, generally the right, leading to the upper flat. In front is an upper wooden balcony, the beams of which are rudely carved, also the doors. The orientation of the door has already been noted.

In approaching the temple-door the visitor must proceed with his right hand to the wall, in conformity with the respectful custom of *pradakshiṇa* widely found amongst primitive people.[5] In niches along the base of the building, about three feet above the level of the path, are sometimes inserted rows of prayer-barrels

---

1 See pp. 271 and 273.

2 Spelt "kñjira," (?) from the Skt., *kanca*, golden.

3 rgyal-mts'an.

4 *Gebi*—cylindrical erections from three feet high and about a foot wide to a greater size, covered by coiled ropes of black yak-hair and bearing a few white bands transverse and vertical, and when surmounted by a trident are called *C'ab-dar*.

5 The Romans in circumambulating temples kept them to their right. The Druids observed the contrary. To walk around in the lucky way was called *Deasil* by the Gaels, and the contrary or unlucky way *withershins* or *widdersinnis* by the lowland Scotch. See JAMIESON'S *Scottish Dict.*; R. A. ARMSTRONG'S *Gaelic Dict.*, p. 184; CROOKE'S *Introd.*; ROCKHILL. *L.*, p. 67.

which are turned by the visitor sweeping his hand over them as he proceeds.

The main door is approached by a short flight of steps; ou ascending which, the entrance is found at times screened by a large curtain of yak-hair hung from the upper balcony, and which serves to keep out rain and snow from the frescoes in the vestibule.

TEMPLE-DOOR DEMON.

Entering the vestibule, we find its gateway guarded by several fearful figures.[1] These usually are—

1. The tutelary demon of the ground, usually a red devil (*Tsän*) a brawny-limbed creature of elaborate ugliness, clad in skins, and armed with various weapons, and differing in name according to the locality.[2]

2. Especially vicious demons or *dii minores* of a more or less local character. Thus, at Pemiongchi is the *Gyal-po S'uk-dên* with a brown face and seated on a white elephant. He was formerly the learned Lāma Söd-nams Grags-pa, who being falsely charged with licentious living and deposed, his spirit on his death took this actively malignant form and wreaks his wrath on all who do not worship him—inflicting disease and accident.[3]

[1] Compare with description of Chinese Budd. temples by EITEL, *Lects. on Buddhism.*

[2] Thus the local devil of Ging temple near Darjiling is called "The Entirely Victorious Soaring Religion" (Ch'os-ldiṅ rnam-rgyal).

[3] Compare with the malignant ghosts of Brāhmans in India. Cf. TAWNEY's *Katha Sarit Sāgara*, ii., 338, 511

3. A pair of hideous imps, one on either side, of a red and bluish-black colour, named *S'em-ba Marnak*,[1] who butcher their victims.

GUARDIAN KING OF THE WEST.
(*Virūpaksha.*)

4. Here also are sometimes portrayed the twelve *Tän-ma*—the aërial fiendesses of Tibet, already figured, who sow disease and who were subjugated by St. Padma.

Confronting the visitor in the vestibule are the four colossal

[1] *rKi-kaṅ.*

images (or frescoes) of the celestial kings of the Quarters, who guard the universe and the heavens against the attacks of the Titans and the outer demons, as described at page 84. They are clad in full armour and are mostly of defiant mien, as seen in their figures over the page and at pages 83 and 330. Two are placed on each side of the doorway.

Sometimes the guardian of the north is given a yellow, and the guardian of the south a green, complexion, thus suiting the complexion of the guardians to the mythic colours of the cardinal points. They are worshipped by the populace, who credit them with the power of conferring good luck and averting the calamities due to evil spirits. And in the vestibule or verandah are also sometimes displayed as frescoes the Wheel of Life and scenes from the Jātakas or former births of Buddha; and here also may be figured the sixteen great saints or Sthavira (*Arhans* or "Rahans").[1]

In the smaller temples which possess no detached chapels for larger prayer-barrels, one or more huge prayer-barrels are set at either end of the vestibule, and mechanically revolved by lay-devotees, each revolution being announced by a lever striking a bell. As the bells are of different tones and are struck alternately, they form at times a not unpleasant chime.

The door is of massive proportions, sometimes rudely carved and ornamented with brazen bosses. It opens in halves, giving entry directly to the temple.

Such grand cathedrals as those of Lhāsa will be described presently. Meanwhile let us look at a typical temple of ordinary size. The temple interior is divided by colonnades into a nave and aisles, and the nave is terminated by the altar—generally as in the diagram-plan here annexed. The whole of the interior, in whichever direction the eye turns, is a mass of rich colour, the walls to right and left being decorated by frescoes of deities, saints, and demons, mostly of life-size, but in no regular order; and the beams are mostly painted red, picked out with lotus rosettes and

1 For their descriptions and titles see p. 376. Amongst the common scenes also represented here are "The Harmonious Four" (mt'un-pa rnam b'zi), a happy family, consisting of an elephant, monkey, rabbit, and parrot; and the long-lived sage (mi-ts'e-riṅ) with his deer, comparable to the Japanese (?) *Ju-rô*, one of the seven genii of Good Luck, and the long-lived hermit, *Se-nin*.

other emblems. The brightest of colours are used, but the general effect is softened in the deep gloom of the temple, which is dimly lit only by the entrance door.

Above the altar are placed three colossal gilt images in a sitting attitude, "The Three Rarest Ones," as the Lāmas call their trinity; though none of the images are considered individually to represent

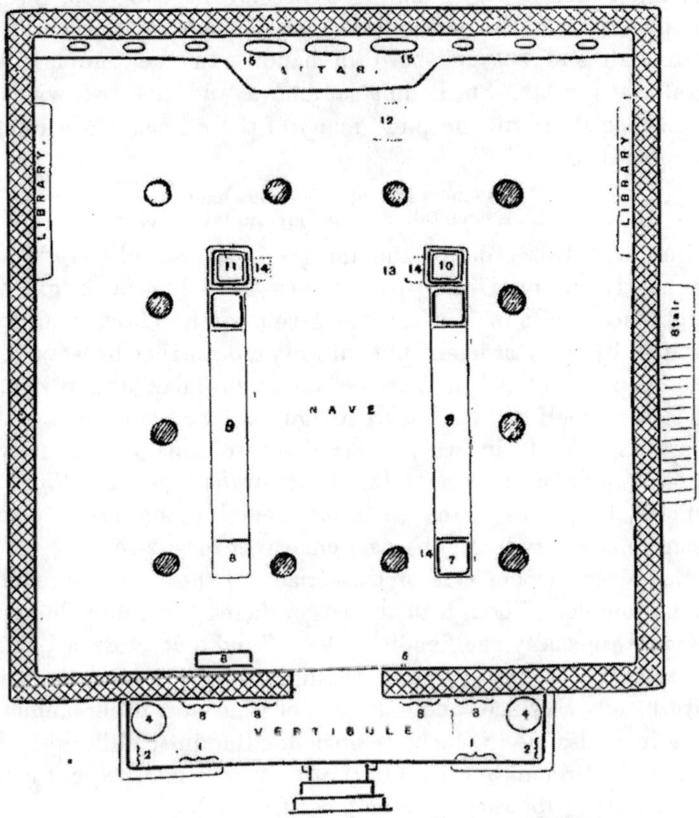

DIAGRAMMATIC GROUND-PLAN OF A TEMPLE IN SIKHIM.

1. Fresco of local demon.
2. Fresco of *Ki-kang Mar-nak* devils.
3. Fresco of guardian kings of quarters.
4. Prayer-barrels.
5. Station of orderlies.
6. Table for tea and soup.
7. Seat of the provost.
8. Seat of the water-giver.
9. Seats of monks
10. Seat of abbot or professor.
11. Seat of choir-leader.
12. Seat of king or visitant head Lāma.
13. Site where lay-figure of corpse is laid for litany.
14. Head Lāmas' tables.
15. Idols.

the two other members of the *Tri-ratna* or "Three Gems," namely *Dharma* or *Sangha*. The particular images of this triad depend on the sect to which the temple belongs ; *Ṣākya Muni* is often given the central position and a saint (Tsoṅ K'a-pa or Padma-sambhava) to the left of the spectator and Avalokita to the right. Particulars and figures of the principal of these idols are given in the chapter on images.

Ṣākya Muni is figured of a yellow colour with curly blue hair, and often attended by standing figures of his two chief disciples, Maugdalayāna on his left and Ṣariputra on his right, each with an alarm-staff and begging-bowl in hand. In the temples of the unreformed sects, St. Padma-sambhava and his two wives are given special prominence, and many of these images are regarded as "self-sprung:"

> "No hammers fell, no ponderous axes rung ;
> Like some tall palm the mystic fabric sprung."[1]

But even this order of the images is seldom observed. Most frequently in the Ge-lug-pa temples Tsoṅ K'a-pa is given the chief place, while in Ñiṅ-ma it is given to the *Guru*, and this is justified by the statement put into his mouth that he was a second Buddha sent by Ṣākya Muni specially to Tibet and Sikhim, as Buddha himself had no leisure to go there. Sometimes Ṣākya's image is absent, in which case the third image is usually the fanciful Buddha of Infinite Light, *Amitābha, or Amitāyus*, the Infinite Life. In many sectarian temples the chief place is given to the founder of the particular sect or sub-sect.

Ranged on either side of this triad are the other large images of the temple. Though in the larger fanes the more demoniacal images, especially the fiendish "lords" and protectors of Lāmaism, are relegated to a separate building, where they are worshipped with bloody sacrifices and oblations of wine and other demoniacal rites inadmissible in the more orthodox Buddhist building. Some of such idol-rooms are chambers of horrors, and represent some of the tortures supposed to be employed in hell.

The alleged existence of images of Gorakhnāth in Tashiding, Tumlong, and other Sikhim temples[2] is quite a mistake. No such image is known. The name evidently intended was "Guru Rinbo-ch'e."

---

[1] HEBER'S *Palestine*.

[2] CAMPBELL, *J.A.S.B.*, 1849 ; HOOKER, *Him. Jours.*, i., 323 ; ii., p. 195 ; Sir R. TEMPLE, *Jour.*, p. 212 ; Sir M. WILLIAMS, *Buddhism*, p. 490.

The large images are generally of gilded clay, and in Sikhim the most artistic of these come from Pá-to or "Paro" in Bhotān. A few are of gilded copper and mostly made by Newaris in Nepal. All are consecrated by the introduction of pellets of paper inscribed with sacred texts as detailed in the chapter on the pantheon.

Amongst the frescoes on the walls are displayed numerous Lāmaist saints and the pictorial Wheel of Life, though this last is often in the vestibule.

There are also a few oil-paintings of divinities framed, like Japanese *Kakemonos*, in silk of grotesque dragon-patterns with a border, arranged from within outwards, in "the primary" colours in their prismatic order of red, yellow, and blue. Some of these pictures are occasionally creditable specimens of art.

The seats for the several grades of officials and the Lāmaist congregation are arranged in definite order. The general plan of a small temple interior is shown in the foregoing diagram. Along each side of the nave is a long low cushion about three inches high, the seat for the monks and novices. At the further end of the right-hand cushion on a throne about 2½ feet high sits the abbot or professor (*Dorje Lô-pön*),[1] the spiritual head of the monastery. Immediately below him, on a cushion about one foot high, is his assistant, who plays the *sĩ-ñen* cymbals. Facing the professor, and seated on a similar throne at the further end of the left-hand cushion, is the *Um-dsé*[2] or chief chorister or celebrant, the temporal head of the monastery; and below him, on a cushion about one foot high, is the deputy chorister, who plays the large *ts'ögs-rol* or assembly-cymbals at the command of the *Um-dsé*, and officiates in the absence of the latter. At the door-end of the cushion on the right-hand side is a seat about one foot high for the provost-marshal, who enforces discipline, and on the pillar behind his seat hangs his bamboo rod for corporal chastisement. During the entry and exit of the congregation he stands by the right side of the door. Facing him at the end of the left-hand cushion, but merely seated on a mat, is the water-man.

To the left of the door is a table, on which is set the tea and soup which is to be served out, by the unpassed boy-candidates, during the intervals of worship.

1 rdo-rje slob-dpon.

2 dbU-mdsad.

THE LĀMAS' TABLES.

To the right front of the altar stands the chief Lāma's table,[1] about two-and-a-half feet in length, and one foot in height, and often elaborately carved and painted with lotuses and other sacred symbols, as figured at page 215. Behind it a cushion is placed, upon which is spread a yellow or blue woollen rug, or a piece of a tiger or leopard skin rug, as a seat. The table of the abbot or professor contains the following articles in the order and position shown in this diagram :—

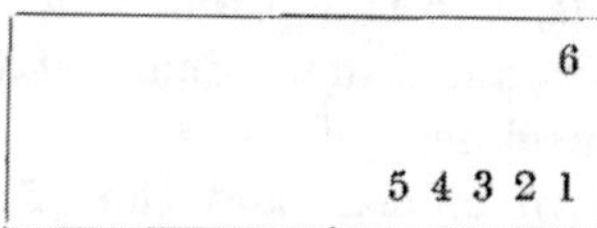

1. Magic rice-offering of universe.
2. Saucer with loose rice (*Ch'en-du* or *ne-sel*) for throwing in sacrifice.
3. Small hand-drum.
4. Bell.
5. *Dorje*-sceptre.
6. Vase for holy-water.

The other two monks who are allowed tables in the temple are the chief chorister or celebrant and the provost-marshal. The chief chorister's table faces that of the abbot, and contains only a holy water vase, bell, *dorje* and the large cymbals. The table of the provost stands in front of the seat of that officer, near the door, and contains an incense-goblet (*sang-bur*), a bell and *dorje*.

At the spot marked "13" on the plan is placed the lay-figure of the corpse whose spirit is to be withdrawn by the abbot. At the point marked "12" is set, in all the larger temples in Sikhim, the throne of the king, or of the re-incarnated Lāma—the "protecting lord"[2]—when either of them visits the temple.

On each pillar of the colonnade is hung a small silk banner with five flaps,[3] and others of the same shape, but differently named,[4] are hung from the roof, and on each side of the altar is a large one of circular form.[5]

THE ALTAR AND ITS OBJECTS.

The altar[6] occupies the upper end of the nave of the temple; and on its centre is placed, as already mentioned, the chief image.

[1] mdúm-lc'og. [2] Kyab-mgon. [3] Ka-'p'an.
[4] Ba-dan. [5] p'ye-p'ur. [6] mch'od s'am.

Above the altar is suspended a large silken parasol,[1] the

ALTAR (DOMESTIC) OF A ÑIṄ-MA LĀMA.

oriental symbol of royalty, which slightly revolves in one or

UMBRELLA-CANOPY.

other direction by the ascending currents of the warm air from

[1] dug.

the lamps. And over all is stretched a canopy, called the "sky"[1] on which are depicted the thunder dragons of the sky.

The altar should have at least two tiers. On the lower and narrow outer ledge are placed the offerings of water, rice, cakes, flowers and lamps. On the higher platform extending up to the images are placed the musical instruments and certain other utensils for worship, which will be enumerated presently.

MAGIC-OFFERING OF THE UNIVERSE.
The Rice-*Maṇḍala*.

In front of the altar, or sometimes upon the altar itself, stands the temple-lamp,[2] a short pedestalled bowl, into a socket in the centre of which is thrust a cotton wick, and it is fed by melted butter. As the great mass of butter solidifies and remains mostly in this state, the lamp is practically a candle. The size varies according to the means and the number of the temple votaries, as it is an act of piety to add butter to this lamp. One is necessary, but two or more are desirable, and on special occasions 108 or 1,000 small lamps are offered upon the altar. Sometimes a cluster of several lamps form a small candelabrum of the branching lotus-flower pattern.

[1] *nam-yul;* but its more honorific title is b*la-bras.*
[2] mch'od-skoṅ.

Below the altar stand the spouted water-jug[1] for filling the smaller water-vessels, a dish to hold grain for offerings,[2] an incense-holder, and a pair of flower-vases. And on the right (of the spectator) on a small stool or table is the magic rice-offering, with its three tiers, daily made up by the temple attendant, and

THE FIVE SENSUOUS OFFERINGS.

symbolic of an offering of all the continents and associated islands of the world.

The ordinary water and rice-offerings are set in shallow brazen bowls,[3] composed of a brittle alloy of brass, silver, gold and pounded precious stones. Their number is five or seven, usually the former. Two out of the five or seven bowls should be filled with rice heaped up into a small cone; but as this must be daily renewed by fresh rice, which in Tibet is somewhat expensive, fresh water is usually employed instead.

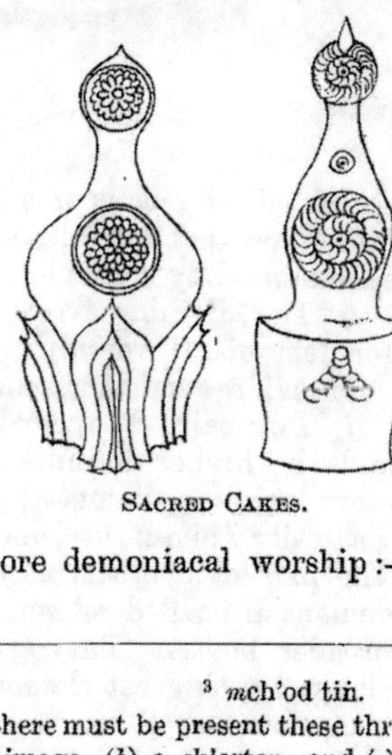

SACRED CAKES.

Another food-offering is a high, conical cake of dough, butter and sugar, variously coloured, named *tormā* or *z'al-zé*, that is, "holy food." It is placed on a metal tray supported by a tripod. To save expense a painted dummy cake is often substituted.

Upon the top of the altar are also usually placed the following objects, though several of them are special to the more demoniacal worship:—

1. A miniature funereal monument.[4]

---

1 ch'ab-bum. 2 nas bzeḍ. 3 *m*ch'od tin.

1 *ch'orten.* In the room in which worship is done there must be present these three essential objects: sku-*g*sum (Skt., *Trikāyā*) (*a*) an image, (*b*) a ch'orten, and (*c*) a holy book, which are symbolic of "the Three Holy Ones." In the early Indian caves this triad seems to have been represented by (?) a *Caitya* for Buddha, and a *Wheel* for Dharma.

2. One or more sacred books on each side of the altar.

3. The Lāmaist sceptre or *Dorje*, typical of the thunderbolt of Indra (Jupiter), and a bell. The *dorje* is the counterpart of the bell, and when applied to the shoulder of the latter should be of exactly the same length as the bell-handle.

4. The holy-water vase[1] and a metal mirror hanging from its spout. The holy-water of the vase is tinged with saffron, and is

SOME ALTAR OBJECTS.
Lamp (inverted), caitya, holy-water jug.

sprinkled by means of a long stopper-rod, which is surmounted by a fan of peacock's feathers and the holy *kusa* grass. Another form is surmounted by a chaplet, etc., as its frontispiece.

5. The divining-arrow bound with five coloured silks called *dādar*[2] for demoniacal worship.

6. A large metal mirror[3] to reflect the image of the spirits.

7. Two pairs of cymbals. The pair used in the worship of Buddha and the higher divinities are called *sī-ñēn*,[4] and are of about twelve or more inches in diameter, with very small central bosses. They are held vertically when in use, one above the other, and are manipulated gently. The pair of cymbals used in the worship of the inferior deities and demons are called *rol-mo*, and are of shorter diameter with very much broader bosses. They are held horizontally in the hands and forcibly clanged with great clamour. Chinese gongs also are used.

8. Conch-shell trumpet (*tuṅ*[5]), often mounted with bronze or silver, so as to prolong the valves of the shell and deepen its note—used with the *sī-ñēn* cymbals.

[1] k'rus-bum. See fig. ROCK., *L.*, 106.
[2] *m*dah-dar.
[3] me-long.
[4] sil-*s*myan.
[5] duṅ.

DEVILS' ALTAR.

9. Pair of copper flageolets.[1]

10. Pair of long telescopic copper horns in three pieces,[2] and often six feet long (see illustration on page 17).

11. Pair of human thigh-bone trumpets.[3] These are sometimes encased in brass with a wide copper flanged extremity, on which are figured the three eyes and nose of a demon, the oval open extremity being the demon's mouth. In the preparation of these thigh-bone trumpets the bones of criminals or those who have died by violence are preferred, and an elaborate incantation is done, part of which consists in the Lāma eating a portion of the skin of the bone, otherwise its blast would not be sufficiently powerful to summon the demons.

12. Pair of tiger thigh-bone trumpets.[4] These are not always present, and the last three instruments are only for the worship of the inferior gods and demons.

13. Drums (ch'os rṅa) :—

(*a*) A small rattle hand-drum or *ṅa-ch'uṅ*[5] or *damāru*, like a large double egg-cup. Between its two faces are attached a pair of pendant leather knobs and a long-beaded flap as a handle. When the drum is held by the upper part of the cloth handle and jerked alternately to right and left the knobs strike the faces of the drum. It is used daily to mark the pauses between different forms of worship.

(*b*) The big drum,called *ch'ö-ṅa*,[6] or religious drum. These are of two kinds, one of which is suspended in a frame and beat only occasionally and in Buddha's worship. The other is carried in the hand by means of a stem thrust through its curved border. These are beaten by drum-sticks with straight or curved handles.

(*c*) The human skull-drum made of *skull-caps*, and of the same style as the smaller drum (*a*) above described.

14. Libation jugs, figured on page 225.

THE CATHEDRAL OF LHĀSA.

The greatest of all the temples of Lāmadom is the great cathedral of Lhāsa, the St. Peter's of Lāmaism, the sketch of which, here given, was drawn for me by a Lāma artist, who visited Lhāsa with this object, and who deliberately sketched the sacred city and its great temple from the hillock about half a mile to the south of the city. And with the description of it[7] we will close our account of temples.

This colossal temple, called "The Lord's House" (*Jo-wo K'aṅ*),

---

1 *r*gye-*g*liṅ. 2 ra*g*-duṅ. 3 *r*kaṅ-*g*liṅ.
4 stag duṅ. 5 rṅa-ch'uṅ. 6 ch'os-*r*na.
7 Summarized from the accounts of Huc, etc., and from Köppen, ii., 334.

stands in the centre of the city of Lhāsa, to which it gives its name, "God's place;[1] and it is also considered the centre of the whole land. All the main roads, which cut through Tibet, run out of it and meet again in it. But it is also the centre of the united Lāmaist church, as it is the first and oldest Buddhist temple of Tibet, the true metropolitan cathedral of Lāmaism. Founded in the seventh century, on commencing the conversion of the gloomy snowland, by king Sroṅ Tsan Gampo, for the preservation of those wondrous images brought to him by his two wives, as before mentioned, it has, no doubt, in the course of a millennium, received many additions and enlargements, and in the seventeenth century it was restored and rebuilt.

Its entrance faces the east, and before it, in a square, stands a flagstaff, about forty feet high with yak's hair, and horns of yak and sheep, tied to its base. The main building is three storeys high, and roofed by golden plates.[2] The entrance is in the shape of a hall, which rests on six wooden pillars, very handsomely decorated with engravings, paintings, and gilding. The walls are covered with rough pictures out of the biography of the founder of the religion. In the centre of the hall is a swing door, which is decorated on the outside with bronze, and on the inside with iron reliefs.

Through this you pass into the ante-court, which is covered by the first storey. In the wall, opposite the entrance, is a second door, which brings you inside, on both sides of which stands the colossal statues of the four great guardian kings; two on the right and two on the left side. This brings us into a large pillared hall, which has the form of the basilica, and is divided by colonnades into three long and two cross-aisles. The light comes from above in the middle or broadest aisle, where a transparent oilcloth serves instead of glass. Through this the whole temple is lighted, because there are no side windows. On the outside of the two

1 The name Lhāsa is properly restricted to the great temple. Sroṅ Tsan Gampo appears to have been the founder of the city now generally known to Europeans as Lhāsa. It is recorded that he exchanged the wild Yarlung valley, which had been the home of his ancestors, for the more central position to the north of the Tsangpo, a village named Rasa, which, on account of the temple he erected, was altered to Lhā-sa, or "God's place." An old form of the name is said to be *l*nga-*l*dan.

2 These plates are said to be of solid gold, and gifted by the son of the princeling Ananmal, about the end of the twelfth century A.D.

side aisles, *i.e.*, on the north and south side, as the entrance is towards the east, is a row of small cells or chapels, fourteen to the right and just as many to the left. The two cross-aisles form the background, and are separated from the long aisle by silver lattice-work. Here are the seats of the lower priests for common prayer-

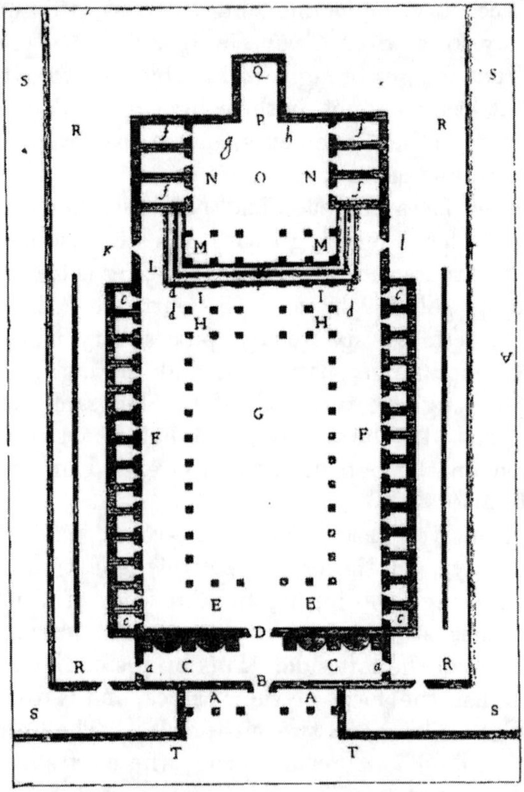

GROUND-PLAN OF LHĀSA CATHEDRAL.[1]

meetings. From the west cross-aisle a staircase leads into the holy of holies. On the left of this we see, by ascending behind silver rods, fifteen plates of massive silver, which are covered with innumerable precious stones, and contain representations of the Buddhist dogmatics and mysticism. We see there, for instance, the Buddhist system of the world, the circle of the metempsychosis

[1] After Giorgi. I have not reproduced the references as they are not sufficiently concise.

with its different states. From the stairs above we come into a cross-aisle, which has just as many pillars as the two lower ones, and is also the inner front hall of the sanctuary. The latter has the form of a square, in which are six chapels, three on each of the north and south flanks. In the middle is the place for the offering altar, which, however, is only erected on certain occasions. On the other side of the altar, on the west side of the holy of holies, also in the lowest depth of the whole edifice, is the quadrangular niche, with the image of Ṣākya Muni. Before the entrance in this, to the left, is raised the throne of Dalai Lāma, very high, richly decorated, and covered with the customary five pillows of the Grand Lāmas. Beside this stands the almost similar one of the Tashi Grand Lāma; then follow those in rotation of the regenerated Lāmas. The abbots, and the whole non-incarnate higher priesthood have their seats in the cross-aisle of the sanctuary. Opposite the throne of Dalai Lāma, on the right from the entrance of the niche, is the chair of the king of the Law, not quite so high as those of the regenerate Grand Lāmas, but higher than those of the others. Behind him are the seats of the four ministers, which are not so high as those of the common Lāmas.

On the west side of the niche stands the high altar, which is several steps high. Upon the top of the higher ones we see small statues of gods and saints made of massive gold and silver; upon the lower ones, as usual on Buddhist altars, lamps, incensories, sacrifices, and so on; upon the highest, behind a silver gilt screen, the gigantic richly-gilded image of Buddha Ṣākya Muni, wreathed with jewelled necklaces as native offerings. This image is named "The gem of majesty" (Jo-vo Rin-po-ch'e), and represents Buddha as a young prince in the sixteenth year of his age. It, according to the opinion of the believers, was made in Magadha during Buddha's lifetime, and afterwards gifted by the Magadha king to the Chinese emperor in return for assistance rendered against the Yavan invaders; and given by the Chinese emperor to his daughter on her marriage with the king of Tibet, in the seventh century A.D. Flowers are daily showered upon it. Beside this one—the highest object of reverence—the temple has also innumerable other idols; for instance, in a special room, the images of the goddess Ṣrī Devi (Pal-ldan Lha-mo). There is also a celebrated image of the Great Pitying Lord—Avalokita—named "the self-created pentad."[1] Also images of historical persons who have made themselves worthy of the church; amongst whom one sees there the aforesaid pious king and his two wives, all three of whom are canonized; also his ambassador, who was sent by him to India to fetch from there the holy books and pictures.[2]

In this large and oldest temple are lodged great numbers of other precious things and holy relics, consecrated presents, gold and silver vessels, which are openly exhibited at the beginning of the third Chinese month.

Round about these stand many wooden or copper prayer-machines. The surrounding wings of the building contain the state-treasures, the magazines, in which are stored everything necessary for divine service, the monks' cells, the lecture-rooms; in the higher storeys also the residences of the highest state officers, and special rooms for the Dalai Lāma. The whole is surrounded with a wall, at which are several Buddhist towers, which, as in the case of the large temple, are covered with gilded plates. No women are allowed to remain within the walls during the night, a prohibition which extends to many Lāmaist cloisters.

[1] raṅ byuṅ *l*ṅa-*l*dan. So called because it is reputed to have formed itself by emanations from: Thug-je ch'enpo (Avalokita), T'ul-ku-geyloṅ—the artist, Sroṅ Tsan Gampo, his Chinese wife, and his Newari wife. And the location of each of these in the image is pointed out.

[2] Köppen says an image of Hiuen Tsiang is also there.

Benedictory Clay Seal of Grand Tashi Lāma, given to Pilgrims.

(Full size.)

LĀMA-POPE BLESSING PILGRIMS.[1]

XIII.

SHRINES, RELICS, AND PILGRIMS.

PILGRIMAGES are most popular in Tibet. The country contains an infinite number of sacred sites, reputed re-incarnated or supernatural Lāmas, self-created images, relics of the Buddhas, holy footprints, sanctified trees, etc., to which the pious throng with gifts of gold and other precious offerings; while many extend their pilgrimages to places outside Tibet, to China, Bhotān, Sikhim, Nepal, Kashmīr, Turkestan, and India, to places hallowed by St. Padma-sambhava, or by Buddha himself.

The most holy of all sites, according to the Lāmas, in common with all Buddhists—like Mecca to the Muhammadans—is the Tree of Wisdom at Buddh-Gayā, in India, with its temple known to Tibetans as Gandhola,[2] where Ṣākya Muni attained his Buddha-

[1] After Giorgi.

[2] drí-gtsaṅ-k'aṅ, or "The Untainted (pure) House." It was built in seven days by the high-priest "Virtue" (*d*ge-ba). See also TĀRANĀTHA, 16, 4, etc. At the Bodhimaṇḍa (byaṅ-ch'ub-sñiṅ-po) is the diamond-throne (vajrāsana, Tib., Dorje-dan), so called on account of its stability, indestructibility, and capacity of resisting all worldly shocks.

hood, and which is believed to be the hub of the world. After this come the site of Buddha's death, Kuṣinagara; and the eight great Caityas which enshrined his bodily relics; the mythical mount Potala[1] in the south; the mythical Shambhala in the north; the Guru's Fairy-land[2] in Udyāna in the west; and "The three hills," or U-tai Shan, in northern China, the original seat of the God of Wisdom, Mañjuṣrī; and Lhāsa, the St. Peter's of the Lāmas, and the seat of Buddha's vice-regent upon earth.

The Indian shrines are seldom visited by Lāmas and Tibetans on account of the great distance and expense. I have listened several times to the prayers of Lāmas and Tibetan laity at the great Buddh-Gayā temple, which, strange to say, is still held by unsympathetic Hindū priests who prey upon the Buddhist pilgrims. These prayers were divided between petitions for temporal prosperity and for "the great ultimate perfection," or Nirvāṇa. They make offerings to the Tree of Wisdom, but their oblations do not take the form of watering it with eau de Cologne and gilding it, as do some of the Burmese.

PILGRIM LĀMAS.

At the shrines under Buddhist management, the pilgrims carry off, as relics, printed charms and fragments of the robes of re-incarnated Lāmas and other holy men, leaves of sacred trees, etc., which are carefully treasured as amulets and fetishes. And these objects and holy water work most miraculous cures in a manner which is not unknown even in Christian Europe.[3]

[1] ri-bo gru-'dsin. [2] mk'ā-'gro gliṅ.

[3] Those Europeans who sneer at the "pagan" superstitions of the East may find

The fullest Tibetan account of Indian shrines is found in the book named *Jambu-gliṅ spyi bs'ad*, a compilation containing a very confused abstract of Hiuen Tsiang's celebrated treatise.[1]

In regard to the site of Buddha's death, the Lāmas have placed it in Asam.

In conversations some years ago with Lāmas and lay Buddhists at Darjiling, I was surprised to hear that Asam contained a most holy place of Buddhist pilgrimage called "*Tsam-ch'ô-ḍuṅ*,"[2] which, it was alleged, next to the great temple at Buddh-Gayā, was the most holy spot a Buddhist could visit. Asam is usually regarded as being far beyond the limits of the Buddhist Holy Land, and the Chinese pilgrims, FaHian and Hiuen Tsiang in the fifth and seventh centuries of our era, to whom we are mainly indebted for our knowledge of ancient Buddhist geography, not only do not mention any holy site in Asam, but Hiuen Tsiang, who visited Gauhaṭī at the invitation of the king of Kāmrūp, positively notes the absence of Buddhist buildings in Asam.[3]

I therefore felt curious to learn further particulars of this important site in Asam, which had apparently been overlooked by geographers.

---

amongst themselves equally grotesque beliefs. For example, the *Holy Coat of Trèves*, and one of the most recent miracles, the *Lady of Lourdes*. Lourdes, as a miracle place, dates from 1858, when a little girl had a vision of "a beautiful and radiant lady." Eighteen times the glorious apparition was seen by the girl; then it was seen no more. Twenty thousand persons by that time had gathered to the *rendezvous*. On one of the last occasions the girl, as if obeying a sign from her visitant, went to a corner of the grotto where the appearances occurred, and scratched in the dry earth. The gaping crowd saw water rise and the girl drink. Then a little streamlet made its way to the river. In a short time the spring gave 120,000 litres a day. And the wonders of miraculous healing effected by this water are the theme of the learned and the ignorant alike. In 1872 the number of pilgrims amounted to 140,000, and this year the same number appeared at the health-giving spring. Over 12,000 brought 1,100 sick. They had come from Paris and the north in seventeen pilgrimage trains, and this year (1894), according to the newspapers, two train-loads steamed out of London for the same convent. There is a band of trained attendants, who do good service, and the sick are dipped by experts and cared for. As the patient is immersed, some of the assistants, with arms uplifted, pray with him. Some of the sick quietly undergo the dip, as if resigned to whatever may befall them. Others beat the water in agony, and clutch at hands near, but all pray—these last with loud cries of despair to heaven: "Cure us, Holy Virgin. Holy Virgin, you *must* cure us." There is great ecclesiastical ceremonial, elevation of the host, priests with lighted tapers, and high dignitaries be-robed and be-mitred. "The cures" are duly certified—they are as marvellous as any by a well-advertised specific.

[1] For a translation of a smaller one see my article in *Proc. A.S.B.*, Feb., 1893.

[2] rTsa-mch'og-groṅ. See *J.A.S.B.*, lxi., pp. 33 *seq.*

[3] *Si-yu-ki*, trans. by BEAL, ii., p. 196.

In Jäschke's Tibetan dictionary[1] I found the name "rTsa-mch'og-groṅ" defined as a "town in west Asam where Buddha died," and this statement, it is noted, is given on the authority of the "Gyalrabs," a vernacular history of Tibet. Csoma de Körös also notes[2] that "the death of Shakya, as generally stated in the Tibetan books, happened in Asam near the city of Kuṣa or Camarūpa (Kāmrūp)."

Here, then, was a clue to the mystery. Buddha's death, it is well known, occurred between two *sāl* trees near *Kuṣinagara* or *Kuṣanagara*, in the north-west provinces of India, thirty-five miles east of Gorakhpur, and about one hundred and twenty miles N.N.E. of Benares; and the site has been fully identified by Sir A. Cunningham[3] and others from the very full descriptions given by Hiuen Tsiang and FaHian. The name *Kuṣanagara* means "the town of Kuṣa grass";[4] and as the early Lāma missionaries in their translation of the Buddhist scriptures habitually translated all the Sanskrit and Pāli names literally into Tibetan, *Kuṣanagara* was rendered in the "Kah-'gyur" canon as "rTsa-mch'og-groṅ," from "*r*tsa-mch'og," kuṣa grass, "grong," a town (=Sskt., *nagara*).

Now, near the north bank of the Brahmaputra, almost opposite Gauhaṭī, the ancient capital of Kāmrūp, is, I find, an old village named *Sāl-Kuṣa*, and it lies on the road between Gauhaṭī and Dewangiri, one of the most frequented passes into Bhotān and Tibet. With their extremely scanty knowledge of Indian geography, the Lāmas evidently concluded that this "town of *Sāl-Kuṣa*" was the "town of Kusa," where Buddha entered into *Nirvāṇa* between the two *sāl* trees—seeing that the word *sāl* was also incorporated with the equivalent of "Tsam-ch'ô-ḍuṅ," and that in the neighbourhood was the holy hill of Hājo, where, as will be seen hereafter, there probably existed at that time some Buddhist remains.

---

1 P. 437.

2 *Asiatic Researches*, xx., p. 295.

3 *Arch. Surv. India Repts.*, i., 76; xvii., 55, etc.

4 Kuṣa grass (*Poa cynosuroides*), the sacrificial grass of the Hindūs, is also prized by the Buddhists on account of its having formed the cushion on which the Boddhisattva sat under the Bodhi tree. It is also used as a broom in Lāmaic temples and as an altar decoration associated with peacock's feathers in the *pumpa* or holy water vase.

No description of this Buddhist site seems to be on record, except a very brief note by Col. Dalton [1] on the modern Hindū temple of Hājo, which shrines a Buddhist image. So as I have had an opportunity of visiting the site, and enjoyed the rare advantage of being conducted over it by a Lāma of eastern Tibet who chanced to be on the spot, and who had previously visited the site several times, and possessed the traditional stories regarding it, I give the following brief description of it in illustration of how the Lāmas, originally misled by an identity of name, have subsequently clothed the neighbourhood with a legendary dress in keeping with the story of Buddha's death, and how this place, with its various associated holy spots, is now implicitly believed by the pilgrims to be the real site of Buddha's *pari-nirvāṇa*. And in this belief, undeterred by the intemperate heat of the plains, Buddhist pilgrims from all parts of Bhotān, Tibet, and even from Ladāk and south-western China visit these spots and carry off scrapings of the rocks and the soil in the neighbourhood, treasuring up this precious dust in amulets, and for placing beside their dead body, as saving from dire calamities during life, and from transmigration into lower animals hereafter. Authentic specimens of this dust, I was informed, commanded in Tibet high prices from the more wealthy residents, who had personally been unable to undertake the pilgrimage.

The Hājo hill, or rather group of hills, where is situated, according to the current tradition of the Lāmas, the spot where Buddha "was delivered from pain," lies to the north (right) bank of the Brahmaputra about nine miles north-west from Gauhaṭī (Kāmrūp), north latitude 26° 11′ 18″ and east long. 91° 47′ 26″, and four or five miles north of *Sāl-Kuṣa.* The hill rises directly from the plain, forming a strikingly bold and picturesque mass; and it is a testimony to its natural beauty to find that the hill has attracted the veneration of people of all religious denominations. The semi-aboriginal Mech and Koch worship it as a deity under the name of Hājo, which means in their vernacular "*the* hill." The Buddhists formerly occupied one of the hillocks, but are now displaced by the Brāhmans, who restored the temple, which is now one of the most frequented Hindū temples in Asam. The Muhammadans also have crowned the summit of the highest peak with a mosque.

The cluster of hills presents a very symmetrical appearance as seen from a distance, forming a bold swelling mass culminating in three

[1] *J.A.S.B.*, 1855, lxxi., p. 8,

trident-like peaks, the central one of which is pre-eminent, and is regarded by the Buddhists as emblematic of Buddha. The high peaks on either side of this are identified with Buddha's two chief disciples, Sāriputra and Maudgalyayāna. This triad of peaks is seen from a great distance, and it is only on near approach that the smaller hillocks are observed. These latter number about sixteen, and are called *Nē-tēn c'u-du*, or "the sixteen disciples" of Buddha.

The most holy site, according to the Buddhists, is a bare flattish shoulder of rock, about eight yards in diameter, situated at the north-west base of the hill. This is stated to be the *Sil-wa ts'al-yi tur-dö*, or "the pyre of the cool grove," where Buddha died, and where his body was cremated. The rock here bears several roughly-cut inscriptions in Tibetan characters of the mystic sentences, "*Om maṇi padme hūṃ*," "*Om ah hūṃ*," "*Om*," etc., and coloured rags torn from the vestments of the pilgrims are tied to the bushes in the neighbourhood. The Hindūs have carved here on the rock a figure of the four-armed Vishnu, which the Brāhman priests call *Dhūbī*, or "the washerwoman of the gods," and the rock they call "*Letai dhupinir pāt.*"

It is worthy of note that the Lāmas, for the benefit of the resident population of Tibet, have made copies of this spot in at least four places in Tibet, viz., at:—

1. *Ra-rgyab*, in the south-east outskirts of Lhāsa city.
2. *P'a-poṅ k'ar*, in the north suburbs of Lhāsa.
3. *P'ur-mo c'he*, about twelve miles to the north-east of Tashi-lhunpo.
4. *Sel-brag.*

These sites were consecrated by placing on them a piece of rock brought from this Asam site, now under report; but the latter spot bears the distinctive prefix of *Gyā-gar*, or Indian, implying that it is the original and genuine site.

A high cliff, close to the west of this spot, is called "the vulture's mound hill," as in Tibet vultures usually frequent the neighbourhood of the *tur-dö* cemeteries, and in belief that it is the Gridha Kuta Giri hermitage of Buddha.[1]

A short distance beyond this spot, in the jungle, is a roughly-hewn stone basin, about six feet in diameter, called by the Lāmas *Saṅ-gyāmā ko-ko*, or the pot in which the *S in-je*—the death-demons—boil the heads of the damned. The Brāhmans, on the other hand, assert that it is the bowl in which *Ṣiva* or *Adi-purusha* brewed his potion of lust exciting Indian hemp, and they point to its green (confervoid) watery contents in proof of this. They also state that a snake inhabits the depths of the bowl; but it was certainly absent at the time of my visit.

Advancing along the pathway, leading up-hill, we pass a few columnar masses of rock lying near the path, which are pointed to as fragments of Buddha's staff with which he unearthed this monster bowl.

---

[1] bya-rgyod p'uṅ poī rī.

Climbing up the hill we reach the temple of Kedāranāth, which is approached by a very steep roughly-paved causeway. At the entrance is a long inscription in granite in old Bengālī characters, those being the characters adopted by the Asamese. Adjoining this temple is the shrine of Kamaleṣvar or "the lord of the Lotus." Here is a tank called by the Lāmas "*Tsŏ mani bhadra*," or "the lake of the notable gem"; and they state that many water-sprites (*Nāga*, serpents or dragons) came out of this pond on the approach of Buddha and presented him with jewels. A small cell by the side of this pond is said to be the place where Buddha set down a mass of butter which had been brought to him as a gift, and the stone *linga* and *yoni* (phallus and its counterpart), now shrined here by the Hindūs, are pointed to as being this petrified butter.

Crowning the summit of the hill is a large masjid built by Lutfullah, a native of Shirāz, in the reign of the emperor Shāh Jahān, in 1656 A.D., with a Persian inscription.[1]

A detached conical hillock, about 300 feet above the plain, lying about half-a-mile to the north-east of the hill, and now crowned by the Hindū temple of Mādhava, is identified with "the great caitya" which was erected over the cremated relics of the Tathāgatha's body.

The present shrine of the temple seems to be the original shrine of an older Buddhist temple, which, according to both Buddhist and Asamese tradition, formerly existed here—the upper portion only is modern. Col. Dalton has described the general details of this building, and he states: "The Brāhmans call the object of worship Mādhab, the Buddhists call it Mahāmuni, the great sage. It is in fact simply a colossal image of Buddha in stone. Its modern votaries have, to conceal mutilation, given it a pair of silver goggle-eyes and a hooked gilt silvered nose and the form is concealed from view by cloths and chaplets of flowers; but remove these and there is no doubt of the image having been intended for the 'ruler of all, the propitious, the asylum of clemency, the all-wise, the lotus-eyed comprehensive Buddha.'"

This large image of Buddha is called by the more learned Lāma-visitors *Munir Muni Mahāmuni, i.e.*, "The Sage of Sages, The Great Sage." It is the original image of the shrine, and is stated by the Brāhmanic priests, who call it *Mādhab*, to be of divine origin and an actual embodiment or *avatār* of the god, in contradistinction to the other images which are called mere "*mūrtis*" or hand-fashioned copies of typical forms of the respective gods represented. This may merely mean that the Brāhmans found this image here, while the others were brought from the neighbourhood or elsewhere. What seems to be the history of the mutilation of this image is found in the account of the invasion of the Koch kingdom of lower Asam by the Musalmans under Mīr Jumlah in 1661 A.D. This chief issued "directions to destroy all the idolatrous temples and to erect mosques in their stead. . . . . To evince his zeal for religion, the general himself, with a battle-axe, broke the celebrated image of Narain, the principal object of worship of the

[1] See *J.A.S.B.*, lxi., p. 37.

Hindūs of that province."[1] Nārāyana is one of the names of Mādhab and a patronymic of the Koch rāja's; and Hājo was a seat of the Koch rājas. And it was at Hājo that Mīr Jumlah took the Koch king prisoner.[2]

The other images, not mentioned by Dalton, but which must have existed at the time of his visit, are also of stone and are placed on either side of the large image. They are four in number and are of considerable size. According to the Lāma-pilgrims they are all Buddhist images; but the crypt was so dimly lit, and the images so enveloped in clothes and wreaths of flowers that I could not distinguish their specific characters, with the exception of the head and peculiar trident of the first, and the head of the second, which were characteristic and justified their recognized names, viz.:—

No. 1.—*Ugyan Guru* to the left of Mahāmuni.
No. 2.—*Dorje Dolö* to the right of Mahāmuni.
No. 3.—*Sākya Thuba* to the right of No. 2.
No. 4.—"*Sencha*" *Muni* to the right of No. 3.

Although Hindū priests, as a rule, are not very methodical in their bestowal of names upon the images which they have appropriated from Buddhist ruins, still I here give the Brāhmanical names as reported by the attendant priests, as, this being a wealthy temple, the priests were more learned than usual, and the names should give some idea of the nature of the images. After stating that the Buddhist pilgrims gave the above noted names to the images, these priests said that the Brāhmanical names were as follows, which, it will be noticed, are Bengali. I give them in the order of the previous list:—

No. 1. Dwitīya Mādhaver mūrti.
No. 2. Lāl Kanaiyā Bankat Vihārer mūrti.
No. 3. Basu Dever mūrti.
No. 4. Hayagrīver mūrti.

In the vestibule are lotus ornamentations and several articles of the usual paraphernalia of a Buddhist temple, including the following: A pyramidal framework or wheeless car like the Tibetan *Ch'aṅ-ga chutuk*, with lion figures at the corners of each tier, such as is used to seat the image of a demon which is to be carried beyond the precincts of the temple and there thrown away. The present frame is used by the priests of this temple to parade in the open air one of the smaller images of the shrine (? Hayagrīver), but the image is again returned to the shrine. Above this throne is stretched a canopy containing the figure of an eight-petalled lotus flower, and has, as is customary, a dependant red fringe. On either side is hung a huge closed umbrella. These articles have been in the temple from time immemorial.

Of the external decoration of the temple, the row of sculptured elephants along the basement, evidently a portion of the old Buddhist temple, has been figured by Col. Dalton in the paper above referred to;

[1] STEWART'S *History of Bengal*, p. 289.
[2] BEVERIDGE, *Cal. Review*, July, 1890, p. 12.

and is identical with the decorative style of the Kailas cave temple of Ellora figured by Fergusson in Plate xv. of his *Cave Temples.* The upper walls are covered with sculptured figures nearly life-size. The ten *avatáras* of Vishnu are represented with Buddha as the ninth. The remaining figures are of a rather nondescript character, but they are mostly male, and nearly every figure carries a trident *(trisula)*—the *khatam* of the Buddhists. The Lāmas state that these figures were formerly inside the temple, but that Buddha ejected them. And it is stated that the temple was built in one night by *Viṣvakarma*, the Vulcan of the Hindūs and Buddhists.

Attached to the temple is a colony of *Naṭī*, or dancing girls,[1] who are supported out of the funds of the temple, and who on the numerous feast days dance naked in a room adjoining the shrine. These orgies are part of the Sākti worship so peculiar to Kāmrūp, but nowhere is it so grossly conducted as at this temple.[2] The *Naṭī* and the idol-car are also conspicuous at the degenerate Buddhist temple of Jagannāth at Puri.

At the eastern base of the hillock, on which this temple stands, is a fine large tank, called by the Lāmas "the lake of excellent water."[3] This pond, it is said, was made by Buddha with one prod of his staff, when searching for the huge bowl already described which he unearthed here. This pond is also said to be tenanted by fearful monsters.

I have been unable to ascertain positively whether any Buddhist building existed here previous to the Lāmas fixing on the site as the Kuṣanagara of Buddha's death. Certainly no monastery existed here at the time of Hiuen Tsiang's visit to the Kāmrūp (Gauhaṭī) court in the seventh century A.D., for he says of this country that "the people have no faith in Buddha, hence from the time when Buddha appeared in the world even down to the present time there never as yet has been built one *Sanghārāma* as a place for the priests to assemble." The reference which Tāranāth[4] makes to the great stūpa of Kuṣanagara as being situated here, in Kāmrūp, was taken from report, and thus would merely show that the present Lāma-tradition was current during his time. Any chaitya or other Buddhist building would seem to have been subsequent to the seventh century; and in all probability marked a site visited by the great founder of Lāmaism, St. Padma-sambhava, or one of his disciples. The different accounts of this saint's wanderings vary considerably, but he is generally credited with having traversed most of the country between lower Asam and Tibet. And in this view it is to be noted that the Bhotān Lāmas call the chief

1 "Asam, or at least the north-east of Bengal (*i.e.*, Kāmrūp), seems to have been in a great degree the source from which the Tantrica and Sākta corruptions of the religion of the Vedas and Purānas proceeded" (H. H. WILSON, Preface to *Vishnu Purāna*).

2 They have their counterpart in the ἱερόδουλοι of the Greek STRABO: viii., 6, p. 20.

3 Yon-ch'ab-mts'o.

4 VASSILIEV's *Le Bouddisme*, trad. du Russe par M. G. A. Comme, p. 44.

image of this shrine *Namo Guru* or "the teacher," one of the epithets of St. Padma-sambhava. And the images on either side of it are also forms of that saint.

The form of Buddhism here represented is of the highly Tāntrik and demoniacal kind, propagated by Padma-sambhava and now existing in the adjoining country of Bhotān. Even this mild form of the image of *Ogyän Guru* has decapitated human heads strung on to his trident. The second image is of a more demoniacal kind. The third image is, of course, Ṣākya Muni. The fourth image, from its Brāhmanical name, is *Tam-din* (Skt., *Hayagrīva*), one of the fiercest forms of demons and an especial protector of Lāmaism. The trident is everywhere conspicuous in the hands of the sculptured figures on the walls, and Shakti rites are more pronounced here than in any other place in northern India.[1]

It is also remarkable to find that the high-priest of the Hājo temple, in common with the other high-priests in Kāmrūp, is called *Dalai*,—a title which is usually stated to have been conferred on the fifth Grand Lāma of Lhāsa by a Mongolian emperor in the seventeenth century A.D.; though the Tibetan equivalent of this title, viz., *Gyam-ts'ó*, or "ocean," is known to have been used by Grand Lāmas previously. As, however, the word is Mongolian, it is curious to find it naturalized here and spontaneously used by Brāhmans. It seems also to be the title of village-headman in the adjoining Garo hills. The *dalai* of this temple is a married man, but the office is not hereditary. He is elected by the local priests from amongst their number, and holds office till death. He resides at the foot of the hill, below the temple, in a large house, the exterior of which is profusely decorated with the skulls of wild buffalo, wild pig, deer, and other big game, etc., like the house of an Indo-Chinese chieftain.

"There does not seem to be in Tibet," says Mr. Fergusson,[2] "a single relic-shrine remarkable either for sanctity or size, nor does relic-worship seem to be expressed either in their architecture or their religious forms," and he supports this by saying that as their deity is considered to be still living, no relics are needed to recall his presence.

Certainly no immense mounds of the colossal proportions common in Indian Buddhism, and in Burma and Ceylon, appear to exist in Tibet, but smaller stūpas are of very common occurrence; and the tombs of the departed Grand Lāmas at Tashi-lhunpo, etc., are special objects of worship.

It is said that Tibet possesses several large stūpas as large as

[1] Dancing girls appear to figure to some extent in certain Lāmaist ceremonies in Bhotān, *vide* TURNER'S *Embassy to Tibet*, p. 32.

[2] *Hist. of Ind. and Eastern Architecture*, p. 311.

the Maguta stūpa of Nepal. This latter is one of the celebrated places of Lāmaist pilgrimage outside Tibet. It is called the *Ja[1]-ruṅ k'a-ṣor ch'ö-rten*, and lies about two miles to the north-east of Khatmandu, and it is figured at page 262. Immense numbers of Tibetans, both Lāmas and laity, visit the place every winter, and encamp in the surrounding field for making their worship and offerings, and circumambulating the sacred spot. It is the chief place of Lāmaist pilgrimage in Nepal, attracting far more votaries than the Svayambhūnāth stūpa,[2] which is not far distant. Its special virtue is reputed to be its power of granting all prayers for worldly wealth, children, and everything else asked for. Dr. Buchanan-Hamilton, in his account of Nepal, written about the beginning of the present century, gives a drawing of the monument, which is of an almost simple hemispherical form, of the type of the earliest stūpas; and Wright,[3] under the title of "temple of Bodhnāth," gives a rough chromo-lithograph of its more modern appearance, with its additional buildings and investing wall. But no description or account of the monument seems to be on record.

As I have obtained a copy of the printed booklet which is sold at the stūpa to the pilgrims, I here give a short abstract of its contents, which are interesting as showing how the stūpa is brought into intimate relation with the chief legendary and historic persons of early Lāmaism. The print is a new revision by Punya-vajra and another disciple of "the great Lāma Z'ab-*d*kar." This latter Lāma, I am informed, lived about thirty years ago, and gilded the short spire of the stūpa and built the present investing wall.

The book states as follows:—

"This stūpa enshrines the spirit of the Buddhas of the ten directions, and of the Buddhas of the three times (*i.e.*, the present, past and future), and of all the Bodhisats, and it holds the Dharma-kāya.

---

1 Spelt *pya*.

2 Called by the Lāmas 'P'ags-pa *Sin Kun* (or ? Zan-bkod); cf. also *Svayambhū purāna*, transld., *J.R.A.S.*, 1894, 297. Another stūpa not far off, namely, about ten miles S.E. of Bhātgaon, and twelve from Khat-mandu, is called sTags-mo-lus-sbyin, and identified as the site where Buddha in a former birth gave his body to a starving tiger, though the orthodox site for this story was really uorthern India, cf. FAHIAN, c. xi.

3 *Nepal*, pp. 22, 100.

"When king Thi-Sroṅ Detsan[1] asked the Guru,[2] at Samyas,[3] to tell him the history of the *Ma-gu-ta* stūpa in Nepal, made by the four sons of 'the bestower of gifts,' named 'the poor mother Pya-*r*dsi-ma (fowl-keeper),' then the Guru thus related (the story):—

"'In a former *Kalpa*—time beyond conception—the Bodhisattva Mahāsattva Avalokiteṣvara, approached the Tathāgatha Amitābha and prayed for the animals immersed in the miry slough, and after saving these he went to mount Potala. There he saw hosts of unsaved animals, innumerable like unto mounds of *murwa*[4] lees, and (seeing this he) wept. Two of his pitying tears were born into Indra's heaven as god's daughters, named respectively Kaṅ-ma and the little Kaṅ-ma or Kaṅ-ch'uṅ-ma. This latter having stolen in heaven some flowers, was as a punishment reborn in earth, in a low pigherd's family in Maguta in Nepal, under the name of Samvara or "the Chief Happiness," her mother's name being Purna. On marriage she had four sons, and her husband's early death left her with the sole care of the family. She with her family undertook the herding and rearing of geese for the wealthy, and having in this pursuit amassed much wealth, she—Ma-pya-*r*dsi-ma (or mother fowl-keeper)—decided to build a large stūpa in honour of the Tathāgatha. She, thereon, went to the king and begged for a site, saying she wanted only so much ground as one hide could cover. The king assented, saying "*Ja-ruṅ*," which literally means "do" + "can," *i.e.*, "you can do (so)."[5] Then she cutting a hide into thin thongs (forming a long rope), enclosed that very large space which now is occupied by this chaitya. And she, with her four sons, and a servant, and an elephant and an ass, as beasts of burden, brought earth and stones, and commenced to build this chaitya by their own personal labour.

"'Then the king's ministers appealed to the king to stop such an ambitious building, as they asserted its magnificence put to shame the religious buildings of the king and the nobles. But the king answered "*K'a-Sor*"—which literally means "mouth + (has) spoken"—and so refused to interfere. (Thus is the name of the stūpa—'*Ja-run K'a-sor*'—accounted for.)

"'After four years, when only the base had been laid, the mother died, but her sons continued the building till its completion. And in the receptacle was placed one Magadha measure (*drona*) of the relics of the Tathāgatha Kāṣyapa. This event was celebrated by the manifestation in the sky, above the stūpa, of Kasyapa himself, and the circles of celestial Buddhas and Bodhisats, and their hosts of retinue, and

---

1 The king of Tibet who introduced Lāmaism.

2 *i.e.*, Padma-sambhava, or Ugyan, the founder of Lāmaism.

3 The first Lāmaist monastery in Tibet.

4 The millet seed (*elusine crocanum*), about the size of mustard seed, from which is made the Himalayan beer.

5 This story, and, indeed, the greater part of the legend, seems to have its origin in a false etymology of the proper names.

amongst showers of flowers the gods contributed divine music and rained perfume. Earthquakes thrice occurred, and through the glory of the assembled divinities there was no darkness for five nights.

"'One of the sons then prayed, "May I in my next re-birth be born as a great scholar (to benefit mankind)"—and he was born as Thunmi Sambhota[1] (the introducer of the so-called "Tibetan" character, and the first translator of Indian Buddhist texts into Tibetan), *circa* 650 A.D.

"'The second son prayed in a similar manner, and was re-born as "The Bodhisattva"[2] (the abbot of the first monastery of Tibet).

"'Then the elephant or *laṅ-po* (hearing these prayers) said, "These two, neglecting me who contributed so much assistance, are asking all the good things for themselves, therefore let me be re-born in a form to destroy them or their work." And he was afterwards re-born as Laṅ-darma (the persecutor of Lāmaism).

"'The third son, hearing the elephant's request, prayed that he might be re-born in a form to neutralize the evil of the elephant's incarnation; and he was born as Lho-luṅ phel kyi *r*dorje (the Lāma who murdered Laṅ-darma, the Julian of Lāmaism).'

"This stūpa is also worshipped by the Nepalese Buddhists, viz., the Newars—the semi-aborigines of the Nepal valley, and the Murmi, a cis-Himalayan branch of Tibetan stock. The name 'Maguta'—pronounced 'Makuta'—is doubtless a contraction for *Makuta bandhana*, the pre-Buddhist 'crested chaitya,' such as existed at Buddha's death at Kusinagara, in the country of the Mallas."

The Gyan-tse Caitya-temple is thus described[3]:—

It is nine storeys high, and is about 100 to 120 feet high and capped by a gilt dome. A magnificent view of Gyantse town and monasteries from top storey. Numberless niches filled with images of Buddha and Bodhisatwas. In the first floor is an image of the religious king Rabtan. The *base* is fifty paces *square*. It is only open to public at the full and new moon.

At those shrines holding or professing to hold relics the fiction of miraculous increase of the relics is frequently enacted. Thus at the Maguta stūpa and Tashiding Ch'orten are sold small granules,[4] alleged to be obtained by miraculous efflorescence on

---

1 Who introduced a written character to Tibet.

2 The Indian monk Ṣanta-rakshita, abbot of the first monastery of Tibet (Samyas).

3 SARAT's Narrative.

4 On the cremation of the body of a Buddha it is believed that no mere ash results, but, on the contrary, the body swells up and resolves into a mass of sago-like granules of two kinds, (*a*) *Phe-duṅ*, from the flesh as small white granules, and (*b*) *ring-srel*, yellowish larger nodules from the bones. It is the former sort which are believed to be preserved at the holiest Caitya of Sikhim, namely, *T'oṅ-wa raṅ grol*, or "Saviour by mere sight." It owes its special sanctity to its reputedly containing some of the funereal granules of the mythical Buddha antecedent to Ṣākya Muni, namely

the surface of the building from the legendary relics of the fictitious Buddha, Kāṣyapa, alleged to be enshrined therein. But this practice is common also to southern Buddhism. In the Burmese chronicles[1] it is stated that the tooth of Buddha, enshrined at Ceylon, yielded in the eleventh century A.D., to the Burmese king, "a miraculous incarnation or mysterious growth of homogeneous substances from the holy tooth," and Col. Phayre adds "and a somewhat similar mission with a like result occurred about twenty years ago (about 1860 A.D.).

And in 1892 similar relics were sent from Ceylon to the Tibetan commissioner at Darjiling. But, after all, such relics are no more spurious than the innumerable "bits of the true cross," holy coats, and keys of St. Peter, of Christendom; nor is their worship more remarkable than the vestiges of relic-worship which still survive in the structural features of our chancels, and the black-letter day of the Holy Cross in the calendar.

The temple of Buddha's tooth at Fu-chau in China is also a known place of Lāmaist pilgrimage. The tooth is evidently an elephant's molar.[2] That one also at the "Clear water P'u-hsein monastery" in western Ssŭ-ch'an seems to be somewhat similar. It is described by Mr. Baber as "dense fossil ivory," "about a foot long, and of a rudely triangular outline."

The sacred mountain of Wu-t'ai or U-tai in northern China, and the alleged birth-place of Manjuṣṛī, now identified with the metaphysical Bodhisat of Wisdom, is a favourite place of pilgrimage. It has been visited and figured by Huc and others.[3]

On mount O in western Ssŭ-ch'an, at an elevation of about 11,000 feet, is to be seen "The glory of Buddha"[4]—a mysterious apparition like the giant of the Brocken,[5] which is seen occasionally by looking over the top of a cliff about 2,000 feet high into the terrible abyss below. It is a radiant halo of rainbow tints and it is deemed an emanation from the aureole of Buddha. The Tibetans visit the place.

Od-sruṅ, or Kāsyapa, the relics having been deposited there by Jik-mi Pawo, the incarnation and successor of St. Lha-tsün.

[1] PHAYRE's *History of Brit. Burma.*

[2] Sir HENRY YULE's *Marco Polo*, iii., ch. xv., where it is figured after Mr. Fortune.

[3] Visited and described also by Rev. J. Edkins (*Religion in China*), Gilmour, Reichthofen, Rockhill, and more fully described by D. Pokotiloff, St. Petersburg, 1893.

[4] In Chinese *Fo-Kuang.* Cf. BABER's *Suppl. Papers Geog. Soc.*, p. 42.

[5] BREWSTER's *Natural Magic*, 1833, p. 130.

The sacred sites of Tibet are cited in considerable detail in the vernacular geography already mentioned. And stories abound of the miraculous efficacy of such pilgrimages, and even of the manifestations of the divine spirit to worthy worshippers.

Thus a story is related regarding the great image of "the Lord" at Lhāsa, which is a parallel to that of the widow's mite: A poor old widow, destitute of friends and of means, made a long pilgrimage to Lhāsa, but had nothing left as an offering. By begging she ultimately obtained a morsel of butter, which she offered in a tiny lamp to the great idol. The god thereupon revealed himself through the idol, which thanked her for her gift, and spoke to her a few words of comfort. On this miracle getting noised abroad, a rich merchant set out for Lhāsa, arguing that if the Lord appeared to a poor woman who presented only one tiny lamp, he would certainly appear to the donor of a host. So he offered many thousands of lamps with tons of butter, but the idol remained impassive and irresponsive.

The circling of the great temple by prostrations on the ground is an essential part of the devotions, not only of the pilgrims but of the residents. The day's devotions begin at Lhāsa with the gunfire about 4 a.m. from the Chinese minister's house, and they close with another gun at 9 or 10 p.m.

After the morning report the people are to be seen in dense crowds on the circular road, all moving in one and the same direction, as with the hands of a watch. A similar circuit is made by the devout in the evening, to say nothing of smaller circuits around individual shrines: at least this is imperative on common folk; as to the great and wealthy,[1] they urge that their presence would only interfere with the piety of the people, so they engage substitutes, who, however, are rigorously required to circumambulate for their masters. But whether done in person or by proxy, a careful reckoning is kept of the number of circuits performed, and these, in occasional cases of excessive devotion, are even executed by the method of successive prostrations full length on the road, each prostration beginning where the preceding one ended, called "Kiāng K'or."

Of the places sacred to the Guru, the most celebrated is the

[1] Says A. K. (HENESSY'S *Abstract*, p. 293).

"Lotus lake" (Ts'o Padma-c'an), on which he is believed to have been born. It is usually stated to be in Udyāna, but other accounts place it near Haridwar.[1] In Nepal at Halāsi on the bank of the Dudh-Kusi is the famous hermitage of the Guru on a hill with many fossil remains, which from their description suggest the outlying Siwaliks range

In the mountains, two days' journey south of Gyang-tse, near the unreformed monastery of Ṣe-kar, is a celebrated rock-cut cave of St. Padma, called Kyil-k'or ta-ḍub. It is thus described[2] :—

> "We took lighted lamps, and after going 120 paces inside the cavern we reached an open flat space about twenty feet square, from which a rock-cut ladder led us up to another open space about ten feet square; thirty paces further brought us to a stone seat, said to be the seat of Guru Padma-sambhava. Behind the seat was a small hole drilled through the rock: through this hole a wooden spoon about two feet long was passed by the sister of the Lāma who accompanied us, and a small amount of reddish dust was extracted which is said to be the refuse of the Guru's food. This we ate and found very sweet to the taste. Then after lighting some sacred lamps and asking a blessing, we descended by another flight of steps to a place where a stream issues from the face of the rock. The total length of the cave from the entrance of the stream is about a quarter of a mile. There are ascents and descents, and many turns and twists through narrow passages where only one man can go at a time, and many people are afraid to risk exploring the place. If the lamp were to go out there would be no finding the way back again."

Colossal images of Jam-pa or "The Loving One" (the Buddha to come), and sometimes of Avalokita are occasionally carved on cliffs. A monster image of the god Maitreya (Jam-pa), three storeys in height, is mentioned by explorer A. K.;[3] the figure is internally of clay, and is well gilded externally; it is seated on a platform on the ground floor, and its body, passing succes-

---

[1] One account given me says that three days from the town in northern India named Nirdun (? Dehra Dun) lies Ramnagar, thence four days Haraduar, where there is a railway station, thence on foot two days to Guruduar, whence Ts'o Padma is eight days distant amongst seven hills, like Mt. Meru. In regard to it, the *Sham-bha-la Lam-yig* contains the following passage: "At the city of the king Da-ya-tse of Pu-rang, in consequence of water striking against coal, at night the coal is seen burning. It is said of this coal and water, that they have the peculiarity that the water, if introduced into the stomach of man or beast, turns into stone."

[2] Lāma U. G. *S.R.*, *loc. cit.*, p. 20.

[3] Henessy, *S.R.*, *loc. cit.*, para 19. An image similar to this, thirty feet high, but of gilt copper, is noted by the Lāma U. G., *loc. cit.*, p. 22. Lake at Roṅch'am Ch'en, near the crossing of the Tangpo, near Yam-dok.

sively through the second and third floors, terminates in a jewelled and capped colossal head above the latter floor ; in all, the figure and platform are said to be seventy or eighty feet high. Now, as an essential feature in Tibetan worship is the performance of circuits around an image, it will be seen that the pilgrim in circling this image of Jam-pa is compelled by circumstances to perform three different series of circumambulations on as many floors ; at first around the god's legs, next around his chest, and lastly around his head.

But, after all, the greatest pilgrimage to which a Lāmaist devotee looks is to the Buddhist-god incarnate at Lhāsa, the Grand Dalai Lāma.

Accounts of the culmination of such a pilgrimage have been recorded by Manning and others. The infant Grand Lāma, who received Manning, was altogether a prodigy. A reception by the Grand Tashi Lāma, one of the many witnessed by Mr. Bogle, is thus described by that gentleman[1] (see figure, page 305):—

"On the 12th November, a vast crowd of people came to pay their respects, and to be blessed by the Lāma. He was seated under a canopy in the court of the palace. They were all ranged in a circle. First came the lay folks. Everyone according to his circumstances brought some offering. One gave a horse, another a cow ; some gave dried sheep's carcasses, sacks of flour, pieces of cloth, etc. ; and those who had nothing else presented a white Pelong handkerchief. All these offerings were received by the Lāma's servants, who put a bit of silk with a knot upon it tied, or supposed to be tied, with the Lāma's own hands, about the necks of the votaries. After this they advanced up to the Lāma, who sat cross-legged upon a throne formed with seven cushions, and he touched their head with his hands, or with a tassel hung from a stick, according to their rank and character. The ceremonial is this: upon the gylongs or laymen of very high rank he lays his palm, the nuns and inferior laymen have a cloth interposed between his hand and their heads ; and the lower class of people are touched as they pass by with the tassel which he holds in his hand. . . . . There might be about three thousand people

[1] *Op. cit.*, p. 85. A grander reception is described by him at p. 98.

—men, women, and children—at this ceremony. Such as had children on their backs were particularly solicitous that the child's head should also be touched with the tassel. There were a good many boys and some girls devoted to the monastic order by having a lock of hair on the crown of the head cropped by the Lāma with a knife. This knife came down from heaven in a flash of lightning. . . . . After the Lāma retired, many people stayed behind that they might kiss the cushions upon which he had sat."

The ordinary receptions by his holiness have been described by the survey spy A. K.[1] Since his worshippers are in thousands, and it is only to those who are wealthy or of high degree that he can afford to address even a brief sentence or two, this is always done in a deep hoarse voice, acquired by training in order to convey the idea that it emanates from maturity and wisdom. Seated cross-legged on a platform some six feet high, he is dressed to be worshipped in the usual colours of priesthood, *i.e.*, red and yellow, and with bare arms, as required of all Buddhist priests, and holds a rod from the end of which hangs a tassal of silk, white, red, yellow, green, and blue. The pilgrim, coming in at the entrance door, advances with folded hands as if in prayer, and resting his head against the edge of the platform above him, mentally and hastily repeats the petitions he would have granted. These unuttered prayers the Dalai Lāma is understood to comprehend intuitively; he touches the pilgrim's head with the bunch of silk in token of his blessing, and the worshipper is hurried out at the east door by attendants, only too happy if he has passed say half a minute in the vicinity of the great priest. This is the common procedure. Persons of rank or substance are permitted to mount the platform and to perform obeisance there, receiving the required blessing by actual touch of the Dalai Lāma's hand; subsequently such worshipper may be allowed a seat below the platform where a few hoarse utterances of enquiry may be addressed to him by the Dalai Lāma, and he may also be given some food.

The account of one of these more select receptions, to which Baber Ṣarat gained admission in disguise, is here abridged from his narrative.

"We are seated on rugs spread in about eight rows, my seat being in

[1] *Loc. cit.*, edited by HENESSY, para. 20.

the third row, at a distance of about ten feet from the Grand Lāma's throne, and a little to his left. There was perfect silence in the grand hall. The state officials walked from left to right with serene gravity, as becoming their exalted rank in the presence of the supreme vice-regent of Buddha on earth. The carrier of the incense-bowl (suspended by three golden chains), the head steward, who carried the royal golden teapot, and other domestic officials then came into his holiness's presence, standing there motionless as pictures, fixing their eyes, as it were, on the tips of their respective noses.

"The great altar, resembling an oriental throne, pillared on lions of carved wood, was covered with costly silk scarves; and on this his holiness, a child of eight, was seated. A yellow mitre covered the child's head, his person was robed in a yellow mantle, and he sat cross-legged, with the palms of his hands joined together to bless us. In my turn I received his holiness's benediction and surveyed his divine face. I wanted to linger a few seconds in the sacred presence, but was not allowed to do so, others displacing me by pushing me gently. The princely child possessed a really bright and fair complexion with rosy cheeks. His eyes were large and penetrating. . . . The thinness of his person was probably owing to the fatigues of the ceremonies of the court, of his religious duties, and of ascetic observances to which he had been subjected since taking the vows of monkhood. . . . When all were seated after receiving benediction, the head steward poured tea into his holiness's golden cup from the golden teapot. Four assistant servers poured tea into the cups of the audience. Before the Grand Lāma lifted his cup to his lips a grace was solemnly chanted. Without even stirring the air by the movements of our limbs or our clothes, we slowly lifted our cups to our lips and drank the tea, which was of delicious flavour. Thereafter the head butler placed a golden dish full of rice in front of his holiness, which he only touched; and its contents were then distributed. I obtained a handful of this consecrated rice, which I carefully tied in one corner of my handkerchief. After grace had been said, the holy child, in a low indistinct voice, chanted a hymn. Then a venerable gentleman rose from the middle of the first row of seats, and, addressing the Grand Lāma as the Lord Avalokita Incarnate, recited the many deeds of mercy which that patron saint of Tibet had vouchsafed towards its benighted people. At the conclusion he thrice prostrated himself before his holiness, when a solemn pause followed; after which the audience rose, and the Grand Lāma retired.

"One of the butler's assistants gave me two packets of pills, and the other tied a scrap of red silk round my neck. The pills, I was told, were Chinlab (blessings consecrated by Buddha-Kashyapa and other saints), and the silk scrap, called sungdû (knot of blessing), was the Grand Lāma's usual consecrated return for presents made by pilgrims and devotees."

XIV.

PANTHEON, SAINTS, AND IMAGES.

"Since we left off to burn incense to the Queen of Heaven and to pour out drink-offerings to her, we have wanted all things and have been consumed by the sword and famine."—*Jeremiah* xliv., 18.[1]

LĀMAIST mythology is a fascinating field for exploring the primitive conceptions of life, and the way in which the great forces of nature become deified. It also shows the gradual growth of legend and idolatry, with its diagrams of the unknown and fetishes; and how Buddhism with its creative touch bodied forth in concrete shape the abstract conceptions of the learned, and, while incorporating into its pantheon the local gods of the country, it gave milder meanings to the popular myths and legends.

The pantheon is perhaps the largest in the world. It is peopled by a bizarre crowd of aboriginal gods and hydra-headed demons, who are almost jostled off the stage by their still more numerous Buddhist rivals and counterfeits. The mythology, being largely of Buddhist authorship, is full of the awkward forms of Hindū fancy and lacks much of the point, force, and picturesqueness of the myths of Europe. Yet it still contains cruder forms of many of these western myths,[2] and a wealth of imagery.

Primitive Buddhism, as we have seen, knows no god in the sense of a Creator or Absolute Being; though Buddha himself

---

[1] Compare with the analogous Buddhist "Queen of Heaven," Tārā or Kwān-yin, pp. 435, etc.

[2] Cf. V. A. SMITH "On the Græco-Roman influence on the Civilization of Ancient India," *J.A.S.B.*, 1891-92, p. 50, etc. Also Prof. GRÜNWEDEL, *loc. cit.*

seems to have been in this respect an agnostic rather than an atheist.

But, however, this may be, the earliest Buddhist mythology known to us gives the gods of the Hindūs a very prominent place in the system. And while rendering them finite and subject to the general law of metempsychosis, yet so far accepts or tolerates the current beliefs in regard to their influence over human affairs as to render these gods objects of fear and respect, if not of actual adoration by the primitive Buddhists.

The earliest books purporting to reproduce the actual words spoken by the Buddha make frequent references to the gods and demons. And in the earliest of all authentic Indian records, the edict-pillars of Aṣoka, we find that model Buddhist delighting to call himself "the beloved of the gods." The earlier Buddhist monuments at Barhut, etc., also, are crowded with images of gods, Yakshas and other supernatural beings, who are there given attributes almost identical with those still accorded them by present-day Buddhists. Every Buddhist believes that the coming Buddha is at present in the Tushita heaven of the gods. And the Ceylonese Buddhists, who represent the purer form of the faith, still worship the chief Indian gods and are addicted to devil-worship and astrology.[1]

But the theistic phase of Buddhism carried objective worship much further than this. For as Buddha himself occupied in primitive Buddhism the highest central point which in other faiths is occupied by a deity, his popular deification was only natural.

In addition to the worship of Buddha, in a variety of forms, the Mahāyāna school created innumerable metaphysical Buddhas and Bodhisats whom it soon reduced from ideal abstractness to idolatrous form. And it promoted to immortal rank many of the demons of the Sivaist pantheon; and others specially invented by

[1] Rhys Davids, *B.*, p. 7. "In the courtyard of nearly all the wihāras (monasteries) in Ceylon there is a small dewāla (or god-temple) in which the Brāhmanical deities are worshipped. The persons who officiate in them are called *Kapavas.* They marry. The incantations they use are in Sanskrit (*East. Mon.*, p. 201). The chief gods worshipped are Vishṇu, Kataragama, Nāta who in the next Kalpa is to become Maitreya Buddha, and Pattini Deva. Other temples belong to tutelaries, *e.g.*, Saman Deva, the tutelary of Buddha's foot-print, Srī-pade (*Rept. Service Tenures Commission*, Ceylon, 1872, p. 62). It is probable that this Pattini is the tutelary goddess of Aṣoka's capital, Patna. Cf. my *Discovery of exact site of Pāṭaliputra*, etc., 1892."

itself as *defensores fidei;* and to all of these it gave characteristic forms. It also incorporated most of the local deities and demons of those new nations it sought to convert. There is, however, as already noted, reason for believing that many of the current forms of Brāhmanical gods were suggested to the Brāhmans by antecedent Buddhist forms. And the images have come to be of the most idolatrous kind, for the majority of the Lāmas and almost all the laity worship the image as a sort of fetish, holy in itself and not merely as a diagram or symbol of the infinite or unknown.

The Lāmaist pantheon, thus derived from so many different sources, is, as may be expected, extremely large and complex. Indeed, so chaotic is its crowd that even the Lāmas themselves do not appear to have reduced its members to any generally recognized order, nor even to have attempted complete lists of their motley deities. Though this is probably in part owing to many gods being tacitly tolerated without being specially recognized by the more orthodox Lāmas.

The nearest approach to a systematic list which I have seen, is the Pekin Lāma's list so admirably translated by the late Mr. Pander,[1] but this, as well as all the other extant lists, is defective in many ways and only fragmentary.

The chief Tibetan treatises on the Lāmaist pantheon according to my Lāma informants, are :—

(*a*) Z'ā-lu Lô-tsa-wa's, "The means of obtaining The Hundred (gods).[2] This is said to be the oldest of the extant systematic works on Lāmaist deities and seems to date from about 1436 A.D., when Z'ā-lu succeeded to the great Pandit Atīsa's chair at Gāh-ldan monastery. Zhā-lu Loch'en, "the great translator," states that he translated his description from one of the three great Indian works by Pandit Bhavaskanda entitled "Slokas on the means of obtaining (tutelary and other deities)."[3] The term "the hundred" which occurs in the title of this and the following treatises refers only to the chief divinities; for the total number described is much greater.

(*b*) Pāri Lô-tsa-was "The Hundred precious Manifestations of Narthang."[4] This work issuing from the great press at Narthang near Tashi-lhunpo is said to deal mainly, if not solely, with those omitted by Z'ālu, and is placed about the sixteenth century A.D.

1 *Das Pantheon des Tschangtscha Hutuktu*, etc.
2 sGrubs-t'ub brgya-rtsa.
3 Sgrub-t'ub ts'ig bc'ad, Skt. ? *Sadanaṅ sloka.*
4 rin-'byuṅ sNar-t'aṅ brgya-rtsa.

(*c*) Tāranātha's "The Hundred precious Appearances."[1] This work by the great historiographer Lāma Tāranātha contains mainly residual deities omitted by the two previous writers; but it is chiefly devoted to the more demoniacal forms.[2] This work dates from about 1600 A.D. and was, I think, printed at Phun-ts'o-ling near Narthang; but I omitted to note this point specially while consulting the book at Darjiling.[3]

(*d*) The Dalai Lāma Ňag-waṅ Lô-zaṅ Gya-ts'ô's "autobiography," written in the latter half of the seventeenth century A.D. In its mythological portion it describes chiefly those aboriginal Tibetan deities which had become grafted upon orthodox Lāmaism.

All the foregoing works have been consulted by me except the second or Narthang text, which seems to be the same book referred to by Pander.[4] The Pekin work translated by Pander and dating from 1800 A.D., seems to have been a compilation from the above sources in regard to those particular deities most favoured by the Chinese and Mongolian Lāmas, though the descriptions with the Pekin list are often meagre and frequently different in many details compared with the earlier work of Z'ā-lu.[5] Another book, also, it would seem, printed in China, was obtained by Mr. Rockhill.[6]

I cannot attempt, at least at present, to give any satisfactory classification of such a disorderly mob, but I have compiled from the foregoing sources a rough general descriptive list, so as to give a somewhat orderly glimpse into this chaotic crowd of gods, demons, and deified saints.

Arranged in what appears to be the order of their rank, from above downwards, the divinities seem to fall under the following seven classes :—

1. *Buddhas.*—Celestial and human.
2. *Bodhisats.*—Celestial and human, including Indian saints and apotheosized Lāmas.
3. *Tutelaries.*—Mostly demoniacal.
4. *Defenders* of the Faith, and *Witches* (Ḍākkinī).
5. *Indian Brāhmanical gods*, godlings, and genii.

---

1 Rin-'byuṅ-brgya rtsa.

2 Gon-po, Skt., Nātha ; and Lha-mo, Skt., Kalī.

3 It may probably be a version of this work which Pander (*Zeitschrift für Ethnologie*, p. 54, Berlin, 1889) refers to as published at Urgya by a successor of Tāranātha *r*Je-*b*tsun *g*dam-pa.

4 *Op. cit.*, p. 63.

5 With these lists may also be compared the illustrated Buddhist pantheon of the Japanese, *Butzu dso-dsui*, reproduced in parts in Prof. J. Hoffman at Leyden in SIEBOLD's *Nippon Archiv zur Beschreibung von Japan*, Vol. v., and by Dr. W. ANDERSON in his admirable *Catalogue of Jap. Paintings in British Museum.*

6 It gives pictures of the gods and saints with their special mantras.

6. *Country gods* (yul-lha) and guardians (sruṅ-ma), and *Local* gods.
7. *Personal gods*, or familiars.

The tutelaries, however, overlap the classes above them as well as the next one below, and some of the "guardians" are superior to the Indian gods. The first four classes, excepting their human members, are mostly immortal,[1] while the remainder are within the cycle of re-births.

Before giving the list of these various divinities, and descriptive details of the images of the more important ones, let us look at the typical forms and attitudes, the material, and methods of execution of images in general.

The immense numbers of images abounding in Tibet are not confined to the temples, but are common in the houses of the laity, in the open air, as talismans in amulet-boxes, and painted or printed as screens, and on the title-pages of books, and as charms, etc.

The artists are almost exclusively Lāmas, though a few of the best idols in Lhāsa are made by Newari artisans from Nepal, who are clever workers in metal and wood. Some also are painted by lay-artists, but such images must be consecrated by Lāmas in order to be duly efficacious as objects of worship, for most of the images are credited with being materially holy, like fetishes, and capable of hearing and answering prayers. The mode of executing the images, as regards the materials, the auspicious times to commence the image, and to form the most essential parts, such as the eyes, are all duly defined in the scriptures, whose details are more or less strictly observed. Many of the more celebrated idols are believed by the people and the more credulous Lāmas to be altogether miraculous in origin—"self-formed," or fallen from heaven ready fashioned.[2]

The images are executed in various ways: as statues or *bas-reliefs* (sku) and medallions, and as pictures (sku-t'aṅ or z'al-t'aṅ).[3] The statues are sometimes of colossal size,[4] especially those of

[1] The Lāmas do not generally, as do the Nepalese Buddhists, restrict immortality to Ādi-Buddha.

[2] The Hindus entertain the same belief as regards their *āp-rupi* idols, which are mostly ancient Buddhist ones.

[3] Lit. = flat + image.

[4] Schlagintweit describes (*Bud.*, p. 220) one of these colossal images at Leh as "the Buddha in Meditation," and as higher than the temple itself, the head going through

Maitreya, or "The coming Buddha," which are occasionally rock-cut; but most are less than life-size.

Of statues the most common form is the plastic,[1] all of which are gilt or coloured. They are often cast, as *bas-reliefs*, in moulds, and are formed of coarse *papier-maché*, or clay, bread-dough, compressed incense, or variously-tinted butter,[2] and the larger ones have a central framework of wood. The plastic image or moulded positive is then dried in the sun—excepting, of course, those made of butter,—and it is afterwards painted or gilt.

The gilt-copper images[3] are more prized. The costly ones are inlaid with rubies, turquoises, and other precious stones. Less common are those of bell-metal,[4] while the poorer people are content with images of brass or simple copper. Wooden images[5] are not common, and stone images[6] are least frequent of all, and are mostly confined to the shallow *bas-reliefs* on slabs, or rock-cut on cliffs. Internal organs of dough or clay are sometimes inserted into the bodies of the larger images, but the head is usually left empty; and into the more valued ones are put precious stones and filings of the noble metals, and a few grains of consecrated rice, a scroll bearing "the Buddhist creed," and occasionally other texts, booklets, and relics. These objects are sometimes mixed with the plastic material, but usually are placed in the central cavity, the entrance to which, called "the charm-place,"[7] is sealed up by the consecrating Lāma.[8] And the image is usually veiled by a silken scarf.[9]

AMITAYUS.
(Gilt-copper from Lhāsa.)

Here also may be mentioned the miniature funereal images or

the roof. "The body is a frame of wood, dressed with draperies of cloth and paper, the head, the arms, and the feet are the only parts of the body moulded of clay."

[1] 'jim-gzugs.

[2] Huc's *Souv.*, ii., p. 95; Rockhill, *Land*, i., p. 69. In Ceylon temporary images are said to be made of rice.—Hardy's *East. Mon.*, 202.

[3] gser-zaṅs-sku. [4] li-ma. [5] S'iṅ-sku. [6] rdo-sku. [7] zuṅ-zhug.

[8] This ceremony is called "rabs-gnas zhug-pa." Cf. Csoma, *A.*, p. 403.

[9] The images of the fierce gods and goddesses especially are veiled. The veil covering the face of *Devi* is called "Lha-moi zhab-k'ebs. It is a white silken scarf, about

caityas, moulded of clay or dough, with or without the addition of relics,[1] and corresponding to the *dharma-ṣarira* of the Indian *stūpas*, and mentioned by Hiuen Tsiang in the seventh century A.D. Small consecrated medallions of clay are also given by the Dalai and Tashi Grand Lāmas to donors of largess, in return for their gifts, one of which is figured as a tail-piece on page 304.

GUARDIAN KING OF THE SOUTH.
Virūdhaka.

The pictures are mostly paintings, seldom uncoloured drawings, and many of them are of considerable artistic merit. The style and technique are, in the main, clearly of Chinese origin. This is especially seen in the conventional form of clouds, water, etc., though the costumes are usually Tibetan, when not Indian. The eye of the Buddhas and the more benign Bodhisats is given a dreamy look by representing the upper eyelid as dented at its centre like a cupid's bow, but I have noticed this same peculiarity in mediæval Indian Buddhist sculptures.

eighteen inches broad, with red borders about a foot wide. And on it are dr wn in colours several of the auspicious symbols, the swastika, elephants' tusks, conch, jewels, also the goad, etc., and the mystic spell *Bhyc-*,.

[1] Called *sa-tsch'a*.

The paintings are usually done on cloth, frescoes[1] being mostly confined to the mural decoration of temples. The colours are very brilliant and violently contrasted, owing to the free use of crude garish pigments, but the general colour effect in the deep gloom of the temple, or when the painting is toned down by age, is often pleasing.

The cloth used is canvas or cotton—seldom silk. It is prepared by stretching it while damp over a wooden frame, to which the margin of the cloth is stitched; and its surface is then smeared over with a paste of lime and flour, to which a little glue is sometimes added. On drying, its surface is rubbed smooth and slightly polished by a stone, and the drawing is then outlined either by hand with a charcoal crayon, or, in the more technical subjects, by a stencil-plate consisting of a sheet of paper in which the pattern is perforated by pin-holes, through which charcoal dust is sifted.

The lines are then painted in with Chinese ink, and the other colours, which are usually crude pigments imported from China or India. The colours are simply mixed with hot thin glue, and as the picture is unvarnished, Lāmaist paintings are especially subject to injury by damp.

On completion, the artist puts a miniature figure of himself in a corner at the bottom in an adoring attitude. The painting is then cut out of its rough easel-frame, and it has borders sewn on to it, consisting of strips of coloured silk or brocade, and it is mounted on rollers with brazen ends, somewhat after the manner of a map or a Japanese *Kakemono*.[2] But it is not so elongated as the latter, nor is it so artistically mounted or finished.

The mounted Tibetan painting has a tricoloured cloth border of red, yellow, and blue from within outwards, which is alleged to represent the spectrum colours of the rainbow, which separates sacred objects from the material world. The outer border of blue is broader than the others, and broadest at its lowest border, where it is usually divided by a vertical patch of brocade embroidered with the dragons of the sky.

A veil is usually added as a protection against the grimy smoke of incense, lamps and dust. The veil is of flimsy silk, often

[1] 'dabs-ris.

[2] Cf. W. Anderson's *Catalogue Japanese Pictures;* Nott and Gliddon, *Indig. Races*, 302.

adorned with sacred symbols, and it is hooked up when the picture is exhibited.

Now we are in a position to consider the detailed description of the images. The various forms of images fall into characteristic types, which, while mainly anthropomorphic, differ in many ways as regards their general form, attitude, features, dress, emblems, etc., yet all are constructed, according to a special canon, so that there is no difficulty in distinguishing a Buddhist image from a Brāhmanical or a Jain.

The forms of images differ broadly, as regards the general type or mode of the image, the posture of the body (sedent or otherwise), and the attitude in which the hands are held, the number of arms, which are emblematic of power, and the symbols or insignia which they bear, as signifying their functions.

The general type of Buddha's image is well-known. It is that of a mendicant monk, without any ornaments and with tonsured hair, and it is also extended to most of the mythical Buddhas. It is called the *Muni* or saint-type,[1] and it is usually represented upon a lotus-flower, the symbol of divine birth.

Extra to this type, the three others most common are:—

1st. "The Mild" calm form (*Z'i-wa*[2]) or Bodhisat type.

2nd. "The Angry" type (*T'o-wo*[3]), of the "Howler" (*Rudra* and *Marut*), or Storm-deity of Vedic times.

3rd. "The Fiercest" fiend type (*Drag-po* or *Drag-s'é*[4]); a fiercer form of No. 2, and including the "lord"-fiends.[5]

These latter two types are confined mainly to Tāntrik Buddhism, which, as with Tāntrik Hindūism, gives each divinity a double or treble nature with corresponding aspects. In the quiescent state the deity is of the mild Bodhisat type; in the active he is of the Angry or Fiercest-fiend type. Thus the Bodhisat Mañjuṣrī, the God of Wisdom, in his ordinary aspect is a "Mild" deity (*Z'i-wa*); as "The Fearful Thunderbolt" (*Bhairava-vajra*), he is an "Angry"

[1] t'ub-bzugs.

[2] Tibeto-Sanskrit dictionaries give "Ṣiva" as well as "Santi" as the Sanskrit equivalent of this word, so it may literally mean a mild form of the Ṣivaist gods.

[3] *K'ro-bo* from the Skt. *Krodha*, anger.

[4] *Drags-po* or *Drags-gs'ed.*

[5] mGon-po—Skt., *Nātha.*

deity (*T'o-wo*); and as "The six-faced dreadful King-demon,"[1] he is of "The Fiercest Fiend" type (*Drag-po*).[2]

To avoid unnecessary repetition in the detailed descriptions, it seems desirable to give here a general note on these typical mild and demoniacal aspects, and also on the attitudes of the body and of the fingers.

The "Mild" (Z'i-wa) deities are of what has been called by some European writers "the Bodhisat type." They are figured as young handsome Indian princes and princesses, seated usually on lotus thrones, and are thus described by Z'ā-lu: The figure looks proud, youthful, beautiful,[3] and refined. The body emits a halo of innumerable rays of light, figured as radiating wavy lines, with tremulous lines alternating. The dress is of the Indian style, with one silk shawl for the lower limbs, and one for the upper, a head ornament (or crown) of precious things, an ear-ring, a close-fitting necklace, and a *doshal* or garland reaching down to the thigh, and a *Semondo* or shorter garland reaching to the navel, an armlet, wristlet, bracelet, anklet, girdle (*'ok-pags*), and a sash (*dar-'p'yaṅ*) with fringes. The above ornaments are accounted thirteen.

AMITĀYUS.
The Buddha of Boundless Life.

1 gdoṅ-drug-ch'an 'jig-byed bdud-las rnam rgyal.

2 According to the rhyme:

rje-btsun 'jam dbyaṅs k'ros-pa-ni
rdo-rje 'jigs byed 'jigs par byed,
k'ro-bor rgyal-po gdoṅ drug c'an.

3 For the (80 or 84) secondary beauties, cf. BURNOUF's *Lotus*, App., viii., HARDY's *Man.*, 367, RAJ. L. MITRA's *Lalita Vist.* For description of Hindū Idols, see Bṛihat Saṃhitā, translated by DR. KERN, *J.R.A.S.*, vi., 322.

The hair of the gods is dressed up into a high cone named ral-pa'-t'or-tshugs, and the forehead usually bears the *tilak* or auspicious mark. The goddesses are given a graceful form with slender waist and swelling breasts, and their hair is dressed into plaits which lie on the hinder part of the neck, and they beam with smiles.

The "Angry" type (*T'o-wo*) is terrible in its elaborate ugliness, with disproportionately large head,[1] scowling brows, and cruel, callous eyes, and usually with a third eye in the centre of the forehead.[2] Z'ā-lu describes them as fat, brawny-limbed, and menacing in attitude, standing or half-seated upon some animal, their lips agape, showing their great canine fangs, and rolling tongue; their wolfish eyes are glaring, the beards, eyebrows, and hair are either yellow, red, reddish-yellow, or greyish-yellow, and the hair is erect, with occasionally a fringe of curls on the forehead, believed by some to represent coiled snakes. The females, as in the annexed figure,[3] except for their full breasts and the absence of beards, do not differ in appearance from the males.

THE SHE-DEVIL *DEVI*.
T., Lha-mo.

[1] Cf. SCHLAG., *B.*, p. 222, for measurements of proportions of several of these images.

[2] Trilôcana, a character also of the Hindū Bhairava and Kālī and their demon troop of followers, the *gana*.

[3] After Pander.

All these fiends have six ornaments of human bones, namely: (1) ear ornament, (2) necklet, (3) armlet, (4) bracelet, (5) anklet (but some have snake-bracelets and anklets), and (6) a garland of circular bodies, fixed to bone-heads (*seralkha*), and corresponding to the *semodo* of the Z'i-wa, and occasionally they have a *doshal* garland. The foregoing is according to the Indian canon, but the Tibetan style enumerates for them thirteen ornaments, namely: (1) the raw hide of an elephant, as an upper covering, (2) skins of human corpses as a lower garment, (3) a tiger skin inside the latter, (4) Brāhma's thread (ts'aṅ-skud), (5 to 10) the six bone ornaments above noted, (11) *Tilak* mark on forehead, of blood, (12) Grease (Z'ag) on either side of mouth, and (13) ashes smeared over body.

The "Fiercest" Fiends—(*Drag-po* and *Gön-po*) closely resemble the above "Angry Deities." They have usually chaplets of skulls encircled by tongues of flames; and they tread upon writhing victims and prostrate bodies.

ṢĀKYA IN MEDITATION.

As regards the *Postures* of the images, the chief sedent postures, and especially characteristic of the several forms of Buddha himself, and secondarily of the celestial Buddhas and Bodhisats are as follows:—

(1) "The adamantine, unchangeable, or fixed pose" (Skt., *Vajra* (?) *Palaṅa*[1]) sedent in the well-known cross-legged Buddha posture. The legs are locked firmly and the soles directed fully upwards. This is the pose of deepest meditation, hence it is also called, when the hands lie loosely in the lap, the "*Dhyāna* or meditative *mudra*."

(2) "The Bodhisat-pose" (Skt., *Satva* (?) *palaṅa*[2]) differs from No. 1 in having the legs looser and unlocked. The soles are scarcely seen. This is the pose of first emergence from meditation.

(3) "The sub-active pose" (Skt. (?) *Niyampalaṅa*)[3] is emerged farther from meditation. It has the legs unlocked, the left being quite under the right, and the soles invisible.

[1] rdo-rje skyil-druṅ. [2] Sems-dpa skyil druṅ. [3] Skyil dkruṅ chuṅ zad.

(4) "The Enchanter's pose" (Skt., *Lalita*[1]), *i.e.*, after the manner of "The Enchanter" Mañjuṣṛī. Here the right leg hangs down with an inclination slightly inwards and the left is loosely bent.

(5) Maitreya's pose.[2] Sedent in the European style with both legs pendant.

The chief attitudes of the hands and fingers (*mudras*[3]) are the following, and most are illustrated in the figures :—

THE FIVE CELESTIAL JINAS (OR BUDDHAS).

Amitābha. Amogha-siddhi. Vairocana. Ratna-sambhava. Akshobhya.

1. "Earth-touching," or the so-called "Witness" attitude (Skt., *Bhūṣparṣa*[4]), with reference to the episode under the Tree of Wis-

[1] rol-ba bzugs. [2] byams bzugs. [3] p'yag-rgya. [4] sa-gnon.

dom, when Ṣākya Muni called the Earth as his witness, in his temptation by Māra. It affects only the right hand, which is pendant with the knuckles to the front. It is the commonest of all the forms of the sedent Buddha, and almost the only form found in Burma and Ceylon. It is also given to the celestial Buddha Akshobhya, as seen in the figure on the preceding page.

2. "The Impartial" (Skt., *Samāhitan*[1]), or so-called "meditative posture" (Skt., *Samādhi*[2]). Resting one hand over the other in the lap in the middle line of the body, with the palms upwards, as in Amitābha Buddha (see the attached figure).

3. "The best Perfection" (Skt., *Uttara-bodhi*[3]). Index-finger and thumb of each hand are joined and held almost in contact with the breast at the level of the heart, as in the celestial Buddha Vairocana in the figure on the opposite page.

4. "Turning the Wheel of the Law" (Skt., *Dharma-cakra*[4]). Dogmatic attitude with right index-finger turning down fingers of left hand, figured at page 134.

5. "The best Bestowing" (Skt., *Varada*[5]). It signifies charity. The arm is fully extended, and the hand is directed downwards with the outstretched palm to the front, as in "the Jewel-born" Buddha Ratnasambhava, who is figured on the opposite page.

6. "The Protecting," or "Refuge-giving" (Skt., *Ṣaraṇ*[6]). With arm bent and palm to front, and pendant with fingers directed *downwards*, as in No. 5.

7. "The Blessing of Fearlessness" (Skt. ? *Abhaya*). The arm is elevated and slightly bent. The hand elevated with the palm to the front, and the fingers directed upwards, as in Amogha-siddha Buddha, figured over page. It is also the pose in the episode of the mad elephant.

8. "The Preaching"[7] differs from No. 7 in having the thumb bent, and when the thumb touches the ring-finger it is called "The triangular[8] (pose), see figure on page 5.

9. "The Pointing Finger."[9] A necromantic gesture in bewitching, peculiar to later Tāntrism.

The halo, or nimbus, around the head is subelliptical, and never acuminate like the leaf of the *pipal* or Bodhi tree (*Ficus religiosa*). The fierce deities have their halo bordered by flames (see figure page 330). An additional halo is often represented as surrounding the whole body, as figured at pages 333 and 335. This consists of the six coloured rays of light, and it is conventionally represented by wavy gilt lines with small tremulous lines alternating.

Colour, too, is frequently an index to the mood. Thus, white

1 mñam-bz'ag. 2 tiṅ-ṅe 'dsin. 3 byaṅ-chub-mch'og.
4 ch'os 'k'or-bskor. 5 mch'og-sbyin. 6 skyab-sbyin.
7 ch'os 'c'ad. 8 pa-dan rtse gsum. 9 sdigs-dsub.

and yellow complexions usually typify mild moods, while the red, blue and black belong to fierce forms, though sometimes light blue, as indicating the sky, means merely celestial. Generally the gods are pictured white, goblins red, and the devils black, like their European relative.

The Buddhas and other divinities, as well as the superior devils, are figured upon a lotus-flower, a symbol of divinity. The lotus-flower, on which the Buddhas and mild divinities are figured, is the red lotus (*Nelumbium speciosum*); while the fiercer divinities, including frequently Avalokita, and all those demons who are entitled to lotus-cushions, should have a pinkish variety of the white lotus (*Nymphœa esculenta*), the petals of which are much notched or divided, so as to resemble somewhat the *Acanthus* in Corinthian capitals. The blue lotus is the special flower of Tārā, but it is conventionally represented by the Lāmas as different from the Utpal (*Nymphœa sp.*), as figured on the opposite page.

A remarkable feature of most Tāntrik Buddhist images is the frequent presence of a Buddha seated on the head of the image

TABLE SHOWING
THE SURMOUNTING *JINAS* IN BUDDHIST IMAGES.

JINAS.	Vairocana.	Akshobhya.	Ratnasambhava.	Amitābha.	Amoghasiddha.
Surmounted BUDDHAS.	Maitreya	Mnni-vajrāsan		Amitāyus	Maitreya
Surmounted BODHISATS.	? Samantabhadra Prajñā-pāramita (pita) Vetuda-Marīcī Mahāsahasrau Vijaya Pita-Vijaya Sita-Ushṇīsha	Vajra-pāṇi Mañju-ghosha (adhicakra) Jñauasattva Mañjuṣri Sita Prajña-pāramitā	Ratna-pāṇi Pita Jambhala Pita Vaisravana Vasudhara "Kan-wa-bhadra"	Avalokita Padma-pāṇi Tārā	Viṣva-pāṇi
Surmounted KRODHA-*fiends.*		Kāla-Yamari Sasmuka-Yama Kāla-Jambhala Acala-Khroda raja Ri-khra-loma-gyon mar "Hun mdsad" Khroda raja "San-nags rje 'dsin-ma" Mahā-pratyangira	Rakta-yakiha	Hayagrīva Krodha Avalokita Pita Bṛikuṭi (? . . . Kalpa) Kuru-kulle "rTogs-pa las-junwa-Kuru-kulla" "gsilba tsal ch'en-mo"	Kuru-kulle Mahā-Mayuri

or amidst the hair. The existence of such surmounting images in the Tāntrik Buddhist sculptures of India was noted by Dr. Buchanan-Hamilton in his survey of Bihar[1] at the beginning of this century, but since his time the subject has attracted only

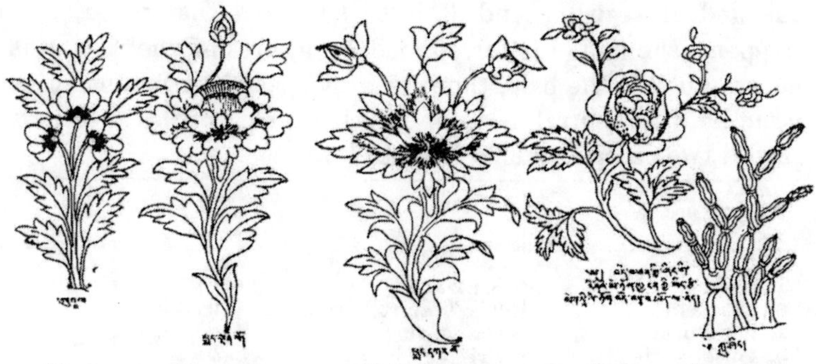

Utpal. Blue Lotus. White Lotus. Asok. Naga-tree.

LOTUSES and other flowers of conventional form.

the merest incidental notice of writers on Indian Buddhist antiquities,[2] who seem to have considered all such images to be figures only of Avalokita, because Hiuen Tsiang mentioned that a certain image of Avalokita had Amitābha seated in his hair.

As the subject is interesting, and of some importance, I give in the table the results of my study of a large series of Lāmaist pictures containing such figures, and descriptions of others extracted from the works of Pandits "gZ'onnu" Gupta, Ṣrītāri, Kalamtāra, Lhan-skyes rolwa-kun-rigs, and Bhavaskandha.

The surmounting image represents the spiritual father of the particular Bodhisat or deity; and he nearly always is one or other of the five *Jinas*, as the Tibetans term them,[3] or the Buddhas of Meditation (*Dhyāni-Buddha*), as they are called by the Nepalese Buddhists. In a few cases the coming-Buddha Maitreya is figured with Ṣākya Muni on his head, as indicating spiritual succession rather than parental relationship, but it is the latter which is the rule.

1 *Eastern India*, i.

2 *India Archæological Survey Repts.*, by Sir A. CUNNINGHAM; *West India Arch. S. Repts.*, by J. BURGESS; *Catalogue of Archæolog. Collection in Indian Museum*, by J. ANDERSON.

3 rgyal-ba rigs-lṅa—or "The Pentad Victors." No one seems to have noticed this constant use by the Lāmas of the word *Jina* for the celestial Buddhas, whom the Nepalese term Dhyāni-Buddha, though it is interesting in regard to Jainism in its relations to Buddhism.

Occasionally the surmounting Jinas are represented by their mystic emblems of a wheel, *vajra*, jewel, lotus, or *viṣva-vajra*, as will be described presently. Thus Ratnasambhava is usually represented by a jewel on the head of his spiritual reflex Jambhala, the god of wealth. And it is to be noted that when, as often happens, the image is surrounded by figures of the five Jinas in an arc outside the halo, then its own special surmounting parent occupies the central position in that arc, whilst the others are placed two on each side at a lower level.

English Name.	Tibetan.	Sanskrit.
1. a pike	K'atvaṅ	*khāṭvānga*
a trident	K'a-'tvaṅ-rtse-gsum	*triṣūla*
2. hand-drum	Da-ma-ru	*ḍamaru*
3. chisel-knife	Gri-gug	*kartrikā*
4. thunderbolt	rDo-rje	*vajra*
5. cross-thunderbolt	sNa-ts'ogs rdo-rje	*viṣva-vajra*
6. rosary	Preṅ-ba	*mālā*
7. Lotus-flower (white or red)	Pad-ma	*padma*
blue lotus [1]	Ut-pal	*utpal*
Aṣoka-flower [1]	Mya-ṅan-med pahi-shiṅ	*aṣoka*
"Nāga's tree" (cactus or coral) [1]	*k*Lu-shin	*nāgā-taru*
8. alarm-staff	'K'ar-gail	*hikile*, or *khakhara*
begging-bowl	'Luṅ-bzed	*patra*
9. wish-granting gem	(Yid bz'in) Norbu	(*cintā-*) *maṇi*
10. flames	Me-ris	
11. snare [2]	z'ags-pa	*pāṣa*
12. bell	dril-bu	*ghanta*
13. wheel	'K'or-lo	*cakra*
14. skull-cup	T'od-k'rag	*kapāla*
15. thunderbolt-dagger	p'ur-bu	*phurbu* (?)
16. spear	gDuṅ	
17. club	Be-con	*gadā*
18. dirk or dagger	'Chu-gri	
19. sword	Ral-gri	*adi*
20. axe	dGra-sta	*paraṣu* (?)
21. hammer	T'o-ba mt'o-ba	*mudgara*
22. iron-goad	lC'ags-kyu	
23. mace	Ben	
24. thigh-bone trumpet	rKaṅ-duṅ	
25. conch-shell trumpet	Dun	*ṣaṅkha*
26. iron-chain	lChags-sgrog	
27. skeleton-staff	dByug-pa	
28. See No. 1 (*a*)		
29. water-pot	Bum-pa	*kalāsa*
anointing vase	sPyi-glugs	
fly-whisk	rÑa-yab	*chauri*
banner	rGyal-mts'an	*dhvaja*

[1] See figures on previous page.

[2] To rescue the lost or to bind the opponents. A symbol of Ṣiva, Varuna, and Lakshmi.

The objects or insignia which the several figures hold in their hands refer to their functions. Thus, Mañjuṣrī, the god of wisdom, wields the sword of the truth in dissipating the darkness of ignorance, and in his left he carries the book of Wisdom

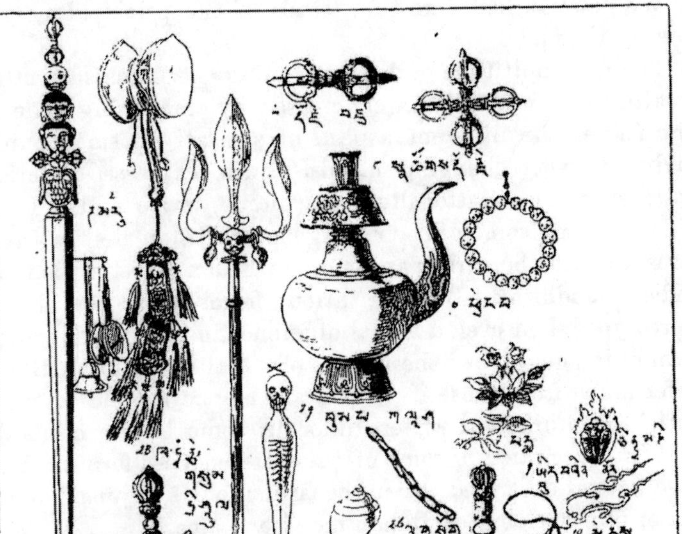

INSIGNIA AND WEAPONS OF THE GODS, ETC.

upon a Lotus-flower, thus symbolizing its supernatural origin; and he rides upon a roaring lion to typify the powerfully penetrating voice of the Law.

The chief of these insignia and other objects held in the hands of the images are shown in the foregoing illustration[1] and are as follows; the numbers in this list correspond to those in the figures.

We now can look into the details of the principal members of the pantheon.

The vast multitude of deities forming the Lāmaist pantheon is, as already mentioned, largely created by embodying under different names the different aspects of a relatively small number of divinities with changing moods. Such expressed relationship, however, seems occasionally a gratuitous device of the Lāmas in order to bring some of their indigenous Tibetan deities into relationship with the earlier and more orthodox celestial Bodhisats of Indian Buddhism. But the various forms have now all become stereotyped, and even a trivial difference in title yields a different form of image. Thus the images of "Maitreya" and "Bhṛikuṭi" differ much from those of "Bhadraka Maitreya" and "Ārya Bhṛikuṭi." And different writers differ in some of the minor details in their description of some of these stereotyped forms. Thus we have images described as "in the fashion of Nāgārjuna," or of some one or other celebrated Indian monk or Lāma.

First in our classification come the Buddhas, human and celestial.

I. The Buddhas.

The innumerable forms of the Buddhas, the fabulous terrestrial, the celestial and metaphysical, are all, with a few exceptions, based upon the five conventional attitudes ascribed to the historical Buddha, as marking the chief episodes of his Buddhahood. And of these "the Witness attitude" is in Tibet, as in Indian and southern Buddhism, the most common. Additional varieties are obtained by giving to these images different colours, ornaments, and symbols. Almost all are sedent in the well-known cross-legged attitude of Buddha's image; few are standing, and the recumbent or dying posture is very rarely seen in Tibet.

The typical Buddha is conventionally represented as a man of

[1] After Pander, *Panth.*, p. 108.

the most perfect form and beauty.[1] The face, usually of Aryan type and unbearded, wears a placid and benign expression. The head is bare, and the hair roughly tonsured and curly,[2] with a protuberance [3] on the crown or vertex upon which is sometimes represented a diadem.[4] He is clad in mendicant's garb, without any jewellery. The shawl [5] usually leaves the right shoulder bare, except when representing him preaching or walking abroad in public. He sits under the *pipal*-tree, the "Tree of Wisdom," upon a cushion of lotus-flowers set upon a throne covered by a mat,[6] supported by lions or other animals, as a sort of heraldic shield. And the throne is sometimes surmounted by a framework bearing at its sides the figures of a rampant lion trampling upon an elephant, and surmounted by a "water-lion," [7] topped by a *garuḍa*-bird as the centre-piece or keystone of the arch.

1. *Ṣākya Muni Bhagavān.*

T., S'ākya-t'ub-pa bc'om-ldan 'das.

This typical form of the Buddha is figured as at page 6, but the right hand should be in the pose of Akshobhya at page 336. It represents Ṣākya Muni at the greatest epoch of his life, namely, under the "Tree of Wisdom," at the instant of his attaining his Buddhahood. He has the general characters of a Buddha as already described. He has a golden complexion, with tonsured indigo-coloured hair, and wears the three robes of a religious mendicant, without any ornaments. He sits in "the indestructible" pose, with right hand in "witness attitude," and sometimes a begging-bowl rests on his lap. He is seated upon a cushion of

---

1 Possessing "the thirty beauties" and "the eighty *secondary* beauties." These include a lotus mark on each palm and sole.

2 The ragged contour of Ṣākya's cropped hair in his images is ascribed to his having on his great renunciation cut off his tresses with his sword. The cut locks of hair were carried to heaven, where the gods enshrined them in "the tomb of the Jewelled Tresses" (*Cuḍamani Caitya*), which is still a regular object of worship witb Burmese Buddhists.

3 Skt., *Ushṇīsha;* Tib., *Tsug-tor.*

4 Skt., *Cuḍa.* The peculiar flame-like process intended to represent a halo of rays of light issuing from the crown, so common in Ceylon images, is not distinctly represented by the Tibetans, and at most by a jewel.

5 Tib., *Lagoi.*

6 Tib., *Ten-kab*

7 Described by HIUEN TSIANG, BEAL's translation of *Si-Yu-Ki*, ii., p. 122.

sacrificial grass,[1] set upon a lion-supported lotus-throne at the spot at Buddh-Gayā, in Gangetic India, afterwards called "the adamantine throne."[2] In this, his final struggle for the Truth, the powers of darkness which assailed him are concretely represented as Māra, the demon of Desire, and his minions, and the "three fires" of desire are still pictured as being above him.

Māra denies the good deeds in this and former lives, which qualified Ṣākya Muni for the Buddhahood, and calls upon him to produce his witness. Whereupon the embryo Buddha touches the ground and instantly the old mother Earth, Dharitri or Dharti Mātā,[3] appears riding upon a tortoise (symbolic of the earth), bearing in her hand a "*pantsa*" garland, and she addresses the saint, saying, "I am your *Witness*,"—hence the name of this attitude of Buddha, the "Earth-touching" or "Witness." The legend goes on to relate that the earth-spirit, wringing her hair, caused a huge river to issue therefrom, which swept away Māra and his hordes. This episode of wringing the hair and the destruction of Māra and his minions is frequently depicted in Burmese temples; and the custom amongst the Burmese of pouring water on the ground at the conclusion of a religious service is, I am informed by a Burmese monk, an appeal to the earth-spirit to remember and bear witness to the particular good deed when men have forgotten it.

In the larger images of this form of Buddha he is frequently figured with his two favourite disciples standing by his side, Ṣāriputra on his right, and Maudgalyayāna on his left.

This title of *Bhagavān*, or "The Victorious,"[4] is in Tibet the most frequently used of all Buddha's titles, after Ṣākya Muni and Tathāgata.

Other recognized forms of Ṣākya's image are:—

(*a*) Ṣākya in the four other sedent attitudes, and the standing and dying, or the so-called "lion"-postures.

(*b*) Jo-wo Rin-po-che, "The Precious Lord," as a young Indian prince of sixteen.

(*c*) Vajrāsan Muni (T'ub-pa rdo-rje gdan tso-'k'or-gsum).

---

1 Kuṣa (*poa cynosuroides*).

2 Vajrāsana (T., rdo-rje-gdan, pron. Dorje-dén).

3 Cf. TAYLOR'S *Primitive Culture*, i., 326; ii., 270.

4 Le bien-heureux (BURN., i., 71; and JAESCH., *D.*, 147).

(*d*) T'ub-pa dam-ts'ig gsum-bkod (PAND., No. 86).
(*e*) Bhagavān ekajata (CSOMA's *An.*, p. 591).
(*f*) Buddha-kapāla (Saṅs-rgyas t'od-pa : PAND., No. 69)—a very demoniacal form.

And here also seem to come the mythological series of "The Six Muni," the presidents of the six worlds of re-birth—see "Wheel of Life." These appear to be identical with "The Six *Jizô*" of the Japanese, though the "*Jizô*" are usually alleged to be forms of *Kshitigarbha.* Here also should probably come "The King of the powerful Nāgas"[1] which seems to represent Buddha defended by the *Nāga* Muchilinda, who seems to be a historic person, a helot (that is Nāga) villager of Muchilinda, a hamlet which adjoins Buddh-Gayā.

2. *The Seven Heroic Buddhas* (*of the Past*)[2] or *Tathāgatas.*[3]

This is a fabulous arrangement of human Buddhas, for none of them are historical except the last, to wit, Ṣākya Muni. Yet it was of early origin, as this series of images, and each of the number with his special tree of wisdom, is found in the Stūpa of Barhut, which is assigned to about 150 B.C., and they are also enumerated in the southern scripture, the *Dīgha-nikāya.*

In keeping with their imaginary character, all are given the most extravagant size and duration of earthly life.[4]

Their number is sometimes extended to nine. The most celebrated of the antecedent Buddhas is *Dīpaṃkara* (Tib., Mar-me-mdsad), "The Luminous." This imaginary Buddha is considered by some of the Lāmas to be the first of the series of the seven earthly Buddhas preceding Ṣākya Muni, but by the Ceylonese he is placed as the twenty-fourth predecessor.[5] He is represented as the first teacher of Ṣākya in one of the former births of the latter, and a favourite Jātaka-tale frequent in the Gāndhāra sculptures in the British Museum, and as a current picture in Burmah shows

1 kLu-dbaṅ-gi-rgyal-po; Skt., Nageṣvara raja.—His face is white and his body blue; he is sitting in rdo-rje skyil-kruṅ. Symb.—His two hands are in the mudra of ṅan-'gre-las-'don-par-mdsad-pa (or causing the animal beings to be delivered from misery) and are held over the heart. He has no ornaments. Behind him is a screen and flower and a seven-hooded snake canopy. Cf. PANDER, p. 71.

2 Saṅs-rgyas dpah-bohiduns.

3 De-bz'in gs'egs-pa.

4 Cf. Cs., *An.*; TURNER, *J.A.S.B.*, viii., 789; HARDY'S *Man.*, 94.

5 The Nepalese place him as the ninth predecessor of the historical Buddha (HODGS., *I.*, p. 135). Cf. HOFFMANN in Siebold's *Nippon Pantheon*, v., 77. "THE TWENTY-FOUR BUDDHAS" are Dīpaṃkara, Kauṇḍinya, Maṅgala, Sumanas, Raivata, Ṣobhita, (?) Ana-

the self-sacrifice of the embryo Ṣākya Muni in throwing himself over a puddle to form a stepping-stone for the Buddha Dīpaṁkara (Sumedh?)—suggestive of Sir W. Raleigh's gallantry to Queen Elizabeth under somewhat similar circumstances.

Dīpaṁkara's image, which is figured in the *Vajracedika*,[1] is frequently perforated by innumerable sockets, into which small lamps are set. This practice is evidently suggested by the concrete rendering of his name as "the burning lamp."

The Seven Buddhas are usually enumerated as:—

1. Vipaṣyin (T., rNam-gzigs); hands "earth-touching" and "impartial."
2. Ṣikhin (T., gTsug-gtor-c'an); hands "best-bestowing" and "impartial."
3. Viṣvabhu (T., T'am-ch'ad-skyob); hands "meditative."
4. Krakucandra (T., K'hor-wa-hjigs); hands "protecting" and "impartial."
5. Kanaka-muni (T., gSer-t'ub); hands "preaching" and "impartial."
6. Kāṣyapa (T., 'Od-sruṅs) has his right hand in "best bestowing"; and the left holds a piece of his robe resembling an animal's ear (see figure on page 5). Each is dressed in the three religious garments, and sits in the "unchangeable or adamantine" pose, or stands.
7. Ṣākya Muni (T., S'ākya t'ub-pa) in "the preaching attitude."

"*The Three Holy Ones*" are seldom, if ever, concretely represented in Tibet by Buddha, Dharma, and Saṅgha; nor have I found such a triad figured in Indian Buddhism, though many writers have alleged the existence of them, without, however, bringing forward any proofs. A triad of large images often occupies the centre of the Lāmaist altar, the central one being usually the founder of the particular sect to which the temple belongs, and the other two varying with the whim of the local Lāma.

THE CELESTIAL BUDDHAS.

The ideal origin of the celestial Buddhas has already been referred to in the chapter on doctrine. The five celestial Buddhas were invented in the earlier theistic stage of Buddhism.

The first of the series seems to have been Amitābha, or "the Boundless Light," a title somewhat analogous to the name of the oldest of the mythical human Buddhas, "the Luminous" (Dīpaṁkara). This metaphysical creation first appears in works about the

vama-darṣin, Padma, Nārada, Padmottara, Sumedhas, Sujāta, Priya-darṣin, Artha-darṣin, Dharma-darṣin, Siddhārta, Tishya, Pushya, Vipaṣyin, Ṣikhin, Visvabhū, Krakucandra, Kanaka-muni (or Koṇāgamana), and Kāṣyapa.

[1] Csoma, *An.*

beginning of our era, and seems to embody a sun-myth and to show Persian influence. For he was given a paradise in the west, to which all the suns hasten, and his myth seems to have arisen among the northern Buddhists when under the patronage of Indo-Scythian converts belonging to a race of sun-worshippers. Indeed, he is believed by Eitel and others to be a form of the Persian sun-god; and he was made the spiritual father of the historical Buddha.

Afterwards he was quintupled, apparently to adapt him to the theory of the five earthly Buddhas, the coming one and the four of the past, as well as to the other mystical groups of five—the five senses, the five *skandhas*, the five virtues, five cardinal points where the centre makes the fifth. And each one of these five celestial Buddhas was made to preside over a particular direction, as already detailed. Images of this series of Buddhas are found amongst the lithic remains of India about the seventh century A.D., if not earlier.

In the more developed theory, tending towards monotheism, a First Great Cause, under the title of the primordial or Ādi-Buddha, is placed above these five celestial Buddhas as their spiritual father and creator. And to this rank was promoted the first and central one of the metaphysical Buddhas, namely, Vairocana, "The Omni-present" or his reflex Samantabhadra, "The All Good."

These three series of Buddhas are arranged according to the mystical theory of the three bodies of Buddha (*Tri kāya*);[1] namely, (*a*) the *Dharma-kāya*, or law-body, which has been termed "*essential* wisdom (Bodhi)" and is self-existent and ever-lasting, and represented by Ādi-Buddha, (*b*) *Sambhoga-kāya* or adorned body, or *reflected* wisdom, represented by the celestial Jinas, and (*c*) *Nirmaṇa-kāya*, or changeable body, or *practical* wisdom represented by Ṣākya Muni and the other human Buddhas. Though in a more mystic sense Ṣākya Muni is considered to be an incarnate aggregate of the reflected *wisdom* of all the five celestial Jinas.

But these five celestial Jinas were latterly held to unite also within themselves both the forms of metaphysical bodies, both the Dharma-kāya and the Sambhoga-kāya. Hence arose two series of their images.

[1] Cf. HODGS., *Ess.*, 27, 58, 64; KÖPPEN, ii., 25; SCHLAG., 51, 210; EITEL, *Handb.*, *passim*.

The original series of these images of the strictly ascetic Buddha-type was by a materializing of the word called the religious (ascetic) or *Dharma* type—and such images may or may not hold begging-bowls; while the other is literally represented as "adorned bodies" (Sambhoga-kāya) in the same postures as the foregoing, but adorned with silks and jewels, and wearing crowns, like kingly Bodhisats. In this latter series, "the five Jinas" bear individually the same names as their prototypes, except the second and fourth, who are named respectively *Vajrasattva* (or "the indestructible or adamantine-souled") and *Amitāyus*, or "the boundless life," instead of *Akshobhya*, "the immovable," and *Amitābha*, "the boundless light." These alternative names, however, it will be seen, empress very similar and almost synonymous ideas.

Side by side with these developments arose the theory of celestial Bodhisat sons. The celestial Jinas absorbed in meditation in heaven could hold no contact with the sordid earth, so as agents for the salvation and protection of mortal men and animals they evolved sons, who, though celestial, were given active functions on the earth.

As in the other developments, this new theory first and most firmly attached to those creations most intimately associated with the historical Buddha. His celestial father, Amitābha, evolved the celestial Bodhisat Avalokita or Padma-pāṇi, who still remains the most popular of all the celestial Bodhisats.

But the popular craving for creative functions in their gods led, in the Tāntrik stage, to the allotment of female energies to these celestial Bodhisats. Thus Tārā, the goddess of Mercy, was given to Avalokita. And the extreme Tāntrik development under the Kāla-cakra system [1] awarded female energies also to each of the celestial Buddhas, and even to the primordial Ādi-Buddha himself.

Thus we have celestial Buddhas and Bodhisats and their female energies. Of the celestial Buddhas there are the following series:—(1) The primordial Buddha-god, or *Ādi-Buddha*. (2) The five celestial Victors (*Jina*). (3) The adorned forms of these latter, like kingly Bodhisats. (4) The Tāntrik forms with energies, mostly demoniacal Buddhas. And from several of these were latterly evolved other forms with special attributes; also medical and other Buddhas.

[1] In its Anuttara-yoga section.

The Primordial Buddha-God.[1]

As found in Lāmaism, he is most actively worshipped by the old or unreformed school, under the title of "The all-good religious body."

Skt., *Dharma-kāya Samantabhadra ;* Tib., Kun-tu bzaṅ-po.

He is figured of a blue colour, and often naked, sitting in Buddha fashion, with his hands in the meditative pose.

The established Lāmaist church gives somewhat similar functions to Vajradhāra, whom, however, they regard as a sort of celestial offshoot of Ṣākya Muni; while others of the semi-reformed sects seem, like the Nepalese, to credit Vajrasattva with supreme power as the primordial Buddha-god.

The Five Celestial Victors or Jina.

Skt., *Pañcajāti Jina ;* T., *r*gyal-ba rig*s*-lṅa.

These are figured on page 336[2]; and for the sake of clearness and convenience of reference, I have tabulated (see following page) the objective characters and relationships of these divinities. All the forms sit in the same Buddha-like attitude,[3] but the pose of the hands is characteristic.

The technical description of their attitudes and colour is as follows :—

Akshobhya (T., Mi-*s*kyod-pa), blue in colour, has his right hand in "witness" attitude and left in "impartial."

Vairocana (T., rNam-*s*naṅ), white with hands in "best perfection" attitude.

Ratnasambhava (T., Rin-'byuṅ), yellow, has his right hand in "bestowing" attitude, and left in "impartial."

Amitābha (T., 'Od-pag-med), red, in "meditative" (Tiṅ-ṅe-'dsin) attitude.

Amogha-siddhi (T., Don-yod-*g*rub-pa), green, has his right hand in "protecting" (skyabs-sbyin) attitude, and left in "impartial."

Each sits in the indestructible or "adamantine" pose, and differs only from the images of the human Buddha in having no begging-bowl in the lap.

In another and more common series, each is adorned with silks and jewels like a kingly Bodhisat, see page 333.

Other Celestial Tāntrik Jinas.

Another series of celestial Buddhas was formed by adorning the five Jinas with a crown, silks, and jewels, like a kingly Bodhisat,

---

[1] t'og-mahi Saṅs-*r*gya*s*.

[2] Conf. also HODGSON's figures from Nepal in *Asiatic Researches, xvi.*

[3] *i.e.,* Vajra-palaṅga. See p. 335.

T

THE OBJEC

THE FIVE CELEST

Direction where located.[1]	Names of the Jinas.	Mode of holding hands. (*Mudrā.*)	Animal as Throne-Support. (*Vahan.*)	Colour. (These seem colours of the five elements—not the quarters.)	Symb Objec Insig
CENTRAL.	*Vairocana* (*r*Nam-par *s*naṅ-*m*dsad).	"Teaching," or, "Turning the Wheel of the Law." *Dharma-cakra.*[3]	Lion.	White = space.	Wh *Ca*
EAST.	*Akshobhya* (Mi-*b*skyo*d*-pa).	"Witness,"—"touching the ground." *Bhūsparsa.*	Elephant.[4]	Blue = air.	Thur bo *Va*
SOUTH.	*Ratnasambhava* (Rin-ch'en' byuṅ-*g*nas).	"Bestowing." *Vara.*	Horse.	Golden-yellow = earth.	Jew *Rat*
WEST.	*Amitābha* (*s*Naṅ-ba *m*tha*h*-yas, or, 'Od-*d*pag-med).	"Meditative." *Dhyāna.*	Peacock.	Red = light.	Red L *Rak* *pad*
NORTH.	*Amogha-siddhi* (Don-yod-'*g*rub-pa).	"Blessing of Fear-lessness." *Abhaya.*	"Shang-shang," a winged dwarf. = ? Kin-nara.	Green = water.	Cro Thur bol *Vis* *va*

N.B.—The Sanskrit names are in italics and the Tibetan equivalents in brack

1 In magic-circles, however, the special form of the celestial Buddha to whic

2 This symbol is represented on the special Tāntrik *vajra*, and bell of each of t

3 This refers to the witness episode of Māra's temptation, see page 344.

4 Being in the teaching attitude, Vairocana Buddha is held to be *the* Buddha

5 He is usually made an emanation from all of the celestial Jinas.

RACTERS OF

)DHAS OR *JINAS*.

tial or erm" ell. ija.)	"Adorned" Active Reflex. (*Sambhogakayā.*)	Female Reflex (? *Saṅghā-prajñam nayā*) or Energy.	*Bodhisat* Reflex, or Spiritual Sons. (*Jinaputra.*)	Earthly Reflex, as Buddha. (*Manushi Buddha.*)
)M.	*Vairocana* 2nd.	*Vajradhātisvari* (nam-*m*kah-*d*byid*s*-p'ug-me).	*Samantabhadra* (Kuntu-zaṅ-po).	*Krakucandra* ('K'or-ba-'jig*s*).
IŪṂ.	*Vajra-sattva* (*r*Do-*r*je-sems-*d*pa).	*Locanā.*	*Vajrapāṇi* (p'yag-*r*dor).	*Kanaka Muni* (*g*ser-t'ub).
AM (or RAM).	*Ratnasambhava* 2nd	*Māmakī.*	*Ratnapāni* (p'ag-rin-ch'en).	*Kāṣyapa* ('Od-sruṅs).
HRI.	*Amitāyus* (Tse-*d*pag-med).	? *Pāndarā* or *Sita* (go*s*-dKar-mo).	*Avalokita*—the common title of *Padma-pāvi* (sbyan ra*s*-zig*s*).	*Ṣākya Muni* (S'ākya-t'ub-pa).[5]
A.	*Amogha-siddhi* 2nd.	. . . *Tārā* (dam-ts'ig-*s*grol-ma).	*Viṣvapāni* (p'ag na-ts'og).	*Maitreya* (Byam-pa).

ṇḍala is addressed occupies the centre.
as and the colour of the *vajra* and bell are the same as that of the *Jina* they symbolize.

ɔecially personifies Wisdom.

of "the mild deity" type. Of these the best known are Amitāyus, Vajradhāra, and Vajrasattva.

"The Buddha of Infinite or Eternal Life," Skt., *Amitāyus* or *Aparimitāyus;* Tib., Ts'e-*d*pag-med. He is, as figured at pages 329 and 333, of the same form as his prototype Amitābha Buddha, but he is adorned with the thirteen ornaments, and he holds on his lap the vase of life-giving ambrosia.

Other forms of Amitāyus are the four-handed white A., the red A., the King A., Tantrācārya A., and Ras-ch'uṅ's A.

The following two divinities, esoteric so-called, are accorded by the Lāmas the position of Buddhas, though they are Bodhisat-reflexes from or metamorphoses of Akshobhya, and they both resemble in many ways their relative and probable prototype Vajrapāṇi :—

"The Adamantine or Indestructible-souled." (Skt., *Vajrasattva ;* T., rDor-je dSems-pa), The Everlasting.

"The Indestructible or Steadfast holder." Skt., *Vajradhāra ;* T., rDorje 'Ch'aṅ).

He is figured at page 61, and holds a vajra and a bell. In the exoteric cults he is called "the concealed lord" (*Guhya-pati*, T., Saṅ-bahi'dag-po). He is a metamorphosis of Indra, and, like him, presides over the eastern quarter, and he seems the prototype of most of those creatures which may be called demon-Buddhas. And though, as above noted, the established church regards this Buddha as a reflex from Ṣākya Muni himself, it also views him as the presiding celestial Buddha, analogous to the Ādi-Buddha of the old school.[1]

Some Tāntrik forms of Amogha-siddha, etc., are :—

Don-yod z'ags-pa (PA., 96).
„ z'ags-pa *s*na-ts'ogs *d*baṅ-po.
„ lc'ag*s*-kyu.
„ mch'od-pa'i ṅor-bu.

Other forms of celestial Buddhas and Bodhisats are :—

*r*Do-rje mi-k'rugs-pa (PA., No. 87).
Vajradhātu : *r*dor-*d*byiṅs (PA., No. 77).
*r*Nam-snaṅ *m*ṅon-byaṅ (PA., No. 83).
Vajragarbha Jina : *r*Gyal-ba *r*Do-rje sñiṅ-po.
„ rin-c'hen-'od-'p'ro.
Surasena Jina : *r*Gyal-ba *d*pa'bo'i-*s*de, etc., etc.

(See PA., p. 71 for about thirty more), and cf. *Butsu dzo-dsui*, p. 62, for "the Secret Buddhas of the 30 days."

[1] Cf. SCHL., 50 ; KÖPPEN, ii., 28, 367 ; HODGS., 27, 46, 77, 83 ; SCHIEF., *Tāra.*, 300 ; PAND., No. 56.

Demoniacal Buddhas.

The later Tāntrik forms include many demoniacal Buddhas:—

Guhya-Kāla (T., gSan-'dus).
Buddha Kapāla, Saṅs-rgyas t'od-pa (PAND., No. 69).
Vajrāsana-mula, rDo-rje gdan-bzhi (PAND., No. 70), etc.

The special relationships of the Buddhas to certain fiends is seen in the foregoing table of surmounting Jinas.

The Thirty-five Buddhas of Confession.

These imaginary Buddhas or Tathāgatas are invoked in the so-called Confession of Sins.[1] Their images are evolved by giving different colours to the Buddhas in the five elementary sedent attitudes. And they, together with "the thousand Buddhas,"[2] may be considered as concrete representations of the titles of the historical human Buddha.

The Highest Healers and Medical Tathāgatas.

T., sMan-bla-bde-gs'egs brgyad.

This is a very popular form of Buddha as "The supreme physician," or Buddhist Æsculapius, and is probably founded upon the legend of the metaphysical Bodhisat, "The medicine-king" (Bhaisajyarājā), who figures prominently in several of the northern scriptures as the dispenser of spiritual medicine. The images are worshipped almost as fetishes, and cure by sympathetic magic. The first of the series, namely, the beryl, or Bedūriya Buddha, is also extremely popular in Japan under the title of "The lord Binzuru" (Binzura Sama), a corruption evidently, it seems to me, of the Indian word "Bedūriya," although the Japanese themselves[3] believe it to be derived from Bharadhvāja, one of the sixteen Arhats.

These Æsculapic Buddhas are much worshipped in Tibet, in ritual by pictures, seldom by images as in Japan, where, as the latter are so much consulted by the people, and also doubtless owing to their essentially un-Buddhist character, they are usually

1 Dig-pa t'am-c'ad s'ag-par ter-choi, details in SCHLAG., p. 123 *seq.* It is not to be confused with the section of the Pratimoksha, properly so called.

2 See list of Buddha's thousand names by Prof. SCHMIDT, B. Ac., St. Petersbg.

3 Banyio Nanjio, CHAMBERLAIN's *Handbook to Japan.*

placed outside the central shrine. The supplicant, after bowing and praying, rubs his finger over the eye, ear, knee, or the particular part of the image corresponding to the patient's own affected spot, and then applies the finger carrying this hallowed touch to the afflicted spot. The constant friction and rubbing of this rude worship is rather detrimental to the features of the god.

This group of medical Buddhas is figured in Schlagintweit's atlas, but erroneously under the title of "Maitreya." They are :—

1. Saṅs-*r*gya*s* sman-gyi *b*la Bedūrya'i 'Od-Kyi *r*gyal-po, or, "King of beryl-light, the supreme physician Buddha." Like all of the series, he is of Buddha-like form, garb, and sedent attitude. He is indigo-coloured; his right hand is in mch'og-sbyin pose, and in his palm he holds the golden Arura fruit (myrobalans). His left hand is in *m*ñam-*b*z'ag pose, and holds a begging-bowl of *Bai-dur-ya* (beryl-stone). Cf. Butsu Yakushi in *Butsu-dzô-dsui*, p. 26; Schf., *Leben*, 84; Pand., No. 142.

2. *m*Non-*m*k'yen-*r*gyal-po is red in colour, with hands in *m*ch'og-*s*byin and *m*ñam-bz'ag pose. Cf. Pand., No. 141.

3. Ch'os-*s*grag*s*-*r*gya-*m*ts'o'i-*d*byaṅ*s* is red in colour, with hands in *m*ch'og-*s*byin and *m*ñam-*b*z'ag pose. Cf. Pand., No. 140.

4. Mya-ṅan-med-mch'og-*d*pal is light red in colour, with both hands in *m*ñam-*b*z'ag pose. Cf. Pand., No. 139.

5. *g*Ser-*b*zaṅ-dri-med is yellowish-white in colour, with right hand in ch'o*s*-'ch'ad mudra, and his left in *m*ñam-*b*z'ag pose. Cf. Pand., No. 138.

6. Rin-ch'en-zla-wa (or *s*gra-*d*byaṅs) is yellow-red in colour; his right hand is in ch'o*s*-'ch'ad, and his left in *m*ñam-*b*z'ag pose. Cf. Pand., No. 137.

7. *m*tsh'an-leg*s* yoṅ*s*-grag*s* *d*pal is yellow in colour. His right hand is in *c*h'o*s*-'ch'ad, and his left in *m*ñam-*b*z'ag pose. Cf. Pand., No. 136.

And in the centre of the group is placed, as the eighth, the image of Ṣākya Muni.

In this relation it is rather curious to note that some celebrated Europeans have come to be regarded as Buddhas. "The common dinner-plates of the Tibetans, when they use any, are of tin, stamped in the centre with an effigy of some European celebrity. In those which I examined I recognized the third Napoleon, the Prince and Princess of Wales, and Mr. Gladstone, all supposed by the natives to represent Buddhas of more or less sanctity."[1]

II. Bodhisats (Celestial).

These are the supernatural Bodhisats, the active reflexes from the relatively impassive celestial Buddhas. The human Bodhi-

[1] Baber, *Supp. Papers*, Royal Geog. Soc., p. 200.

sats, or the saints, are referred by me to the end of the pantheon, though the Lāmas usually place them above the *dii minores*, and many of them next to the celestial Bodhisats themselves.

The Lāmas head the list with the metaphysical Bodhisat of wisdom, Mañjuṣrī; but following what appears to be the order of development of these divinities, I commence with Maitreya, the coming Buddha, who, indeed, is the only Bodhisat known to primitive Buddhism and to the so-called "southern" Buddhists of the present day, the Burmese, Ceylonese, and Siamese; though the Lāmas place him fourth or later in their lists, giving priority to the especially active Bodhisats which the Mahāyāna created, the mythical Mañjuṣrī, Vajrapāṇi, and Avalokita, whom they have made their *defensores fidei* of Lāmaism, with the title of "The three lords"[1] and given functions somewhat like the analogous triad of Brāhmanism, Brahmā, Ṣiva and Vishṇu.

The female Bodhisats, Tārā, etc., are given towards the end of the list, though they might more naturally have been placed beside their consorts.

MAITREYA, "The loving one," the coming Buddha or Buddhist Messiah. T., *Byams-pa* (pr. "Jam-pa" or "Cham-pa.")

He is usually represented adorned like a prince,[2] and sitting on a chair in European fashion with legs down, teaching the law.[3] He is at present believed to be in the Tushita heaven. His image is frequently rock-carved or built in colossal form several storeys high in Tibet, as he is credited with gigantic size.

MAÑJUṢRĪ or *Mañjughosha*, "The sweet-voiced," the god of wisdom or Buddhist Apollo, and figured at page 12. T., *'Jam-pahi* dbyaṅs (pr. Jam-yang).

He is Wisdom deified, and seems a purely metaphysical creation unconnected with any of his later namesakes amongst the Buddhist monks in the fourth or fifth centuries of our era, or later. His chief function is the dispelling of ignorance. He presides over the law, and with his bright sword of divine knowledge[4] cuts all knotty points, and carries in his left the bible of transcendental Wisdom, the Prajñā-pāramitā, placed upon a lotus-flower.[5] He is the especial patron of astrology. In keeping with his pure character he is strictly celibate, one of the few of the

1 Rig-sum mgon-po, the Lāmaist *Trimurti*.
2 Of the mild, z'i-wa type.
3 Cf. PAND., No. 151.
4 *Ses-rab ral-gri*
5 Cf. KÖPPEN, ii., 21.

Mahāyāna deities who is allotted no female energy.[1] He usually sits, as in the figure, in the Buddha attitude. He is given several other modes.

Most of the countries where northern Buddhism prevails have their own special Mañjuṣrī. Thus China has a quasi-historical Mañjuṣrī of about the fifth century A.D., located near the U-tai Shan shrine; and Nepalese Buddhism has another of the same name as its tutelary saint.[2]

VAJRAPĀṆI, "The wielder of the thunderbolt," a metamorphosis of Jupiter (Indra)[3] as the spiritual son of the second celestial Buddha, Akshobhya. T., p'yag -na-rdo-rje (pronouced chāna-dorje or chak-dor.)

He is figured at page 13, and of the fierce fiend type, black or dark blue in colour, and wields a Vajra (*rdo-rje*) in his uplifted right hand, while in his left he holds a bell or snare or other implement according to his varying titles, of which there are fifteen or more.[4] Hiuen Tsiang mentions his worship in India in the seventh century A.D.[5]

AVALOKITA (or *Avalokiteṣvara* or *Mahākaruṇa*), "The keen seeing lord, the great pitier and lord of mercy." T., spyan-ras-gzigs (pr. *Chä-rä-zi*), T'ugs-rje-ch'en-po.

His origin and various forms I have described in some detail elsewhere.[6] The spiritual son of the celestial Buddha Amitābha, he is the most powerful and popular of all the Bodhisats, and the one which the Dalai Lāmas pretend to be the incarnation of. Other forms of this deity are *Padma-pāṇi*, the Lotus-handed *Khasarpāṇi*, *Siṅhanada* (T., seṅ-ge-sgra), the Roaring Lion, Hala-hala, Arya-pāla ("Aryabolo"), etc.

Avalokita, being a purely mythological creation, is seldom like Buddha represented as a mere man, but is invested usually with monstrous and supernatural forms and attributes. The earliest Indian images of Avalokita yet found by me, dating to about the

1 Though the Prajnā must be somewhat of this character.

2 Cf. *Archæol. W.Ind.*, 9, xxvi., 18. PA., No. 145.

3 *Dyaush-pitar*, or heavenly father of the Hindūs, becomes "Jupiter" or "Diespiter" of the Romans, and "Zeus" of the Greeks.

4 Cf. for more common form, *Arch. W.Ind.*, 9, xxvii., 23, and PA., 84, 146, 169, 170, 171.

5 BEAL's trans., ii.

6 *J.R.A.S.*, 1894, p. 51, *et seq.*, where twenty-two forms are described.

sixth century A.D., clearly show that Avalokita's image was modelled after that of the Hindū Creator *Prajāpati* or Brāhma; and the same type may be traced even in his monstrous images of the later Tāntrik period, and his images usually bear Brahmā's insignia, the lotus and rosary, and often the vase and book. His commonest forms found in Tibet are:

The Four-handed form, see figure on page 228. This represents him as a prince, with the thirteen ornaments, of white complexion, and sitting in the Buddha posture with the front pair of hands joined in devotional attitude (and often as clasping a jewel); while the upper hand holds a crystal rosary, and the left a long-stemmed lotus-flower, which opens on the level of his ear.[1]

His monstrous eleven-headed form is figured at page 15. It is usually standing. In addition to the double pair of hands, it has others carrying weapons to defend its votaries. It represents the wretched condition of Avalokita when his head split into pieces with grief at seeing the deplorable state of sunken humanity. But this form, too, seems based on the polycephalic Brāhma.[2]

The eleven heads are usually arranged, as in the figure, in the form of a cone, in five series from below upwards, of 3, 3, 3, 1 and 1, and the topmost head is that of Amitābha, the spiritual father of Avalokita. Those looking forward wear an aspect of benevolence; the left ones express anger at the faults of men; while the right faces smile graciously at the good deeds or in scorn at evil-doers.

This form is frequently given a thousand eyes, a concrete materialistic expression of the name *Avalokita*, "He who looks down" or *Samanta-mukha*, "He whose face looks every way."[3] The fixing of the number of eyes at one thousand is merely expressive of multitude, and has no precise numerical significance. And unlike the thousand-eyed god of Brāhmanic mythology—Indra—Avalokita's extra eyes are on his extra hands, which are symbolic of power, and most of their hands are stretched forth to save the wretched and the lost. The eye, which is ever on the look-out to

1 Cf. *A.W.I.*, xxvi., p. 17; PA., No. 147 and my Art. *J.R.A.S.*, *loc. cit.*

2 Cf. my art. above cited. The head-splitting is associated with the presence of an obstacle, in early Buddhist works. Thus in the Dialogues of Menander (*Milinda*, RHYS DAVIDS' trans., p. 222), in regard to the raiser of an obstacle it is said, "then would his head split into a hundred or into a thousand pieces."

3 Cf. BURNOUF'S *Lotus*, p. 428; BEAL'S *Catena*, 384.

perceive distress, carries with it a helping hand—altogether a most poetic symbolism. Of this type there are many modes, differing mainly in colour and degrees of fierceness.

The other supernatural male Bodhisats[1] are not so commonly met with. The chief are:

SAMANTABHADRA, "The all good." T., Kuntu-bzaṅ-po.

He is figured at page 14,[2] and is the son of the celestial Buddha Vairocana, and is to be distinguished from the Ādi-Buddha of the same name. He is of the "mild" type, and usually mounted on an elephant, and he is frequently associated with Mañjuṣrī[3] as attendant on Buddha.

KSHITIGARBHA, "The matrix of the earth."[4]
T., Sa-yi sñiṅ-po.

Ākāṣagarbha, "The matrix of the sky."
T., Nam-k'ahi-ñiṅ-po.[5]

Sarva nivarana vishkambhini.
T., sgRib-pa rnam sel.[6]

(? *Jñānaguru*), Master of divine foreknowledge.[7]
T., Ye-s'es bla-ma.

(? *Prabhāketu*), The crown of light.[8]
T., 'Od-kyi-tog.

Pranidhānamati.
T., sMon-lam blo-gros.[9]

Ṣāntendra, The foundation of power.[10]
T., dbAṅ-po z'i.

FEMALE BODHISATS.

The chief and most active of the supernatural female Bodhisats or "energies" are Tārā and Marīcī.

TĀRĀ, The saviour, or deliverer. T., sgRol-ma (pr. *Dö-ma*). She is the consort of Avalokita, who is now held to be incarnate in the Dalai Lāmas, and she is the most popular deity in Tibet,

[1] For description of some of these in the Ajaṇṭa caves, see art. by me in *Ind. Antiquary*, 1898.

[2] From the Japanese *Butzu Dzô-dsui*, p. 127. The form figured, which is generally like that in Lāmaism, is entitled Samantabhadra-Yama. Cf. also W. ANDERSON'S *Cat.*, p. 81, No. 57.

[3] Cf. PAND., No. 152, and No. 55. The Japanese call him Fugen.

[4] Fig. PAND., No. 148.

[5] Fig. PAND., No. 150.

[6] Fig. PAND., No. 149.

[7] Fig. PAND., No. 153.

[8] Fig. PAND., No. 154.

[9] Fig. PAND., No. 155.

[10] Fig. PAND., No. 156.

both with Lāmas and laity. She corresponds to the goddess of mercy and queen of heaven (*Kwan-yin*)[1] of the Chinese, and has her literal analogy in biblical mythology (see the heading to this chapter), and she has several analogies with "the Virgin;"[2] but she is essentially Indian in origin and form.

Her most common form is "the green Tārā," and much less common is "the white Tārā," whose worship is almost confined to the Mongols. Her other numerous forms, of which the names of "the twenty-one" are daily on the lips of the people, are seldom pictured, except the fiendish form *Bhṛikuṭi*.[3]

The green Tārā. T., sgRol-ma ljaṅ-k'u—pronounced *Döl-jang.*

She is represented (see the figure) as a comely and bejewelled Indian lady with uncovered head, and of a green complexion, seated on a lotus, with her left leg pendant, and holding in her left hand a long-stemmed lotus-flower.

TĀRĀ, THE GREEN.

The white Tārā. T., sgRol-ma dkar-po—or sgRol-dkar (pr. Dö-kar).

She is figured (see p. 23) as an adorned Indian lady with a white complexion, seated Buddha-like, and the left hand holding a long-stemmed lotus-flower. She has seven eyes, the eye of foreknowledge in the forehead, in addition to the ordinary facial pair, and also one in each palm and on each sole. Hence she is called "The seven-eyed white Tārā." She is believed by the Mongols to be incarnate in the White Czar.

Tārā with the frowning brows—Bhṛikuṭi Tārā. T., kKo-gñer-gyo-ba-hi sgRol-ma (pronounced T'o-nyer-chän).

1 Or in Japanese *Kwan-non*, a translation of "Avalokita."

2 For note on Tārā's origin, see my article in *J.R.A.S.*, 1894, pp. 63, etc.

3 For detailed description of twenty-seven forms, see *ibid.*

This Tārā is dark indigo-coloured, and usually with three faces, all frowning.

THE TWENTY-ONE TĀRĀS.

The list of the names of "the twenty-one Tārās" given below,[1] and known to almost all lay Tibetans, indicates many of her attributes.

[1] Titles of "The Twenty-one Tārās."

1. Tārā, the supremely valiant (*Prasura Tārā*).
2. ,, of white-moon brightness (*Candrojasa Sita Tārā*).
3. ,, the golden coloured (*Gauri T*).
4. ,, the victorious hair-crowned (*Ushnishahiaya T.*).
5. ,, the "Huṅ"-shouter (*Hūṃdā T*).
6. ,, the three-world best worker.
7. ,, suppressor of strife.
8. ,, the bestower of supreme power.
9. ,, the best providence.
10. Tārā, the dispeller of grief.
11. ,, the cherisher of the poor.
12. ,, the brightly glorious.
13. ,, the universal mature worker.
14. ,, with the frowning brows (*Bhṛikuṭi Tārā*).
15. ,, the giver of prosperity.
16. ,, the subduer of passion.
17. ,, the supplier of happiness (*Sarsiddhi T.*).
18. ,, the excessively vast.
19. ,, the dispeller of distress.
20. ,, the advent or realization spiritual power (*Siddhārtā Tārā*).
21. ,, the completely perfect.

MARĪCĪ, The resplendent. T., 'Od-zer 'c'an-ma.

She was originally the queen of heaven, a Buddhist Ushas, or goddess of the dawn, a metamorphosis of the sun as the centre of energy, curiously coupled with the oriental myth of the primæval productive pig. In another aspect she is a sort of Prosperine, the spouse of Yama, the Hindū Pluto. While in her fiercest mood she is the consort of the demon-general, "The horse-necked *Tamdin*," a sort of demoniacal centaur. In another mode she is "The adamantine sow" (Skt., *Vajra-vārāhī;* T., rDo-rje P'ag-mo), who is believed to be incarnate in the abbess of the convent on the great Palti lake,[1] as already described.

འོད་ཟེར་ཅན་མ་

MARĪCĪ, OR VĀRĀHĪ.
(or "The Diamond Sow.")

In her ordinary form she has three faces and eight hands, of which the left face is that of a sow. The hands hold various weapons, including an *araju*, axe, and snare. She sits in "the enchanting pose" upon a lotus-throne drawn by seven swine,[2] as in the figure.

III. TUTELARIES.

Although the tutelaries (T., *Yi-dam*) belong to different classes of divinities, it is convenient to consider them together under one group.

The important part played by tutelaries in every-day life, their worship, and the mode of coercing them, have already been described.

The qualifications demanded in a tutelary are activity combined with power over the minor malignant devils. Thus most of the superior celestial Buddhas and Bodhisats may be, and are, tutelaries. But the favourite ones are the great demon-kings,

[1] Cf. Chapters x. and xi., and also Giorgi.

[2] Cf. PAND., No. 163, whose figure is reproduced above.

and also some of the inferior fiends who have been promoted in diabolic rank for their adherence to the cause of Buddhism.

All the five celestial Jinas are tutelaries, but it is their Tāntrik forms, such as Vajrasattva and Vajradhāra, and Amitāyus, which are especially utilized in this way; and most common of all are those who have consorts (*sakti*), as these are considered to be most energetic.

Of the Bodhisats, those most common as tutelaries are Avalokita and Mañjuṣrī, the demon Vajrapāṇi, Tārā, and Marīcī.

The demon-kings, however, are the favourite ones. They are repulsive monsters of the type of the Hindū devil Ṣiva.[1] These morbid creations of the later Tāntrism may be considered a sort of fiendish metamorphoses of the supernatural Buddhas. Each of those demon-kings, who belong to the most popular section of Lāmaist Tāntrism—the *Anuttara yoga*—has a consort,[2] who is even more malignant than her spouse.

There are several of these ferocious many-armed monsters, all of the fiercest fiend type already described, and all much alike in general appearance. But each sect has got its own particular tutelary-demon, whom it believes to be pre-eminently powerful.

Thus the established church, the Ge-lug-pa, has as its tutelary Vajra-bhairava, though several of the individual monks have Sambhara and Guhyakāla as their personal tutelaries.

VAJRA-BHAIRAVA, or "The Fearful thunderbolt." (T., rDo-rje-'jigs-byed). See figure on opposite page.

This is a form of Ṣiva as the destroyer of the king of the dead, namely, as *Yamāntaka*. Yet with truly Lāmaist ingenuousness this hideous creature is believed to be a metamorphosis of the mild and merciful Avalokita. His appearance will best be understood from his picture here attached.[3] He has several heads, of which the lowest central one is that of a bull. His arms and legs are innumerable, the former carrying weapons, and the latter trample upon the enemies of the established church.

It will be noticed that these writhing victims are represented

[1] As in the type also of the "Pancha Raksha."

[2] Skt., *Matrikā*, or mother; T., *Yum*, and the pair are called "the father-mother," T., *Yab-yum*.

[3] After PANDER, No. 61, which see for some details.

of the four ancient classes of beings, namely, gods, men, quadrupeds, and birds.

Others of these tutelary devils are :—

Ṣamvara (T., bDe-mch'og[1]), the chief of happiness, also called dpal-'k'or-lo-sdom-pa

Guhyukāla (T., gSan-'dus[2]), "the secret time."

Vajra-phurba, the *phurba*-thunderbolt.

Dub-pa-kah-gye (or ? dGyes-pa-dorje).

These are the tutelary fiends of the Kar-gyu, Sa-kya, and the unreformed Ñiṅ-ma sects respectively. Others are Hé-vajra (Kye-

VAJRA-BHAIRAVA.
(Tutelary fiend of established church.)

rdorje), Buddhakapāla (Saṅs-gyas-t'od-pa), Yāma (gsin-rje), but they do not here require special description.

IV. Defenders of the Faith.

Skt., *Dharmapāla* ; T., Ch'os-skyoṅ.

These are the demon-generals or commanders-in-chief who execute the will of the tutelaries—the demon-kings. In appear-

---

1 PAND., No. 63, and CSOMA, *An.*, p. 498. 2 PAND., Nos. 62 and 68.

ance they are almost as hideous and fierce as their fiendish masters, and each commands a horde of demons.

They are of the fiercest fiend type (the *Drag-po* and *To-wo*) already described. The females are metamorphoses of the Hindū fiendess, *Kāli Devi.* A few local country gods have also been promoted to the position of defenders of the faith.

Of those of the *Drag-po* or *To-wo* type, the chief are:—

"The horse-necked (fiend)," Skt., *Hayagrīva ;* T., *r*Ta-*m*grin, pron. *Tam-din.*

ཧོ་ཁྲོའི་ལྷྲུ་ཀྱི་རྟ་མགྲིན

TAM-DIN.

(General tutelary of established church.)

He is figured as shown here,[1] with a horse's head and neck surmounting his other heads. There are many varieties of him[2]; see also his figure at p. 62.

"The immoveable," Skt., *Acala ;* T., Mi-gyo-ba.

He is also found in the Japanese Buddhist pantheon as "*Fu-do.*"[3]

"The slayer of the death-king," Skt., *Yamamāri,*[4] T., yS'in-rje gs'ed, a form of Bhairava, and held to be incarnate in the Dalai Lāma as the controller of metempsychosis.

"THE GODDESS or The queen of the warring weapons." *Lha-mo* (or pal-ldan-Lha-mo); Skt., *Devi* (or *Srī-Devi*). And also, in Tibetan, dMagzor rgyal-mo.

This great she-devil, like her prototype the goddess Durga of Brāhmanism, is, perhaps, the most malignant and powerful of all the demons, and the most dreaded. She is credited with letting loose the demons of disease, and her name is scarcely ever mentioned, and only then with bated breath, and under the title of "The great queen"—Mahā-rāni.

She is figured, as at page 334,[5] surrounded by flames, and riding

---

1 After Pander.

2 Cf. PA., No. 166, 167, 168, 213.

3 Cf. CHAMBERLAIN'S *Handbook to Japan.* PAND., No. 174.

4 Cf. PANDER, No. 212.

5 After PANDER, No. 148. Cf. SCHLAG., 112.

on a white-faced mule, upon a saddle of her own son's skin flayed by herself. She is clad in human skins and is eating human brains and blood from a skull; and she wields in her right hand a trident-rod. She has several attendant "queens" riding upon different animals.

She is publicly worshipped for seven days by the Lāmas of all sects, especially at the end of the twelfth month, in connection with the prevention of disease for the incoming year. And in the cake offered to her are added amongst other ingredients the fat of a black goat, blood, wine, dough and butter, and these are placed in a bowl made from a human skull.

THE LORD-DEMONS.

T., mGön-po; Skt., *Nātha.*[1]

These form a class of demon-generals, of the fiercest Drag-po type. Each Lāmaist sect has chosen one as its defender, whom it claims to be pre-eminently powerful, thus:—

"The six-armed lord,"[2] T., mGon-po p'yag-drug, is the chief minister of the tutelary fiend of the established church.

"The lord of the black cloak," or "The four-armed lord," T., mGon-po *Gur*, is the general of the tutelary Samvara of the Kar-gyu-pa sect. And he is the fiend-general of the old unreformed sect—the Ñiṅ-ma-pa. He is figured at page 70.

These "lords" are said to number seventy-five. Several of them are referred to in regard to their masks in the chapter on the mystic play. The highest is the bird-faced Garuḍa. Other important ones are:—

"The lord of foreknowledge," T., ye-ses mGon-po; Skt., *Jñananātha;* and formerly called "The devil *Mata-ruta.*"

"The black lord." T., mGon-po Nag-po; Skt., *Kālānātha.*

"The great potent sage." T., bLo-c'an dban-p'ug-ch'en-po. Both of these latter bear titles of the Hindū Ṣiva, Mahākāla.

---

[1] This name suggests relationship with the "*Nāts*" of the Burmese Buddists, though most of these *Nāts* are clearly Hindū Vedic deities, and as their number is said to be 37, probably they are the 33 Vedic gods of Indra's heaven *plus* the four-fold Brāhma or the four guardians of the quarter. For list of the *Nāts* cf. App. by Col. Sladen in ANDERSON'S *Mandalay to Momein*, p. 457.

[2] PAND., No. 230.

Ḍākkinīs, or Furies.

T., mkah-'gro-ma, or "Sky-goer"; Skt., *Khecara*.

These Ḍākkinīs are chiefly consorts of the demoniacal tutelaries, and the generals of the latter. Many of them seem to be of an indigenous nature like the Bön-pa deities. One of the most common is "The lion-faced" (Seṅ-gehi-*g*doṅ-c'an). Several others are described and figured by Pander.[1]

Here also may be placed the eight goddesses, who are probably metamorphoses of "the eight mothers." They encircle the heavens and are figured in many of the magic-circles, usually of beautiful aspect and with the following characters:—

1. *Lāsyā* (T., *s*Geg-mo-ma), of white complexion, holding a mirror and in a coquettish attitude.
2. *Mālā* (T., Preṅ-ba-ma), of yellow colour, holding a rosary.
3. *Gītā* (T., *g*Lu-ma), of red colour, holding a lyre symbolizing music.
4. T., *Gar-ma*, of green colour, in a dancing attitude.
5. *Pushpa* (T., Me-tog-ma), of white colour, holding a flower.
6. *Dhupā* (T., *b*Dug-*s*pös ma), of yellow colour, holding an incense-vase.
7. *Dipa* (T., *s*Naṅ-*g*sal-ma), of red colour, holding a lamp.
8. *Gandha* (T., Dri-ch'a-ma), of green colour, holding a shell-vase of perfume.

V. Godlings and Angels.

These *Dii minores* are the gods and lesser divinities of Aryan and Hindū mythology, degraded to this low rank on account of their inclusion within the wheel of metempsychosis, and from their leading lives only partially devoted to Buddhist duties. The morality of these gods is, generally, of a higher order than their counterparts in the Greek or Roman mythology.

Collectively they are called "The eight classes," and are made subordinate to the tutelary-fiends and their generals; and in the order of their rank, are thus enumerated[2]:—

1. The Gods—Skt., *Deva;* T., Lha.
2. Serpent-demigods (mermaids)—*Nāgā;* kLu.

[1] Nos. 127, 187, 188, 189, 191, 192, 223, 224, 226, 227, 228.

[2] Cf. Bournouf, i., 87.

3. Genii—*Yaksha*; gNod-sbyin.
4. Angels—*Gandharva*; Dri-za.
5. Titans—*Asura*; Lha-ma-yin.
6. Phœnix—*Garuḍa*; Namk'ah-ldiṅ.
7. Celestial musicians—*Kinnara*; Mi-'am-c'i.
8. The Great Reptiles (creepers), *Mahoraga*; lTo-'bye-ch'en-po.

The GODS are the thirty-three Vedic gods, which have already been described as regards their general characters.[1] They are usually figured, like earthly kings of the "mild deity" type, on lotus-thrones. The chief gods are made regents or protectors of the quarters; though in the later legends they have delegated these duties to subordinates, the "kings of the quarters"; see page 84.

The great Indra (Jupiter, T., brGya-byin), on the east.
Yama (Pluto, T., gSin-rje), on the south.
Varuṇa (Uranus, T., Ch'u-'lha[2]), on the west.
Kuverā (Vulcan[3], T., gNod-sbyin), on the north.

The remainder of the ten directions are thus apportioned:—

S.E. to Agni (Ignis, the fire-god; T., Me-lha), or Soma the moon or Bacchus.
S.W. to Nririti (the goblin; T., Srin-po).
N.W. to Marut (the storm-god; T., rLuṅ-lha).
N.E. to Isa (T., dbAng-ldan).
Nadir to Ananta (or "mother-earth"; T., 'Og-gis-bdag).
Zenith to Brahmā (Ts'aṅs-pa[4]).

The first and the last of the above, namely, Indra and Brāhma, are represented as attendant on Buddha at all critical periods of his earthly life—the former with a third and horizontal eye in the forehead, acting as his umbrella-carrier, and the latter usually four-handed and headed, carrying the vase of life-giving ambrosia. The Brāhmanical god Vishṇu is called K'yab-'jug.

Yama (T., S'in-rje), the Hindū Pluto, the judge of the dead and controller of metempsychosis, is the most dreaded of these

---

[1] They comprise eleven Rudras, eight Vasus, and twelve Adityas.

[2] The god of the Waters, formerly the god of the Sky.

[3] Kuvera or Vaiṣrāvaṇa "the renowned" is identified by Genl. Cunningham with the Greek Hephaestus, and the Homeric epithet Periklutos always applied to Vulcan.

[4] Also Me-mjad kyi bdag-po, or Master of the Universe.

divinities. He is represented in the Wheel of Life as the central figure in hell; but he too has to suffer torment in his joyless realm. His special emblem is a bull; thus the great tutelary demon Vajra-bhairava, by having vanquished the dread Yama, is represented with the head of a bull under the title of Yamāntaka or "the conqueror of Yama."

The most favourite of the godlings is the god of wealth, *Jambhala*, a form of Kuvera or Vaiṣrāvana. He is of portly form like his relative or prototype, the Hindū Ganeṣa. In his right hand he holds a bag of jewels, or money, or grain, symbolic of riches, and in his left an ichneumon or "mongoose,"[1] which is the conqueror of snakes—the mythical guardians of treasure.

The Nāga or Dragon-demigods are the mermen and mermaids of the Hindū myth and the demons of drought. They are of four kinds: (1) *celestial*, guarding the mansions of the gods; (2) *aërial*, causing winds to blow and rain to fall for human benefit; (3) *earthly*, marking out the courses of the rivers and streams; (4) *guardians of hidden treasures*, watching the wealth concealed from mortals.

The Nāgas are usually given the form of snakes, as these inhabit the bowels of the earth, the matrix of precious stones and metals; while in their character of rain-producers they are figured as dragons. From their fancied association with treasure they are often associated with the god of wealth, Vaiṣrāvana and his mode Jambhala. Indeed, the great Nāga king Mahākāla, the "Dai Koko" of the Japanese, seated on his rice-bales, like our chancellor of the exchequer on his wool-sack, and his attendant rats as symbols of prosperity, form almost a facsimile of the Buddhist god Jambhala, who, like his prototype Ganeṣa, seems of Nāga origin. Indeed, one of his titles is "lord of the water" (*Jalendra*).[2] The Nāga community, like the human, is divided into kings, nobles, and commoners, Buddhists and non-Buddhists.[3]

---

[1] Skt., *Nakula;* T., Ne-'ule. *Herpestes sp.* (?pharaonis). It is figured vomiting jewels.

[2] Cf. also BEAL's *Catena*, 417.

[3] The Nāga kings Nanda, Upananda, Sagara, Dritarasa, and Anävätaptu are Buddhists and therefore exempt from attack by Garuḍas. For many particulars regarding Nāgas, cf. *Megha-Sutra*, transl. by Prof. C. BENDALL, *J.R.A.S.*, 1880, pp. 1 *seq.*; BEAL's *Catena*, 50, etc.; SCHIEFNER's trans. of the kLu-'bum dKar-po; also my list of Nāga kings and commoners, *J.R.A.S.*, 1894.

Of the remaining classes, the Yaksha and Asura have already been described. The female Yaksha—the Yakshini—are the "witch-women," the stealer of children of general myths. In addition there are also the malignant spirits and demons,[1] of whom among the Rakshas, the already mentioned she-devil Hāriti, "the mother of the *Daitya*-demons," is the chief.[2]

VI. The Country-Gods.

The country-gods (Yul-lha), and the country-guardians (Sruṅ-ma) are of course all indigenous, though some of them have been given quasi-Buddhist characters. Ruling over a wider sphere, they occupy a higher rank than the more truly local genii, the locality- or foundation-owners—the Z'i-bdag of the Tibetans.

These indigenous gods, godlings, and demons are divided after the Indian fashion, roughly into eight classes, namely:—

1. Gods (Lha), all male, white in colour, and generally genial.
2. Goblins or Ghosts (Tsan), all male, red in colour. These are usually the vindictive ghosts of Lāmas, discontented priests; and they are vindictive. They especially haunt temples.[3]
3. Devils (bDud), all male, black in colour, and most malignant.[4] These are the ghosts of the persecutors of Lāmaism, and cannot be appeased without the sacrifice of a pig.[5]
4. Planets (gZah), piebald in colour (Kra-bo).
5. Bloated fiends (dMu), dark-purple colour (smug-po).[6]
6. Cannibal fiends (Srin-po), raw flesh-coloured (sā-za), and blood-thirsty.
7. King-fiends (rGyal-po), the wealth-masters (dkor-bdag), white (? always) in colour, the spirits of apotheosized heroes.

---

1 The malignant spirits are also divided into:

Preta (T., Yi-dvag).
Kumbhanda (Grul-bum).
Pisācha (Sa-za).
Bhūta ('Byuṅ-po).
Pūtana (*S*rul-po).
Katapūtana (Lus *s*rul-po).
Unmāda (sMyo *b*yed).
Skanda (T., sKyem *b*yed).
Apsmāra (*Brjed-byed*).
C'hāyā? (Grib *g*non).
Rāksha (Srin-po).
Revati grahā (Nam gru hi *g*don).
S'akuni grahā (Bya hi *g*don).
Brāhma Rākshasa (Bram-zehi-srin-po).

2 On Hāriti, cf. p. 99, and EITEL, *Handbk.*, p. 62.

3 Cf. JAESCHKE, p. 423.

4 The 'Dre are especially virulent. Cf. JAESCHKE, p. 269 and 434.

5 Cf. also JAESCHKE, p. 423.

6 Cf. also JAESCHKE, p. 284.

8. Mother-she-devils (Ma-mo), black coloured, the "disease mistresses" (näd-bdag). They are sometimes the spouses of the foregoing malignant demons, and cannot be very sharply demarcated from the other she-devils.

The greatest of the country-gods and guardians have been made defenders of Lāmaism. They are chiefly the spirits of the larger mountains, and deified ghosts of heroes and ancestors.

The former are figured either as fierce forms of Vaiṣrāvana, the god of wealth, but clad in Tibetan costume, and riding on lions, etc., and carrying banners of victory, such, for example, as mount Kanchinjunga, mount Langch'enṅa, of western Tsang, etc., as in annexed figure; or they are figured as fiendesses, as for example, the *Tän-ma*, or as mild nymphs, as the five sisters of mount Everest.[1]

རྣམ་སྲས་མདུང་དམར་ཅན་

THE RED GOD OF WEALTH.

The mountain Kanchinjunga, on the western border of Tibet. is known to most visitors to Darjiling and northern Bengal. This graceful mountain, second in height only to Everest, was formerly in itself an object of worship, as it towers high above every other object in the country, and is the first to receive the rays of the rising sun and the last to part with the sun-set. *Kanchinjunga*[2] literally means "the five repositories or ledges of the great snows," and is physically descriptive of its five peaks—the name having been giving by the adjoining Tibetans of Tsang, who also worshipped the mountain. But the Sikhim saint, Lha-tsün Ch'enbo, gave the name a mythological meaning, and the mountain was made to become merely the habitation of the god of that name, and the five "repositories" became real store-houses of the god's treasure. The peak which is most conspicuously gilded by the rising sun is the treasury of gold; the peak which remains in cold grey shade is the silver treasury, and the other peaks are the

[1] Tse-riṅ mc'ed-lṅa. They are higher in rank than the Tän-ma.

[2] Properly Kaṅ-ch'en-mdsod-lṅa.

stores of gems and grain and holy books. This idea of treasure naturally led to the god being physically represented somewhat after the style of "the god of wealth," as figured on the opposite page. He is of a red colour, clad in armour, and carries a banner of victory, and is mounted on a white lion. He is on the whole a good-natured god, but rather impassive, and is therefore less worshipped than the more actively malignant deities.

The four greatest deified mountains of Tibet are alleged to be T'aṅ-lha on the north, Ha-bo-gaṅs-bzaṅ or gNod-sbyin-gaṅ-bza on the west, Yar-lha z'aṅ-po on the east, and sKu-la k'a-ri on the south; but mount Everest, called by the Tibetans Lap-c'i-gāṅ, is not included here.

The twelve furies called *Tän-ma* have already been referred to and figured in connection with St. Padma-sambhava's visit. They are divided into the three groups of the four great she-devils, the four great injurers, and the four great medicine-females,[1] of which the last are relatively mild, though all are placed under the control of Ekajati, a fiendess of the Indian Kālī type, who rides on the thunder-clouds.

The deified ghosts of heroes and defeated rivals are pictured usually of anthropomorphic form, and clad in Tibetan style, as for example, "The holy rDorje Legs-pa," figured at page 26, and others at page 385. Though some are pictured of monstrous aspect, and of the fiercest-fiend type already described, as for instance, Pe-har,[2] the especial patron of the sorcerers of the established church.

Pe-har is a fiend of the "king" class, and seems to be an indigenous deified-hero, though European writers identify him with the somewhat similarly named Indian god, *Veda* (Chinese wei-to), who is regularly invoked by the Chinese Buddhists[3] for monastic supplies and as protector of monasteries (—*Vihar;* hence, it is believed, corrupted into Pe-har), and chief of the army of the four guardian kings of the quarters.

VII. Local Gods and Genii.

The truly "local gods" or *Genii loci*, the "foundation owners"[4]

---

[1] bdud-mo ch'en-mo bzhi, gnod-sbyin ch'en, etc.; sman-mo ch'en, etc.

[2] See his figure in Schlagintweit's *Atlas*.

[3] Rémusat's *Notes in Foe-Koue-Ki*; Edkin, *Chin. Buddh.*, Sarat., *J.A.S.B.*, 1882, page 67.

[4] (gZ'i-bdag).

of the Tibetans, are located to a particular fixed place, and seldom conceived of as separate from their places.

In appearance they are mostly Caliban-like sprites, ill-tempered and spiteful, or demoniacal, like the temple-door fiend figured at page 288; and, unlike the higher spirits, they have no third or "heavenly eye of second sight or omniscience."

The majority are of the "earth owner" class (sa-*b*dag), occupying the soil and lakes like plebeian Nāgās of the Hindūs. Others more malignant, called "gÑan," infest certain trees, rocks, and springs, which reputed haunts are avoided as far as possible, though they are sometimes daubed with red paint or other offering to propitiate the spirit.

In every monastery and temple the image of the *genius loci*, as an idol or fresco, is placed within the outer gateway, usually to the right of the door, and worshipped with wine, and occasionally with bloody sacrifice, and it is given a more or less honorific name. The local demon of the red hill near Lhāsa, surnamed Potala, and the residence of the Grand Lāma, is called gÑan-ch'en Taṅ. The one at Darjiling is already referred to at page 288.

THE HOUSE-GOD.

The House-god of the Tibetans seems to be the same as the "Kitchen-god" (Tsan-küin) of the Chinese, who is believed to be of Taoist origin, but adopted into the Chinese Buddhist pantheon[1] as a presiding divinity of the monastic diet. He also has much in common with the Door-god of the Mongols.[2]

The Tibetan House-god, as shown in his figure at page 573.

---

[1] EDKINS, *Chin. Buddh.*, 207. His official birthday is the twenty-fourth day of the sixth month.

[2] The Mongol Door-gods are thus described by Galsang Czomboyef, a recent Russo-Mongol writer, quoted by Yule (*Marco Polo*, i., 250): "Among the Buryats (who retain to greatest extent the old customs of the Mongols), in the middle of the hut, and place of honour is the *Dsaiagaçhi*, or 'Chief Creator of Fortune.' At the door is the *Emelgelji*, the tutelary of the herds and young cattle, made of sheep-skins. Outside the hut is the *Chandaghatu*, a name implying that the idol was formed of a white hare-skin, the tutelary of the chase and perhaps of war. All these have been expelled by Buddhism except Dsaiagachi, who is called *Tengri* (= Heaven), and introduced among the Buddhist divinities" as a kind of Indra. Those placed at side of door are not prayed to, but are offered a portion of the food or drink at meal times by greasing the mouths of the fetishes, and sprinkling some of the broth by them.

is anthropomorphic, with a piggish head, and flowing robes. He is called "the inside god,"[1] and is a *genius loci* of the class called by the Tibetans "earth-masters" (Sab-dag).

As he is of a roving disposition, occupying different parts of the house at different seasons, his presence is a constant source of anxiety to the householders; for no objects may invade or occupy the place where he has taken up his position, nor may it be swept or in any way disturbed without incurring his deadly wrath. Thus it happens that an unsophisticated visitor, on entering a Tibetan house and seeing a vacant place near at hand, sets there his hat, only, however, to have it instantly snatched up by his host in holy horror, with the hurried explanation that the god is at present occupying that spot.

It is some satisfaction, however, to find that all the house-gods of the land regulate their movements in the same definite and known order. Thus in the first and second months he occupies the centre of the house, and is then called "The *Gel-thuṅ* house-god."

In the third and fourth months the god stands in the doorway and is called "the door-god of the horse and yak."

In the fifth month he stands under the eaves, and is called "ya-ngas-pa."

In the sixth month he stands at the south-west corner of the house.

In the seventh and eighth months he stands under the eaves.

In the ninth and tenth months he stands in the fire-tripod or grate.

In the eleventh and twelfth months he stands at the kitchen hearth, where a place is reserved for him. He is then called "the kitchen-god."

His movements thus bear a certain relation to the season, as he is outside in the hottest weather, and at the fire in the coldest.

Formerly his movements were somewhat different; and according to the ancient style he used to circulate much more extensively and frequently.[2]

---

[1] *Naṅ-lha.*

[2] As detailed in my article on the subject in *Journ. Anthropological Institute*, London, 1894.

The other precautions entailed by his presence, and the penalties for disturbing him, are these :—

In the first and second months, when the god is in the middle of the house, the fire-grate must not be placed there, but removed to a corner of the room, and no dead body must be deposited there. While he is at the door, no bride or bridegroom may come or go, nor any corpse. Should, however, there be no other way of ingress or egress, such as by a window or otherwise, and there be urgent necessity for the passage of a bride, bridegroom, or corpse, then the images of a horse and a yak must be made with wheaten flour, and on each of them is placed some skin and hair of each of the animals represented. Tea and beer are then offered to the god, who is invited to sit on the images thus provided for him. The door is then unhinged and carried outside, and the bride, bridegroom, or corpse passes, and the door is restored to its place.

When he is at the kitchen fire, no part of the hearth can be removed or mended, and no corpse may be placed there, nor must any marriage then take place. And should any visitor arrive, he must be screened off from the fireplace by a blanket, and a scripture (the "ch'ös-mge-khri") read to avert his wrath.

When he is in the verandah he gives very little trouble. Only at that time no one may whitewash or repair the outside of the house.

And as a general precautionary measure once every year, and at extra times, whenever any suspicion arises that the god may have been slighted or is offended, it is necessary to get the Lāmas to propitiate him by doing "The water sacrifice for the eight injurers."

VIII. Personal Gods or "Familiars."

These are comparable to the *daimon* or familiar-spirits of the Greeks. But in Tibet the body of each individual is beset by a number of personal sprites.[1]

Each Tibetan carries the following familiar spirits extra to the two Buddhist angels, good and bad, which sit upon the right and left shoulder respectively and prompt to good deeds or to sins, namely,

[1] Cf. my *Lāmaism in Sikhim*.

the *p'o*, ma, z'aṅ, *da*, or enemy (-defeating) god, vulgarly called *dab-lha.* This enemy-god sits on the right shoulder of every Tibetan.

Worship of the *p'o-lha* secures long life and defence against accident; by worshipping the *da-lha* enemies are overcome. Worship of the *ma-lha* and *z'aṅ-lha* procures physical strength; worship of the *yul-lha* glory and dominion, and of the *nor-lha* wealth.

The greatest of these gods is the Enemy (-defeating) god, a sort of Hercules, who resembles in many ways the war-god of the Chinese—Kwan-te, an apotheosized hero—though the Lāmas endeavour to identify him with the Buddhist Māra, the god of passion. As seen from his figure, in the upper compartment of the Wheel of Life at page 102, he is of un-Indian aspect:—

He is of a white colour clad in golden mail and flying on a white horse through the clouds. In his uplifted right hand he holds a whip with three knots and in his left hand a spear with a stream of the five-coloured silks. The blade of the spear is blue, bordered by flames, and at its base the two divine eyes, and below the blade is a ring of yak-hair-bristle. His bow-sheath is of a leopard hide and his quiver of tiger skin. A sword is thrust into his waist-belt, and from each shoulder springs a lion and a tiger. The mirror of fore-knowledge is suspended from his neck. He is accompanied by a black dog, a black bear, and a man-monkey; and birds circle around his head.

Each class of these local and personal gods has its particular season for popular worship, thus:—

The Earth-gods (sa-*gz*'i mi-rig-gi lha) are worshipped especially in the spring.

The Ancestral gods (*s*mra z'an ch'uṅ-gi lha) are worshipped in the summer season.

The three Upper gods (*s*tod-sum pahī lha) in the autumn; and

The royal Ancestor of the Tibetan or Sikhim king (*s*ton mi-ñag-gi lha) in the winter. The first king of Mi-ñag in eastern Tibet was a son of Thi-Sroṅ Detsan, and the Sikhim king is alleged to be of the same ancestry.

It is beyond the scope of our present subject to refer to the heterodox duties of the aboriginal or Bön-pa order. But it may be stated that this latter religion having existed for centuries side by side with the more favoured Lāmaism, it has now come to model its deities generally on the Buddhist pattern. A reference to one of the Bön gods, namely, the Red-Tiger devil, will be found in the chapter on the mystic play.

The Saints.

The saints of Lāmaism may be divided into the Indian and the Tibetan, inclusive of a few Chinese and Mongolian. They are usually figured with a halo around their heads, and when attended by disciples they are always represented much larger in size than the latter ; and, in keeping with the later fiction of re-incarnate Lāmas, they are usually surrounded by a few scenes of their so-called former births.

Of the Indian saints the chief are :—

I. The Ten Chief Disciples of Buddha.

The highest of these is "the model pair," Ṣāriputra and Mahā-Maugdalayāna, the right- and left-hand disciples of Buddha, and generally represented in a standing posture, carrying a begging-bowl and alarm-staff, or with the hands joined in adoration of Ṣākya Muni.[1] After these the best known are Mahā-kāṣyapa, the president of the first council and the first "patriarch," Upāli, Subhuti, and Buddha's cousin and favourite attendant, Ananda.

II. The Sixteen *Sthavira*, or Chief Apostles or Missionaries.

T., gNas-brtan = "The Steadfast Holders (of the Doctrine)."

These are called by the Chinese and Japanese "the sixteen Rahan" (= Skt., Arhat), or "Lohan."

Several of them lived after Buddha's day; and latterly two other saints were added to the list, namely, Dharmatrāta and Hvashang, bringing the number up to eighteen. Other conventional groups of Arhats are the 108, 500, 1,000, etc.[2]

Each of these *Sthavira* or *Arhats* is figured in a fixed attitude, and each has his distinctive symbol or badge, like our apostles, as Mark with a lion, Luke with a book, etc.

The descriptive list of these sixteen *Sthavira* is briefly[3] :—

1. *Angira-ja* (T., Yan-lag 'byun), "the limb-born." Holds incense censer and cow-tail fly-whisk fan. He went as missionary to the Te-Se mountains around Manasrovara lake (Jaesch., *D.*, 203), or to mount Kailās (Schief., *Lebensb.*).

2. *Ajita* (T., Ma-p'am-pa), "the unconquered." Hands in the

---

[1] Cf. Csoma's *An.*, 48 ; Raj. Lal Mitra's trans. *Lalita Vist.*, 10.

[2] For descriptions of many of these see Tāranātha's *mDsad-brgya*, and his *Hist. of Ind. Budd.*, trans. by Schiefner ; also Eitel's *Handbk.*, and Pander's *Panth.*

[3] For their figures and some details cf. Pander's *Panth.* (*loc. cit*), pp. 83 *et seq.*

"impartial" attitude. A *rishi*, or sage, of mount Usira (Nos-se-la).[1] His statue is one of the few which is prepared singly.

3. *Vana-vāsa* (T., Nags-na-gnas), "forest-dweller." Right hand in sdigs-Me dsub attitude; left holds a cow-tail fly-whisk. He went to "The seven-leaves mountain" (Loma-bdun). According to Schief., he remained at Ṣrāvastī.

4. *Kālika* (T., Dus-ldan-rdorje), "timely." Wears a golden earring as a badge. He went to Tāmradvīpa (= ? Tamluk in S.W. Bengal).

5. *Vajraputra* (T., rDo-rje-mo'-bu) "son of the thunderbolt." Right hand in sDigs-mdsub attitude, and left carries fly-whisk. He went to Ceylon.

6. *Bhadra* (T., bZaṅ-po) "the noble." Right hand in preaching, and left in meditative attitude—the latter hand usually bearing a book. He went to Yamunādvīpa.

7. *Kanaka-vatsa* (T., gSer-be'u), "golden calf." Carries a jewelled snare. He went to the Saffron-peak in Kashmīr.

8. *Kanaka-bhara-dvaja.* Hands in "impartial" attitude. He went to Apara-Gōdhānya (Nub-kyi-ba glaṅ spyod-glin).

9. *Vakula*, carries an ichneumon (Ṅakula) like the god of riches. On this account, Pander notes (p. 86) that the Tibetans probably knew this saint as "Nakula." He went to Uttarakuru (byaṅ-gi-sgra-mi-sñan).

10. *Rāhula* (T., sGra-c'an-zin [? 'dsin]). Holds a jewelled crown. Pander believes that this simile is probably suggested by interpreting the name as "sgra-rgyan-'dsin," or "holding a crown." He went to Pri-yan-gu-dvīpa (= ? Prayag, or Allahabad).

11. *Cuda-panthaka* (T., Lam-p'ran-bstan). Hands in "impartial" pose. He went to Gridrakuta hill in Magadha.[2]

12. *Bharadvaja* (T., Bha-ra-dva-dsa-bsod-sñoms-len). Holds book and begging-bowl. Went to the eastern Videka. He is usually identified with the "Binzuru" of the Japanese.

13. *Panthaku* (T., Lam-bstan). Hands in preaching attitude with a book.

14. *Nāgasena* (T., kLu'i-sde). Holds a vase, and an alarm-staff. He went to "the king of mountains," Urumunda (Ṅos-yaṅs). This seems to be the Arhat who is known to southern Buddhists as the author of the celebrated dialogues with Menander (Milinda).

15. *Gōpaka* (T., shed-byed), holds a book. Went to Mt. Bi-hu.

16. . . . . (T., Mi-p'yed) Holds "the *caitya* of perfection." He went to the Himalayas.

The additional pair of saints who are usually associated with the above are:—

Dharmatrāta or Dharmatala (T., dGe-bsñen dharma). Holds a vase and fly-whisk and carries on his back a bundle of books, and he gazes at a small image of Buddha Amitābha. As he is only a lay-devotee he has long hair. He was born in Gāndhāra and seems to be the uncle of

[1] SCHIEF., *Lebensb.*, 92.

[2] Cf. JAESCH., *D.*, 372.

Vasumitra. Of his seven works the chief are the Udānavarga (translated by Rockhill), and the Samyuktābhidharma Ṣāstra.

Hvashang corresponds to the Chinese "Huo-shang" or priest with the sack.[1] He is a sort of lay-patron or "dispenser of alms" to the disciples; and is represented as a good-natured person of portly dimensions, in a sitting position. His attributes are a sack, a rosary in his right hand and a peach in his left, while little urchins or goblins play around him. The name in Chinese is said by Pander to be also rendered "the dense-smoke Maitreya Buddha," and he is explained as the last incarnation of Maitreya who is at present enthroned in the Tushita heavens. In the entrance hall of all the larger temples in China we find the colossal statue of this big-bellied, laughing Maitreya surrounded by the four kings of the universe.

III. Other Mahāyāna Saints.

The other Indian saints of the Mahāyāna school who are most worshipped by the Lāmas are: Aṣvaghosha, Nāgārjuna (kLu-grub), Arya-deva (P'ags-pa-lha), Kumārala, Asaṅga (T'ogs-med), Vasubandhu (dByig-gñan), Dharma-kīrti (Ch'os-grags), Candra-kirti (zla-wa-grags); and the more modern Ṣānta-rakshita and Atīṣa-Dipaṃkara. Figures of most of these have already been given.[2]

IV. Tāntrik Wizard-Priests.

T.'Grub-t'ob ch'en or "grub-c'hen (Skt., *Siddha* or *Mahāsiddha*).

This degraded class of Indian Buddhist priest (see figure on page 16) is most popular with the Lāmas. They are credited with supernatural powers, by being in league with the demons. They are usually figured with long untonsured locks, and almost naked.

The chief of these Indian priests is St. Padma-sambhava, the founder of Lāmaism. Others are

Sāvari (Sa-pa-ri-pa), Rāhulabhadra or Saraha (Sa-ra-ha-pa), Matsyōdara (Lu-i-pa), Lalita-vajra, Kṛishṇcārin or Kālācārita (Nag-po-spyod-pa); and more modern Telopa or Tila and Nāro.[3] These latter two are apparently named after the Indian monasteries of Tilada and Nalanda.

St. Padma-sambhava receives more active worship than any of the others. Indeed, he is deified. He is most commonly worshipped in the form shown in the centre of the plate on page 24. He sits dressed as a native of Udyāna, holding a thunderbolt in his right

[1] Cf. Pander, *Panth.*, p. 89.

[2] For additional details see Tāranātha's *History* (Schiefner's transl.), and Pander's *Panth.*, pp. 47, etc. These first four, cf. Julien's *Hiuen Tsiang*, ii., 214.

[3] For some details and figures see Pander, *Panth.*, pp. 50, etc.

hand and a skull of blood in his left, and carrying in his left arm-pit the trident of the king of death. The top of this trident transfixes a freshly decapitated human head, a wizened head, and a skull. And the saint is attended by his two wives, offering him libations of blood and wine in skull-bowls, while before him are set offerings of portions of human corpses.

He is given seven other forms, wild or demoniacal, which are shown surrounding him in that picture.

These, his eight forms, together with their usual paraphrase, are here numerated:—

I.—*Guru Pädma Jungnä*,[1] "Born of a lotus" for the happiness of the three worlds, the central figure in the plate.

II.—*Guru Pädma-sambhava*, "Saviour by the religious doctrine."

III.—*Guru Pädma Gyëlpo*, "The king of the three collections of scriptures" (Skt., "Tripitaka").

IV.—*Guru Dôrje Dô-lö*,[2] "The *Dorje* or diamond comforter of all."

V.—*Guru Ñima Od-zer*,[3] "The enlightening sun of darkness."

VI.—*Guru S'akya Seṅ-ge*, "The second Ṣākya—the lion," who does the work of eight sages.

VII.—*Guru Seṅg-ge dā dok*,[4] The propagator of religion in the six worlds—with "the roaring lion's voice."

VIII.—*Guru Lô-tén Ch'og-Se*,[5] "The conveyer of knowledge to all worlds."

These paraphrases it will be noted are mostly fanciful, and not justified by the title itself.

As he is the founder of Lāmaism, and of such prominence in the system, I give here a sketch of his legendary history:—

The Guru's so-called history, though largely interwoven with supernatural fantasies is worth abstracting,[6] not only for the

---

[1] *guru pad-ma 'byuṅ gnas*. Cf. GIORGI, p. 242, and figure p. 552.

[2] rdo-rje *gro-lod*.

[3] *nyi-ma 'od zer*.

[4] *Sen-ge* s*gra* s*grogs*.

[5] b*lo*-l*dan* m*ch'g*-S*red* (or ? *Srid*).

[6] The account here given is abstracted from the following Tibetan works, all of which are of the fictitions "revelation" order, and often conflicting, but dating, probably, to about six or seven hundred years ago, namely: *Padma-bkah-t'an* (or "The displayed Commands of the Lotus-one"); *Than-yig gser-'p'ren* (or "The Golden Rosary of Displayed-letters"); *Than'-yig-sde-la* (or "The Five Classes of Displayed-letters"), and a Lepcha version, entitled *Tashi Sun*, or "History of the Glorious One," written by the Sikhim king (? Gyur-mei Nami-gyal), who, about two centuries ago, invented the so-called Lepcha characters by modifying the Tibetan and Bengālī letters.

historical texture that underlies the allegorical figures, but also for the insight it gives into the genesis and location of many of the demons of the Lāmaist pantheon and the pre-Lāmaist religion of Tibet. The story itself is somewhat romantic and has the widest currency in Tibet, where all its sites are now popular places of pilgrimage, sacred to this deified wizard-priest:—

The Legendary History of the Founder of Lāmaism.

Once upon a time, in the great city of Jatumati[1] in the Indian continent, there dwelt a blind king named Indrabodhi,[2] who ruled over the country of Udyāna or Urgyan. The death of his only son plunges the palace in deepest sorrow, and this calamity is followed by famine and an exhausted treasury. In their distress the king and people cry unto the Buddhas with many offerings, and their appeal reaching unto the paradise of the great Buddha of Boundless Light —Amitābha—this divinity sends, instantly, like a lightning flash, a miraculous incarnation of himself in the form of a red ray of light to the sacred lake of that country.

That same night the king dreamt a dream of good omen. He dreamt that a golden thunderbolt had come into his hand, and his body shone like the sun. In the morning the royal priest Trignadhara[3] reports that a glorious light of the five rainbow-tints has settled in the lotus-lake of Dhanakosha, and is so dazzling as to illuminate the three "unreal" worlds.

Then the king, whose sight has been miraculously restored, visits the lake, and, embarking in a boat, proceeds to see the shining wonder, and finds on the pure bosom of the lake a lotus-flower of matchless beauty, on whose petals sits a lovely boy of eight years old, sceptred and shining like a god. The king, falling on his knees, worships the infant prodigy, exclaiming: "Incomparable boy! who art thou? Who is thy father and what thy country?" To which the child made answer: "My Father *I* know! I come in accordance with the prophecy of the great Ṣākya Muni, who said: 'Twelve hundred years after me, in the north-east of the Urgyan country, in the pure lake of Kosha, a person more famed than myself will be born from a lotus, and be known as *Padma-sambhava*, or "the Lotus-born," [4] and he shall be the teacher of my esoteric *Mantra*-doctrine, and shall deliver all beings from misery.'"

On this the king and his subjects acknowledge the supernatural

---

1 *mDses-ldan.*

2 This is the form found in the text, while another MS. gives Indrabhuti; but its Tibetan translation also given is *Spyan-med-'byor-ldan*, or "The Eyeless Wealthy One," which could give an Indian form of Andhara-basuti.

3 *Trig-na-'dsin.*

4 Also an epithet of Brāhma.

nature of the Lotus-born boy, and naming him "The Lake-born *Vajra*,"[1] conduct him to the palace with royal honours. And from thenceforth the country prospered, and the holy religion became vastly extended. This event happened on the tenth day of the seventh Tibetan month.

In the palace the wondrous boy took no pleasure in ordinary pursuits, but sat in Buddha fashion musing under the shade of a tree in the grove. To divert him from these habits they find for him a bride in p'Od-'c'aṅ-ma,[2] the daughter[3] of king Candra Gomashi, of Singala.[4] And thus is he kept in the palace for five years longer, till a host of gods appear and declare him divine, and commissioned as the Saviour of the world. But still the king does not permit him to renounce his princely life and become, as he desired, an ascetic. The youthful Padma-sambhava now kills several of the subjects, who, in their present or former lives, had injured Buddhism; and on this the people complain of his misdeeds to the king, demanding his banishment, which sentence is duly carried out, to the great grief of the king and the royal family.

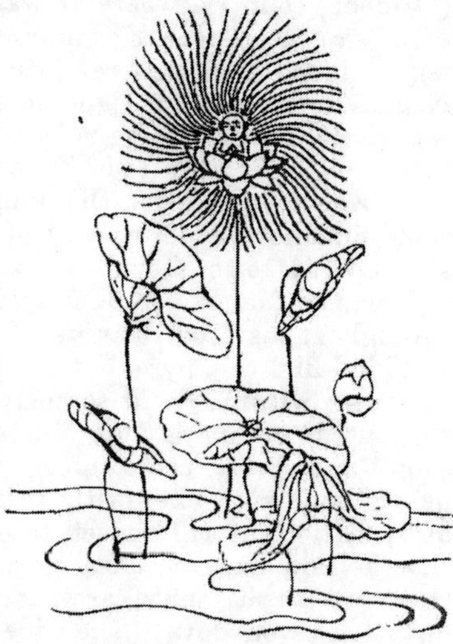

THE LOTUS-BORN BABE.

The princely pilgrim travels to the Shitani cemetery of the cool grove,[5] where, dwelling in the presence of the dead as a *Sosāniko*[6] he seeks communion with the gods and demons, of whom he subjugates many. Thence he was conducted by the Ḍākkinīs or witches of the four classes to the cave of Ajñapāla,[7] where he received instruction

[1] mTs'o-skyes rdo-rje; Skt., *Saroruha-vajra*.

[2] Skt., *Bhasudhara* or "The Light-holder."

[3] The text gives "wife."

[4] This is probably the Siṅhapura of Hiuen Tsiang, which adjoined Udayāna or Udyāna; or it may be Sagāla.

[5] bSil-ba ts'al. This is said to lie to the east of India and to be the abode of *Hungkara*, the greatest of the eight great sages or rig-dsin. For a Mahāyāna Sūtra delivered here by Buddha, see CSOMA, *An.*, p. 517.

[6] *Sasānika* is one of the twelve observances of a Bhikshu, and conveys just ideas of the three great phenomena, impermanence, pain, and vacuity, by seeing the funerals, the grieving relatives, the stench of corruption, and the fighting of beasts of prey for the remains. Buddha in the Dulva (ROCK., *B.*, p. 29) is also stated to have followed the ascetic practice of a *Sosāniko*, or frequenter of cemeteries.

[7] bkāh-skyoṅ, or command + protector; it may also be Sanskritized as *pudarsanā-pāla*.

in the *Asvaratna abaṅkāra*, after which he proceeded to the countries of Pañchā, etc., where he received instruction in the arts and sciences direct from old world sages, who miraculously appeared to him for this purpose.

Other places visited by him were the cemeteries of the Biddha (? Videha) country, where he was called "the sun's rays," the cemetery of b*De-ch'en* br*dal* in Kashmīr, where he was called "the chief desire sage" (*blo-ldan mch'og-sred*), the cemetery of *Lhun-grub*-br*tsegs-pa* in Nepal, subjugating the eight classes of Dam-sri at Yaksha fort, where he was named "the roaring voiced lion," and to the cemetery of *Laṅka* br*tsegs-pa* in the country of Zahor, where he was named Padma-sambha.

At Zahor (? Lahore), the king's daughter, a peerless princess who could find no partner worthy of her beauty and intellect, completely surrendered to the Guru—and this seems to be the "Indian" princess-wife named Mandārawā Kumāri Devi, who was his constant companion throughout his Tibetan travels. At Zahor the rival suitors seize him and bind him to a pyre, but the flames play harmlessly round him, and he is seen within seated serenely on a lotus-flower. Another miracle attributed to him is thus related: Athirst one day he seeks a wine-shop, and, with companions, drinks deeply, till, recollecting that he has no money wherewith to pay his bill, he asks the merchant to delay settlement till sunset, to which the merchant agrees, and states that he and his comrades meanwhile may drink their fill. But the Guru arrests the sun's career, and plagues the country with full day-light for seven days. The wine-seller, now in despair, wipes off their debt, when welcome night revisits the sleepy world.

The leading details of his defeat of the local devils of Tibet are given in the footnote.[1]

[1] When the Guru, after passing through Nepal, reached *Maṅ-yul*, the enemy-god (*dgra-lha*) of *Z'an-z'un*, named *Dsa-mun*, tried to destroy him by squeezing him between two mountains, but he overcame her by his *irdhi*-power of soaring in the sky. He then received her submission and her promise to become a guardian of Lāmaism under the religious name of r*Do-rje Gyu-bun-ma*.

E-ka-dsa-ti.—When the Guru reached g*Nam-t'an*-mk'*ar-nag*, the white fiendess of that place showered thunderbolts upon him, without, however, harming him. The Guru retaliated by melting her snow-dwelling into a lake; and the discomfited fury fled into the lake *T'an-dpal-mo-dpal*, which the Guru then caused to boil. But though her flesh boiled off her bones, still she did not emerge; so the Guru threw in his thunderbolt, piercing her right eye. Then came she forth and offered up to him her life-essence, and was thereon named *Gans*-d*kar-sha-med*-r*Do-rje*-s*Pyan-gcig-ma*, or "The Snow-white, Fleshless, One-eyed Ogress of the Vajra."

The twelve Tän-ma Furies.—Then the Guru marched onward, and reached *U-yug-bre-mo-snar*, where the twelve b*stan-ma* (see figure, page 27) furies hurled thunderbolts at him, and tried to crush him between mountains; but the Guru evaded them by flying into the sky, and with his "pointing-finger" charmed their thunderbolts into cinders. And by his pointing-finger he cast the hills and mountains upon their snowy dwellings. Thereupon the twelve b*stan-ma*, with all their retinue thwarted and subdued, offered him their life-essence, and so were brought under his control.

Dam-c'an-rDor-legs.—Then the Guru, pushing onward, reached the fort of *U-yug-bye-*

The Tibetan and other non-Indian canonized saints may generally be recognized by their un-Indian style of dress, and even when they are bare-headed and clad in the orthodox Buddhist robes they always wear an inner garment extra to the Indian fashion.

The various Tibetan saints, excluding the apotheosized heroes already referred to, are held in different estimation by the different sects, each of whom holds its own particular sectarian

---

tshan'-rdson, where he was opposed by dGe-b*sñen* r*Do-rje-legs-pa* (see figure, p. 26) with his three hundred and sixty followers, who all were subjected and the leader appointed a guardian (b*srung-ma*) of the Lāmaist doctrine.

Yar-lha-sham-po.—Then the Guru, going forward, reached *Sham-po-lun*, where the demon *Yar-lha-sham-po* transformed himself into a huge mountain-like white yak, whose breath belched forth like great clouds, and whose grunting sounded like thunder. Bu-yug gathered at his nose, and he rained thunderbolts and hail. Then the Guru caught the demon's nose by "the iron-hook gesture," bound his neck by "the rope gesture," bound his feet by "the fetter-gesture"; and the yak, maddened by the super-added "bell-gesture," transformed himself into a young boy dressed in white silk, who offered up to the Guru his life-essence; and so this adversary was subjected.

Tan'-lha the great g*Ñan.*—Then the Guru proceeded to *Phya-than-la* pass, where the demon g*Nan-ch'en-t'an-lha* transformed himself into a great white snake, with his head in the country of *Gru-gu*, and his tail in g*Yer-mo-than* country, drained by the Mongolian river Sok-Ch'u, and thus seeming like a chain of mountains he tried to bar the Guru's progress. But the Guru threw the *lin-gyi* over the snake. Then the T'an'-lha, in fury, rained thunderbolts, which the Guru turned to fishes, frogs, and snakes, which fled to a neighbouring lake. Then the Guru melted his snowy dwelling, and the god, transforming himself into a young boy dressed in white silk, with a turquoise diadem, offered up his life-essence, together with that of all his retinue, and so he was subjected.

The Injurers.—Then the Guru, proceeding onwards, arrived at the northern Phan-yul-thang, where the three Injurers—s*Ting-lo-sman* of the north, s*Ting-sman-zor gdon-ma*, and s*Ting-sman-ston*—sent hurricanes to bar the Guru's progress. On which the Guru circled "the wheel of fire" with his pointing-finger, and thus arrested the wind, and melted the snowy mountains like butter before a red hot iron. Then the three g*Nod-sbyin*, being discomfited, offered up their life-essence and so were subjected.

The Black Devils.—Then the Guru, going onward, reached g*Nam-gyi-shug-mthon-glang-sgrom*, where he opened the magic circle or *Maṇḍala* of the Five Families (of the Buddhas) for seven days, after which all the commanders of the host of b*Dud-Devil* offered their life-essence and so were subjected.

The-u-ran.—Then the Guru went to the country of g*La-wa-rkan-c'ig-ma*, where he brought all the *The-u-ran* demons under subjection.

The Mi-ma-yin Devils.—When the Guru was sitting in the cave of *Senge-brag-phug*, the demon *Ma-sans-gyah-spang-skyes-shig*, desiring to destroy him, came into his presence in the form of an old woman with a turquoise cap, and rested her head on the Guru's lap and extended her feet towards *Gye-mo-than* and her hands towards the white snowy mountain *Ti-si.* Then many thousands of *Mi-ma-yin* surrounded the Guru menacingly; but he caused the Five Fierce Demons to appear, and so he subjected the *Mi-ma-yin*.

Ma-mo, etc.—Then he subjected all the *Ma-mo* and b*Semo* of *Ch'u-bo-ri* and *Kha-rak*, and going to *Sil-ma*, in the province of *Tsang*, he subjected all the s*Man-mo*. And going

founder to be pre-eminent. Thus the established church gives the chief place to Tsoṅ-K'ā-pa and the chief pupils of Atīṣa; the Kar-gyu sect to Mila-ras-pa, the Sa-kya-pa to Sa-kya Paṇḍita, and so on. And each sub-sect has canonized its own particular chief. The innumerable Lāmas who now pose as re-incarnations of deceased Lāmas, also receive homage as saints, and on their decease have their images duly installed and worshipped. Some saints are

---

to the country of *Hori* he subjected all the *Dam-sri*. And going to *Rong-lung-nag-po* he subjected all the *Srin-po*. And going to central Tibet (db*Us*) towards the country of the lake *Manasarova (mal-dro)*, he subjected all the *Nāgās* of the *mal-dro* lake, who offered him seven thousand golden coins. And going to *Gyu-'dsin-phug-mo*, he subjected all the *Pho-rgyud*. And going to *Dung-mdog-brag-dmar*, he subjected all the smell eating *Driza (? Gandharva)*. And going to *Gan-pa-ch'u-mig*, he subjected all the d*Ge-sñen*. And going to *Bye-ma-rab-khar*, he subjected all the eight classes of *Lha-srin*. And going to the snowy mountain *Ti-si*, he subjected all the twenty-eight *Nakshetras*. And going to *Lha-rgod-gans*, he subjected the eight planets. And going to *Bu-le-gans*, he subjected all the *'dre* of the peaks, the country, and the dwelling-sites, all of whom offered him every sort of worldly wealth. And going to g*Lo-bor*, he subjected all the nine l*Dan-ma-spun*. Then he was met by *Gaṅs-rje-jo-wo* at *Pho-ma-gans*, where he brought him under subjection. Then having gone to r*Tse-lha-gaṅs*, he subjected the r*Tse-sman*. And going to s*Tod-lung*, he subjected all the b*Tsan*. Then having gone to *Zul-p'ul-rkyaṅ-gram-bu-t'sal*, he remained for one month, during which he subjugated *gzah-bolud* and three *Dam-sri*.

And having concealed many scriptures as revelations, he caused each of these fiends to guard one apiece. With this he completed the subjection of the host of malignant devils of Tibet.

Then the Guru proceeded to Lhāsa, where he rested awhile, and then went towards s*Tod-lun*. At that time *mṅah-bdag-rgyal-po* sent his minister, *Lha-bzaṅ-klu-dpal*, with a letter and three golden *Pata*, silken clothes, horses, and divers good presents, accompanied by five hundred cavalry. These met him at s*Tod-luṅ-gzhon-pa*, where the minister offered the presents to the Guru. At that time all were athirst, but no water or tea was at hand, so the Guru touched the rock of s*Tod-luṅ-gzhon-pa*, whence water sprung welling out; which he told the minister to draw in a vessel. Hence that place is called to this day *gz'on-pai-lha-ch'u* or "The water of the God's vessel."

From *Hao-po-ri* the Guru went to *Zuṅ-k'ar*, where he met King mṄah-*b*dag-rgyal-po, who received him with honour and welcome. Now the Guru, remembering his own supernatural origin and the king's carnal birth, expected the king to salute him, so remained standing. But the king thought, "I am the king of the black-headed men of Tibet, so the Guru must first salute me." While the two were possessed by these thoughts, the Guru related how through the force of prayers done at *Bya-ruṅ-K'a-shor* stūpa in Nepal (see p. 315) in former births, they two have come here together. The Guru then extended his right hand to salute the king, but fire darted forth from his finger-tips, and catching the dress of the king, set it on fire. And at the same time a great thunder was heard in the sky, followed by an earthquake. Then the king and all his ministers in terror prostrated themselves at the feet of the Guru.

Then the Guru spoke, saying, "As a penance for not having promptly saluted me, erect five stone stūpas." These the king immediately erected, and they were named *z'uṅ-m'kar-mch'od-rten*, and exist up till the present day.

entirely of local repute, and the ghosts of many deceased Lāmas are worshipped in the belief that they have become malignant spirits who wreak their wrath on their former associates and pupils.

Amongst the earlier Tibetans who are generally accorded the position of saints are king Sroṅ Tsan Gampo, his two wives and minister Ton-mi, who were associated with the introduction of Buddhism to Tibet, king Thi-Sroṅ Detsan, who patronized

DEMONIFIED TIBETAN PRIESTS.[1]

the founding of Lāmaism, the earlier translators of the scriptures, and especially those associated with St. Atīṣa.

One of the popular saints is the famous engineer, T'aṅ-toṅ rGyal-po, whose image or picture is often found in Lāmaist temples. He lived in the first half of the fifteenth century A.D., and is celebrated for having built eight iron-chain suspension-bridges over the great river of central Tibet, the Yaru Tsaṅ-po; and several of these bridges still survive.[2]

---

[1] After Pander.

[2] Regarding his image in the cathedral of Lhāsa, the sacristan related the following legend to Sarat: T'aṅ-toṅ feared the miseries of this world very much, having inhabited it in former existences. Accordingly he contrived to remain sixty years in his mother's womb. There he sat in profound meditation, concentrating his mind most earnestly on the well-being of all living creatures. At the end of sixty years he began to realize that, while meditating for the good of others, he was neglecting the rather prolonged sufferings of his mother. So he forthwith quitted the womb, and came into the world already provided with grey hair, and straightway commenced preaching.

Certain titles have come to be restricted to particular saints. Thus "(His) Precious Reverence" (Je-rin-po-c'e) is St. Tsoṅ K'a-pa, "(His) Reverence" (Je-tsün) is St. Mila-raspa, "(His) Holy Reverence" (Je-tsun dam-pa) is Tāranātha, "The Teacher" (sLob-dpön) is St. Padma-sambhava, and the Sakya Lāma is "(His) Highness."

MYSTIC MONOGRAM.

(Nam-c'u-vaṅ-dan.)

See p. 142, f.-n. 6.

Garuḍa *Yantra* Charm.

XV.

SACRED SYMBOLS AND CHARMS.

MOST religions of the present day teem with symbolism, which is woven so closely into the texture of the creeds that it is customary to excuse its presence by alleging that it is impossible to convey to the people spiritual truths except in material forms. Yet we have only to look at Muhammadanism, one of the great religions of the world, and still actively advancing, to see that it appeals successfully to the most uneducated and fanatical people, although it is practically devoid of symbolism, and its sanctuary is a severely empty building, wholly unadorned with images or pictures. People, however, who are endowed with artistic sense, tend to clothe their religion with symbolism.

The symbols proper, extra to the symbolic representations of the deities dealt with in the preceding chapter, are conventional signs or diagrams, or pictures of animals, mythological or otherwise, or of plants and inanimate objects; and in Tibet they are very widely met with. They are painted or carved on houses and furniture, and emblazoned on boxes and embroidery, and on personal ornaments, trinkets, charms, etc.

The extremely rich symbolism found in Lāmaism is largely of Indian and Chinese origin. Its emblems are mainly of a conventional Hindū kind, more or less modified to adapt them to their Buddhist setting. Others are derived from the Chinese, and a few only are of Tibetan origin. These latter are mostly of a very crude kind, like the *rebuses* common in mediæval England for the use of the illiterate.

In this place, also, we can most conveniently glance at the mystic value of numbers; the "magic-circle" offering in effigy of the universe, etc., which enters into the daily worship of every Lāma; and the charms against sickness and accidents, ill-luck, etc., and the printed charms for luck which form the "prayer-flags," and the tufts of rags affixed to trees, bridges, etc.

THE LOTUS.—Most of the sacred emblems, as well as the images of divinities, it will be noticed, are figured upon a lotus-flower. This expresses the Hindū idea of super-human origin. The lotus upon the lake seems to spring from the body of the waters without contact with the sordid earth, and, no matter how muddy the water may be, the lotus preserves its own purity undefiled.

The various kinds of lotuses figured at page 339 are given special uses. The red lotus is common to most deities and divine symbols; the white lotus is special to Avalokita; the blue one to Tārā; and when a demon is figured upon a lotus the latter is a pinkish variety of the white form, with the petals much notched or divided.

THE THREE GEMS (*Tri-ratna*[1]), symbolic of the Trinity: Buddha, his Word, and the Church. These are usually figured (as in No. 2 on next page) as three large egg-shaped gems, with the narrow ends directed downwards, and the central member is placed slightly above the other two, so as to give symmetry to the group, which is usually surrounded by flames.

[1] Tib., dKon-mch'og-gsum, or "The rarest ones."

THE SVASTIKA,[1] or "fly-foot cross," is a cross with the free end of each arm bent at right angles to the limbs. It is one of the most widely diffused of archaic symbols, having been found at Troy by Schliemann, and among ancient Teutonic nations as the emblem of Thor. In Buddhism, the ends of the arms are always bent in the respectful attitude, that is, towards the left; for the Lāmas, while regarding the symbol as one of good augury, also consider it to typify the continuous moving, or "the ceaseless becoming," which is commonly called Life. Sir A. Cunningham believed it to be a monogram formed from the Aṣoka characters for the auspicious words *Su* + *Asti*, or "that which is good."[2] It was especially associated with the divinity of Fire, as representing the two cross pieces of wood[3] which by friction produce fire. The Jains, who seem to be an Indian offshoot of Buddhism,[4] appropriate it for the seventh of their mythical saints.[5] The heterodox Tibetans, the Bön, in adopting it have turned the ends in the reverse direction.

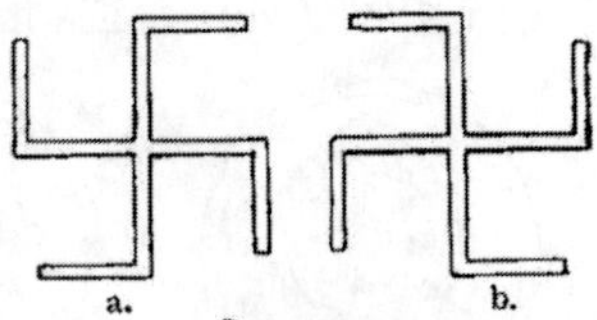

SVASTIKA.
a. Orthodox form.
b. Unorthodox form.

THE SEVEN GEMS.[6] These are the attributes of the universal monarch,[7] such as prince Siddhārta was to have been had he not become a Buddha. They are very frequently figured on the base of his throne, and are:—

1. The Wheel.[8] The victorious wheel of a thousand spokes. It also represents the symmetry and completeness of the Law. It is figured in the early Sanchi Tope.[9]

2. The Jewel.[10] The mother of all gems, a wish-procuring gem (Cintamaṇi).

1 Yun-druṅ. Chinese, *Chu'-Vang*, or "The ten thousand character"; cf. also *Indian Antiquary*, ix., 65, etc., 135, etc., and numerous references in DUMOUTIER, *op. cit.*, 22-23.

2 Su, meaning "good" or "excellent" (in Greek, *eu*), and *Asti* is the third person singular present indicative of the verb *As*, "to be," and *Ka* is an abstract suffix.

3 Skt., *Arani*.

4 But see JACOBI'S works.

5 Namely, the Jina *Su-parṣva*.

6 Skt., *Sapta-ratna*. T., Rin-ch'en sna-bdun; cf. HARDY'S *Man*, p. 130, and ALABASTER'S *Wheel of the Law*, p. 81.

7 *Cakra-vartin Rāja*.

8 Skt., *Cakra;* T., *'K'or-lo*.

9 FERGUSSON, *Tree and Serp. Wors.*, pl. xxix., Fig. 2.

10 Skt., *Ratna;* T., *Norbu*.

3. The jewel of a Wife.[1] "The Jasper-girl" who fans her lord to sleep, and attends him with the constancy of a slave.

4. The gem of a Minister,[2] who regulates the business of the empire.

5. The (white) Elephant.[3] The earth-shaking beast, who as a

THE SEVEN GEMS.

symbol of universal sovereignty the Buddhist kings of Burma and Siam borrowed from Indian Buddhism. It seems to be Indra's elephant Airāvata.[4]

6. The Horse.[5] It seems to symbolize the horse-chariot of the sun, implying a realm over which the sun never sets, as well as the celestial *Pegasus*-steed,[6] which carries its rider wherever the latter wishes.[7]

7. The gem of a General,[8] who conquers all enemies.

---

[1] Skt., *Stri*; T., *Tsun-mo.*

[2] Skt., (?) *Girti* or *Mahājana*; T., *bLon-po.*

[3] Skt., *Hasti*; T., *glañ-po.*

[4] This elephant is frequently represented as a miniature bronze ornament or flower-stand on the Lāmaist altar. Mr. Baber records (*R. G. Soc. Suppl.*, paper, p. 33) a colossal elephant with six tusks, cast in silvery-bronze, in western Ssu-ch'uan. It is of artistic merit, and carries on its back, in place of a howdah, a lotus-flower, in which is enthroned an admirable image of Buddha.

[5] Skt., *Aṣva*; T., *rTa-mch'og.*

[6] Aṣwin or Uchchaihsravas.

[7] Compare with the divine horse named "Might of a Cloud," from the thirty-three heavens, which delivered the merchants from the island of Rākshasis.—See HIUEN TSIANG'S *Si-Yu-Ki.*

[8] Skt., *Kshatri* or *Sena-pati*; T., d*Mag*-d*pön.*

And to these the Lāmas add an eighth, namely, the Vase,[1] for storing all the hidden riches of the three regions of life.

THE SEVEN (ROYAL) BADGES.[2]

1. The precious	House (palace).	(Kaṅ-saṅ	Rinpoch'e)
2. ,, ,,	royal Robes	(Gös	,,
3. ,, ,,	Boots (embroidered).	(Lham	,,
4. ,, ,,	Elephant's tusk.	(Laṅ-ch'en ch'em	,,
5. ,, ,,	Queen's earring.	(Tsunmo na-ja	
6. ,, ,,	King's earring.	(Gyalpo na-ja	
7. ,, ,,	Jewel.	(Norbu	

The above list seems somewhat confused with "The seven world-

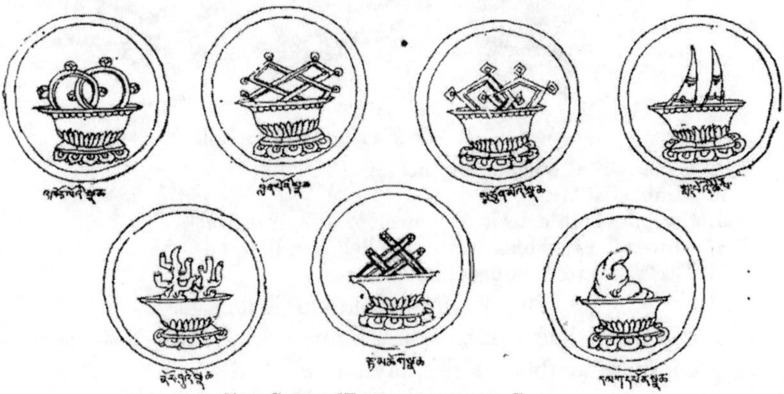

THE SEVEN WORLD-RAVISHING GEMS.

ravishing Gems" here figured.[3]

THE SEVEN PERSONAL GEMS.[4]

1. The Sword-jewel—confers invincibility.
2. The Snake (*Nāga*)-skin jewel. It is ten miles long by five broad; water cannot wet it, nor the wind shake it; it warms in the cold weather and cools in the hot; and shines brighter than the moon.
3. The Palace-jewel.
4. The Garden-jewel.
5. The Robes.
6. The Bed-jewel.
7. The Shoe-jewel. Conveys the wearer one hundred miles without fatigue and across water without wetting the feet.

[1] *Bum-pa-ter;* Skt., *Kalaṣa.*

[2] Gyal-ts'an sna bdun.

[3] 'Jigs-yoṅs-gyi rin-po-ch'e, namely, *bSeru*, conch-shell curd, king's earring, queen's earring, jewelled tiara, three-eyed gem, and the eight-limbed coral. Another enumeration gives Padmaraga, indranila, baidurya, margad, vajra, pearl, and coral.

[4] Ne-wai rin-poch'e sna bdun.

A selection of four of these, with the addition of the royal umbrella, is termed "The five Royal Insignia,"[1] namely:—

THE SEVEN PERSONAL GEMS.

1. Ornamental cushion or throne.
2. Umbrella.
3. Sword—emblematic of power of life and death
4. Cow-tail Fly-whisk with jewelled handle.
5. Parti-coloured embroidered shoes.

THE EIGHT GLORIOUS EMBLEMS.[2]

These auspicious symbols are figured in Buddha's footprints,[3] and on innumerable articles, lay and clerical.

THE EIGHT GLORIOUS EMBLEMS.

[1] Cf. CSOMA'S *An.*, p. 76; JAESCHKE'S *Dict.*, p. 454.

[2] Skt., *Ashta-maṅgala*; T., bkra-s'i rtags-brgyad.

[3] Said to be symbols of the Vita-rāga. HODGSON'S *L.L.*, p. 136; also *J.A.S.B.*, art. "*Naipālya Kalyāṇa*"

	SKT.	TIB.
1. The Golden Fish[1]	matsya	gser-ña
2. The Umbrella ("Lord of the White Umbrella"[2])	chatra	gdugs
3. Conch-shell Trumpet—of Victory ...	ṣaṅkha	duṅ
4. Lucky Diagram[3]	ṣrīvatsa	dpal-be
5. Victorious Banner	dhvaja	rgyal-mts'an
6. Vase	kalaṣa	bum-pa
7. Lotus	padma	padma
8. Wheel	cakra	'k'or-lo

THE EIGHT GLORIOUS OFFERINGS.[4]

1. *Mirror.*—The light-holding goddess-form offered a looking-glass to Buddha Bhagavāt when he was turning the wheel of religion,

THE EIGHT GLORIOUS OFFERINGS.

and he blessed it and rendered it holy. (Compare with the mirror in the Shinto religion of Japan.)

2. The intestinal concretion (*gi-ham* or *gi-'vaṅ* found in the entrails

[1] The credulous Lāmas of north-eastern Tibet credited Mr. Rockhill with having captured the golden fish in the Tosu lake. "When I came back from Tosu-nor to Sbang, the Khanpo (abbot), a Tibetan, asked me where I proposed going; 'To Lob-nor,' I replied, not wishing to discuss my plans. 'I supposed that was your intention,' he rejoined; 'you have caught our horse and fish of gold in the Tosu-nor, and now you want to get the frog of gold of the Lob-nor. But it will be useless to try; there is in the whole world but the Panchen Rinpoche, of Tashi-lhunpo, who is able to catch it" ("A Journey in Mongolia and Tibet," *The Geog. Journ.*, May, 1894, p. 376). The Japanese use a wooden fish as a gong.

[2] In Sanchi Tope. FERGUS., *Tree and Serp. Worship*, pl. xxxv., Fig. 2.

[3] Also the symbol of the tenth Jina (*Sītala*) of the Jāins. Compare with "Buddha's entrails," see number 2 of next list, also on this page.

[4] bkras's-rdsas brgyad. These, together with the foregoing, may be compared with the *Navakosa* or *Navanidhi*, or nine treasures of Kuvera, the god of riches, namely, Padma, Mahapadma, Makara, Kacchapa, Mukunda, Nanda, Nila, Kharwa. And these are related to the so-called Nāga kings, "the nine Nandas" of Magadha.

of certain animals and on the neck of an elephant. The land-guarding elephant offered this to Buddha, and he blessed it.

3. Curds (źo).—The farmer's daughter (legs-skyes-ma) offered Buddha curdled milk, and he blessed it.

4. *Darwa grass.*—Mangalam, the grass-seller, offered Buddha *darwa* grass, which he blessed.

5. The *Bilwa* fruit (Ægle marmelos).—Brahma offered him *bilwa*, which he blessed as the best of fruits.

6. Conch-shell.—Indra offered him a white conch-shell, and he blessed it.

7. *Li-khri.*—The Brahman "King-star," offered him Li-khri, and he blessed it as the overpowering knowledge.

8. The white turnip.—Vajrapāni, "the Secret Lord," offered him a white turnip (yaṅ-dkar), which he blessed as the demon-defeating turnip.

The Five Sensuous Qualities.[1]

These are figured at page 297. They seem to be a Buddhist adaptation of the Hindū "eight enjoyments" (*Ashtabhoga*), namely, a grand house, a bed, fine clothes, jewels, wives, flowers, perfumes, areca-nut and betel. They are offered on the altars and are :—

1. Pleasing form (*Rupa*).
2. Sound (*Sapta*).
3. Perfumes (*Gandhe*).
4. Luscious eatables (*Naiwete*).
5. Pleasing-touch and feelings (*Sparsa*).

Distinctly Chinese in origin are the Trigrams and the following symbolic animals.

The Trigrams are especially used in astrology, and are described in the chapter on that subject. They are based upon the very ancient Chinese theory of the *Yin-Yang* or "the great extreme" ("Tai-Ky"[2]), where two parallel lines, in a circle divided spirally into two equal tadpole-like segments, represent, as in the doctrine of the Magi, the two First Causes and great principles, or contrary influences (*Yin*+*Yang*); such as

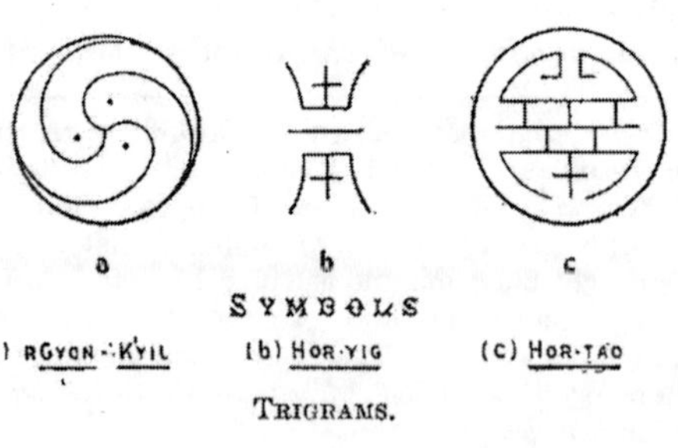

Trigrams.

[1] Skt., *Kāmaguna*, T., 'dod-yoṅs.

[2] Dumoutier, *Les Symboles, etc., Annamites.*

light and darkness, good and evil, male and female, heat and cold, movement and repose, and so on.

The circular diagram[1] is divided by the Lāmas, like the Japanese, into three segments (as in the annexed figure *a*); and it will be noticed that the tails are given the direction of the orthodox fly-foot cross, for it too, according to the Lāmas, signifies ceaseless change or "becoming."

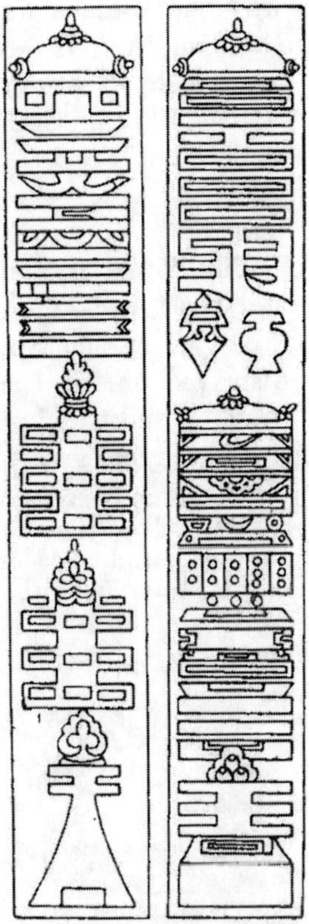

TRIGRAMS AS CHARMS.

The LONGEVITY-trigram or hexagram, in both its oblong and circular forms (fig. *b* and *c*), is a modification of the Chinese symbol for longevity called *Tho.*[2]

The Lāmas have also incorporated the four greatest amongst the Chinese symbolic animals, to wit, the Tortoise, the Phœnix, Dragon, and Horse-dragon, as well as the Chinese Tiger, and the Bats.

THE TORTOISE symbolizes the universe to the Chinese as well as the Hindūs. Its dome-shaped back represents the vault of the sky, its belly the earth, which moves upon the waters; and its fabulous longevity leads to its being considered imperishable.

THE DRAGON[3] seems to perpetuate the tradition of primæval flying saurians of geologic times, now known only through their fossilized remains. The Lāmas and Chinese Buddhists have assimilated them with the mythical serpents (Nāga) of Indian myth.

THE HORSE-DRAGON figures, as it seems to me, very prominently in the prayer-flags of Tibet, as we shall presently see.

THE PHŒNIX (or "*Garuḍa*"). This mythical "sky-soarer"[4] is the great enemy of the dragons, and has been assimilated to

[1] Called rGyan-'k'yil, probably a corruption of the Chinese name.

[2] Cf. DUMOUTIER, *op. cit.*, p. 21.

[3] Tib., 'drug; Chinese *Long.*

[4] Tib., nam-K'ah-ldiṅ. The Chinese call it Con-phu'ong (DUMOUTIER, p. 48).

the Indian *Garuḍa*, the arch-enemy of the Nāgas. And anyone who has, like myself, seen the bird popularly called *Garuḍa* (namely the Adjutant or Stork) devouring snakes, must realize why the Indians fixed upon such a homely simile to represent their myth. It seems to be analogous to the Thunder-bird of the North American Indians. In a more mystic sense the Lāmas, like the Chinese, believe it to symbolize the entire world; its head is the heaven, its eyes the sun, its back the crescent moon, its wings the wind, its feet the earth, its tail the trees and plants.[1]

THE TIGER is a deity of the pre-Lāmaist religion of Tibet; and the "Red-Tiger," as already noted, appears to me to be the prototype of the favourite Lāmaist demon (Tām-din). The tiger is displayed on all the Tibetan prayer-flags in contest with the dragon,[2] and the five tigers (see figure, page 519) are conspicuous in the Chinese symbolism prevalent in Annam.[3]

The group is mystically reputed to symbolize the five elements: the central yellow tiger is the earth, the upper right blue one is wood, the lower right red one is fire (also the south), the upper left black one is water (also the north), and the lower left is metal (also the west).

THE BATS, five in number, have come by a confusion of homonyms to symbolize the five good Fortunes,[4] namely, Luck, Wealth, Long life, Health, and Peace. They are embroidered on dresses of high Lāmas, sorcerers, maskers, etc.[5]

THE FIVE BATS OF FORTUNE.

Astrology also uses many other symbols, as will be seen hereafter.

The symbolism of colours is referred to in the chapter on images and incidentally elsewhere.

SYMBOLIC WORDS USED AS NUMERALS IN CHRONOGRAMS.

In chronograms and astronomical and other works, symbolic names are often used instead of numerals. The rationale of the

---

1 Cf. also DUMOUTIER, p. 48.

2 Ngu Ho, see figure, p. 413.

3 DUMOUTIER, p. 55.

4 Chinese *Ngu Phư'o'c*; cf. DUMOUTIER, p. 51.

5 See also their form on page 4.

use of such names is generally obvious; thus the individual's body, the moon, the (one-horned) rhinoceros, express unity from their singleness. The hand, the eye, wings, twins, denote a pair. And many of the others are derived from the mythology of the Hindūs. The following are some additional illustrations[1] :—

3 = the world—*i.e.*, the three Buddhist worlds of Kāma, Rūpa, Arupa.
= quality—*i.e.*, the three *Guna.*
= fire—evidently from its triangular tongue.
= top—probably from the Chinese ideograph of a hill.
4 = a lake or sea—*i.e.*, the idea of fluid requiring to be hemmed in on all four sides.
5 = the senses—the five senses.
= an element—the five elements.
= an aggregate—the five *Skandha.*
7 = a sage—the seven *Ṛishi.*
8 = a snake—the eight great Nāgas.
9 = a treasure—the nine treasures of Kuvera and the Nandas.
10 = points—the ten points or directions.
12 = the sun—with its twelve signs of the Zodiac.
24 = Jina or victor—the twenty-four *Jina* and *Tirthaṅkara.*
32 = tooth—the human set of thirty-two teeth.
0 = sky—the "empty" space.

THE "MAṆḌALA" OR MAGIC CIRCLE-OFFERING OF THE UNIVERSE.

It is almost a matter of history how the great emperor of Aṣoka thrice presented India to the Buddhist church, and thrice redeemed it with his treasure. But it seems to be little, if at all, known that the Lāmas systematically ape Aṣoka in this particular gift; and they are much more magnificently generous than he. For every day, in every temple in Lāmadom, the Lāmas offer to the Buddhas (as well as to the saints and demons) not only the whole of India, but the whole universe of Jambudvīp and the three other fabulous continents of Hindū cosmogony, together with all the heavens and their inhabitants and treasures. And although this offering is made in effigy, it is, according to the spirit of Lāmaism, no less effective than Aṣoka's real gifts, upon which it seems to be based.

The mode of making this microcosmic offering of the universe in effigy is as follows; but to fully understand the rite, reference

[1] Taken mostly from CSOMA's *Grammar*, pp. 150, *et seq.*

should be made to the illustrated description of the Buddhist universe, already given at page 79.

MODE OF OFFERING THE MAṆḌALA.

Having wiped the tray with the right arm or sleeve, the Lāma takes a handful of rice in either hand, and sprinkles some on the tray to lay the golden foundation of the universe. Then he sets down the large ring (see figure, p. 296), which is the iron girdle of the universe. Then in the middle is set down a dole of rice as mount Meru (Olympus), the axis of the system of worlds. Then in the order given in the attached diagram are set down a few grains of rice representing each of the thirty-eight component portions of the universe, each of which is named at the time of depositing its representative rice. The ritual for all sects of Lāmas during this ceremony is practically the same. I here append the text as used by the Kar-gyu sect.

During this ceremony it is specially insisted on that the performer must mentally conceive that he is actually bestowing all this wealth of continents, gods, etc., etc., upon his Lāmaist deities, who themselves are quite outside the system of the universe.

The words employed during the offering of the Maṇḍala are the following, and it should be noted that the figures in brackets correspond to those in the diagram and indicate the several points in the magic circle where the doles of rice are deposited during this celebration or service.

"*Om! Vajra bhummi ah Hūṃ!*"

"On the entirely clear foundation of solid gold is *Om! bajra-rekhe ah Hūṃ.*

"In the centre of the iron wall is *Hūṃ* and Ri-rab (Meru), the king of Mountains (1).

"On the east is Lüs-'p'ag*s*-po (2),

"On the south 'Jam-bu-gliṅ (3),

"On the west Ba-laṅ-*s*pyöd (4), and

"On the north Gra-mi-*s*ñan (5).

"On either side of the eastern continent are Lüs (6) and Lüs-'p'ag*s* (7).

"On either side of the southern continent are rNa-yab (8) and rNa-yab-gz'an (9).

"On either side of the western continent are Yonten (10) and Lam-mch'og-'gra (11).

DIAGRAM
showing
THE COMPOSITION OF THE MANDALA
OFFERING OF THE UNIVERSE

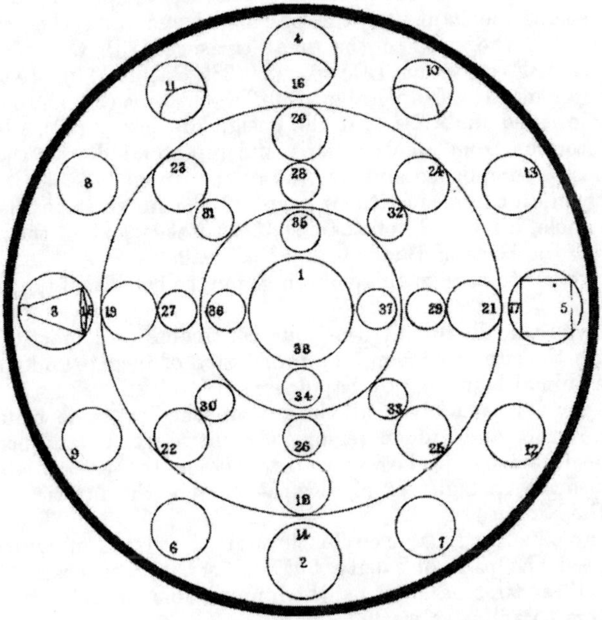

FRONT.

The numbers are in the order of the procedure.

1	Ri Gyalpo Ri-rabe.	
2.	Shar-lü Phag-po.	THE GREAT CONTINENTS
3	Hlô Jam-bu-ling.	THE GREAT CONTINENTS
4.	Nub Pa-lang Jö.	THE GREAT CONTINENTS
5	Chang ḍa-mi nyen.	THE GREAT CONTINENTS
6	Lü	THE SATELLITE CONTINENTS
7	Lü phag.	THE SATELLITE CONTINENTS
8	Nga-yab	THE SATELLITE CONTINENTS
9	Nga-yab zhén.	THE SATELLITE CONTINENTS
10	Yô-dén	THE SATELLITE CONTINENTS
11	Lam-chhog dô.	THE SATELLITE CONTINENTS
12	Ḍa-mi nyen	THE SATELLITE CONTINENTS
13	Ḍe-mi nyen kyi da.	THE SATELLITE CONTINENTS
14.	Rin-pochhe-ī ri-wô.	THE 4 WORLDLY TREASURES.
15	'Pg-sam Kyi Shing	THE 4 WORLDLY TREASURES.
16.	Dod jô-ī-loo.	THE 4 WORLDLY TREASURES.
17	Ma-mō pa-ī lô thog	THE 4 WORLDLY TREASURES.

18.	Khor-lo.	THE SEVEN PRECIOUS THINGS.
19	Nor-bu.	THE SEVEN PRECIOUS THINGS.
20.	Tsün-mo.	THE SEVEN PRECIOUS THINGS.
21.	Lön-po.	THE SEVEN PRECIOUS THINGS.
22	Lang-po.	THE SEVEN PRECIOUS THINGS.
23.	Tam-chhog.	THE SEVEN PRECIOUS THINGS.
24.	Mag-pōn.	THE SEVEN PRECIOUS THINGS.
25.	Ter chhen-po-ī Bum-pa.	
26	Geg-mo-ma.	THE 8 MATRI GODDESSES.
27.	Theng-wa ma.	THE 8 MATRI GODDESSES.
28.	Lu-ma.	THE 8 MATRI GODDESSES.
29	Gar-ma.	THE 8 MATRI GODDESSES.
30.	Me-tog ma.	THE 8 MATRI GODDESSES.
31	Dug-pö ma.	THE 8 MATRI GODDESSES.
32.	Nang sol-ma.	THE 8 MATRI GODDESSES.
33.	Di chhab ma.	THE 8 MATRI GODDESSES.
34.	Nyi-ma	SUN AND MOON.
35.	Da-wa	SUN AND MOON.
36.	Rinpo-chhe-ī dug.	
37.	Chhog-lé nam-par Gyal-wa-ī Gyal-tshén.	
38.	Nam-par Gyal-wa-ī Khang zang.	

"And on either side of the northern continent are sGra-mi-sñan (12) and sGra-mi-sñan-gyi-mda (13).

"There are mountains of jewels (14), wish-granting trees (15), wish-granting cows (16), unploughed crops (17), the precious wheel (18), the precious *Norbu* jewel (19), the precious queen (20), the precious minister (21), the precious elephant (22), the precious horse (23), the precious battle-chief (24), the vase of the great treasure (25), the goddesses sgeg-pa-ma (26), 'P'reṅ-wa-ma (27), gLu-ma (28), Gar-ma (29), Me-tog-ma (30), bDug-spös-ma (31), sNaṅ-gsal-ma (32), Dri-ch'al-ma (33), the sun (34), moon (35), jewelled umbrella (36), the ensign of victory (37), which is entirely victorious from all directions, and in the middle are the gods (38), the most accomplished and wealthy of the beings!

"I offer you all these constituent parts of the universe in their entirety, O! noble, kind, and holy Lāma! O! tutelary gods of the magic-circle, and all the hosts of Buddhas and Bodhisats!

"I beg you all to receive these offerings for the benefit of the animal beings!

"I offer you O! Buddhas! the four continents and mount Meru adorned with the sun and moon on a foundation of incense and flowers. Let all the animal beings enjoy happiness!

"I offer you O! assembly of all the accomplished supreme beings of the outside, inside, and hidden regions, the entire wealth and body of all these ideal regions. I beg you all to give us the best of all real gifts, and also the real gift of *r*Dsogs-pa-ch'en-po (the mystic insight sought by the Ñiṅ-ma)!

"I offer up this fresh magic-circle, through the virtue of which let no injury beset the path of purity, but let us have the grace of the Jinas of the three times, and let us, the innumerable animal beings, be delivered from this illusive world!

"I offer up salutations, offerings, confessions of sins, and repentance. What virtue has been accumulated by myself and others, let it go to the attainment of our great end. *Idam-ratna maṇḍala kamnir-yaiteyāmi!*

"I humbly prostrate myself three times to all who are worthy of worship, with my whole heart and body." Let glory come![1]

But the commonest use of sacred symbols is as talismans to ward off the evils of those malignant planets and demons who cause disease and disaster, as well as for inflicting harm on one's enemy. The symbols here are used in a mystical and magic sense as spells and as fetishes, and usually consist of formulas in corrupt and often unintelligible Sanskrit, extracted from the Mahāyāna and Tāntrik scriptures, and called *dhāraṇi*,[2] as they are believed to "hold" divine powers, and are also used as incantations. Shorter

[1] For details of the rest of this service, see my *Lāmaism in Sikhim*, p. 105.

[2] *z'uṅs.*

forms of these, consisting often of a single letter, are also used as representing the essence or "germ" of these spells or *mantras*, and hence named *vīja*. And the mystic diagram in which they are often arranged is named *Yantra*, as in Hindū Tāntrism.[1]

The forms of these talismans and amulets are innumerable. The majority are luck-compelling, but different diseases, accidents and misfortune have each their special kinds.

The eating of the paper on which a charm has been written is an ordinary way of curing disease, as indeed it had been in Europe till not so many centuries ago, for the mystic ℞ heading our prescriptions is generally admitted to have had its origin in the symbol of Saturn, whom it invoked, and the paper on which the symbol and several other mystic signs were inscribed constituted the medicine, and was itself actually eaten by the patient. The spells which the Lāmas use in this way as medicine are shown in the annexed print, and are called "the edible letters" (*za-yig*).

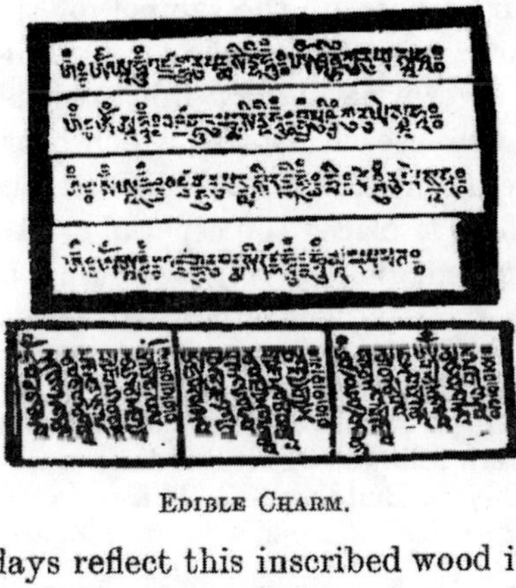

EDIBLE CHARM.

A still more mystical way of applying these remedies is by the washings of the reflection of the writing in a mirror, a practice not without its parallels in other quarters of the globe.[2] Thus to cure the evil eye as shown by symptoms of mind-wandering and dementia condition—called "byad-'grol"—it is ordered as follows: Write with Chinese ink on a piece of wood the particular letters and smear the writing over with myrobalams and saffron as varnish, and every twenty-nine days reflect this inscribed wood in a mirror, and during reflection wash the face of the mirror with beer, and collect a cupful of such beer and drink it in nine sips.

[1] MONIER WILLIAMS'S *Hinduism*, 127.

[2] "In Gambia," writes the colonial surgeon in his report for 1890 (quoted in *Nature*) "the treatment relied upon for cure, and much practised in the country, is to call in a man who is supposed to be a 'doctor,' who, after looking at the patient, sits down at his bedside and writes in Arabic characters on a wooden slate a long rigmarole, generally consisting of extracts from the *Koran*. The slate is then washed, and the dirty infusion is drunk by the patient."

But most of the charms are worn on the person as amulets. Every individual always wears around the neck one or more of these amulets, which are folded up into little cloth-covered packets, bound with coloured threads in a geometrical pattern. Others are kept in small metallic cases of brass, silver, or gold, set with turquoise stones as amulets, and called "*Ga-u.*" These amulets are fastened to the girdle or sash, and the smaller ones are worn as lockets,[1] and with each are put relics of holy men—a few threads or fragments of cast-off robes of saints or idols, peacock feathers, sacred Kuṣa grass, and occasionally images and holy pills. Other large charms are affixed overhead in the house or tent to ward off lightning, hail, etc., and for cattle special charms are chanted, or sometimes pasted on the walls of the stalls, etc.[2]

Most of these charms against accident, disease, and ill-fortune are in the form figured on the opposite page, which is called "The Assembly of all the Lāmas' Hearts," as it is believed to contain the essence of all that is most powerful in the Lāmaist spells.

It consists of a series of concentric circles of spells surrounded by flames, amid which in the four corners are the symbols of the Buddhist trinity symbolized as three gems, a lotus-flower, a thunder-bolt sceptre, and a flaming dagger with a *vajra*-hilt. In the interior is an eight-petalled lotus-flower, each petal of which bears mystic syllables, and in the centre of the flower is a circular space of about an inch in diameter, in which is placed the especial mystic charm, prepared as presently described, and varying according to the purpose for which the charm is wanted. The outer spells are:—

In the Outmost Circle.—Guard the Body, Mind, and Speech of this charm-holder! *Rakhya rakhya kuruye svāhā! Angtadyatha! Om muni muni mahamuniye svāhā.* (Here follows "The Buddhist creed" already given; followed by the Dhyāni Buddhas:—) *Vairocana Om vajra Akshobhya Hūṃ, Ratna-sambhava Hri, Bargudhara Hri, Amoga-siddha Ah!*

In Second Circle.—Om! Nama Samanta Buddhanam, Nama Samanta Dharmanam, nama Samanta Saṁghanam. Om Sititabatrai. Om Vimala, Om Shadkara, Om Brahyarigar Vajra ustsikhatsa krawarti sarvayana manta mūla varma hana dhanamhā. Namkil-

---

1 Figured on page 571. The kidney-shaped ones are called *Ga-u ke-ri-ma.*

2 Cf. also Csoma and W. E. Carte, *J.A.S.B.*, ix., 904. See figures of some of these charms at pages 568, 571, and 572.

anibā makriayena keni chatkramtamtata sarban rātsin rātsin dakhinda bhinda tsiri tsiri giri giri mada mada hūṃ hūṃ phat phat.

In Third Circle.—Guard the Body, Mind, and Speech of this charm-holder! *Mama rakya rakhya kuruye swāhā.* (Here follows the letters of the alphabet:—) Ang, a, ā, i, ī, u, ū, ri, rī, li, lī, e, ai, o. au, ang, a, k, kh, g, gh, ṅ, ts, tsh, ds, dsā, ñ, ta, th, d, dh, n, p, ph, b, bh, m, y, r, l, w, ṣ, sh, s, h, aṃ!

In Fourth Circle.—*Hūṃ, Hūṃ*, etc.

In Fifth Circle.—*Hri, Hri*, etc.

THE GENERAL CHARM PRINT.
Entitled "The Assembly of Lāmas' Hearts."
(Reduced ½.)

In Sixth Circle.—*Om! A! Hūṃ! Hri! Guru! Deva! Ḍākkinī! Sarvasiddhipala Hūṃ! A!*

The special charm, which occupies the centre of the diagram, varies according to the object for which the charm is required. It consists of a monogram or mystic letter (Sanskrit, *vīja*, or seed), which represents the germ of a spell or *mantra*. This letter is often in the old Indian character of about the fourth or fifth century A.D., and is inscribed in cabalistic fashion with special materials as prescribed in the manual on the subject.

As most of these specific charms are of the nature of sympathetic magic, and evidently derived from very ancient Indian sources, probably dating back to Vedic times when the ritual consisted largely of sympathetic magic,[1] I give here a few examples:[2]—

Thus to make the

Charm against Bullets and Weapons.—The directions are as these: With the blood of a wounded man draw the annexed monogram (D Ɑ) and insert in the vacant space in the centre of the aforesaid print of "The Assembly of the Hearts of the Lāmas." The sheet should then be folded and wrapped in a piece of *red* silk, and tie up with a piece of string and wear around the neck or an unexposed part of your breast immediately next the skin, and never remove it.

Charm for Clawing Animals (*i.e.*, tigers, cats, bears, etc.).—On a miniature knife write with a mixture of myrobalans and musk-water the monogram (? ZAH) and tie up, etc. (Here the knife seems to represent the animal's claw.)

For Domestic Broils.—Write the monogram (? RE) and insert in print and fold up and bind with a thread made of the mixed hairs of a dog, goat, sheep, and enclose in a mouse-skin, and tie, etc. (This seems to represent union of domestic elements.)

For Kitchen Cooking Smells offensive to the House-Gods.—With the blood of a hybrid bull-calf write the monogram GAU (= cow), and insert it in the print, and fold up in a piece of hedge-hog-skin. (Compare with the western Aryan myth of the Greek hearth-god Vulcan, whose mother *Hera* as Io is represented as a cow.)

For Cholera (or "the vomiting, purging, and cramps").—With

---

1 Cf. BERGAIGNE'S *La religion védique;* also FRAZER.

2 For a fuller account, with illustrations, see my article in *Jour. Anthrop. Institute*, 1894.

the dung of a black horse and black sulphur and musk-water write the monogram (? ZA), and insert in the print, and fold up in a piece of snake-skin, and wear, etc. (Here the dung seems to represent the purging, the horse the galloping course, the black colour the deadly character, and the snake the virulence of the disease.)

CHARM AGAINST PLAGUES.

This charm, figured at the head of this chapter, consists of a monster figure of the Garuḍa, the king of birds, with a snake in its mouth, and each of its outstretched plumes bears a text, and it also contains the "Buddhist creed." The inscription runs:—

Om! Bhrum satrirbad namkhamjamram.
Om! bisakhrilimili hala svāhā!
Om! bisakhrilimilihalayā skachig!

Guard the holder (*i.e.*, the wearer) of this from all the host of diseases, of evil spirits and injuries, including contagious diseases, sore-throat, cough, rheumatism, the black "rgyu-ghgyel," brum-bu, and all kinds of plague of the body, speech, and mind! [Here follows the Buddhist creed.] *Habatse habatse hūṃ sod. Suru suru hūṃ sod. Sukarjuka hūṃ sod. Sati karur hūṃ sod. Kularakhyi hum sod. Merumthuntse hūṃ sod. Mahakuruṇa guru triga gurunam nagashara ramram duldul nagatsịta pho naga chunglinga shag thumamnyogs sos.*

Guard the holder.

Om! thamitharati sadunte dswaramghaye svāhā!

Another charm for disease is given at page 62, where the fierce demon Tam-din, clad in human and animal skins, bears on his front a disc with concentric circles of spells.

SCORPION-CHARM AGAINST INJURY BY DEMONS.

This charm, figured at page 474, is in the form of a scorpion, whose mouth, tipped by flames, forms the apex of the picture. On its shoulder are seated the especial demons to be protected against. The inscription runs:—

Ayama durur cashana zhamaya.
Hūm! Om! A! Hūṃ! Artsignirtsig!
Namo Bhagavāti Hūṃ! Hūm! Phat!

A guard against all the injuries of "*r*gyalpo," "drimo" (a malignant demon specially injuring women), "*b*tsan" (or red demons), "sa-dag" (or earth-demons), *k*lu (or *nāga*), including "*g*ñan" (a plague-causing subordinate of the *nāga*).

Against injury by these preserve!

And the figures are hemmed in by the mystic syllables: *Jsa! Hūṃ! Hūṃ! Bam! Hô!*

The huge Tibetan mastiffs are let loose at night as watch-dogs, and roaming about in a ferocious state are a constant source of alarm to travellers, most of whom therefore carry the following charm against dog-bite. It consists of a picture of a dog fettered and muzzled by a chain, terminated by the mystic and all-powerful thunderbolt-sceptre; and it contains the following inscribed Sanskrit *mantras* and statements: "The mouth of the blue dog is bound beforehand! *Omriti-sri-ti swāhā! Omriti-sri-ti*

CHARM AGAINST DOG-BITE.

swāhā!" And this is repeated along the body of the dog, followed by:—

Om Vajra ghana kara kukuratsa sal sal nan marya smugs smugs kukuratsa khathamtsa le tsa le mun mun sar sar rgyug kha tha ma chhu chhinghchhang maraya rakkhya rakkhya! (It is) fixed! fixed!

CHARM AGAINST EAGLES AND BIRDS OF PREY.

Eagles play havoc with the young herds of the pastoral Bhotiyas of the Sikhim uplands and Tibet. For this the people use the annexed charm, which they tie up near their huts. The central figure is a manacled bird, representing the offending eagle or other bird of prey; and around it is the following text:—

"A guard against all injuries of the covetous, sky-soaring monarch bird. (It is) fixed! fixed! *Om smege smege bhum bhummu!*"

CHARM FOR KILLING ONE'S ENEMY.

The necromantic charms for killing one's enemy are resorted to mostly in inter-tribal feuds and warring with foreigners. I have given details of these rites elsewhere.[1] They require the following objects :—

1. An axe with three heads, the right of which is bull-headed, the left snake-headed, and the middle one pig-headed.

2. On the middle head a lamp is to be kept.

3. In the pig's mouth an image of a human being made of wheaten flour (a *linga*). The upper part of the body is black and the lower part red. On the side of the upper part of the body draw the figure of the eight great planets, and on the lower part of the body the twenty-eight constellations of stars. Write also the eight *parkha* (trigrams), the nine *mewa*, the claws of the Garuḍa in the hands, the wing of the eagles and the snake tail.

EAGLE-CHARM.

4. Hang a bow and an arrow on the left and load him with provisions on the back. Hang an owl's feather on the right and a rook's on the left; plant a piece of the poison-tree on the upper part of the body, and surround him with red swords on all sides. Then a red Rgyangbu wood on the right, a yellow one on the left, a black one in the middle, and many blue ones on divers places.

5. Then, sitting in quiet meditation, recite the following :—

"*Hūm!* This axe with a bull's head on the right will repel all the injuries of the Ṅag-pas and Bön-pos—sorcerers; the snake on the left will repel all the classes of plagues; the pig's head in the middle will repel the *sa-dag* and other earth-demons; the *linga* image in the mouth will repel all the evil spirits without remainder, and the lamp on the head will repel the evil spirits of the upper regions. O! the axe will cleave the heart of the angry enemy and also of the hosts of evil spirits ! ! ! etc., etc., etc., etc.

During the Sikhim expedition of 1888, near Mt. Paul on the Tukola ridge, where the final attack of the Tibetans was made, there was found one of the mystic contrivances for the destruction of the enemy. It consisted of an obliquely carved piece of wood,

[1] My *Lāmaism in Sikhim.*

about fourteen inches long, like a miniature screw-propeller of a steamer, and acted like the fan of a windmill. It was admittedly a charm for the destruction of the enemy by cleaving them to pieces, a device for which there are western parallels. And on it was written a long, unintelligible Bön spell of the kind called *z'aṅ-z'uṅ*, followed by a call for the assistance of the fierce deities Tam-ḍin, Vajrapāṇi, and the Garuḍa, and concluding with "*phat, phat*"—Break! Destroy! It may also be mentioned here that the bodies of all the Tibetans slain in these encounters were found to bear one or more charms against wounds, most of them being quite new; and some of the more elaborate ones, which contained in their centre figures of the other weapons charmed against, swords, muskets, etc., had cost their wearers as much as twenty-five rupees a-piece.

And for torturing one's enemy short of death, there is the same popular practice which is found amongst occidentals,[1] namely, of making a little clay image of the enemy and thrusting pins into it. The directions for this procedure are:—

Take some of the earth from his footprints; or better from the house of some wrecked person, and mixing with dough prepare a small figure of a man. On its head put thorns. Through the heart's region thrust a copper needle. Then say following spell: *Om Ghate Jam-mo hāmo hādsam*; during the recital of which move the needle briskly over the region of the heart. If this process is long continued then the bewitched person will surely die within the day; but if done only for a time, and the needle and thorns are again withdrawn, and the image-body and needles are washed, the enemy who is thus bewitched will only suffer temporary anguish, and will recover (for it is against Buddhist principles to take life).

"Prayer-Flags."

The tall flags inscribed with pious sentences, charms, and prayers, which flutter picturesquely around every Lāmaist settlement, curiously combine Indian with Chinese aud Tibetan symbolism.

It seems a far cry from Aṣoka pillars to prayer-flags, but it is not improbable that they are related, and that "the Trees of the Law," so conspicuous in Lāmaism, are perverted emblems of Indian Buddhism, like so much of the Lāmaist symbolism.

Everyone who has been in Burma is familiar with the tall masts

[1] Cf. Virgil, *Bucol.* viii.; Theocritus, *Pharmaceutria*.

(*tagūn-daing*),[1] with their streaming banners, as accessories of every Buddhist temple in that country. Each mast in Burma is surmounted by an image of one or more Brāhmani geese, and the streamers are either flat or long cylinders of bamboo framework pasted over with paper, which is often inscribed with pious sentences. The monks whom I asked regarding the nature of this symbol believed that it was borrowed from Indian Buddhism.

Now, the resemblance which these posts bear to the Aṣoka pillars is certainly remarkable. Both are erected by Buddhists for the purposes of gaining merit and displaying aloft pious wishes or extracts from the law; and the surmounting geese form an essential feature of the abacus of several Aṣoka pillars. The change from pillar to post could be easily explained, as great monoliths were only possible to such a mighty emperor as Aṣoka; but every-one could copy in wood the pious practice of that great and model Buddhist who had sent his missionaries to convert them.

Such wooden standards may have been common in Indian Buddhism, as some Burmese believe, and yet, from their perishable nature, have left no trace behind. At most of the old rocky Buddhist sites in Magadha I have seen sockets in the rock, some of which may have been used for such standards, although many of the smaller sockets were doubtless used for planting umbrellas to shelter the booth-keepers in their sale of flower and other offerings for the shrines. Most also of the clay models of Caityas in relief, dug out of the earlier Indian Stūpas, show streamers tied to the top of the Caityas; and in Ceylon the old Stūpas are surrounded by what seems to be similar posts.[2]

Lāmaism, which, more than any other section of Buddhism, has, as we have seen, substituted good words for the good works of the primitive Buddhists, eagerly seized upon all such symbolism, as for instance, Aṣoka's historic gifts in their daily rice-offerings. The decided resemblance of its "prayer-flags" to the *tagūn-daing* of the Burmese is[3] not more striking, perhaps, than the apparent

[1] Mr. St. A. St. John kindly informs me that the etymology is *ta*, something long and straight + *gun*, bark or husk + *daing*, a post.

[2] See figures in FERGUSON'S *History of India and Eastern Architecture.*

[3] These instances seem something more than the simple cloths and banners as propitiatory offerings, which, of course, are found in most animistic religions—from the "rag-bushes" of India to the shavings of the Upper Burmese and the Ainos. And the hypothetical relationship between the Burmese and the Tibetans, based on the affinity

homology which they present to the Aṣoka pillars. They are called by the Lāmas *Da-cha*,[1] evidently a corruption of the Indian *Dhvaja*, the name given by the earlier Indian Buddhists to the votive pillars offered by them as railings to Stūpas.[2]

The planting of a Lāmaist prayer-flag, while in itself a highly pious act, which everyone practises at some time or other, does not merely confer merit on the planter, but benefits the whole country-side. And the concluding sentence of the legend inscribed on the flag is usually "Let Buddha's doctrine prosper"—which is practically the gist of the Aṣoka inscriptions.[3]

CHINESE *LONG*-HORSE.
Or Horse-Dragon, "Long-ma."

But the Lāmas have degraded much of their Indian symbolism, and perverted it to sordid and selfish objects.

The prayer-flags are used by the Lāmas as luck-commanding talismans; and the commonest of them, the so-called "Airy

of their languages, does not count for much, as no real racial relation has yet been proved. Probably related to these prayer-flags are the stone pillars called *musts* or poles (wei-kan), found in western Su-Ch'uan in China, and figured by Mr. Baber ("A Journey," etc., *Roy. Geog. Soc. Suppl. Papers*, i., p. 19).

1 dar-lch'og.

2 CUNNINGHAM'S *Stupa of Barhut*.

3 As the legend usually bears a lion and a tiger in its upper corners, while below are a Garuḍa-bird and dragon (Nāga), it seems not impossible that these may be related to the surmounting lion and the so-called geese of Aṣoka's pillars. The rites related to the erection of the Lāmaist standard are somewhat suggestive of the Vedic rite of "raising Indra's banner," which in its turn is probably the original of our Maypole, and Aṣoka's pillars seem to have been somewhat of the nature of the *Jayastambha*.

horse," seems to me to be clearly based upon and also bearing the same name as "The Horse-dragon" of the Chinese.

This Horse-dragon or "*Long*-horse" is one of the four great mythic animals of China, and it is the symbol for *grandeur*. It is represented, as in the figure on the opposite page, as a dragon-headed horse, carrying on its back the civilizing Book of the Law.

The Tibetan *Lung*-Horse.

Now this is practically the same figure as "The *Lung*-horse" (literally "Wind-horse") of the Lāmaist flag, which also is used for the expressed purpose of increasing the *grandeur* of the votary; indeed, this is the sole purpose for which the flag is used by the Tibetan laity, with whom these flags are extremely popular.

And the conversion of "The Horse-dragon" of the Chinese into the Wind-horse of the Tibetans is easily accounted for by a confusion of homonyms. The Chinese word for "Horse-dragon" is *Long-ma*,[1] of which *Long* = Dragon, and *ma* = Horse. In Tibet, where Chinese is practically unknown, *Long*, being the radical word, would tend to be retained for a time, while the qualifying word, *ma*, translated into Tibetan, becomes "rta." Hence we get the form "Long-rta." But as the foreign word *Long* was unintelligible in Tibet, and the symbolic animal is used almost solely for fluttering in the *wind*, the "Long" would naturally become changed after a time into *Lung* or "wind," in order to give it some meaning, hence, so it seems to me, arose the word Lung-rta,[2] or "Wind-horse."

In appearance the Tibetan "*Lung*-horse" so closely resembles its evident prototype the "Horse-dragon," that it could easily be mistaken for it. On the animal's back, in place of the Chinese civilizing Book of the Law, the Lāmas have substituted the Buddhist emblem of the civilizing Three Gems, which include the Buddhist Law. But the Tibetans, in their usual sordid way, view these objects as the material gems and wealth of good luck which this horse will bring to its votaries. The symbol is avowedly a luck-commanding talisman for enhancing the grandeur[3] of the votary.

Indian myth also lends itself to the association of the horse with luck; for the Jewel-horse of the universal monarch, such as Buddha was to have been had he cared for worldly grandeur, carries its rider, *Pegasus*-like, through the air in whatever direction wished for, and thus it would become associated with the idea of realization of material wishes, and especially wealth and jewels. This horse also forms the throne-support of the mythical celestial Buddha named *Ratna-sambhava*, or "the *Jewel*-born One," who is often represented symbolically by a jewel. And we find in many of these luck-flags that the picture of a jewel takes the place of the horse. It is also notable that the mythical people of the northern continent, subject to the god of wealth, Kuvera, or Vaiṣravana, are "horse-faced."

The flags are printed on the unglazed tough country paper,

---

[1] DUMOUTIER, *op. cit.*, p. 30.

[2] rLuṅ-rta; another form of spelling sometimes, though rarely, met with, is kLuṅ rta, where *kLuṅ* is said to mean "year of birth."

[3] T., rgyas.

and are obtainable on purchase from the Lāmas, but no Lāma is necessarily needed for the actual planting of the flag and its attendant rites.

These luck-commanding or "prayer-flags" are of four kinds :—

I. The *Lung-ta* proper, as above figured. It is almost square in form, about four to six inches long, and contains in the centre the figure of a horse with the mystic jewel *Norbu* on its back. It is

War of the Tiger and Dragon.

hung upon the ridges of the houses, and in the vicinity of dwellings. The printed text of this sort of flag varies somewhat in the order in which the deified Lāmas are addressed, some giving the first place to St. Padma, while others give it to the celestial Bodhisat, Mañjurṣī ; but all have the same general form, with the horse bearing the jewel in the centre, and in the four corners the figures or the names of the tiger, lion, the monstrous *garuḍa*-

bird, and the dragon—the tiger being opposed to the dragon, in accordance with Chinese mythology, as figured over the page.

A translation of one of the prayer-flags is here given :—

TIGER. | Hail ! *Vagishwari mum* ! (*i.e.*, yellow Mañjuṣrī's spell.) | LION.

Hail ! to the jewel in the Lotus ! *Hūṃ* ! (*i.e.*, Avalokita's spell).

Hail ! to the holder of the Dorje ! Hūṃ ! (*i.e.*, Vajrapāṇi's spell).

Hail ! to Vajrasattva (The Diamond-souled one !)

Hail ! *Amarahnihdsiwantiye swāhā.*

[The above is in Sanskrit. Now follows in Tibetan :—]

Here ! May all of the above (deities whose spells have been given) prosper. . . . . . . [here is inserted the year of birth of the individual], and also prosper—

the *Body* (*i.e.*, to save from sickness),
the *Speech* (*i.e.*, to give victory in disputations),
and the *Mind* (*i.e.*, to obtain all desires);
GARUḌA. of this year-holder [above specified] DRAGON.
and may Buddha's doctrine prosper !

Here it will be noted that the three great celestial *defensores fidei* of Lāmaism are invoked through their spells, namely :—

1. *Mañjuṣrī*, who conveys wisdom ; 2. *Avalokita*, who saves from fear and hell; and 3. *Vajrapāṇi*, who saves from accident and bodily injury. And in addition to the above are also given the spells of: 4. *Vajrasattva*, who purifies the soul from sin; and 5. *Amitāyus*, who confers long life.

It is interesting to compare with these Tibetan luck-flags the somewhat similar prayer-flags[1] which the Burmese Buddhists offer at their shrines. "These," says Mr. Scott,[2] "are fancifully cut into figures of dragons and the like, and in the centre contain, in Pāli or the vernacular, sentences like these :—

"By means of this paper the offerer will become very strong.

"By the merit of this paper Wednesday's children will be blessed by spirits and men.

"May the man born on Friday gain reward for his pious offering.

"May the man born on Monday be freed from Sickness and the Three Calamities."

---

[1] Kyet sha-taing.

[2] *The Burman*, i., p. 225.

THE LARGE LUCK-FLAG "THE VICTORIOUS BANNER."
(Reduced ⅓.)

The second form of the Tibetan luck-flag is called *chö-pén.*[1] It is of a long, narrow, oblong shape, about eight to ten inches in length. This sort of flag is for tying to twigs of trees or to bridges, or to sticks for planting on the tops of hills. Its text has generally the same arrangement as form No. 1, but it wants the horse-picture in the centre. Its Tibetan portion usually closes with "May the entire collection (of the foregoing deities) prosper the power, airy horse, age and life of this year-holder and make them increase like the waxing new moon."

Very poor people, who cannot afford the expense of the printed charms, merely write on a short slip of paper the name of the birth-year of the individual, and add "May his *lung-horse* prosper."

One *lung-horse* for each member of a household must be planted on the third day of every month (lunar) on the top of any hill near at hand, or on the branch of a tree near a spring, or tied to the sides of a bridge; and on affixing the flag a stick of incense is burned. And a small quantity of flour, grain, flesh, and beer are offered to the *genius loci* of the hill-top by sprinkling them around, saying, *So! So!* Take! Take!

A more expanded form of the luck-flag is the *Gyal-tsan dse-mo*, or "Victorious banner,"[2] which is generally of the same form as that first mentioned, but containing a much larger amount of holy texts, and also usually the eight glorious symbols, of which the lotus forms the base of the print. It prospers not only luck in wealth, but also the life, body, and power of the individual, and seems to contain also spells addressed to the goddess Durga, Ṣiva's spouse.

The Vast Luck-flag. This fourth form of Lung-ta is named "*gLañ-po stob ryyas*," or "That which makes vast like the Elephant."[3] It is pasted to the walls of the houses, or folded up and worn around the neck as a charm for good luck. It consists of crossed *vajras* in the centre with a Garuḍa and a peacock, the jewelled elephant and the jewelled horse, each bearing an eight-leaved lotus-disc on which are inscribed the following Sanskrit and Tibetan texts. The other symbols are "the eight glorious symbols" already described.

---

1 *s*byod-pan.

2 Sometimes rendered into Sanskrit as Arya dhvaja agra-keyur rana maharani.

3 gLañ-po stob-*r*gyas.

And around the margin is the familiar legend "the Buddhist creed," repeated several times, also the letters of the alphabet, together with the words "May the life, body, power, and the 'airy horse' of the holder of this charm prosper his body, speech, and wishes, and cause them to increase like the growing new moon; may he be possessed of all wealth and riches, and be guarded against all kinds of injury."

In the upper left hand disc: "May the *life* of this charm-holder be raised sublimely (like the flight of the garuḍa here represented). *Om! sal sal hobana sal sal ye swāhā! Om! Om! sarba kata kata sata kaṭa sala ya nata sah wa ye swāhā! Om! kili kili mili mili kuru kuru hūṃ hūṃ ye swāhā!* O! May the life of this charm-holder be raised on high!

In the upper right-hand disc: "May the *body* of this charm-holder be raised sublimely (like the flight of the peacock here represented). *Om! yer yer hobana yer yer ye svāhā! Om! sarba Tathagata bhiri bhiri bata bata miri miri mili mili ae bata sarba gata-gata shramana sarba gata-gata shramana sarba!* O! May the body of this charm-holder be raised on high."

In lower left-hand disc: "May the power of this charm-holder be raised sublimely (like the precious elephant here represented). *Om! Mer mer hobana mer mer ye swāhā! Om sarva dhara dhara bara dhara ghi kha ye swāhā! Sarva kili kili na hah kang li sarba bhara bhara sambhara sambhara!* O! May the power and wealth of this charm-holder be increased and all the injuries be guarded against.

In lower right-hand circle: "May the 'Airy horse' of this charm-holder be raised sublimely (with the celerity of 'the precious horse' here represented). *Om! lam lam hobana lam lam lam swāhā! Om! Sarva kara kara phat! Sarbha dhuru dhuru na phat! Sārbā kata kata kata na phat! Sarba kili kili na phat! Sarbha mala mala swāhā!* O! May the '*Lung*-horse' of the charm-holder be raised on high and guarded against all injury."

In the central disc over the junction of the cross *Dor-je* is written: "*Om! neh ya rani jiwenti ye swahā!* O! May this charm-holder be given the undying gift of soul everlasting (as the adamantine cross *Dor-je* herein pictured)."

In planting these luck-flags a special form of worship is observed. And the planting of these flags with the due worship is advised to be done when ever anyone feels unhappy and down in luck, or injured by the earth-demons, etc. It is called "The great statue of the Lung-horse," and is as follows:—

First of all is made a rice-offering of the universe, under a yellow canopy, but screened on the four sides by curtains of different colours, blue on the east, red on the south, white on the west, and black on the north. The canopies are to be fixed in the ends of a perfect square set in the four directions, around which are the twelve-year cycle, the nine cakes (*bs'ös*) representing the nine Mewas, eight lamps representing the eight parkha, eight planets, twenty-eight constellations of stars, five *Tormas*, five *glüd* (small balls of wheaten flour offered to demons as ransom), five arrows with silk streamers (mda-dar) of the five different colours, and many more *mdā rgyan-bu* and *'p'aṅ*. The above must be arranged by a practical man, and then the ceremony begins with the fingers in the proper attitude of the twelve cycle of years, and recitation of the following in a raised and melodious voice :—

"*Kye! Kye!* In the eastern horizon from where the sun rises, is a region of tigers, hares, and trees. The enemy of the trees is the Iron, which is to be found in the western horizon, and where the enemy, the life-cutting bdüd-devil, is also to be found. In that place are the demons who injure the life, body, power, and the '*Lung*-horse.' The devil who commands them also lives in the occidental region : he is a white man with the heads of a bird and a monkey, and holds a white hawk on the right and a black demon-rod on the left. Oh! Bird and monkey-headed demon! Accept this ransom and call back all the injuring demons.

"*Kye! Kye!* In the southern horizon is a region of horses, snakes, and fire. The enemy of the fire is the water, etc., etc. O! Rat and pig-headed demon! Accept this ransom and call back all the injuring demons." . . . .

"*Kye! Kye!* In the boundary of the south-eastern horizon is a yellow dragon-headed demon. O! Dragon-headed devil! Accept this ransom and call back all the injuring devils.

"*Kye! Kye!* In the boundary of the south-western horizon is a yellow sheep-headed woman. O! Sheep-headed she-devil! Accept this ransom and call back all the injuring demons.

"*Kye! Kye!* In the boundary of the north-western horizon there is a yellow dog-headed demon. O! Dog-headed devil! Accept this ransom and call back all the injuring demons.

"*Kye! Kye!* In the boundary of the north-eastern horizon there is a yellow bull-headed demoness. O! Bull-headed she-devil! Accept this ransom and all back all the injuring demons!

"O! Upset all the injuring evil spirits, the ill-natured devils, the demons who injure the life, body, power, and the *Lung*-horse, the wandering demons, the ill-luck of bad '*Lung*-horses,' the fearful goblins, the bad omens, the doors of the sky, and the earth, and the injuries of all malignant devils.

"May we be freed from all kinds of injuries and be 'favoured with the real gift, which we earnestly seek!'"

"May virtue increase!'

"GLORY!"

THE "VAST" LUCK-FLAG.
(Reduced ½.)

DOUGH SACRIFICIAL EFFIGIES OF THE TIBETAN BÖN RELIGION.
(Reduced ¼.)

XVI.

WORSHIP AND RITUAL.

WORSHIP and priestcraft had no place in primitive Buddhism. Pious regard for admirable persons, such as Buddha and the elders, and for ancient cities and sacred sites, was limited to mere veneration, and usually took the form of respectful circumambulation (usually three times), with the right hand towards the admired object, as in western ceremonial,[1] and this veneration was extended to the other two members of the Buddhist trinity, namely, Buddha's Word or *Dharma*, and the Assembly of the Faithful.

After Buddha's death such ceremonial, to satisfy the religious sense, seems soon to have crystallized into concrete worship and sacrifice as an act of affection and gratitude towards the Three

---

[1] For instance, as in the Scotch highlands, "to make the *deazil*," or walk thrice in the direction of the sun's course around those whom they wish well (GORDON-CUMING, *From the Hebrides to the Himalayas*, ii., 164). We also follow the same rule in passing decanters round our dinner-tables; and it is the direction in which cattle tread out the corn.—Cf. *Pradakshina*, p. 287

Holy Ones; and it was soon extended so as to include the worship of three other classes of objects, namely (1), Bodily relics (*Ṣarīrika*); (2), Images of Buddha's person, etc. (*Uddesika*); and (3), Vestments, utensils, etc. (*Paribhogika*). And in justification of such worship the southern Buddhists quote the sanction of Buddha himself,[1] though of course without any proof for it.

And we have seen how, in the objective phase of Buddhism, and especially in its Tāntrik development, ritual is elevated to the front rank in importance, and binds the votaries in the bonds of sacerdotalism and idolatry. Even in southern Buddhism there is a good deal of priestcraft. The monks draw out horoscopes, fix auspicious days for weddings, etc., and are sent for in cases of sickness to recite the scriptures, and the *pirit* as a charm against snakes, and evil spirits, and devil dances.[2]

A Lāma Priest.[3]

But in Lāmaism the ritualistic cults are seen in their most developed form, and many of these certainly bear a close resemblance outwardly to those found within the church of Rome, in the pompous services with celibate and tonsured monks and nuns, candles, bells, censers, rosaries, mitres, copes, pastoral crooks, worship of relics, confession, intercession of "the Mother of God," litanies and chants, holy water, triad divinity, organized hierarchy, etc.[4]

It is still uncertain, however, how much of the Lāmaist symbolism may have been borrowed from Roman Catholicism, or

1 Hardy's *East. Mon.*, 216.

2 "After the conclusion of the perahera (in the month of Ehala [July] in the god's temples), the officers, etc., engaged in it, including the elephants, have ceremonies for the conciliation of lesser divinities and evil spirits performed, called Balibat-néṭima, Garáyakun-néṭima, and Waliyakun-néṭima. The Balibat-néṭima is a devil dance performed for five days after the perahera by a class of persons, named *Balibat Gammehela*, superior to the Yakdesso or devil-dancers."—*Report of Service Tenure Commissioners*, Ceylon, 1872, p. 60-82.

3 After Giorgi.

4 Cf. Huc, ii., 50.

vice versâ. Large Christian communities certainly existed in western China, near the borders of Tibet, as early as the seventh century A.D.[1]

Thus has it happened, in a system which acknowledged no Creator, that the monks are in the anomalous position of priests to a host of exacting deities and demons, and hold the keys of hell and heaven, for they have invented the common saying, "without

---

[1] At Si-ngan-fu, near the eastern border of Tibet, is an edict stone, erected by the Chinese emperor Tetsung, 780-783 A.D., which contains an account of the arrival of the missionary Olopan (probably a Chinese form of Rabban-monk) from Tat'sin (Roman empire), in the year equivalent to A.D. 635, bringing sacred books and images; of the translation of the said books; of the imperial approval of the doctrine, and permission to teach it publicly. There follows a decree of the emperor Taitsung, a very famous prince, issued in 638 in favour of the new doctrine, and ordering a church to be built in the square of Peace and Justice at the capital. The emperor's portrait was to be placed in the church (in the royal garden of Inifan). Kaotsung (650-683, the devout patron also of the Buddhist traveller Hiuen Tsiang) continued to favour it.—See YULE in *Marco Polo*, ii., 23, where a photograph of the inscription is given. The edict also states (KIRCHER's *China Illustrata*) that in the years 699 and 713, the Bonzes, or Buddhist idolatrous priests, raised a tumult against the Christians, which was quelled by order of the emperor Yven-Sun-ci-tao.

The Muhammadan traveller, Abu Zeid al Hassan, writing in the ninth century (RENAUDOT's transl., Lond., 1733, p. 42), states that "thousands of Christians" were massacred in *S. W. China*.

In the twelfth century Jenghiz Khan and his successors were well inclined to Christianity; his principal wife was the daughter of king Ung Khan, who was a Christian.

In the thirteenth century Marco Polo found in the north of Yunnan a few Nestorian Christians.—YULE, *M.P.*, ii., 52.

"In 1246," writes Huc (*Chinese Empire*, i., p. 141), "Plan-Carpin was sent to the great Khan of the Tartars by pope Innocent the Fourth. At Khara Khoroum, the capital of the Mongols, he saw, not far from the palace of the sovereign, an edifice on which was a little cross; 'then,' says he, 'I was at the height of joy, and supposing that there must be some Christians there, I entered, and found an altar magnificently adorned; there were representations of the Saviour, the Holy Virgin, and John the Baptist, and a large silver cross, with pearls and other ornaments in the centre: and a lamp with eight jets of light burned before the altar. In the sanctuary was seated an Armenian monk of swarthy complexion, very thin, wearing nothing but a coarse tunic reaching only down to the middle of his leg, and a black mantle fastened with iron clasps.'"

And in 1336 letters reached pope Benedict XII. from several Christian Alans holding high office at the court of Cambaluc, in which they conveyed their urgent request for the nomination of an archbishop in succession to the deceased John of Monte Corvino. John Marignalli says of these Alans that in his day there were 30,000 of them at the great Khan's service, and all at least nominally Christians.—YULE, *M.P.*, ii., 164.

And in the fourteenth century, still before Tsong Khopa's era, not only were missionaries of the Roman Church established in the chief cities of China, but a regular trade was carried on overland between Italy and China by way of Tana, Astracan, Otrar, and Kamul.—YULE's *Marco Polo*, i., 135; Conf. also *The Nestorians and their Rituals*, by Dr. BADGER.

a Lāma in front (of the votary), there is (no approach to) God." And so instilled is such belief in the minds of the laity that no important business is undertaken without first offering worship or sacrifice.

The necessity for offerings at the shrines of the images, etc., is now insisted on in all the forms of Buddhism.

The regular offerings will be detailed presently. But there is no limit to the variety of things that are offered. Wealthy votaries offer art objects, rich tapestries, gold and silver vessels, jewels, and the plunders of war, including weapons. In Burma, some of the earliest knitting and embroidery efforts of young girls are devoted to Buddha's shrine, along with American clocks and chandeliers, tins of jam and English biscuits, sardines, and Birmingham umbrellas. And most of these, and still more incongruous objects, are offered on Lāmaist altars; even eggs are sometimes given.

We have already seen the general form of daily service as practised at Potala and lesser cathedrals and temples, and by isolated monks in hermitage. Here we shall look at some details of particular acts of worship and celebrations.

Personal ablution is enjoined, as a sacerdotal rite preparatory to worship, on the principle of purity of body being emblematic of purity of heart. But this ceremonial purification seldom extends to more than dipping the tips of the fingers in water, and often even not that, for the Tibetans, like most mountaineers, are not remarkable for their love of water or soap.

Before commencing any devotional exercise, the higher Lāmas perform or go through a manœuvre bearing a close resemblance to "crossing oneself," as practised by Christians. The Lāma gently touches his forehead either with the finger or with the bell, uttering the mystic Om, then he touches the top of his chest, uttering Ah, then the epigastrium (pit of stomach), uttering Hūṃ. And some Lāmas add Svā-hā, while others complete the cross by touching the left shoulder, uttering Dam and then Yam. It is alleged that the object of these manipulations is to concentrate the parts of the *Sattva*, namely, the body, speech and mind, upon the image or divinity which he is about to commune with.[1]

[1] The Svāhā, etc., are held to mean knowledge (Yon-ton) and a kind of *Karma* ('p'rin-las), and the five syllables are mystically given the following colours from above downwards: white, red, blue, yellow and green.

In the worship of every Buddhist divinity there are seven recognized stages,[1] evidently framed on a Hindū model.[2] The stages are[3] :—

1. The Invocation—Calling to the feast or sacrifice.
2. Inviting the deity to be seated.
3. Presentation of offerings, sacred cake, rice, water, flowers, incense, lamps, music, and occasionally a *maṇḍala* or magic-circle offering, for which there is a special manual.
4. Hymns in praise.
5. Repetition of the special spell or *mantra*.
6. Prayers for benefits present and to come.
7. Benediction.

Many of the Lāmaist offerings are of the nature of real sacrifice. Some of the objects are destroyed at the time of offering. Ceremonies to propitiate demons are usually done after dark, and the objects are then commonly thrown down "*delibare*." Frequently the sacrifice is given the form of a banquet, and accompanied by games and sacred plays and dances.

What are called "the Essential Offerings or Sacrifice"[4] seem to represent the earlier and purer offerings of Indian Buddhism, and are little more than the fresh-cut flowers and incense which were

---

[1] Tib., Yan-lag-bdun.

[2] In the Hindū worship of a deity there are sixteen stages of ceremonial adoration following on the Invocation to come (*āvāhan*), and the Invitation to be seated (*āṣan*), and in each stage *mantras* are chanted. I have italicized those stages which are found in the above Lāmaist ritual :—

1. *Pādya*, washing the idol's feet.
2. Azgha, washing the idol's hands.
3. Achmana, offering water to rinse mouth.
4. Snāna, bathing the idol.
5. Vastra, dressing the idol. [4 and 5: The Lāmas dress and bathe their idols only once or twice a year.]
6. Chandan, offering sandal wood, saffron, or *holi* powder.
7. Akshat, offering rice.
8. *Pushpa*, offering flowers.
9. *Dhupa*, offering incense.
10. *Dipa*, offering lamp.
11. *Naividya*, offering food.
12. Achmana, second offering of water to rinse mouth.
13. Tāmbula, offering betel.
14. Supāri or puga, offering Areca nuts
15. Dakshana, offering money.
16. Nizājan, waving lights or camphor.

It may also be compared with the Jaina ritual by Dr. J. BURGESS, *Indian Antiquary*, i., 357, etc.

[3] Another enumeration gives : 1, Salutation ; 2, Offering ; 3, Confession of sins (sdig-'s'ags) ; 4, Rejoicing (yid-rangs) ; 5, Exhortation ('skul-wa) ; 6, Prayers for temporal and other blessings (gsol-gdeb) ; 7, Prayers for spiritual blessing (bṣṅo-ba).

[4] Ner-spyod mch'od-pa.

customary offerings even in the seventh century, at the time of Hiuen Tsiang. These offerings are set upon the altar already described, before the image worshipped, accompanied by the rhythmic recital of incantations and music.

These "essential" or necessary offerings, which are needed

DOUGH SACRIFICIAL EFFIGIES of the Lāmas.

in every service of worship, are seven in number, and each bears a special Sanskritic name descriptive of its nature,[1] and must be

[1] 1. *Ar-gham* (in Tibetan *cŏ-yŏn*), or excellent drinking river water.
2. *Pā dyam* (Tib., *zāb-sel**), or the cool water for washing feet.
3. *Pukh-pe* (Tib., *me-tok†*), flower.
4. *Dhu-pe* (Tib., *du-pŏ*), incense fumes.
5. *A-loke* (Tib., *snaṅ-gsal‡*), lamp.
6. *Gan-dhe* (Tib., *ti-chab*), perfumed water for anointing body.
7. *Nai-vi-dya* (Tib., *zāl-zé‖*), sacred food.
8. *Shabta* (Tib., *rol-mo§*), cymbals.

This order is reversed in established church and *Kar-gyu-pa* temples when doing a certain kind of tutelary deity's worship. The Lāmaist account of the history of these offerings, is that each was offered to Buddha by some celestial or other person, namely :—

Ar-gham.—Indra, the king of gods, offered this, the water of eight-fold virtues, to the Buddha for general use.

Pā dyam.—gTsug-na-rin-ch'en, the king of the Nāgas, offered *z'abs-gsil*, the purifying water, to the Buddha for washing his feet.

Pukh-pé.—Ganga Devi, the fiendess, offered a flower-rosary to the Buddha for decorating his head.

Dhu-pé.—"The glorious Kheu," the incense-seller, offered sweet-smelling incense to the Buddha.

A-loké.—The gold-handed king offered the darkness-clearing light for invigorating his eyes.

* mch'od yon. † z'abș g-sil. ‡ dug-spoș. ‖ dri-ch'ab. § zal-zaș.

placed in the bowls already described,[1] and in line in the above order. In the third and fourth bowls on the top of the rice heaps should be placed respectively a flower[2] and a stick of incense; and in the sixth bowl should be placed perfumed water; and lastly a cake, into which have been incorporated a few filings of the precious metals[3]; but these details are only observed on special occasions. Ordinarily all of the bowls are filled with plain water. On placing the above offerings in position in the order noted, the benefit of a full service of worship is obtained by merely chanting the following hymn :—

A-va-tā-ya, A-va-tā-ya. Om vajra! Argham, Pā-dyam, Pūkh-pe, Dhū-pe, A-loke, Gan-dhe, Nāi-vi-dya, Shab-ta, Prāti-dsa-yī Swāhā! Which being interpreted is: "Come! Come! Om! The Thunderbolt! Partake of these offerings: Excellent river water for drinking, cool water for washing your feet, flowers for decking your hair, pleasing incense fumes, lamps for lighting the darkness, perfumed water for anointing your body, sacred food, the music of cymbals! (here the cymbals are sounded). Eat fully! *Swāhā!*"

But the high-church Lāma, or Ge-lug-pa monk, must chant a longer service, which is noted below.[4]

Gan-dhé.—Zur-phud-lnga-pa, the King of Gandarvas, offered *Dri-ch'al*, the soothing scent, to the Buddha for refreshing his body.

Nai-wi-dya.—Mgön-Anātha-med-dānu athara data zas-sbyin (the lordless+food+give) the house-owner, offered the food of hundred tastes to the Buddha for supporting his health.

Shapta.—The divine and Nāga-smiths offered *Gsil-snyan*, the pleasant music, to the Buddha for cheering his ears. The Buddha blessed each of the offerings, and since then they are considered sacred.

[1] See p. 297.

[2] The flowers most commonly used for this purpose at Lhāsa and sold in booths near the temples, are the common marigold (*Calendula*—Tib., gur-Kum me-tog), and white and blue asters (skal-bzaṅ), and hollyhocks.

[3] See annexed figure for the block containing these metals (named Rin-ch'en brdar-ru, [or p'yema]); the metals are usually gold, silver, copper, brass and iron.

[4] *Namo ratnatrayaya! Namo Bhagawate vajra sara foramardu Tathagataya arhate samayagasa budhhaya! Tadyatha! Om Vajra Vagra! Mahabodhitsattva Vajre! Mahabodhimandop asam Kramana Vajra! Sarbo karma awarana bigodhana vajra swāhā!* This mantra invites all the Jinas and their (celestial) sons). *Om! Namo bhagawate puhpe ketu rajaya! Tathagataya! Arhate samayaka san Budhaya! Tadyatha! Om! puhpe puhpe swāhā! puhpesu puhpesu puhpesudbhawe! puhpe awakarane swāhā!* This should be repeated seven times, after which the magic-circle and food grains should be offered. When the lamp is offered, the following should be repeated :—

"I arrange this lamp with great reverence, and offer it to the Buddha, the Law, and

It is customary for every votary on special occasions to offer one hundred and eight lamps, together with an equal number of

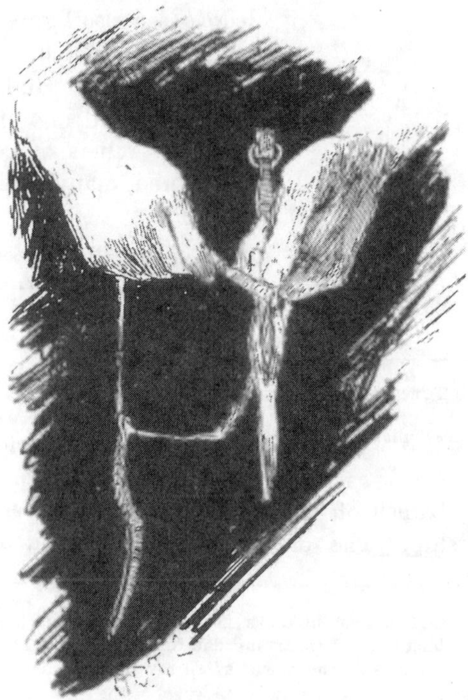

FILING THE FIVE PRECIOUS METALS
for the sacrifice.

vessels of rice and of cake. These are placed in four rows, the

---

the Order. Through the power of this virtuous deed, let me be possessed of illuminating knowledge, and let the animal beings be cleared of the misty impurities which surrounds them."

Then he must rise up, and joining his hands in devotional attitude, chant "The Invitation":—

"I beg you O Patrons of the animal beings! Demon-vanquishing gods! Jinas and your retinues! to approach this humble dwelling. I beg you, merciful owners of miracles, to approach this humble dwelling and receive these offerings."

[Then holding hands horizontally, bow down and say:—] "I bow down before the Lāmas of the three times and of the ten directions, and before the precious Three Holy Ones with greatest reverence and oceans of praise." *Om! Namo Mañjuṣriye! Namassce Shriye! Namo uttamshriyesloaha!* [bow down at once at each recitation of this *mantra*].

The Presentation of offerings: "I here offer up all the most excellent offerings of

order of which from before backwards is rice, water, lamps, and cakes. And for the great demoniacal tutelary's service extra cakes used on a separate altar with five ledges (see also figure on page 299), on each of which are set a series of one hundred and eight of the offerings noted, and on special feasts great bas reliefs of coloured butter are offered, many of them of artistic designs.[1]

OFFERINGS TO TUTELARY-FIEND.

1. Great cake.
2. Wine or blood in a skull.
3. Rice.
4. Cake.
5. Butter.
6. Lamps.

A still more elaborate arrangement of food-offerings is seen in the banquet to the whole assembly of the gods and the demons, entitled Kön-ch'og - chī - dü, or "sacrifice, to the whole assembly of Rare Ones," which is frequently held in the temples. This feast is observed by Lāmas of all sects, and is an interesting sample of devil-worship. The old fashion is here detailed, but it

holy drinking water, foot-washing water, flowers, incense, lamp, scented toilet water, food and music, which I have here arranged in full, to you with all my heart.

"I confess all my past sins and repent of all my sinful deeds. I beg you to bless me with mahabodhi, so that I may turn the wheel of the Law and be useful to all the animal beings.

"I have here arranged the flowers on the pure soil of incense, and the Mt. Meru, decked with sun, moon, and the four continents, all of which I offer up to the Buddhas with my whole heart.

"May all the animal beings be blessed with perfection and purity, and be born in brighter regions. *Idam Guru ratna mandala kam niryata yami!* [Then offer up the magic-circle in suitable manner, for description of which see previous chapter, and continue.]

"May my Lāma, tutelary deity and the Holy Ones, and the potent Mahā-Vajradhāra remain inseparably with the Kumuda flower.

"May all the animal beings be freed from re-births by being born into the pure regions.

"May I be endowed with firm resolve and ability to rescue animal beings from the worlds of woe.

"May I be endowed with an unfailing ocean of knowledge to enable me to advance the holy religion among both orthodox and heterodox.

"May my misty ignorance be cleared by the bright rays of Mañjuṣrī from on high.

"May my desires be all realized through the grace of the Jinas and their celestial sons, and the auspicious breath of the Supreme Ones.

[1] Cf. HUC, ii., 42; ROCKHILL, *L.*, 70.

differs from that of the reformed or high church only in providing for a slightly larger party of demoniacal guests; the Ge-lug-pa inviting only the following, to wit, their chief Lāma, St. Tsoṅ-

ARRANGEMENT OF
THE BANQUET TO THE WHOLE ASSEMBLY OF THE GODS AND DEMONS.

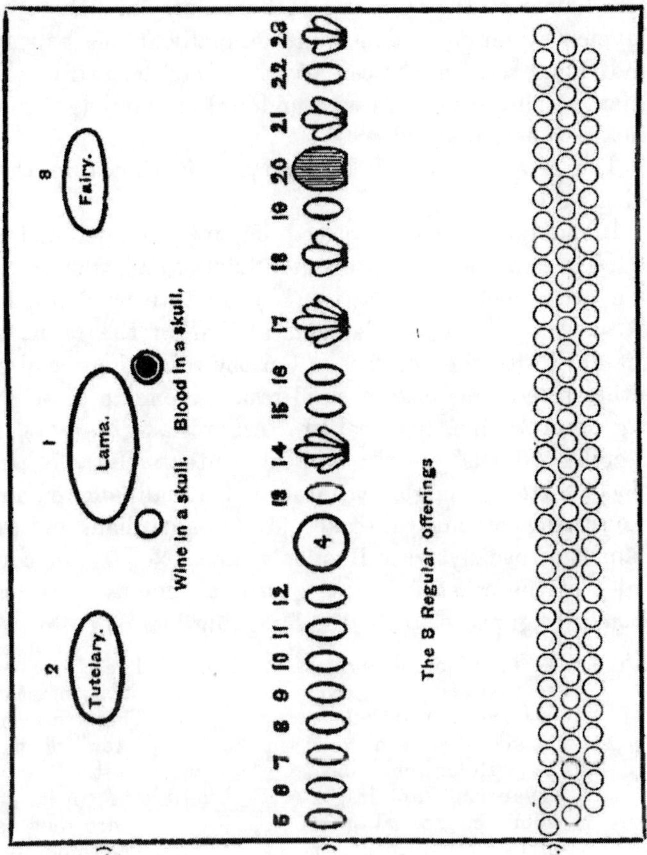

K'a-pa, their tutelary deity Vajra-bhairava, Vajrasattva Buddha, the deified heroes, the fairies, the guardian demons of the Ge-lug-pa creed, the god of wealth, the guardian demons of the caves where the undiscovered revelations are deposited, the five sister sprites of mount Everest, the twelve aërial fiendesses (Tän-ma), who sow disease, and the more important local gods.

This sacrifice should be done in the temples for the benefit of the Lāmas on the 10th and 15th of every month. On behalf of laymen it must be done *once* annually at the expense of every individual layman who can afford it; and on extra occasions, as a thanksgiving for a successful undertaking, and as a propitiation in sickness, death, and disaster.

The arrangement of the banquet is shown in the foregoing diagram :—

In the inmost row are placed the large coloured and ornamented *Baling* cakes for (*a*) the chief Lāma-saint, who in the case of the old school is *St. Padma*, (*b*) the tutelary deity, in this case *Guru tak-po*, a fierce demoniacal form of the saint, and (*c*) the she-devil with the lion-face. For the saint there is also placed on either side of his cake a skull-cap, the one to his right containing country wine, here called "Ambrosia" (*amrita*), in Tibetan literally "devils' juice"; and the contents of the other are called blood (*rakta*), though tea-infusion is usually offered instead. In the second row are the cakes for the guardians and protector of Lāmaism, usually with Buddha's cake (No. 4) in centre. The order of the cakes for these guardian demons is as follows—the attached figures relate to the foregoing diagram :—

No. 5. The Lion-faced demoness.
,, 6. The four-armed "Lord," a form of Mahākāla.
,, 7. The god of wealth.
,, 8. The "Ruler of Tibet's guardian" (and in Sikhim the special guardian of the *Ña-dukpa* monasteries).
,, 9. The demon blacksmith (red and black colour, rides a goat and carries an anvil and a bellows, was made a protector of Lāmaism by St. Padma).
,, 10. The Lord of the Rākshas devils.
,, 11. The Locality protector.
,, 12. The *Nāga* demi-gods, white and black.
No. 13. The Nun-fiendess of Dikung monastery.
,, 14. The five everlasting sisters of mount Everest.
,, 15. The spirits of the tank-drowned persons.
,, 16. The homestead demon-owner.
,, 17. The country-god Kang-chen-dsönga (mountain).
,, 18. The black devil, red devil and *Nāga* of Darjiling or special locality of temple.
,, 19. The demons who cause disease.
,, 20. The twelve aërial fiendesses of disease (*Tän-ma*)

No. 21. The demon owners of the "Ter" caves where the hidden revelations are deposited.	No. 22. The black and red devils and *Nāga* of parent monastery of the priests of this temple.

In the third row are placed the "essential offerings" already described, which are especially intended for the superior gods.

In the fourth and outmost row are an indefinite number of *T'sog*-cakes, which are especial dainties as an extra course for all. These cakes contain ordinary *torma* cake of cooked rice or barley, with the addition of some wine, and a mixture of cooked flesh and all sorts of eatables available.

The stages of the worship in this feast are as follows:—

1st. Invitation to the deities and demons to come to the feast (Skt., *āvāhan*). This is accompanied by great clamour of drums, cymbals, horns and fifes, so as to attract the attention of the gods and demons.

2nd. Requesting the guests to be seated (Skt., *āsan*).

3rd. Begging them to partake of the food offered.

4th. Praises the goodness and admirable qualities of the guests. This is done while the guests are partaking of the essence of the food.

5th. Prayers for favours immediate and to come.

6th. The especial delicacy, the *T'sog*-cake, is then offered to all, on four plates, a plate for each row of guests, and one plateful is reserved for the Lāmas themselves.

Then is done the ceremony of "Expiation for religious duties left undone,"[1] which wipes off all arrears of religious duty. Here the sacristan throws skywards, amid great clamour of wind and brass instruments, several of the *T'sog*-cakes to all the demi-gods and demons not specially included in the feast. One *T'sog*-cake is then given to each Lāma in the order of his rank, from the highest to the lowest, as the food has been consecrated by the gods having partaken of it.

Each Lāma must, however, leave a portion, which is collected carefully, in a plate, in order, from the lowest to the head Lāma. And on the top of these collected fragments is placed a whole cake. Then a celebration called *Lhak-dor* is done, and the whole of these crumbs—the leavings of the Lāmas—are contemptuously thrown down on to the ground, outside the temple-door to the

[1] bsKaṅ-gso.

starveling ghosts and those evil-spirits who have not yet been subjected by St. Padma or subsequent Lāmas.

The efficacy of these cake-offerings is urged at length in the manual of the established church.[1]

The special rites and celebrations are usually detailed in separate manuals; but each Ge-lug-pa monk has a general manual of worship, etc., entitled "the monk's timely Memoranda,"[2] and seems to correspond in some measure to the Dina Chariyāwa of the Ceylonese,[3] in which are given directions for personal and general devotions as well as for monastic conduct, from which I have already made extracts in the chapter on the order.

The service is mostly in Tibetan, which is like the Latin of the papal mass-books used throughout Mongolia and Lāmaist temples in China, the only exception being the privileged temple at Pekin.[4] Music is much used, though it is in the main an ear-piercing din of drums, loud trumpets, horns, and clashing cymbals.

The leaders of the choir also have a psalter or score in which the swelling, rising, and falling notes are curiously represented by curves, as shown in the annexed photograph; and the points at which the several instruments join in the choir are also duly noted therein. The pauses are marked by bells and cymbals, and the effect at times of the noisy din and clamour suddenly lapsing into silence is most solemn, and even impressive in the larger cathedrals with their pious and sombre surroundings.[5]

---

1 The Ge-lug-pa manual says:—

The advantages to the chanter of the above service are that: His wishes will be all realized; wealth and luck will increase according to his wishes; he will obtain power, and all his sins will be blotted out; he will subject the evil spirits and will duly perform charity, and the *preta* will obtain deliverance by being re-born in the heavens, and he himself will also obtain heaven, and it has been said that he will ultimately obtain Buddhahood.

The burnt-offering of incense, analogous to the Vedic *Homa*, but specially intended for demons, includes by name the Tän-ma and other Tibetan fiends. It is a mixture of incense and butter heated to ignition on coals. The celebration is detailed above. Cf. also Schlag., p. 249; Jaesch., p. 210, for kinds of cakes.

2 dGe-slon-gi dus dran.

3 *East Mon.*, 24, and also "the Daily Manual of the Shaman" of the Chinese. Beal's *Catena*, 239.

4 Cf. Köppen, ii., 228.

5 Although the instruments are wielded with great clamour, each is manipulated strictly according to rule. Thus with the cymbals, at the word *Argham* the cymbals are held horizontally and struck with mid-finger erect. On *Pargham*, held below waist and the upper cymbal is made to revolve along the rim of the lowest, etc., etc.

LÁMA'S MUSICAL SCORE.

The daily celebrations of the high church monk, or the Ge-lug-pa Lāma, comprise the following services :—

1. The "Refuge-formula" (mT'un-moṅ).
2. mT'uṅ-moṅ ma-yiṅ-pa.
3. The four-fold prayer for the Animals (Sems-bskyed).
4. Another prayer for Animals (K'yad-par gyi smes-bskyed).
5. Prayer for the Earth (Sa-gz'i byin brlabs).
6. Sacrificial offerings (mCh'od-pa byin brlabs).
7. Invocation to the Jinas (Spyan-'dren).
8. Offering of bathing water to the Gods and Jinas (K'rus-gsol. "*Tui-Sol*).")
9. Salutation to Buddhas, Saints and Lāmas (P'yag-'t'sal).
10. Offerings of "the necessary things" (mCh'od-pa).
11. Offerings of "five sensuous things" ('Dod-yon-lṅa).
12. Offerings of "seven precious things" (rgyal-sri sna bdun).
13. Confession of Sins (bS'ag*s*-pa).
14. In praise of the Jinas and Buddha-putras (rJes-su yi-raṅ*s*).
15. Turning the Wheel of the Law (Ch'os-'k'or bskor-wa).
16. Prayer for attaining Nirvāṇa (Mya-ṅan las-mi 'das was gsol-wa 'debs-pa).
17. Prayer for Blessing (bsṅo-wa).
18 Magic-circle—Offering of the Universe.
19. Prayer to Lāma-tutor.[1]
20. The Tutelary's invocation—Yamāntaka, etc. (for Ge-lug-pa) and Guru Tak-po Kah-gye, etc., for Ñiṅ-ma.
21. Sacrificial worship (ch'oga) to the demons, after dark with cake (torma), incense and wine with the libations (gSer-skyems) the Kang-sô banquet.[2]

We will illustrate a few of these services by some abstracts and extracts :—

A good sample of the worship of a Lāmaist divinity is seen in that of Tārā, the Virgin of northern Buddhism, and the "Goddess of Mercy."

The manual of Tārā's worship[3] is one of the commonest booklets in Tibet, and is in the hands of nearly all laymen, most of whom can repeat her hymn and chief service by heart.[4]

[1] La-mai-gsol-'debs. [2] See p. 429.

[3] Abstracted by me in considerable detail in *J.R.A.S.*, 1894, p. 68, etc.

[4] The book is entitled "sGrol-ma dkar sṅon-gyi bstod-pa gzuṅs," or "The praise and spells (*Dhāraṇī*) of The Pure Original Tārā." And in some editions she is termed "Mother of the *Jinas*" (rgyal-yum), also "Mother of the Tathāgathas." The manual extends to thirty-eight or forty pages of five lines each. The greater portion, including "The Exhortation" and "The Hymn," is alleged internally to have been composed by "The great Vairocana-Buddha of the Ultimate Perfection" [dsog,-pai saṅs-rgyas rnam

Tārā's Worship.

Tārā's worship, like that of most of the Mahāyāna and Tāntrik deities, is divided into the seven stages already mentioned.

The service is chanted in chorus, and the measure used in chanting the hymn, namely trochaic in eight-syllabled lines, I have indicated in a footnote to the hymn.

A portion of the manual is here translated—

"If we worship this sublime and pure-souled goddess when we retire in the dusk and arise in the morning, then all our fears and worldly anxieties will disappear and our sins be forgiven. She—the conqueror of myriad hosts—will strengthen us. She will do more than this! She will convey us directly to the end of our transmigration—to Buddha and Nirvāṇa!

"She will expel the direst poisons, and relieve us from all anxieties as to food and drink, and all our wants will be satisfied; and all devils and plagues and poisons will be annihilated utterly; and the burden of all animals will be lightened! If you chant her hymn two or three or six or seven times, your desire for a son will be realized! Or should you wish wealth, you will obtain it, and all other wishes will be gratified, and every sort of demon will be wholly overcome."

Invocation.

"Hail! O! verdant Tārā!
The Saviour of all beings!
Descend, we pray Thee, from Thy heavenly mansion, at Potala,
Together with all Thy retinue of gods, titans, and deliverers!
We humbly prostrate ourselves at Thy lotus-feet!
Deliver us from all distress! O holy Mother!"

Presentation of Offerings (Sacrificial).

"We hail Thee! O rever'd and sublime Tārā!
Who art adored by all the kings and princes
Of the ten directions and of the present, past and future.

par snaṅ-mdsad ch'en-po] and usually interpreted by the Lāmas as referring to Vairochana, the first of the mythical Jina-Buddhas; but it may probably be the Kashmīr Monk Vairocana, of the "Great Ultimate Perfection (*Maha-utpanna*)" form of the Buddhist doctrine, who lived in the eighth century A.D., and a noted translator of Sanskrit Scriptures into the Tibetan. An appendix is signed by Gedun Ḍub, The Grand Lāma, who built Tashi-lhunpo monastery *circâ* 1445 A.D.

We pray Thee to accept these offerings
Of flowers, incense, perfumed lamps,
Precious food, the music of cymbals,
And the other offerings!
We sincerely beg Thee in all Thy divine Forms [1]
To partake of the food now offered!
On confessing to Thee penitently their sins
The most sinful hearts, yea! even the committers of the
Ten vices and the five boundless sins,
Will obtain forgiveness and reach
Perfection of soul—through Thee!
If we (human beings) have amassed any merit
In the three states,[2]
We rejoice in this good fortune, when we consider
The unfortunate lot of the poor (lower) animals
Piteously engulphed in the ocean of misery.
On their behalf, we now turn the wheel of religion!
We implore Thee by whatever merit we have accumulated
To kindly regard all the animals.
And for ourselves!
When our merit has reached perfection
Let us not, we pray Thee,
Linger longer in this world!"

HYMNS IN TĀRĀ'S PRAISE.[3]

(The translation I have made almost literal. Each separate stanza is addressed to a special one of Tārā's twenty-one forms—the name of which is given in the margin for reference.)

(Tārā, the Mother.) Ārya Tārā! Hail to Thee!
Our Deliveress sublime!

---

[1] The polymorphism already referred to.
[2] Kāma, Rūpa, and Arupa.
[3] As this hymn is so popular amongst Lāmaist people in Tibet, Sikhim, etc., I give here in the Lhāsa dialect its second stanza, which is the proper commencement of the hymn, in order to show its metre.

Ch'ag ts'al | Ḍö-ma | ñur-ma | pa-mô |
Ch'en-ni | ké-c'ig | log-taṅ | ṭa-ma |
Jig-ten | sum gön | c'u kyé | z'al-gyi |
Ke-sar | c'e-wa | le-ni | juṅ-ma | .

Avalok'ta's messenger
Rich in power and pity's store.

(1. Tārā, the Supremely Courageous.)

Hail O Tārā! quick to Save!
Lotus-born of pitying tear
Shed down by The Three-World-Lord,
(Grieving sad for sunken souls.)

(2. Tārā, of White-moon Brightness.)

Hail! to Thee with fulgent face,
Brilliant as a hundred moons
Of harvest gleaming in the light
Of myriad dazzling stars.

(3. Tārā, the Golden-Coloured.)

Hail! to Thee whose hand is decked
By the lotus, golden blue.
Eager Soother of our woe,
Ever tireless worker, Thou!

(4. Tārā, the Grand Hair-piled.)

Hail! to Thee with pil'd-up hair,
Where Tathāgata sits shrin'd,
Victor[1] of the universe.
Thou a saintly victor too!

(5. Tārā, the "*Huṅ*" Shouter.)

Hail to thy "*tut-tārā-huṅ*,"[2]
Piercing realms of earth and sky,
Treading down the seven worlds,
Bending prostrate everyone!

(6. Tārā, the best Three-World Worker.)

Hail! adored by mighty gods,
Indra, *Brāhma*, Fire and Wind,
Ghostly hordes and *Gandharvas*
Al unite in praising Thee!

(7. Tārā, the Suppressor of Strife.)

Hail! with Thy dread "*tre*" and "*phat*"[3]
Thou destroyest all Thy foes:
Striding out with Thy left foot
Belching forth devouring fire!

8. Tārā, the Bestower of Supreme Power.)

Hail! with fearful spell "*tu-re*"
Banishing the bravest fiends,
By the mere frown of Thy brows,
Vanquishing whole hordes of foes!
etc., etc., etc., etc.

---

[1] rgyal-wa = Sanskrit *Jina*.
[2] This is a portion of Tārā's spell, for which see over page.
[3] Mystic spells used by wizards—*phat* means break or smash!

TELLING THE ROSARY.

[Here is repeated on the rosary 108 times, or as often as possible, the spell or *mantra* of Tārā, namely: *Om! Tā-re-tu-tā-re tu-re Svā hā!*

The *mantra* of Sīta Tārā is *Om! Tā-re tu-tā-re ma-ma ā-yur-pun-ye jna-na-push-tin ku-ru Svā-hā!*

The rosary used in Sīta Tārā's worship is a *Bodhitse*, while Tārā requires either a *Bodhitse* or turquoise one.[1]]

PRAYERS FOR BLESSINGS.

We implore thee, O! Revered Victorious *Bhagavāti*[2] and Merciful One! to purify us and all other beings of the universe thoroughly from the two evil thoughts; and make us quickly attain the perfection of Buddhahood. If we cannot attain this perfection within a few life cycles, then grant us the highest earthly and heavenly happiness and all knowledge. And preserve us, we beseech Thee, from evil spirits, plague, disease, untimely death, bad dreams, bad omens, and all the eight fears and accidents. And in our passage through this world grant unto us the most perfect bliss, beyond possibility of increase, and may all our desires be realized without exertion on our part.

Let the holy religion prosper. And in whatever place we dwell, we beg thee to soothe there disease and poverty, fighting and disputes, and increase the Holy Religion.

And may Thy benign[3] face always beam on us and appear large like the waxing moon in forwarding our heart's desire of admission to the heavenly circle and *Nirvāṇa*.

Let us obtain the favourite gods[4] of our former lives and entry into the prophesied paradise of the Buddhas of the past, present and future!

BENEDICTION.

Now! O! Thou! The Great Worker!
Thou Quick Soother and Gracious Mother,
Holding the *uptal* flower!
Let Thy glory come. *Maṅgalam!*[5]

The offering of the universe as a so-called "magic-circle" is an essential part of the daily service of the Lāmas, and has been described in the previous chapter.

The following hymn in praise of the Three Holy Ones is recited at noon with the presentation of the offering of rice.

---

[1] But see page 206 for details on "Lāmaist Rosaries."
[2] bc'om-ldan-'das-ma, pronounced "chom-den-dé-ma."
[3] In contradistinction to "fury-face" (khro-bo; Skt. *krodha*).
[4] sGrub-bahi-lha.
[5] bgra-shis shok, pronounced "*Tā-shi-sho.*"

Hymn to the Three Holy Ones.

OM! Salutation to the Omniscient Ones! Buddha, The Law and The Church!

Salutation to Buddha Bhagavān, the Victorious and All-wise Tathāgata Arhat, who has gone to happiness!

He is the guide of gods and men!
He is the root of virtue.
He is the fountain of all treasure.
He is adorned with perfect endurance.
He is adorned with all-beauty.
He is the greatest flower of all the race.
He is admirable in all his actions.
He is admirable in the eyes of all.
He delights in the faithful ones.
He is The Almighty Power.
He is The Universal Guide.
He is The Father of all the Bodhisats.
He is The King of all the revered Ones.
He is The Leader of all the dead.
He owns infinite knowledge.
He owns immeasurable fortitude.
His commands are all-perfect.
His melodious voice is all-pleasing.
He is without equal.
He is without desires.
He is without evil.
He delivers all from sorrow.
He delivers all from sin.
He is free from worldliness.
His senses are the sharpest.
He bravely cuts all knots.
He delivers all from deepest misery.
He delivers all from this woeful world.
He has crossed the ocean of misery.
He is perfect in fore-knowledge.
He knows the past, present and future.
He lives far from death.
He lives in the pure blissful land where, enthroned, he sees all beings!

Salutation to the Holy Law!—(*Dharma*)

It was the virtue of the ancient times.
It was the virtue of the middle ages.
It is the virtue of the present hour.
It has excellent sense.
It has excellent words.
It is unalloyed Law.
It is all-perfect and illuminating.
It is the all-pure Law.
It is perfectly clear.
It is free from disorder.
It is everlasting.
It points the direct path.
It realizes the desires of all.
It benefits the wisest men.

The Law has been well ordered and taught in the *Vinaya* by Bhagavān. It brings all to perfection! It fulfils all desires! It is an all-sufficient support, and it stops re-birth.

Salutation to The Assembly or Clergy (*Saṅgha*) of the Mahāyāna!

They live in peace.
They live in wisdom.
They live in truth.
They live in unison.
They merit respect.
They merit glory.
They merit the grandest gifts.

The goodness of Buddha is immeasurable!
The goodness of The Law is immeasurable!
And the goodness of The Clergy is immeasurable!
By planting our faith on The Immeasurable Ones we shall reap immeasurable fruit in the land of bliss.

Salutation to the Tathāgata! The Merciful Patron, the omniscient Guide, the ocean of knowledge and glory.

Salutation to the softening *Dharma!* the pure gift of the heart, the deliverer from evil, and the best of Truth.

Salutation to the Assembly! the deliverer, and guide to the true faith, the teacher of pure wisdom, and the possessor of the holy knowledge for cultivating the (human) soil.

THE "REFUGE-FORMULA" OF THE LĀMAS.

The "Refuge-formula" of the Lāmas, which I here translate, well illustrates the very depraved form of Buddhism professed by the majority of Lāmas; for here we find that the original *triple* Refuge-formula (Skt., *Triṣaraṇa;* Pāli, *Ṣaraṇagamana*) in the Three Holies, the *Triratna*—Buddha, The Word, and The Assembly—has been extended so as to comprise the vast host of deities, demons and deified saints of Tibet, as well as many of the Indian Mahāyāna and Yogācārya saints.

The version here translated is that used by the Kar-ma-pa and Ñiṅ-ma sects of Lāmas, but it is practically the same as that in general use in Tibet, except among the reformed Lāmas of the established church—who address a less extensive circle of saints and demons, and who substitute St. Tsoṅ-K'a-pa for St. Padmasambhava. It is extracted from the manual of worship entitled the sKyabs-'gro, commonly pronounced "Kyamdô,"[1] which literally means "the going for protection or refuge"; and its text is as follows:—

"We—all beings—through the intercession of the Lāma,[2] go for refuge to Buddha!

"We go for refuge to Buddha's Doctrine (*Dharma*)!

"We go for refuge to the Assembly of the Lāmas (*Sangha*)![3]

"We go for refuge to the Host of the Gods and their retinue of tutelaries and she-devils, the defenders of the Religion, who people the sky!

---

[1] Contributed to *Ind. Antiq.* 1893.

[2] It is a Lāmaist axiom, as already noted, that no layman can address the Buddhas except through the medium of a Lāma.

[3] The Ge-lug-pa formula begins thus: bdag sogs nam-mkah daṅ mñams-paī sems-c'ạn t'ams-c'ad bLa-ma la skyabs su mch'io, Saṅs-rgyas-kyi skyabs-su mch'io Ch'os-kyi skyabs su mch'io, dGe-'dun-gyi skyabs su-mch'io.

"We go for refuge to the victorious Lāmas, who have descended from heaven, the holders of Wisdom and the Tāntras!

"We go for refuge to the Buddhas of the Ten Directions, and to the primordial *Samantabhadra.* Buddha with his spouse!"

Then the following deities and saints are addressed as refuges: The Incarnate Saṁbhoga-kāya, the Mild and Angry Loving One the *Nirmāṇa-kāya Mahā Vajradhara;* the Diamond-souled Guide—*Vajrasatva;* the Jina—the Victorious *Śākya Muni;* the most pleasing Vajra Incarnate; the Fierce Holder of the Thunderbolt—*Vajrapāṇi;* the Goddess-Mother, *Marīcī Devi;* the Learned Teacher, *Acārya-Mañjuśrī;* the Great *Paṇḍita Śrī Siṅha;* the *Jina Suda;* the Great *Paṇḍita Bimala Mitra;* the Incarnate Lotus-born Dharmakāya *Padmasambhava;* (his wife) the Fairy of the Ocean of Fore-knowledge; the Religious King, Thi-Sroṅ-deu-Tsan; the Noble Apocalypse-Finder, Myaṅ-ban; the Teacher's disciple, the Victorious *Sthavira* Dang-ma; the Reverend Sister, the Lady *Siṅheṣwara;* the Incarnate Jina "Zhang-tön"; the Guru, clever above thousands; the Religious Lord (*Dharma-nātha*) *Guru Jo-Ber;* the Illusive Lion *Gyāba;* the Great Siddhi, the Clearer of the Misty moon—grub-ch'en zla-wa-mün-sel; the Sage *Kumaraja;* the Prince, *Bimāla Bhāskara;* the renowned *Candrakīrti;* the Three Incarnate Kind Brothers; the Bodhisat, The noble Ocean; the Incarnate Sage, the Holder of the religious *vajra;* the Entirely accomplished and renowned Speaker; the Great Teacher *Mahāguru Dharmarāja;* the Revelation-Finder *T'ig-po-liṅ;* the Religious King of Accomplished Knowledge[1]; the Banner of Obtained Wisdom; the Peerless active *Vajra;* the Radical (Skt., *Mūla*) Lāma Aṣoka;[2] the Lāma of the *Mūla Tantra* of the Three Times; the Sage, the Accomplished Soul; the Religious Loving King, the Holder of the Doctrines[3]; the Reverend Abbot, the Sky *Vajra;* the Noble Jewelled Soul—"Pal-zaṅ"; the Assembly of Mild and Angry tutelary Deities; the Holy Doctrine of the Great End—*Mahotpanna!*

"We go for refuge to the Male and Female Saints of the Country!

"O! Lāma! Bless us as You have been blessed. Bless us with the blessings of the *Tāntras!*—

"We beg You to bless us with OM, which is the (secret) Body. We beg You to purify our sins and pollutions of the body. We beg You to increase our happiness without any sickness of the body. We beg You to give us the real undying gift of bodily life!

"We beg You to bless us with AH, which is the (secret of the) Speech. We beg You to purify the sins and pollution of our Speech.

---

1 The first Bhotiya king of Sikhim, *circ.* 1650 A.D.

2 This may be a reference to the great emperor Aṣoka, or his confessor Upagupta, the fourth patriarch of the early Buddhist church in India, or it may be only the title of a Lāma. Several also of the foregoing titles which I have translated are proper names.

3 The sixth Bhotiya king of Sikhim, *circ.* 1770-90 A.D.

We beg You to give us the power of Speech. We beg You to confer on us the gift of perfect and victorious Speech!

"We beg You to bless us with HŪṂ (pronounced "*hūṃ*") which is the (secret) THOUGHT. We beg You to purify the pollution and sins of our Mind. We beg You to give us good understanding. We beg you to give us the real gift of a pure heart. We beg You to empower us with The Four Powers (of the heart)!

"We pray You to give us the gifts of the True *Body*, *Speech*, and *Mind*.[1] OṂ! AH! HŪṂ!

"O! Give us such blessing as will clear away the sins and defilement of bad deeds!

"We beg You to soften the evils of bad causes!

"We beg You to bless us with the prosperity of our body (*i.e.*, health)!

"Bless us with mental guidance!

"Bless us with Buddhahood soon!

"Bless us by cutting us off from (worldly) illusions!

"Bless us by putting us in the right path!

"Bless us by causing us to understand all things (religious)!

"Bless us to be useful to each other with kindliness!

"Bless us with the ability of doing good and delivering the animal beings (from misery)!

"Bless us to know ourselves thoroughly!

"Bless us to be mild from the depths of our heart!

"Bless us to be brave as Yourself!

"Bless us with the *Tāntras* as You Yourself are blessed!"

"Now! we—the innumerable animal beings—conceiving that (through the efficacy of the above *dharaṇīs* and prayers, we have become pure in thought like Buddha himself; and that we are working for the welfare of the other animal beings; we, therefore, having now acquired the qualities of the host of the Gods, and the roots of the *Tāntras*, the *Z'i-wa*, *rGyas-pa*, *dBaṅ* and *P'rin-las*, we desire that all the other animal beings be possessed of happiness, and be freed from misery! Let us—all animals!—be freed from lust, anger, and attachment to worldly affairs, and let us perfectly understand the true nature of The Religion!

"Now! O! Father-Mother—*Yab-yum*—the *Dharmakāya Samantabhadra!* The *Sambhogakāya Ṣānti Khrôdaprasaraka*, mild and angry Loving Ones! The *Nirmāṇa-kāya*, Sages of the skull-rosary! And the *Mūla-tāntra* Lāma! I now beg You all to depart!

"O! Ghosts of Heroes! Witches! Demoniacal Defenders of The Faith! The holy Guardians of the Commandments! And all those that we invited to this place! I beg You all now to depart!!

"O! most powerful King of the Angry Deities! The powerful *Isvara*, and the host of the Country Guardian Gods! And all those

[1] This triad refers to the mystic Yoga or union of "The three secrets," which the Japanese call, San-mitsu-sō-ō.

others that we invited to this place, with all their retinue! I beg You all now to depart!!! May glory come! *Tashi-shok!* and Virtue! *Ge-o! Sarva-maṅgalam!*"

Confession of Sins.

The Confession of Sins[1] is done twice a month in public assembly, in presence of the abbot and senior monks. It is no proper confession, only a stereotyped form chanted in chorus. The full form is practically the same as in southern Buddhism.[2] The shortest form is here given :—

"I here confess the sins which I may have committed by the body, speech and mind, and through lust, anger and stupidity.

"Listen to me, O! great *Vajra*-holding Lāmas[3] and all the Buddhas and Bodhisats of the ten directions! I repent of all the sinful acts which I have committed from the time of my birth up to the present, such as: committing the ten unvirtuous deeds and the five waverings, transgressing the vows of deliverance, the teachings of the Bodhisats, the vows of the secret *mantras*, irreverence, and want of faith in The Three Rarest Ones, irreverence and want of faith in the abbots and teachers; separation from the holy religion and the best commands; want of reverence to the revered clergy; want of reverence to parents, and want of reverence to one's faithful fellow-mortals. In short, I here confess to all the *Vajra*-holding Lāmas, the Buddhas and Bodhisats of the ten directions, all the sins which hinder my reaching the heaven of deliverance; and I promise never again to commit these sins."

There are also numerous rites on the same lines or by magic-

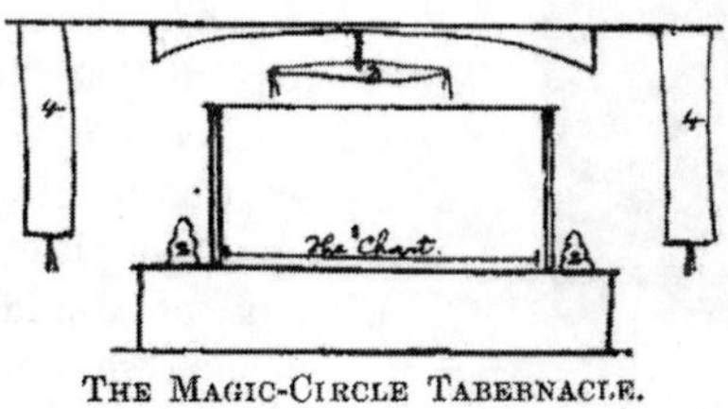

THE MAGIC-CIRCLE TABERNACLE.

1. Chart or Mosaic. . Umbrella.
2. Cakes. 4. Banners.

circles, posturing and mummery, for obtaining supernatural powers

[1] gso-byoṅ. See pages 323 and 501; and cf. SCHLAGINTWEIT, p. 123.

[2] Cf. *Pratimoksha sūtra*, "The Book of Deliverance" and its Tibetan version, trans. by ROCKHILL.

[3] Probably mythical Buddha, Vajradhara.

and for purposes of sorcery. Some of these latter I have abstracted in the chapter on necromancy.

Of special celebrations it will suffice to refer only to one of the most interesting, which some Europeans who witnessed its pompous and solemn service, have compared to the Christian Eucharist.

THE EUCHARIST OF LĀMAISM.

THE "EUCHARIST" OF LĀMAISM.[1]

This Lāmaist liturgy, the celebration of which is pictured as the frontispiece, on account of its dispensation of consecrated wine and bread, has been compared by Huc and others to the Christian Eucharist, although it is in reality, as here shown, a ceremony for gratifying the rather un-Buddhistic craving after long earthly life. Still, it nevertheless presents many parallels to the Christian rite for conferring on the worthy recipient "the life everlasting."

It is entitled "The Obtaining of (long) Life,"[2] and is a very good sample of the Lāmaist blending of Buddhists' ideas with demon-worship. It seems to incorporate a good deal of the pre-Lāmaist ritual, and its benedictions and sprinkling of holy water are suggestive of Nestorian or still later Christian influences.

This sacrament is celebrated with much pomp at stated

[1] In the *Asiatic Quarterly*, 1894, part of this article was published by me.

[2] Tib. Ts'e-grub.

periods, on a lucky day, about once a week in the larger temples, and attracts numerous votaries. Crowds throng to the temple to receive the coveted blessing. Its benefits are more particularly sought in cases of actual illness, and when death seems imminent; but every village must have it performed at least once a year for the life of the general community, and after its performance any prolongation of life is credited to this service; while a fatal result is attributed to the excessive misdeeds of the individual in his last life or in previous births.

The chief god addressed is Buddha *Amitāyus* or *Aparamita*,[1] "The (god of) infinite Life," or "The Eternal." Unlike the Chinese Buddhists the Lāmas never confuse *Amitābha* (the Buddha of infinite Light) with his reflex *Amitāyus*; they represent these differently, and credit them with different functions. The other gods specially identified with life-giving powers are "The five long-Life Sisters,"[2] mountain nymphs presiding over the everlasting snows, and to a less degree the white Tārā, and Ushṇīsharāni; and even *Yama*, the Lord of Death himself, may occasionally be propitiated into delaying the day of death.

The priest who conducts this ceremony for propitiation of *Amitāyus* and the other gods of longevity must be of the purest morals, and usually a total abstainer from meat and wine. He must have fasted during the greater part of the twenty-four hours preceding the rite, have repeated the *mantras* of the life-giving gods many times, 100,000 times if possible, and he must have secured ceremonial purity by bathing. The rite also entails a lot of other tasks for the preparation of the consecrated pills and the arrangement of utensils, etc., and extends over two or three days.

The arrangements are as follow:—

Upon an altar, under the brocaded dragon-canopy, within the temple or in a tent outside, are placed the following articles:—

1. *Las-bum*, the ordinary altar water-vase.
2. *Ti-bum*, the vase with pendant mirror and containing water tinged with saffron.
3. *dBaṅ-bum*, the "empowering vase" with the chaplet of the Five Jinas.
4. *Ts'e-bum*, the "vase of Life," special to *Amitāyus*, with a banner of peacock's feathers and sacred Kuṣa-grass.
5. *Ts'e-ch'aṅ*, or "the wine of Life," consisting of beer in a skull-bowl.
6. *Ts'e-ril*, or the "pills of Life," made of flour, sugar and butter.
7. *Chi-mar*, or wafers of flour and butter and rice.
8. *mDah-dar*, or sacred divining-dagger with silk tassels.
9. *rdor-jehi gzuṅ t'ag*, or the divining-bolt, a *vajra* or thunderbolt-sceptre with eight ridges to which a string is attached.

In the preliminary worship the pills are made from buttered dough, and the ambrosia or *amrita* (Tib., *dud-tsi* or "devil's juice") is brewed from spirit or beer, and offered in a skull-bowl to the great image of

[1] Tib., Ts'e-pag-med.

[2] Ts'e-riṅ-che-ṅa.

Buddha *Amitāyus*. Everything being ready and the congregation assembled, the priest, ceremonially pure by the ascetic rites above noted,[1] and dressed as in the frontispiece, abstracts from the great image of Buddha *Amitāyus* part of the divine essence of that deity, by placing the *vajra* of his *rdor-jehi gzuṅ-t'ag* upon the nectar-vase which the image of *Amitāyus* holds in his lap, and applying the other end to his own bosom, over his heart. Thus, through the string, as by a telegraph wire, passes the divine spirit, and the Lāma must mentally conceive that his heart is in actual union with that of the god *Amitāyus*, and that, for the time being, he is himself that god.[2] Then he invokes his tutelary-fiend, and through him the fearful horse-necked *Hayagrīva* (Tamdin), the king of the demons. The Lāma, with this divine triad (namely, the Buddha and the two demon kings) incorporate in him, and exhibiting the forms of all three to spiritual eyes, now dispenses his divine favours. He takes up the *Las-bum*-vase and consecrates its contents, saying,

"*Om! namo Tathāgata Abhi-khita samayasriri hūṃ! Namu candra vajra krodha Amṛita hūm phat!*"

Then he sprinkles some of the water on the rice-offerings (*gtor-ma*) to the evil spirits, saying, "I have purified it with *svabhava*, and converted it into an ocean of nectar within a precious *Bhum*-bowl. *Om akaromu-kham! Sarva dharma nantyanutpanna tatto! Om! A! Hūṃ! phat! Svāhā!* I now desire to bestow the deepest life-power on these people before me; therefore, I beg you demons to accept this cake-offering, and depart without doing further injury."

Here the Lāma, assuming the threatening aspect of the demon-kings, who are, for the time being, in his body, adds, "Should you refuse to go, then I, who am the most powerful *Hayagrīva* and the king of the angry demons, will crush you—body, speech and mind—to dust! Obey my mandate and begone, each to his abode, otherwise you shall suffer. *Om sumbhani*," etc. Now, the Lāmas and the people, believing that all the evil spirits have been driven away by the demon-king himself, shout, "The gods have won! the devils are defeated!"

The Lāma then proceeds to secure for himself the benedictory power of life-conferring. He first meditates on "the guardian-deities," murmuring thus: "The upper part (of the divine abode) is of thunderbolt

[1] He usually wears a mantle (stod-gyog), on which are embroidered mystic Chinese emblems of luck, including the *Bat*, etc. See pp. 394, 396.

[2] In southern Buddhism is found a very similar instance of ceremonial union with a Buddhist fetish. At the pirit (*paritta*) celebration "a sacred thread, called the *pirit nūla*, is fastened round the interior of the building, the end of which, after being fastened to the reading platform, is placed near the relic (of Buddha). At such times as the whole of the priests who are present engage in chanting in chorus, the cord is untwined, and each priest takes hold of it, thus making the communication complete between each of the officiating priests, the relic, and the interior walls of the building." —HARDY'S *E. Monachism*, p. 241.

tents and hangings; the lower part of earth-foundation and adamantine-seat; and the walls are of thunderbolts. The entire building is a great tent, protected by precious charms, so that the evil spirits can neither destroy it, nor can they gain entry. *Om! vajra rakhya rakhya sūtra tikhtha vajraye svāhā!*"

Then the magic-circle (*maṇḍala*) is offered up, saying:—

"If I fail to refer to the successive Lāma-saints, my words and deeds will count for nothing. Therefore must I praise the holy Lāmas to secure their blessing towards the realization of my plans. O holy *Padma-sambhava*,[1] in you are concentrated all the blessings of the present, past and future! You are the Buddha of the great final Perfection (*Maha-utpanna*) who beheld the face of Lord *Amitāyus*. O Saint possessed of the gift of undying life, of life lasting till the worlds of re-births are emptied! You hid away from us, in the snowy regions, the revelation upon the true essence of the five hundred 'Obtainings of Life.' The one which we now perform is 'the iron palace of the attainment of life' (*Ts'e-grub lc'ags-kyi-pho-braṅ*), and is extracted from *dKon-mch'og-spyi-'dus*. It was discovered by the saint *'Dsah-Ts'on-sñiṅ-po* in the cave where you hid it; and this mode of endowering a person with life has come down to me through many generations of saints. Now, O Lord *Amitāyus* and the host of radiant gods! I beg you to sustain the animal beings, vast as the starry host, who now, with great reverence and praise, approach you. *Om a hūṃ!* O holy shrine of our refuge! *Hri!*[2] O Hosts of the Bright World of Light! *Pad-ma t'od-phreṅ-rtsal-vajrasa-mayaja siddhi phala hūṃ!*"

Then here is repeated "*Ts'e-'gug*," or "The Invoking of Life," thus:

"O Lord *Amitāyus*, residing in the five shrines whence glittering rays shoot forth! O! *Gandharva* in the west! *Yama* in the south! *Nāga rāja* in the west! *Yaksha* in the north! *Brāhma* and *Indra* in the upper regions! and *Nanda* and *Taksha* in the lower regions! And especially all the Buddhas and Bodhisatwas! I beg you all to bless me and to gratify my wishes by giving me the gift of undying life and by softening all the injuries of the harmful spirits. I entreat you to grant life and implore you to cause it to come to me. *Hrī!* I beg your blessing, O Buddhas of the three times. (Dipaṅkara, Ṣākya Muni and Maitreya).

At this stage the celestial Buddhas, Bodhisats, and other gods are now supposed to have consecrated the fluid in the vase and transformed it into immortal ambrosia. Therefore the priest intones the following chant to the music of cymbals: "This Vase is filled with the immortal ambrosia which the Five celestial Classes have blessed with the best Life. May life be permanent as adamant, victorious as the king's banner. May it be strong like the eagle (*Gyuṅ-druṅ*) and last for ever. May I be favoured with the gift of undying life, and all my wishes be realized.

"*Buddha! Vajra! Ratna! Padma! Karma, Kapālamāla. Hrī mahārinisaayu siddhi phala hūṃ! Om A Hūṃ vajra Guru Padma siddhi ayukke Hūṃ nijā!*"

The priest now bestows his blessing as the incarnate *Amitāyus* as well as the other gods of longevity, by laying-on of hands, and

[1] A Lāma of the established church would usually invoke St. Tsoṅ-K'a-pa, and the subsequent prayer would be slightly different.

[2] The *Vija-mantra* of *Avalokita* and *Amitābha*.

he distributes the consecrated water and food to the assembled multitude. When the crowd is great, the votaries file past the holy Lāma. In smaller congregations the Lāma, with the *Ti-bum* vase in hand, walks along the rows of kneeling worshippers near the temple door, and pours a few drops of the holy fluid into the hands of each votary. With the first few drops the worshipper rinses his mouth, and with the next few drops he anoints the crown of his head, and the third few drops are reverently swallowed.

Then the Lāma brings the vase of Life and places it for an instant on the bowed head of each of the kneeling votaries, reciting the spell of Amitāyus (*Om Amarani jivantiye svāhā*), which all repeat. Then the Lāma touches the head of each one with the power-conferring vase; and afterwards, in similar manner, with the divining-dagger, saying: "The life which you now have obtained is unfailing like the *vajra*-armour. Receive it with reverence! As the *vajra* is unchangeable, so now is your life. *Vajra rakhya rakhya svāhā!* Worship Amitāyus, the god of boundless Life, the chief of all world-rulers! May his glory come, with virtue and all happiness." And all the people shout, "Glory and all-happiness!"

Each worshipper now receives from the skull-bowl a drop of the sacred wine, which he piously swallows; and each also receives three of the holy pills, the plateful of which had been consecrated by the touch of the Lāma. These pills must be swallowed on the spot. They are represented as beads upon the vase which the image of the god of Infinite Life holds in his lap.

The Lāma then takes a seat on a low throne, and the votaries file past him offering him a scarf and any money presents they may have to make; the majority pay in grain, which is piled up outside the door of the temple. Each then receives a benediction from the Lāma, who places his hand on their heads and repeats the spell of *Amitāyus;* and on its conclusion he throws over their shoulder a knotted white scarf (*Tsim-tu*) from a heap of consecrated scarves lying at his side. The colours of the scarves are white for the laity and red for the priests.

Other ceremonies for prolonging life, especially resorted to in severe sickness, are "The Saving from Death" (*'ch'i-bslu*); the "Ransoming of another's Life" (*srog-bslu*); Substitution-offering to the devils of an effigy of the patient, or as a sacrifice for sin (*Ku-rim*[1]) as in the illustration given on the opposite page; Libation of wine to the demons (*gSer-skyems*); *gyal-gsol*, etc. All of these services are more or less mixed up with demonolatry.

Numerous other ceremonies have already been referred to in other chapters, such as the "Water Baptism" ("Tüi-Sol"),[2] "The Calling for Luck" (Yaṅ-gug),[3] etc., "The Continued Fast" (Ñuṅ-gnas).[4]

[1] sKu-rim: cf. JAESCH., *D.*, 22; GIORGI'S *Alphab. Tib.*, p. 442; ROCKHILL'S *L.*, p. 114.

[2] bKrus-gsol = ablution + to pray or entreat; see SCHLAGINTWEIT, *Budd.*, p. 239.

[3] See p. 447; also SCHLAG., p. 263.

[4] SCHLAG., p. 240.

The rites for the attainment of supernatural powers, and for downright demonolatry, are detailed in the chapter on sorcery and necromancy. And it is evident that the Lāmas or professing

A GUILT-OFFERING AT TANKAR.[1]

Buddhists are conscious of the unorthodoxy of these practices, for the so-called reformed Lāmas, the Ge-lug-pa, do their demoniacal worship mostly after dark.

[1] After Rockhill.

GEOMANTIC TRIGRAMS.

XVII.

ASTROLOGY AND DIVINATION.

"That mendicant does right to whom omens, planetary influences, dreams, and signs are things abolished; he is free from all their evils."—*Sammā Paribbājaniya Sutta*, 2.

LIKE most primitive people, the Tibetans believe that the planets and spiritual powers, good and bad, directly exercise a potent influence upon man's welfare and destiny, and that the portending machinations of these powers are only to be foreseen, discerned, and counteracted by the priests.

Such beliefs have been zealously fostered by the Lāmas, who have led the laity to understand that it is necessary for each individual to have recourse to the astrologer-Lāma or *Tsi-pa* on each of the three great epochs of life, to wit, birth, marriage, and death; and also at the beginning of each year to have a forecast of the year's ill-fortune and its remedies drawn out for them.

These remedies are all of the nature of rampant demonolatry for the appeasing or coercion of the demons of the air, the earth, the locality, house, the death-demon, etc.

Indeed, the Lāmas are themselves the real supporters of the demonolatry. They prescribe it wholesale, and derive from it their chief means of livelihood at the expense of the laity.

Every large monastery has a *Tsi-pa*,[1] or astrologer-Lāma, recruited from the cleverest of the monks.

And the largest monasteries may have as astrologer a pupil of the great government oracle-Lāma, the Ch'o-c'oṅ.

The astrologer-Lāmas have always a constant stream of persons coming to them for prescriptions as to what deities and demons require appeasing and the remedies necessary to neutralize these portending evils.

The nature of these prescriptions of worship will best be illustrated by a concrete example. But to render this intelligible it is necessary to refer, first of all, to the chronological nomenclature current in Tibet, as it is used for indicating the lucky and unlucky times, as well as much of the worship. And it will be seen to be more Chinese than Indian in nature. The Chinese calendar is said to have been introduced by king Sroṅ Tsaṅ's Chinese wife, but the first sixty-year cycle does not begin until 1026 A.D.[2]

The Tibetan system of reckoning time, derived from China and India, is based upon the twelve-year and sixty-year cycles of Jupiter.[3] The twelve-year cycle is used for short periods, and the particular year, as in the Chinese style, bears the name of one or other of the twelve cyclic animals :—

1. Mouse.	5. Dragon.	9. Monkey.
2. Ox.	6. Serpent.	10. Bird.
3. Tiger.	7. Horse.	11. Dog.
4. Hare.	8. Sheep.	12. Hog.

And in the case of the sixty-year cycle these animals are combined with the five elements (namely: Wood, Fire, Earth, Iron, and Water), and each element is given a pair of animals, the first being considered male and the second female. I append a detailed list of the years of the current cycle as an illustration, and for reference in regard to the horoscopes which I shall translate presently.

THE TIBETAN CHRONOLOGICAL TABLE.

The table here given differs from that of Schlagintweit (*op. cit.*, p. 282) in making the initial year of the current sixty-year cycle, namely, the fifteenth

---

[1] rTsis-pa—the *Chebu* of HOOKER's *Himalayan Jours.*

[2] CSOMA, *Gr.*, 148. The Chinese "*Description of Tibet*," translated by KLAPROTH (*Nouv. Jour., Asiat.*, iv., 138), states that the Chinese system was introduced by the Chinese wife of Sroṅ Tsan Gampo, in 642 A.D.

[3] There is also a cycle of 252 years seldom used. Conf. GIORGI, 464-69. HUC, ii., 368, and SCHLAG., 284.

cycle (*Rab-juṅ*), coincide with the year 1867 A.D., as this is alleged by the learned astrologer Lāma of Darjiling to be the true epoch, and not the year 1866.

Year A.D.	Tibetan Era.			Year A.D.	Tibetan Era.		
	Cycle No.	Cyclical Year.	Year-name.		Cycle No.	Cyclical Year.	Year-name.
1858	XIV.	52	Earth-Horse	1890	XV.—	24	Iron-Tiger
1859	,,	53	,, -Sheep	1891	*contd.*	25	,, -Hare
1860	,,	54	Iron-Ape	1892	,,	26	Water-Dragon
1861	,,	55	,, -Bird	1893	,,	27	,, -Serpent
1862	,,	56	Water-Dog	1894	,,	28	Wood-Horse
1863	,,	57	,, -Hog	1895	,,	29	,, -Sheep
1864	,,	58	Wood-Mouse	1896	,,	30	Fire-Ape
1865	,,	59	,, -Ox	1897	,,	31	,, -Bird
1866	,,	60	Fire-Tiger	1898	,,	32	Earth-Dog
1867	XV.	1	,, -Hare	1899	,,	33	,, -Hog
1868	,,	2	Earth-Dragon	1900	,,	34	Iron-Mouse
1869	,,	3	,, -Serpent	1901	,,	35	,, -Ox
1870	,,	4	Iron-Horse	1902	,,	36	Water-Tiger
1871	,,	5	,, -Sheep	1903	,,	37	,, -Hare
1872	,,	6	Water-Ape	1904	,,	38	Wood-Dragon
1873	,,	7	,, -Bird	1905	,,	39	,, -Serpent
1874	,,	8	Wood-Dog	1906	,,	40	Fire-Horse
1875	,,	9	,, -Hog	1907	,,	41	,, -Sheep
1876	,,	10	Fire-Mouse	1908	,,	42	Earth-Ape
1877	,,	11	,, -Ox	1909	,,	43	,, -Bird
1878	,,	12	Earth-Tiger	1910	,,	44	Iron-Dog
1879	,,	13	,, -Hare	1911	,,	45	,, -Hog
1880	,,	14	Iron-Dragon	1912	,,	46	Water-Mouse
1881	,,	15	,, -Serpent	1913	,,	47	,, -Ox
1882	,,	16	Water-Horse	1914	,,	48	Wood-Tiger
1883	,,	17	,, -Sheep	1915	,,	49	,, -Hare
1884	,,	18	Wood-Ape	1916	,,	50	Fire-Dragon
1885	,,	19	,, -Bird	1917	,,	51	,, -Serpent
1886	,,	20	Fire-Dog	1918	,,	52	Earth-Horse
1887	,,	21	,, -Hog	1919	,,	53	,, -Sheep
1888	,,	22	Earth-Mouse	1920	,,	54	Iron-Ape
1889	,,	23	,, -Ox.	1921	,,	55	,, -Bird.

It is by giving a realistic meaning to these several animals and elements, after which the years are named, that the Lāma-astrologers arrive at their endless variety of combinations of attraction and repulsion in regard to their casting of horoscopes and their prescriptions of the requisite worship and offerings necessary to counteract the evils thus brought to light. The animals are more or less antagonistic to each other, and their most unlucky combinations are as follows :—

Mouse and Horse. Hare and Bird.
Ox and Sheep. Dragon and Dog.
Tiger and Monkey. Serpent and Hog.

But it is with the five elements that the degrees of affinity and antagonism are most fully defined, according to certain more or less obvious inter-relations of the elements. The recognized degrees of relationship are: (1) *mother*, or greatest affection; (2) *son*, or neutrality; (3) *friend*, or mediocre affection, and (4) *enemy* or antagonism. The relationships of the elements are thus stated to be the following:—

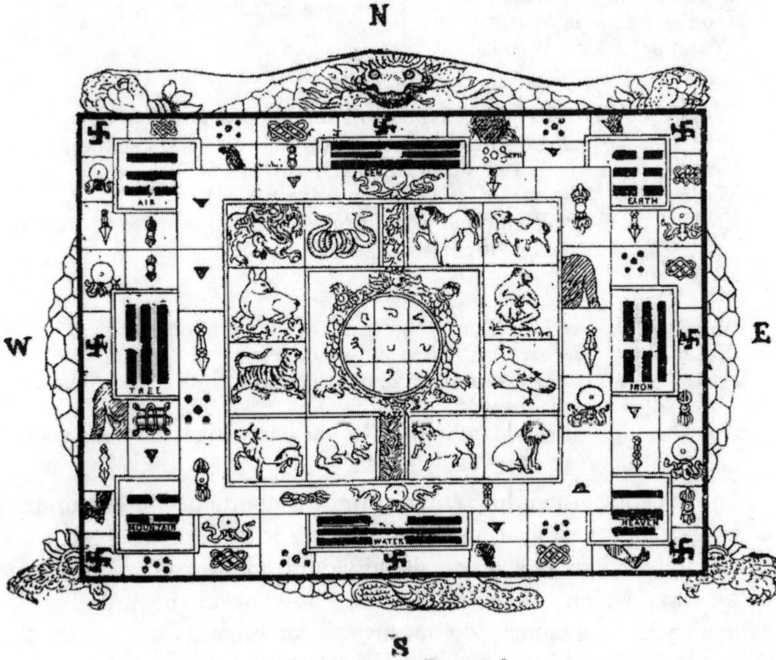

Astrological Figures.[1]
(On the Tortoise.)

Maternal.

Wood's *mother* is Water (for wood cannot grow without water).
Water's ,, is Iron (for water-channels for irrigation cannot be made, and therefore water cannot come, without iron).
Iron's ,, is Earth (for earth is the matrix in which iron is found).

[1] Modified from Sarat's figure.

Earth's *mother* is Fire (for earth is the ash-product of fire).
Fire's ,, is Wood [for without wood (carbon) fire is not].

FILIAL.

Wood's	*son*	is Fire	This is merely a reverse way of presenting the above details.
Fire's	,,	is Earth	
Earth's	,,	is Iron	
Iron's	,,	is Water	
Water's	,,	is Wood	

HOSTILE.

Wood's *enemy* is Iron (as Iron instruments cut down wood).
Iron's ,, is Fire (as fire melts iron and alters its shape).
Fire's ,, is Water (as water extinguishes fire).
Water's ,, is Earth (as earth hems in water).
Earth's ,, is Wood (as wood grows at the expense of and impoverishes earth).

AMICABLE.

Wood's *friend* is Earth (as wood can't grow without earth).
Water's ,, is Fire (as it warms water).
Fire's ,, is Iron (as it absorbs heat, and thus assists the continuance of the fire).
Iron's ,, is Wood (as it supplies the handles to iron-weapons and is non-conducting).

The Tibetan year is lunar, and numbers nominally three hundred and sixty days; so that in order to bring it into keeping with the moon's phases one day is occasionally omitted, and as it is the unlucky days which are omitted, and these occur irregularly, the Tibetan year and months do not always correspond exactly with the Chinese months and years. And the solar difference is compensated by inserting seven intercalary months (Da-s'ol) every nineteen[1] years.

The year begins in February with the rise of the new moon. The months (Da-wa)[2] are named first, second, etc., and the word Da-wa prefixed thus, Da-wa-tang-po, "first month." The week is divided into seven days (Za), bearing, as with us (for the Lāmas adopted the Aryan system), the names of the sun, moon, and the five planets, two being allotted to each day, and is represented by a symbol (see figure) which is a concrete picture of the name.

[1] So says SCHLAG., *op. cit.*, 288. The intercalary month seems to be added at less intervals. According to the Baidyur-Kar-po in 1891 the duplicated month was the tenth.

[2] Zla-wa = moon.

Name.	Celestial Body.	Its Symbol.
Sunday (Tib., *Nima*)	Sun	A sun.
Monday (*Da wa*)	Moon	Crescent moon.
Tuesday (*Mig mar*)	Mars	A red eye.
Wednesday (*L'ag-pa*)	Mercury	A hand.
Thursday (*P'ur-bu*)	Jupiter	A thunderbolt.
Friday (*Pā-saṅ*)	Venus	A garter.
Saturday (*Pen-ba*)	Saturn	A bundle.

The different days of the week are associated with the elements; thus Sunday and Tuesday with Fire, Monday and Wednesday with Water, Thursday with Air, and Friday and Saturday with Earth.[1]

Each hour and day of the week possesses a lucky or unlucky character, and the days of the month according to their order in troduce other sets of unlucky combinations. Thus the individual days of the week are divided: Monday and Thursday are best. Sunday and Tuesday are rather "angry." Saturday and Wednesday are only good for receiving things (Yang-sa) and not for giving away. Saturday is not quite so gloomy and malignant as in Western mythology.

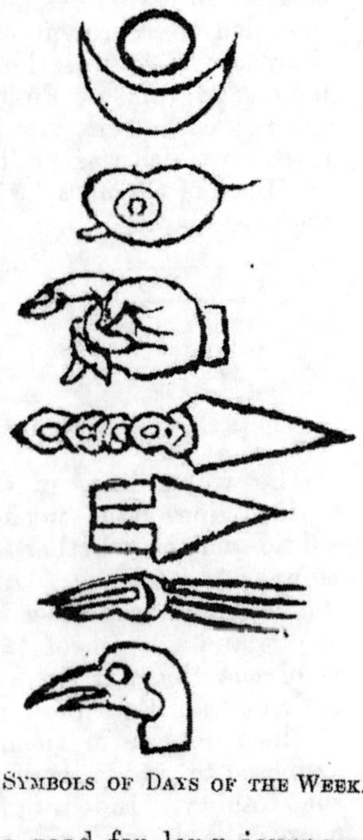

SYMBOLS OF DAYS OF THE WEEK.

The days of the month in their numerical order are unlucky *per se* in this order. The first is unlucky for starting any undertaking, journey, etc. The second is very bad to travel. Third is good provided no bad combination otherwise. Fourth is bad for sickness and accident (Ch'u-'jag). Eighth bad. The dates counted on fingers, beginning from thumb and counting second in the hollow between thumb and index finger, the hollow always comes out bad, thus second, eighth, fourteenth, etc. Ninth is good for long journeys but not for short (Kut-da). Fourteenth and twenty-fourth are

1 According to the rhyme:

"Ñi-ma mik-mar me K'am; Da-wa lhak-pa Ch'u- r K'am;
P'ur-bu dā-c'en luṅ-i K'am; Pasaṅ p'em-ba Sa-i K'am."

like fourth. The others are fairly good *cæteris paribus.* In accounts, etc., unlucky days are often omitted altogether and the dates counted by duplicating the preceding day.[1]

Chinese geomantic figures, the Pu-Kwā (*Par-k'a*) and the *Mewa*, enter largely into the calculations of the Lāma astrologer, and these are usually figured on the belly of a spread tortoise, as in the above figure, whose paws sometimes grasp a pole surmounted by or transfixing a frog.[2]

The Pu-Kwa or Par-k'a symbolize the great productive and antagonistic powers of nature, as summarized in a most interesting manner by Dr. Legge.

The first character, pū, is the Chinese symbol for divining by the lines produced through a certain process on the back of a tortoise-shell. It consists of two lines,[3] which may possibly, says Dr. Legge, have been intended to represent the lines appearing on the shell. The second character, *Kwā*, was the symbol for divining by means of the eight famous trigrams of Fū-hsī, themselves called "the eight Kwā." They are not characters, but lineal figures composed of whole and divided lines, on which was built up the mysterious book called the Yī-Kiṅ, or "Book of Changes," with its sixty-four hexagrams. The eight trigrams are here shown :—

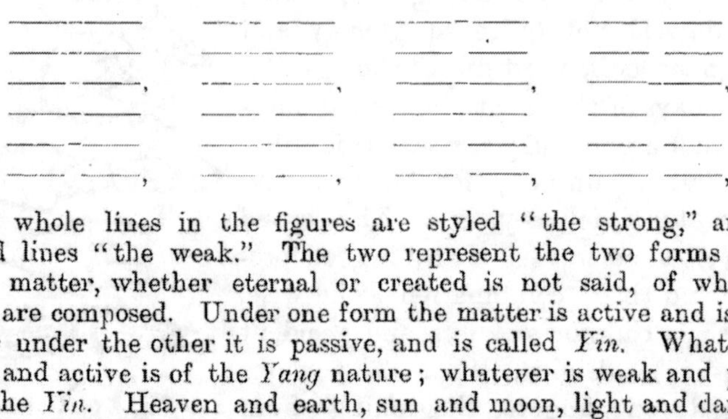

The whole lines in the figures are styled "the strong," and the divided lines "the weak." The two represent the two forms of the subtle matter, whether eternal or created is not said, of which all things are composed. Under one form the matter is active and is called *Yang ;* under the other it is passive, and is called *Yin.* Whatever is strong and active is of the *Yang* nature ; whatever is weak and passive is of the *Yin.* Heaven and earth, sun and moon, light and darkness, male and female, ruler and minister, are examples of these antinomies. The aggregate of them makes up the totality of being, and the *Yi* is supposed to give in its diagram a complete picture of the phenomena of that totality. It does not give us a sexual system of nature, though of course the antinomy of sex is in it ; but the lines on which it is con-

[1] Klaproth, iv., 137 ; Huc, ii., 370.

[2] This may be the sacred three-legged frog. Cf. also my article (*Ind. Antiq.*, 1893) on "Frog Worship among the Newars."

[3] Legge's *The Relig. of China*, p. 14, do. 15.

structed embrace other antinomies as well. Authority and power on one side; inferiority and docility on the other.

Further, the hidden operation in and through which the change takes place in nature is said to be that of the *Kwei shan*,[1] usually meaning "spirits," but here held to be technical. "Shan is *Yang*, and indicates the process of expanding; *Kwei* is *Yin*, and indicates the process of contracting." The fashion of the world is continually being altered. We have action and reaction, flux and reflux, and these changes are indicated in the diagrams, which are worked in divination by manipulating a fixed number of stalks of a plant called shih (*Ptarmica Sibirica*), and, indeed, the form of the trigrams themselves is suggestive of divination by *twigs*.

The usual geomantic arrangement of the Par-k'a is given in figure. Individually they are named Heaven, Earth, Fire, Thunder, Mountains, Celestial Water, Terrestrial Water, though the fourth and eighth are sometimes called Iron and Tree. And Mountain, Iron, and Water are said to be sons of the Earth and Heaven, while Wind, Fire, and Tree are their daughters.

It is remarkable, however, that while the Chinese use only the hexagrams for divination purposes, the Tibetans use only the trigrams in this way.[2]

The Nine *Mewa*[3] are arranged in the form of a quadratic square or circle, and the figures usually, as in a magic square, so disposed as to give the same total in all directions.

4	9	2
3	5	7
8	1	6

The spirits of the seasons also powerfully influence the luckiness or unluckiness of the days. It is necessary to know which spirit has arrived at the particular place and time when an event has happened or an undertaking is entertained. And the very frequent and complicated migrations of those aërial spirits, good and bad, can only be ascertained by the Lāmas. The most malignant of these evil spirits are a black dog, a monster with a dragon-tail, a man on horseback, and the fabulous Phœnix; and the seasons are specially assigned to these in the order of spring, summer, autumn, and winter respectively.[4]

The almanac which the Lāmaist astrologer uses, gives for each

[1] LEGGE, *op. cit.*, p. 39.

[2] Cf. Prof. DE LA COUPERIES' *Ancient Chinese Divination Manual*—The Yi King.—Paris, 1889.

[3] *s*Me-ba = a blot. Cf. PALLAS, *Mong.*, ii., 229; SCHLAG., 297.

[4] SCHLAG., 299.

day the six presiding influences. Thus the page of the almanack for the first day of the third month of 1891 (Iron-horse) gives:—

Cyclic Animal	*Par-kha*	*Nidāna*
Tiger	Li	Nāmarūpa
	Mewa	
	C'ikar	
Week-day		*Star*
5		26
P'urba (Thursday) (giving Wind).		She-sa (giving Water).

And the general record for the particular month is: This month's star is moderate and the celestial Mansion is the sheep. *Nidana*, Avidya. Element is mid-summer, and named Great Fire-Horse. It is time for plants budding and marshes, thunder and birds. The empty vase is in the east (∴ do not go E.). On the 15th day the Teacher taught the *Kālācakra;* it is a holiday. Thursday, Sunday, and Tuesday are good. Friday, Saturday, Monday, and Wednesday are bad. The "Yas" road (*i.e.*, the road on which cake and the devil's image are to be thrown) is N.W. The "Zin-p'uṅ" (a kind of *genius loci*) in the Ox and Sheep days at dawn passes from W. to E. (∴ at that time be careful).

Lāmaist Horoscopes.

The Lāmaist horoscopes or *Tsis* are of several kinds. Those most commonly sought are for: (a) *Birth* [1] (b) *Whole-Life Forecast* [2] (c) *Marriage* [3] (d) *Death* [4] and the (e) *Annual.*[5]

They are written in cursive characters on a long sheet of paper, and attested by the stamp of the astrologer. Such manuscript divinations usually called Suṅ-ta, are in the case of the more wealthy clients mounted on silk. A preliminary fee or present is usually given to the astrologer at the time of applying for the horoscope, in order to secure as favourable a presage as possible.

Each of the various horoscopes takes into account the conflict or otherwise of the elementary and astral influences dominant at the time of the person's birth, as compared with the existing influences

[1] sKyed-rtsis [2] ts'-rabs las rtsis. [3] pag-rtsis. [4] gs'in-rtsis.

[5] sKag-rtsis. Other horoscopes for general and extra divinations are: Gab-tsi or "Concealed," and Grub-tsi or "the perfect" Astrology; and the Chinese system is termed *Nak-tsi* in distinction to the Indian or *Kar-tsi*.

at the time consulted. The ordinary horoscope is usually arranged under the following six heads, namely :—

1. The year of birth of the individual in its auspicious or inauspicious bearings.
2. His *Park'a,* influences.
3. His "Reversed calculation" of age (*Log-men*). This is evidently introduced in order to afford a further variety of conflicts.
4. "The Seizing-Rope of the Sky."—This seems to refer to a popular idea of ultimate ascent to the celestial regions by means of an invisible rope.
5. "The Earth-dagger."—This is an invisible dagger, and is for the individual the emblem of stability and safety so long as it is reported to be fixed firmly in the earth.
6. The *Mewa.*

And each of these several heads is separately considered in detail with reference to its conflicts in regard to—(*a*) the Life (or *srog*); (*b*) the Body (or *lus*); (*c*) the Power or capability (*ban-t'an*); (*d*) the Luck-horse (or *rlun-rta*); and (*e*) the Intelligence (*bla*).

The particular *Parkha* and *Mewa* for the several times are found by reference to the Lāma's almanac as above noted; but the other details are elicited by divers calculations made upon the astrologer's board,[1] and in consultation with the various manuals on the subject.

[1] The astrologer's board consists of a large napkin on which are drawn squares and the other necessary geomantic figures, all in a definite and convenient relation to each other. This napkin is spread on a table, and the calculations are made with coloured buttons as counters which are kept in a bag—the several elements having each a recognized colour: thus wood is *green,* fire is *red,* earth is *yellow,* iron is *white,* and water is *blue.* These counters are placed on the coloured squares as in a chess-board, and are moved according to rule, either transversely from right to left or *vice versâ,* or longitudinally over the requisite number of squares. In the top row of the board are the sixty squares of the sixty-year cycle, all named and in the proper colour of their elements. And the succeeding rows of squares are those of the Life, Body, Power, Luck, and Intelligence series, each with its appropriate series of coloured elements. The other divisions relate to the Parkhas and Mewas.

The calculations are made according to rule backwards or forwards a certain number of years in the row of the sixty-year cycle squares, and the secondary results come out of the vertical columns of the Life, Body, etc., series according to the conflict of their respective elements; the results being noted by white or black seeds or buttons, which have the following values :—

The seven recognized degrees of affinity or repulsion are expressed in the astrological accounts by the following signs of circles and crosses, and during the calculation the circles are represented by white buttons and the crosses by black buttons or seeds :—

When the conflict of the elements comes out—*Mother, i.e.,* the *best* degree = ○○○

" " " " *Friend, i.e.,* the *better* " = ○○

" " " " {*Water* + *Water* / *Earth* + *Earth*} *i.e., a harmless mixture and ∴ good.* = ○

(*Continued over page.*)

These manuals have their signs inscribed on the belly of a tortoise (see page 453), and the Mewa occupies the centre.

With this explanation I now give here a sample of a horoscope for one family for one year's ill-luck, in which the prescribed worship is italicized. I have added in footnotes some further explanations which may be consulted by those interested in knowing in more detail the methods by which the Lāmaist-astrologer makes his calculations.

"THE MISFORTUNE ACCOUNT OF THE FAMILY OF ———— FOR THE EARTH-MOUSE YEAR (*i.e.*, 1888 A.D.)."

Salutation to MAÑJUṢRĪ ![1]

A.—FOR THE FATHER OF THE FAMILY.

I.—According to the BIRTH-CONFLICT.

This male, aged 26 years, being born in the Water-Hog year, that year conflicts with the Earth-Mouse year (the present year) as follows :—

Life	=	○,	or *good.*[2]
Body	=	○○,	or *better.*[3]
Power	=	××,	or *worse.*
Luck-horse	=	○○○,	or *best.*
Intelligence	=	×,	or *bad.*

1. *As modified by "Parkha."*—His *Park'a* for the year is *Khon,* which gives the Earth-Sheep year and the following conflict :—

Life	=	worse.
Body	=	better.

When the conflict of the elements comes out *Son, i.e., neutral* = ○×

" " " " { *Wood* + *Wood* / *Fire* + *Fire* / *Iron* + *Iron* } *i.e., unmiscibility, and ∴ opposition and bad* = ×

" " " " *Enemy, i.e., worse* = ××

" " " " *Deadly* hate, *i.e., worst* = ×××

For example, water meeting iron, *i.e.*, its "*mother,*" is the very best and .. = ○○○ and the same would be true of fire meeting wood. But wood meeting earth would = "*friend,*" and therefore = ○○; but should earth meet wood, then it would be "*enemy,*" and therefore = ××; and water meeting wood = "*neutrality,*" or ○×. While fire meeting water = "*deadly hate,*" and therefore = ×××. Then the average of the total is taken as the average result of the conflict. And the several remedies necessary to avoid each and all of the calamities thus foretold are specified categorically in the astrologers' books.

[1] The metaphysical Bodhisat Mañjuṣrī is the presiding divinity of the astrologers, and he is always invoked at the head of astrologic prescriptions.

[2] The year of his birth being the Water-Hog, gives, according to the astrologic table, Water as the *srog* for that year, and the present year being the Earth-Mouse year, its *srog*, according to the table, is also Water. Therefore Water meeting Water = ○, *i.e.*, "good."

[3] The *lus* of these two years are found by the table to give the elements respectively of Water and Fire. Therefore Water meeting its friend Fire = ○○ or "better," *i.e.*, good of the second degree

Power = worse than bad.
Luck-horse = bad.
Intelligence = worse.

2. *As modified by "Reversed Age Calculation."*—This gives a "good" result,[1] ∴ = ○.
3. *As modified by "The Seizing-Rope of the Sky."*—This gives "good,"[2] ∴ = ○. [If it were bad, then prescribed "The closure of the door to the sky" (spirits)].[3]
4. *As modified by "The Earth dagger."*—This gives a medium average, [If it were bad would have to do "The closure of the door to the earth" (spirits)].[4]

Thus the summary of the year's conflict as to birth, together with its prescribed remedies is :—

"Life" has black in excess ; ∴ to procure long life *have read very much The Sutra and Dhāraṇīs for Long Life.*

"Body" has white in excess ; ∴ the Body will be free from sickness (*i.e.*, only as regards this one aspect of the calculation).

"Power" has black in excess ; ∴ Food shall be scanty, and crops suffer, and cattle die or be lost. To neutralize it (a) *have read very much* "Yaṅ-gug" *or the Luck-Bestowing and* "Nor-zaṅ" (*the Best Wealth*) ; (b) *offer holy cakes ;* (c) *also give food and sweets to monks and children.*

"Luck" has black in excess ; ∴ be careful not to provoke a law-suit or go on a long journey. To neutralize this (a) *do* "*Du-kar*" 100 *times ;* (b) *plant as many* "*Luṅ-ta'-flags*" *as years of your age ;* (c) *offer in the temple* 13 *lamps with incense, etc.* ; (d) *have read the* "*mDo-maṅ*" *very much ;* (e) *make an image of yourself* (*of cooked barley or rice*) *and throw it towards your enemy ;* (f) *also make an earthen Caitya.*

"Intelligence" has black in excess ; ∴ *have read the* "*La-guk*" *or worship for recalling the Intelligence.*

II.—According to PARK'A—

His Park'a for the year being "*khon*," he cannot during the year excavate earth or remove stones. The Nāgas and the Earth master-demons are opposed to him. He is especially liable to the diseases of stiffened joints and skin disorders In the second month he is especially subject to danger. The N. and E. and S. directions are bad for him ; he must not go there. *For removing*

---

1 This *Log-men* or "Reversed + downwards" is a more abstruse calculation according to the saying :—

"skyes-pa pu-yi stag t'og nas lo grańs t'ur,
"bud-med ma-yi sprel-t'og nas lo grańs gyen."

For *males*—the *sons* of elements—begin from *Tiger* and count age *downwards*.
For *females*—the *mothers*—begin from *Ape* and count age *upwards*.

Thus the birth-year of this individual being Water-Hog, and he being a male, and the *son* of Water being Wood, gives us for his *Log-men* the Water-Tiger year (which = 1854 A.D.). And as he is male, on counting *downwards* from the Wood-Tiger the number of years of his age (*i.e.*, 26), we get the year Earth-Hare (*i.e.*, 1879 A.D.). And according to the Log-men Manual, the Earth-Hare year is "'byor-pa" or *Riches*, which is given the value of "good," *i.e.*, = ○.

2 This is calculated on the *srog* of the *Log-men* year, minus five years. In this case we have seen *Log-men* year is the Earth-Hare year. Counting back to the fifth year gives the Wood-Hog, which has its *srog* the element water, and the *srog* of the present 1888 A.D. year, viz., Earth-Mouse, being also Water, therefore = ○ or good for the "sky-seizing Rope."

3 See next chapter.

4 See next chapter.

these evils (a) *have read the "Gyé-tong-ba" section of the Prajña Pāramitā, and* (b) *do the worship of "Gya-zhi-tong"* [= "The 400," *i.e.*, 100 *torma* or holy cakes, 100 *lamps and* 100 *rice and* 100 *water offerings*], *and* (c) *offer a lamp daily in worship.*

III.—According to MEWA—

His mewa is *Dün-mar* (= the 7 reds) : therefore the Tsen and Gyalpo demons give trouble. Dreams will be bad. The gods are displeased. Head, liver, and heart will give pain, and boils will ensue. To prevent these evils (a) *make a "Tsen mdos" and a "Gyal mdos" (this is somewhat like the Sā-gô,*[1] *but without the ram's head)*; (b) *The favourite gods and guardians (srung-ma) of individual : Do their worship energetically ;* and (c) *ransom a sheep from the butchers.*

B.—FOR THE WIFE.

I.—According to BIRTH-CONFLICT—

This female born in Iron-Monkey year (*i.e.*, 29 years ago). That year compared with the Earth-Mouse year (*i.e.*, 1888 A.D.) gives :—

Life	= ○ ×
Body	= ○ ×
Power	= ○ ○ ○
Luck	= ×
Intelligence	= ○ ×

1. *As modified by her Parkha, which is Li.* These come out respectively, × ×, ○ ○, × ×, ○, × ×.
2. *As modified by "Reversed Age Calculation"* = ×
3. *As modified by "The Sky-rope"* = ○ ×
4. *As modified by "The Earth-dagger"* = ○ ○ ○

The total of the year's conflict is . . :—

Life and Intelligence are bad, like No. 1, and must be treated accordingly, and in addition to No. 1.

Body and power are good.

Luck is neutral ; therefore the good people will be kind to you ; and the bad people will trouble ; therefore it is necessary *to do very much "Mikha ṭa-ḍot," to drive away scandal* (from) *men's mouth.*

The Sky-seizing Rope is interrupted (*i.e.*, cut) ; therefore—

(1) *do very much "te-gyed," and "ser-k'yem"* (or oblation of wine to the gods) ;

(2) *prepare a "nam-go" to close breach in the sky-connection.*

The conjunction of her year (Monkey with Mouse) is not good ; ∴ she cannot journey far. And if she does any business she will suffer ; ∴ *have read "Tâshi tsig-pa."*

II.—According to PARK'A—

The Park'a being *Li*, she must not try to build or repair a house or allow any marriage in her house or spill any water on the hearth. The devil-spirit of a dead person is offended with her. Headache and eyeache will occur ; ∴ (*a*) do not look at fresh flesh meat or blood ; (*b*) in the 8th month will be especially bad ; (*c*) must not go W. or N.W. ; (*d*) *have read the "Dô-mang" and "Gye-tong ;"* (*e*) be careful not to provoke quarrels.

III.—According to MEWA—

Her Mewa is "*some thing*" ; therefore will occur sudden domestic quarrels of great seriousness, lying reports of infidelity, also grief among relatives, and dropsy. To prevent these do—

(a) *Gya zhi* (*i.e.*, 100 *lamps*, 100 *rice*, 100 *water*, *and* 100 *torma*) ; (b) *Lu-tor*, or offering of cake to the *Nāgas* and *Dug-kar* (= white umbrella-god with 1,000 heads) ; (c) *Also ransom a goat.*

[1] *Vide* p. 150.

C.—For the Daughter, aged 7.

I.—According to Birth-conflict—

This female, born in the Water-Horse year, 7 years ago. That year conflicted with the Earth-Mouse year as follows:—× ×, ○ ×, × ×, ○ ○, × ×.

1. *As modified by her "Parkha,"* which is *zin*. It is:—○ ○ ○, ○ ○ ○, ○ ×, × ×, ○ ○ ○.
2. *As modified by her "Reversed Age Calculation"* = ○
3. *As by "Sky-rope"* = ○ ×
4. *As by "The Earth-dagger"* = ○ ×

The total of the year's conflict ∴ is, Life, Intelligence, Body, and Luck are good of 2nd degree, Power is bad; therefore *do as for her father No. 1, previously noted.*

"Sky-seizing Rope" and Earth-dagger" are neutral. For evil Sky-seizing Rope, *have read the Sutra* "Akasgarbha."
And for Earth-dagger have read "Sa-yi snying po-ī mdo,"
and repeat as frequently as years of age, i.e., 7 times.

The conjunction of her birth year, the Horse, with that of the present year, the Mouse, is very bad, as these two are enemies; *for this have read* the Chinese "zloṅ-gaṅ-maṅ."

II.—According to Park'a—

Her Park'a is *zin*. Be careful not to break a twig or demolish any tree sacred to the Nāgas or other deities (*gnyan*), and don't handle a carpenter's tool for the same reason. In 2nd month when buds come out, it is somewhat bad for you, as the Nāgas are then pre-eminent. The West and N.W. directions are bad, and have to be avoided. *For these evils have read the "Dô-mang."*

III.—According to Mewa—

Her Mewa is *like her father's (No. 1), and therefore do accordingly.*

D.—For the Son, aged 5.

I.—According to Birth-conflict—

This male (son), born in the Wood-Ape year, 5 years ago. That year compared with the Earth-Mouse year gives:—○ ×, ○ ○, ○ ○, ×, ○ ×.

1. *As modified by his "Parkha,"* which is *kham*. It is ○ ×, ○, ○ ○ ○, ○ ○ ○, ○ ○ ○.
2. *As by "Reversed Age Calculation"* = ×
3. *As by "Sky-rope."* = ○ ○
4. *As by "Earth-dagger."* = × ×

The total of the year's conflict ∴ is:—

Body, Power, and Luck are good.
Life and Intelligence are neutral or middling.
The Sky-rope is *not broken*, and therefore good.
The Earth-dagger is withdrawn, and therefore bad.

For the latter—

(a) *make as many clay Chaityas as possible;*
(b) *the torma-cake of the earth-goddess (Sa-yi-lha-mo); and*
(c) *give also torma-cake to the Nāga demigods.*

II.—According to "Park'a"—

His Park'a being *k'am*, don't go to a large river, and to pools and other waters reputed to be the abode of water-spirits. Don't stir or *disturb* the water. Don't go out at night. Don't eat fish. The Tsan fiends are ill disposed towards you. These spirits are especially malevolent to you in the 6th month; ∴ be careful then. Don't go in a S.W. and N.E. direction. *Have read* (1) *kLu 'bum and* (2) *Ser-'od dampa 'don.*

III.—According to MEWA—

This Mewa is *ku-mar.* The Mamo and Tsan fiends are ill disposed towards you. For this as (a) *make "de-gñis kyi mdos gtoṅ,"* which is like the *Sa-gô* and "Sky-door" with threads and masts, and (b) *have read well "gser-'od gyaṅ skyabs."*

General Note on the Grand Average of the above.

The *Mewa* is excessively red. It thus betokens shedding of blood by accident. *Therefore make "Tsan mdos" and the* bloody *"Mamo mdos"* masts (see page 464). *And have read as much as possible*—(1) *stobs po-ch'e-ī-gsuṅs,* (2) *gzā-ī yum,* (3) *nor-rgyun-ma-ī gzuṅs gaṅ-man sgrogs.*

The extravagant amount of worship prescribed in the above horoscope is only a fair sample of the amount which the Lāmas order one family to perform so as to neutralize the current year's demoniacal influences on account of the family inter-relations only. In addition to the worship herein prescribed there also needs to be done the special worship for *each* individual according to his or her own life's horoscope as taken at birth; and in the case of husband and wife, their additional burden of worship which accrues to their life horoscope on their marriage, due to the new set of conflicts introduced by the conjunction of their respective years and their noxious influences; and other rites should a death have happened either in their own family or even in the neighbourhood. And when, despite the execution of all this costly worship, sickness still happens, it necessitates the further employment of Lāmas, and the recourse by the more wealthy to a devil-dancer or to a special additional horoscope by the Lāma. So that one family alone is prescribed a sufficient number of sacerdotal tasks to engage a couple of Lāmas fairly fully for several months of every year!

A somewhat comical result of all this wholesale reading of scriptures is that, in order to get through the prescribed reading of the several bulky scriptures within a reasonable time, it is the practice to call in a dozen or so Lāmas, each of whom reads aloud, but all at the same time, a different book or chapter for the benefit of the person concerned.

So deep-rooted is the desire for divination even in ordinary affairs of every-day life, that, in addition to these elaborate horoscopes, nearly every Lāma, even the most ignorant, and most of the laity, especially the poorer class who cannot afford the expense of spiritual horoscopes, seek for themselves presages by more simple methods, by cards, by rosary beads or pebbles, by dice, by sheep's shoulder blades,[1] by omens, etc. And the results are allowed to determine the movements of the individual, as every traveller who has had to do with Tibetans knows to his cost. It is a sort of fortune-telling, which, however, is not resorted to for the mere idle curiosity of ascertaining fortune long beforehand, but seriously to find the issues of undertakings in hand or those immediately contemplated by the consulter.

For the purposes of divination most families possess a small divining manual called *mô* or "*mô-pe.*"[2] These books show the portent attached to the particular number which is elicited and also the initiatory spells.

The cards used for most divination purposes are small oblong strips of cardboard, each representing several degrees of lucky and unlucky portents suitably inscribed and pictorially illustrated, and to each of these is attached a small thread.

In consulting this oracle, an invocation is first addressed to a favourite deity, frequently the goddess Tārā, and the packet is held by the left hand on a level with the face, and, with closed eyes, one of the threads is grasped, and its attached card is drawn out. The best out of three draws is held to decide the luck of the proposed undertaking, or the ultimate result of the sickness or the other question of fortune sought after.

Divination by the rosary is especially practised by the more illiterate people, and by the Bön priests. A preliminary spell is chanted:—

"*gSol! ye dharma! Om Sha-kya Muneye svā-hāh! Kramuneye svā-hāh! Madahshumuneye svāhāh!*" After having repeated this, breathe upon the rosary and say "*Namo-Guru!* I bow down before the kind, merciful and noble Lāma, the three Holy Ones, the *yidam* (tutelary deity), and before all the collections of Ḍākkinīs, religious protectors and guardians of the magic-circle, and I beg that you will cause the truth to descend on this lot. I also beg you, O! religious protectors and guardians, Brāhma, Indra, the others of the ten directions Nanda and Takshaka, the Nāga kings, including the eight great Nāgas, the sun, the eight planets, the twenty-eight constellations of stars, the twelve great chiefs of the injurers, and the great locality gods, to let the true light descend on my lot, and let the truth and reality appear in it."

After repeating the above, the rosary is taken in the palm and rolled between the two revolving palms, and the hands clapped

[1] See description by PALLAS, quoted by ROCKHILL (*L.*, p. 341).

[2] *I.e.*, short for "mô-pecha," or "The *mô* book.'

thrice. Then, closing the eyes, a portion of the rosary is seized between the thumb and finger of each hand, and opening the eyes the intervening beads are counted from each end in threes. And according as the remainder is 1, 2, or 3 depends the result. Thus:—

(1) *If One as a remainder comes after One* as the previous remainder, everything is favourable in life, in friendship, in trade, etc.

(2) *If Two comes after Two* it is bad: "The cloudless sky will be suddenly darkened, and there will be loss of wealth. So Rim-'gro must be done repeatedly, and the gods must be worshipped, which are the only preventions."

(3) *If Three comes after Three* it is very good: "Prosperity is at hand in trade and everything."

(4) *If Three comes after One* it is good: "Rice plants will grow on sandy hills, widows will obtain husbands, and poor men will obtain riches."

(5) *If One comes after Two* it is good: "Every wish will be fulfilled and riches will be found; if one travels to a dangerous place one will escape every danger."

(6) *If One comes after Three* it is good: "God's help will always be at hand, therefore worship the gods."

(7) *If Two comes after Three* it is not very good, it is middling: "Legal proceedings will come."

(8) *If Three comes after Two* it is good: "Turquoise fountains will spring out and fertilize the ground, unexpected food will be obtained, and escape is at hand from any danger."

(9) *If Two comes after One* it is bad: "Contagious disease will come. But if the gods be worshipped and the devils be propitiated, then it will be prevented."

The most ordinary mode of divination is by counters of seeds or pebbles in sets of ten, fifteen, or twenty-one, which may be used with or without a dice-board. If a dice-board be used, it consists of small squares drawn on paper to the number of fifteen or of twenty-one, and each square has got a number within a circle corresponding to a number in the *mô-pe* or divination-book. The set of ten is called "The Ten Fairy Circle,"[1] and requires a board bearing the outline of an eight-petalled lotus arranged as pairs of petals which correspond to the Tāntrik symbols of the five Jinas (vajra, gem, etc.), the fifth being in the centre, and its pair of petals is named the "Consort" of the Jina and the Sākti.[2] The

1 *m*Kal-'gro-ma.

2 Thus *r*Dorje Kahgro, rdo-rje shug*s*-'gro, the former having higher rank and better prognosis.

counters are white and black pebbles or seeds, only one black one to each series. And after the invocation to the special deity and shaking up and mixing all the seeds in the closed palm they are then told out between the forefinger and thumb of the still closed palm on to the squares in the numerical order of the latter, and the number on which the black seed comes out determines by means of the *mô-pe* book the divination result of the particular fortune sought for.

The set of fifteen squares is called "Gya-nag-sman-ch'u," or "The Chinese medicinal water." It consists of a triple series of five squares, with the numbers arranged as in the sketch. But properly, as its name implies, the seeds should be dropped into a vessel of water, and no dice-board is then needed. This kind of divination is used especially in sickness, hence it is called "medicinal." But the manual most commonly consulted for the prognosis and treatment of sickness is "The calculation of the eight goddesses." This book gives a fixed prognosis and prescriptions of remedial worship for the month in series of fours. Thus for its reference, only the day of the month is needed, and no dice or seeds are necessary.[1]

15	14	13	12	11
6	7	8	9	10
5	4	3	2	1

The set of twenty-one squares is called "The twenty-one Tārās," after the twenty-one forms of that obliging goddess. Above the centre of the diagram is a figure of that goddess, who is specially invoked in this divination. The numbers run as in the diagram here given. As a sample of the oracles I give here a few of the divination-results from Tārā's series. If the black seed falls on 1, 2, 8, or 9, the divination is as follows:—

Image of Dölma.

17	18	19	20	21
16	15	14	13	12
7	8	9	10	11
6	5	4	3	2 1

No. 1. *The Jewel.*—If you do not go to sea then you will get the jewel. For merchants' and thieves' adventures it is good. For your own house and soul it is excellent. But if you

[1] Another manual named Dus-ts'od-rtsis gives similar information in regard to the particular time of the day of the occurrence in question.

are sick it is somewhat bad. For travelling you should first feed people and dogs. You will obtain a son and get temporal power. Your wishes will ultimately be gratified. You have a thief as an enemy.

No. 2. *The Turquoise Spring.*—The dried valley will yield springs, and plants will become verdant, and timely rain will fall. The absent will soon return. Do the dPaṅ-bstod worship of the enemy god, and the worship of your own special god (mch'od lha). It is good for marriage.

No. 8. *The Conch Chaitya.*—In the supreme *'Og-min* heavens it is good for the lower animals. In the three worlds of existence is long life and auspicious time. Your desires will be realized. Life is good. If you are ill, whitewash the Caitya and worship in the temple. The enemy is somewhat near. For merchants the time is rather late, but no serious loss will happen. For health it is good.

No. 9. *The Invalid.*—If an actual invalid it is due to demon of grand-parents. Agriculture will be bad. Cattle will suffer. To prevent this offer the "black" cake of the three heads (*g*Tor nag *m*gô sum) and do "calling for luck." For your wishes, business, and credit it is a bad outlook. For sickness do "obtaining long life." Mend the road and repaint the "*Maṇi*" stones. Household things and life are bad. For these read the "dô mang" spells, also Du-Kar and Dok. The ancestral devil is to be suppressed by Srignon. Avoid conflict with enemy and new schemes and long journeys.

The titles of the other numbers indicate somewhat the nature of their contents, namely :—

3. Golden *Dorje.*
4. Painted vase.
5. Turquoise parrot.
6. Verdant plants.
7. Lady carrying child.
10. White lion.
11. Golden vase.
12. Turquoise dragon.
13. Garuda.
14. Tigress.
15. Sun and moon.
16. Enemy with bow and arrows.
17. Fiendess with red mouth.
18. 'Gong king-devil.
19. Peacock.
20. Glorious white conch.
21. The great king.

The foregoing are the forms of dice-boards used by the laity and the lower clergy. The more respectable Lāmas use a circular disc with twenty-eight divisions in the form of three concentric lotus-flowers, each of the petals of the two outer whorls bearing a number which corresponds to a number in the divining manual which is called "The one who sees all actions."[1] The margin of the disc is surrounded by flames. This more artistic arrangement is shown in the accompanying figure. As a sample of this oracle I give here the detail of No. 1 and list of the presiding divinities of the other numbers.

[1] "Las-bye*d* *m*t'oṅ-ba kun-*l*dan."

No. 1., *Bhagavān* (a title of Buddha). You are of the wise class, or if not you will get a wise son. Your god needs to be worshipped fully, and what you desire will be realized, and you will obtain long life and freedom from sickness. And if you are a male this blessing will last for nine years. If you are a female then nine monks must be

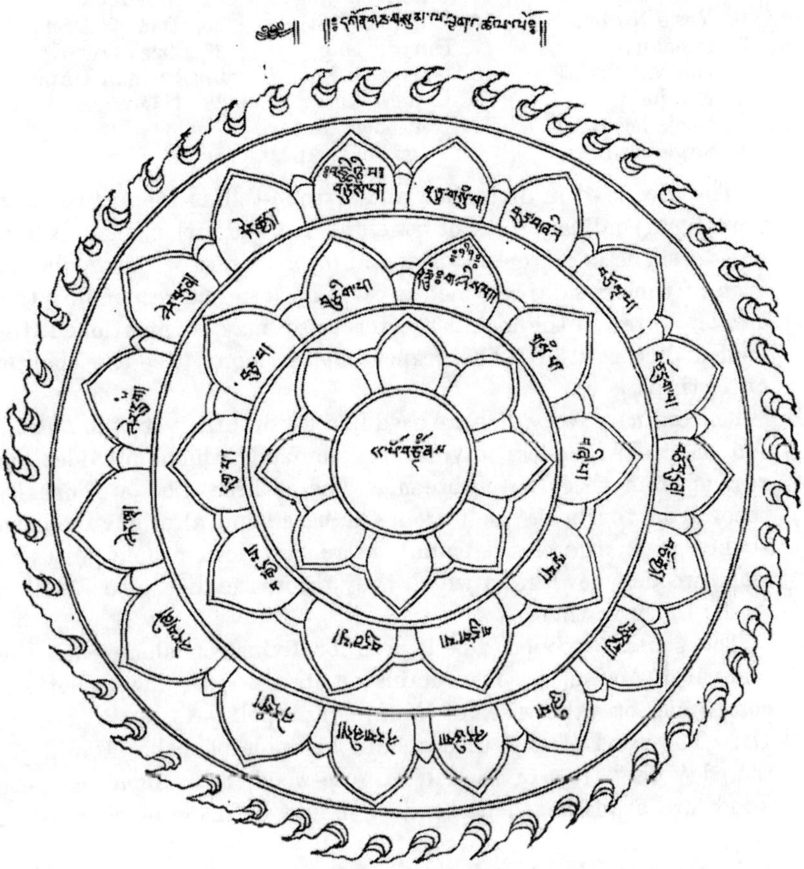

LOTUS DICE-BOARD.

engaged to read the *Ñyīthi Abidharma*, and four monks must do the *dok-pa*, clapping of hands to drive away the evil spirits; for in the south is a king demon who is angry with you and your heart is disturbed and your temper bad. On this account do the worship of the king demon and wear his charm. In your house children will be unsafe, but they will not die. Your valuable goods are likely to go, therefore do the worship of *Nor-t'ub* or "the obtaining of wealth."

The names of the divinities of the other numbers, which give some indication of the nature of the divination, are:—

2. Avalokita.
3. Ugyen Rinboch'e.
4. Tārā.
5. Vajrapāṇi.
6. Yes'e Norbu.
7. Candan.
8. Indra.
9. Mañjuṣrī.
10. Dorje leg-pa.
11. Sirge Ṣāshi.
12. Dorje Gya-t'am.
13. Yuduk Nonmo.
14. Toṅ-ṅan Lhamo.
15. Tamch'en Nagpo.
16. Lungpa Kyithik.
17. Durpag Nag.
18. Garwa Bishū.
19. Gyacha kua.
20. Nad-bdak Remati, god of sickness.
21. Tsunpa.
22. Ch'ui Lhamo.
23. Tuk-zig-pa.
24. Sipi Kukhor.
25. Damc'a Dzema.
26. Dreo Dagyak.
27. Purnan Ukpu.
28. Ṅāg-nag.

The dice used in divination and fortune-telling are of two sorts, namely, (*a*) ordinary ivory or bone dice marked with black dots from one to six as in European dice, and (*b*) a solitary wooden cube, on each of the six sides of which is carved a letter corresponding to a similar letter in the manual. Here also may be mentioned the loaded dice used in "The scape-goat ceremony," see the chapter on festivals.

The ordinary ivory dice are used in a set of three with the *Lhamo Mô* or "The goddess' divination manual," which provides for results from three to eighteen. These three dice are usually thrown on the book itself from the bare hand after having been shaken up in the closed palm. More luxurious people possess a small wooden bowl from which they throw the dice, also a pad on which to throw them.

The solitary wooden dice is used for divination along with the manual of Mañjuṣrī. It contains on its six sides the six letters, compound or otherwise, of Mañjuṣrī's spell—A, R, P, TS, N, DI. The wood of this dice should be made of either Mañjuṣrī's sacred "bla" tree, or sandal, or rose-wood, or if none of these woods are available, then the dice should be made of conch-shell or glass.

In the manual of this dice the portent of each letter is divided into the following sections, namely—House, Favours, Life, Medical, Enemy, Visitors, Business, Travel, Lost property, Wealth, Sickness, etc., which cover all the ordinary objects for which the oracle is consulted. As an example I here extract the portents of A:—

"'A' is the best of all for great Lāmas and for lay officers, and what you will perform will have a good result. For low people it means a little sadness; therefore worship your favourite god.

"*House section.*—All your household will be happy and lucky, and for a time your house will be safe; but where the cattle dwell, there a thief and rogue will perhaps come. To avoid this repeat, or get repeated (by Lāmas), 10,000 times the spell of Marīcī.

"*Favours section.*—The favours you wish will be got gradually. To remove the difficulty in the way of getting these repeat, or get repeated, 100,000 times the spell of gra-lṅa, and also of Devi lô-gyön-ma (this latter is *Om! pisha-tsi par-na-sha-wa-ri sarba dsô-la-ta-sha-ma-na-ye swa-hā!*), and do the *Dug-kar* with its contained *b*zlog-*b*sgyur (clapping of bands) celebration.

"*Life* (*Srog*).—This is good. But the *g*Dön demon from the east and south came with a blue and black article you got. To clear away this cloud do, or get done, 100,000 grib-sel, and do the Nāga worship and read, or get read, 1,000 times Sherab-Ñiṅpo.

"*Medical.*—Taking the medicine prescribed for you for a long time secretly you shall recover. Also burn a lamp nightly from sunset to sunrise as an offering to the gods.

"*Enemy.*—You shall not suffer, as your god is strong and will protect you.

"*Visitors*—probable.—They are coming, or news of their visit will soon be received.

"*Business.*—If you quickly do business it shall be profitable—delay shall be unprofitable.

"*Travel.*—The actual leaving of your house shall be difficult, but if you persevere you shall travel safely.

"*Lost property.*—If you go to the north-west you shall get the lost property, or news of it."

A most peculiar application of the dice is for determining the successive regions and grades of one's future re-births. Fifty-six or more squares of about two inches wide are painted side by side in contrasted colours on a large sheet of cloth, thus giving a chequered area like an ordinary draught or chess-board. Each square represents a certain phase of existence in one or other of the six regions of re-birth, and on it is graphically depicted a figure or scene expressive of the particular state of existence in the world of man, or beast, or god, or in hell, etc., and it bears in its centre the name of its particular form of existence, and it also contains the names of six other possible states of re-birth which ensue from this particular existence, these names being preceded by one or other of the following six letters: A, S, R, G, D, Y, which are also borne on the six faces of the wooden cube which forms the solitary dice for this divination.

Starting from the world of human existence, the dice is thrown, and the letter which turns up determines the region of the next

RE-BIRTH DICE-BOARD.

re-birth. Then proceeding from it the dice is again thrown and the letter turned up indicates the next state of re-birth from this new existence, and so on from square to square *ad infinitum.*

Thus for the Lāmaist layman there appear only six states of re-birth ordinarily possible, namely:—

A. The path of the sorcerer; S. Many days' journey (Ñiṅ ts'og lam); R. The "bent goers," *i.e.*, the beasts; G. The Unorthodox, *i.e.*, a follower of the Bön or pre-Lāmaist form of religion in Tibet; D. an Indian heretic; Y. a ghostly state in Limbo.

The dice accompanying my copy of this board seems to have been loaded so as to show up the letter Y, which gives a ghostly existence, and thus necessitates the performance of many expensive rites to counteract so undesirable a fate. But in addition to the ordinary six states of possible re-birth are the extraordinary states of re-birth to be obtained by the *grand coup* of turning up the letter A five times in succession or the letter S thirteen times in succession. The former event means direct re-birth in the paradise of St. Padma and his mythical primordial god, Samantabhadra, while the latter event is re-birth immediately into the grander paradise of the coming Buddha, Maitreya.

Every year has its general character for good or evil foretold in the astrological books (like Zadkiel's),[1] but like most oracular utterances, these prophecies are couched in rather ambiguous terms, and as there are four or five versions of these forecasts for each year of the twelve-year cycle in addition to a separate set for each year of the sixty-year cycle, there is thus considerable latitude allowed for accounting for most phenomena.

In 1891, during that great visitation of locusts which swarmed over India and into Sikhim as well, the local Lāmas were in great glee on finding that the plague of locusts[2] was down in the Lāmaist

---

[1] The ordinary Lāmaist forecast for 1891 ran as follows: During this year of the Iron-Hare, there is fear for the cattle. The valuable crops will be moderate. Dew and hail excessive. Birds and mice destructive. Robbery and loss of land, fleeing inhabitants. Slowly crops may recover. Black (seeded crops) good, white not good. Human sickness excessive. In early summer water scanty, with hail and heat afterwards. Slowly progress. If those who otherwise shall certainly die, do "the Life Ransom," the "Death Ransom" (*e.g.* releasing small fish from the fishmongers), and the "Ceremony to Obtain Life," then they shall be safe, etc., etc.

[2] The great oriental locust is well-known to the Nepalese and Sikhim highlanders as an occasional visitant, and I am told that a few of the swarms occasionally pass actually into Tibet. The Nepalese during this last visitation were to be seen catching basketfuls of these insects, which they cooked and ate like shrimps with much relish.

forecast for that year. I examined the old printed books and found that in one of the more common versions of the twelve-year cycle a plague of *ch'aga* was foretold for that year, and *ch'aga* is a short form of the word for "locust." And it seemed that it could not have come out in the forecaste oftener than about once in six years.

The more demoniacal forms of divination practised by the professional oracles and wizards are described in the following chapter.

SCORPION CHARM
AGAINST INJURY BY DEMONS

1. *Naga* snake-spirit.
2. *Tsan* devil.
3. *Ma-mo* fiendess.
4. "King"-fiend.

A Black-hat Sorcerer.

XVIII.

SORCERY AND NECROMANCY.

> "He drew the mystic circle's bound
> With skull and cross-bones fenced around;
> He traced full many a sigil there;
> He muttered many a backward prayer
> That sounded like a curse."

WITH the Lāmas, as with the ancient Greeks and Romans, the oracle is a living and highly popular institution. Dwelling in an atmosphere of superstition, the Lāmas, like the alchemists of old, do not recognize the limitation to their powers over Nature. They believe that the hermits in the mountains, and the monks in their cloisters, can readily become adepts in the black art, and can banish drought, and control the sun, and stay the storm; and many of their necromantic performances recall the scene of the "witches' cauldron" in Macbeth.

Magic, and this mostly of a sympathetic kind, seems to have crept into Indian Buddhism soon after Buddha's death. In the form of *irdhi*, or the acquisition of supernatural power, it is a recognized attribute of the Arhats, and even among the primitive Hīnayāna Buddhists. The *Paritta* ("pirit") rite of the Southern Buddhists is essentially of the character of exorcism,[1] and portions of the text of the Saddharma Puṇḍarīka, dating to about the first century of our era, are specially framed for this purpose.

But the Indian cult does not appear ever to have descended to the gross devil-dancing[2] and Shamanist charlatanism of the Lāmas; though even the Lāmas seldom, if ever, practise such common tricks as swallowing knives and vomiting fire, with which they have been credited. They find plenty of scope for their charlatanism in playing upon the easy credulity of the people by working themselves into the furious state of the "possessed," so as to oracularly deliver auguries, and by the profitable pursuits of necromancy and sorcery.

Every orthodox monastery in Tibet, even of the most reformed sects, keeps or patronizes a sorcerer, and consults him and follows

---

[1] "*Pirit*," as practised by the southern Buddhists, is a reading of certain scriptures as an exorcism against evil spirits in sickness. It addresses itself to "all spirits here assembled," and says: "therefore hear me, O ye spirits! Be friendly to the race of men; for every day and night they bring you their offerings; therefore keep diligent watch over them. Ye spirits, etc." (HARDY'S *E. Mon.*). Nagasena in *Milinda* (*circa*, 150 A.D.) is made to say, "The blessed one, O king . . . sanctioned Pirit. And Rhys Davids (*Milinda*, p. 213), commenting on this remark, states: This is the oldest text in which the use of the service is referred to. But the word Parittā (Pirit) is used *Kullavagga*, v., 6, on an asseveration of love; for snakes to be used as what is practically a charm against snake-bite, and that is attributed to the Buddha. The particular Suttas, Ratana Sutta, Khanda-paritta, Mora paritta Dhagagga-paritta, and the Atānāṭiya-paritta, and the Aṅguli-mala paritta, and passages here referred to are all in the Pitakas.

Cf. also a manual of exorcism used in Ceylon, entitled Piruwana-pota.—HARDY'S *East Mon.*, p. 26, 30.

[2] It will be interesting to find whether the dancing orgies of the Ceylon Buddhists are in any way related to those of northern Buddhism. The descriptions of Callaway are insufficient for this purpose. They show, however, that Yama the Death king figures prominently in the dances.

his dictates upon most matters; and there are some cloisters near Lhāsa specially devoted to instruction in this art. Such are, Moru, Ramo-ch'e, and Kar-mas'a.

The chief wizards are called "Defenders of the faith" (*ch'os-skyoṅ*), and the highest of these, namely, Nä-ch'uṅ, is the government oracle, and is consulted on all important state occasions and undertakings. But every monastery of any size has its own sorcerer, who, however, in the case of the poorer sects, is not usually considered a member of the brotherhood, and he is allowed to marry. They possess no literature, and deliver their sayings orally.

Their fantastic equipment and their frantic bearing, as in figure at page 475, their cries and howls, despite their name, can scarcely be of Sivaite origin, but seem clearly to identify them with the Bön— the grossest of Shamanist devil-dancers. The belief both in ghosts and witchcraft and the practice of exorcism was so deep-rooted in the country, that Padma-sambhava gave it a prominent place in his system, and even Tsoṅ-K'ā-pa could not do otherwise than take them over into his yellow sect. And that position within the Lāmaist priesthood once granted to the heathen sorcerer it naturally became dogmatic and scholastic,[1] and seems to have been given its present organized shape by the fifth Grand Lāma, Ṅag Waṅ, in the seventeenth century; though even now it is satisfactory to find that some of the more intelligent and respectable Lāmas despise such gross exhibitions as an unholy pandering to the vulgar taste for the marvellous.

The chief sorcerers are called "The revered protectors of religion," *Ch'o-kyoṅ* or *Ch'o-je*, and are believed to be incarnations of the malignant spirit called "kings,"[2] who seem to be spirits of demonified heroes, and still the object of very active popular worship.[3]

These king-fiends are alleged to have been originally five brothers,[4] who came from Ch'ad-dumiṅ northern Mongolia,

[1] KÖPPEN, ii., 260.

[2] rgyal-po.

[3] The mode of worshipping these "kings" and the offerings most acceptable to them are detailed in the book *Ku-ṅa gyal-pou Kaṅ-Ṣag*. "Confession to the five sacred Kings" and "Confession (*Kan-Sag*) to the Incarnate Great *Ch'o–Kyoṅ*."

[4] rgyal-po-sku-nga. These are said to have been the kings of the east, mystically called "the Body" and resident at Sam-yä, the king of the west, entitled the Speech,

though now only two (or three) of them seem to be known, and these are represented by the oracles of Nä-ch'uṅ, Karma-s'ar, and Gadoṅ.

The chief of these necromancers was first brought into the order of the Lāmas by the fifth Grand Lāma, who seems to have felt, like the Roman governors, the necessity for placing the divination for government service under the control of the priests, and he doubtless realized the political advantages of having so powerful an instrument entirely within the order. He admitted the augur of Nä-ch'uṅ[1] to the brotherhood, and made him the state-oracle.

The Necromancer-in-Ordinary to Government.
The Nä-ch'uṅ Oracle.

The Necromancer-in-Ordinary to the government is the Nä-ch'uṅ sorcerer. The following details regarding him I have obtained from a resident of his temple, and also from several of his clientèle.[2]

This demon-king was originally a god of the Turki[3] tribes, and named "The White Overcast Sky."[4] and on account of his Turki descent the popular epic of the famous prince *Kesar*, who had conquered the Turki tribes, is not permitted to be recited at De-pung, under whose ægis the Nä-ch'uṅ oracle resides for fear of offending the latter.

He was brought to Tibet by Padma-sambhava in Thi-Sroṅ Detsan's reign, and made the Ch'o-Kyoṅ or religious guardian of the first monastery, Sām-yä. There he became incarnate, and the man possessed by his spirit was styled "The Religious Noble" or Ch'ö-je, and he married and became a recognized oracle with hereditary descent.

This demon-king is thus identified with Pe-har (usually pronounced *Pé-kar*),[5] although other accounts make him the fourth and younger brother of Pe-har.

---

resident at Nä-ch'uṅ, the king of the north, the Deeds, resident at Norbu-gaṅ and of the south, the Learning, resident at Gāh-dong, eight miles west of Lhāsa, and of the centre (? Lamo). Schlagintweit (p. 157) names them, "Bihar Ch'oichoṅ Da-lha Luvaṅ and Tokchoi," but this seems to include divinities of other classes.

1 About seven miles west of De-pung.

2 Cf. also the vernacular literature: gSer-p'reṅ; gyu p'reṅ; dṅul p'reṅ, and the deb-ther of Nä-ch'uṅ temple, and of Reting gyal po.

3 Hor-pa lha of the Bādā *s*gom-kaw order.

4 *g*Nam-t'b dKar-po.

5 Although he is specially associated with monasteries it is unlikely that his name is a corruption of Bihar (*Vihara*), as it is spelt *d*pe-har, and he has Tibetan attributes.

Many centuries later Pe-har's spirit is said to have transferred itself to Ts'al-guṅ-t'aṅ, about four miles E.S.E. of Lhāsa, on the way to Gah-dan, and thence in a miraculous manner to its present location.[1]

In the time of the Grand Lāma Ñag-Waṅ, in the seventeenth century, when he extended the Ge-lug-pa order wholesale, he made the Nä-ch'uṅ ch'o-je a Lāma of the yellow sect, and gave him the monastery called De-yang ta-tsaṅ,[2] and made him the state oracle. The reason alleged for the pre-eminence thus conferred is said to be that he frustrated an attempt of the Newars or Nepalese merchants of Lhāsa to poison the tea-cistern at the great festival, by driving a knife through the vessel, and thus discharging the alleged poison.

Since his promotion within the ranks of the established church he and his successors have been celibate and educated. His monastery, which is richly furnished and surrounded by gardens, including a conservatory with stuffed birds, and leopards, and other animals, now contains one hundred and one monks, many of whom are real Ge-longs, observing the two hundred and fifty-three *Vinaya* rules, and from amongst these his successor is chosen—the succession passing by breath and not by heredity, and it is said that these sorcerers are very short-lived on account of their maniacal excitement; and they probably are addicted to Indian hemp. He has the title of *Kung* from the Chinese emperor, a title which is seldom bestowed even on the Sha-pe or governors (dukes) of Tibet.

He is dressed like a Ge-lug-pa monk, usually in red robes, but wears a lotus-shaped hat of a yellow colour relieved by red and topped by a ruby button.

---

1 The legend states that the spirit of Pehar entered into a resident of Ts'al-guṅ-t'aṅ, and said to a Lāma named Z'aṅ, "Let us go to Udyāna (the country of Padma-sambhava)." The Lāma then shut up the possessed man in a box, which he flung into the river Kyi. Now the abbot of De-puṅg had prophesied the previous day to his pupils, saying, "A box will float down the river, go find it and seize it." The pupils found the box and brought it to the spot where the Nä-ch'uṅ temple now stands, namely, about one mile to the S.E. of De-pung, and there they opened it, and lo! a great fire came out and disappeared into a tree, and the dead body of a man was found in the box; but by the prayers of the abbot the spirit consented to return to the body. And the resuscitated corpse, refusing to enter the pure monastery of De-pung on the plea of being uncelibate, requested to be granted "a small dwelling" where he stood—hence the name of the place Nä-ch'uṅ or "the small dwelling." And the identical tree is still to be seen there.

2 *b*de-yaṅs gra-*g*tsan.

This state-sorcerer proceeds in great pomp to Lhāsa once a year, on the second day of the first month, attended by the magistrate[1] of De-pung, and is accommodated in a special temple close to the east of the great Jo-wo temple, where he prophesies the events of the year. His rank is so high that he only visits the Dalai Lāma. Government officials require to visit him when seeking information in regard to government projects, war, sickness, etc. And when he is at home his minister[2] acts as the government go-between on ordinary occasions, and he and other sorcerers accompany troops to battle and interpret the portents of the omens of birds, animals, etc.

He is also consulted by private people who can afford the expense. In addition to any presents in kind, a money fee of from ten to 1,000 *taṅkas* (silver coins about sixpence) or more are needed, and these are applied to the support of his large establishment.

The applicant to the oracle must have his request presented in writing, and when a sufficient number of applications have accumulated, the augur is disclosed in a wildly ecstatic state. He throws rice at the applicants, and becoming more inflamed by fury, he falls down in convulsions and then replies to questions addressed to him. The replies are noted down by attendant scribes, and the document is afterwards sealed—it is said by the sorcerer himself on his recovery.

The utterances are often couched in poetry or allegory, with the brevity and ambiguousness of an oracular response.

One of the *Nä-ch'uṅ* sorcerer's responses which I have seen bears a circular red seal of crossed thunderbolts. It is interesting rather as a sample of the kind of questions addressed to the oracle than for the oracular deliverance itself, which is of the ordinary prosaic kind.

"To the exalted throne (made of the corpses of infidels) on which rest the feet of the great Religious Protector, the Incarnate Victor-God of the enemies in all the three worlds,—The Lamp of Wisdom!

"I, this child (Sra*s*), believing in you, with my ten fingers resting on my heart, petition thus:—

"1. What is the evil accruing this year on the following persons, and what the necessary worship (to counteract the evil)?

ts'ogs-ch'en z'al-'ṅo.

[2] Entitled Lon-po rdo-rje drag-ldan.

The Governor	birth year,	Iron-Monkey.
Male	,,	Earth-Hare.
Male	,,	Fire-Tiger.
Female	,,	Earth-Ox.
Male	,,	,, Tiger.
Female	,,	Iron-Bird.
Female	,,	Fire-Hare.
Female	,,	Fire-Dog.

"2. What is the evil, now and hereafter, accruing to the Guide (Teacher) of Sikhim and Gang-ljong (=*Cis*-Tibet) from the foreign harmers? And what can be done?

"3. At the Tibetan farm of Dô-ta (near Khamba-jong) the fields for several seasons have yielded no crops on account of 'dew from want of clouds.' What remedy is for this?

"Pray relieve our anxiety. You, who are the best of gods, do not ever abandon us; but ever protect us on all sides as by a thick 'tent!' Save us! We worship Thee! And we offer you this god-like silken robe; also this pair of fowls (male and female)!

"This applicant's name is——— "

The Reply.

"Hri! 1. Read Tārā's ritual, and plant 'prayer-flags' (in number) according to your age.

"2. Worship Tārā much, and plant as many of the largest 'prayer-flags' as possible.

"3. Read the *Bum* (Prajña pāramitā) and (St. Padma's) T'aṅ-yig, the three roots (Lāma, tutelary and Buddha); make the Ts'ogs offering, also one to Dorje Nam-ch'uṅ, and Yul-K'rus (sprinkling holy water to purify the country); and mollify the country-gods by the Gya-ṅan Sruṅ-ma."

THE KARMA-S'AR ORACLE.

But the Karma-s'ar[1] oracle seems to have been the original one, and it still is one of those most popularly resorted to. Its sorcerer is also held to be possessed by the demon-king Pe-har. It is within Lhāsa, and is specially under the ægis of the Serra monastery, and this indeed is said to have been a chief reason why the Grand Lāma Ṅag-waṅ eclipsed it by attaching the state oracle to his own and rival monastery De-pung.

Yet Karma-s'ar too receives some direct countenance from

[1] Or rKar-ma-K'ya.

government, for on the seventh month of each year its sorcerer proceeds to Serra and delivers there his fore-warnings of portending danger to the church and state for the forthcoming year. He is not celibate, but has received some education and is able to read and write, and has a large following of pupils.

He is extensively consulted about political events, and his deliverances, which are posted up at the south door of his residence at Lhāsa as well as at Serra, excite much notice. I quote here a few examples of his oracular responses :—

The dog is unlikely to catch the fox though both may wear off their tails (advice to give up pursuing some small though wily party).

The prancing steed thinking only of himself falls over the cliff (compare with "pride meets a fall").

The eagle's wings bring the fishes under its power.

The fox will become greater than a mountain-like elephant (fortelling advancement of a crafty underling).

The path of the voracious wolf is barred by a serpent.

The grunting pig with upturned tusks frightens the hawk. (This is an excuse for evading reply to the question for fear of offending the authorities.)

A more inferior type of sorcerer is the Lhā-Ka (probably Lhā-K'a or "God's mouth-piece," also called Ku-t'em-ba. Such are found frequently in western Tibet, and may be females,[1] and in which case the woman may marry without hindrance to her profession. These wizards are especially resorted to for the relief of pain.

This exorcist puts on the mirror over the heart, the masker's cope, with the five Bats of Fortune, and the five-partite chaplet of the five Jinas, topped by skulls, a silken girdle (paṅ-den), and placing a cake on his head, he calls upon Buddha and St. Padma, and offers a libation[2] and incense to the demons, and beating a large drum (not a tambourine or hautboy) and cymbals, calls on the several country-gods by name, saying: *Nä-K'aṅ dira c'é-den su-so-so!* and the advent of the deity is believed to be seen in the mirror. The first to come is the *tutelary*, who then brings

[1] They somewhat resemble the *Ñan-jorma* and *Pa-o* of Sikhim, but are not devil-dancers like the latter. Compare also with the witch-like priestesses called "Day-gals" of the Hunza tribes mentioned by Dr. Leitner as the mediums of the divine pleasure and supernatural presence being manifest by ringing of bells, etc.

[2] ser-skyem.

the *Nāgas*, dragon-demi-gods and the *Dré*, which are the most malignant of all demons.

The divining-arrow is then taken from the plate of flour which had been offered to these demons, and its blunted point is put on the affected part. The Lhā-ka exorcist now applies his mouth half-way down the shaft, and sucks forcibly. On this a drop of blood appears over the painful part, without any abrasion of skin, and evidently dropped by sleight of hand from the parti-coloured ribbons of the arrow. It is, however, considered a miracle, and the patient is led to believe that the demon has been expelled from the part.

The commonest sorcerer is called *Ńag-pa* or "the Expert in Incantations." These are very numerous and are more nearly allied than the *Ch'ö-je* to the original type of the Tibetan devil-dancer. But they are not admitted into any of the monasteries of the reformed and semi-reformed sects.

They are usually illiterate, they marry and wear a peculiar dress, the most characteristic part of which is the tall conical hat like that of the orthodox western witch, and pictured at page 475. It has, however, added to it a broad rim of yak-hair and on either side a coiled serpent, and it is surmounted by a *vajra*-topped skull and peacock feathers with long streamers of the five-coloured silks such as are used with the divining-arrow.

Their special weapons[1] for warring with the demons are:—

1. The Phurbu, a dagger of wood or metal to stab the demons. The central portion is in the form of a *vajra*-thunderbolt which is the part held in the wizard's hand, and the hilt-end is terminated either by a sample fiend's-head, or by the same surmounted by a horse's head, representing the horse-headed tutelary-devil Tam-ḍin.
2. A sword with thunderbolt-hilt.
3. Sling, bows and arrows.
4. The divining-arrow (Dah-dar). This is inserted into a plate of flour offered to the demons. Other appliances are the magic triangle (huṅ-huṅ) containing talismanic sentences within which the wish of the votary is inscribed and called *liṅ-ga*.

A sash of human bones (rus-rgyan) carved with fiends and mystic symbols is also worn, and as a breast-plate a magic mirror of metal which probably is identical with that found in Taoism and Shintoism.

1 They are called *zor*, and the edge or point directed against the demons is Zor-kha.

The commonest necromantic rites are "the closing of the doors to the demons of the earth and sky," the exorcising of the disease-demon, the death ceremonies as a whole, expelling the death-demon, the lay figure of the deceased and its rites, etc., and the exorcising of ghosts. And I here give some details of these rites.

Barring the Door against the Earth-Demons.

The Tibetan *genii loci* are worshipped in a way presenting many parallels to the Roman worship of their *Lares*, the horse-shoe above the door of our old-fashioned houses, and the skull-trophies of the Indo-Chinese.[1]

The local earth-spirits are named "Master Earth" or "Earth-Masters,"[2] and are comparable to the terrestrial Nāgas of the Hindūs. The most malignant are the "*gñan*," who infest certain trees and rocks, which are always studiously shunned and respected, and usually daubed with paint in adoration.

The earth-demons are innumerable, but they are all under the authority of "Old mother *Khön-ma*."[3] She rides upon a ram, and is dressed in golden yellow robes, and her personal attendant is "Sa-thel-ṅag-po." In her hand she holds a golden noose, and her face contains eighty wrinkles.

The ceremony of "closing the door of the earth," so frequently referred to in the Lāmaist prescriptions, is addressed to her.

In this rite is prepared an elaborate arrangement of masts, and amongst the mystic objects of the emblem the strings, etc.; most prominent is a ram's skull with its attached horns, and it is directed *downwards* to the earth.

Inside the ram's skull is put some gold leaf, silver, turquoise, and portions of every precious object available, as well as portions of dry eatables, rice, wheat, pulses, etc.

On the forehead is painted in ochre-colour[4] the geomantic sign

---

[1] Certain Himalayan tribes (*e.g.* the Limbu), and the Lushais (Riebeck's *Chittagong Hill Tribes*, Lond., 1882), place skulls of animals outside their dwellings. These, I believe, are intended less as trophies than as charms against spirits.

[2] Sa-bdag-po.

[3] Apparently derived from the Chinese name of the *Pa-Kwa* for "earth."

[4] The symbolic colour of the earth.

EMBLEMS TO BAR THE DEMONS.

For the earth-demons. For the sky-demons.

of the park'a *Khön*, on the right jaw the sun, and on the left jaw the moon, and over it are placed masks, around which are wound coloured threads in geometric patterns; also pieces of silk (*tarzab*) rag, and Chinese brass coins (Ang., "cash") and several wool-knobbed sticks (*phan-k'ra*).

PARK'A KHÖN.

Along the base are inserted on separate slips of wood the following images, etc.: 1, a man's picture; 2, a woman's picture with a spindle in her hand; 3, a house picture; 4, a tree picture (*k'ram-s'in*); 5, figures of the geomantic signs eight *Parkha* and the nine *Mewa*.

The whole erection is now fixed to the outside of the house above the door; the object of these figures of a man, wife and house is to deceive the demons should they still come in spite of this offering, and to mislead them into the belief that the foregoing pictures are the inmates of the house, so that they may wreak their wrath on these bits of wood and so save the real human occupants.

Then when all is ready and fixed, the Lāma turns to the south-west and chants:—

"O! O! *ke! ke!* Through the nine series of earths you are known as Old Mother Khön-ma, the mother of all the Sa-dak-po. You are the guardian of the earth's doors. The dainty things which you especially desire we herewith offer, namely, a white skull of a ram, on whose right cheek the sun is shining like burnished gold, and on the left cheek the moon gleams dimly like a conch-shell. The forehead bears the sign of *Khön*, and the whole is adorned with every sort of silk, wool, and precious things, and it is also given the spell of *Khön* (here the Lāma breathes upon it). All these good things are here offered to you, so please close the open doors of the earth to the family who here has offered you these things, and do not let your servant Sa-thel ngag-po and the rest of the earth spirits do harm to this family. By this offering let all the doors of the earth be shut. *O! O! ke! ke!* Let not your servants injure us when we build a house or repair this one, nor when we are engaged in marriage matters, and let everything happen to this family according to their wishes. Do not be angry with us, but do us the favours we ask." Here the priest claps his hands and shouts:—

"*Om kharal dok! Om khamrhil dok!*[1] *Benneu swāhā!*"

[1] "The images of men and women made of wool were hung in the streets, and so many balls made of wool as there were servants in the family, and so many complete images as there were children (*Festus pud Lil. Gyr*). The meaning of which custom

DEMONS OF THE SKY.

The local-demons of the sky are under the control of "the grandfather of the three worlds"—Old father Khen-pa—who is represented as an old man with snow-white hair, dressed in white robes and riding on the white dog of the sky, and in his hand he carries a crystal wand. He is the "master" of the sky, and the ceremony named *nam-gô*, or "the closing of the doors of the sky," so frequently prescribed by the astrologers, is addressed to him.

In it is an arrangement of masts, threads, images, etc., exactly similar to that used for the Earth-demons, the only difference being that in this case a dog's skull is used (note that the dog was especially associated with the analogous *Lares* worship of the Romans,[1]) and it is directed upwards, pointing to the sky; and the sign of the *parkha* painted on the forehead is that of *Khen*, and is in blue colours. And the ceremony is the same except in its prelude and in the name of the chief servants:—

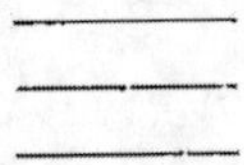

PARKHA KHEN.

"O! O! we turn towards the western sun, to the celestial mansion where the sky is of turquoise, to the grandfather of the three worlds—Old Khen-pa, the master of the sky. Pray cause your servant, the white Nam-tel, to work for our benefit, and send the great planet Pemba (Saturn) as a friendly mes-enger," etc., etc.

Another common ceremony of a necromantic character is that entitled "Prevention from injury by the eight classes (of demons)." These eight classes of spirits have already been noted, and the detailed account of their worship has been given by me elsewhere.[2]

The demons who produce disease, short of actual death, are called Shé, and are exorcised by an elaborate ceremony in which a variety of images and offerings are made.[3] The officiating Lāma invokes his tutelary fiend, and thereby assuming spiritually the

was this: These feasts were dedicated to the Lares, who were esteemed infernal gods; the people desiring hereby that these gods would be contented with these woollen images and spare the persons represented by them. These Lares sometimes were clothed in the skins of *dogs* (*Plutarch. in Prob.*) and were sometimes fashioned in the shape of dogs (*Plautus*), whence that creature was consecrated to them."—TOOKE's *Pantheon*, p. 280.

1 The meaning of the "*dok*" is "let all evils be annihilated!"

2 *Lāmaism in Sikhim.*

3 gsed.

dread guise of this king evil, he orders out the disease-demon under threat of getting himself eaten up by the awful tutelary who now possesses the Lāma. The demons are stabbed by the mystic dagger *purba*. Charmed seeds and pebbles, consecrated by muttering spells over them, are thrown at the demon. The charmed seeds are stored in a small horn (*t'uṅ-rva*), carved with scorpions, caityas and various other symbols in relief.[1]

EXORCISER'S HORN.

The ritual itself is a curious mixture of Indian magic circles with Chinese astrology and necromancy, and has been detailed by me elsewhere.[2]

DEATH CEREMONIES.

As the rites in connection with a death include a considerable amount of devil worship, they may be noticed in this place.

On the occurrence of a death the body is not disturbed in any way until the Lāma has extracted the soul in the orthodox manner. For it is believed that any movement of the corpse might eject the soul, which then would wander about in an irregular manner and get seized by some demon. On death, therefore, a white cloth is thrown over the face of the corpse, and the soul-extracting Lāma (*'p'o-bo*) is sent for. On his arrival all weeping relatives are excluded from the death-chamber, so as to secure solemn silence, and the doors and windows closed, and the Lāma sits down upon a mat near the head of the corpse, and commences to chant the service which contains directions for the soul to find its way to the western paradise of the mythical Buddha—Amitābha.

[1] For the Tartar mode of exorcising disease-demons, cf. Huc., i., 75.

[2] *Lāmaism in Sikhim.*

After advising the spirit to quit the body and its old associations and attachment to property, the Lāma seizes with the fore-finger and thumb a few hairs of the crown of the corpse, and plucking these forcibly, he is supposed to give vent to the spirit of the deceased through the roots of these hairs; and it is generally believed that an actual but invisibly minute perforation of the skull is thus made, through which the liberated spirit passes.

The spirit is then directed how to avoid the dangers which beset the road to the western paradise, and it is then bid god-speed. This ceremony lasts about an hour.

In cases where, through accident or otherwise, the body of the deceased is not forthcoming, the operation for extraction of the soul is done by the Lāma in spirit while he sits in deep meditation.

Meanwhile the astrologer-Lāma has been requisitioned for a death-horoscope, in order to ascertain the requisite ages and birth-years of those persons who may approach and touch the corpse, and the necessary particulars as to the date and mode of burial, as well as the worship which is to be done for the welfare of the surviving relatives.

The nature of such a horoscope will best be understood by an actual example, which I here give. It is the death-horoscope of a little girl of two years of age, who died at Darjiling in 1890.

HAIL TO LĀMA MAÑJUṢRĪ!

The year of birth of this female was the Bull-year, with which the Snake and the Sheep are in conflict; therefore those individuals born in the Snake and the Sheep year cannot approach the corpse. The death-demon was hiding in the house inside certain coloured articles, and he now has gone to a neighbouring house where there is a family of five with cattle and dogs (therefore that other family needs to do the necessary worship). The death-demon will return to the house of the deceased within three months; so there must be done before that time the "za-de-kha-gyur" service.

Her PARK'A being *Dvā* in relation to her death, it is found that her spirit on quitting her body entered her loin girdle and a sword. [In this case the affected girdle was cast away and the sword was handed over to the Lāma.] Her life was taken to the east by Tsān and king demons, and her body died in the west; therefore, small girls, cousins, sisters and brothers in that house will be harmed. The deceased's death was due to Iron. And the death-demon came from the south and has gone to the east.

Her Mewa gives the "3rd Indigo blue." Thus it was the death-demon of the deceased's paternal grandfather and grandmother who caused her death; therefore take (1) a Sats-ts'a (a miniature earthern caitya), and (2) a sheep's head, and (3) earth from a variety of sites, and place these upon the body of the deceased, and this evil will be corrected.

The Day *of her Death* was Friday. Take to the north-west a leather bag or earthern pot in which have been placed four or five coloured articles, and throw it away as the death-demon goes there. The death having so happened, it is very bad for old men and women. On this account take a horse's skull,[1] or a serpent's skull[2] and place it upon the corpse.

Her Death Star is *Gre.* Her brother and sister who went near to her are harmed by the death-messenger (s'in-je). Therefore an ass's skull and a goat's skull must be placed on the corpse.

Her Death Hour was soon after sunset. And in the twelfth month her life was cut. The death-demon therefore arrived in the earthern cooking pot and bowl of a man and woman visitor dressed in red who came from the south. Thus the deceased's father and mother are harmed, and especially so if either is born in the Sheep-year.

Precautions to secure a Good Re-birth.—It is necessary to prepare an image of Vajrapāṇi, Vajrasattva, and before these to have prayer[3] done for the good re-birth of the girl's spirit. If this be done, then she will be re-born in the house of a rich man in the west.

For deceased's Spirit.—It is necessary to get the Lāmas to read the service (*s*mon-lam) praying for re-birth in the Paradise of Sukhāvatī.

For Survivors *of family.*—It is necessary to have read the prayers for long life, viz., "ts'e-*m*do" and "ts'e-*g*zuṅs."

Directions for Removal of Corpse.—Those who remove the corpse must have been born in the *Dog* or the *Dragon* year. The body must be taken outside of the house on the morning of the third day following the death, and it must be carried to the south-west, and be *buried* (not burned, or abandoned to birds or dogs).

On obtaining this death-horoscope the body is tied up in a sitting posture by the auspicious person indicated by the horoscope, and placed in a corner of the room which is not already occupied by the house-demon.

Notice is sent to all relatives and friends within reach, and these collect within two or three days and are entertained with food of rice, vegetables, etc., and a copious supply of *murwa* beer

[1] A fragment of such a skull or its image made of dough is usually all that is used.

[2] Dough also will do.

[3] It has frequently been asserted that *no* prayer is practised in Lāmaism. This is not true: real prayer is frequently done; the word used here in *g*sol-wa-*g*tab.

and tea. This company of visitors remain loitering in and around the house, doing great execution with hand-prayer-wheels and muttering the "*Om-maṇi*," until the expulsion of the death-demon, which follows the removal of the body, and in which ceremony they all have to join. The expense of the entertainment of so large a company is of course considerable.

During this feasting, which is suggestive of an Irish "wake," the deceased is always, at every meal, offered his share of what is going, including tobacco, etc. His own bowl is kept filled with beer and tea and set down beside the corpse, and a portion of all the other eatables is always offered to him at meal times; and after the meal is over his portion is thrown away, as his spirit is supposed to have extracted all the essence of the food, which then no longer contains nutriment, and is fit only to be thrown away. And long after the corpse has been removed, his cup is regularly filled with tea or beer even up till the forty-ninth day from death, as his spirit is free to roam about for a maximum period of forty-nine days subsequent to death.

And to feed the *manes* of the deceased is done a sacrifice for the dead, called *Tiṅ-s'ag*, suggestive of the Indian Buddhist practice of *Avalambana*[1] and the Hindū rite of *Sradh*.[2] In this sacrifice a cake and a quantity of rice are thrown into the nearest stream or river, after having called the spirits by means of a small gong struck by a horn, and the chanting by six or more Lāmas of the cake-offering-service,[3] followed by the repetition by them of a *mantra* to the number if possible of 100,000 times.[4]

The soul is now assisted in winging its way to the western paradise by a group of Lāmas who chant by relays all night and day the litany for sending the soul directly to that paradise. And

[1] As a festival (in China on the fifteenth day of the seventh month), cf. EITEL Handb. "Ulamba"; BEAL, *The Oriental*, Nov. 6th, 1875, showing that the Avalambana sutra of sacrifice for the dead was translated into Chinese, *circa* 265 A.D. Also in Ceylon, HARDY's *Man.*, p. 59. It is still kept in Europe: "Even at the cemetery of Père Lachaise, they still put cakes and sweetmeats on the graves; and in Brittany the peasants do not forget to make up the fire, and leave the fragments of the supper on the table for the souls of the dead of the family who will come to visit their home." TYLOR's *Anthrop.*, p. 351.

[2] *Theatre of the Hindus*, i., 322, *n*.

[3] Namo sarva Tāthāgata Avalokita om Sambhara hūm.

[4] On feeding the corpse, cf., TAYLOR's *Prim. Cult.*, i., 482; SPENCER's *Sociology*, i., 157, 206; FARRER's *Primitive Manners*, 21; Lady WILDES, *Irish Legends*, 118, 140.

a special reading of this service by the assembled monks in the neighbouring monastery is also arranged for by those who can afford the expense.

One or more Lāmas also read over the corpse the guide[1] for the spirit's passage through the valley of horrors intervening between death and a new re-birth. This passage is somewhat suggestive of Bunyan's "Pilgrim's Progress," only the demons and dangers which beset the way are much more numerous and awful. Full

SUMMONING THE HUNGRY DEMONS.

directions are read out for the benefit of the deceased as to how to avoid these pitfalls and ogres, and how to find the proper white coloured path which alone leads to a good re-birth.

It is, however, rather incongruous to find that while the Lāma reading this service is urging the spirit to bestir itself to the necessary exertions for a good re-birth, the other Lāma by his side in the *De-wa-chan* service is sending the spirit direct to the western paradise—a non-Buddhist invention which is outside the regions of re-birth.

[1] t'os-grol.

At this stage it often happens, though it is scarcely considered orthodox, that some Lāmas find, as did Maudgalayāna by his second-sight, consulting their lottery-books, that the spirit has been sent to hell, and the exact compartment in hell is specified. Then must be done a most costly service by a very large number of Lāmas. First of all is done "virtue" on behalf of the deceased; this consists in making offerings to the Three Collections, namely: To the *Gods* (sacred food, lamps, etc.); to the *Lāmas* (food and presents); to the *Poor* (food, clothes, beer, etc.).

The virtue resulting from these charitable acts is supposed to tell in favour of the spirit in hell. Then many more expensive services must be performed, and especially the propitiation of "The Great Pitying One," for his intercession with the king of hell (a form of himself) for the release of this particular spirit. Avalokita is behind to terminate occasionally the torment of tortured souls by casting a lotus-flower at them. Even the most learned and orthodox Lāmas believe that by celebrating these services the release of a few of the spirits actually in hell may be secured.[1] But in practice every spirit in hell for whom its relatives pay sufficiently may be released by the aid of the Lāmas. Sometimes a full course of the necessary service is declared insufficient, as the spirit has only got a short way out of hell,—very suggestive of the story of the priest and his client in Lever's story,—and then additional expense must be incurred to secure its complete extraction.

Before removing the corpse from the house, an especial feast of delicacies, including pork and drink of sorts, are set before it. And a Lāma presenting a "scarf of honour" to the corpse thus addresses it:—

> "You! (and here the deceased's name is stated) now have received from your relatives all this good food and drink; partake freely of its essence, as you shall not have any more chances! For you must understand that you have died, and your spirit must be gone from here, and never come back again to trouble or injure your relatives. Remember the name of your Lāma-teacher, which is . . . . . , and by his aid take the right path—the white one. Come this way!"

Then the Lāma with a thigh-bone trumpet in the one hand and a hand-drum in the other, and taking the end of a long white

[1] Cf. page 98 for Maudgalayāna releasing his mother.

scarf,[1] the other end of which has been tied to the corpse, he precedes the carrier of the corpse blowing his trumpet and beating the drum and chanting a liturgy. This scene is figured in the Wheel of Life, in the upper part of its human compartment.

He frequently looks back to invite the spirit to accompany the body, which he assures it is being led in the right direction. And the corpse-bearer is followed by the rest of the procession, some bearing refreshments, and last of all come the weeping relatives. The ceremony of guiding the deceased's spirit is only done for the laity—the spirits of deceased Lāmas are credited with a knowledge of the proper path, and need no such instruction. The body is usually carried to the top of a hillock for burial or cremation.

The corpse is cremated with much ceremony, including some interesting worship of the Fire-god *Agni*, as well as of Avalokita, the Great-hearted Pitying Lord.[2]

But the cremation or interment of the corpse does not terminate the death-rites. There needs still to be made a masked lay figure of the deceased, and the formal burning of the mask and the expulsion from the house of the death-demon and other rites.

Expelling the Death-Demon.

This rite for expelling from the house and locality the demon who caused the death must be done within two days after the removal of the corpse. It is called "The turning away of the face of the Destroying Devil."[3]

This ceremony, of the nature of a sacrifice, as well as exorcism, has been detailed by me elsewhere.[4]

---

[1] The scarf used in the funeral procession may probably represent the Chinese *hurin-fan*, or "soul's banner," which is carried before the coffin in China.

[2] As detailed in the book "the deliverance of the entire animal (world) by the revered Great Pitying One ('gro-wa-Kun-grol)."

[3] Za-'dre K'a-sgyur.

[4] *Lāmaism in Sikhim*; part of its ritual is the following:—

On a small wooden platform is made the image of a tiger by means of the grass and mud plaster; it is fashioned in a walking attitude, with mouth wide open. The mouth and tusks are made of a dough, and the body is coloured with yellow and brown stripes, in imitation of a tiger's markings, and around its neck is tied a rope of threads of five colours.

Then a small image of a man is made by kneaded dough, in which are incorporated filings from the alloy of the five precious things. Into the belly of this image, which is called "the eating-demon," is inserted a piece of paper, on which is written the following banishing spell: "Go, thou devouring devil, having your face turned

THE LAY FIGURE OF DECEASED, AND ITS RITES.

The day on which the corpse was removed a lay figure of the deceased is made by dressing a stool or block of wood in the clothes of the deceased, and as a face a mask is inserted of printed

---

to the enemy!" It is then clad in pieces of silk, and is placed sitting astride the tiger's back.

Another figure is of human form, but with the head of a bird. Its face is painted red, in its belly is inserted paper on which is written, "You devouring devil, don't remain in this village, but go to the enemy's country." It is then placed in front of the tiger, and is made to hold the free end of the rope attached to the tiger's neck, as a groom.

Another figure of human shape, but with an ape's head, is placed behind as driver. . .

Then around these figures strew morsels of every kind of eatables, grains, fruits, spices, including raw meat and wine; also a few small coins of silver and copper.

The following weapons are then enchanted for the conflict, viz., pieces of iron, copper, small stones, preferably of white and black colours, grains, the root of rampu for the use of the Lāmas. And for the lay army of the household and neighbours, a sword, knives, reaping hook, yak's tail, a rope of yak's hair with hook at end as figured with the fierce *Gon-pa*-demons.

When these preparations are completed *and the sun has set*—for demons can only move in the darkness—then the ceremony begins. The head Lāma invokes his tutelary deity to assist him in the expulsion of the death-demon. And with an imprecatory gesture blows his breath spiritualized by his tutelary deity upon the images. And the other Lāmas loudly beat a large drum, cymbals and a pair of thigh-bone trumpets. And the laymen armed with the aforementioned weapons loudly shout and wildly cut the air with their weapons, crying "*Begone!*"

After a long incantation the Lāma concludes: "O death-demon do thou now leave this house and go and oppress our enemies. We have given you food, fine clothes and money. Now be off far from here! Begone to the country of our enemies!! Begone!!!" And the Lāma smites his palms together, while the other Lāmas beat their drums, etc., and the laymen wield their weapons, shouting "Begone!" "Begone!" Amid all this uproar the platform containing the image and its attendants is lifted up by a layman, one of the relatives, selected according to the astrologer's indications, who holding it breast high, at arm's length, carries it outside, attended by the Lāmas and laity, shouting "Begone!" and flourish their weapons. And it is carried off for about one-eighth of a mile in the direction prescribed by the astrologer of the enemy of the people, and deposited, if possible, at a site where four roads meet.

Meanwhile, to make sure that the demon is not yet lurking in some corner of the room, the sorcerer-Lāma (Ṅgag-pa) remains behind with a *dorje* in his right hand and a bell in his left, and with the *dorje* he makes frantic passes in all directions, muttering spells, and with the forefinger and thumb of the right hand, without relinquishing the *dorje*, he throws in all directions hot peebles which have been toasted in the fire, muttering his charms, and concludes:—

"Dispel from this family all the sorceric injury of Paṇḍits and Bons!! etc. Turn all these to our enemy! Begone!" Afterwards the Lāma, addressing the people, says, "Now by these angry spells the demon is expelled! *O! Happiness!*" Then the people triumphantly shout: "God has won! The Demons are defeated!!"

paper,[1] here figured. Schlagintweit, in giving a specimen of one form of this print,[2] has mistaken its meaning. The figure in the centre is not "the Lord of the Genii of Fire," but it is merely intended to represent the spirit of the deceased person who sits or kneels, and sometimes with the legs bound, in an attitude of adoration. And before this paper figure, occupying the position of the face, are set all sorts of food and drink as was done to the actual corpse.

THE EFFIGY OF THE DEAD PERSON.
1. Mirror. 3. Lyre.
2. Conch. 4. Vase with flowers.
5. Holy Cake.

This seems essentially a Bön-pa rite, and is referred to as such in the histories of St. Padma, as being practised by the Bön, and as having incurred the displeasure of St. Padmasambhava, the founder of Lāmaism.

The Lāmas then do the service of the eight highest Buddhas

---

[1] mts'an-spyaṅ, or "*Jan-ku.*" Compare with the mortuary masks of ancient Greeks, North American Indians, and E. R. EMERSON'S *Masks, Heads, and Faces*, pp. 152, etc. Its inscription usually runs:—

"I, the world-departing One, . . . (and here is inserted name of the deceased), adore and take refuge in my Lāma-confessor, and all the deities, both mild and wrathful, and 'the Great Pitier' forgive my accumulated sins and impurities of former lives, and show me the right way to another good world!"

And in the margin or adown the middle of the figure are inscribed in symbolic form —by the initial letter of the Sanskrit title—the sixth states of rebirth, viz., SU = *Sura*, a god; A = *asura*, NA = *Nara* or man, TRI = *Triyak* or beast, PRE = *preta* or *Ghost*, HUṂ = hell. (This also is a mystic interpretation of Avalokita's mantra, the sixth syllable of which is made to mean hell, and is coloured black.)

Around the figure are depicted "the five excellent sensuous things," viz., (1) body (as a mirror), (2) sound (as cymbals, a conch, and sometimes a lyre), (3) smell (a vase of flowers), (4) essence or nutriment (holy cake), (5) dress (silk clothes, etc.).

[2] *Op. cit.*, p. 252.

of Medicine, and also continue the service of the western paradise.

Next day the Lāmas depart, to return once a week for the repetition of this service until the forty-nine days of the ghostly limbo have expired; but it is usual to intermit one day of the first week, and the same with the succeeding periods, so as to get the worship over within a shorter time. Thus the Lāmas return after six, five, four, three, two, and one days respectively, and thus conclude this service in about three weeks instead of the full term of forty-nine days.

Meanwhile the lay figure of the deceased remains in the house in its sitting posture, and is given a share of each meal until the service is concluded by the burning of the mask.

On the conclusion of the full series of services, the paper-mask is ceremoniously burned in the flame of a butter-lamp, and the spirit is thus given its final *congé*. And according to the colour and quality of the flame and mode of burning is determined the fate of the spirit of deceased, and this process usually discovers the necessity for further courses of worship.[1]

The ashes of this burned paper are carefully collected in a plate and are then mixed with clay to form one or more miniature Caityas named Sa-tsch'a.[2] One of these is retained for the

[1] The directions for noting and interpreting the signs of this burning paper are contained in a small pamphlet which I have translated, entitled: "*The mode of Divining the signs of The Flames during the Burning of the 'Chang' paper*," which I have translated in full in *Lāmaism in Sikhim*. It begins :—

Salutation to "Ch'e-*m*ch'og, Heruka," or the "The most Supreme Heruka!" The marking of the five colours of the flames is as follows :—

If the flames be white and shining, then he has become perfect and is born in the highest region of Ok-min (*i.e.*, The supreme paradise).

If the flames be white and burn actively with round tops, then he has become pious and is born in the eastern "*m*ngön-*d*gah," or "The Paradise of Real Happiness."

If they burn in an expanded form, resembling a lotus (*padma*), then he has finished his highest deeds and has become religious.

If they be yellow in colour and burn in the shape of "*r*gyal-*m*tshan," or "Banner of Victory," then he has become religious nobly.

If they be red in colour and in form like a lotus, then he has become religious and is born in *b*de-wa-chan, or "The Paradise of Happiness."

If they be yellow in colour and burn actively with great masses of smoke, then he is born in the region of the lower animals, for counteracting which a *g*tsug-lag-khang, or "An Academy," and an image of the powerful and able Dhyani Buddha (*s*nang-par-*s*nang-*m*dsa*d*) should be made; then he will be born as a chief in the middle country (*i.e.*, The Buddhist Holy Land in India). . . . .

[2] Representing the *dharma sarira* of Indian Buddhism.

household altar, and the others are carried to any hill near at hand, where they are deposited under a projecting ledge of a rock, to shelter them from the disintegrating rain.

On the burning of this paper the lay figure of the deceased is dismantled, and the clothes are presented to the Lāmas, who carry them off and sell them to any purchasers available and appropriate the proceeds.

After the lapse of one year from death it is usual to give a feast in honour of the deceased and to have repeated the service of the medical Buddhas. On the conclusion of this service, should the deceased have left a widow or widower, the latter is then free to re-marry.

To Exorcise Ghosts.

The manes of the departed often trouble the Tibetans as well as other peoples,[1] and special rites are necessary to "lay" them and bar their return. A ghost is always malicious, and it returns and gives trouble either on account of its malevolence, or its desire to see how its former property is being disposed of. In either case its presence is noxious. It makes its presence felt in dreams or by making some individual delirious or temporarily insane. Such a ghost is disposed of by being burned.[2]

For the foregoing necromantic services the dough images required as sacrificial effigies are made from wooden moulds, and the practice is evidently borrowed from the Bön-pa rites which entailed sacrifices of animal life. But instead of the animals

[1] On barring the return of ghosts, cf. Wilson's *Essays*, ii., 292; Tyler's *Prim. Cult*, ii., 126; Spencer's *Principles of Sociology*, i., 147. The Chinese call the Dead or *Manes* of men Kwei, alleged to mean the malicious two-legged ghost (Jas. Legge, *The Religs. of China*, p. 13), showing that they did not think that man when he was dead had all ceased to be.

[2] For this purpose a very large gathering of Lāmas is necessary, not less than eight, and a "burnt offering" (sbyin-sregs) is made. On a platform of mud and stone outside the house is made, with the usual rites, a magic circle or "kyil-'*kh*or," and inside this is drawn a triangle named "huṅ-luṅ." Small sticks are then laid along the outline of the triangle, one piled above the other, so as to make a hollow three-sided pyramid, and around this are piled up fragments of every available kind of food, stone, tree-twigs, leaves, poison, bits of dress, money, etc., to the number of over 100 sorts. Then oil is poured over the mass, and the pile set on fire. During the combustion additional fragments of the miscellaneous ingredients reserved for the purpose are thrown in, from time to time, by the Lāmas, accompanied by a muttering of spells. And ultimately is thrown into the flames a piece of paper on which is written the name of the deceased person—always a relative—whose ghost is to be suppressed. When this paper is consumed the particular ghost has received its quietus, and never can give trouble again.

themselves only their dough-images are now offered. At page 424 are given ink prints from the original dough moulds, reduced to one-fourth of their size; the moulds are carved in longitudinal series on the four faces of a block of wood. The Bön-pa moulds are called "The God's food to go to the Thousand."[1]

Rain Compelling.

Even the so-called reformer of Lāmaism, Tsoṅ-K'a-pa, seems himself to have practised sorcery. The orthodox mode of compelling rain in use by the established church is identified with his name; and is done according to the instructions contained in a book[2] of which he is the accredited author, and which seems to be based upon the Nāga worship as contained in the Sūtra "on asking Rain of the Great Cloud,"[3] and may be compared with the method used by the Mongols.[4]

The officiating Lāma bathes and cleans the place of worship and sets down an image of Tsoṅ-K'a-pa and non-poisonous flowers, grains and a white cake, and a jewelled vase (or if no jewelled vase a pure white one may be used washed over with chalk and sandal wood), and inside the vase place pellets made of dough, spice and flowers, and over each ball say the mantra of Yama or Tsoṅ-K'ā-pa[5] one hundred and eight times (or twenty-one or seven times), and blow over it and insert all the pellets in the vase and cover it by a red cloth and thus address the Nāgas:—

"O! all ye Nāgas great and small I come not to harm you but to ask rain for the good of the world, and especially for this place. It is the command of Tsoṅ-K'ā-pa that ye obey. And if you do not, then by my *mantra* spells I will break your heads to atoms. Give it therefore without delay and leave not this place till rain falls."

Then he places three stones at each of the four corners and repeats the names of the *Jinas* or celestial Buddhas of the four

---

[1] sTtoṅ-rgyas lha-bsaṅs.

[2] dmigs brtse-mai las ts'ogs.

[3] bc'ig las c'ar 'bebs skor. Compare with *The Mahāmegha Sutra*, translated by Prof. C. Bendall, *J.R.A.S.*, xii., pp. 288-311.

[4] Among the Mongols the soothsayers throw bezoar stones on the water and these produce vapor, which it is pretended is the element of clouds—but they don't operate unless the sky looks rainy, and if they fail they excuse themselves on the plea that other magicians have counteracted them. E. Rehatsek, *Bombay Br. R. A. S. Jour.* xiii., p. 188.

[5] The so-called *Mig-tse-ma*:—

dmig*s* med brtse pahi gter ch'en *s*pyan-ras gzigs
Dri-med *m*k'yen-pahi dbang po 'jam-pai '*b*yaṅ*s*
Gaṅ*s* ch'an mk'as pai gtsug rgyan Ts'oṅ-k'a-pa
bLo-bzaṅ grag*s* pahi z'ab*s* la gsol-wa-'deb*s*.

directions. And he conceals the vase and its pellets in the water of a spring in such a way that it cannot be seen; and he erects in front a small white tent, within which he places St. Tsoṅ-K'ā-pa's image, and the five kinds of offerings (cake, water, flowers, lamps, fruit and grain). And he calls on the location-god for assistance and goes on repeating Tsoṅ-K'ā-pa's *mantra* and conceives that on each lamp a glorious image of Tsoṅ-K'ā-pa appears seated upon a Nāga and raining down cleansing ambrosia upon them, and that they sparkle with delight and dart their lightning into the sky where clouds gather and the thunder-dragons roar, and rain falls. Then, naively adds the scripture, real rain will certainly come.

THUNDER-DRAGONS OF THE SKY.

XIX.

FESTIVALS AND HOLIDAYS.

THE regular Buddhist festivals[1] are all found in Lāmaism, and many more besides of an indigenous and local origin, related to demonist cults, or the worship of Nature.

Originally, in Buddha's day, the days of the new[2] and full moon were set apart for fasting, confession, and listening to the Law, and this institution is strictly observed in Lāmaism.

On the first and fifteenth days of each lunar month no animal food should be taken, even by the laity, and no animal killed,[3] and only on these days are many of the great cathedrals and temples in Tibet open to the public. These days, however, were afterwards increased to three or four,[4] so that many monks observe a fast four days monthly, and hence has arisen the idea of some writers that there is a Tibetan Sabbath [5]; though the public service and con-

---

1 'dus-ch'en. nam-gaṅ.

On the reconversion of the Mongols to Buddhism in the sixteenth century, in the treaty between the Dalai Lāma and Altun Khan, it was stipulated that on the monthly fast days the hunting or slaughter of animals would be prohibited.

4 Hiuen Tsiang speaks of six fasts every month, and Julien quotes a Chinese authority giving the days as the eighth, fourteenth, fifteenth, twenty-third, twenty-ninth, and thirtieth. FaHian notes that in Ceylon preaching occurred on the eighth, fourteenth, and fifteenth days of the month. On the fourteenth, fifteenth, twenty-ninth and thirtieth (says KÖPPEN, ii., 139, 307), "by rule, among the Lāmas nothing should be tasted but farinaceous food and tea, the very devout refrain from all food from sunrise to sunset. The temples are decorated, and the altar-tables set out with the holy symbols, with tapers, and with dishes containing offerings in corn, meal, tea, butter, etc., and especially with small pyramids of dough or of rice or clay, and accompanied by much burning of incense-sticks. The service performed by the priests is more solemn, the music louder and more exciting, than usual. The laity make their offerings, tell their beads, and repeat 'Ommani padme huṅ.'"

5 *Guṅ-saṅ.*

fession[1] (*Uposatha*) are only done as a rule twice a month.[2] But every month is held a high mass or celebration of divine service in honour of a special deity or saint. And in addition are the great festivals in which the laity also take part.

The special feasts for the deities and saints of the established church at Lhāsa are here enumerated. The Tibetan year, it should be remembered, begins about the end of January, so that the Tibetan month is thus about one month later than ours.

First month.—On the eighth day is *Tagon*, and from the ninth to fifteenth the liturgy of the great tutelary fiend *Bhairava*.

Second month.—On the eighth is *Tagon*, and from the ninth to fifteenth is the liturgy of "The Medical Buddhas."

Third month.—On the fifteenth is *Tagon*, and from the sixteenth to twenty-second is the celebration of Tu-K'or.

Fourth month.—On the eighth is *Tagon*, and from the ninth to fifteenth the worship of "The Great Pitier."

Fifth month.—On the third is *Tagon*, and from the fourth to tenth is the liturgy of the tutelary fiend Sambhara.

Sixth month.—On the first is *Tagon*, and from the second to fourth rab-*g*nas, and from ninth to fifteenth is the "white Tārā's" liturgy.

Seventh month.—On the eighth is *Tagon*, and from the ninth to fifteenth is the liturgy of Mi-'krugs-pa.

Eighth month.—On the eighth is *Tagon*, and from the ninth to fifteenth the liturgy of "The nine gods of Immortality."

Ninth month.—From the first to fifteenth the Kah-gyur scriptures are read, and from the seventeenth to twenty-third is the service of "The Dead Saints," the *Sthavira*.

Tenth month.—On the eighth is *Tagon*, and from the ninth to fifteenth is the worship of the tutelary fiend Guhyakāla, and on the twenty-fifth is the service of "The Five" of Gāh-ldan monastery.

Eleventh month.—On the twenty-second is *Tagon*, and from the twenty-third to twenty-ninth is the celebration of the Tor-gyak of the fiendish lords.

Twelfth month.—On the twenty-second is *Tagon*, and on the twenty-ninth day of the month begins the great carnival and masquerade of "Drug-*b*c'u lchags-mk'ar-gyi gtor rgyags."

An interesting glimpse into the Lāmaist feasts of saints and divinities as current in the thirteenth century is given by Marco Polo. The Venetian traveller says:—

When the idol festivals come round these Bacsi (Lāmas) go to the prince and say, "Sire, the feast of such a god is come (naming him).

[1] T., gSo-sbyoṅ. Mongol.—*Mazak*.
[2] Including the Tu-i-sol cleansing ceremony before referred to.

My lord, you know that this god, when he gets no offerings, always sends bad weather and spoils our seasons. So we pray you to give us such and such a number of black-faced sheep, and we beg also that we may have such a quantity of incense, etc., etc., that we may perform a solemn service and great sacrifice to our idols, and that so they may be induced to protect us and all that is ours." The great kaan then orders the barons to give everything the Bacsi have asked for. And when they have got those articles they go and make a great feast in honour of their god, and hold great ceremonies of worship, with grand illuminations, and quantities of incense of a variety of aromatic odours. And they cook the meat and set it by the idols, and sprinkle the broth hither and thither, saying that in this way the idols get their bellyful. Thus it is that they keep their festivals. Each of the idols has a name of his own and a feast-day, just as our saints have their anniversaries.

It is not easy to give a categorical list of the great popular festivals of the Lāmas, for the Tibetans, unlike the Chinese[1] and Japanese, do not seem to possess printed lists of their feast-days, and the particular event which certain of the days devoted to Buddha is intended to commemorate is not generally known.

As much confusion has been caused by the official new year differing in its epoch from the popular styles, and further disorder is introduced by the official Tibetan style differing from the Chinese, the order of the months in the latter being about two months earlier, the following list, therefore, has been compiled by me from somewhat conflicting information supplied by different Lāmas, and can only be considered approximate. Some of the feasts, such as the Water-festival, are moveable, as mentioned in the text.

LIST OF THE CHIEF LĀMAIST FESTIVALS.

Month.	Day.	Festival.
1st.	1st.	Carnival.
	15th.	Buddha's Incarnation or Conception.[2] Feast of Flowers.
2nd.	29th.	Chase and Expulsion of the "Scape-goat," Demon of Bad Luck.

[1] See EDKINS' *Chinese Buddhism*, 206-210, for list of Chinese Buddhist festivals.

[2] Saṅgyas-sku-*bl*tams-pa, or Chums-su zugs-paĉ dus mch'od. [Sacrificial festival of the Conception (of Buddha)].

Month.	Day.	Festival.
3rd.	15th.	The *Kalacakra* Revelation[1] and Sacred Masquerades.
4th.	8th.	"Attainment of Buddhahood." Great Renunciation.[2]
	15th.	Buddha's Death, or *parinirvana*.[3] Feast of the Dead, "All Souls Day."
5th.	5th.	The Medical Buddhas.[4]
	10th.	Birth of St. Padma-sambhava.[5]
6th.	4th.	Buddha's Birth and Preaching,[6] and "The Picture Feast."
7th.	10th.	Birth of St. Padma-sambhava (according to Sikhim style).
8th.	8th.	The Water-festival, *Rib-Chi.*
9th.	22nd.	Descent from Heaven.[7]
10th.	25th.	St. Tsoń-K'ā-pa's Ascension.[8] Feast of Lanterns.
11th.	1st.	New Year, *Old* Style.
12th.	29th.	Pantomime and expulsion of Old Year.

The Tibetan new-year was formerly celebrated about the winter solstice in what is now the eleventh month, when the larders were full,[9] and no field work possible in the snow-bound country, and the days first show signs of lengthening. The return of the sun, so to say, has at such a season been celebrated by every nation of any culture. This was the period for popular festivity and general joy.

Since the government adopted a later date for the new year, namely, about the beginning of February,[10] most of the people have transferred their festivities to the new date, which is known

---

1 dus-'k'or gsuns-pa.

2 rab-tu byuṅ-ba, "The highest Being or Becoming."

3 mya-ṅ'an las-'das-pa.

4 Saṅgyas sman bla (=*Skt.*, Bhaiṣyaguru Buddha) of the Eastern World.

5 ch'os-gsuṅ-pa (*lit.*,=Religious Speech).

6 Orgyan rin-po ch'e sku bltams-pa.

7 lha-babs.

8 dgā-ldan *l*ṅ'a *m*ch'od.

9 The grain has been stored since two months, and the yak and sheep-flesh since four to six weeks.

10 In 1892 it was on the 29th February.

as the "royal new year"[1] in contradistinction to the old style, now called "The cultivators' new year."[2]

This altered date, February to the beginning of March, makes the "new year" a spring festival. Its gay carnival is doubtless an expression of the self-same feelings, inspired by spring upon the animate and inanimate world, which prompted the analogous Roman festivals of Lupercalia, the Festum Stultorum, the Matronalia Festa, the worship of the goddess Anna Perenna, and the festival of Bacchus, all held about the same season, during the month of February and the first fortnight of March, and represented in India by the Holi festival.

With new-year's eve commences a grand carnival, which lasts the greater part of the first month. The people decorate their doorways and houses with boughs of juniper, etc., prepare puddings, and lay in a stock of wine, and pass the time eating, drinking, dancing,[3] singing, and games,[4] combined with as much praying as they may feel inclined for. The people flock from the smaller villages into the larger towns, and the Lāmas contribute to the general amusement by masquerades and pompous processions, in the intervals of their worship for the general welfare.

The new year is ushered in with high carousal, and first footing and health-drinking are the order of the day, and everyone is pressed to partake of sweet cakes and puddings, more or less gaily decorated, and beer and wine *ad libitum.*[5]

And while this festivity lasts, that is, during the first four or six weeks of the year, the temporal government of the city of Lhāsa is removed from its usual custodians, and placed in the hands of the priests of De-pung monastery, the chief of whom becomes for the time *rex sacrorum*, as with the Romans. It is possible that this is a political sop to the most powerful monastery

1 rgyal-po lö-gsar.

2 So-nam lô-gsar. It is popular in Ladāk (RAMSAY's *Dict.*, p. 43), and in Sikhim.

3 The dancing is usually done in lines, the men and women apart.

4 The games include archery; putting the stone (and called Liṅ-siṅ ch'en gyal-po), in which the losers pay forfeits; acrobats, in the Lhāsa festivals these come usually from Shigatse (Tsang-jo-mo-Kha-rag), and slide down long ropes of yak-hair from the gilt umbrellas on the top of Potala to the foot of the edict pillars.

5 According to the current saying "The Tibetan New-Year is Wine, the Chinese is Paper, and the Nepalese is Noise," with reference to the Chinese celebrating their festivals by display of red paper flags, and the Nepalese by clamour of noisy instruments. Cf. Huc's description of these gala days.

of the established church in Tibet to reconcile it to its exclusion from the ordinary government of the country, which is now restricted to the four monasteries in Lhāsa called Lings.

The Lāma, who is chief judge [1] of De-pung, proceeds to Lhāsa in state on the third day of this month, and assumes the sovereignty of the city. He is received with regal honours, and incense is burned before him wherever he goes; and on his arrival at Lhāsa all prisoners are set free except those convicted of the most aggravated crimes.

During his dominion he holds absolute power over property, life, and death; and assisted by thirty deputies, he inflicts severe punishments and heavy fines for trifling offences, to the financial benefit of his monastery. It is said that many of his retainers commit excesses, so that such of the richer classes as may have incurred, or have reason to believe that they have incurred, the displeasure of De-pung Lāmas, leave the city and live in its suburbs during this period of priestly rule.

The poorer classes, usually so dirty, now sweep and whitewash their houses through fear of punishment by Lāmas for uncleanness. So long as these Lāmas govern Lhāsa they are feasted at the public expense or by the richer people,[2] and are entertained with sports.

One of the duties of this Rex Sacrorum is to deliver a series of lectures to the assembled monks on religious history, philosophy, and polity; and he is credited with divine powers.

Lhāsa, during this festival, contains, it is said, over 30,000 monks,[3] from Serra, De-pung, Gāh-ldan, etc., so that the city seems red with the red cloaks of the Lāmas. They are engaged the greater part of the day in worship for the general welfare of the country and people.

---

[1] His title is Tshogs-ch'en-z'al-ṅgo.

[2] Everyone is expected on the last day of the old year to bring to the monasteries half a month's rations for the monks, in flesh, grain, butter, etc.

[3] The stupendous size of the cooking arrangements and the size of the tea-cauldrons for such a multitude may be imagined. Each monk receives refreshments at each of the three daily assemblies at the Lhāsa cathedral. After the first assembly at six a.m., each monk gets tea and soup at government expense, and one penny. At the second assembly, at eleven a.m., he again gets similar refreshment and one or two *tankas* (silver coins value about sixpence), and at three p.m. further refreshment. During this festival each Lāma receives about twenty to twenty-five *tanka* coins, which money is mainly provided by the Tengyeling regent.

Public worship is done daily in the great cathedral of Lhāsa during the first half of the month, from before dawn till after dark, and clouds of incense fill the air. The especially holy days are the third, eighth, tenth, thirteenth, and the fifteenth, or full moon, which latter day is the greatest *gala* day of the year, and seems to be considered the anniversary of Buddha's conception, and "the goddess" evidently intended for Buddha's mother, Maya Deva, is worshipped with red flowers,[1] and it is believed that divine blessings if then asked for are more readily granted at this season than at any other.

People don their gayest dress and jewellery on that day, and exchange presents freely, and the carnival reaches its climax. The laity wear masks of coloured cloth, with fringes of hair, in imitation of beards. And the Dalai Lāma is especially worshipped on this day, and receives many presents.

On the second day of the month the state sorcerer of Nä-ch'uṅ enters Lhāsa, as already noted, and his entry is like that of the archaic god-king, for none dare look at him, and even high state officials have been fined for looking at him whilst passing.

On the twenty-sixth day are horse-racing and shooting, and on the twenty-seventh a grand review of the troops by the Chinese Amban, and the procession of the holy sceptre from the Serra monastery for solemn salutation by the Dalai Lāma, the officials, and people, as already mentioned.

During the latter half of the month the demons are worshipped, and on the thirtieth day Tārā's celebration concludes the feasts.

The anniversary of Buddha's death is held on the full moon (or fifteenth day) of the fourth month, and is evidently combined with the old Nature-festival in honour of the commencement of summer and the propitiation of the rain-deities.

In the first half of this month (known as Sa-ḍa-wa) the people do more worship than in any other season of the year. They count their beads and ply their prayer-wheels with more energy than usual, and at the larger temples of Lhāsa, Tashi-lhunpo, etc., the devotees go round the holy buildings by measuring their length on the ground.

From the tenth to the fifteenth even the laity abstain from

---

[1] For an account of this "Feast of the Flowers," see Huc, ii., 39.

flesh, and give away as much alms in charity as they can afford; and there appears also to be some idea of ancestor-worship in the ceremonial. Certainly deceased ancestors and relatives are often prayed for at this time, which is not many weeks removed from the great Japanese feast of the dead.

During this feast many of the monks encamp in tents, and colossal pictures are displayed. Thus at Tashi-lhunpo the pictures are hung from the great tower named Kiku.[1]

At this festival, held there on June 30th, 1882, Lāma Ugyen Gyats'o informs us, a great picture of Dipaṁkara Buddha was displayed about a hundred feet long, in substitution for other pictures of the previous days. Next day it was replaced by one of Ṣākya Muni and the past Buddhas, and the following day by one for Maitreya (Jam-pa). On this day women are admitted to the monastery shrines, from which they are at other times excluded, and all the people seek the benediction of the Coming Buddha, by touching the lower border of the picture with their heads.

The rain-deities, the dragons, or Nāgas of the sky, are also propitiated on the fifteenth day of the fourth month. A procession is formed by the lay governors of Lhāsa,[2] and the high official Lāmas,[3] and some other officers, who proceed from the court at Potala to the great Lhāsa cathedral, where the great image of Buddha is worshipped, and the officers feed the temple-lamp by pouring into it melted butter in silver ladles.

Then one of the governors and a secretary of state, with about thirty retainers, go to the Ramo-ch'e temple, *viâ* the Gyambum K'aṅ Caitya, where they also feed the great lamp of the chief shrine; and here they distribute largess, in the shape of bits of brick-tea to the paupers, who are here assembled in rows to receive the customary bounty.

From Ramo-ch'e the procession passes round the great circular road, dispensing tea as it goes, *viâ* the Mende bridge to the Nāga or dragon-temple. The governor and party here embark in four or five small boats of hide with wooden frame work, and are rowed round the moat once in the respectful Pradakshina direction. They then disembark and ascend the hillock on which stands the dragon-temple, where, in an inner sanctuary, they deposit

[1] Figured at p. 273. Its base is sixty paces long, and its height greater.—UGYEN GYATS'O.

bkāh-blon Tsi-tung.

offerings of gold and silver among the snake-idols, and this room is then locked and sealed, only to be opened again the following year.

The laity are now permitted by payment to be rowed round the moat, and cheer lustily as they go. The avowed object of this ceremony is to conciliate the Nāga demi-gods, so as to secure timely and sufficient rain for the benefit of crops and animals. And if, as sometimes happens, rain does fall, it is considered an extremely lucky omen.

The anniversary of the birth of Padma-sambhava is observed mainly by the older party of the Lāmaist church. It is held in Sikhim on the tenth day of the seventh month; but in many parts of central and eastern Tibet, as at Sam-yäs and mCh'og-*g*ling, near Gyantse, and also at Ladāk,[1] it is held on the tenth day of the fifth month, and the tenth day of every month is sacred to him and called "Ts'e-*b*chu."

On the day previous to this anniversary are held masked dances of the black-hat Lāmas and of the fiends and fiendesses, as fully detailed hereafter in the chapter on the mystic plays, followed on the tenth by representations of the saint in his eight forms, and the "Ging," father and mother demons. And if rain now happens, it is deemed of good augury, and due to these pious celebrations.

The Water-Festival marks the commencement of the autumn, and usually falls about September.[2] It is a thanksgiving feast. Water, especially of springs, becomes holy and sacred, a veritable *elixir vitæ;* as the water sprites now set free their sacred water. At this season the Tibetans, though not particularly fond of washing and bathing, indulge in this luxury more than usual.[3]

This festival depends on the appearance above the horizon, about the eighth month, at early dawn, of the star named Rikhi or Rishi-agastya, or "Rib-chi," which Colonel C. Strahan, of the Indian

[1] RAMSAY'S *Dict.*, p. 44.

[2] In 1891 it happened on the fourteenth day of the eighth month, *i.e.*, on the 17th September.

[3] It is said that Buddha Æsculapius, the founder of medical science according to the Tibetans, bathed at this season, hence the custom (see JAESCHKE'S *Dict.*, p. 20). the cessation of the rains, when nature, having reached her womanhood, decks her-With this may be compared the so-called Cocoa-nut festival of the Hindus, held at self in all her wealth of leafy charm, when the grateful people cast thousands of cocoa-nuts and flowers into the sea to the sea-gods in gratitude, and to secure patronage and new enterprises during the current year.

survey, informs me must be Canopus[1] or Sirios, the Dog-star. The Tibetans consider this fixed star to be a saint who dwells in heaven in deep meditation, but who appears in the sky in the beginning of the eighth month, before dawn[2] in the southern quarter, and through his influence the water at early dawn becomes ambrosia or life-giving nectar.

Before dawn, therefore, the Tibetans throng to springs and lakes, and watch eagerly for a glimpse of this star to enable them to snatch a draught of the glorified water.

And the Lāmas go in procession to the lakes and rivers, and partake in this practice. They cast in offerings to the water-nymphs and dragon-spirits of the water, and draw and drink the life-giving and sin-cleansing water, attended by much popular festivity.[3] Tents are erected in the neighbourhood for about two weeks, during which the multitude drink and bathe in the water, dance, sing, masquerade, and give vent to their joy, in what may be considered a cleansing or atonement feast, as well as a thanksgiving. And monastic discipline even is relaxed during this festival, and many monks are allowed to go home on leave.

"The descent of the gods" is evidently founded on the legend of Ṣākya Muni's descent from heaven, where he had gone to preach the saving Law to his regenerated saintly mother; and he descended thence by a ladder—a glorified sort of Jacob's ladder. It also marks the end of the rainy season (*Varsha*), the Buddhist Lent,[4] which Buddha was wont to spend in retirement, in fasting, praying, and holy exercises.

The anniversary of Tsoṅ-K'ā-pa's ascent to heaven is the special festival of the established church, of which Tsoṅ-K'ā-pa was the founder. It is a Feast of Lanterns, and takes place in winter, about the beginning of our December, when the days are near their shortest, and it probably is associated with the great nature-festival found in other nations at this season, to emphasize the loss of light, and desire for the return of the sun.

---

1 Arabic *Suhail*, "to be level."

2 dbugs (literally "breath").

3 KÖPPEN, ii., 313, speaks of the Lāmas blessing or consecrating the waters, but this seems to be a mistake.

4 This, according to General CUNNINGHAM (*Indian Eras*, 3), on account of the extension latterly of the Indian year, must, in the time of Alexander and Aṣoka, have commenced in June instead of July, and lasted till October.

It is celebrated on the twenty-fifth day [1] of the tenth Tibetan month, by a general illumination [2] of both lay and religious buildings, like the analogous Dewali festival of the Hindūs, and the lamp (Chirāgh) feast of the Muhammadans, and the festival of Buddha the Burning Lamp (Dipaṁkara) of the Chinese Buddhists,[3] which also are celebrated about this time.

On this day, in the year 1417, Doctor Tsoṅ-K'ā-pa died, or was transfigured as is now believed. The legend says that he appeared on the stone altar in front of the throne at his monastery at Gāh-ldan, and having addressed the assembled multitude, and prophesied the future greatness of his church, he ascended into the Tushita heavens.

The anniversary of this event is called Gah-dan Nam-ch'od, and is celebrated with great joy and torchlight processions. Altars and stages are for this purpose erected beforehand, and decorated with hundreds of lamps and ornamental cakes. On the evening of the feast is a great procession, before which is carried the image of Tsoṅ-K'ā-pa, and torches and lamps, and if they burn brilliantly, much happiness is prophesied.

Advantage also is taken of this day, at the onset of winter, to visit the Dalai and other high Lāmas, and present them with bundles of new warm robes, thus corresponding to the ancient Buddhist "Robe-month" (Chīvara Māsa), which was the month following the end of the rains, and on which the mendicants were provided with new robes on the approach of the cold weather.

In addition to these great feasts are innumerable minor and local ones, as Lāmaism is not behind the Catholic church in accommodating herself to the customs of the people. The Mongols have their Fire and other special festivals all in Buddhist dress. The worship of the mountain-god Kaṅ-ch'en-dsö-ṅa [4] has already been referred to as peculiar to the Sikhimite form of Lāmaism, in addition to which are other local feasts.[5]

---

1 On the twenty-fourth, or preceding day, the monks of the Serra monastery observe a special illumination in honour of the decease of their great Lāma, rJe-byams ch'en-ch'os rje-gzegs-pu.

2 bzhi-mch'od.

3 On the twenty-second day of the eighth Chinese month.—Edkins' *Chinese Budd.*, p. 210.

4 It is held on the fifteenth day of the seventh month. In 1891 it happened on the nineteenth of August. It lasts for three days; and the fifteenth of every month is sacred to this god.

5 Among the local feasts in Sikhim are the Thanksgiving and Prayer-festival (*rub-gnas*) for the welfare of the country, held in the ninth month of every year at the To'ṅ-

A somewhat droll and almost dramatic feast is the chase of the demon of ill-luck, evidently a relic of a former demonist cult.[1] It is called "Chongju Sewang," and is held at Lhāsa on the twenty-ninth and thirtieth days of the second month, though it sometimes lasts about a week. It starts after divine service. A priest represents a Grand Lāma,[2] and one of the multitude is masqueraded as the ghost-king. For a week previously he sits in the market-place with face painted half black and half white, and a coat of skin is put on his arm and he is called "King of the Years'" (? head).[3] He helps himself to what he wants, and goes about shaking a black yak's tail over the heads of the people, who thus transfer to him their ill-luck.

This latter person then goes towards the priest in the neighbourhood of the cloister of La-brang and ridicules him, saying: "What we perceive through the five sources (the five senses) is no illusion. All you teach is untrue," etc., etc. The acting Grand Lāma contradicts this; but both dispute for some time with one another; and ultimately agree to settle the contest by dice; the Lāma consents to change places with the scape-goat if the dice should so decide. The Lāma has a dice with six on all six sides and throws six-up three times, while the ghost-king has a dice which throws only one.

When the dice of the priest throws six six times in succession and that of the scape-goat throws only ones, this latter individual, or "*Lôjon*" as he is called, is terrified and flees away upon a white horse, which, with a white dog, a white bird, salt, etc., he has been provided with by government. He is pursued with screams and blank shots as far as the mountains of Chetang, where he has to remain as an outcast for several months in a narrow haunt, which, however, has been previously provided for him with provisions.

We are told[4] that, while *en route* to Chetang, he is detained

wa-roṅ-grol Caitya, at Tashiding monastery; and the tenth month the anointing and blessing of the Sikhim king by the head Lāma of Pemioṅchi.

[1] What seems a version of this ceremony is celebrated in Ladāk (at the village of Māsho) under the name "Nagh-rang," and described by RAMSAY, *Dict.*, p. 44.

[2] I did not enquire into the personality of this Lāma and his relationship, if any, to the temporary Lāma-king of De-pung monastery. Pandit Nain Sing connects this Scape-goat ceremony with the termination of the De-pung Lāma-regent's rule, and makes its Lāma identical with the latter, while Lāma U. G. (*loc. cit.*, 32), states that the dice-throwing Lāma belongs to the Chang-chub-Ling monastery.

[3] Lo-gon gyal-po.

[4] Pandit A. K.'s *Survey Rept.*

for seven days in the great chamber of horrors at Sam-yäs monastery filled with the monstrous images of devils and skins of huge serpents and wild animals, all calculated to excite feelings of terror. During his seven days' stay he exercises despotic authority over Sam-yäs, and the same during the first seven days of his stay at Chetang. Both Lāma and laity give him much alms, as he is believed to sacrifice himself for the welfare of the country. It is said that in former times the man who performed this duty died at Chetang in the course of the year from terror at the awful images he was associated with; but the present scape-goat survives and returns to re-enact his part the following year. From Chetang, where he stays for seven days, he goes to Lho-ka, where he remains for several months.

At the beginning of the third month an exhibition is held of the holy vessels and precious things in the La-brang temple, also the hanging out of pictures on Potala. There are sowing and harvest and other non-Buddhist festivals, and special rogation days of supplications in case of war, famine, and pestilence.

The old year with all its bad luck is despatched with rites of a clearly demonistic character, and the ceremony, named the "Throwing away of the Dead Year,"[1] is combined with a devil-dance, as described in the next chapter.

Every household contributes to "ring out the old" and "ring in the new" year. On the 22nd day of the 12th month each family prepares a dough image weighing about four pounds, and on it stick pieces of cloth, woollen or silken, and coins, etc., according to the wealth of the house-owner, and the demon of ill-luck is invoked to enter into the image, which is then worshipped, and on the 29th day, or the last but one of the old year, a Lāma is sent for, who carries the image out of the house and beyond the village to a place where four paths meet, and there he abandons it.

But for the general community a huge image is prepared, and attached to its top are many threads, and in front of it on the 29th day a grand dance of the death-devils, etc., takes place, as detailed in the chapter on the mystic plays. And when it is carried off and abandoned the laity vie with one another in snatching the threads,

---

[1] Lo-s'i sKu-rim.

which are treasured as most potent charms, while the Lāmas return to the temple and perform a service to complete the expulsion of the dead old year.

And so they go on, feast following feast, till the end of the year, when the pantomime and carnival commence.

SOME ACTORS IN THE MYSTIC PLAY.[1]

XX.

MYSTIC PLAYS AND MASQUERADES.

FANCY-DRESS balls and the masked carnivals of Europe find their counterpart in Tibet, where the Lāmas are fond of masquerading in quaint attire; and the populace delight in these pageants, with their dramatic display and droll dances. The masked dances, however, are essentially religious in nature, as with the similar pageants still found among many primitive people, and probably once current even among the Greeks and Egyptians.[2]

The Lāmas reserve to themselves the exclusive right to act in "the Mystery-Play," with its manifestations of the gods and demons, by awe-inspiring masks, etc., while they relegate to lay actors the sacred dramas, illustrating the former births of Buddha and other saints, the *Jātakas*.

---

[1] From a photograph by Mr. Hoffmann.

[2] The myth of the snaky-haired Gorgon, and the death-masks found in ancient tombs of Mycenæ, Kertch, Carthage, Mexico, etc.

"The Mystery-Play of Tibet," the name by which the acted pageant of the Lāmas is known to many Europeans, has been seen by several travellers in Tibet and adjoining Lāmaist lands; but the plot and motive of the play seem never to have been very definitely ascertained, owing, doubtless, to the cumbrous details which so thickly overlay it, and the difficulty of finding competent interpreters of the plot, as well as the conflicting accounts current amongst the Lāmas themselves in regard to its origin and meaning.

As I have had opportunities for studying the various versions of the play with the aid of learned Lāmas of several sects, I give here a brief sketch of what I have elicited regarding what appears to have been its original character and subsequent developments.

Originally it appears to have been a devil-dancing cult for exorcising malignant demons and human enemies, and associated with human sacrifice and, probably, cannibalism.

Afterwards, during the Buddhist era, the devil-dance, like that of the Ceylonese, was given a Buddhist dress, which was not difficult, as somewhat analogous displays representing the temptation of Buddha, seem to be found in Indian Buddhism, as seen in the annexed figure of a frieze from Gāndhāra.[1] And several leading indigenous names lent themselves readily to perversion into Buddhist names or titles, by a process already practised by the Brāhmans in India, who Sanskritized aboriginal Indian names in order to bring them within the mythological pale of Hindūism.

The unsophisticated Tibetans still call the mystery-play the "Dance of the Red-Tiger Devil,"[2] a deity of the Bön or pre-Buddhist religion of Tibet. The original motive of the dance appears to have been to expel the old year with its demons of ill-luck, and to propitiate with human sacrifice and probably cannibalism the war-god and the guardian spirits, most of whom are demonified kings and heroes, in order to secure good-luck and triumph over enemies in the incoming year.

Human sacrifice seems undoubtedly to have been regularly practised in Tibet up till the dawn there of Buddhism in the seventh century A.D. The glimpses which we get of early Tibet through the pages of contemporary Chinese history, show, as Dr. Bushell

[1] Figured by GRUENWEDEL, *Buddh. Kunst in Ind.*

[2] sTag-dmar-ch'am.

DEMONS OF MĀRA IN GĀNDHĀRA SCULPTURES.
(Lahore Museum.)

translates,[1] that "at the new year they (the Tibetans) sacrifice men or offer monkeys," and so late as the seventh century the annual rites in connection with the defence of their country were triennially accompanied by human sacrifice.[2]

Actual cannibalism is, indeed, attributed to the early Tibetans,[3] and the survival of certain customs lends strong colour to the probability of such a practice having been current up till about the middle ages. The Tibetans themselves claim descent from a man-eating ancestry, and they credit their wilder kinsmen and neighbours of the lower Tsang-po valley with anthrophagous habits even up to the present day. Vestiges of cannibalism appear to be preserved in the mystery-play. And of similar character seems to be the common practice of eating a portion of the human skin covering the thigh-bone in preparing the bone trumpets, and also, probably, of like origin is the common Tibetan oath of affirmation, "By my father's and mother's flesh."[4]

The Lāmas, however, as professing Buddhists, could not countenance the taking of life, especially human. So, in incorporating this ancient and highly popular festival within their system, they replaced the human victims by anthropomorphic effigies of dough, into which were inserted models of the larger organs, and also fluid red pigment to represent the blood. This substitution of dough images for the living sacrifices of the Bön rites is ascribed by tradition to St. Padma-sambhava in the second half of the eighth century A.D. And these sacrificial dough-images, of more or less elaborate kinds, now form an essential part of the Lāmaist daily service of worship.

The Lāmas also, as it seems to me, altered the motive of the play to hang upon it their own sacerdotal story for their own glorification and priestly gain. Retaining the festival with its Bacchanalian orgies for expelling the old year and ushering in good-luck for the new, they also retained the cutting-up of their enemies in effigy; but they made the plot represent the triumph of the Indian missionary monks (*Acārya*) under St. Padma-sambhava over the indigenous paganism with its hosts of malignant fiends and the black-hat devil-dancers, and also over the Chinese heretics.

1 *J.R.A.S.*, New Ser., xii., p. 440.

2 *Idem*, p. 441.

3 YULE's *Cathay*, 151, and *Marco Polo*, i., 303.

4 a-pe-s'a a-me-s'a.

The voracious man-eating devils of Tibet were mostly assimilated to the Ṣivaite type of fiend in mediæval Indian Buddhism, with which they had so much in common. And the title was accordingly altered from *tag-mar*, "the (dance) of the red Tiger (devil)" to its homonym *tag-mar* (spelt *drag-dmar*), or "the red fierce ones." Thus Yama, the Death-king, and his minions form a most attractive feature of the play, for it is made to give the lay spectators a very realistic idea of the dreadful devils from whom the Lāmas deliver them; and they are familiarized with the appearance of these demons who, according to the Lāmas, beset the path along which the disembodied soul must hereafter pass to paradise.

As this tragedy is so intimately identified with Padma-sambhava, the founder of Lāmaism, it is acted in its most gorgeous style on the birthday of that saint, namely, on the tenth day of the fifth Tibetan month.

But latterly both plot and date were again altered by the established church of Tibet, the Ge-lug-pa sect. This reformed sect, which dissociates itself as far as possible from St. Padma-sambhava, who now is so intimately identified with the unreformed sects, transferred the festival from the end of the old Tibetan year, that is the eleventh month of the present style, to the end of its own year according to the new official year.

And it has also, in its version, altered the motive of the tragedy, so as to make it represent the assassination of the Julian of Lāmaism (Laṅ-darma) by a Lāma disguised as a Shamanist dancer, and this is followed by the restoration of the religion by the aid of Indian and Chinese monks, and the subsequent triumph of Lāmaism, with its superior sorcery derived from Buddhist symbolism.

This version of the play calls the central episode "the strewing food of the sixty iron castles,"[1] and it still further alters, as I take it, the title of the chief character to its further homonym of "*Tag-mar*,"[2] the red horse-headed *Hayagrīva*, a name borrowed from Hindū mythology, but evidently, as it seems to me, suggested by the cognomen of their old familiar fiend, *Tag-mar*, the red Tiger-devil, of the pre-Lāmaist Bön priests. Tiger-devils are also well-

1 Drug-bchu-lchags mk'ar-gyi gtor-rgyags.

2 sTag-(mgrm)-dmar.

known to Chinese mythology,[1] while Hayagrīva, as a Buddhist creation, appears to be known only to the Lāmaistic form of Buddh-

RED TIGER-DEVIL OF THE BÖN.

ism, and his Tāntrik book is admittedly of Tibetan composition.

But even as thus adapted by the established church, the purest of all the Lāmaist sects, the play still retains, as will be presently

TIGER-DEVILS
(of the Chinese. The lower right-hand one is the Red-tiger; the central one is yellow).

shown, the devil-dancing Shamanist features, as well as vestiges of human sacrifice, if not of actual cannibalism.

---

[1] See page 396, and compare also their relatives, the Cat-devils, which latter take the only form of the cult in Japan.

Let us first look at the mystery-play or tragedy as acted by the Lāmas of the old school, at Himis, in Ladāk, in Sikhim, Bhotān, etc., and afterwards refer to the versions as acted by the reformed and established church.

This play is acted, as already mentioned, by all sects of Lāmas, on the last day of the year when the community is *en fête*, by many of the unreformed sects on St. Padma-sambhava's day.

When acted at the end of the year it forms part of the ceremony called "The sacrificial body of the dead year,"[1] and is held on the last two or three days of the old year, from the 28th to the 30th of the twelfth month. As the performance is conducted at the Himis monastery, in Ladāk, in a much grander style than was witnessed by me in Sikhim, and more in the style seen in Tibet, and as it has been there witnessed and described by several travellers,[2] I shall take the Himis performance as the basis of my description, and amplify the descriptions of it where necessary.

As the day for the play draws near, the villagers flock in from the country-side; and on the morning of the day fixed for the performance, the people, decked in holiday attire, throng to the temple many hours before that fixed for the performance, to secure good points of view. Seats are provided and reserved only for the gentry and high officials and visitors. The king and other grandees have state boxes.

The performance is held *al fresco* in the courtyard of the temple (see the photograph on page 528). The orchestra is sometimes screened off from view, and the maskers assemble either in the temple or in yak-hair tents, and are treated to refreshments often, and soup between the acts.

A shrill bugle-call, from a trumpet made out of a human thigh-bone,[3] notifies the commencement of the play.

The gongs and shawms strike up a wailing sort of air, which the musicians accompany by a low chant, and out come trooping a

---

[1] Lô-s'i sku-rim. The term sKu-rim is applied to certain indigenous sacrificial ceremonies, usually with bloody offerings, in contradistinction to the more truly Buddhist ceremonial offerings, which are named "mch'od" and "ch'oga."

[2] Notably H. H. GODWIN-AUSTEN (*J.A.S.B.*, 1861, 71 *seq.*); H. A. JAESCHKE, *ibid.*, p. 77; SCHLAGT., p. 233; KNIGHT, *loc. cit.*, where several fine photographs of the play are given; A. B. MELVILLE, *Proc. B.A.S.*, 1864, p. 478; and RAMSAY'S *West. Tibet.*, p. 43.

[3] Kaṅ-liṅ.

crowd of the pre-Lāmaist black-mitred priests, clad in rich robes of China silk and brocade, and preceded by swingers of censers. They make the mystic sign of "The Three," and execute a stately dance to slow music.

Stretching out the right hand and left alternately, the leaders turn to the right, and the last in line to the left, both advancing and retiring towards each other several times, and, reforming the circle and making the sign of the Trident, they retire.

After these have gone out, then enter a troupe of the man-eat-

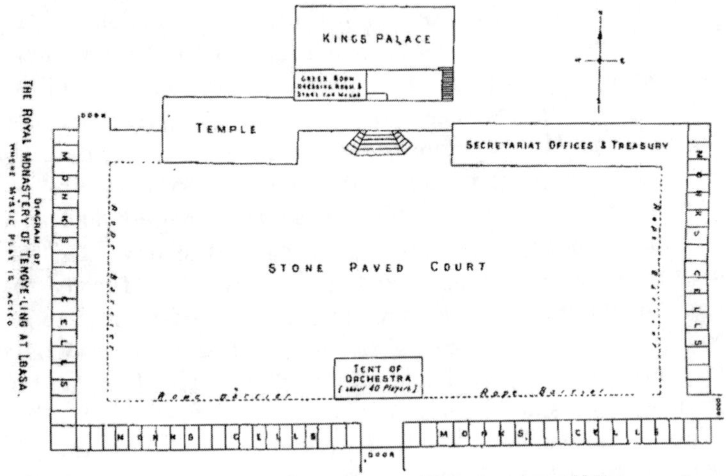

DIAGRAM OF ROYAL MONASTERY AT TENG-GYE-LING, Lhāsa (where mystic play is acted).

ing malignant demons,[1] who, with their hordes, vex and harass humanity. They infest the air, the earth, the water, and are constantly seeking to destroy man, not unlike their better-known relative, who, "as a roaring lion, walketh about seeking whom he may devour."[2] These hordes of demons are intended to illustrate the endless oppression of man by the powers of evil, against whom he can of himself do nothing, but occasionally the exorcisms or prayers of some good Lāma or incarnator may come to his assistance and shield him, but even then only after a fierce and doubtful contest between the saints and the devils. And only for a time, too, can this relief from persecution endure, for all the ex-

[1] Tib., mGon-pa.

[2] I. Peter, v. 8.

orcisms of all the saints are of little avail to keep back the advancing hordes. The shrieking demons must close in upon the soul again.[1]

These demons, now incorporated in Tibetan Buddhism, are regarded as forms of Durga (Devi), Ṣiva (Nātha), and the king of

DEMON-MASKERS.[2]

the Dead (Dharmarāja or Yama).[3] "Flames and effigies of human skulls were worked on their breasts and other parts of their raiment. As their hoods fell back, hideous features of leering satyrs were disclosed."[4]

"In their right hand they hold a bell or fan, and in their left a bowl cut out of a human skull, and round the edge of which are attached narrow streamers of silk and some plaited ends of hair. This ghastly ladle is called Bundah. Some of the maskers hold in the right hand a short stick, with red and blue streamers

[1] KNIGHT, *loc. cit.*, p. 201.

[2] After GODWIN-AUSTEN in *J.A.S.B.*, *loc. cit.*

[3] The chief of these fiends are Devi, Hayagriva, Khyetapala, Jinamitra, Ḍākkirāja, *b*dud-gontrag-sag, lha-ch'en brgya-po, gzah-ch'en-brgyad-po, kLu-ch'en, brgyad-po, etc.

[4] KNIGHT, p. 203.

of silk; these and the spoons majestically waved about as they go round in their solemn dance had the most curious effect I ever saw."[1]

To these monsters (now coerced by Buddhism) the Lāmas offer a libation of beer, and some rice or mustard-seed, and to all the beings of the six classes, and especially including the demons, and the rice or seeds are thrown about freely;[2] and each Lāma present inwardly prays for the realization of his desire.

At a signal from the cymbals the large trumpets (eight or ten feet long) and the other instruments, pipes and drums, etc., and shrill whistling (with the fingers in the mouth), produce a deafening din to summon the noxious demons and the enemies. "The music became fast and furious, and troop after troop of different masks rushed on, some beating wooden tambourines, others swelling the din with rattles and bells. All of these masks were horrible, and the malice of infernal beings was well expressed on some of them. As they danced to the wild music with strange steps and gesticulations, they howled in savage chorus. . . . The solemn chanting ceased, and then rushed on the scene a crowd of wan shapes, almost naked, with but a few rags about them. . . . They wrung their hands despairingly, and rushed about in a confused way as if lost, starting from each other in terror when they met, sometimes feeling about them with their outstretched hands like blind men, and all the while whistling in long-drawn notes, which rose and fell like a strong wind on the hills, producing an indescribably dreary effect. These, I was told, represented the unfortunate souls of dead men which had been lost in space, and were vainly seeking their proper sphere through the darkness. . . . The variously masked figures of Spirits of Evil flocked in, troop after troop—oxen-headed and serpent-headed devils; three-eyed monsters with projecting fangs, their heads crowned with tiaras of human skulls; Lāmas painted and masked to represent skeletons; dragon-faced fiends, naked save for tiger-skins about their loins, and many others. Sometimes they appeared to be taunting and terrifying the stray souls of men—

[1] GODWIN-AUSTEN, *loc. cit.*, p. 73.

[2] Compare with the *confetti* pellets and odoured powders thrown about at western carnivals.

grim shapes who fled hither and thither among their tormentors, waving their arms and wailing miserably, souls who had not obtained Nirvāṇa and yet who had no incarnation. . . . . Then the demons were repelled again by holy men; but no sooner did these last exorcise one hideous band than other crowds came shrieking on. It was a hopeless conflict. . . . At one period of the ceremony a holy man . . . blessed a goblet of water by laying his hands on it and intoning some prayer or charm. Then he sprinkled the water in all directions, and the defeated demons stayed their shrieking, dancing, and infernal music, and gradually crept out of the arena, and no sound was heard for a time but the sweet singing of the holy choir. But the power of exorcism was evanescent, for the routed soon returned in howling shoals."[1]

DEATH-SKELETON MASKER.

The superior effect of Buddhism over the indigenous Shamanism is now shown by the arrival on the scene of the Indian monk, Padma-sambhava, and his assistants, or his eight forms; or sometimes these are represented as Buddha himself, or the group of the "Seven Buddhas."[2]

---

[1] KNIGHT, *op. cit.*, p. 207.

[2] Cf. page 345. The same motive appears in the Burmese religious dramas at Arakan.—HARDY, *East. Monachism*, p. 236.

This scene is thus described: "The loud music suddenly ceased, and all the demons scampered off shrieking as if in fear, for a holy thing was approaching. To solemn chanting, low music and swinging of censers, a stately procession came through the porch of the temple and slowly descended the steps. Under a canopy, borne by attendants, walked a tall form in beautiful silk robes, wearing a large mask representing a benign and peaceful face. As he advanced, men and boys, dressed as abbots and acolytes of the church of Rome, prostrated themselves before him and addressed him with intoning and pleasing chanting. He was followed by six other masks,

DEVILS FLEEING FROM THE BUDDHIST SAINTS.

who were treated with similar respect. These seven deified beings drew themselves in a line on one side of the quadrangle and received the adoration of several processions of masked figures, some of abbots, and others beast-headed, or having the faces of devils."[1]

These last are the demon-kings who have been coerced by Buddhism into becoming guardians and *defensores fidei* of that religion. And amongst the worshippers are the Pa-wo or "heroes" with green masks, surmounted by triangular red flags, and girdles, and anklets of bells; and the solemnity is relieved by a few

[1] KNIGHT, p. 204. These seven masks were, says Mr. Knight, variously explained as being the Dalai Lama and his previous incarnations, while another "explained that these were intended for the incarnations of Buddha, and not the Dalai Lāma."

Acaryas, or jesters, who play practical jokes, and salute the holy personages with mock respect.

The enemy of Tibet and of Lāmaism is now represented in effigy, but before cutting it to pieces, it is used to convey to the people a vivid conception of the manner in which devils attack a corpse, and the necessity for priestly services of a quasi-Buddhist sort to guard it and its soul.

Some days previous to the commencement of the play, an image[1] of a young lad is made out of dough, in most elaborate fashion, and as life-like as possible. Organs representing the heart, lungs, liver, brain, stomach, intestines, etc., are inserted into it, and the heart and large blood-vessels and limbs are filled with a red-coloured fluid to represent blood. And occasionally, I am informed on good authority, actual flesh from the corpses of criminals[2] is inserted into the image used in this ceremony[3] at the established church of Potala.

This effigy of the enemy is brought forth by the four cemetery-ghouls,[4] and laid in the centre of the square, and freely stabbed by the weapons, and by the gestures and spells of the circling hosts of demons, as in the illustration here given.

The necromantic power of the Lāmas is here shown much in the same way as in the Burmese sacred play at Arakan.[5] On three signals with the cymbals, two Indian monks (Acāryas) come out of the monastery, and blow their horns and go through a series of droll antics, and are followed by two or more Lāmas who draw around the effigy on the pavement of the quadrangle a magic triangle and retire. Then rush in the ghosts, death-demons, "figures painted black and white to simulate skeletons, some in chains, others bearing sickles or swords, engaged in a frantic dance around the corpse. They were apparently attempting to snatch it away or inflict some injury on it, but were deterred by the magic effect of the surrounding triangle and by the chanting and censer-swinging of several holy men in mitred and purple copes. . . .

"A more potent and very ugly fiend, with great horns on his head

---

1 Named *liṅ-ka or*.

2 Preserved and stored for this purpose at the Ragyab cemetery—in such cases, the Ge-lug-pa Lāmas are said not to touch this defiling flesh.

3 The ceremony is called drag-las.

Tur-t'od-bdag-po. Cf. HARDY's *E. Mon.*, p. 236.

and huge lolling tongue, ran in, hovered threateningly over the corpse, and with a great sword slashed furiously about it, just fail-

DANCE OF THE DEATH-DEMONS IN HEMIS MONASTERY.[1]

ing by little more than a hair's-breadth to touch it with each sweep of the blade. He seemed as if he were about to overcome

[1] After Mr. KNIGHT.

the opposing enchantment when a saint of still greater power than he now came to the rescue. The saint approached the corpse and threw a handful of flour on it, making mystic signs and muttering incantations. This appeared from his mask to be one of the incarnations of Buddha. He had more control over the evil spirits than any other who had yet contended with them. The skeletons, and also he that bore the great sword, grovelled before him, and with inarticulate and beast-like cries implored mercy. He yielded to their supplications, gave each one a little of the flour he carried with him, which the fiends ate gratefully, kneeling before him; and he also gave them to drink out of a vessel of holy water."[1]

This usually concludes one day's performance.[2] On the following day adoration is paid to the *Jina*, by whom unreformed Lāmas seem to intend St. Padma-sambhava. And mustard-seed is blessed and thrown at the enemy with singing, dancing, and incantations. And then occurs the ceremony of stabbing the enemy by the *phurbu* or mystic dagger.

Four ghouls bring in an object wrapped in a black cloth, and placing it on the ground, dance round it with intricate steps, then raising the cloth disclose a prone image of a man, which has been made in the manner previously described.

Then enter the demon-generals and kings, including the demon Tam-ḍin, and they dance around the image. They are followed by the fiendesses, including the twelve Tän-ma, under *Devi*. These are followed by the black-hat devil-dancers, and these are, in the established church version, held to represent the Lāma who assumed this disguise to assassinate king Laṅ-darma. The four guards now hold the door to prevent entry of any enemies or evil spirits. The black-hats dance round thrice and are succeeded by the god of Wealth, fiendesses, and butchers, the five great "*kings*,"[3] and their queens and ministers, also the state sorcerer of Nä-ch'uṅ, and his eight-fold attendants.[4]

---

1 KNIGHT, *op. cit.*, p. 208.

2 Mr. KNIGHT (*op. cit.*, p. 209) notes that "Three horses and three dogs were smeared over with red paint, and thenceforth dedicated for life to the temple, explained as scape-goats for the sins of the people," the red paint being held to represent the sins.

3 These are gyal-ch'en sku lha, yum-lha, Sprul-pu-na and blon-pa.

4 gnas-ch'uṅ, and rdorje grags-ldan—the attendants are male and female with dishevelled hair.

Then enters a fearful fiend named "The holy king of Religion,"[1] with the head of a bull, holding in his right hand a dagger with silk streamers, and in his left a human heart (in effigy) and a snare, attended by a retinue of fiends and fiendesses, bearing weapons and dressed in skins,[2] human beings, tigers and leopards; and the last to enter are tiger-skin-clad warriors with

THE RELIGIOUS KING-DEVIL.

bows and arrows. This part of the Demon-king can only be taken by a monk of the purest morals, and the costly dress which this actor wears at the play at Potala is one presented by the emperor of China.

[1] Dam-ch'an ch'os-rgyal. By some regarded as Vajrabhairava and by others as Yama or Heruka. *On Bull-headed Demons in S. India*, cf. *Ind. Ant.*, p. 19.

[2] These are made of painted calico or silk.

The King-devil, surrounded by his fiendish hordes, dances and makes with dagger the gesture of "The Three"; he stabs the heart, arms and legs of the figure, and binds its feet by the snare. He then rings a bell, and seizing a sword, chops off the limbs and slits open the breast and extracts the bleeding heart, lungs and intestines.

A troupe of monsters, with the heads of deer and yaks, rush in and gore the remains and scatter the fragments with their horns and hands to the four directions.[1]

Underling fiends now collect the fragments into a huge silver basin shaped like a skull, which four of them carry to the Demon-king in a pompous procession, in which the black-hat devil-dancers join. The Demon-king then seizes the bleeding fragments, and, eating a morsel, throws them up in the air, when they are caught and fought for by the other demons, who throw the pieces about in a frantic manner, and ultimately throwing them amongst the crowd, which now takes part in the orgie, and a general melée results, each one scrambling for morsels of the fragments, which some eat and others treasure as talismans against wounds, diseases and misfortunes.

The service, which is done by the priest who represents the saint Padma-sambhava, is here summarized. It is called "The Expelling Oblation of the hidden Fierce Ones."[2]

"Salutation to Padma-sambhava! I here arrange to upset the hosts of demons, by the aid of the hidden Fierce Ones. In bygone ages you guarded the Buddha's doctrines and upset all the harmful spirits. Now the charge has come to me, O! St. Padma! Instruct me as you did prince Pearl and your fairy wife—the Victorious Ocean of Foreknowledge. You wrote the rite and hid it away in the cave. *Samaya! rgya!* The sealed secret!"

Then arrange as a square magic *maṇḍala* the cemetery, as the abode of the eight classes of demons. And set down poison, blood, and four lotus leaves with a red trident in the centre. And draw fire-flames, doors, etc., according to rule. Above it place a small table and on it a vessel filled with black grains, and a three-headed cake. Cover it up with an umbrella and put inside this house a linka (image of wheaten flour), which represents the injuring demon. Then arrange everything com-

[1] According to the reformed Lāmas, these animals have to be considered as representing the Lāma who assassinated Laṅ-darma, and the Demon-king represents the god Mahākāla, who delivered Laṅ-darma into the Lāma's hands; and the graveyard ghouls are the scavengers who carried off the king's corpse.

[2] gTor-zlog and is extracted from the *pu* volume of bLa-ma-norbu-rgya-mts'o.

plete with the various sorts of offerings, and then do the necessary rites.

First of all invoke one's own tutelary thus:—

"*Hūṃ!* O! Chief of fiercest thunderbolts, immovable and vast as the sky, the overruling angry one! I invoke you who are possessed of supreme strength, and able to subjugate all three empty worlds to do my desires. I invoke you to rise from the burning sky. I, the spell-holder, invoke you with great reverence and faith. You must ripen all the fruits of my desires, otherwise you shall suffer, O! tutelary![1] Arise from the sky and come forth with all your retinue, and quickly route the demons."

Then here offer a libation of wine.

Now the mantra-holder must mentally conceive that the house is full of clouds and that he is sitting in the presence of his tutelary; while the fire of anger burns outside, the mist of poison floats inside; the Las-byed-gs'ed-ma is killing the animals, and the evil spirits are wandering about. The devil now must assume a sorrowful state owing to his separation from his patron and protector.

Then recite the following:—

"*Namo!* The commands of the Lāma are true, the commands of the Three Holy Ones true; and so are those of the fierce Thunderbolt Lāma, etc., etc. Through the power of the great truths, Buddha's doctrines, the image of the noble Lāma, the riches of wealthy people and all the lucky times, let the hosts of demons of the three regions come forth and enter this *linka* image. *Vajra-Agushaja!*"

Then chant the following for keeping the demons at bay:—

Hūṃ! Through the blessing of the blood-drinking Fierce One, let the injuring demons and evil spirits be kept at bay. I pierce their hearts with this hook; I bind their hands with this snare of rope; I bind their body with this powerful chain; I keep them down with this tinkling bell. Now, O! blood-drinking Angry One, take your sublime seat upon them. *Vajor-Agu-cha-dsa! vajora-pasha-hūṃ! vajora-spo-dava! vajora-ghan-dhi-ho!*"

Then chant the following for destroying the evil spirits:—

"Salutation to Heruka, the owner of the noble Fierce Ones! The evil spirits have tricked you and have tried to injure Buddha's doctrine, so extinguish them. . . . . . Tear out the hearts of the injuring evil spirits and utterly exterminate them."

Then the supposed corpse of the linka should be dipped in Rakta (blood), and the following should be chanted:—

"*Hūṃ!* O! ye hosts of gods of the magic-circle! Open your mouths as wide as the earth and sky, clench your fangs like rocky mountains, and prepare to eat up the entire bones, blood, and the entrails of all the injuring evil spirits. *Ma-ha mam-sa-la kha hi! Ma-ha tsitta-kha-hi! maha-rakta kha-hi! maha-go-ro-tsa-na-kha-hi! Maha-bah-su-ta kha-hi! Maha-keng-ni ri ti kha hi!*"

1 Compare this threat with the killing of the gods—in FRAZER's *Golden Bough.*

Then chant the following for upsetting the evil spirits:—

"*Hūṃ! Bhyo!* The black grains and a three-headed cake are duly set on the Buddha's plate: the weapons flash; the poisonous vapour flows; the Fierce Ones thunder their mantras; the smell of the plague is issuing; but this three-headed cake can cure all these disasters, and can repress the injuring demon spirits.

"*Bhyo! Bhyo!* On the angry enemies! On the injuring demon spirits! On the voracious demons! turn them all to ashes!

"*Mah-ra-ya-rbad bhyo!* Upset them all! Upset! Upset!

"'Let glory Come' and Virtue! *Sādhu!*"

A burnt sacrifice is now made[1] by the Demon-king. He pours oil into a cauldron, under which a fire is lit, and when the oil is boiling, he ties to the end of a stick which he holds an image of a man made of paper, and he puts into the boiling oil a skull filled with a mixture of arak (rum), poison, and blood, and into this he puts the image; and when the image bursts into flame, he declares that all the injuries have been consumed.

This rite is followed by a procession to abandon a large three-headed image of dough,[2] to the top of which many threads and streamers are tied. This procession of monks is preceded by the maskers, numbering several hundreds in the larger monasteries,[3] clanging noisy cymbals and blowing thigh-bone trumpets, etc. The laity follow in the rear, brandishing guns and other weapons, and shouting "*Drag-ge-puṅ c'am.*" And when the image is abandoned the crowd tear it to pieces and eagerly fight for the fragments, which are treasured as charms. A gun is then fired amid general shouts of joy, and the Lāmas return to the temple for a celebration of worship.

The play is now practically over. The black-cap devil-dancers again appear with drums, and execute their manœuvres, and the performance concludes with the appearance of the Chinese priest,

1 Named Hom-*bsreks*; Skt., *Homa.* Cf. VASIL., 194; SCHLAG., 251.

2 gtor-gyak.

3 At the monastery of Tiṅ-ge, to the west of Tāshi-lhunpo, and where this play is conducted, as at other Ge-lug-pa monasteries, at government expense, this procession, I am informed, consists of six pairs of thigh-bone trumpet blowers, five censer-swingers, two pairs of long horn players, several skull libationers, 100 maskers with small drums, 100 maskers with cymbals, and 100 with large drums, behind whom walk the ordinary monks, shouting and clapping their hands, followed by the laity armed with guns and other weapons, and forming a procession over a mile in length.

entitled Hwashang, who was expelled from Tibet by St. Padma. This Chinese priest is represented with a fatuous grinning large-mouthed mask (see fig. 3, page 536), and attended by two boys like himself. They go through a form of worship of the images, but being unorthodox, it is ridiculed by the spectators.

This mystic play is conducted at all monasteries of the established church, at government expense. The greatest of these performances are held at Potala, Muru Tasang,[1] and Tashi-lhunpo at the end of the old year, and at the priest-king's palace of Teng-gye-ling on the twenty-ninth day of the eighth month.

At Potala it is held in the courtyard of the Grand Lāma's chapel royal, the Nam-gyal temple-monastery. The dough-images and cakes begin to be prepared from the second day of the twelfth month, and from the third to the ninth the whole convent is engaged in the worship of the terrible guardian-demons[2] of the country, and of Ye-she-Gon-po or Mahākāla.

The rest of the month till the eventful day is occupied in rehearsals and other preparations. Before dawn on the twenty-ninth, the play-manager, after worshipping the demons, arranges the banners, instruments, and carpets.[3] At the first blast of the great conch-shell trumpet, the populace assemble. On the second blast the state officials enter and take their seats, the Shab-pe or state ministers, Duṅ-k'or, and Tse-duṅ. And on the third blast, the Tibetan king-regent enters with all his attendants, and he invites the attendance of his Defending Majesty,[4] the Dalai Lāma, who enters a small state-box[5] named "The world's transparency."

The orchestra, which is screened off in a tent, begins by blowing a thigh-bone trumpet thrice, followed by the great cymbals[6] and drums; then out troop the black-hatted Shamanist dancers, and the play proceeds as above detailed. In the concluding ceremony the large cake, surmounted by a human head, is burned, and is considered to typify the burning of the present enemies of Lāmaism.

But the grandest display takes place at the king-regent's own monastery of Teng-gye-ling, of which I have given a sketch-plan of the buildings, etc., from information supplied to me by a monk who has taken part frequently in the play there. The

1 This is chiefly attended by old women and children.
2 *b*Sruṅ-ma.
3 p'an-rgyal-mts'an p'ye-p'ur, s'am-bu, ba-ran.
4 kyab-*m*gon rin-po-ch'e.
5 zim-ch'uṅ.
6 "The glorious great cymbals."

Lāma who acts as regent is the *de facto* ruler of Tibet, and is generally known as "the King"[1] and also called "The country's Majesty."[2] The superior guests and nobility who have received invitations are permitted to pitch their tents upon the roof of the monks' quarters, and the populace are kept outside the arena by a rope barrier.

An account of the play at Tashi-lhunpo has been given by Mr. Bogle.[3] It took place in a large court under the palace, and the surrounding galleries were crowded with spectators. Another short account[4] describes the court as surrounded by pillared balconies, four storeys high. The Grand Lāma's seat was on the second storey. The other seats in the lower balcony were occupied by the families of chiefs and nobles. In the upper were pilgrims and merchants. The stage manager held a *dorje* and bell-like Dorje-ch'aṅ, but had an abbot's hat. After a prayer there entered a figure representing "the celebrated Dharmatala, who invited the sixteen Sthaviras to China for the diffusion of Buddhism." His mask was dark with yawning mouth to mean ecstasy. Numerous scarves were thrown to him by the spectators, which were picked up by his two wives, with painted yellow complexions. Then came the four kings of the quarters, dressed in barbaric splendour. Following these came the sons of the gods, about sixty in number, dressed with silk robes, and glittering with ornaments of gold, precious stones, and pearls. Following these were Indian acharyas, whose black-bearded faces and Indian dress excited loud laughter among spectators. Then followed the four warders of the cemeteries in skeleton dress. Afterwards "the body of the devil in effigy was burnt, a pile of dry sedge being set on fire upon it." Incense was burnt on the hill-tops in the neighbourhood.

The masks used in this play deserve some notice. In Tibet the great masks[5] are made of mashed paper and cloth, and occasionally of gilt copper.[6] In Sikhim and Bhotān, etc., where wood is abundant, and the damp climate is destructive to *papier-maché*, they are carved out of durable wood.[7] In all cases they are fantastically

---

1 *r*gyal-po. 2 bde-mo rin-po-che. 3 MARKH., p. 106.
4 On the 17th February, 1882, by ṢARAT, in *Narrative*.
5 *u*'bag. 6 gser-saṅ.
7 In Sikhim they are made from the giant climber called "*zar*."

painted, and usually provided with a wig of yak-tail of different colours.

Some Masks.

1. Ghoul.
2. Bull-headed K'ang.
3. Hwashang.
4. A fiendess.
5. A locality genius.
6. A "Teacher."
7. Hwashang's son.

The masks may be broadly classed into the following five groups [1]; though the so-called reformed Lāmas have modified some of these, as already noted.

I.—King of the Ogres (*sKu*)

1. *Drag-mar*,[2] or "The Terrible Red One." Sometimes called Guru Drag-s'ed, or Yes'e-Gon-po, and "Religious Protector,"[3] and regarded as the god of Death, Mahākāla, and also as a form of St. Padma-sambhava. His mask is of hideous anthropomorphic appearance and huge size, with great projecting tusks and three eyes; the vertical eye on the centre of the forehead is the eye of fore-knowledge. And it bears a chaplet of five skulls, with pendants of human bones.

The Ten Awful Ogres, and the Ten Ogresses. These are generally like the above. The females only differ in having no beards nor horns. The chief are:–

II.—The Angry Ogres (To-wo).

2. *Lha-mo dMag-zor-ma*, identified with Kāli, the consort of Mahākāla, and of a blue colour; measly lips. As Raṅ-'byuṅ-ma she is green, and her mouth is shut and not gaping as in the former.
3. *Ts'e-ma-ra.*[4] Red like number one.
4. The Bull-headed (Laṅ). Black in colour with three eyes and bearing a banner[5] on its forehead. It is also called "ma-c'an."[6]
5. The Tiger-headed (sTag), brown and yellow-striped.
6. The Lion (Seṅ-ge). White.
7. The Roc, or Garuḍa (Kyuṅ). Coloured green.
8. The Monkey (spre-ul). Ruddy-brown.
9. The Stag (S̓'a-ba).[7] Fawn-coloured.
10. The Yak. Coloured black.

III.—The Ghouls

11. *Tur*, or grave-yard ghouls, with skull masks and clothes representing skeletons.

---

[1] Excluding those of the Buddhas, which are not essential to the play, and seldom appear.

[2] According to some the Garuḍa (bya-*m*'kyuṅ) or Roc should occupy the highest place. It is yellow, with a bird's beak, yak's horns, and erect hair, forming a spiked crest. It is said to be even superior to the sixteen great saints, the Sthavira.

[3] He is also identified with forms known as Na-niṅ-nag-po, Legs-ldan nag-po, Ber-nag-po.

[4] Ch'os-skyoṅ brtse-dmar-ra.

[5] rgyal-mts'an.

[6] dma-c'an c'os-rgyal.

[7] This seems intended for the Indian *Sambhar*.

IV.—The Earth-Master-Demons.	12. *Sa-bdag* Genii. These have large hideous masks but only one pair of eyes, as representing their subordinate position. Their chief is called "The great guardian King,"[1] and he is attended by red demons (*Tsan*) and black ones (*Dud*), etc.
V.—The Teachers.	13. *Acāryas.* These have small cloth masks of ordinary size, and of a white, or clay, or black colour ; and their wives are red- or yellow-complexioned. The hair of these "Teachers" is blue in colour, and done up into a chignon on the crown as with Indian *Yogis.* Although they represent the early Indian priests who brought Buddhism to Tibet, they are, as in ancient India, the buffoons and jesters of the play.
	14. *Hva-shang.* This is a huge, fatuous, round mask of a red colour, to represent a historical Chinese Buddhist monk of the eighth century. And he is attended by several of his sons[2] with similar masks.

The dresses of the King-demon and Ogre maskers are of the most costly silk and brocade, and usually with capes, which show Chinese influence.[3] Those of the others are usually woollen or cotton. And the robes of those actors who represent the demons, who get severely cudgelled by their superiors, are thickly padded to resist the blows which fall on them.

Where there are a number of one class going in processions or dancing, those dressed alike go in pairs. The weapons carried by the maskers have already been referred to. Most are made of wood carved with thunderbolts. The staves of the skeleton maskers are topped by a death's-head. The sword made by stringing together Chinese brass coins ("*Cash*") is called the *Siling tun,* from the province of Siling in western China, whence these coins come to Tibet.

Another religious pantomime, performed, however, by lay actors, is the Lion-Dance. It is not enacted at the new year, but at other seasons, when the people are *en fête.*

---

1 rgyal-ch'en-po bsrung*s* bstan-po, and seems related to, or identical with the "Five Kings" and Heroes (*d*pa-o).

2 Ha-p'ug.

3 These capes generally show the trigrams and other symbols of luck and long life including the *Bat.*

The plot is based upon the mythical lion of the Himalayan snows, which is believed to confer fortune on the country where it resides. One of these lions was enticed to China by a wizard, and, somewhat like *La Mascotte*, the crops and cattle prospered as long as it lived, and when it died the Chinese stripped off its skin, with which they conduct this dance. The lion is represented as about the size of an ox. Its head and shoulders are formed by a framework, which one man manipulates from the interior, while another man occupies its hind-quarters. A harlequin mummer with a variety of rough-and-tumble

LION-DANCE.

antics introduces the beast, which enters with leaps and bounds and goes through a variety of manœuvres, including mounting on a table, and the performance is diversified by the capers of clowns and acrobats.

THE SACRED DRAMAS.

The sacred dramas, which are based upon the *Jātakas* or former births of Buddha, are very popular. They are performed by professional lay actors and actresses, generally known as "A-lche-lha-mo," though this title "goddess-sister" is strictly applicable only to the actresses who take the part of the goddesses or their incarnations. Strolling parties of these actors travel about Tibet, especially during the winter months, and they frequently act in the presence of the Grand Lāma himself.

The play is usually performed *al fresco*, without a stage frame to the picture, but to obtain the due sense of illusion it is usually done at night by lantern-light. The plot is presented in the form of a chanted narrative, comparable to the chorus of the Greek plays, in the course of which the several leading characters, dressed in suitable costume, come forth and speak for themselves. It is thus somewhat like the narration of a novel with the conversational parts acted. Some buffoonery is given as a prelude and to also fill up the intervals between the acts. These buffoons usually are

ACTORS OF THE VIṢVANTARA-PLAY.

the so-called hunters[1]; but sometimes, as in the old Hindū dramas, the buffoons are Brāhmans.

The most popular of all the dramas which they play are the Viṣvantara (Vessantara) Jātaka, or the last great Birth of Buddha, and the indigenous drama of Nań-sa, or The Brilliant Light. But they also at times play amongst other pieces the Sudhāna Jātaka,[2] the marriage of king Sroṅ Tsan Gampo,[3] the Indian king (?) Amoghasiddha,[4] and the fiendess Dô-ba-zań-mo.[5]

1 rṅon-pa blue masks adorned with cowries, and have kilts of Yak's-hair ropes which fly round at right angles as the men pirouette like dancing dervishes.

2 Ch'os-rgyal-nor-bzań.

3 rgya-za pal-za.

4 rgyal-po don-grub.

5 'rgo-ba-bzań-mô, the consort of Kāleṣvara.

VIṢVANTARA.

THE GREATEST OF BUDDHA'S FORMER BIRTHS.

Throughout the Buddhist world the story of prince Viṣvantara is the most favourite of all the tales of Buddha's former births.[1] It represents the climax of the virtuous practice (the *pāramita*) of charity, in which the princely Bodhisat, in order to attain Buddha-hood, cuts himself loose from all worldly ties by giving away not only all his wealth, but also his children and even his beloved wife.

It is one of the most touching of the legendary tales of its class, and still exercises a powerful fascination for orientals, moving many to tears. Even the rough Indo-Scythian tribes, who invaded India about the beginning of the Christian era, could not refrain from tears when they saw the picture of the sufferings of this prince.[2] It is sculptured on the Sanchi Topes at Bhilsa, and it is also the most favourite of all the sacred plays with the southern Buddhists[3]; though, as Mr. Ralston observes, "such acts of renunciation as the princely Bodhisat accomplished do not com-

---

[1] Of the ten Great (former) Births (Mahājātaka) this is considered the greatest, and it was the last earthly birth but one of the Bodhisat. It purports to have been narrated by Buddha himself at the monastery of the Fig-tree (Nigrodha, *Ficus Indica*) in Buddha's native country of Kapilavastu, *à propos* of the over-weening pride of his own kindred. The *Milinda* dialogues (*loc. cit.*), written about 150 A.D., contain many references to it.

[2] Sung Yun's history, translated by S. BEAL, *Records*, p. 201.

[3] See HARDY'S *Man.*, pp. 116-124. The late Captain Forbes, in his work on *British Burma and its People*, says: "One of the best I think, and certainly the most interesting performances I have seen in Burma, was that of a small children's company in a village of about two hundred houses. The eldest performer was about fourteen, the daughter of the head man, a slight pretty girl; the others boys and girls, younger. The parents and villagers generally were very proud of their talents, and they were regularly trained by an old man as stage-manager, prompter, etc. Their principal piece was the Way-than-da-ra, the story of one of the previous existences of Gan-da-ma, in which he exemplified the great virtue of alms-giving, and in itself one of the most affecting and beautifully written compositions in Burma. . The little company used to perform this piece capitally, but the acting of the little maid of fourteen in the part of the princess could not be surpassed. She seemed really to have lost herself in her part; and her natural and graceful attitudes heightened the effect. The first time I witnessed the performance in going round and saying a word to the tiny actors, when I came to the little fellow of ten or eleven who had acted the part of the surly and greedy Brahmin, I pretended to be disgusted with his cruelty to the two poor infants. This the little man took in earnest, so much to heart that as I learnt, on my next visit, nothing would induce him to act the part again, and it was not till his father almost forcibly brought him to me and I had soothed him by what was deemed most condescending kindness and excited his vanity, that I could obtain a repetition of the play." Captain Forbes also states that he has seen men moved to tears by the acting of this play.

KEY TO PICTURE OF VIṢVANTARA JĀTAKA.

34
30 37 35
27 33 36
38 32 31
28 29 39
40 16
26
41 42
25 9a
24 43 15
49
23 45
44
22 46
21 14
48
8
20 13
4 10 17 1
18
3 47 9 7 2
11 12
6 19

1 The sonless king and queen bewailing their lot.
2. A son is obtained after worshipping the Buddhas.
3. A princess sought for his wife.
4. His suit urged by princess's father.
5. Bride leaving her father's palace.
6. Viṣvantara meeting his bride.
7. Their family.
8. Giving charity.
9. Brāhman sent for the Wishing Gem.
9a. Brāhman begging the gem.
10. Prince hesitating to give it.
11. Leads Brāhman to his treasury.
12 Brāhman refusing other jewels.
13. Prince giving up gem.
14. Placing it on white elephant.
15. Arrival of Brāhman with jewel.
16. Its deposit in the enemy's palace.
17. Prince upbraided by his family.
18. Minister urging king to kill prince.
19. Prince saved from lynching.
20. His banishment.
21. Citizens bidding him farewell.
22. Brāhmans beg his elephants.
23. Brāhmans beg his chariots.
24. He and family proceed on foot.
25. Miraculous crossing of river.
26. Travelling to forest of banishment.
27. In forest.
28. Brāhman begging for the children.
29. Children leave-taking.
30. Brāhman beating the children.
31. Takes them to his home.
32. Engaged as drudges.
33. Forest hut.
34. Princess gathering food.
35. Birds assisting her.
36. She is begged by Indra (Jupiter).
37. And is given and taken off.
38. Prince visited by 1,000 Buddhas.
39. Worship by animals, Nāgas, etc.
40. His departure from forest with restored wife.
41. Gives his eyes to blind beggar.
42. The restored blind man's gratitude.
43. The blind prince led onwards.
44. The Buddhas restore his sight.
45. The wicked king begs forgiveness.
46. The Brāhman returns the jewel.
47. Prince's joyous reception.
48. The prince and family at home again.
49. The prince's re-birth as St. Padma, the founder of Lāmaism.

THE GREAT FORMER BIRTH OF BUDDHA AS THE CHARITABLE PRINCE VIṢVANTARA.

[*To face p.* 542.

mend themselves to the western mind. An oriental story-teller can describe a self-sacrificing monarch as cutting slices of flesh out of his own arms and plunging them in the fire in honour of a deity, and yet not be afraid of exciting anything but a religious thrill among his audience. To European minds such a deed would probably appear grotesque."[1]

The text of the story, as found in the Tibetan canon,[2] agrees generally with the Pāli[3] and Burmese[4] accounts. I give here an abstract of the version[5] which is currently acted in western Tibet. It differs in several details from the canonical narrative and in the introduction of some incidents, such as the bestowal of his eyes, which are usually regarded as pertaining to other Jātakas, and it also is given a local Tibetan application, and the founder of Lāmaism, St. Padma, is made to appear as a reincarnation of the prince Viṣvantara. To illustrate the text, I give its pictorial representation as a reduced tracing from a Tibetan painting.

THE OMNIPOTENT PURE ONE,[6] OR THE PRINCE OF CHARITY.

Salutation to the Sublime Lord of the World![7]

Long long ago, in the city of Baidha,[8] in India, there reigned a king named Gridhip,[9] who, after propitiating the gods and dragons, had a

---

1 *Tibetan Tales*, p. lvii.

2 Kah-gyur, iv., ff. 192-200, translated by Schiefner and Englished by Ralston, in "*Tibetan Tales*," p. 257, who also traces its comparative aspect, p. lvii. In the following account those portions which are identical with the canonical version are put in quotation marks when given in Ralston's words.

3 *Wessantara Jātaka*, HARDY's *Manual*, 116-124, and *East. Monach.*, 83-428. *Milinda loc. cit.*; UPHAM, *Hist. and Doct. of Buddhism*, p. 25; S. DE OLDENBURG, *J.R.A.S.*, 1893, p. 301.

4 "*The Story of We-than-da-ya*," Englished from the Burmese version of the Pāli text by L. A. Goss, Rangoon, American Bap. Mission, 1886.

5 Translated from the MS. of a company of Tibetan actors from Shigatse. It generally agrees with the version in the Manikah-bum.

6 Dri-med-kun-*l*dan (pronounced *Ti-med Kün-den*).

7 *Nāmo aryalokeṣvara.*

8 In the Mani-kah-bum it is called "The Sounding" (*s*Gra-chan). In the Kah-gyur "*Viṣvanagara*." It is believed by Tibetans to be the ancient Videha which they identify with the modern "Bettiah" in northern Bengal, but it was evidently in northern India.

9 According to the Kah-gyur, Viṣvamitra; the Maṇi-kah-'bum gives "the Voice of the Drum-Sound" (*s*gra-*d*byang-*r*nga-*s*gra), and the Pāli "*Sanda*" and Burmese "*Thain See*."—GOSS, *loc cit.*, p. 7.

son born unto him by his favourite queen, "The Pure Young Goddess,"[1] and the prince was named by the Brāhmans the "Omnipotent Pure Lord of the World" [but we shall call him by the better known name of Viṣvantara]. This prince grew luxuriantly, "like a lotus in a pool," and soon acquired all accomplishments. He was "addicted to magnanimity, bestowing presents freely and quite dispassionately and assiduous in giving away." When men heard of his excessive generosity, numberless crowds flocked to beg of him from all directions, and he sent none of them away without having fully realized their expectations, so that after a few years of this wholesale almsgiving, no poor people were left in the country—all had become rich.

Now, this country owed its prosperity to an enchanted wish-granting gem,[2] which was kept in the custody of the king, and by virtue of which the stores in his treasury, notwithstanding the enormous amounts which were daily given away by his son, never grew less. The traditional enemy of this country, the greedy king[3] of a barren land,[4] hearing of the prince's vow to bestow any part of his property on anyone who asked for it, secretly instructed one of his Brāhmans to go and beg from the prince the enchanted gem.

So the Brāhman having arrived at the gate of the palace, threw himself before the prince, exclaiming, with outstretched hands: "Victory to thee, O prince! our land is famished for want of rain, therefore give unto me the enchanted Jewel!"

Now, prince Viṣvantara was deeply distressed at hearing such a request, and he hesitated to give away this precious gem, through fear of offending his father, the king, and the people; but finding that the Brāhman would accept nothing less than this gem, and reflecting that if he refused to give away any of his property which had been asked from him, his charitable merit would cease, he besought the blessing of the gem by placing it on his head, and then gave it away without regret, saying, "May I, by this incomparable gift, become a Buddha." And the Brāhman carried off the gem on a white elephant to the foreign king, their enemy, who by virtue of the gem waxed rich and threatened to invade the country, which now became afflicted by famine and other disasters.

The prince's father and the people, hearing of the loss of the enchanted gem, were furious with vexation, and the enraged minister,

1 Lha-ch'ung dri-ma med-pa.

2 Tib., Nor-bu *d*gos-'dod-dbung-'jom.; Skt., *Cintāmaṇi*. Its properties are analogous to *La Mascotte*. The Lāmas say it was given to Buddha Amitābha by a white Nāga of the ocean. In the Burmese version (*loc. cit.*, p. 12), it is made to be the white elephant; but the word Nāga means both elephant and the serpent-dragons, or mermen, the guardians of treasure.

3 Shiṅ-thi-bstan.

4 mt'a-'k'ob bye-ma-s'iṅ druṅ. Kaliṅga (on the west of the Bay of Bengal). The Ceylon version (HARDY's *Manual*, p. 116) makes the rain-producing elephant be brought from Jayaturā, the capital of Sibi, by Brāhmans sent by the king of Kaliṅga.

Tara-mdses, seized the prince and handed him over to the scavengers[1] for lynching, and he was only rescued by the entreaties of the good minister Candrakirtī and of his wife and children—for he had, when of age, married the beautiful princess, "The Enlightening Moon-Sun,"[2] better known as "Madrī," by whom he had two[3] children, a son and daughter. The ministers decided that the person who informed the prince of the arrival of the Brāhman should lose his tongue; he who brought the Jewel from its casket-box should lose his hands; he who showed the path to the Brāhman should lose his eyes; and he who gave away the Jewel should lose his head. To this the king could not consent, as it meant the death of his beloved son, so he ordered the prince to be banished for a period of twenty-five years to "the black hill of the demons resounding with ravens."[4]

Then the prince prayed his father's forgiveness, and the king, filled with sorrow at parting, besought his son, saying, "O, son, give up making presents and remain here." But the prince replied, "The earth and its mountains may perhaps be overthrown, but I, O! king, cannot turn aside from the virtue of giving."

And the good prince implored his father's permission to devote seven more days to almsgiving, to which the king consented.

Prince Visvantara, addressing the princess, besought her to cherish their darling children, and to accept the hand of a protecting consort worthy of her incomparable virtue and beauty. But the princess, feeling hurt even at the suggestion of her separation, refused to part from him, and inspired by a desire to comfort the prince, paints in glowing colours the amenities of life in the forest of banishment, though the prince protested that it was a wilderness of thorns, beset by tigers, lions, venomous snakes, and scorpions and demons, excessively hot during the day, and rigorously cold at night, where there are no houses or even caves for shelter, and no couch but grass, and no food but jungle fruits.

The princess, however, replies, "Be the dangers what they may, I would be no true wife were I to desert you now," and thus refuses to part from him; so they set out accompanied by their children,[5] riding in a three-horse chariot and on one elephant.

"When the prince, together with his wife and children, had reached

---

1 Skt., *Chandal.*

2 Ñi-zla-sgron-ma, daughter of king Grags-pa (=Skt., *Kirti*). Another account says he also married "The Lamp of the Sky" (Namk'ai sgron-ma), daughter of king Dri-ma-Med-pa, of the "Lotus" country. And these two are said to have been first met by him carrying *udumwara* flowers on one of his charitable rounds of visiting the temple of Buddha Yes'e-*h*od-mdsad-tok, or "the Buddha of the Light Diadem of fore-knowledge." The Burmese version states (Goss' trans., p. 11) that he visited "The Six Temples" six times every month, mounted on his white elephant Pis-sa-ya.

3 Another version gives three children.

4 The place of banishment, according to the Pāli, was Vankagiri.

5 Named 'Od-zer-tok, and Utpalmaṇi. The southern version gives the name of the son as Jālin and of the daughter as Krishnājinā.

the margin of the forest, all the people who formed his retinue raised a loud cry of lament. But so soon as it was heard, the Bodhisat addressed the retinue which had come forth from the good city, and ordered it to turn back, saying,—

"'However long anything may be loved and held dear, yet separation from it is undoubtedly imminent. Friends and relatives must undoubtedly be severed from what is dearest to them, as from the trees of the hermitage wherein they have rested from the fatigues of the journey. Therefore when ye recollect that all over the world men are powerless against separation from their friends, ye must for the sake of peace strengthen your unsteady minds by unfailing exertion.'

"When the Bodhisat had journeyed three hundred yojanas, a Brāhman came to him, and said, 'O Kshatriya prince, I have come three hundred yojanas because I have heard of your virtue. It is meet that you should give me the splendid chariot as a recompense for my fatigue.'

"Madrī could not bear this, and she addressed the begging Brāhman in angry speech: 'Alas! this Brāhman, who even in the forest entreats the king's son for a gift, has a merciless heart. Does no pity arise within him when he sees the prince fallen from his royal splendour?' The Bodhisat said, 'Find no fault with the Brāhman.' 'Why not?' 'Madrī, if there were no people of that kind who long after riches, there would also be no giving, and in that case how could we, inhabitants of the earth, become possessed of insight. As giving and the other Pāramitās (or virtues essential to a Buddhaship) rightly comprise the highest virtue, the Bodhisats constantly attain to the highest insight.'

"Thereupon the Bodhisat bestowed the chariot and horses on that Brāhman with exceeding great joy, and said, 'O Brāhman, by means of this gift of the chariot, a present free from the blemish of grudging, may I be enabled to direct the car of the sinless Law directed by the most excellent Rishi!'

"When Visvantara had with exceeding great joy bestowed on the Brāhman the splendid chariot, he took prince Krishna on his shoulder, and Madrī took princess Jalīnī.[1] They went forth into the forest, proceeding on foot, when five Brāhmans appeared and begged for their clothes, which were at once taken off and given to them. The prince and his family then clothed themselves with leaves, and trudged along painfully for about a hundred miles, until a mighty river barred their progress. The prince then prayed, 'O! Great river, make way for us!' Then the torrent divided, leaving a lane of dry land, across which they passed. On reaching the other side, the prince, addressing the river, said, 'O! river, resume your course, otherwise innumerable animal beings lower down your course will suffer misery from drought!' On which the river straightway resumed its course.

"Then, journeying onwards, they reached the forest of penance

[1] In HARDY'S *Southern Recension*, the boy is called Jāliya and the girl Krishnāyina (*Manual*, p. 116).—SCHIEFNER.

among snowy-white mountains and forest-clad[1] hills; and by the aid of two mendicants of the Mahāyāna creed whom they accidentally met, they fixed on a hillock for their abode. And the prince dwelt there in a separate cell like a celibate monk, and took the vow which pleased his heart, and it was not altogether an unpleasant life. The water welled out of the ground conveniently near, and flowers and most luscious fruits appeared in abundance, and the parrots assisted the princess and children in gathering fruit by nipping the stem of the best fruits on the highest trees. And the carnivorous animals left off preying on animals and took to eating grass. The most pleasing songsters amongst the birds settled near by, and the wild animals treated the young prince and princess as playmates, and rendered them useful aid. Thus the young prince riding on a deer, fell off and bruised his arm, when a monkey at once carried him to a lake and bathed and soothed the wound with healing herbs.

"One day, when Madrī had gone to collect roots and fruits in the penance-forest, a Brāhman[2] came to Visvantara, and said, 'O prince of Kshatriya race, may you be victorious! As I have no slave, and wander about alone with my staff, therefore is it meet that you should give me your two children.' As the Bodhisat, Visvantara, after hearing these words, hesitated a little about giving his beloved children, the Brāhman said to the Bodhisat,—

"'O prince of Kshatriya race, as I have heard that you are the giver of all things, therefore do I ask why you still ponder over this request of mine. You are renowned all over the earth as the possessor of a compassion which gives away all things: you are bound to act constantly in conformity with this renown.'

"After hearing these words the Bodhisat said to the Brāhman, 'O great Brāhman, if I had to give away my own life I should not hesitate for a single moment. How, then, should I think differently if I had to give away my own children? O great Brāhman, under these circumstances I have bethought me as to how the children, when given by me, if I do give away these two children who have grown up in the forest, will live full of sorrow on account of their separation from their mother. And inasmuch as many will blame me, in that with excessive mercilessness I have given away the children and not myself, therefore is it better that you, O Brāhman, should take me.'

"The Brāhman presses his petition and says, 'It is not right that I, after having come to you, should remain without a present, and all my cherished hopes be brought to nought.' On hearing this the prince, though torn by paternal emotion, gave the children, saying, 'May I, by virtue of this gift, become a Buddha.'

"Meanwhile, Madrī had set off for the hermitage, carrying roots and fruits, and when the earth shook, she hurried on all the faster towards

[1] The chief trees were "Ka-det" (*Cratæva Roxburghii*).

[2] "Zoo-za-ga" of Don-nee-wee-ta in Kalinga, according to the Burmese (Trans., *loc. cit.*, p. 35).

the hermitage. A certain deity who perceived that she might hinder the surrender which the Bodhisat proposed to make for the salvation of the world, assumed the form of a lioness and barred her way. Then Madrī said to this wife of this king of the beasts, 'O wife of the king of the beasts, full of wantonness, wherefore do you bar my way? In order that I may remain truly irreproachable, make way for me that I may pass swiftly on. Moreover, you are the wife of the king of the beasts, and I am the spouse of the Lion of Princes, so that we are of similar rank. Therefore, O queen of the beasts, leave the road clear for me.'

"When Madrī had thus spoken, the deity who had assumed the form of a lioness turned aside from the way. Madrī reflected for a moment, recognizing inauspicious omens, for the air resounded with wailing notes, and the beings inhabiting the forest gave forth sorrowful sounds, and she came to the conclusion that some disaster had certainly taken place in the hermitage, and said, 'As my eye twitches, as the birds utter cries, as fear comes upon me, both my children have certainly been given away; as the earth quakes, as my heart trembles, as my body grows weak, my two children have certainly been given away.'

"With a hundred thousand similar thoughts of woe she hastened towards the hermitage. Entering therein she looked mournfully around, and, not seeing the children, she sadly, with trembling heart, followed the traces left on the ground of the hermitage. 'Here the boy Krishna and his sister were wont to play with the young gazelles; here is the house which they twain made out of earth; these are the playthings of the two children. As they are not to be seen, it is possible that they may have gone unseen by me into the hut of foliage and may be sleeping there.' Thus thinking and hoping to see the children, she laid aside the roots and fruits, and with tearful eyes embraced her husband's feet, asking, 'O lord, whither are the boy and girl gone?' Viṣvantara replied, 'A Brāhman came to me full of hope. To whom have I given the two children. Thereat rejoice.' When he had spoken these words, Madrī fell to the ground like a gazelle pierced by a poisoned arrow, and struggled like a fish taken out of the water. Like a crane robbed of her young ones she uttered sad cries. Like a cow, whose calf has died, she gave forth many a sound of wailing. Then she said, 'Shaped like young lotuses with hands whose flesh is as tender as a young lotus leaf.[1] My two children are suffering, are undergoing pain, wherever they have gone. Slender as young gazelles, gazelle-eyed, delighting in the lairs of the gazelles, what sufferings are my children now undergoing in the power of strangers? With tearful eyes and sad sobbing, enduring cruel sufferings, now that they are no longer seen by me, they live downtrodden among needy men. They who were nourished at my breast, who used to eat roots, flowers, and

[1] Properly, "lotus arrow." According to Maximowicz the young lotus leaves are reed-like or arrow-like in appearance.—SCHIEFNER.

fruits, they who, experiencing indulgence, were never wont to enjoy themselves to the full, those two children of mine now undergo great sufferings. Severed from their mother and their family, deserted by the cruelty of their relatives, thrown together with sinful men, my two children are now undergoing great suffering. Constantly tormented by hunger and thirst, made slaves by those into whose power they have fallen, they will doubtless experience the pangs of despair. Surely I have committed some terrible sin in a previous existence, in severing hundreds of beings from their dearest ones.'

"After gratifying the Bodhisat with these words, the king of the gods, Sākra, said to himself: 'As this man, when alone and without support, might be driven into a corner, I will ask him for Madrī.' So he took the form of a Brāhman, came to the Bodhisat, and said to him: 'Give me as a slave this lovely sister, fair in all her limbs, unblamed by her husband, prized by her race.' Then in anger spake Madrī to the Brāhman: 'O shameless and full of craving, do you long after her who is not lustful like you, O refuse of Brāhmans, but takes her delight according to the upright law?' Then the Bodhisat, Viṣvantara, began to look upon her with compassionate heart, and Madrī said to him: 'I have no anxiety on my own account, I have no care for myself; my only anxiety is as to how you are to exist when remaining alone.' Then said the Bodhisat to Madrī: 'As I seek after the height which surmounts endless anguish, no complaint must be uttered by me, O Madrī, upon this earth. Do you, therefore, follow after this Brāhman without complaining. I will remain in the hermitage, living after the manner of the gazelles.'

"When he had uttered these words, he said to himself with joyous and exceedingly contented mind: 'This gift here in this forest is my best gift. After I have here absolutely given away Madrī too, she shall by no means be recalled.' Then he took Madrī by the hand and said to that Brāhman: 'Receive, O most excellent Brāhman, this is my dear wife, loving of heart, obedient to orders, charming in speech, demeaning herself as one of lofty race.'

"When in order to attain to supreme insight, he had given away his beautiful wife, the earth quaked six times to its extremities like a boat on the water. And when Madrī had passed into the power of the Brāhman, overcome by pain at being severed from her husband, her son, and her daughter, with faltering breath and in a voice which huskiness detained within her throat, she spoke thus: 'What crimes have I committed in my previous existence that now, like a cow whose calf is dead, I am lamenting in an uninhabited forest?' Then the king of the gods, Sākra, laid aside his Brāhman's form, assumed his proper shape and said to Madrī: 'O fortunate one, I am not a Brāhman, nor am I a man at all. I am the king of the gods, Sākra, the subduer of the Asuras. As I am pleased that you have manifested the most excellent morality, say what desire you would now wish to have satisfied by me.'

"Rendered happy by these words, Madrī prostrated herself before

Sākra, and said: 'O thou of the thousand eyes, may the lord of the three and thirty set my children free from thraldom, and let them find their way to their great grandfather.' After these words had been spoken the prince of the gods entered the hermitage and addressed the Bodhisat. Taking Madrī by the left hand, he thus spoke to the Bodhisat: 'I give you Madrī for your service. You must not give her to anyone. If you give away what has been entrusted to you fault will be found with you.'[1]

"The king of the gods, in accordance with his promise, caused angels every night to unloose and nurse the unfortunate children of the illustrious recluse when the wicked Brāhman fell asleep, and only re-tied them just before he awaked. Afterwards he deluded the Brāhman who had carried off the boy and girl, so that under the impression that it was another city, he entered the self-same city from which they had departed, and there set to work to sell the children. When the ministers saw this they told the king, saying: 'O king, your grand-children, Krishna and Jalīnī, have been brought into this good city in order to be sold, by an extremely worthless Brāhman.' When the king heard these words, he said indignantly, 'Bring the children here, forthwith.'"

When this command had been attended to by the ministers, and the townspeople had hastened to appear before the king, one of the ministers brought the children before him. When the king saw his grand-children brought before him destitute of clothing and with foul bodies he fell from his throne to the ground, and the assembly of ministers, and women, and all who were present, began to weep. Then the king said to the ministers: "Let the bright-eyed one, who, even when dwelling in the forest, delights in giving, be summoned hither at once, together with his wife."

Then the king sent messengers to recall his son; but the latter would not return until the full period of his banishment was over.

On his way back he meets a blind man, who asks him for his eyes, which he immediately plucks out and bestows on the applicant, who thus receives his sight.[2] The prince, now blind, is led onwards by his wife, and on the way meets "The Buddhas of the Three Periods,"—the Past, Present, and Future, namely, Dipaṁkara, Ṣākya,[3] and Maitreya, who restore the prince's sight.

Journeying onwards he is met by the hostile king who had been the cause of all his trouble, but who now returns him the gem, and with it much money and jewels, and he implored the prince's forgiveness for having caused his banishment and sufferings, and he prayed that when the prince became a Buddha he might be born as one of his attendants. The prince readily forgave him, and accorded him his other requests, and they became friends.

---

1 RALSTON, *op. cit.*

2 Cf., The "*Sibi* Jātaka."

3 This is rather absurd, as it is supposed to have happened before Sākya's birth.

On the approach of the prince to the capital, the old king, his father, caused the roads to be swept and strewn with flowers, and sprinkled with sweet perfume, and met him with flags and joyous music. And he gave again into his son's charge all the treasure and jewels.

The prince, thus restored to his former position, resumed his wholesale bestowal of charity as before, and everyone was happy. The young princess, Utpalmaṇi, married the son of the Brāhman chief, named Ksheman. And the young prince married the beautiful princess Mandhara, daughter of king Lja-wai-tok; and succeeding to the throne, he left his father free to indulge in his pious pursuit, Charity.

The play concludes by the chief actor, who takes the part of the charitable prince, giving the piece a local Tibetan application.

He states: I, "The Lord of the World," am afterwards king Sroṅ-Tsan Gampo (the introducer of Buddhism into Tibet), and my two wives are afterwards his Chinese and Newari princess-consorts. The two Bhikshus, who assisted me, are afterwards Thonmi Sambhota (the minister of king Sroṅ-Tsan, who introduced writing to Tibet), and Mañjuṣrī (the introducer of astrology and metaphysics), the demon who obstructed the two queens is Srī Vajrapāṇī. *And five generations later, I, Sroṅ-Tsan Gampo, appeared as Padma-sambhava,* the founder of Lāmaism. The prince 'Od-zer-tok is Norbu 'Dsin-pa, the princess Utpalmaṇi is Lhamo dbyan Chan-ma (Saraswati devi). That Brāhman is the black devil Tharba, and his wife is *g*Nod *s*byin-ma, or "The injuring Yakshinī." That uninhabited wilderness of the demons, resounding with the croaking of ravens, is the snowy region of Tibet. The dwelling place there of the king is Yar-luṅ*s* gyalwaī-k'ra-'buk; and that great river is the Yar-chab Tsaṅ-po (The "Tsanpu" or Brahmāputra). Thus history repeats itself! *Maṅgalam*! [and here the people all shout "*Maṅgalam*—All Happiness."].

Another popular play is the *Sudhāna Jātaka*, which is mentioned by FaHian,[1] and is also met with in southern Buddhism.[2] The Tibetan version is here given.[3]

The Sudhāna Jātaka.

Its chief *dramatis personæ* are the following:—

Nor-zaṅ ch'os-skyoṅ, The Prince Sudhāna, without a mask.
Mende-zaṅ-mo, the beautiful fairy Kinnara and two other goddesses.
A black-hat sorcerer.
Ṅon-ba, a hunter in a blue mask holding a jewel.

1 Beal's *Records*, etc., 157, chap. xxxviii.; also Raj Mitra, *Nepalese Skt. Lit.*, p. 62.
2 By Upham, under name Sudāna or Sutāna; cf. Spence Hardy's *Manual*, p. 116.
3 Nor-bzaṅ.

Ma-cho Ya-ma gen-te, the chief wife of the prince. Wears mask having right side white (= divine colour) and left side black (= satanic), to represent her composite disposition.

Luk-zi ch'un-me tak-gye, in sheep-skin coat, flour-smeared face, carrying reel of wool thread, and a sling.

The seven S'em-pa brothers, armed with swords, etc., two-eyed, ferocious, with mouth agape.

The Hermit Lāma Toṅ-soṅ ch'en bo, with a yellow mask, and carrying a rosary.

The plot is as follows: A serpent-charmer endeavours by incantations to capture the Nāga which confers prosperity on his enemy's country. The Nāga, alarmed at the potency of the sorcerer's spells, appeals to a hunter, who kills the sorcerer, and is presented with a magic noose as a reward for his services. This noose he bequeaths to his son, Utpala or Phalaka, who one day in the forest near Valkalāyana's hermitage at Hastinapura, hearing a celestial song sung by a marvellously beautiful *Kinnari* fairy, he captured the fairy with his magic noose. The Kinnari to regain her liberty offered him her jewelled crown, which conferred the power of traversing the universe. Meanwhile a young prince of Hastinapura named Sudhāna, or Maṇibhadra,[1] engaged on a hunting expedition, appears upon the scene. He gets the jewel, marries the Kinnari, and gives her his entire affection. His other wives, mad with jealousy, endeavour to kill her during his absence, but she escapes to her celestial country, leaving, however, with the hermit a charmed ring for the prince should he seek to follow her to her supernatural home. The prince pursues her, overcoming innumerable obstacles, and finally gains her, and also obtains her father's consent to their marriage, and to their return to the earth, where they live happy ever after.

This story, which is translated in detail by Mr. Ralston, presents many parallels to western folk-tales. Mr. Ralston remarks in this regard that "One of these is the capture by the hunter Palaka of the celestial maiden, the Kinnari Manoharā, who becomes Sudhāna's bride. This is effected by means of a 'fast binding chain' which the hunter throws around her when she is bathing in a lake. Her companions fly away heavenwards, leaving her a captive on earth. This incident will at once remind the reader of the capture of 'swan-maidens' and other supernatural nymphs, which so frequently occur in popular romances. . . . Mano-

[1] CSOMA. *Analy.*, p. 542.

harā is captured by means of a magic chain. But her power of flying through the air depends upon her possession of a jewel. . . . . Sudhāna's visit to the palace of his supernatural wife's father, and the task set him of recognizing her amid her ladies, bear a strong resemblance to the adventure which befall the heroes of many tales current in Europe. A mortal youth often obtains, and then for a time loses, a supernatural wife, generally represented in the daughter of a malignant demon. He makes his way, like Sudhāna, to the demon's abode. There tasks are set him which he accomplishes by means of his wife's help, and the Russian story of 'The Water King,' Grimm's 'Two Kings' Children,' the Norse 'Mastermaid,' and the Scottish Highland 'Battle of the Birds,' are shown to be European variants or parallels to this tale."[1]

Of indigenous Tibetan plays the chief is :—

NAṄ-SA ;
OR,
"THE BRILLIANT LIGHT."

This drama, now translated from the Tibetan[2] for the first time, is one of the most popular plays in Tibet, and its popularity is doubtless owing, not a little, to its local colour being mainly Tibetan, though, like most of the other plays, it is moulded on the model of the Buddhist Jātakas.

Its chief scene is laid at Rinang, a few miles to the south-east of Gyaṅ-tse,[3] the well-known fortified town between Tashi-lhunpo and Lhāsa, where the several sites of the story are still pointed out, and an annual fair held in honour of Naṅ-sa's memory. It also well illustrates the current mode of marriage in Tibet, by planting an arrow[4] on the girl's back, so clearly a survival of the primitive form of marriage by capture.

---

[1] *Op. cit.*, xlviii.

[2] I obtained the MS. from a strolling company of actors who visited Darjiling under the auspices of the Tibetan commissioner. I have curtailed it in places, on account of the inordinate length of the original narrative.

[3] The Tibetan words are romanized according to Csoma de Körös' method of transliteration.

[4] The arrow was the primitive national weapon of the Tibetans ; and their military chief or general is still called *m*Dah-*d*pon, or "Commander of the Arrows" ; and a golden or gilt arrow is a symbol of military command in Tibet.

Dramatis Personæ.

Nań-sa ("The Brilliant Light").
Kun-zań de-ch'en ("The Nobly Virtuous")—*Nań-sa's father* (wears a red mask).
Myań-sa-sal-dön ("The Lamp of Bliss")—*Nań-sa's mother.*
Dag-ch'en duk dag-pa ("The Roaring Dragon")—*Lord of Rinang.*
Sö-nam pal-Kye—*his minister.*
Lha-pu-dar-po ("The Gentle Divinity")—*Nań-sa's son.*
Ani Nemo—*Lord Rinang's sister.*
Lāma Shakyai gyal-ts'an—*Monk in beggar's guise.*
Shin-je Ch'ö-wa—*The King of the Dead.*
Servants, Soldiers, etc.

Act I.

The Re-births of the Deer—A Story of Nań-sa's former Births.

Scene—India. *Time*—Immemorial.

Om! Salutation to the Revered and Sublime Tārā![1]

In bygone times, far beyond conception, there lived in the revered country of India an old couple of the Brāhman caste who during their youth had no children, but when they waxed old and feeble, a daughter was born unto them.

This child was secluded till her fifteenth year, when, peeping outside one day, she for the first time saw the landscape of the outer world. And as she observed the different classes of people cultivating their plots, whilst her own family-plot lay neglected, she ran to her mother and said: "Mother, dear! the giver of my body! Listen to me, your own daughter! All the different classes of people are busy tilling their fields while our family-land lies neglected. Now as the time for cultivation has come, permit me, mother, to cultivate our fields with our servants!"

The mother, having granted her request, the daughter proceeded to work with the servants, and they laboured on till breakfast-time, but no one brought them food. This neglect caused the girl uneasiness, not so much on her own account as on that of the servants; but in the belief that food would be sent, she laboured on till sunset, when she and her companions returned home starving.

As they neared the house the girl met her mother bringing some refreshment for them; and she asked her why she had so long delayed, as the servants were quite famished. The mother explained that in entertaining some visitors who had called during the day, she had quite forgotten the food for her daughter and servants.

Then the daughter petulantly exclaimed, "Mother! you are inconsiderate like a grass-eating beast!" On this the mother cried out: "O! ungrateful one! I your mother! who have reared you, and clad and fed you with the best, you now in return call me *a beast!* May you in your next re-birth be born as an ownerless grass-eating beast!"

[1] Nań-sa is held to be an incarnation of the Buddhist goddess Tārā.

So after a time the girl died and was re-born as a deer, according to the curse of her mother.

In course of time her deer-parents died, and the young doe was left alone in strict accordance with her mother's curse.

While in such a plight, a handsome young hart, with a mouth like a conch-shell, came up to her and said: "O, ownerless orphan doe! hear me, the hart Dar-gyas, 'The Vast Banner!' Where is your mate in grazing during the three months of spring? Where is your companion to tend you down to the river? Where is the partner who will remain with you through life?"

The young doe, timidly raising her head, said: "O, master hart! pray be off! I graze during spring without a partner! I go down to the river without a comrade. Gambolling on the hills and dales, I place my faith on The Three Holy Ones alone!"

The hart then replied: "O, noble and virtuous doe! pray hear me! I am the ornament of all the herds! won't you become my mate? I will be your companion when you eat grass. I will be your comrade when you go to the river; and I will support you in all your difficulties. So from this time forth let us be bound in wedlock inseparably, for doubtless we have been brought together here through the deeds and fate of our former lives."

Then the doe consenting, these two became partners and lived together most happily; and not long afterwards the doe gave birth to a fawn who was named *s*Kar-ma-p'un-ts'og*s*, or "The accomplished Star."

One night the doe dreamt a most inauspicious dream; and at midnight she awoke the hart, saying: "Hearken! O deer, Dar-gya*s*! I dreamt as I slept a dreadful dream! This Yal-wa mountain-ridge was overspread by a terrible thundering noise, and I saw several hunters appear. I saw the dogs and hunters pursuing you—the hart—towards the left ridge of the hill, and I, with our child, the fawn, fled by the right ridge of the hill. I dreamt again that the decapitated head of a deer was arranged as a sacrifice, and the skin was stretched out to dry on the meadow, and oh, the blood! it flowed down and formed an awful pool like many oceans! O, deer! Sleep no longer! but arise and let us fast escape to the highest hills."

But the hart refused to listen to the advice of his mate; and saying that "the words of females are like unto the dust," he fell asleep.

Not long afterwards, a ring-tailed red hunting dog seemed to be approaching from the distant barks which now were to be heard distinctly by all the awakened deer.

Too late, the hart then realized that the vision of his doe must have indeed been true; therefore he hurriedly gave the following advice to the doe and the fawn, feeling great pity for them: "O! poor doe and fawn! flee by the left ridge and make good your escape! and if we do not meet again in this life, let us meet in our next life in the pure kingdom of righteousness!" On so saying the hart fled; and the mother and the fawn made their escape by the left ridge.

Meanwhile, the hart, hotly pursued by the hunting-dog, was chased into a narrow gorge where he could not escape; and at that critical moment a man with his hair bound up, bearded and fearfully fierce-looking, with pointed eyebrows, and carrying a noose and a bow and arrow, descended from the top of the cliff, and catching the hart in the noose he killed it with one shot from his bow.

Thus everything happened exactly according to the doe's dream.

The deceased hart was afterwards re-born in a respectable family of Ri-naṅ-*d*paṅ-k'a, and named Grag-pa-*b*sam-grub, or "The famous Heart"; while the doe after death was reborn in *l*Jaṅ-p'al-k'uṅ-naṅ-pa, and was named *s*Nan-sa-'Od-'bum, or "brilliant above a hundred thousand lights." The fawn after death was re-born as their son, and assumed the name of Lha-bu-dar-po, or "the gentle divinity."

[Here endeth the first act dealing with "The Re-births of the Deer."]

Act II.

The Life, Marriage, and Death of Naṅ-sa.

Scene—Rinang. *Time*—Latter end of eleventh century A.D.

Om! Ma-ṇi pad-me Hūṃ! Om! the Jewel in the Lotus! *Hūṃ!*

Long ago, there lived a father named Kun-bzaṅ-bde-ch'en and a mother named Myan-sa-gsal-sgron in *l*Jaṅ-ph'aṅ-k'uṅ-Nan-pa, on the right of Myaṅ-stod-s'el-dkar-rgyal-rtse (Gaṅ-tse).

The mother once had a strange vision, regarding which she thus addressed her husband: "O, great father! Listen! Whilst asleep, I dreamt a most auspicious dream! I dreamt that a lotus-flower blossomed forth from my body, to which many fairies made offerings and paid homage. And a ray of light in the form of the letter *Tam*, of the revered goddess Tārā's spell, entered my head!" On hearing this the father was overjoyed, and exclaimed, "O! Myan-sa-gsal-sgron-ma! Mark my words; by God's blessing, through our making offerings unto Him, and as the fruit of our charity to the poor, an incarnate Bodhisat is about to come unto us! We must again offer thanks unto God and do the several ceremonies."

In course of time a divine-looking daughter was born unto them. She was peerlessly beautiful, and so was named Naṅ-sa, "the brilliant above a hundred thousand lights," and a grand festival was given at her birth.

By her fifteenth year Naṅ-sa was fully educated, and matchlessly beautiful; and though she was most pious, practising fully all the religious rites, she was most modest, and forgot not her filial love and duty.

In the fourth month of that year, during the summer season, a grand tournament was given by the king, to which everyone was invited, and the whole population of the neighbouring countries, young and old, flocked to *r*Gyal-rtse-sger-tsa to see the sports.[1] The games

[1] Known as *g*Ñas-sñiṅ-*b*Zuṅ-'p'hrug.

were held by order of the great king of Myan-stod-ni-nan-pa for the selection of a bride fit for his son. The king himself was of a fiery temper, long like a river, round like a pea, and slender like a stick.

Naṅ-sa also, having taken leave of her parents, set out for the sports. Her moon-like face was white as milk, and her neatly-dressed hair looked like a bouquet of flowers. Thus went she, "the princess," as she was called, to see the grand spectacle, accompanied by her servants, carrying the needful presents.

As she neared the market, where the great gathering was held, the king and prince were looking down from the balcony of their palace, and the prince at once caught sight of her, and his eyes remained rivetted on the princess. Whilst the multitude gazed at the players, the prince followed only the movements of the princess.

The prince being fascinated by the beauty of the princess, soon despatched to her his chief minister, named *b*Sod-nam-dpal-*s*kyed, who, in compliance with his master's order, brought the princess before the prince, just as the eagle Khra carries off a chicken.

And the prince, drawing the princess by her shawl with his left hand and offering her wine with his right, addressed her, saying,—

"O! pretty one! sweet and pleasing-mouthed! possessed of the five sensuous qualities! Tell me truly, whose daughter are you? Are you the daughter of a god or a *Nāga*, or are you an angelic Gandharva? Pray hide nothing from me. What is your father's name? What is your birth-giver's name? Who are your neighbours? I am the overruling lord of Mzang-*s*tod-ri-nang! and called 'The famous Roaring Dragon!' or Da-c'hens-'brug-grag-pa.[1] My family is the Grag-pa-bsam-'grub! I am the jewel of these sheltering walls! My age is six times three (18). Will you consent to be my bride?"

Naṅ-sa now thinking escape impossible, though she had desired to devote herself to a religious life, answered the lord Da-ch'en: "*Om!* Tārā, have mercy on a poor girl void of religion! O! lord Da-ch'en, I am called 'The Brilliant above a Hundred Thousand Lights,' and am of a respectable family. But a poisonous flower, though pretty, is not a fit decoration for an altar vase; the blue *Dole*, though famous, cannot match the turquoise; the bird *l*chog-mo, though swift, is no match for the sky-soaring T'an-dkar-eagle, and Naṅ-sa, though not bad-looking, is no match for the powerful lord of men."

On hearing this reply of Naṅ-sa, the minister took up the turquoise sparkling in rainbow tints, and, tying it to the end of the arrow of the five-coloured silks, handed it to the prince, saying, "As the proverb runs, 'Discontented youths are eager to war, while discontented maidens are eager to wed.' Thus, while this maid feigns disqualifying plainness, she is really anxious to comply with your wishes; her pretended refusal is doubtless owing to modesty and the publicity of such a crowd. Do thou, then, O powerful king! plant the arrow with the five-coloured streamers on her back, and thus fix the marriage tie."

[1] dgr*a* ch'en.

The prince, thinking that the advice was good, addressed Nań-sa, saying, "O! angelic princess! on whom one's eyes are never tired of gazing, pray hear me. O! pretty one, brilliant amongst a thousand lights! I, the great lord sGra-ch'en, am far-famed like the dragon! I am the most powerful king on earth! And whether you choose to obey my commands or not, I cannot let you go! We have been drawn here by the bonds of former deeds, so you must become my mate for ever. Though the bow and bow-string be not of equal length and materials, still they go together; so you must be my mate for ever, as we have certainly been brought together here through fate and former deeds. The great ocean-fish consort with the affluent river fish, so must you live with me. Though I and you differ much in position, you must come with me. And from this day forth the maiden Nań-sa is mine."

So saying, he planted the arrow with its five rainbow-coloured streamers on her back, and set the turquoise diadem on her forehead. And she, being duly betrothed in this public fashion, returned to her own home with her servants.

Nań-sa endeavoured to evade the betrothal and enter a convent instead, but her parents pressed the match upon her and forced her to accept the prince, and the nuptials were duly celebrated with great feasting.

Seven years later, Nań-sa bore a son, whose beauty excelled the gods, hence he was named Lha-bu-Dar-pu, "The god's son," and a grand festival was held in honour of his birth. And Nań-sa, so clever in all the arts, so pretty and befitting her position, and so universally kind, that all the subjects loved her, now became endeared to everyone even more than before. And the three, the prince-father, the princeling, and Nań-sa, were never separated even for a moment. But Nań-sa was the jewel of them all, and she was given the keys of the treasury which had formerly been held by the prince's elder sister, Ani-Nemo-Ne-tso.

Now this old Ani-Nemo, on being deprived of her keys, became madly jealous of Nań-sa, and began contriving means to injure her reputation in the eyes of the prince, her husband.

Ani-Nemo helped herself to the best food and clothes, leaving the very worst to Nań-sa, who was too mild and good to resent such treatment. Ultimately Nań-sa began to feel vory sad, and though engaged in worldly affairs, she felt keenly the desire to devote herself wholly to religion, but she was afraid to reveal her thoughts to her husband and son.

One day while sad at heart, she went to the garden carrying the young prince, and they all sat down together, the lord resting his head on Nań-sa's lap. It was autumn, and the summer flowers had ceased blossoming, and the gold and turquoise-coloured bees had gone. Then Nań-sa wept on thinking that she could not realize her religious desires, and that she was separated from her parents, and subject to the torture of Ani's jealousy. But her lord comforted her, saying,

"O! beloved Naṅ-sa, you shall have a chance of seeing your parents soon, so do not feel sorry. Have patience to remain till the harvest is gathered. Let us now go to *b*Z'un-z'in-rin-ma with our servants and collect the harvest, as the time is now far advanced." Then they went there with their servants and Ani.

Now, there arrived at that place the devotee, Dor-grags-Ras-pa,[1] and his servant, and the devotee addressed Naṅ-sa thus,—

"*Om!* Salutation to our spiritual father, the Lāma!

"O! Naṅ-sa! You are like the rainbow on the eastern mead, the rainbow beautiful and pleasing to see, but quickly vanishing. Now the time for devoting yourself to religion has arrived.

"O! Naṅ-sa! you are like the warbling bird of the southern forest, whose voice, though pleasing and cheery, is ephemeral. Now the time for devoting yourself to religion has come.

"O! Naṅ-sa! you are like the Nāga-dragon of the western ocean; the Nāga possessing vast wealth, but without real substance. Now the time for your devotion to religion, which is the only true reality, has arrived. On death nothing can save you but the real refuge of religion. The bravest hero and the wisest man cannot escape. Now as there is no alternative, you should avail yourself of this great chance, for once lost it may never be refound."

On hearing this speech Naṅ-sa was overpowered with grief. And as she had nothing to offer the holy man as alms, for everything was in charge of Ani, she, with faltering voice, said: "Though I am anxious to offer you whatever alms you need, yet am I possessed of nothing, but pray go to that house over there, where you will find Ani with a sleek face, and seek alms from her."

The devotee and his servant accordingly went and requested Ani-Nemo to give them some alms, but she replied: "O! you beggars! why have you come begging of me! you plundering crew! you steal at every chance! You neither devote yourself to religious purposes in the hills, nor do you work in the valleys. If you want alms go to that person over there with the peacock-like prettiness, and the bird-like warbling voice, and the rainbow-like lofty mind, and with a mountain of wealth, for I am only a poor servant and cannot give you anything."

The two devotees, therefore, returned to Naṅ-sa, and told her what Ani had said. So Naṅ-sa gave alms to the devotees in spite of her fear of displeasing Ani. The holy man replied, "It will be an auspicious meeting an event to look forward to, when Naṅ-sa and we two meet again." On this Naṅ-sa became more cheerful, and giving more alms to the devotees, bowed down before them and requested their blessings.

Now these proceedings did not escape the wary eye of Ani-Nemo, who, waxing wroth, came out with a cane in her hand, and thus abused Naṅ-sa:

[1] A wandering Lāma of the Kar-gyu-pa sect and contemporary of the great Mila-raspa in the eleventh century A.D.

"You look lovely, but your heart is black and venomous! Listen to me, O peacock-like she-devil Naṅ-sa! In those high mountains the holy Buddha and the great Indian sages sat, but whence came and go devotees like these Ras-pas? If you give alms to all of them according to their requests I would cut you even though you were my own mother! In the S'oṅ-z'iṅ-riṅ-mo of this country the chief products are barley and peas. Now you have given away as alms all these men asked for, more than your own portion; and thus as you, too, are a beggar, go and accompany these others," and so saying, she began to beat Naṅ-sa.

Naṅ-sa, imploring mercy, said: "What else could I do? I gave them alms to avoid scandal according to the saying, which runs, 'beggars carry bad news to the valleys, crows flesh to the peaks.' The giving of alms to the poor and blind and offerings to the holy ones is a most important duty of every rich family; for wealth collected by avarice, like the honey collected by house-bees, is of no use to oneself. Do not, therefore, call these venerable Ras-pas 'beggars,' but respect and honour them; and call not a girl a devil for being piously inclined, or hereafter you may repent it." But Ani only beat her more mercilessly, and tore her hair, which was like delicate Sete-lJang-pa grass. And Naṅ-sa, left alone, wept bitterly, thinking of her misfortunes.

Meanwhile Ani-Nemo went to the lord, her brother, and said, "Hear, O! lord! Our mistress Naṅ-sa without doing any of those things she ought to, does the opposite. This morning a devotee, beautiful and of pleasing voice, came up to this place accompanied by his servant, and Naṅ-sa, fascinated by his beauty, fell madly in love with him and behaved too immodestly for me even to describe it to you. As I was unable to tolerate such conduct I ran down to stop this intercourse, but was beaten and driven off. Therefore, O! lord! have I informed you so that you can take such steps as you think fit."

The lord rather discredited this story, but remembering the proverb "women and sons must be well brought up when young, otherwise they will go wrong," he went to seek Naṅ-sa, and found her shedding torrents of tears in solitude. On seeing her he said, "Ah! *Lah-se!* Listen to me! you naughty Naṅ-sa! *Lah-se*, why have you exceeded all the bounds of propriety! *Lah-se!* Why did you beat my young sister! who gave you authority to do that? *Lah-se!* Like a dog tied on the house-top, barking at and trying to bite the stars of heaven! What has the fiendess Naṅ-sa to say in her defence?"

Naṅ-sa meekly replied, "My lord! were I to relate all that happened it would only make matters worse, and our subjects shall be shown such strife as was unknown before. Therefore I refrain from grieving you, O! my lord, with any details."

But the lord interpreting the reticence of Naṅ-sa as sufficient proof of her guilt, he seized her by the remaining hair, and beat her so unmercifully that no one but Naṅ-sa could have endured it. And he dragged her along the ground and inflicted the deepest pain by pricking reeds. Just then the male-servant *b*Sod-nam-*d*pab-*s*kyed and the female servant 'Dsom-pa-skyid-po came to Naṅ-sa's aid and besought their master saying,—

"O! Great and powerful Lord! Listen to us, your slaves! What can have maddened your majesty to have inflicted such chastisement on your life-partner? The lovely face of our lady Naṅ-sa, which shone like the moon of the fifteenth day, is now bruised and bleeding by your hands. O! Lord of Myaṅ-*s*tod-Ri-nang! Pray stay your wrath, and you, O! lady, cease to weep!"

Then the lord and his lady allowed themselves to be led away, each to their own room.

At that time, Lāma-S'akyahi-rgyal-mts'an, versed in the doctrine of "The Great Perfection," lived in the monastery of sKyid-po-se-rag-ya-luṅ in the neighbourhood. And perceiving that, according to the prophecy of the great reverend Mila-ra*s*, the princess Naṅ-sa was really a good fairy, he thought fit to advise her to pursue her holy aims. So dressing himself in the guise of a poor beggar, though his appearance rather belied him, and taking a young monkey which knew many tricks, he went to the window of Naṅ-sa's chamber and sang this song,—

"O! lady! surpassing the godesses in beauty, pray sit by the window, and cast your eyes hither, so that you may be amused at the tricks of this young monkey, and lend me your ear to hear clearly the songs of a poor travelling beggar, who now stands in your presence.

"In the green forests of the eastern Kong-bu country dwell the monkeys with their young, the wisest of whom climb the high trees, but the foolish ones roam recklessly on the ground, tasting the fruits according to their whims, and one of these unlucky young ones fell into the clutches of a passing beggar, who tied him by the neck as it deserved (through its Karma), and subjected it to various tortures in teaching it his tricks.

"In the forests of the southern craggy Mon country the birds rear their young, of whom the wisest and the strongest soar into the sky, while the foolish ones perch on the lower trees. Thus the speech-knowing parrot comes within the grasp of the king who imprisons it and chains it by the feet, as it deserved; and it is tortured and troubled when being taught to speak.

"In the western country of Nepal, the country of rice, the bees breed their young, of whom the fortunate ones sip the juice of the rice-flowers, while the foolish ones, smelling the rice-beer, come, as they deserved, within the grasp of the cruel boys, who tear them in their hands for the sake of their honey.

"In the northern country of Tsa-kha, the sheep bring forth lambs, of whom the fortunate ones graze on the green meadow, frolicking and skipping in their wild joy, while the unlucky ones come within the grasp of the butchers, who kill them without mercy.

"In the middle country of Myaṅ-*s*tod-*g*ser-*g*z'oṅ-riṅ-mo, the mothers have children, of whom the wisest spend their lives in the country; while the unlucky ones stay with their parents, but the most unlucky of all the pretty girls is married to a lord, and Ani-Nemo treats her as she thinks she deserves. Now if this girl fails to remember the inconstancy of life, then her body, though pretty, is only like that of the peacock of the plains. If she does not steadfastly devote herself to religion, her voice, though pleasing, is like the vain cry of the 'Jolmo bird in the wilderness."

Here the man paused, while the monkey began to play many wonderful tricks, which amused the young prince; while Naṅ-sa, deeply agitated by the song, ordered the beggar to enter her chamber, and addressing him said, "O! traveller in the guise of a beggar! Listen to me! My earnest wish indeed is to devote my life to religion; I have no earthly desires whatever; I was forced to become the manager of a worldly house only through filial obedience to the dictates of my parents. Now pray tell me, which is the most suitable convent for me to enter, and who is the most learned Lāma as a spiritual father?"

The beggar gave her the information she desired. And Naṅ-sa, in her gratitude, bestowed upon him all her silver and golden ornaments.

Now, it so happened that just at this time, the lord arrived, and hearing the voice of a man in his wife's chamber he peeped in and, to his great surprise, saw Naṅ-sa giving a beggar all her jewels, while the young prince was playing with the beggar's monkey.

Furious at the sight, he entered the chamber, just as the beggar and his monkey left; and thinking that Ani's story must indeed be true, and that his wife had bestowed his property on the devotees, and had scandalously brought beggars even inside her private chamber, he seized Naṅ-sa by the hair and began to beat her most unmercifully, and Nemo also came and assisted in beating her. They tore the young prince away from her, and the lord and Ani-Nemo continued beating Naṅ-sa until she died.

ACT III.

Naṅ-sa's return from the Dead.

Om ma-ṇi-pad-me Hūṃ! The young prince, unable to bear separation from his mother, stole to her room after the tragedy and found her lying dead. Rushing to his father with the dreadful news, his father, in alarm, ran to her prostrate figure, but thinking that Naṅ-sa was merely shamming, he exclaimed, "O! fair Naṅ-sa, arise! The starry heaven betimes is obscured by clouds; the lovely flowers die at winter's approach; you have been harshly treated, but your time has not yet come; so, pray arise!" But the corpse lay still, for its spirit long had fled.

Then the lord repented him bitterly, but being powerless to revive her, he had to consent to the customary funeral offerings being made to The Three Holy Ones, and he gave alms to the poor and blind, and feasts to the priests. And the death-astrologer was called and he ordered that the body should be kept for seven days exposed on the eastern hill, and care taken that no animal should destroy it, and that after the eighth day it should be cremated or thrown into a river or lake. Naṅ-sa's body was therefore wrapped in a white blanket and bound on a four-footed bed, and taken to the eastern grassy hill, where it was deposited in solitude.

Now Naṅ-sa's spirit on her death had winged its way, light as a feather, to the ghostly region of the intermediate purgatory, *Bardo*, where the minions of the Death-king seized it and led it before the dreaded judge-king of the dead.

At that tribunal Naṅ-sa's spirit was terrified at seeing many wicked souls condemned and sent down for torture to the hells, in cauldrons of molten metal, or frozen amongst the ice; while she was pleased to see the souls of several pious people sent to heaven.

But in her fear she threw herself before the great judge of the

Dead and with joined hands prayed to him: "Have mercy upon me! O! holy mother Tārā! And help and bless me, ye host of fairy she-devils! O! Judge of the Dead! who separates the white virtuous from the black sinful ones, hear me, O! great king! I longed to benefit the animals, but could do little during my short stay in the world. When I learned that the birth must end in death, I cared not for my beauty; and when I saw that wealth collected by avarice was useless to oneself I gave it away to the poor and blind. Have mercy upon me!"

Then the judge of the Dead ordered her two guardian angels—the good and the bad—to pour out their white and black deed-counters. On this being done, it was found that the white virtuous deeds far exceeded the black sinful ones, which latter were indeed only two in number; and the judge having consulted his magical mirror and found this record to be correct, and knowing that Naṅ-sa was of intensely religious disposition, and capable of doing much good if allowed to live longer in the human world, he reprieved her and sent her back to life, saying:—

"O! Naṅ-sa, brilliant above a hundred thousand lights! Listen! *Lah-se!* Listen to king Yama, the master of Death! I separate the white deeds from the black, and send the persons in whom the white virtue preponderates to the heavens; in this capacity I am named Ārya Avalokiteṣvara ('p'ags-pa-spyan-ras-*g*zigs-*d*baṅ). But when I send the sinful persons to hell, I am named *Mrityupati Yama-rāja* ('ch'i-*b*dag-s'in-*r*jehi-*r*gyal-po)! *Lah-se!* I am the inexorable fierce king who always punishes the wicked! I never save an oppressive king, no matter how powerful; nor will I let any sinful Lāma escape. No one can ever escape visiting this my bar of Justice. But you, O Naṅ-sa! are not a sinful person: you are a good fairy's incarnation, and when a person sacrifices her body for a religious purpose, she obtains paradise, and if she is profoundly pious, she shall obtain the rank of Buddhaship, though the former state is much to be preferred. So stay no longer here, but return to the human world, and recover your old body! *Lah-se!* Be a 'death-returned person,'[1] and benefit the animal beings!"

Naṅ-sa, now overjoyed, bowed down before his Plutonic majesty, and besought his blessing, and after receiving it, she departed by the white heavenly path, and then descending to this world, resumed her former body lying in its white blanket-shroud, and folding her hands in the devotional attitude, she lay with her feet flexed, like a holy thunderbolt. And flowers rained down from heaven upon her, and a rainbow shed its halo round her. And she prayed to the fairies and she-devils:—

"I prostrate myself before the triad assembly of the Lāmas, the tutelaries, and the Ḍākkinī—she-devils and fairies—to whom I pray for deliverance from the circle of re-births. O! eastern fairy of the *Vajra* class, white as the conch-shell, sounding the golden drum (*ḍamaru*) in your right hand, '*tô-lô-lo*,' and ringing the silver bell in your left, '*sī-lī-lī*,' surrounded by hundreds of mild and white-robed attendants, pray forgive all my short-comings! O! southern fairy of the Jewel race, golden-yellow, sounding," etc., etc.

Now the men who had come to remove the corpse, being terrified at

[1] 'das-log.

hearing the dead body speak, dared not approach. The more frightened amongst them fled, while the braver ones prepared to defend themselves by throwing stones, in the belief that the ghost of Naṅ-sa was agitating her dead body. Then Naṅ-sa cried out, saying "I am not a ghost, but a 'death-returned person';" and the men being astonished, drew near and bowed down before her, and paid profound reverence to the resuscitated one.

The good news of Naṅ-sa's return from the dead soon reached the lord and the prince, who hurried to the spot, and throwing themselves before her, implored her forgiveness, and conducted her back to their home; not, however, without protests from Naṅ-sa, who had decided to become a nun. She only consented to resume domestic life on the ardent entreaties of her son.

But soon her excessive piety again subjected her to the ill-treatment of her husband as before, and forced her to flee to her parents' home, where, however, she met with no better reception, but was beaten and expelled. And now driven forth from home, a wanderer for religion's sake, she seeks admission into a convent, where, throwing herself at the Lāma's feet, she prays him, saying,—

"*Om!* Salutation to our spiritual father, the Lāma, and the host of Fairy-mothers! I have come in deep distress in order to devote myself to religion; and I appeal to you, good Lāma, for help and permission to stay here (at *g*Ser-rag-gya-luṅ), O Lāma! I beg you to catch me, insignificant fish as I am, on your hook of mercy; for otherwise the pious resolves of this poor girl will perish, and the injury you thereby will inflict shall be my utter ruin, and make me wretched like a jackal haunting a cave. O! Lāma of the red Lotus-cap, if you fail to help me now, then I am indeed undone! I adore The Holy Religion with all my heart, and I crave your blessing!" and so saying she took off her rich robes and jewels, and offered them to him. And the Lāma, pitying her, blessed her, and gave her the vow of a novice.

The news of Naṅ-sa's entry to the convent soon reached the ears of the lord of Rinang, who waxed wroth and went to war against the monastery. Arriving there with his men he cried unto the Lāma, saying: "*Lah-se!* You fellow, why have you made a nun of Naṅ-sa? Unless you give full satisfaction, I will crush you and all your convent like butter!" And so saying he seized the Lāma and pointed his sword to his heart.

Now Naṅ-sa, driven to despair on seeing that the life of her Lāma was thus threatened for her sake, she, in the dress of a novice, ascended the roof of the convent, and in the sight of all, sailed away, Buddha-like, through the sky, vanishing into space like the rainbow.

Then the lord of Rinang with all his retinue, dismayed at the sight of Naṅ-sa's miraculous flight, fell to the ground. And stung by remorse at their sacrilege, they offered up all their arms and armour to the Lāma; and promising never again to molest him, they returned home gloomy and sad; and Naṅ-sa was seen no more.

May glory come! *Tashi-s'o!* May virtue increase! *Ge-leg-'p'el!!*

And here all the people forming the audience joyfully shout: "*Maṅgalam!!!* All happiness!!!" And the play is over.

The people, old and young, now discuss amongst themselves the theme of the play and its moral lessons. They are profoundly impressed by the self-sacrifice of Naṅ-sa and the other pious persons, and by the vivid pictures drawn of the way in which evil-doers must inexorably pay the penalty of their misdeeds. Thus even these crude Tibetan plays point, in their own clumsy way, very much the same moral lessons as are taught by the Western Stage.

SOME ACTORS OF THE PLAY OF NAṄ-SA.

XXI.

DOMESTIC AND POPULAR LĀMAISM.

LĀMAISM is not merely a monastic brotherhood; it is a truly popular religion, deeply pervading and dominating the life of the people.

LĀMA RECEIVING HOMAGE OF CHILDREN.[1]

On it the Tibetan builds his daily fears and hopes, and it is not without some elevating influence. The current of Buddhism which runs through its tangled paganism has brought to the Tibetan most of the little civilization which he possesses, and has raised him correspondingly in the scale of humanity, lifting him above a life of wild rapine and selfishness, by setting before him higher aims, by giving milder meanings to his mythology, by discountenancing sacrifice, and by inculcating universal charity and tenderness to all living things.

Unlike, however, the Buddhism of the Burmese, it is not an educational factor, for the Lāmas restrict their learning to themselves, as indeed did the Brāhmans, and most priestly orders of old, and they contemptuously call the laity "the dark (ignorant) people,"[2] "the worldly ones,"[3] or "the givers of alms."[4] And certainly the last epithet is well deserved, for the Tibetans, while,

---

[1] After Giorgi, *op. cit.*

[2] mi-nag-pa.

[3] 'jig-rten-pa.

[4] sbyin-bdag, "owners of alms," cf. KÖPP., i., 487.

perhaps, the most priest-ridden people in the world, are amongst the most pious and the most lavish in their religious gifts. The popular name for a Lāma is "Father," as with Roman priests.

It is surprising, in view of the excessive amount of non-Buddhist elements in Lāmaism, to find how deeply the everyday life and notions of the laity are leavened by the Buddhist spirit.

The doctrine of metempsychosis and its *Karma* enters into the ordinary habits and speech of the people. Their proverbs, folk-lore,[1] songs, and lay dramas, are full of it. Friendships also are explained by them on this principle.

More than once have I been told by some worthy Tibetan that it could not have been mere chance which had brought us together, across so many thousand miles of land and sea; but that we must, in a former life, have been friends, who now have met again in this life, through the force of *Karma*. Similarly as regards the lower animals. A Tibetan seeing my dog and pony playing good-naturedly together, explained the situation by saying that in a former birth these two must have been mates.

Even practices which are clearly dishonest and sinful, are at times justified on the same principle, or rather by its abuse. Thus the more sordid Tibetan reconciles cheating to his conscience, by naïvely convincing himself that the party whom he now attempts to defraud, had previously swindled him in a former life, and that justice demands retribution.

Congenital defects such as blindness, dumbness and lameness, and accidents, are viewed as retributions which are due to the individual having, in a previous life, abused or sinned with the particular limb or organ presently affected. Thus a man is blind because he sinned with his eye in a former life. Indeed this is a common dogma of Buddha's own teaching, and forms the basis of the *Jātakas* or tales of the previous Births of Buddha.

For a like reason, cattle and all other dumb animals are humanely treated; life is seldom wantonly taken. Indeed, the taking of animal life is rather strictly prohibited in Tibet, except in the case of the Yaks and sheep needed for food, for in such a cold climate flesh forms an essential staple of diet, but the butchers[2] being thus professional sinners, are the most despised

[1] Cf. my art. on Cats in *Indian Antiquary*, Dec., 1892.

[2] gDol-pa. Originally, says JAESCHKE (*D.*, p. 268), these were probably fishers.

of all classes in Tibet. Wild animals, and even small birds, are seldom killed, nor fish, on account of the religious penalties attached to this crime, hence game is so extremely abundant in the country. Yet human prisoners are, at times, most cruelly tortured; though this probably is owing, in some measure, to the example set by the Chinese, as well as the necessity for some violent punishment to check the commission of crime. Nearly every offence, even to the most heinous, the murdering of a Lāma, may be condoned by a fixed scale of fine; but failing the payment of the fine and the extra blackmail to the officials, the prisoner, if not actually killed, is tortured and mutilated, and then usually set free, in order not only to avoid the expense of detainment in jail, but also to serve as a public warning to others. Thus many of the maimed beggars who swarm about Lhāsa are criminals who have had their eyes put out or their hands cut off in this way.

TIBETAN LAYMEN.

The tolerant spirit of Buddhism has, however, stamped more or less distinctly the national character, the mildness of which contrasts strongly with the rough exterior and semi-barbarous state of the people. Bogle's high testimony to this trait has already been referred to. Huc, writing of the lay regent of Lhāsa,[1] describes him as a man "whose large features, mild and remarkably pallid, breathed a truly royal majesty, while his dark eyes shaded by long lashes were intelligent and gentle." And Rockhill and others who have been brought into intimate contact with the people have remarked an unexpected amount of mildness of temper; and my own experience is similar.

The spirit of consideration for others expresses itself in many graceful acts of genuine politeness. A stirrup-cup of wine[2] is presented to the departing visitor or traveller, bidding him God-speed, and adding, "May we be able to present you with another as welcome on your return." The seller of any article, other than eatables, always gives his blessing to the buyer, in terms such as these: "May good come upon you; may you live long; may no sickness happen; may you grow rich"[3]; to which the buyer replies with "thanks."[4]

The personal names of both boys and girls are largely borrowed from mystical Buddhism, for instance "The Thunderbolt of Long-Life" (Dorje-ts'e-riṅ), "Dölma" (the Indian goddess of Mercy, Tārā); and the influence of the religious habit is also seen in several of the names of places.

The common oaths are mainly of a Buddhist character. The oath so much in the mouth of the merchants, and used at times by most of the laity as an asseveration in ordinary conversation, is "(by) the precious Lord (Ṣākya Muni)!"[5] or "(by) The Three Rarest Ones!"[6] Though others also are in use.[7]

---

1 Named "Pe-chi" (the "She-te Shaffee" of Edgar?). 2 C'aṅ-kyel.

3 yag-po byaṅ-pa s'og, ts'e-riṅ-pa-s'og, nad-med-pa s'og, p'ug-po yoṅ-wa s'og.

4 t'ug-rje-ch'e, literally = "great mercy," compare with French *merci*, used on similar occasions. 5 Jo-wo Rin-po-ch'e. 6 dK'on-mch'og sum.

7 The other *Oaths* used in Tibet are: "May I die ere sunset" (ñi-ma 'di-las ts'e-t'uṅ); "may my mother be separated" (a-ma-daṅ bral). In Tsang a common oath is "May my life be separated" (srog-daṅ bral; *pron.* hrok ta-te). The monks of De-pung Serra, etc., swear by their own tutelary Tamdin, or Vajra-bhairava: "May Tamdin devour me" (rta-mgrin-*b*s'e*s*). And in the courts when the great oath is taken, which is seldom, it is done by the person placing a holy scripture on his head, and sitting on the reeking hide of an ox and eating a part of the ox's heart. The expense of this ceremony is borne by the party who challenges the accused. In Sikhim the common oaths are: "May I die" (s'i-ge); "May I go to hell" (na-rak-kan); "May I carry all your ill-luck" (bgeg*s*-chi k'ur-rgyu); "May I be deprived of succession" (mi-rab*s*-ch'ad); "May the mountain-god Kangch'endsonga or the Darjiling *Tsan*-devil have first taste of my red blood" (rdo-rje gliṅ-dgon-btsan sha-k'rag-dmar phuṅ kyi-bs'e*s* bchug).

But both Lāmas and people are so steeped in pagan superstition and idolatry that their un-Buddhist features and practices are most conspicuous. As the Tibetans see nature in its ultimate stronghold, in all its pitiless force and fury, terrorizing the brave as well as the timid, their child-like character impels them to worship the more proximate agents which seem to visibly wreck their fields and flocks, and vex them as with disease and disaster.

Charm to bind Disease-devils.
(Reduced ⅓.)

Their inveterate craving for material protection against those malignant gods and demons has caused them to pin their faith on charms and amulets, which are to be seen everywhere dangling from the dress of every man, woman, and child.

These charms, as we have seen, are mostly sentences of a Sanskritic nature borrowed from mystical Buddhism, and supplemented by relics of holy Lāmas, by which they muzzle and bind the devils, as in the illustration here given.

But these appliances, however good in theory, are found in practice to be deplorably deficient. The priests must constantly be called in to appease the menacing devils, whose ravenous appetite is only sharpened by the food given to stay it.

A more cheerful and graceful side to their demon-worship is seen in the practice of planting the tall prayer-flags, which picturesquely flutter around every village, and the strings of flaglets which flaunt from house-tops, bridges, passes, and other places believed to be infested by malignant sprites.

The people live in an atmosphere of the marvellous. No story is too absurd for them to credit, if only it be told by Lāmas. They are ever on the outlook for omens, and the every-day affairs of life are governed, as we have seen, by a superstitious regard for lucky and unlucky days. Though special divinations are sought from professed astrologers, in the more serious events of life, in birth, marriage, sickness, and death, and often in sowing, reaping, building, etc., each layman determines for himself the auguries for the more trivial matters of his ordinary business, for travelling, buying and selling, mending, etc.

Aud implicit reliance is placed on all these auguries. When I was forced to send a party of Sikhimite Tibetans on a long

AMULETS.[1]

excursion upon a day which was unlucky for travelling, and in consequence of which my men were unwilling to start, I at once secured a revival of their spirits and their ready departure by making the head-man draw, in orthodox fashion, a good augury from the pack of divining-cards, from which, however, I had previously, unknown to them, withdrawn all the unlucky ones.

Pilgrimages are most popular. Every opportunity is seized to visit celebrated shrines, and to circumambulate the numerous holy buildings and sacred spots in their neighbourhood.

[1] Reduced ⅓. See also photograph on next page, by Mr. Hoffmann.

Prayers ever hang upon the people's lips. The prayers are chiefly directed to the devils, imploring them for freedom or release from their cruel inflictions, or they are plain naïve

A TIBETAN LADY WITH AMULETS.

requests for aid towards obtaining the good things of this life, the loaves and the fishes. At all spare times, day and night, the people ply their prayer-wheels, and tell their beads, and mutter the mystic six syllables—*Om ma-ṇi pad-me Hūṃ!* "Om! the Jewel in the Lotus, Hūṃ!"—the sentence which gains them their great goal, the glorious heaven

Hand-Prayer-"Wheels"
(Reduced ⅓. The one on the right has its case removed.)

of eternal bliss, the paradise of the fabulous Buddha of boundless Light—Amitābha.

Still, with all their strivings and the costly services of their priests, the Tibetans never attain peace of mind. They have fallen under the double ban of menacing demons and despotic priests. So it will be a happy day, indeed, for Tibet when its sturdy over-credulous people are freed from the intolerable tyranny of the Lāmas, and delivered from the devils whose ferocity and exacting worship weigh like a nightmare upon all.

Finis.

THE HOUSE-DEVIL.

Appendix I.

Chronological Table.[1]

	B.C.
Buddha's death	477–370[2]
Alexander the Great invaded India	325–327
Candragupta, king of Magadha	315
Aṣoka, emperor of India, adopts Buddhism	263–259
Buddhism introduced to Ceylon	241
Menander (Milinda) of Sagala	150
Scriptures (*piṭaka*) first reduced to writing in Ceylon ...	82
	A.D.
Buddhism introduced to China	62
King Kanishka (Kanerkes), patron of Buddhism ...	78 *circa*
Council of Jalandhar	100 *circa*
Buddhism introduced to Korea	372
FaHian's pilgrimage in Magadha	404
Buddha-ghosha's commentary in Pāli	420
Sung-yun's pilgrimage in India	518
Buddhism introd. to Japan	552
Hiuen Tsiang's pilgrimage in India, from	637
Buddhism introd. to Tibet under king Srong Tsan Gampo	638
Arrival of the Chinese princess Wen-cheng in Tibet ...	640[3]
Building of the first Buddhist temple in Tibet, the *P'rul-snaṅ* at Lhāsa	651
Birth of king K'ri-Srong Deu Tsan	728
Arrival of St. Padma-sambhava in Tibet	747

[1] The dates of the Tibetan events are taken mainly from Csoma (*Gram.*, p. 181 *et seq.*), and supplemented to a slight extent by those of Sum-pa or Yšes-dpal-'byor (trans. by Ṣarat, *J.A.S.B.*, 1889, 37, etc.), except where otherwise specified. I have reduced, by one year, the dates of Sum-pa as given by Ṣarat, as the Lāma who compiled his paper included the current year in his calculations.

[2] The usually accepted date is 477 B.C. (Fergusson, Max Müller in *Sacred Books of the East*, x., xxxix.), though Rhys Davids adopts 412 (*Budd.*, p. 213, and *Numismata Orientalia*, 55); and Westergaard (*Uber Buddha's Todesjahr*, p. 74), Kern and others place it about 370 B.C. The Tibetans follow the popular Chinese accounts in giving it an extravagant antiquity (*see* Csoma's *Gram.*, p. 199 for details).

[3] Bushell, *loc. cit.*

	A.D.
Building of the first Lāmaist monastery, Sam-yäs	749
Birth of Laṅ-darma, the Julian of Lāmaism	861
His persecution of Lāmaism	899
His murder	900
Kālacakra system introduced to India	950
St. Atīṣa, born	980
'Brom-ston, his disciple, born	1002
gSol-nag-t'aṅ monastery founded	1015
'K'on dKon-mc'og-rgyal-po, the founder of Sa-skya monastery, born	1033
St. Atīṣa arrived at mNā-rigs	1038
St. Milaraspa born	1038
Atīṣa died	1053
Rva-sgren mon. founded by 'Brom-ston	1055
The Translator bLo-ldan-S'es-rab born	1057
*l*C'e-stom Nan-pa's Ñiṅ-ma revelation (lCe-btsun)	1066
Saskya and gSang-phu mon. founded	1071
Lha-rje sgam-po-pa of Drag-po born	1077
Ras-c'uṅ-pa born	1082
Kun-gah-sñin Sa-skya Lāma born	1090
Karma dus-sum-mK'an-po born	1109
More Ñiṅ-ma revelations discovered	1117
Milaraspa died	1122
C'ag, translator, born	1152
sNar-t'ang monastery founded	1152
'Bri-guṅ monastery founded	1177
sTag-luṅ monastery founded	1178
Sa-skya Paṇḍita born	1180
Buddhism expelled from Magadha by the Muhamadans, under Ba*kh*tyār *Kh*iljī	1195
S'akya-ṣrī, the Kashmīri Pandit, arrived in Tibet	1202
Karma Bakshi born	1202
Ter-ton Guru Ch'os-dbaṅ	1210
Kublai Khan born	1214[1]
'Gro-mgon-'pags-pa born	1233
He becomes master of Tibet	1251
Bu-ston, the chronologist, born	1288
Friar Odoric reaches ? Lhāsa	1330
rTses-taṅ monastery founded	1349
St. Tsoṅ-K'a-pa born	1355
T'aṅ-stoṅ rgyal-po (the great bridge-builder) born	1383
dGe-'dun-grub-pa born	1389
Ses-rab rin-ch'en (or sTag), the translator, born	1403
Tsoṅ-K'a-pa established the Lhāsa prayer-feast (*smon-lam*), and founded dGah-ldan monastery	1407
Panch'en bzaṅ-po bkra-sis (latterly of Tashi-lhunpo) born	1408

[1] According to Lāmaist (Sum-pa's) data.

	A.D.
Ḍe-pung (dBras-spuṅ) monastery founded	1414
Ṡerra monastery founded	1417
Tsoṅ-K'a-pa died	1417
Nor monastery (of Sa-skya-pa sect) founded	1427
Ch'ab-mdo-byams-gön monastery founded	1435
Z'a-lu legs-pa-rgyal-mts'an, succeeds to Ga-ldan chair ...	1436
Ch'os-skyoṅ-bzaṅ-po, the translator, born	1439
Tashi-lhunpo monastery founded by dGe-'dun-grub ...	1445
The Lāma of the Mongols (Hor-sTon or Nam-mK'ah-dpal) died	1445
bZaṅ-po-bkra-sis becomes abbot of Tashi-lhunpo	1473
dGe-'dun-grub died...	1473
dGe-'dun-rgya-mts'o born	1474
bZaṅ-po bkra-sis died, and succeeded by Luṅ-rig rgya-mts'ô	1476
rTa-nag tdub-bstan-rnam-rgyal monastery founded ...	1476
Panch'en blo-bzaṅ don-grub born	1503
dGe-'dun-rgya-mts'o becomes Grand Lāma of Tashi-lhunpo	1510
The *Ḍug-pa* Lāma Padma-dKar-po born	1510
dGe-'dun-rgya-mts'o died	1540
bSod-nams rgya-mts'o born	1541
Mongol (or "Moghul") invasion of Northern Tibet ...	1546 *circa*
S'va-lu Lotsava died	1562
Tārānātha (Kun-sñiṅ) born	1573
Grand Lāma bSod-nam proceeds to Mongolia on invitation of prince Althun Khan	1575
Kum-bum monastery founded	1576
Lāma bSod-nam died	1586
His successor (Yon-tan) born in Mongolia	1587
Kum-bum subordinated to Tsang	1610
Yon-tan-rgya-mts'o died	1614
Ṅag-dbaṅ-blo-bzaṅ rgya-mts'o born	1615
The Tsang army invades Serra and Ḍepung monasteries, "killing many thousand monks"	1616
Ṅag-dbaṅ became priest-king of Tibet by aid of the Mongol prince Gusri Khan	1640
He built Potala palace near Lhāsa	1643
He visited Chinese emperor	1650
He returned to Tibet	1651
He retires to self-communion, leaving government with the viceroy (sDe-srid), Sans-rgyas rgya-mts'o, said to be his natural son	1675
He died	1680
His successor, Tsaṅs-dbyaṅs born...	1681
But proving dissolute, he is deposed and assassinated ...	1703
Dalai Lāma sKal-bzaṅ born at Lithang	1706
The Mongol armies of C'un-gar restore Gelug-pa Lāma to kingship	1716

	A.D.
Civil war, during which the Chinese troops destroy many monasteries in restoring order	1722
Nepalese army sacks Tashi-lhunpo	1768
Mr. Bogle's friendship with Tashi Grand Lāma... ...	1778
Capt. Turner received by succeeding Tashi Grand Lāma	1783
Mr. Manning reaches Lhāsa and meets the Dalai Lāma	1811
MM. Huc and Gabet enter Lhāsa	1845
Messrs. Rockhill's, Bonvalot's, Prince Henry of Orleans', and Bowers' traverses of eastern and northern Tibet	1887–92
Anglo-Tibetan hostilities on Sikhim frontier	1887
The Tibet Sikhim trade treaty concluded	1893

APPENDIX II.

BIBLIOGRAPHY.

The following list comprises most of the books bearing upon Lāmaism, supplementary, in the main, to the earlier register given by Schlagintweit (*op. cit.*, pp. 331, etc.).

ANDERSON (W.).—Description and Historical Catalogue of a Collection of Japanese and Chinese Paintings in the British Museum. London, 1886.

ARNOLD (E.).—The Light of Asia; or, The Great Renunciation; being the Life and Teaching of Gautama, Prince of India and Founder of Buddhism. 8vo. London, 1883.

ATKINSON (E. T.).—Notes on the History of Religion in the Himalaya of the North-Western Provinces of India. Calcutta, 1883.

AYNSLEY (H. G. M. M.).—Visit to Ladakh. 8vo. London, 1879.

BAILEY (H. V.). Dorje-Ling. 8vo. Calcutta, 1838.

BARTH (A.).—The Religions of India. Translated by J. Wood. 8vo. London, 1882.

BASTIAN (A.).—Der Buddhismus in seiner Psychologie. 366 pp., 8vo. Berlin, 1882.

BEAL (S.).—Catena of Buddhist Scriptures. From the Chinese. 8vo. London, 1878.

— Romantic Legend of Sakya Buddha. From the Chinese. 8vo. London, 1875.

— Buddhist Literature in China. 8vo. London, 1882.

— Texts from the Buddhist Canon known as Dhammapada. With accompanying Narratives. From the Chinese. Pp. viii. and 176. China, 1878.

— Buddhism. 12mo., pp. 263. London, 1884.

— Fo-sho-hing-tsan-King. A Life of Buddha, by Aṣvaghosha Bodhisattva. From the Chinese. 8vo.

— Travels of Fa Hian, etc. 12mo. 1869.

— Si-Yu-Ki. Record of Western Kingdoms, by Hiuen Tsiang. 2 vols., 8vo., pp. 250 and 378. 1884.

BENDALL (C.).—A Journey in Nepal and North India. 8vo. Cambridge, 1886.

— Cat. Buddh. Skt. MSS. 8vo., pp. xii., lxi., 225. Camb., 1883.

BHAGVANLĀL INDRAJI. Appendix to Archæological Survey West India, I. (No. 9). Bombay, 1879.

BIGANDET (P.).—The Ways to Neibban, and Notice on the Burmese Monks. 2 vols., 8vo. London. 1880.

BONVALOT (G.)—Prince Henry of Orleans. Across Thibet. 2 vols, 8vo. Paris and London, 1891.

BOWER (H.).—Diary of a Journey across Tibet. 1894.

BUCHANAN-HAMILTON (F.).—Account of the Kingdom of Nepal. London, 182—.

— Eastern India, ed. Martin. 3 vols. London, 1839.

BURGESS, see *Fergusson.*
BURNOUF (E.).—Introduction à l'Histoire du Buddhisme indien. Vol. I., 4to. 2nd ed. Paris, 1876.
— Le Lotus de la bonne Loi, traduit du Sanscrit, accompagné d'un Commentaire et de vingt et un Mémoires relatifs au Buddhisme. 4to. Paris, 1852.
BUTSU-ZÔ-DSU-I, or The Buddhist Pantheon of the Japanese. 5 fasc. Kyoto, 1887.
BUSHELL (S. W., *M.D.*).—The Early History of Tibet from Chinese sources. J.R.A.S., XII. (1880), p. 435, *et. seq.*
CONWAY, (W. M.).—Climbing and Exploration in the Karakoram Himalayas. 8vo., pp. 709. London, 1894.
COWELL (E. B.).—Mahāyāna Texts. Sacred Bk. East, Vol. XLIX., etc.
— The Jātaka, translated from the Pāli. Cambridge, 1894.
CSOMA DE KÖRÖS (A.).—Grammar of the Tibetan Language. 4to., 204 pp., 40 pp. *lithogr.* Calcutta, 1834.
— Dictionary, Tibetan and English. 4to., 351 pp. Calcutta, 1834.
— Analysis of the Kah-gyur, etc. Asiatic Researches. Vol. XX., pp. 41, etc., 4to. Calcutta, 1820.
CUNNINGHAM (Sir A.).—Coins of Ancient India from the earliest times down to the seventh century A.D. 8vo. London, 1891.
— Ladāk, physical, statistical and historical. London, 1854.
— Mahābodhi, or the Great Buddhist Temple under the Bodhi Tree of Bodh Gayā, *with* 31 *photographs.* 4to. 1892.
DALTON (Col. E. T.).—Descriptive Ethnology of Bengal. Calcutta, 1872.
D'ALVIELLA (Count G.).—The Migration of Symbols. Eng. trans. Lond., 1894.
D'ANVILLE (J. B.).—Nouvel Atlas de la Chine, de la Tartarie Chinoise et du Thibet. Folio. La Haye, 1737.
DAVIDS (T. W. RHYS).—Buddhism; being a Sketch of the Life and Teachings of Gautama, the Buddha. 12mo. London, 1878.
— Buddhist Birth Stories; or Jātaka Tales, being the Jātakatthavannaná. Translation. Vol. I., 8vo. London, 1880.
— Buddhist Sūtras, translated from Pāli. (Vol. XI. of F. Max Müller's Sacred Books of the East.) 8vo. Oxford, 1881.
— The Hibbert Lectures, 1881. Lectures on the Origin and Growth of Religion as illustrated by some points in the history of Indian Buddhism. 8vo. London, 1881.
— Article "Lāmaism" in Encyclopædia Britannica.
— And OLDENBERG (H.)—Vinaya Texts, translated from the Pāli. Part I. The Pâtimokkha. The Mahâvagga, I.-IV. (Vol. XIII. of Sacred Books of the East.) 8vo. Oxford, 1881.
DAVIS (E.).—"Remarks on the Religious and Social Institution of the Bouteas." Trans. R.A.S., Vol. II. 496.
DE MILLOUÉ (L.).—Catal. du Musée Guimet. Lyon, 1883, and Paris, 1894.
DE LACOUPERIE, see *Lacoupérie.*
DESGODINS (Père).—Le Tibet, etc. 8vo., p. 475. 1885.
DOUGLAS (R. K.).—Confucianism and Taoism. London, 1888.
DUKA (T.).—The Life and Works of Alexander Csoma de Körös, between 1819 and 1849. By T. Duka. Pp. 234. London, 1885.
DUMOUTIER (G.).—Les Symboles, les Emblem. du culte chez les Annamites. Paris, 1891.
DUNMORE (Lord).—The Pamirs. 2 vols., sm. 8vo. London, 1893.
EDEN (Honble. A).—Report on the State of Bootan and of the Progress of the Mission of 1863-64. Calcutta, 1864.
EDGAR (J.).—Report on a Visit to Sikhim and the Tibetan Frontier. Calcutta, 1874.
EDKINS (J.).—Chinese Buddhism. Pp. 454. 1880.
EITEL (E. J.).—Buddhism: its Historical, Theoretical, and Popular Aspects. 3rd edition, revised. 8vo. London, 1873.
— Handbook for the Student of Chinese Buddhism. 8vo. pp. 231. 2nd edition. Hong-Kong, 1888.
ELIAS (N.).—Reports on Leh and Central Asia.
FEER (L.).—Introduction du Buddhisme dans le Kashmir. 8vo. Paris, 1866. Pam.
— Études Bouddhiques. Première Série. 8vo. Paris, 1870.
— Étude sur les Jâtakas. 8vo. Paris, 1875.
— Analyse du Kandjour et du Tandjour. Annales du Musée Guimet. Tome 2.

FEER (L.).—Le Tibet. Paris, 1886.
— Extraitcs du Kandjour. Annales du Mus. Guimet.
FERGUSSON (J.).—History of Indian and Eastern Architecture. 8vo. London, 1876.
— and BURGESS (J.).—Cave Temples of India. London, 188—.
FOUCAUX (Ph. E.).—Rgya-tch'er-rol-pa ou Développement des Jeux, contenant l'Histoire du Bouddha Cakya Mouni, traduit sur la version Tibétaine du Bkah hgyour, et revu sur l'original Sanscrit (Lalitavistara). 2 vols., 4to. Paris, 1847-48.
— Parabole de l'Enfant Egaré, formant le chapitre IV. du Lotus de la Bonne Loi, publiée pour la première fois en sanscrit et en Tibétain, et accompagnée d'une traduction française d'après la version Tibétaine du Kanjour. 8vo. Paris, 1854.
— Le Trésor des Belles Paroles, choix de sentences composées en Tibétain par le Lāma Saskya Pandita; suivies d'une élégie tirée du Kandjour, traduites pour la première fois en Français. 8vo. Paris, 1858.
— La Guirlande Précieuse des Demandes et des Réponses publiée en Sanskrit et en Tibétain, et traduite pour la première fois en Français. 8vo. Paris, 1867.
— Le Lalita Vistara traduit du Sanskrit. Annales du Musée Guimet Tome Sixième., pp. 290. Paris, 1884.
FRANKS (Sir A. W.).—Brit. Mus. Art. Catalogues (on Chinese Symbolism).
GARNIER (F.).—De Paris au Tibet. 8vo., pp. 422. Paris, 1882.
GEDDIE (J.).—Beyond the Himalayas. 8vo., pp. 256. London, 1882.
GIORGI (A. A.).—Alphabetum Tibetanun. Romæ, 1762.
GILL (W.).—The River of Golden Sand. 2 vols., 8vo. London, 1880.
GILMOUR (J.).—Among Mongols. London, 189—.
GRUENWEDEL (A).—Buddhistische Kunst in India. Hanb. d. Königlichen Mus. Berlin, 1893.
HARDY (R. Spence).—Eastern Monachism; an Account of the Origin, Laws, Discipline, etc., of the Order of Mendicants founded by Gotama Buddha. Compiled from Singhalese MSS. and other Sources. 8vo. London, 1850.
— A Manual of Buddhism in its Modern Development. Translated from Singhalese MSS. 2nd ed. 8vo. 1880.
— The Legends and Theories of the Buddhists compared with History and Science. 8vo. 2nd ed. 1881.
HEWITT (J. F.).—The Ruling Races of Pre-historic Times. In India, etc. Lond., 1894.
HODGSON (B. H.).—Essays on the Languages, Literature, and Religion of Nepal and Tibet; together with further papers on the Geography, Ethnology, and Commerce of those Countries. 8vo. London. Reprint. 1874.
HOLLOWAY (L. C.).—Buddhist Diet-Book. 8vo., pp. 80. New York, 1886.
HOOKER (J.).—Himalayan Journals. Notes of a Naturalist in Bengal, the Sikkim and Nepal Himalayas, the Khasia Mountains, etc. 2 vols. With Plates. 8vo. London, 1854.
HOWORTH (Sir H. H.).—History of the Mongols from the 9th to the 19th Century. Part I.:—The Mongols Proper and the Kalmuks. Part II.:—The So-called "Tartars" of Russia and Central Asia. 8vo. London, 1876-80.
HUC (M.).—Travels in Tartary, Thibet, and China, during the years 1844-5-6. Translated from the French by W. HAZLITT. 2 vols., 8vo. London (? 1850).
HUNTER (Sir W. W.).—A Comparative Dictionary of the Languages of India and High Asia. 4to. London, 1868.
— Statistical Act of Bengal. Vol. Darjiling, etc. London, 1877.
— The Indian Empire: its History, People, and Products. 8vo. London, 1882.
HUTH (G.).—Geschichte des Buddhismus in der Mongolei. Aus dem Tibetischen des oJigs-med nam-mk'a herausgegeben, uebersetzt und erläutert. Vol. I.: Vorrede. Text. Kritische Anmerkungen. 8vo., pp. x., 296. Strassburg, 1892.
Hor Ch'os Byung.—Geschichte des Buddhismus. *Trans. Ninth Intern. Congress, Orient.*, London, 1893.
JAESCHKE (H. A.).—A Tibetan-English Dictionary. With special Reference to the Prevailing Dialects. To which is added an English-Tibetan Vocabulary. 8vo., cloth, pp. xxii., 671. London, 1881.
JAMETEL (M.).—L'Epigraphie chinoise au Tibet. 8vo. Peking, 1880, etc.
KERN (H.).—Geschiedenis van het Buddhisme in Indie. 2 vols., royal 8vo., *half calf.* Haarlem, 1882-4.

KERN (H.).—Der Buddhismus. 8vo., 2 vols. Liepzig, 1882, etc.
— Saddharma Pundarika, or the Lotus of the True Law. Translated into English, Vol. XXI., Sac. Books of East. 8vo. London.
— The Jātaka-Mālā, or Bodhisattvāvadāna-Mālā by Arya-çūra (Harvard Oriental Series, Vol. I.). 8vo. Boston, Mass., 1891.

KIRCHER (A.).—China Monumentis, quà Sacris quà Profanis, nec non variis Naturæ et Artis Spectaculis, aliarumque rerum memorabilium Argumentis illustrata. Fol. Amstelodami, 1667.

KIRKPATRICK (Col.).—An account of the Kingdom of Nepaul, being the substance of observations made during a mission to that country in the year 1793. 4to. London, 1811.

KLAPROTH (J.).—Description du Tibet traduite du Chinois, etc. Nouv., Jour. Asiat., Vol. IV., etc. Paris, 1831, etc.

KNIGHT (E. F.).—Where Three Empires Meet. London, 1893.

KRISHNA (A. K.).—Account of the *Pandit's* Journey in Great Thibet from Leh in Ladākh to Lhāsa, and of his return to India *viâ* Assam. 8vo. Vol. 47 of Royal Geographical Society, 1877.

KOEPPEN (C. F.).—Die Religion des *Buddha* und ihre Entstehung, und die *Lamaische Hierarchie und Kirche*, Vols. I.-II., 8vo. Berlin, 1857-59.

KREITNER (Lt.-G.).—*In Fernen Osten*, Vienna, 1881.

LACOUPERIE (TERRIEN DE).—Western Origin of the Early Chinese Civilization, 1894.

LEWIN (Major T. H.).—A Manual of Tibetan. Being a Guide to the Colloquial Speech of Tibet, in a Series of Progressive Exercises. Pp. xi., 176. Calcutta, 1879.

LILLIE (A.).—Buddhism in Christendom. 8vo., pp. 410. London, 1887.
— Koot Hoomi Unveiled ; Tibetan "Buddhists." pp. 24. London, 1884.

MACAULAY.—Report on a Mission to Sikhim. Calcutta, 1885.

MACKENZIE (A.).—Report on the Tribes of the North-Eastern Frontier of Bengal. Calcutta, 1884.

MARKHAM (C. R.).—Narrative of the Mission of George Bogle to Tibet, and of the journey of Thomas Manning to Lhāsa, with notes, etc. 8vo. 2nd edition. London, 1879.

MARX (KARL).—History of Ladakh. J.A.S.B. pp. 97, *et. seq.* Calcutta, 1891.

MAYERS.—Chinese Reader's Manual.

MIKHAILOOSKII (V. M.).—Shamanstoo (Shamanism in Siberia and European Russia). Translated in Jour. Anthrop. Inst. London, 1894.

MONIER-WILLIAMS (Sir).—Buddhism, in its Connection with Brāhmanism and Hinduism, etc. 8vo., pp. 583. London, 1889.

MONTGOMERIE (T. G.).—Journey to Shigatze, in Tibet, and return by Dingri-Maidan into Nepaul in 1871, by the Native Explorer, No. 9. Vol. 45 of Roy. Geog. Soc. London, 1875.

MUELLER (F. MAX).—The Dhammapada, a Collection of Verses ; and the Sutta Nipata, a Collection of Discourses ; being two of the Canonical Books of the Buddhists. Translated from Pāli. Vol. X., Sacred Books. 8vo. London.
— Buddhist Māhāyana Texts. Sac. B. East., Vol. XLIX. 1894.

NANJIO (BUNYIO).—A catalogue of the Chinese Translation of the Buddhist Tripitaka, the Sacred Canon of the Buddhists in China and Japan. 4to. Oxford, 1883.
— A Short History of the Twelve Japanese Buddhist Sects. Tokyo, 1886.

OLDENBERG (HERMANN).—Buddha ; his Life, his Doctrine, his Order. Translated from the German by William Hoey, *M.A.* London, 1888.

OLDFIELD (H. A.).—Sketches from Nipal, Historical and Descriptive, etc., to which is added an Essay on Nepalese Buddhism, and illustrations of Religious Monuments, etc. 2 vols., 8vo. London, 1880.

OLLIVIER BEAUREGARD (G. M.).—Kachmir et Tibet. 8vo., pp. 144. Paris, 1883.

OTTO AND RISTNER.—Buddha and His Doctrine. London, 1869. [Contains a bibliographical list.]

PANDER (E.).—Das Pantheon des Tschangtscha Hutuktu ein beitrage zur Iconographie des Lāmaismus. Könl. Museen, Berlin. 4to. 1890.

PEMBERTON (R. B.).—Report on the Eastern Frontier of British India. 8vo. Calcutta, 1835.
— Report on Bootan. With maps. 8vo. Calcutta, 1839.

PREJEVALSKI (Col. N. M.).—The Tangut Country and the Solitudes of Northern Tibet, being a Narrative of Three Years' Travels in Eastern

High Asia. Translated by E. D. Morgan, with introduction and notes, by Col. Henry Yule, *C.B.* 2 vols. 8vo. London, 1876.

PREJEVALSKI (Col. N. M.).—Reisen in Tibet. 8vo., pp. 281. Jena, 1884.

PRINSEP (H. T.).—Tibet, Tartary and Mongolia, their Social and Political Condition, and the Religion of Boodh, as there existing. 8vo. London, 1851.

RĀJENDRA LĀL MITRA.—The Sanskrit Buddhist Lit. of Nepal. Calcutta, 1882.

RALSTON (W. R. S.).—Tibetan Tales, from Indian Sources, translated from the German. Shiefner, with Introduction. Pp. lxvi. and 368. London, 1892.

RAMSAY (W.).—Western Tibet: A Practical Dictionary of the Language and Customs of the Districts included in the Ladak Wazarat. Lahore, 1890.

RENNIE (Dr.).—The Bhotan and Dooar War. London, 1866.

RISLEY (H. H.).—Tribes and Castes of Bengal. 2 vols. Calcutta, 1891.

RITTER (C.).—Erdkunde, Vol. VI. Berlin.

ROCKHILL (W. W.).—Udanavarga, a Collection of Verses from the Buddhist Canon. Compiled by Dharmatrata. The Northern Buddhist version of Dhammapada. Translated from the Tibetan of Bkahgyur. Pp. vii. and 244. 1883.

— The Life of the Buddha, and the Early History of his Order. From Tibetan Works in the Bkah-hgyur and Bstan-hgyur. With Notices on the Early History of Tibet and Khoten. Pp. 284. 1884.

— The Land of the Lāmas. London, 1891.

ROERO (O.).—Ricordi dei Viaggi al Cashemire Medio Thibet. 8vo., 3 vols. Torino, 1881.

SARATCANDRA DĀS.—Narrative of Travels in Tibet. Calcutta, 1885.

SCHIEFNER (F. A.).—Tibetische Studien. St. Peterb. Bull. Hist. Phil. Vol. viii.

— Târanâtha's Geschichte des Buddhismus in Indien aus dem Tibetischen übersetzt. 8vo. St. Petersburg, 1869.

— Herrn Professor Wassiljew's Vorrede zu seiner Russischen Uebersetzung von Târanâtha's Geschichte des Buddhismus in Indien, Deutsch mitgetheilt. 8vo., St. Petersburg, 1869. Pam.

— Buddhistische Triglotte, d. h. Sanskrit-Tibetisch-Mongolisches Wörterverzeichniss. Oblong 4to., pp. 73. St. Petersburg, 1859.

— Kālacakra tantrarāja, Handschr. aus dem Nachlasse des Akademikers.

SCHLAGINTWEIT (E.).—Buddhism in Tibet, illustrated by literary documents and objects of religious worship, with an account of the Buddhist systems preceding it in India. 8vo. London, 1868.

— Le Bouddhisme au Tibet. Pp. 292, 1881 (Annales du Musée Guimet, tome 3).

— Ladak Gyal-rabs. Leipzig.

SCHLAGINTWEIT—SAKUENBIENSKI (H. VON).—Das Kaiserreich Ostindien und die angrenzenden Gebirgslander. 8vo., pp. 639. Jena, 1884.

SCHMIDT (J. J.).—Dsanglun, der Weise und der Thor, aus dem Tibetischen übersetzt und mit dem Original-texte herausgegeben. 4to. St. Petersburg, 1843.

— Geschichte der Ostmongolen und ihres Fürstenhauses Verfasst von Ssanang Ssetsen. St. Petersburg, 1829.

SCHOPENHAUER (A.).—The World as Will and Idea. English translated by Haldane and Kemp. 3 vols. London, 1883.

SENART (E.).—Essai sur la Légende de Buddha. 8vo., pp. 496. Paris, 1882.

SINNETT (A. P.).—Esoteric Buddhism. 8vo., pp. 215. London, 1883.

Survey of India Reports. Various. Calcutta.

TAWNEY (C. H.)—Katha Sarit Sāgara, or Ocean of the Streams of Story. Calcutta. 1880.

TEMPLE (Sir R. and R. C.).—Journals kept in Hyderabad, Kashmir, Sikhim, and Nepal. 2 vols., 1887.

TROTTER (Captain H.).—Account of Pandit Nain Sing's Journ. (in 1865, etc.). J. R. Geogr. Soc., Vol. 47. 1887.

TURNER (S.).—An account of an embassy to the Court of the Teshoo Lāma in Tibet, containing a narrative of a journey through Bootan, and part of Tibet. 4to. Lond. 1806.

VASSILIEF.—See Wassiljew.
WADDELL (L. A.).—Lāmaism in Sikhim, Part II. of Gazetteer of Sikhim. 4to., pp. 171. Calcutta, 1893.
WASSILJEW (W.).—Der Buddhismus, seine Dogmen. Geschichte und Literatur. St. Petersburg, 1860.
— Le Bouddisme; ses dogmas, son histoire et sa littérature. Première partie:—Aperçu général. Traduit du Russe par M. G. A. Comme. 8vo. Paris, 1865.
WILSON (A.).—The Abode of Snow. London, 1875.
WRIGHT (D.).—History of Nepāl. Cambridge, 1877.
YULE (Sir H.).—Cathay and the Way Thither. Vol. 36. Hakluyt Soc. 8vo. London, 1868.
The Book of Ser Marco Polo. 2nd edition. 2 vols. 8vo. London, 1875.

APPENDIX III.

MUHAMMADAN MASSACRE OF LĀMAISTS.

An interesting glimpse into the religion of Northern Tibet during the sixteenth century, and of the Moghul holy war against the Lāmas of that period, is got from the *Tarikh-i-Rashidi* by Mirza Haidar, Dughlát of Kashgar: a book recently discovered by Mr. Ney Elias, C.I.E., to whom I am indebted for the following extract, illustrative of Muhammadan fanaticism. The work dates to about 1546 A.D., and it is to be hoped that Mr. Elias' translation of it will soon be published.

The general, Mirza Haidar, writes: "On the day appointed, I approached the fort (of Mutadār in Nubra), and the talons of Islam seizing the hands of Infidelity, the enemy were thrown into disorder and routed. Having deserted the fort, they fled in confusion and dismay, while the Musalmāns gave them chase as far as was possible, so that not one of these bewildered people escaped. Burkápa was slain, together with all his men, and their heads formed a lofty minaret, so that the vapour from the brains of the infidels of that country reached to the heavens. Thenceforth no one dared offer resistance."

INDEX.

Abacus (of Aṣoka-pillars), 409.
Abbess, 233, 245, 275.
Abbot, 172.
Ābhasvarā (devā), 86.
Abhi-dharma, 159.
Ablutions (ceremonial), 214, 423, 445.
Abstinence, 134, 138, 445.
Ābū, Mt., 95.
Acala, 131, 364.
Acanthus, 338.
Ācārya, 538.
Act-force, 30, 100.
Adam, 226.
Ādi-Buddha, 126, 130, 348.
Ādityas, 367.
Admission (to order), 173.
Æsculapius (Buddha), 353, 498, 509.
Afghan fanatics and Indian Buddhism, 16.
Afghanistan, 8, 26, 197.
Agni, 367, 494, 496.
Agnostic views, 7, 122.
Ajaṇṭa caves, 108, 128.
A. K., Pandit, 322.
Akanishṭhā (devā), 85, 86.
Ākāṣagarbha, 358.
Akshobhya, 349, 350.
Ālala, 356.
Alasaddā, 9.
Ālaya, or pantheistic soul-basis, see Ātman.
Alchemy, 165.
Allahabad, 377.
Almanack, 458.
Alms (giving), 135, 138.
Alms-bowl, 211, 212.
Alphabet (introduced into Tibet), 21.
Altar, 294, 428; (offerings), 423, 425; (devils'), 299.
Altun Khan, 501.
Amban, 254.
Amdô, 43, 266.
Amitābha (Buddha), ix., 12, 127, 335, 336, 338, 347, 348, 349, 350; (paradise of), 127, 217.
Amitāyus, 348, 352, 444.
Amogha-pāṣa, 352.
Amogha siddha, 349, 350, 352.
Amṛita (ambrosia), 87.
Amṣuvarman, 20.
Amulets, 571.
Anabhraka (devā), 86.
An-āgamī, 136.
Ānanda, 8, 108.
Anātmaka, 111.
Ancestor-worship, 375.
Anger, 109.
Ani (title of nuns), 160, 170, 202.
Aniccam, 111.
Animals (ransomed), 265; killing of, 211, 213.
Animism, 19, 26, 34, 55, 409.
Anitya, 111.
Antara-vāsaka, 201.
Aparagodhana, see godhanya.
Apramāṇabhā (devā), 86.
Apsaras, 86.
Arahattam, 105, 137, 376.
Archbishop, 187.
Architecture, 260.
Arhant, 105, 137, 376.
Arhatship, 137.
Armenian Christians (influence of), 422.
Arrows in ceremonies, 445, 483, 553.
Arūpa, 85.
Arūpa-loka, 85, 86.
Aryabolo, 356.
Ārya-devā, 8.
Ārya-pāla, 356.
Asam (shrines), 307.
Asañasatya (devā), 86.
Asaṅga, 14, 141.
Ascension, feast of, 504, 510; (of Buddha), 510; (of St. Tsoṅ-K'a-pa), 510.
Asceticism, 6.
Ashṭa maṅgalam, 392.
Ashṭa ratna, 393.
Aṣoka, 8 76. 442; (gifts of), 397; (pillars), 409; (railing of), 11.
Aṣoka (tree), 338.
Assembly-hall, 260, 282.
Astrology, 450.
Asura (Titans), 81.
Aṣva-ghosha, 8, 10.
Atapā-devā, 86.
Atīṣa, 35, 54.
Ātman (or soul), 76, 111, 112, 121, 126, 141.
Attitudes (of fingers), 141, 337; (of body), 335.
Aureole, 337.
Auspicious (days), 455.
Avadāna, 162.
Avalambana Sūtra, 98.
Avalokita, 15, 39, 356; (four-handed), 229, 357; (eleven-headed), 15, 357; (thousand-armed), 357; (female), see Tārā.

Avalokiteṣvara, see Avalokita.
Avataṅsaka, 69, 125.
Avatāra-Lāma, 227.
Avīci (hell), 95.
Avidyā, 110, 119.
Avrihā (devā), 86.

Bactria, 8, 108, 541.
Baidurya-kar-po (chronology), 20.
Baikal (lake), 43.
Bairotsana, 29.
Bakshi, 56, 502, see also Bhikshu.
Balti, 266.
Baṇa, 156.
Banāras, 134.
Bandya, 171.
Baptism, 448, 510.
Bardo (interval between death and re-birth), 113, 491, 562.
Barhut, stupa, 345.
Bas-reliefs, 239.
Bathing (ceremonial), 214, 423, 445, 510; (of images), 424, 427.
Bats of good luck, 4, 395.
Beads, see Rosaries.
Becoming (of). 121.
Beduriya (Buddha), 353.
Beings (classes of), 101.
Bel (tree), 394.
Bells (prayer), 298, 475.
Benares, 134.
Benediction (Cha-wa), 239, 245, 305, 322.
Benedictive attitude (of images), 237.
Berkeley, 107, 121.
Besārh (Vaiṣāli), 10.
Bhagavān, 344.
Bhagavatī, 438.
Bhairava-vajra, 62, 131, 362.
Bhaisajyarāja, 353.
Bhaṇa, 156.
Bharadvāja, 353.
Bharhut (stūpa), 345.
Bhava, 110, 117.
Bhavacakra, 109.
Bhavanam, 117.
Bhikshu, 170, 213.
Bhikshuṇī, 160, 170, 202.
Bhīmmitra, 51.
Bhoga, 394.
Bhotān, 44, 226, 284, (sect), 55, 68.
Bhṛikuṭi, 20, 23, 359.
Bihar-gyäl-po
Binzuru Sama, 353.
Birth, 110, 117.
Birth-stories, 101, 533.
Bishop, 187.
Blessing, 239, 245, 306, (attitude of), 237, (before food), 214.
Blind (curing of), 550.
Böd (= Tibet).
Bodhi (perfect Wisdom).
Bodhi-dharma, 8, 138.
Bodhi-druma, see Bodhi-tree.
Bodhisat (Bodhisattva), 10, 137; (celestial), 348, 354.
Bodhisatship, 138; (stages), 139.
Bodhi-tree, 6, 305, 343.
Böd-pa (= Tibetan).
Body (three-fold of Buddha), 127, 347, (luciform), 127.
Bogle (Mr.), 236.
Bön (religion), 19, 55, 389; (opposing Lāmaism), 29; (extent), 41; (devils), 27; (priests), 26, 34, (sacrifices), 420.
Bone (trumpets), 300, 493; (ornaments), 483, see Skull.
Bonze, 171, 422, and see Bön.
Books (sacred), 60.
Bowl (alms), 211, 212.
Boy-pupil, 173.
Brāhma (god), 85; (heavens of), 86.
Brāhmaṇas, 6.
Brāhmaṇi geese, 200, 409.
Brāhmanism, 6, 17.
Bram-ze = Brāhman.
Bre-pung, see De-pung.
Bribsun, 23, 359.
Bri-kung, see Di-kung.
Brom Bakshi, 36.
Brom-ton, 36.
Brugpa, see Ḍug-pa.
Buddha, see Ṣakya Muni; (coming), see Maitreya.
Buddhas, 123, 342; (celestial), 12, 342; (Pratyeka), 123.
Buddha Gayā, 36, 305; temple, 11; (railing at), 11.
Buddha-palīta, 139.
Buildings (religious), 254.
Bum (book), 161.
Burial, 7, 305, 420.
Buriat (tribes), 41, 43, 282, 372.
Burma, 8; (gods), 365; (Mahāyāna element in), 123, 142, 476; (monks as schoolmasters), 566; (prayer-flags), 409, 414; (sacred plays), 527, 541.
Burnt-offering, 432, 533.
Bu-ston, 20.
Butan, see Bhotān.
Butter (candles), 296, bas-reliefs, 239.
Byam-pa, 355.

Caitya, 261.
Cakes, 219, 223, 297, 299, 429, 449.
Cakra, 390, 392.
Cakravartin, 389.
Calendar, 454.
Candles, 296.
Candragupta, 575.
Candrakīrti, 36, 139, 378.
Canon, 12, 54, 157; (Nepalese), 159; (Southern), 10.
Canopus (star), 510.
Canopy, 295.
Caps (of monks), 194; (of nuns), 199.
Cardinals, 187.
Car-procession, 312.
Cathedrals, 287, 300.
Cats, 520.
Catur-mahārājakāyika, 84, 290.
Cauldron, 533.
Causal nexus, 105.
Causation, chain of, 105.
Cave (hermitages), 254.
Celebrations, 434.
Celibacy, 193.
Cemetery-dweller, 381.
Cenotaphs, 262.
Censer, 323.
Ceremonies, 212, 420.
Ceylonese Buddhism, 9, 123, 142, 476; (ceremonial union and fetishes in), 446; (rice images in), 329.
Chab-lug, 201.
Chaḍāyatana, 110, 115.
Chag-dor, 356.

Chag-na dorje, 356.
Chag-wa (hand-blessing), 239, 245, 305, 322.
Chag-z'i-pa = 4-handed.
Chain of Causation, 105, 119.
Chaitya, 261.
Chalice-cup, 225.
Champa (Buddha), see Maitreya.
Cham-pahi Ch'ö-ṅa, 128.
Chana-dorje, 356.
Changachelling, see Sang-ṅa-ch'oling.
Changes in Buddhism, 9.
Ch'ang-skya, 243, 252.
Chän-rassig, see Avalokita.
Charity, 138, 398, 493, 566; (by words), 133, 146.
Charms, 387, 571.
Chase of Scape-goat of ill-luck, 512.
Checbuling, see Ts'e-ch'og-ling.
Chemiling, see Tso-moling.
Chenresi, see Avalokita.
Chetang (mon.), 412, 576.
Chiamdô, 278, 577.
China, 8, 20, 43, 247.
Chinha, 341.
Ch'i-ñer, 188.
Chin-lab, 176, 434.
Chinsreg (burnt offering), 432, 498, 533.
Ch'ö (= Dharma), 132, 156.
Ch'oga, 434.
Ch'öi-de, 255.
Ch'oikyong, 363, 477.
Ch'ö-je, 186, 477.
Ch'o-k'ang, see Jo-k'ang.
Ch'orten, 262.
Ch'os-kyoṅ (demons), 363, sorcerers, 477.
Choir-master, 188.
Chom-dan-däs (Buddha), 344.
Chongju Sewang, 512.
Christian (miracle-mongering), 307; (relic-worship), 318; (ritual), 422.
Christians, Nestorian, influence of, 421.
Christmas-tree, 81.
Chronology, Tibetan, 20, 397; (table), 452, 575.
Chryse, 36.
Chuṛamaṇi, 263, 343.
Church, 169, 287.
Chutuktu, 232.
Cinha, 341.
Cintāmaṇi.
Circumambulation, 287, 420.
Clairvoyance, 477.
Clapping hands, 486.
Clergy, see Order and Hierarchy.
Clock (water-), 218.
Cloister, see Monastery.
Clothes, 200, 511.
Clothes of images (nab-ze), 424.
Colleges, 178.
Colossal images, 320.
Colours, 331, 337.
Commandments, 134.
Commentaries, 164.
Conception (festival of), 503.
Conch-shell (trumpet), 298.
Confession, 160.
Consciousness, 110.
Contemplation, 138, 141.
Continuity (of becoming); 112.
Corea, 8.
Cosmology, 77.
Costumes, 200, 511.
Council (great), 9; (of Rājagriha), 159; (Vaiṣāli), 10; (Kanishka), 9.
Country-gods, 369.
Court-ceremonies (at Lhāsa), 322; (at Tashi-lhunpo), 321.
Cow-god, 404.
Cowls, 195.
Creed (the Buddhist), 105, 133.
Cross, 30, 389.
Crossing (oneself), 423.
Cūḍā-mani, 263, 343.
Cycle of Life, 105.
Czar, 167; (as the goddess Tārā), 359.

Ḍaba (a monk), 178.
Dab-chad (magical figure), 153.
Dab-lha, see War God.
Da-dar (arrow), 445, 483, 553.
Dāgarbha, 262.
Dagger (necromantic), 445, 483.
Dagoba, 262.
Dag-po, 330.
Dah-dar (arrow), 445, 483, 553.
Dah-pön, 553.
Dai Koko, 368.
Ḍākkinī, 129, 340, 366, 562.
Dalai Lāma, 39, 227, 305; (list of), 233.
Ḍa-lha, 88, 374.
Ḍamaru, 48.
Ḍam-c'an, 371, 382.
Dāna, 138.
Dance (devil), 34, 477; (lion), 539; (sacred), 515.
Dante's Inferno, 93.
Ḍapung, 63, 269.
Ḍāra Eke, see Tārā.
Dar-c'og, 410.
Darjeeling, 258, 288, 370, 430.
Darṣana (*ta-wa*), 61.
Dartya, 99, 369.
Darwinian descent, 21.
Dasa bhūmiṣvara, 139.
Dasa-ṣīla, 134.
Daughters (of Māra), 6, 109.
Days, names and symbols for, 455.
Dé, see Dre, 494.
Death, 100; (god of), see Yama; (ceremonies), 488.
Debang, see De-pung.
Deb-rāja, 242.
Decalogue, 134.
Deer (lord of), 134, 360; (masks of), 531, 537.
Deer-park, 134.
Degrees, 185.
Deities, 324.
Delhi (Hastināpura), 552.
De-lok, 100.
Dem-ch'og, 163, 363.
Demerit, 101, 567.
Demo-jong or Den-jong (Sikhim).
De-not sum, 159.
Depa-rāja, 242.
De-pung (monastery), 63, 189, 228, 269.
Der-chok, see (Darc'og), 410.
Der-ge, 159, 202, 278.
Descent (from heaven), 504, 510.
Desid, 40, 240, 253.

Desire, 109, 110, 116 (see Māra).
De-srid, 40, 240, 253, 577.
Destiny, 30.
Deva (gods).
Deva (monk), 8.
Deva-chan, 127, 139.
Deva-loka, 87.
Devi (she-devil), 364.
Devils, 93, 99, 363, 369; (dance), 34, 477; (disease causing), 405; (exorcising), 369, 494.
De-wa-chan, 127, 139.
De-wa z'uṅ, 254.
De-z'iṅ-s'eg-pa, 345, 353.
Dhamek (stūpa), 134.
Dhamma-pada, 162.
Dhaṇa, 138, 493.
Dhana Nanda, 393.
Dhāraṇī, 141.
Dharītrī (mother-earth), 344.
Dharma, 133.
Dharma-cakra, 337.
Dharma-kāya, 127, 347.
Dharma-kīrti, 30, 378.
Dharma-pada, 162.
Dharma-pālas (devils), 363.
Dharma-rāja (of Bhotān), 226, 233, 242; (of Lhāsa), 303.
Dharmatrāta, 377.
Dharma ṣarīṛa, 320, 497.
Dharmāṣoka, 8, 76, 398.
Dhatu-garbha, 144.
Dhṛita-rāshṭra, 84.
Dhyāna, 136, 138.
Dhyāni-Bodhisats, 130.
Dhyāni - Buddhas, 130, 336, 349.
Dialectic, 184.
Dialects (Buddha's sermons in), 159.
Diamond (souled), 352; (throne), 305, 344.
Dice, 466, (leaded), 512.
Diet of Lāmas, 225.
Dikung (monast.), 38, 55, 69, 276.
Dina-cariyāwa, 511.
Ding-pön, 3.
Dīpaṃkara, Buddha, 345, 511.
Dīpaṃkara (monk), 35, see Atīṣa.
Ḍipa-nam-sel, 358.
Disciples, 376 (the Sixteen), 376.
Discipline, 187, 192.
Disease (remedies for), 401, 405.
Divination, 450; (by cards), 465; (by beads), 465; (by dice, 466).
Divisions, 54.
Divyāvadāna, 108.
Dô, 159.
Doctrine, 132.
Dogras destroying mons., 282.
Dogs (metempsychosed men) 567; (bite charm), 406.
Dol-jang, 359.
Dol-kar, 359.
Dol-ma, 358.
Dö-ma, 358.
Dô-mang, 163.
Ḍom-bakshi, 36.
Domestic Lāmaism, 566.
Ḍom-ton, 36
Ḍor-je (Vajra), 298, 341; (ch'aṅ), 352; (dän), 305; (dän-z'i), 344, 353; (jig-je), 62; (kyil-ḍuṅ), 335; (legs), 371, 382; (lô-pön), 293; (p'ag-mo), 233, 245, 275; (sem-pa), 352; (ṭak), 55, 73, 277.
Dor-ma, 297.
Dragon (thunder), 395.
Drag-po, 330.
Drag-s'é, 330.
Drama, 539, (Burmese), 541.
Dra-pa (monks), 178.
Drawings and paintings, 239.
Dress (monastic), 194, 200.
Dril-bu (bell), 298, 341.
Dri-med kun-dan (Jātaka play), 540.
Drink (tea), 215, (spirituous), 225.
Dri-zä, 84, 367.
Drugs (mystic words as), 401.
Drum (sacred), 48, 300.
Dsog-ch'en, 47, 72; (a monk), 47.
Dub-ch'en, 378.
Duck (Brāhmani), 200, 409.
Düd, 93, 99, 363, 369.
Düd Dub-jed, 153.
Düd-tsi (ambrosia), 87.
Ḍug-pa (sect), 55, 66, 68, 242; (southern), 55.
Dü-k'ang (assembly hall), 260, 287.
Dukkha, 111.
Duk-pa, see Ḍug-pa.
Dul-va, 159.
Durgā, 129, 364.
Dur-k'rod (graveyard ghouls), 537.
Dyaus-pitar, 356, 367.
Dying, 100, 448.

Earth (spirits), 344; (demons), 484.
Eating charms, 401.
Ecstatic state, 128.
Education, 173; (of laity), 566.
Eggs (on altar), 423.
Ego, 100, 112, 121, 124.
Eightfold (path), 133; (division of relics), 306; (division of gods), 366, 369.
Ekotībhāva, 112.
Elder (monks), 174.
Election of Grand Lāmas, 246.
Elements (five), 453; (of body), 263.
Elephant (white), 390; (episode), 337.
Eleven-headed Avalokita, 15, 357.
Emanation, 347.
Empedocles, 109.
Endowments, 194.
Energy (female), 129.
Entrance to order, 171.
Epidemic (remedies for), 405.
Established Church, 54.
Ether, 77, 264.
Ethics, 119, 132.
Eucharist of Lāmaism, 444.
Europe (Lāmaism in), 9, 282.
Everest (Mt.), 371, 430.
Examination (candidates' orders), 182; (physical), 173; (for degrees) 182; (test books), 174, 183; (of Grand Lāma), 216.
Excrescence (on skull), 343.
Exercising death-devil, 494
Exoteric Buddhism, 128.

Expiring breath (exercise), 145.
Expulsion from Order, 192.
Eye (bestowing of), 550; (thousand), 357.
Eye-shades, 306.
Eye-tooth of Buddha, 318.

Fa Hian, 551.
Faith (salvation by), 12, 146, 153, 499.
Familiars (spirits), 374.
Family cults, 372, 566.
Fan (palm-leaf), 195.
Fan (tribe), 33.
Fasting, 501.
Fatalism, 30, 567.
Father (title of Jupiter), 356, 487; (title of Lāmas), 566.
Features (of Buddha), 343; (of gods), 333; (of demons), 334.
Feet (of Buddha), 335.
Festivals, 501; (monthly), 502; (annual), 50.
Fetishes, 238, 446.
Fig-tree (sacred), 343.
Filigree work, 572.
Fines, 192.
Fire (sacred), 296.
Fish (ransoming), 448.
Five (groups of), 347, 397.
Flags (luck or "prayer"), 409.
Flames (from head), 343; (enveloping body), 337; (in hell), 93; (thirst as), 97.
Flesh (sacrifice), 495, 529.
Flower-offerings, 297, 425.
Flowers (conventional forms of), 339.
Flux (life as a), 121.
Flying-horse, 390, 410.
Fo, see Buddha.
Food offerings, see Cakes, Oblations
Footprints, 392.
Foretelling, 458.
Forms of prayer, 435.
Formula (of causal nexus), 105; (spells for rosary), 150.
Fortune-telling, 458.
Foundation of buildings, 259.
Four paths, 133.
Four truths, 132.
Frog (three-legged), 456.
Full moon (day), 501.
Funeral (rites), 488.

Gah-dan or Gah-ldan (monastery), 61, 189, 268.
Gah-rab dor-je, 73.
Gambling, 470
Games (of chance), 465.
Gāndhāra, 14, 517.
Gandharvas, 84, 367.
Gandhola (temple), 305.
Ganesa, 368.
Garbha, 260.
Garlands, 297, 425.
Garlic (forbidden to monks), 225.
Garma-khia, 272, 477, 481.
Garuḍa, 81, 367, 387.
Gāthā, 162.
Gati, 101.
Gautama, see Ṣākya,
Gayā, 305, 344.
Ge-dun (clergy), 169.
Gedun-ḍub, see Gedun-grub.
Gedun-grub, 38, 63, 230, 233.
Gedun-gya-ts'ô, 233.
Ge-k'o (officer), 188, 193.
Ge-loṅ (ordained Lāma), 171, 213.
Geloṅ-ma, 160, 170, 202.
Gelong, see Geloṅ.
Gelug-pa (sect), 36, 38, 54, 59.
Geñen, 171.
Genii, 367; (local), 371.
Ge-s'o, 185.
Gets'ul, 171.
Ghosts, 498.
Gifts, 138, 398, 493, 566.
Giorgi, 2.
Glacier (torture), 95; (gods of), 370.
Goblins, 369.
Godhanya, 80.
Gods, 86, 324.
Golden-fish, 393.
Gömpa (monastery), 255, 287.
Gon-po (devil), 365.
Gorakhas, 53, 578.
Gorakhuth, 292.
Goṣīrsha, 394.
Gotama, see Ṣākya.
Graces (before meat and drink), 214.
Grades of monkhood, 171.
Grain, consecrated, 323, 488.
Grand Lāma, 37, 233, 303, 305; (list of Dalai), 233; (Tashi-lhunpo), 235; (Sakya), 241; (Urgya), 240; (Bhotan), 226, 242; (receptions), 321.
Greek art-influence, 13.
Gṛidhra-kūṭa, 161, 377.
Grol-ma, see Tārā.
Grub-pa, 141, 152, 378.
Guard ans(supernatural), 369, 374.
Guhyapati, 61, 352.
Guilt-offering, 449.
Gujarāt, 80.
Gupta characters, 22.
Gur-gön, 70.
Guru Padma (or Rimboch'e), see Padma-sambhava.
Gusri-khan, 39.
Gya-jin, see Indra.
Gyal-ch'en, 84, 290, 538.
Gyal-gön rimpo-ch'e, 235.
Gyal-po (king-devils), 369.
Gyalts'an (banner), 408.
Gyal-wa-rimpo-ch'e, 39, 228.
Gyamtshô, 227, 233.
Gyantse (mon.), 278, 317
Gyé-bo (Gyal-po), 369.
Gyud (Tantra), 129.

Hair (of Budda), 343; (tonsure of candidates), 179.
Halo, 318, 337.
Hanle (monastery), 283.
Hanumān, 19.
Hare, in moon, 102.
Haritī, 99.
Harsha-vardhana, 20.
Hartmann, 107, 121.
Hastināpur, 552.
Hastings (Warren), mission of, 236.
Hats, 194; (red), 68, 73, 195; (yellow), 61, 195; (black), 61.
Haya-griva, 62, 164, 364, 529.

Heart (the sacred), 147.
Heavens, 84; (Brahmā's), 86; (Indra's), 85, 87.
Hells, 90; (cold), 95; (hot), 93.
Hemis (monastery), 282; (play at), 521, 528.
Heraclitus, 121.
Hercules, 374.
Heredity, 100.
Hermits, 223.
Heruka, 51, 131, 496, 530.
He-vajra, 131, 363.
Hexagrams, 456.
Hierarchical Buddhism, 227.
Hierarchy, 227; (female), 226.
Himavat, 19.
Himis (mon.), 282; (play at), 521.
Hīna-yāna, 10, 123.
Hindū (mythology), 76.
History, nebulous, x., 19.
Hiuen Tsiang, 15, 19, 26, 56, 108, 307, 330, 338, 501, etc.
Hoblighan, 232.
Hodgson (Brian H.), 12.
Hog (symbolizing stupidity), 109.
Holies (the three), 388, 390.
Holy days, 501.
Holy plays, 515.
Holy-water, 298.
Homa, 432, 498, 533.
Homeric views, 367.
Honouring persons or things, 287, 420.
Hor tribe (Turki).
Horn (exorciser's), 488.
Horoscopes, 459; (annual), 460; (special), 481; (death), 489.
Horse (car celestial), 32; (dragon), 410; (flying), 390; (flags), 409.
Hoshang, 31, 378, 534.
Hospitals, 269.
Houris, 86.
Houses (of Lāmas), 260; (god of), 372.
Howling devil-dancer, 477.
Hrī, invocation to Avalokita, 147, 324, 402.
Hsuan-chuang, see Hiuen Tsiang.
Hublighan, 227.
Huc, Pere, 2.
Hūṃ, mystic ejaculation.
Human (bones), 300, 483, 493; (sacrifices), 516, 518.
Hung, see Hūṃ.
Hunterian spelling, xviii.
Hutuktu, 232.
Huxley on *Karma*, 100.
Hwa Shang, 31, 378, 534.
Hymn-book score, 433.
Hymns (to Tārā), 435; (to Trinity), 439.
Hypnotism (self-), 141.

Ichneumon, 368, 377.
Iddhi, 128, 141.
Iddhi-pāda, 141.
Identity (personal), 112, 121.
Idolatry, 12, 13, 15, 324.
Ignorance, 105, 110, 119.
Illusion, 7, 101, 107, 121.
Images, 13, 15, 291, 324; (colossal), 320; (insignia of), 341; (self-created), 292, 304; (stone), 278, 339; (union with), 446.
Image-worship, origin of, 13, 324.
Incantations, 141.
Incarnate deities, 40.
Incarnate Lāmas, see Reincarnation.
Incense 222, (butter), 222.
India (origin of Buddhism in), 5; (changes), 9; (expulsion from), 16.
Indian (gods), 76, 367; (monks), 376; (shrines), 305; (? Vedic charms), 401.
Individuality, 112, 124.
Indra, 86, 356, 367; (as a Yaksha), 369.
Induction-ceremony, 178.
Inferno, 90; (source of Dante's), 94.
Initiation, 178, 185.
Inspiration (physical in Yoga), 145.
Instruments, 298, 300.
Intercalation of days and months, 454.
Investure, 178, 185.
Io (goddess), 373, 404.
Irdhi, 128, 141.
Iron-tower (in S. India), 15.
Iṣhta-devata, 152.
Islām, 16, 387, 583.
Iṣvara, 141.
Itinerancy, 211, 212.

Ja, see Tea.
Jacob's ladder, 510.
Jagannāth (idol car), 313.
Jainism, 4, 339, 424; (saints), 389, 393, 397.
Jai-yung, see Mañjuṣrī.
Jālandhara, 9.
Jalendra, 368.
Jambhala (god), 151, 368.
Jambu tree, 80.
Jambudvīpa, 80.
Jambu-ling, see Jambudvīpa.
Jam-pa, see Maitreya.
Jam-yang, 355.
Japan, 9, 27, 136, 145, 327, 345, 352, 353, 393, 395; (God of Wealth), 368; (rosaries), 202.
Jarāmarana, 110.
Jātakas (former births), 101; (as plays), 533.
Jāti, 110.
Jengiz Khān, 37.
Je rin-po-ch'e, see Tsoṅ-K'a-pa.
Jetavana, 135.
Je-tsun dampa, see Tāranātha.
Jewel (the three), 33, 388, 390; (wish-granting), 544.
Jig-ten-ba (= worldly).
Jina, 130, 267, 336, 349.
Jizo, 345.
Jñāna, 138.
Joll, 263.
Jo-naṅ, 55, 70.
Jong-ni, 49.
Jo-rin-po-ch'e, 345.
Jo-wo-K'ang (cathedral), 23, 281, 300.
Judgment of dead, 91, 113.
Jugglery, 476.
Junior monks, 177.
Jupiter, 86, 356, 367; (planet), 451; (Pluvius), 269; (thunder-bolt), 27; (heavens of).
Jyoti, 263.

Ka-che, 266.
Kadam-pa (sect), 36.
Kah-chan (Kab-chu), 186.
Kah-dam-pa, 36, 54.
Kah-gyur (canon), 157.
Kah-gro, 129, 366, 429, 562.
Kah-lon, 254.
Kailāsa (mount), 19, 78, 80.
Kaiser, see Kesar.
Kālacakra, 15, 131, 163, 269.
Kāla-devi, 129, 334, 364, 537.
Kālanātha, 151, 363, 365, 537.
Kālasūtra (hell), 94.
Kālī, 14, 129, 131, 334, 364, 537.
Kalimpong, 284.
Kaliṅga, 269, 544.
Kalmuk (Tartars), 9, 42.
Kalpa, 76, 111.
Kalpa tree, 86.
K'am (eastern Tibet).
Kāma, 84.
Kamala-sīla, 31.
Kāma-loka, 84.
K'am-ts'an, 189.
Kanaka-muni, 346, 351.
Kanchinjunga (mountain), 49, 370, 430 511.
Kan-dô, 366, 429, 562.
Kang-gyur, 157.
Kang-s'ag, 221, 477.
Kanishka (Kanerkes), 8, 9, 12, 108, 573.
Kanjur, 157.
K'an-po (an abbot), 172.
Kant, 107.
Kapāla, 341, 353, 363.
Kapilavastu, 541.
Kargyu-pa (sect), 55, 63.
Karma (act-force), xviii., 30, 100, 106, 222, 567; (Huxley on), 100.
Karma (sect), 45, 52, 55.
Karma-bakshi, 67.
Karma-kya (mon.), 272, 477; (oracle), 481.
Karma-mārga, 57.
Karmashar (mon.), 272, 477; (oracle), 481.
Kart'og-pa, 55, 73.
Kar-tsis (astrology), 450.
Karuna, 356, and see Avalokita.
Ka'sarpāṇi, 356.
Kāshgar, 583.
Kashmīr, 8, 11, 26, 163, 377.
K'äs-ṭub-je, 59.
Kāṣyapa (Buddha), 346; (monk), 8, 346, 350.
Kaṭak, 269.
Kauṇḍinya, 345.
Kavaca (amulet), 148, 401, 573.
Ken-düling (Kun-de-ling monastery), 253, mon.
Kesar (King), 20, 167, 478.
Kevalātma, 76.
Kha-ba-c'an (Himalayas), 19.
Khakkara, 211.
Khalka (Tartars), 70.
Khalsa, 163.
Khandha, 114.
Khan-po (abbot), 172.
Khas-grub-je, 59.
Kha-s'or ch'orten, 315.
Khatmaṇḍu (K'o-bom), 315.
Khāṭvāṅga, 341.
Khecara, 366.
Khorlo, see Cakra.
Khoten, 44.
Khri Srong de-tsan, 24, 245.
Khroda, 332, 334.
Khrüs-sol, 448, 502, 510.
Khublai Khan (king), 37, 227.
Kublaighan (incarnations), 233.
Khutuktu, 232.
Kilang (monastery), 384.
Kinchinjunga, 49, 370.
Kings (4 guardian), 84; (5 great), 369, 477, 538.
Kinnara, 367, 552.
Kirghis, 43.
Kitchen (god), 373, 404; (monastic), 191.
Knowledge (true), 133.
Kobo Daishi, 27, (way of).
Koko, Dai, 368.
Koko-Nor, 227.
Könch'og-gyalpo.
Kön-ch'og-sum (the three Gems, see Triratna).
Koot Hoomi, 129.
Kraku-cchanda, 346, 351.
Kṛashi-Lunpo, see Tashilhunpo.
Krishṇa, 378.
Kro-bo, 332, 334.
K'rodha, 332, 334, 438.
Kshatriya, 390.
Kshitigarbha, 181, 345, 358.
Kshitipati, 358, 372.
Ku (see body and image).
Kublai Khan, 37, 227.
Kuchar Khanpo, 323.
Kuku Khotun, 43, 282.
Kuku Nor, 227.
Kumārila, Brāhmanical opponent of Buddhism.
Kumbhāṇḍa, 84, 369.
Kumbum, 158, 280, 577.
Kun-de-ling, 253.
Ku-ñer, 188.
Kun-gah-wo, see Ānanda.
Kun-tu-zaṅ-po, 349.
Kurim, 449, 521.
Kuru, 80.
Kurun (or Urgya), 281.
Kushok, 232.
Kuṣi-nagara, 307.
Ku-s'ok, 232.
Kuṭila letters, 22, 149.
Kuvera, 368.
Kwan-non, 249, 356, 359, 435.
Kwan-she-yin, 356, 359.
Kwan-yin, 249, 356, 359, 435.
Kyab-gön, 244.
Kye-lang (monast.), 384.
Kyil-k'or, 319.

La-brang (mon.), 258, 512.
Ladāk, 43, 171, 265, 282, (mystic play), 521.
Lag-na-Dorje, see Vajrapāṇi.
Lahūl, 284.
Laity, 170, 566.
La-k'ang, 287.
Lalita (posture), 336.
Lalita-vistara, 162.
Lāma (meaning of word), 28; (the first), 29; (order), 170; (numbers), 41; (Grand), 226.
Lāma Yuru (monast.), 283.
Lāmaism, 17, 19, 30, 41; (reformation), 36; (sects of), 54.
Lāmas (order of), 169.
Lāmaseries, 255.
Lam-dé, 57.
Lam-ḍön (sgron), 57.
Lamps, 296, 298; (festival of), 511.

Lam-rim (dogmatic by Tsoṅ-K'a-pa), 57.
Lañca (letters), 149.
Laṅ-darma, 34, 54; (assassin of), 520, 529.
Laṅka, see Ceylon.
Lanterns (feast of), 511.
Lapcha (cairn), 283, 285.
Lapis lazuli, 81.
Lares, 215, 484.
Latsün Ch'embo, 45, 55.
Law, see Dharma; (true), 126.
Lay-brothers, 170.
Laymen, 170, 566.
Leh, 282.
Lepchas, 285, 286, 379.
Letters (Tibetan), 22, 149.
Levitation of body, 128, 141.
Lha (gods), see Deva.
Lha-k'a (sorcerer), 482.
Lha-k'aṅ, 287.
Lha-mayin, 81.
Lha-mo (she-devil), 334.
Lhāsa (name), 23; (cathedral), 23, 309; (Potala), 229; (red hill), 229, see Marpo-ri; (vicar apostolicus of), 2.
Lhato (cairn), 283, 285.
Lha-t'o t'o-ri, 19.
Lhatsün Ch'en-bo, 45, 48, 55; (introd. Lāmaism to Sikhim), 49-51.
Lhô-Ḍug-pa (sect), 68.
Libation to devils, 215, 225.
Library, 168.
Licchavi tribe, 19.
Life, 102, (elixir of), 81; (eternal), 443; (ransoming), 265, 448.
Limbu (tribe), 484.
Ling (royal monastery), 253.
Linga (offering to devils), 423, 428, 483.
Ling-k'a, 423, 483, 532.
Lion (pillars), 409, 414; (posture), 343; (throne), 336, 343; (voiced), 151, 356, 379.
Litanies, 444.
Literature, 155.
Liturgy, 444.
Living,
Li-yul, 44.
Lob-nor, 393.
Lôb-pön, 188, see Padmasambhava.
Lob-ta (school), 260.
Lob-zang tak-pa, see Tsoṅ-K'apa.
Locanā, 350.
Lô-Ḍug-pa (sect), 68.
Lokāntarika, 96.
Lokeṣvara (princes), 333.
Lok-pāl, 84.
Long (dragon), 410.
Lô-pön, 188.
Lô-tsava, 187.
Lotus (symbol of perfection, etc.), 338, 339, 388; (birth from), 86, 381.
Love (brotherly), 136.
Lô-zang, see Tsoṅ-K'apa.
Lu, see Nāga.
Lu-'bum.
Luck (ill), (scapegoat of), 512.
Lucky days, 455, 457.
Lung-ta, 409.
Lung-tog Yam-Thso, 233.
L'un-se (begging-bowl), 211, 212.
Lust, 109, 115, 119.

Mādhyamika (schools), 11, 124.
Maḍros (Mal-gro), 266, 376.
Magi, doctrine of, 394.
Magic-circles, see Maṇḍala, (-sentences), 142.
Magic (sympathetic), 401, 404, 446.
Ma-gom, 74.
Maguta (stūpa), 315.
Mahā-deva, 151, 363, 537.
Mahā-jātaka, 540.
Mahā-kāla, 151, 221, 363, 365, 537.
Mahā-Kāṣyapa, 8, 159, 160.
Maha-Maugdalyāyana, 8, 98, 108, 376.
Mahā-purusha, 129.
Maha-parinirvāṇa sūtra, 162.
Mahā-rajas (of quarters), 84.
Mahārāni, 364.
Mahā-raurava (hell), 95.
Mahā-saṅghika, 10, 123.
Mahā-siddha, 378.
Mahā-ṣravaka, 378.
Mahā-sthavira, 378.
Mahātma, 3.
Mahā-utpanna, 72.
Mahā-vagga, 123.
Mahā-yāna doctrine, 10, 124, 137.
Mahoragas, 367.
Maitreya (Buddha), 122, 320, 355.
Maitrī (love), 136.
Makara, 391.
Makuta Stūpa, 315.
Mallas, crested Stūpa of, 317.
Māmakī, 350.
Mamo (she-devils), 370, 383.
Manasarôvara, 266, 376.
Manchu (dynasty), 49, 254.
Manchuria, 43.
Maṇḍala, 144, 163, 181, 217, 266, 296, 397, 444.
Mandarawa, 382.
Mandong, 261.
Manes, 96.
Maṅgala (ashta), 392.
Maṅgala-sutta, 135.
Mang-ja, 189.
Mang-yul, 260.
Maṇi (mystic prayer), 148; (prayer-cylinders), 149; (stone-walls, 261.
Maṇi-Kah-'bum, x., 19, 166.
Mañju-ghosha, 355.
Mañju-ṣrī (god of Wisdom), 12, 161, 339, 355, 460; (incarnations), 35, 231.
Män-la (medical Buddhas), 353.
Man-mo (spirits), 371.
Manning (Mr.), 2.
Mantra (spells), 141, 149; (for rosary), 150; (vehicle), 128, 151.
Mantrayāna, 15, 128, 143, 151.
Manu (date of), 92.
Manushi or human Buddhas, 350.
Māra (god of desire), 6, 88, 344, 375; (his daughters), 109; (his devils), 6, 517.
Marīcī, 219, 361.
Mar-me-dsäd, see Dipaṃkara.
Mar-pa, 55, 64.
Marpo-ri (hill), 21.
Marriage (by capture), 553; (horoscopes), 458.

Mars (planet), 455.
Marut (storm-gods), 332.
Masho (vill.), 512.
Masks (for actors), 536; (mortuary), 496, 497.
Masquerades, 515.
Materialism, 76.
Mati-dhvaja, 38.
Mātrikā (yum), 129, 163, 362.
Matter (views of), 77.
Maudgalyāyana, 8, 98, 108, 376.
Māyā (illusion), 7, 101, 107, 121.
Māyā (Buddha's mother), 507.
May-pole, 410.
Mayūrāsana (peacock throne), 336, 350.
Mayūri, 340.
Me-ba (geomantic figures), 457.
Medical Buddha-gods, 353, 498, 509.
Medicine (sympathetic), 401, 404, 446.
Meditation (Dhyāna), 136, 138, 335.
Meditative (attitude), 335.
Me-lha (fire-god), 367, 496, 533.
Melong (mirror), 393.
Menander, 124, 357, 541.
Mendicant Lāmas, 48.
Men-dong, 261.
Merchant monks, 224.
Mercury (planet), 199.
Mercy (god of), 356; (goddess of), 359, 435.
Merit (action of), 101.
Meru (mount), 78, 398, 400.
Mesmerism, 129.
Metamorphosis, 100.
Metaphysics, 76, 159.
Metempsychosis, 100, 226.
Mewa, 457.
Middle-path, 11, 124.
Mig-mar (Mars), 455.
Mig-tse-ma, 190.
Mila-räspa (saint), 55, 64, 167.
Milinda, 124, 357, 476, 541.
Milinda pañha, 124.
Milinda praşna, 124.
Mind, 114.
Mindolling, 55, 73, 173, 277.
Ming (dynasty), 38.
Miracles, 247, 249; (Christian), 307.
Mirror (magical), 393, 445, 482.
Misery, 110, 132; (of gods), 90.
Missals, 157.
Missionaries (Buddhist), 8, 376; (Roman, in Lhāsa), 2.
Mitre, 24, 197.
Mô (divination), 465.
Moha, 109, 113.
Monasteries, 255; (list of), 266.
Mongol, patronage of Lāmaism, 37, 39.
Mongolia (Lāmaism introd. to), 38, 43, 70; (re-introd.), 501.
Mongolian (alphabet and scriptures), 38, 158; (Lāma), 45.
Monkeys, origin from, 19; (symbol), 115.
Monkhood, 170.
Monlam (celebrations), 422.
Month (festivals of), 502.
Monuments (religious), 261.
Moral conduct, 133; (rules), 134.
Morality, 132.
Moru monastery, 477.
Moulmein, 36.
Mountain-gods, 370.
Mriga-dāva, 134.
Mucalinda (Nāga) 345.
Mudrā (attitudes), 141, 335.
Muhammadan (expulsion of Buddhism), 16, 583.
Mummers, 515.
Mummery, 144, 224.
Muni (sage), 5, 311, 345.
Music, 432.
Musical instruments, 298, 300; (notation), 433.
Musician (heavenly), 83.
Mystery-play, 515.
Mystic (sentences), 141, 146, 148.
Mystical Buddhism, 128, 142.
Mysticism, 124, 128, 142.
Mythology, 76, 324; (of Hindūs), 77, 324, 366.
Nä-ch'uṅ (oracle), 478, 521.
Ṅa-dag-pa, 55, 73.
Nä-dän 376.
Nāga, 11, 84, 104, 164, 156, 289, 368; (worship), 164, 267, 499, 508.
Nāga-raja, 289.
Nāgāsena, 124, 377, 476.
Ṅag-pa (sorcerer), 209, 475, 479, 483.
Nag-po Ch'en-po (Māhakāla), 365.
Ṅag-waṅ Lô-zaṅ Gya-ts'o, 39, 47, 227, 233, 253, 327.
Ṅah-dag, 73.
Ṅah-t'i-tsan-po, 19.
Nail-parings of Lāmas (as charms), 402.
Nain Siṅgh, 266, 512.
Nājārjuna, 8, 10, 11, 15, 69, 125 164, 378.
Nakula, 377.
Nālanda, 24, 64.
Nal-jor (= Yogācārya), 141.
Nāma-rūpa, 110, 115.
Namchi (monastery), 259, 285.
Nam-c'u vaṅ-dan, 142.
Names of Buddha, 203, 353.
Names of monasteries, 257, 266.
Nam-go (masts), 487.
Namgyal (monast.), 253, 272.
Nam-t'o-sräs, 84, 370.
Ṅän (devil), 372.
Nanda (nāga), 368.
Nandas (the nine), 393.
Naṅ-sa (play of), 553.
Naraka (hell), 90.
Ṅari-K'or-sum, 265, 266.
Nāro, 16.
Narthang (mon.), 156, 158, 159, 327.
Nātha, 365.
Nāts (of Burmese), 365.
Navakosa, 393.
Navaniddhi, 393.
Navang Lobsang, see Nag-waṅ.
Nava-ratna, 393.
Nayabliṅ, 81.
Nāyakas, 180.
Ne-chung (oracle), 478, 521.

Necromancers, 478.
Ne-ḍen (chu-tug), 376.
Ñen-nä, 170.
Ñen-t'ö, 170.
Neophyte, 178.
Nepal, 8, 20, 44, 260, 284, 315, 382, 470; (canon), 139.
Nestorian influence in China and Tibet, 421.
Netan c'u-drug, 376.
Newars, 328, 456, 470.
New-moon (day), 501.
New Year (festival), 513.
Nibbāna, see Nirvāṇa.
Nidāna, 105, 107, 110.
Nihilism (sophistic), 125.
Nimbus, 337.
Ñiṅ-ma-pa, 55, 68, 72.
Nirmāṇa-kāya, 127, 347.
Nirvāṇa, 10, 119, 124, 163.
Ñi-t'i (book), 161.
Nomen Khan, 253.
Non-Ego, 124.
Norbu (gem), 389.
Nor-pa, 55, 70.
Northern school, 9.
Nostril (closing), 145.
Nothingness, 125.
Novice, 178.
Novitiate (admission), 178.
Number of Lāmas, 41-52.
Numerals, symbolic use of, 367.
Nuns, 160, 170, 202, 274, 275, 286.
Nya-thi-tsanpo (king), 19.
Nying-ma-pa (sect), 55, 68, 72.
Nyi-thi, 161.

Oaths, 570.
Oblations, 215, 225.
Occultism, 128.
Ocean jewels, 88.
Ocean-Lāma, 228.
Odantapura vihāra, 28, 36.
'Od-pag-med, 349.
'Od-ser, 219, 361.
Offerings, 296, 423.
Officials, 187.
Og-min (heaven), 85, 497.
Olympus, 77, 78, 86.
Om, 142, 148, 160, 165.
Om maṇi padme hūṃ, 139, 148.
'O-pa-me, 349.
Oracles, 475; (of government), 478.
Order (of Lāmas), 168.
Order, 168.
Ordination, 185.
Organs (sense), 115.
Original sin, 115, 160, 222.
Orisons, 219.
Otantipura (vihāra), 28, 36, 266.

Paccaya, 106.
Padma, 95.
Pädma-juṅ-nä, see Padma-sambhava.
Pädma-Kar-po, 68.
Padma-pāṇi, see Avalokita.
Padma-sambhava (saint), (founded Lāmaism), x, 24, 29, 55, 68, 73, 195, 292; (departure from Tibet), 32; (deification), 33, 73, 312, 340, 379, 518, 525, 531, 543, 551; (disciples), 31; (visit to Sikhim), 44; (to Bhotān), 68.
Padmāsana (lotus-seat), 338.
P'ag-mo, see Dorje-p'ag-mo.
Paintings, 331.
Palace-monastery, see Ling.
Pal-dan, title of Atīṣa, Lhamo, Yes'e, etc.
Pāli (scriptures), 156, 159.
Palingenesis, 100, 121, 227.
Pañca-bala, 131.
Pañca-rakshasa, 131.
Pañca-sīla, 134.
Pañca-tantra, 163.
Panch'en Lama, 235.
Panch'en Rim-po-ch'e, 235.
Paṇḍita, 186.
Paṇḍurā, 351.
Pantheism, 122, 129.
Pantheon, 324.
Paradise (Buddha's), 127, 217; (Indra's), 86; (St. Padma's), 32.
Pāramitā (virtues), 138, 541.
Paraṣu, 341.
Pari (Lāma), 326.
Pāribhogika, 420.
Pari-nirvāṇa, 11, 120, 122.
Paritta, 142, 446, 476.
Parivrājika, 178, 185.
Parkha (signs), 456.
Paro (monastery), 44, 278, 284, 293.
Pārṣva (monk), 8.
Patañjali, 128, 141.
Paternal Buddhas, 339.
Path (eight-fold), 133.
Paticca-samuppādo, 105.
Pātimokkha, 160.
Paṭo (mon.), 44, 278, 284, 293.
Patriarchs (list of), 8.
Paṭṭinī (goddess), 325.
Peacock, 88; (feathers), 298, 445; (throne), 336, 349.
Pedong, 284.
Pehar (King-devil), 371, 479.
Peking, 43, 158, 279, 327; (Lāma), 243.
Pelong, 29, 237.
Pemakoi, 279.
Pemiongchi, 50, 173, 258, 265, 285, 512.
Penance, 6; (by proxy), 319.
Penates, 484.
Perfumes, 394.
Personality, 112, 121.
Peshāwar, 14.
Pessimism, 122.
Phag-mo, see Dorje-p'agmo.
Pha-pa, title of Avalokita, etc.
Philistinism (of Muhammadans), 16.
Phungi, 30.
Phur-bu, 51, 341, 488.
Phylacteries, 402, 531.
Pictures, 331.
Pig (symbol of stupidity), 109.
Pilgrims, 305, 278.
Pindar, 109.
Pingala, 99.
Pīpal-tree, 337.
Pirit (ceremony), 142, 446, 476.
Piṭaka, 159.
Pittuk (mon.), 284.

Planets, 199, 454.
Plato, 10, 107, 109.
Plays, 515.
Plotinus, 141.
Pluto, 90, 367.
Pön-ba, see Bön.
P'ongi (Burmese monk etymol), 30.
Pope (Lāmaist), 37; and see Grand Lāmas.
Popular Lāmaism, 566.
Postures, 145.
Potala palace, 21, 39, 40, 229.
Pradakshina, 287, 420.
Prajñā, 125, 161, 356.
Prajñā-pāramitā, 11, 125, 160.
Prasanga-mādhyamika, 139.
Prasenajit, 19.
Pratimoksha, 160.
Pratītya Samutpāda, 105.
Pratyeka (Buddhas), 123, 137.
Pravrajyā, 178.
Prayāg, 377.
Prayer, 12, 15, 141, 213, 435.
Prayer-barrels, 149.
Prayer-cylinders, 149, 172, 218.
Prayer-flags, 408.
Prayer-formula, 141, 213, 435.
Prayer-machines, 149, 172, 218.
Prayer-wheels, 149, 172, 218, 573.
Preaching attitude, 337.
Precentor, 188.
Precepts, 134.
Precious things, 389.
Preta, 96.
Priest, see Order and Worship.
Priestcraft, 18, 153, 217.
Priest-king, 227.
Printing, 157, 219, 327.
Procession, 168.
Pronunciation (rules), xvii.
Proverbs, 175.
Pu-kwa, 456.
Punakha (mon.), 44, 284.
Puṇḍarīka, 96.
Pungī, 30.
Punishments, 193.
P'unts'o-ling, 71, 274.
Punya, 30.
Pupil, 173.
Purang, 260.
P'ur-bu, 51, 341, 483, 488.
Purgatory, 90.
Purusha, 129.

Quarters (Kings of), 84.
Quietists, 141.

Rab-jam-pa, 186.
Radeng (Lāma), 235.
Raḍeng (mon.), 56, 274.
Rāga, 109.
Rag-bushes, 409.
Rahan, 376.
Rahat, see Arhant.
Rāhu, 82, 269, 455.
Rāhula, 82, 377.
Rain-bow (cordon), 103, 331.
Rain (compelling), 499; (worship), 508.
Raivata, 345.
Rāja-gṛiha, 108.
Rākshasa, 32, 81, 369.
Ralung, 68.
Rammoch'e (monastery), 23, 272, 477, 508.
Ransoming (life), 265, 448.
Ratna (gem), 389.
Ratna-kūṭa Sūtra, 99, 161.
Ratna-paṇi, 351.
Ratna-sambhava, 349, 350.
Rāvaṇa, 32.
Rays (of light), 337, 343.
Re-birth, 101, 109; (of Grand Lāmas), 229.
Red-hats, 73; (sect), 68, 73.
Refectory, 189, 214.
Reformation (Lāmaist), 36.
Refreshments in church, 214, 220.
Refuge formula, 440.
Refuges (three), 440.
Regenerated Lāmas, 227.
Regent, 235, 240, 253.
Re-incarnation, 100, 121, 227.
Relics, 305, 318, 330; (of Buddha), 7, 319, 420; (of Grand Lāmas), 253.
Reting (Lāma), 235.
Retreat (in rains), 223.
Revelations, 56, 165.
Rhinosceros, 397.
Rice-offerings, 295; (of universe), 296; (images in Ceylon), 329.
Rinang, 553.
Rin-ch'en-na-dün, 389.
Ri-rab (Mt.), 78, 398, 400.
Rites, 420.
Ri-wo-ch'e (mon.), 279.
Road to heaven, 492.
Robes, 200; (giving of), 511.
Rol-pa (Mañjuṣrī), 336.
Rol-pahi dorje, 243.
Roman Church (analogies), xi.
Rosaries, 202; (spells for), 150.
Routine, 212.
Rudra (god), 209, 332.
Rugs, 294.
Rules (moral), 134, 138, 160; (thirty-six), 171, 179; (two hundred and fifty-three), 171; (of monasteries), 188.
Rūpa (form), 84, 115.
Russia (Lāmaism in), 9, 41, 282.

Sabdag (local genii), 371, 484.
S'ab-duṅ (title), 179.
Sacrifice, 425; (flesh), 495, 527; (burnt), 432, 533; (dogs), 529; (human), 516.
Saddharma - puṇḍarīka, 126, 138, 142, 162.
Sa-gô masts, 484.
Saints, 376.
Saint-worship, 33, 376.
Ṣakra, see Indra.
Ṣakrid-āgāmā, 136.
Ṣakti (female energy), 129.
Sakya (monastery), 69, 274; (sect), 37, 55, 69.
Sakya (pandita), 37, 69, 227.
Ṣākya-muni, 5; (image), 343; (death), 7, 163, 308; (temptation), 6; (the "Second"), 379.
Sakya-pa (sect), 37, 55, 69.
Sāla (tree), 7, 185, 308.
Samādhi, 138, 141.
Saman (God in Ceylon), 325.

Sāmanera, 136.
Samanta-bhadra, 14, 72, 131, 349, 358.
Sambhala, 283, 306.
Ṣambhara, 151, 163, 363.
Sambhoga-kāya, 127, 347.
Sam-bhota, 21.
Saṃsāra, 10, 109, 126.
Ṣamvara, 151, 163, 363.
Śamyak-Sambuddha (title of Ṣākya Muni).
Sam-yäs (monast. founding), 28, 108, 266, 478, 513.
Sandal (rosary), 207.
Sangacheling (monast.), 50, 258.
Saṅgha, 169.
Saṅghārāma, 261.
Saṅghāṭī, 200.
Sang-kar, 266, 278, 283.
Saṅ-gyäs, see Buddha.
Saṅsāra, 10, 109, 126.
Saṅskāra, 106, 110.
Ṣānta-rakshita, 28, 315.
Śapataratna, 390.
Saptaparna, 377.
Sarana, 337.
Sāraṅga-nāth, 360.
Ṣāriputra, 8, 376.
Ṣārīra, 330, 420.
Śārnāth, 134, 360.
Sarvāstivada, 124.
Sas-kya (monast.), 69, 274; (sect), 37, 55, 69.
Satscha, 330, 497.
Sattva, 112, 423.
Saturn, 455.
Sautrānta, 162.
Scales (ordeal of), 113.
Schools (northern and southern), 9.
Schopenhauer, 107, 120.
Scorpion (charm), 405; (exorcism), 488.
Scriptures, 155.
Sculpture, 239.
Scythian, 8, 108, 541.
Seal, 202; (Grand Lāma's), 242, 304.
Seas (seven), 78.
Sects, 54.
Sedent (postures), 335.
Selenginsk, 282.
Self, 112.
Self-consciousness, 110.
Self-extinction, 138.
Self-sacrifice, 138.
Self-sprung (images), 328.
Seṅ-c'en rimpo-ch'e, 243.
Seng-dong-ma (devil), 430.
Sermons (Buddha's), 135.
Serpent, see Nāga; (charmer), 552.
Serra (mon.), 63, 189, 269.
Seven (jewels, etc.), 389, 391.
Shab-ḍung (title), 179.
Shadow (of Buddha), 318.
Shakya-thuba, 343.
Shamanism, 19, 26, 29, 55, 420.
Sha-mar, 81.
Shambhala, 283, 306.
Sham-ch'o-ḍuṅ, 307.
Shaving head, 179.
Sheep's shoulder-blades (divining by), 465.
Sheldrake, 200.
Shen-rab (god), 30.
Sher-chin, see Prajñā pāramitā.
Shi-je-pa, 74.
Shin-je, see Yama.
Shintoism, 27, 393.
Shrines, 305.
Siam, 8, 9.
Siberia, 43, 282.
Sibi (Jātaka), 550.
Sickness (curing), 401.
Siddha, 152, 271.
Siddhārta, 5.
Siddhi, 141, 152, 378.
Sikhim (intro. of Lāmaism to), 44, 51, 52, 284; (Lāmas of), 45, 244; (king), 341, 379.
Ṣikhin, 346.
Ṣīla (moral rules), 134.
Ṣīladitya, 138.
Silk (robes), 200.
Sin (word for), 175.
Siṅhanada, 151, 267, 356.
S'inje, see Yama.
Sirios (dog-star), 510.
Sitā (Tārā), 359.
Ṣiva, 14, 330.
Sixfold (states of life), 101.
Six-syllabled spell, 148.
Skandha, 114.
Skull-bowl, 299.
Skull-drum, 300.
Sky-demons, 487.
Sling, 341, 375, 483.
Snake-demigods, 368.
Soap, 214.
So-bön, 188, 237.
Sod-nam Gya-ts'o, 233.
Sol-pön, 188, 237.
Sooth-sayers, 451, 475.
Sorcery, 475.
Sorrow, 132.
Sosānika, 381.
Soul, 111, 112, 121, 126, 141.
Soup in church, 220.
Southern school, 9.
Space, 77, 264.
Sparṣa, 110.
Spells, 150.
Spinoza, 122.
Ṣrāddha, 99.
Śrag-dharā, 81.
Srāmana, 136.
Srāmanera, 136.
Ṣrāvaka (hearer), 136.
Ṣrāvastī, 135, 161.
Śrong-tsan-gam-po, 19, 22, 551.
Srot-āppanna, 136.
Staff (mendicants'), 211.
Stars (influence of), 450.
Statues, 339.
Stature of mythical Buddhas, 345.
Sthavira, 171; (sixteen), 376.
Storm (-god), 332.
Stūpa, 262.
Styx (Buddhist), 92.
Su-darṣana, 88.
Sudhāna Jātaka, 551.
Suffering (origin of), 133.
Sukhāvatī, 127, 139.
Sumatikīrti (Tsoṅ-k'a-pa).
Sumedha, 346.
Sumeru, 78, 398, 400.
Sum-pa k'anpo, 20.
Sunday (Buddhist), 501.
Sung-Yun, 541.
Sun-worship, 13, 127, 347.
Sūnyatā, 125.
Supernatural (powers), 141, 152, 378.
Surmounting Buddhas (on images), 338.
Sūtra, 159, 162.
Sūtrānta, 123, 162.
Suvarnadvīpa, 36.
Svastika (cross), 30, 389.
Svayambhunāth (stupa), 315.
Swan maidens, 552.
Syllables (mystic), 142.
Symbols, 341, 387; (in hats), 197.

Tables (of Lāmas), 294.
Tachog, see Flags, and Hayagrīva.
Ta-erh-ssu (mon.), 280.
Tag-mar c'ham, 516.
T'ag-p'u (caves), 257.
Tag-ten (monast.), 70.
Tale Lāma, 39, 227.
Talismans, 402, 531.
Talung (sect), 55, 69.
Tamch'og, see Hayagrīva.
Tamdin, see Hayagrīva.
Tam-ze (=Brāhman).
Tangut, 266, 581.
Tän-gyä-ling, 253; (plan of), 522.
Tangyur (commentaries), 157, 164.
Tañhā, 110, 116.
Tanjur, 157.
Tän-ma (she-devils), 27, 371, 382, 529.
Tantalized souls, 96.
T'añ-t'oñ-gyäl-po, 385.
Tantra, 129, 152, 163.
Tāntrism, 14.
T'añ-yig (books), 165.
Taoism, 19.
Tārā, 22, 23, 258, 360, 551; (worship of), 435.
Tāranātha, 43, 55, 70, 240, 282, 327.
Tartars, 9.
Tāshiding, 50, 53, 258, 285, 512.
Tāshi-gô-mañ, 264.
Tāshi Lāma, 230.
Tāshi-lhunpo, 63, 189, 260, 270, 535.
Tāshi-rab-ka, 49.
Tāshisudon (monast.), 44, 284.
Tathāgata, 122, 345, 353.
Tats'in (Rome), 422.
Tawa, 61.
Tea service (general), 191, 215.
Tea-drinking, 214.
Teaching attitude, 134.
Teeth (relics), 308.
Telopa (monks), 64.
Temples, 287.
Temptation (Buddha's), 6, 344.
Ten (prohibitions), 134.
Ten-del (Nidāna), 105.
Tengri, 372.
T'eng-pa, 10.
T'eng-wa, 202.
Ten-gye-ling, 253; (plan of), 522.
Tent (god), 70; (tabernacle), 282.
Terma (revelations), 57, 58, 165.
Terminology (Buddhist), 165.
Ter-pa-ling, 239.
Teshu Lāma, 230.
Text-books, 174.
Thang Chu (record), 20.
Thang-kar pass, 1, 2.
Thañ-yig ser-t'eñ, 45.
Theg-pa (yāna), 10.
Theistic Buddhism, 126.
Theogony, 122.
Theosophy, 128.
Thigh-bone trumpets, 48, 300.
Thin-le-Gya-ts'o, 233.
Thi-Srong-de-tsan, 24, 30, 245.
Tho, 330.
Tho-ling (mon.), 283.
Thonmi-Sambhoṭa, 21, 22.
Thor, 88.
Tho-wo, 330.
Three gems, 346, 388, 390, 443.
Three Holies, 346, 443.
Three Refuges, 440.
Thug-je-ch'en-po, 356.
Thui-sol, 434, 448, 502, 510.
Thumi Sambhota, 21, 22.
Thunderbolt, 15, 25, 27, &c
Tibet (pre-Buddhist), 19.
Tiger-devils, 516.
T'ig-se, 266, 283.
Tilopa (monk), 64.
Timed Kun-dän (Jātaka play), 540.
Tiñge (mon.), 274, 533.
Tisri, 240, 577.
Titans, 81.
T'o, 330.
Tô-lung (monast.), 51.
Tonsure, 179.
Tope, 262.
Top-knot, 179.
Tor-ma cakes, 297.
Tortoise, 395.
Torture, 568.
T'o-t'ori-ñan-tsan, 19.
Trading monks, 224.
Transcendental wisdom, 160.
Transmigration, 100, 226.
Trayastriñsa, 86.
Tree (of heaven), 81, 86, 88, 96; (Christmas), 81.
Trigrams, 394.
Tri-kāya, 127, 347.
Tri-murti (of Lāmaism), 355.
Trinity, 346, 347.
Tri-piṭaka, 159.
Tri-ratna, 33, 388, 390.
Tri-ṣarana, 340.
Trishṇā, 110, 116.
Triṣūla, 342.
Trividagni, 114.
Tri-vidya, 111.
Trumpets, 298.
Truths, 132.
Tsa-cha, 330, 497.
Tsam-ch'ö-duñ, 307.
Tsa-mo-ling, 253.
Ts'e-gug, 447.
Ts'e-mch'ūling, 253.
Ts'e-pag-med, 348.
Ts'e-ring che-ña, 370.
Tsi-pa, 451.
Tsoñ-K'a-pa, 38, 54, 59, 198, 223, 227, 268, 280, 292.
Tsug-tor (Ushṇīsha), 360.
T'uba (=Ṣākya).
T'ug, 147.
T'ug-je ch'en-po, 356.
Tui-sol, 434, 448, 502, 510.
T'ul-ku, 232.
Tung-rampa, 186.
Tun-moñ, 434.
Turquoises, 209, 239, 557.
Tushita (heaven), 77, 86, 128.
Tutelaries, 152, 361; (sectarial), 58, 62, 65, 69, 72.

U, province, 265.
Udānas, 162.
Udānavarga, 162.
Udandapura, 28, 36, 266.
Uddesika, 420.
Udyāna, 26, 197, 306, 380.
Umbrella, 392, 393.
Um-dse (officer), 188, 293.
Universe (Buddhist), 77; (offering of), 296, 397; see Maṇḍala.
Upādāna, 110.
Upādhyāya, 31, 171, 172.
Upagupta, 8, 120, 442.
Upāli, 159, 376.

Upa-me, 349.
Upananda, 368.
Upāsakā, 170.
Upasampadā (full ordination), 185.
Upāsika, 170.
Uposatha (fast days), 178.
Uranus, 367.
Urga, 43, 70, 240, 281.
Urgyän-gya-ts'o (Lāma), xii, 45.
Urgyän-pa (sect).
Utai-shan, 279.
Utpalā, 95.
Uttara (title), 28.
Uttarakuru, 80, 377.
Uttara saṅga, 201.

Vagīṣvara, 414.
Vāibhāshika, 123.
Vaipula, 161, 162.
Vairocana Buddha, 15, 127, 349.
Vairocana (Lāma), 29, 435.
Vaiṣālī (council), 10, 123.
Vaiṣravanā, 84, 368, 370.
Vaitaraṇī, 92.
Vajra, 15, 25, 27, etc.
Vajra-bhairava, 62, 131, 362.
Vajrācārya, 151, 179.
Vajracedika, 161.
Vajra-ḍākkinī, 366.
Vajra-dhara, 61, 130, 352.
Vajra-dhatu, 144, 145.
Vajra-garbha, 144, 145.
Vajra-pāṇi, 13, 86, 150, 356, 365.
Vajra-p'urba, 70, 72, 363.
Vajrāsana, 305.
Vajra-sattva, 15, 352.
Vajra vārāhī, see Dorje-p'agmo.
Vajra-yāna, 15, 151.
Vajrīputra (? Vasuputra), 377.
Vakula, 377.
Vandya (? Bande), 171.
Vanishing, 141, 564.
Vārāhī, 150, 163.
Varsha, 223.
Varuna, 367.
Vasubandhu, 13, 69, 128.
Vasu-mitra, 8.
Vasuputra, 57, 69.
Veda (god), 371; (scriptures), 6.
Vedanā, 110.
Vedānta, 122.
Vedic charms, 401.
Vehicles, 10, 15.
Veṇuvana, 108, 161.
Vessantara (tale enacted), 541.
Vestments, 194.
Via media, 11.
Vicar apostolicus of Lhāsa, 2.
Vidarbha, 11.
Videha, 80, 543.
Vihāra (mon.), 255.
Vijñāna, 110.
Vinaya, 60, 159.
Virgil, 100.
Virtues (practice of), 138.
Virūḍhaka, 83, 84, 330.
Virūpāksha, 84, 289.
Visions (four), 91.
Viṣva-bhu, 346.
Viṣva-karma, 313.
Viṣvantara, 138; (play), 540.
Viṣva-pāṇi, 350.
Vitaraga, 392.
Volga, 182.
Votive offerings, 133.
Vulcan, 313, 367, 404.
Vulture's-peak, 161.

War-god, 89, 374.
Water (festival), 509; (holy), 298; (offerings), 427.
Way, the true, 133.
Weapons (magical), 483.
Week (days), 454.
Wench'eng princess, 20, 23.
Wheel (symbol), 389; (of the Law), 134, 337, 390; (of Life), 102.
Widow's mite, 319.
Will (unconscious), 113, 119.
Wine, 221, 225; (oblations), 225, 495.
Wisdom (deified), 12, 35, 161, 339, 355; (transcendental), 11, 125, 160.
Wish-granting (cow), 87; (tree), 81, 86, 88, 96.
Witch-women, 366, 369.
Witness (attitude), 336, 344.
Wizard-priests, 24, 378.
Works, 30, 100, 106, 222, 567.
Worlds, 84, 101.
Worship (objects), 324, 387; (celebrations), 17, 420; (feast days), 501.
Wu-tai shan, 279.

Xylographs, 157.

Yab-yum (conjugal deities), 129, 362.
Yak (god), 373; (mask), 537.
Yaksha, 81, 84, 369; (Indra as a), 84, 86.
Yakshini, 369.
Yama, 86, 90, 367.
Yama-mari, 364; (heavens), 86.
Yamāntaka, 90, 362.
Yama rocks, 81.
Yam-dog-ts'o (lake), 233, 275.
Yaṅ-c'an-ma (= Sarasvatī).
Yaṅ-gug, 448.
Yantra, 144, 387.
Yarlung, 20.
Yellow-hat (sect), 61.
Ye-s'e-gon-po, 365.
Yidag, 96.
Yidam, 361.
Yoga, 13, 128, 141.
Yogācārya, 14, 128, 147.
Yogi, 13, 128, 141.
Yong-grub.
Yön-tan, 222.
Yul-k'or-rung, 84.
Yum, 129, 163, 362.
Yun-drung, 389.
Yunnan, 254.

Z'al-thang, 328.
Z'alu (Lāma), 326, 333.
Zang-Kar, 266, 283, 278.
Zeus, 86, 356, 367.
Z'i-je-pa, 74.
Z'i-wa (mild deity), 333.
Z'ung (spells), 141, 402, 486.

CATALOGUE.

ARTHUR PENRHYN STANLEY, D.D. (Dean of Westminster).

Scripture Portraits and other Miscellanies collected from his Published Writings. By Arthur Penrhyn Stanley, D.D. Crown 8vo, gilt top, 5s.

Uniform with the above.

VERY REV. FREDERICK W. FARRAR, D.D., F.R.S. (Archdeacon of Westminster).

Words of Truth and Wisdom. By Very Rev. Frederick W. Farrar, D.D., F.R.S. Crown 8vo, gilt top, 5s.

Uniform with the above.

SAMUEL WILBERFORCE, D.D. (Bishop of Winchester).

Heroes of Hebrew History. Crown 8vo, gilt top, 5s.

Uniform with the above.

CARDINAL NEWMAN.

Miscellanies from the Oxford Sermons of John Henry Newman, D.D. Crown 8vo, gilt top, 5s.

CAPTAIN JAMES ABBOTT.

Narrative of a Journey from Herat to Khiva, Moscow, and St Petersburgh during the late Russian invasion at Khiva, with Map and Portrait. 2 vols., demy 8vo, 24s.

Throughout the whole of his journey, his readers are led to take the keenest interest in himself, and each individual of his little suite. The most remarkable anecdote of this part of his journey is concerning the prosecution of the Jews, for an alleged insult to Mohammedanism, not unlike the pretext of Christian persecutors in the days of the Crusaders.

From St Petersburgh, Captain Abbott returned to England, where he gives an amusing account of the difficulties, and mental and physical distresses of his Afghan follower. The book concludes with the author's return to India, and with notices of the fate of some of the individuals in whom we have been most interested by his narrative.

"The work will well repay perusal. The most intrinsically valuable portion is perhaps that which relates to the writer's adventures in Khaurism, and at the Court of Khiva; but the present time imparts a peculiar interest to the sketches of Russian character and policy."—*London Economist.*

MRS R. K. VAN ALSTINE.

Charlotte Corday, and her Life during the French Revolution. A Biography. Crown 8vo, 5s.

"It is certainly strange that when history is ransacked for picturesque and interesting subjects, no one has yet told in English—for so Miss van Alstine remarks, and our own recollection supports her negatively—the romantic story of Charlotte Corday. The author has carefully studied her authorities, and taken pains to distinguish fact from fiction, for fiction, it need hardly be said, has mixed itself plentifully with the story of Charlotte Corday. Miss van Alstine has been able to add to this story several genuine details that greatly heighten its effect."—*Spectator.*

EDWARD L. ANDERSON.

How to Ride and School a Horse, with a System of Horse Gymnastics. Fourth Edition, revised and corrected, crown 8vo, 2s. 6d.

"An admirable practical manual of riding."—*Scotsman.*

"The book deserves perusal by all who have dealings with horses."—*Birmingham Gazette.*

"Though practice is of course essential, it is equally necessary that the practice should be guided by some principle, and the aspirant who adopts the methods explained and recommended by Mr Anderson is not likely to regret his choice of an instructor."—*Morning Post.*

D. T. ANSTED and R. G. LATHAM.

The Channel Islands. Revised and Edited by E. Toulmin Nicolle. Third Edition, profusely illustrated, crown 8vo, 7s. 6d.

"A useful and entertaining book. The work is well done, and to those who have not even paid a flying visit to this beautiful group it is calculated to cause a strong desire to explore and enjoy its attractions."—*Daily Chronicle.*

"We are extremely glad to see a new edition of this fascinating work. . . . All who know the Channel Islands should read this admirable book; and many who read the book will certainly not rest until they know the Channel Islands."—*Black and White.*

PROFESSOR D. T. ANSTED.

Water, and Water Supply. Chiefly with reference to the British Islands. With Maps, 8vo, 18s.

Towns and their water-supply is becoming a clamant grievance.

MAJOR J. H. LAWRENCE-ARCHER, Bengal H.P.

The Orders of Chivalry, from the Original Statutes of the various Orders of Knighthood and other Sources of Information. With 3 Portraits and 63 Plates, **beautifully coloured and heightened with gold, 4to,** coloured, £6. 6s., Plain, £3. 3s.

"Major Lawrence-Archer has produced a learned and valuable work in his account of 'The Orders of Chivalry.' He explains that the object of the book is to supply a succinct account of the chivalric orders in a convenient form. The literary form of the work is amply convenient for reference and study. Its material form could be convenient only to some knight of the times when armour was worn in the field, and men were stronger in the arm than they are now. It is a handsome volume. The size of the book is doubtless due to the introduction of a series of engraved plates of the badges and crosses of the various orders described. These plates are executed in a finished style, and give the work an exceptional value for students of heraldic symbolism. The author may be congratulated on the successful issue of a laborious and useful task."—*Scotsman*, 14th May 1888.

SIR EDWIN ARNOLD, M.A., Author of "The Light of Asia," &c.

The Book of Good Counsels, Fables from the Sanscrit of the Hitopadésa. With Illustrations by Gordon Browne. Autograph and Portrait, crown 8vo, antique, gilt top, 5s.

—— The Same. Superior Edition, beautifully bound, 7s. 6d.

"It is so long since Sir Edwin Arnold's Indian fables were in print that they may practically be regarded as a new book. In themselves they are almost the fathers of all fable, for whereas we know of no source whence the 'Hitopadésa' could have been borrowed, there are evidences of its inspiration and to spare in Bidpai, in Æsop, and in most of the later fabulists."—*Pall Mall Gazette.*

"Those curious and fascinating stories from the Sanskrit which Sir Edward Arnold has retold in 'The Book of Good Counsels' give us the key to the heart of modern India, the writer tells us, as well as the splendid record of her ancient gods and glories, quaint narratives, as full of ripe wisdom as the songs of Hiawatha, and with the same curious blending of statecraft and wood-magic in them."—*Daily Telegraph.*

"A new edition comes to hand of this delightful work—a fit companion to 'Æsop's Fables' and the 'Jungle Book.' Sir Edwin has done well to republish this record of Indian stories and poetical maxims from the Sanskrit. And the illustrations, a specimen of which we give here, what shall we say of them? Simply that they are equal to the text. No more pleasant series of 'Good Counsels' is it possible to find, and we are convinced that it is not an ill counsel—far from it—to advise our readers to forthwith get this charming work. They will derive not a little pleasure, and perchance instruction, from a perusal of the story of the jackal, deer, and crow, of the tiger and the traveller, of the lion, the jackals, and the bull, of the black snake and golden chain, of the frogs, and the old serpent, and of all the other veracious chronicles herein set forth."—*Whitehall Review.*

S. BARING-GOULD, M.A., Author of "Mehalah," &c.

In Troubadour Land. A Ramble in Provence and Languedoc, with Illustrations by J. E. Rogers. Medium 8vo, 12s. 6d.

"The title of Mr Baring-Gould's book only indicates one of the many points of interest which will attract the intelligent traveller during a tour in Provence and Languedoc. Besides troubadours, there are reminiscences of Greek colonisation and Roman Empire, of the Middle Ages, and of the Revolution. . . . The illustrations which adorn the pages of this very readable volume are decidedly above the average. The arm-chair traveller will not easily find a pleasanter *compagnon de voyage.*"—*St James's Gazette.*

"A most charming book, brightly written, and profusely illustrated with exquisite engravings."—*Glasgow Herald.*

"A charming book, full of wit and fancy and information, and worthy of its subject."—*Scotsman.*

SIR E. C. BAYLEY.

The Local Muhammadan Dynasties, Gujarat. Forming a Sequel to Sir H. M. Elliott's "History of the Muhammadan Empire of India," demy 8vo, 21s.

WYKE BAYLISS.

The Enchanted Island, the Venice of Titian, and other studies in Art, with Illustrations. Crown 8vo, 6s.

"Richly imaginative and full of eloquent and frequently highly poetical thought." —*Standard.*

"A charm which would render it difficult for any one to lay the book aside till the last page is reached."—*Art Journal.*

"A clever lecturer might pick more than one chapter as a good bit for evening readings."—*Graphic.*

The Higher Life in Art. Crown 8vo, with Illustrations, 6s.

"The style has the grace which comes by culture, and no small share of the eloquence bred of earnest conviction. Mr Bayliss writes as a man who, having seen much, has also read and thought much on fine art questions. His views are therefore entitled to that respectful attention which the pleasant dress in which he has clothed them renders it all the easier to accord."—*Scotsman.*

"The writing is that of a scholar and a gentleman, and though the critical faculty is often evinced in a subtle and discriminating form, all allusions to individuals are made with so much of the kindliness of true good taste, that we are almost conscious of a reluctance in disagreeing with the author."—*The Spectator.*

"Mr Wyke Bayliss is at the same time a practical artist and a thoughtful writer. The combination is, we regret to say, as rare as it is desirable. . . He deals ably and clearly—notably so in this present book—with questions of the day of practical and immediate importance to artists and to the Art public. . . We prefer to send the reader to the volume itself, where he will find room for much reflection."—*The Academy.*

"One of the most humorous and valuable of the general articles on Art is Mr Wyke Bayliss' 'Story of a Dado.'"—*The Standard.*

MISS SOPHIA BEALE.

The Churches of Paris from Clovis to Charles X., with numerous Illustrations. Crown 8vo, 7s. 6d.

CONTENTS:—Notre Dame; Notre Dame des Champs; Notre Dame de Lorette; Notre Dame des Victoires; Geneviève; Val de Grace; Ste. Chapelle; St Martin; St Martin des Champs; Etienne du Mont; Eustache; Germain l'Auxerrois; Germain des Prés; Gervais; Julien; Jacques; Leu; Laurent; Merci; Nicolas; Paul; Roch; Severin; V. de Paul; Madeleine; Elizabeth; Sorbonne; Invalides.

"An interesting study of the historical, archæological, and legendary associations which belong to the principal churches of Paris."—*Times.*

"A comprehensive work, as readable as it is instructive. The literary treatment is elaborate, and the illustrations are numerous and attractive."—*Globe.*

"For the more serious-minded type of visitor who is capable of concerning himself in the treasures of art and store of traditions they contain, Miss Beale has prepared her book on the *Churches of Paris.* It is more than an ordinary guide-book, for it mingles personal opinion and comment with curious information drawn from the old and new authorities on the history and contents of the more ancient and celebrated of the Paris churches."—*Scotsman.*

"A monument of historical research and judicious compilation is *The Churches of Paris from Clovis to Charles X.,* by Sophia Beale (Allen and Co.). This valuable work, copiously and gracefully illustrated by the author, is destined to serve as a complete vade-mecum to those British visitors to the French capital who take a special interest in ecclesiastical architecture and in the curious mediæval lore connected with several of the venerable Parisian fanes that have survived wars and sieges, revolutions and spasms of urban 'improvement,' throughout from six to eight centuries."—*Daily Telegraph.*

MONSEIGNEUR BESSON.

Frederick Francis Xavier de Merode, Minister and Almoner to Pius IX. His Life and Works. Translated by Lady Herbert. Crown 8vo, 7s. 6d.

"The book is most interesting, not only to Catholics, but to all who care for adventurous lives and also to historical inquirers. De Merode's career as an officer of the Belgian army, as a volunteer in Algeria with the French, and afterwards at the Papal Court, is described with much spirit by Monseigneur Besson, and Bishop of Nimes, who is the author of the original work. The book, which is now translated, was written with permission of the present Pope, and is, of course, a work agreeable to the authorities of the Vatican, but at the same time its tone leaves nothing to be desired by those who are members of the communions."—*Athenæum.*

SIR GEORGE BIRDWOOD, M.D., K.C.I.E., &c.

Report on the Old Records of the India Office, with Maps and Illustrations. Royal 8vo, 12s. 6d.

"No one knows better than Sir George Birdwood how to make 'a bare and short-hand' index of documents attractive, instructive and entertaining, by means of the notes and elucidatory comments which he supplies so liberally, and so pleasantly withal, from his own inexhaustible stores of information concerning the early relations of India with Europe."—*Times.*

"The wonderful story (of the rise of the British Indian Empire) has never been better told. . . . A better piece of work is very rarely met with."—*The Anti-Jacobin.*

"Official publications have not as a rule any general interest; but as there are 'fagots and fagots' so there are reports and reports, and Sir George Birdwood's Report on the Old Records of the India Office is one of the most interesting that could be read." —*Journal des Debats.*

HENRY BLACKBURN, Editor of "Academy Notes."

The Art of Illustration. A Popular Treatise on Drawing for the Press. Description of the Processes, &c. Second edition. With 95 Illustrations by Sir John Gilbert, R.A., H. S. Marks, R.A., G. D. Leslie, R.A., Sir John Millais, R.A., Walter Crane, R. W. Macbeth, A.R.A., G. H. Boughton, A.R.A., H. Railton, Alfred East, Hume Nisbet, and other well-known Artists. 7s. 6d.

A capital handbook for Students.

"We thoroughly commend his book to all whom it may concern, and chiefly to the proprietors of the popular journals and magazines which, for cheapness rather than for art's sake, employ any of the numerous processes which are now in vogue."—*Athenæum.*

"Let us conclude with one of the axioms in a fascinating volume: 'Be an artist *first*, and an illustrator afterwards.'"—*Spectator.*

"'The Art of Illustration' is a brightly written account, by a man who has had large experience of the ways in which books and newspapers are illustrated nowadays. . . . As a collection of typical illustrations by artists of the day, Mr Blackburn's book is very attractive."—*The Times.*

"Mr Blackburn explains the processes—line, half-tone, and so forth—exemplifying each by the drawings of artists more or less skilled in the modern work of illustration. They are well chosen as a whole, to show the possibilities of process work in trained hands."—*Saturday Review.*

"Mr Blackburn's volume should be very welcome to artists, editors, and publishers."—*The Artist.*

"A most useful book."—*Studio.*

E. BONAVIA, M.D., Brigade-Surgeon, Indian Medical Service.

The Cultivated Oranges and Lemons of India and Ceylon. Demy 8vo, with oblong Atlas volume of Plates, 2 vols., 30s.

"The amount of labour and research that Dr Bonavia must have expended on these volumes would be very difficult to estimate, and it is to be hoped that he will be repaid, to some extent at least, by the recognition of his work by those who are interested in promoting the internal industries of India."—*Home News.*

"Dr Bonavia seems to have so thoroughly exhausted research into the why and wherefore of oranges and lemons, that there can be but little left for the most enthusiastic admirer of this delicious fruit to find out about it. Plunging into Dr Bonavia's pages we are at once astonished at the variety of his subject and the wide field there is for research in an everyday topic. Dr Bonavia has given a very full appendix, in which may be found a few excellent recipes for confitures made from oranges and lemons."—*The Pioneer.*

R. BRAITHWAITE, M.D., F.L.S., &c.

The Sphagnaceæ, or Peat Mosses of Europe and North America. Illustrated with 29 plates, **coloured by hand, imp. 8vo,** 25s.

"All muscologists will be delighted to hail the appearance of this important work . . . Never before has our native moss-flora been so carefully figured and described, and that by an acknowledged authority on the subject."—*Science Gossip.*

"Mosses, perhaps, receive about as little attention from botanists as any class of plants, and considering how admirably mosses lend themselves to the collector's purposes, this is very remarkable. Something may be due to the minuteness of the size of many of the species, and something perhaps to the difficulties inherent in the systematic treatment of these plants; but we fancy the chief cause of comparative neglect with which they are treated is to be sought in the want of a good illustrated English treatise upon them. In the work which is now before us, Dr Braithwaite aims at placing the British mosses on the same vantage-ground as the more favoured classes of the vegetable kingdom; and judging from the sample lately issued, he will succeed in his endeavours."—*Popular Science Review.*

"TOM BOWLING."

Book of Knots (The). Illustrated by 172 Examples, showing the manner of making every Knot, Tie, and Splice. By "TOM BOWLING." Third Edition. Crown 8vo, 2s. 6d.

Edited by JAMES BURROWS.

Byron Birthday Book. 16mo, cloth, gilt edges, 2s. 6d.
A handsome book.

B. CARRINGTON, M.D., F.R.S.

British Hepaticæ. Containing Descriptions and Figures of the Native Species of Jungermannia, Marchantia, and Anthoceros. **With plates coloured by hand.** Imp. 8vo, Parts 1 to 4, all published per set, 15s.

S. WELLS WILLIAMS, LL.D., Professor of the Chinese Language and Literature at Yale College.

China—The Middle Kingdom. A Survey of the Geography, Government, Literature, Social Life, Arts, and History of the Chinese Empire and its Inhabitants. Revised Edition, with 74 Illustrations and a New Map of the Empire. 2 vols., demy 8vo, 42s.

"The work now before us is second to none in thoroughness, comprehensiveness, and all the tokens of accuracy of which an 'outside barbarian' can take cognisance."—A. P. PEABODY.

SURGEON-MAJOR L. A. WADDELL, M.B.

The Buddhism of Tibet. With its Mystic Cults, Symbolism, and Mythology, and in its relation to Indian Buddhism, with over 200 Illustrations. Demy 8vo, 600 pp., 31s. 6d.

SYNOPSIS OF CONTENTS:—Introductory. *Historical*—Changes in Primitive Buddhism leading to Lamaism—Rise, Development, and Spread of Lamaism—The Sects of Lamaism. *Doctrinal*—Metaphysical Sources of the Doctrine—The Doctrine and its Morality—Scriptures and Literature. *Monastic*—The Order of Lamas—Daily Life and Routine—Hierarchy and Reincarnate Lamas. *Buildings*—Monasteries—Temples and Cathedral—Shrines (and Relics and Pilgrims). *Mythology and Gods*—Pantheon and Images—Sacred Symbols and Charms. *Ritual and Sorcery*—Worship and Ritual—Astrology and Divination—Sorcery and Necromancy. *Festivals and Plays*—Festivals and Holidays—Mysic Plays and Masquerades and Sacred Plays. *Popular Lamaism*—Domestic and Popular Lamaism. *Appendices*—Chronological Table—Bibliography—Index.

"By far the most important mass of original materials contributed to this recondite study."—*The Times.*

"Dr Waddell deals with the whole subject in a most exhaustive manner, and gives a clear insight into the structure, prominent features, and cults of the system; and to disentangle the early history of Lamaism from the chaotic growth of fable which has invested it, most of the chief internal movements of Lamaism are now for the first time presented in an intelligible and systematic form. The work is a valuable addition to the long series that have preceded it, and is enriched by numerous illustrations, mostly from originals brought from Lhasa, and from photographs by the author, while it is fully indexed, and is provided with a chronological table and bibliography."—*Liverpool Courier.*

"A book of exceptional interest."—*Glasgow Herald.*

"A learned and elaborate work, likely for some time to come to be a source of reference to all who seek information about Lamaism. . . . In the appendix will be found a chronological table of Tibetan events, and a bibliography of the best literature bearing on Lamaism. There is also an excellent index, and the numerous illustrations are certainly one of the distinctive features of the book."—*Morning Post.*

"Cannot fail to arouse the liveliest interest. The author of this excellently produced, handsomely illustrated volume of nearly six hundred pages has evidently spared no pains in prosecuting his studies. . . . The book is one of exceptional value, and will attract all those readers who take an interest in the old religions of the far East."—*Publishers' Circular.*

"The author is one of few Europeans who have entered the territory of the Grand Lama, and spent several years in studying the actualities of Lamaism as explained by Lamas. A Lamaist temple with its fittings was purchased, and the officiating priests explained in full detail the symbolism and the rites as they proceeded. Other temples and monasteries were visited and Lamas employed for copying manuscripts, and searching for texts bearing upon the author's researches. Enjoying special facilities for penetrating the reserve of Tibetan ritual, and obtaining direct from Lhasa and Tashi-lhunpo most of the objects and explanatory material needed, much information has been obtained on Lamaist theory and practice which is altogether new."

"The internal developments and movements of Lamaism are now for the first time presented in an intelligible and systematic form. Details of the principal rites, mystic and other deep-rooted demon worship and dark sorcery, the religious Plays and Festivals, are given fully."

With numerous illustrations from originals brought from Lhasa, and from photographs by the author.

M. C. COOKE, M.A., LL.D.

*** For fuller notices of Dr Cooke's works see under Scientific, pp. 29, 30.

The British Fungi: A Plain and Easy Account of. With Coloured Plates of 40 Species. Fifth Edition, Revised, crown 8vo, 6s.

Rust, Smut, Mildew, and Mould. An Introduction to the Study of Microscopic Fungi. Illustrated with 269 Coloured Figures by J. E. Sowerby. Fifth Edition, Revised and Enlarged, with Appendix of New Species. Crown 8vo, 6s.

Handbook of British Hepaticæ. Containing Descriptions and Figures of the Indigenous Species of Marchantia, Jungermannia, Riccia, and Anthoceros, illustrated. Crown 8vo, 6s.

Our Reptiles and Batrachians. A Plain and Easy Account of the Lizards, Snakes, Newts, Toads, Frogs, and Tortoises indigenous to Great Britain. New and Revised Edition. With **Original Coloured Pictures of every species, and numerous woodcuts**, crown 8vo, 6s.

F. C. DANVERS.

Report to the Secretary of State for India in Council on the Portuguese Records relating to the East Indies, contained in the Archivo da Torre de Tombo, and the Public Libraries at Lisbon and Evora. Royal 8vo, sewed, 6s. net.

REV. A. J. D. D'ORSEY, B.D., K.C., P.O.C.

Portuguese Discoveries, Dependencies, and Missions in Asia and Africa, with Maps. Crown 8vo, 7s. 6d.

CONTENTS.

Book I.

Introductory.
The Portuguese in Europe and Asia.
Portugal and the Portuguese.
Portuguese Discoveries in the Fifteenth Century.
Portuguese Conquests of India in the Sixteenth Century.
The Portuguese Empire in the Sixteenth Century.

Book II.

The Portuguese Missions in Southern India.
Early History of the Church in India.
First Meeting of the Portuguese with the Syrians.
Pioneers of the Portuguese Missions.
The Rise of the Jesuits.
The Jesuits in Portugal.
St Francis Xavier's Mission in India.
Subsequent Missions in the Sixteenth Century.

Book III.

The Subjugation of the Syrian Church.
Roman Claim of Supremacy.
First Attempt, by the Franciscans.
Second Attempt, by the Jesuits.
The Struggle against Rome.

Book III.—*continued*

The Archbishop of Goa.
The Synod of Diamper.
The Triumph of Rome.

Book IV.

Subsequent Missions in Southern India, with special reference to the Syrians.
Radiation of Mission of Goa.
The Madura Mission.
Portuguese Missions in the Carnatic.
Syrian Christians in the Seventeenth Century.
Syrian Christians in the Eighteenth Century.

Book V.

The Portuguese Missions, with special reference to Modern Missionary efforts in South India.
The First Protestant Mission in South India.
English Missions to the Syrians 1806-16.
English Missions and the Syrian Christians.
The Disruption and its Results.
Present State of the Syrian Christians.
The Revival of the Romish Missions in India.

C. L. EASTLAKE.

Notes on the Principal Pictures in the Royal Gallery at Venice. Crown 8vo, 3s. 6d.

VERY REV. FREDERICK W. FARRAR, D.D., F.R.S.
(Archdeacon of Westminster).

Words of Truth and Wisdom, by Very Rev. Frederick W. Farrar, D.D., F.R.S. Crown 8vo, gilt top, 5s.

CONTENTS.

Christian Statesmanship.
Legislative Duties.
The Use of Gifts and Opportunities.
The Brotherhood of Man.
Energy of Christian Service.
Christianity and the Human Race.
Christianity and Individual.
The Victories of Christianity.
The Christian Remedy against the Frailties of Life.
Prayer, the Antidote of Sorrow.
The Conquest over Temptation.
Too Late.
The Souls of the Departed.
What Heaven is.
No Discharge in the War against Sin.
The Dead which die in the Lord.
The Resurrection of the Dead.
The Blighted Life.
Wisdom and Knowledge.
The Voice of History.
The Monks.
The Early Franciscans.
The Hermits.
The Missionaries.
The Martyrs.
Seneca.
Seneca and St Paul.
Gallio and St Paul.
Roman Society in the days of St Paul.
Sanskrit.
Greek and Hebrew.
Aryan Migrations.
Words.

"In theological views he might be described as standing between the Evangelical party and the Broad Church; but his knowledge, coloured by a poetic temperament, his superabundant fertility, and eloquent luxuriance of style, have gained for him a unique position in the theological thought of the last twenty years."—*Celebrities of the Century.*

GENERAL GORDON, C.B.

Events in the Taeping Rebellion, being Reprints of MSS. copied by General Gordon, C.B., in his own handwriting; with Monograph, Introduction, and Notes, by A. Egmont Hake, Author of "The Story of Chinese Gordon." With Portrait and Map, demy 8vo, 18s.

"The publication of this volume completes what may be called the personal narrative of General Gordon's eventful life told in his own words."—*Manchester Guardian.*

"There is no doubt that a wide circle of readers will like to read the story in the very words of the gallant leader of the 'Ever Victorious Army.'"—*Daily Graphic.*

A handy book of reference.

Companion to the Writing Desk; or, How to Address, Begin, and End Letters to Titled and Official Personages. Together with a Table of Precedence, copious List of Abbreviations, Rules for Composition and Punctuation, Instructions on Preparing for the Press, &c. 32mo, 1s.

A useful manual which should be in every office.

BARON CUVIER.

The Animal Kingdom, with considerable Additions by W. B. Carpenter, M.D., F.R.S., and J. O. Westwood, F.L.S. New Edition, Illustrated with 500 Engravings on Wood and **36 Coloured Plates,** imp. 8vo, 21s.

M. GRIFFITH.

India's Princes, short Life Sketches of the Native Rulers of India, with 47 full-page Illustrations. Demy 4to, gilt top, 21s.

The contents are arranged in the following order:—THE PUNJAUB—H.H. The Maharaja of Cashmere, H.H. The Maharaja of Patiala, H.H. The Maharaja of Kapurthalla. RAJPUTANA—The Maharaja of Ouidpur, The Maharaja of Jeypore, The Maharaja of Jodhpur, The Maharaja of Uwar, The Maharaja of Bhurtpur. CENTRAL INDIA —H.H. The Maharaja Holkar of Indore, H.H. The Maharaja Scindia of Gwalior, H.H. The Begum of Bhopal. THE BOMBAY PRESIDENCY—H.H. The Gaikwar of Baroda, H.H. The Rao of Cutch, H.H. The Raja of Kolhapur, H.H. The Nawab of Juarrghad, H H. The Thakore Sahib of Bhavnagar, H.H. The Thakore Sahib of Dhangadra, H.H. The Thakore Sahib of Morvi, H.H. The Thakore Sahib of Gondal. SOUTHERN INDIA—H.H. The Nizam of Hyderabad, H.H. The Maharaja of Mysore, H.H. The Maharaja of Travancore, &c.

"A handsome volume, containing a series of photographic portraits and local views with accompanying letterpress, giving biographical and political details, carefully compiled and attractively presented."—*Times.*

GEORGE GRESSWELL.

The Diseases and Disorders of the Ox. Second Edition, demy 8vo, 7s. 6d.

"This is perhaps one of the best of the popular books on the subject which has been published in recent years, and demonstrates in a most unmistakable manner the great advance that has been made in Bovine and Ovine Pathology since the days of Youatt. . . . To medical men who desire to know something of the disorders of such an important animal—speaking hygienically—as the Ox, the work can be recommended."—*The Lancet.*

C. HAMILTON.

Hedaya or Guide, a Commentary on the Mussulman Laws. Second Edition, with Preface and Index by S. G. Grady, 8vo, 35s.

The great Law-Book of India, and one of the most important monuments of Mussulman legislation in existence.

"A work of very high authority in all Moslem countries. It discusses most of the subjects mentioned in the Koran and Sonna."—MILL's Mohammedanism.

"A valuable work."—ALLIBONE.

JOSEPH HAYDN.

Book of Dignities, containing lists of the Official Personages of the British Empire, Civil, Diplomatic, Heraldic, Judicial, Ecclesiastical, Municipal, Naval, and Military, from the Earliest Periods to the Present Time, together with the Sovereigns and Rulers of the World from the Foundation of their respective States; the Orders of Knighthood of the United Kingdom and India, and numerous other lists. Founded on Beatson's "Political Index" (1806). **Remodelled and brought down to 1851 by the late Joseph Haydn. Continued to the Present Time, with numerous additional lists, and an Index to the entire Work, by Horace Ockerby, Solicitor of the Supreme Court.** Demy 8vo, 25s.

"The most complete official directory in existence, containing about 1,300 different lists."—*Times.*

"The value of such a book can hardly be overrated."—*Saturday Review.*

"A perfect monument of patient labour and research, and invaluable for many purposes of reference."—*Truth.*

"This valuable work has cost its editor, Mr Horace Ockerby, a great deal of labour, and does infinite credit to his research and industry."—*World.*

Rev. H. R. HAWEIS, M.A., Author of "Music and Morals."

Sir Morell Mackenzie, Physician and Operator, a Memoir, compiled and edited from Private Papers and Personal Reminiscences. New Edition, with Portrait and copy of Autograph Letter from the Queen, crown 8vo, 3s. 6d.

CONTENTS.

Family Tree.	Private Practice.	The Respite.
Surroundings.	Leisure Hours.	The Last Voyage.
Boyhood.	The Emperor.	Last Glimpses.
A Vocation.	The German Doctors.	The End.
The Throat Hospital.	The Book.	

"Mr Haweis writes not only fearlessly, but with remarkable freshness and vigour. He is occasionally eloquent, and even pathetic. In all that he says we perceive a transparent honesty and singleness of purpose."—*Saturday Review.*

"A deeply interesting book, and one which challenges in a most striking and fearless manner the stern verdict which Sir Morell's own profession so generally passed upon his conduct before and after the death of his illustrious patient the Emperor. . . The volume is full of absolutely interesting details, many among them new."—*Daily Telegraph.*

HOWARD HENSMAN, Special Correspondent of the "Pioneer" (Allahabad) and the "Daily News" (London).

The Afghan War, 1879-80. Being a complete Narrative of the Capture of Cabul, the Siege of Sherpur, the Battle of Ahmed Khel, the March to Candahar, and the defeat of Ayub Khan. With Maps, demy 8vo, 21s.

"Sir Frederick Roberts says of the letters here published in a collected form that 'nothing could be more accurate or graphic.' As to accuracy no one can be a more competent judge than Sir Frederick, and his testimony stamps the book before us as constituting especially trustworthy material for history. Of much that he relates Mr Hensman was an eye-witness; of the rest he was informed by eye-witnesses immediately after the occurrence of the events recorded. There could, therefore, be little doubt as to the facts mentioned. Credibility might be concurrent with incorrect deductions, but we are assured by Sir Frederick Roberts that Mr Hensman's accuracy is complete in all respects. Mr Hensman enjoyed singular advantages during the first part of the war, for he was the only special correspondent who accompanied the force which marched out of Ali Kheyl in September 1879. One of the most interesting portions of the book is that which describes the march of Sir Frederick Roberts from Cabul to Candahar. The description of the Maiwand disaster is given with combined clearness, simplicity, and power, and will be read with the utmost interest. Indeed, the book is in every respect interesting and well written, and reflects the greatest credit on the author."—*Athenæum.*

SIR JOHN F. W. HERSCHEL, Bart., K.H., &c., Member of the Institute of France, &c.

Popular Lectures on Scientific Subjects. New Edition, crown 8vo, 6s.

"We are reminded of the rapid progress made by science within the last quarter of a century by the publication of a new edition of Sir John Herschel's *Popular Lectures on Scientific Subjects.* In 1861, spectrum analysis, as applied to the heavenly bodies, was referred to as a possibility; now it is not only an accomplished fact, but the analysis of the gases contained in the sun has led to the discovery of one of them, helium, upon the earth. Some of the lectures, such as that on light, are practically popular treatises on the particular subject to which they refer, and can be read with advantage even by advanced students."—*The Westminster Review.*

REV. T. P. HUGHES.

Dictionary of Islam. Being a Cyclopædia of the Doctrines, Rites, Ceremonies, and Customs, together with the Technical and Theological Terms of the Muhammadan Religion. With numerous Illustrations, royal 8vo, £2. 2s.

"Such a work as this has long been needed, and it would be hard to find any one better qualified to prepare it than Mr Hughes. His 'Notes on Muhammadanism,' of which two editions have appeared, have proved decidedly useful to students of Islam, especially in India, and his long familiarity with the tenets and customs of Moslems has placed him in the best possible position for deciding what is necessary and what superfluous in a 'Dictionary of Islam.' His usual method is to begin an article with the text in the Koran relating to the subject, then to add the traditions bearing upon it, and to conclude with the comments of the Mohammedan scholiasts and the criticisms of Western scholars. Such a method, while involving an infinity of labour, produces the best results in point of accuracy and comprehensiveness. The difficult task of compiling a dictionary of so vast a subject as Islam, with its many sects, its saints, khalifs, ascetics, and dervishes, its festivals, ritual, and sacred places, the dress, manners, and customs of its professors, its commentators, technical terms, science of tradition and interpretation, its superstitions, magic, and astrology, its theoretical doctrines and actual practices, has been accomplished with singular success; and the dictionary will have its place among the standard works of reference in every library that professes to take account of the religion which governs the lives of forty millions of the Queen's subjects. The articles on 'Marriage,' 'Women,' 'Wives,' 'Slavery,' 'Tradition,' 'Sufi,' 'Muhammad,' 'Da'wah' or Incantation, 'Burial,' and 'God,' are especially admirable. Two articles deserve special notice. One is an elaborate account of Arabic 'Writing' by Dr Steingass, which contains a vast quantity of useful matter, and is well illustrated by woodcuts of the chief varieties of Arabic script. The other article to which we refer with special emphasis is Mr F. Pincott on 'Sikhism.' There is something on nearly every page of the dictionary that will interest and instruct the students of Eastern religion, manners, and customs."—*Athenæum.*

Dictionary of Muhammadan Theology.

Notes on Muhammadanism, by Rev. T. P. Hughes. Third Edition, revised and enlarged. Fcap. 8vo, 6s.

"Altogether an admirable little book. It combines two excellent qualities, abundance of facts and lack of theories. . . . On every one of the numerous heads (over fifty) into which the book is divided, Mr Hughes furnishes a large amount of very valuable information, which it would be exceedingly difficult to collect from even a large library of works on the subject. The book might well be called a 'Dictionary of Muhammadan Theology,' for we know of no English work which combines a methodical arrangement (and consequently facility of reference) with fulness of information in so high a degree as the little volume before us."—*The Academy.*

"It contains *multum in parvo*, and is about the best outlines of the tenets of the Muslim faith which we have seen. It has, moreover, the rare merit of being accurate; and, although it contains a few passages which we would gladly see expunged, it cannot fail to be useful to all Government employés who have to deal with Muhammadans; whilst to missionaries it will be invaluable."—*The Times of India.*

"It is manifest throughout the work that we have before us the opinions of one thoroughly conversant with the subject, and who is uttering no random notions. . . . We strongly recommend 'Notes on Muhammadanism.' Our clergy especially, even though they are not missionaries, and have no intention of labouring amongst Muhammadans, or consorting with them, ought to have at least as much knowledge of the system as can be most readily acquired, with a very little careful study, from this useful treatise."—*The Record.*

SIR W. HUNTER.

Bengal MS. Records. A Selected List of Letters in the Board of Revenue, Calcutta, 1782-1807, with an Historical Dissertation and Analytical Index. 4 vols., demy 8vo, 30s.

A Statistical Account of Bengal. 20 vols., demy 8vo, £6.

J. HUNTER, late Hon. Sec. of the British Bee-keepers' Association.

A Manual of Bee-keeping. Containing Practical Information for Rational and Profitable Methods of Bee Management. Full Instructions on Stimulative Feeding, Ligurianising and Queen-raising, with descriptions of the American Comb Foundation, Sectional Supers, and the best Hives and Apiarian Appliances on all Systems. Fourth Edition, with Illustrations, crown 8vo, 3s. 6d.

"We are indebted to Mr J. Hunter, Honorary Secretary of the British Bee-keepers' Association. His Manual of Bee-keeping, just published, is full to the very brim of choice and practical hints fully up to the most advanced stages of Apiarian Science, and its perusal has afforded us so much pleasure that we have drawn somewhat largely from it for the benefit of our readers."—*Bee-keepers' Magazine (New York).*

"It is profusely illustrated with engravings, which are almost always inserted for their utility. . . . There is an old saying that 'easy writing is hard reading,' but we will not say thus much of Mr Hunter's book, which, taken as a whole, is perhaps the most generally useful of any now published in this country."—*The Field.*

MAJOR LEIGH HUNT, Madras Army, and ALEX. S. KENNY, M.R.C.S.E., A.K.C., Senior Demonstrator of Anatomy at King's College, London.

On Duty under a Tropical Sun. Being some Practical Suggestions for the Maintenance of Health and Bodily Comfort, and the Treatment of Simple Diseases; with remarks on Clothing and Equipment. Second Edition, crown 8vo, 4s.

"This little book is devoted to the description and treatment of many tropical diseases and minor emergencies, supplemented by some useful hints on diet, clothing, and equipment for travellers in tropical climates. The issue of a third edition proves that the book has hitherto been successful. On the whole we can commend the hints which have been given for the treatment of various diseases, but in some places much has been left to the knowledge of the reader in the selection and application of a remedy."—*Scottish Geographical Magazine.*

"Is written more especially for the rougher sex, and is only less important than Tropical Trials' because it has had many more predecessors. It is now in a third edition, and contains practical suggestions for the maintenance of health and bodily comfort, as well as the treatment of simple diseases, with useful remarks on clothing and equipment for the guidance of travellers abroad."—*Daily Telegraph.*

Tropical Trials. A Handbook for Women in the Tropics. Crown 8vo, 7s. 6d.

"Is a valuable handbook for women in the East, and, we are glad to see, now in its second edition. It does not treat theoretically of the maladies incidental to Europeans in hot climates, or go deeply into those matters which properly belong to the experienced doctor, but it gives plain, wholesome advice on matters of health, which, were it scrupulously followed, it is not too much to say would add fifty per cent. to the enjoyment of our countrywomen abroad. She could scarcely have a better guide as to what to do and what not to do than this excellent handbook, which deserves to be included in every woman's foreign outfit."—*Daily Telegraph.*

JOHN H. INGRAM.

The Haunted Homes and Family Traditions of Great Britain. Illustrated. Crown 8vo, 7s. 6d.

Epitomised in One Volume by R. O'BYRNE, F.R.G.S., &c.

James' Naval History. A Narrative of the Naval Battles, Single Ship Actions, Notable Sieges, and Dashing Cutting-out Expeditions, fought in the days of Howe, Hood, Duncan, St Vincent, Bridport, Nelson, Camperdown, Exmouth, Duckworth, and Sir Sydney Smith. Crown 8vo, 5s.

MRS GRACE JOHNSON, Silver Medallist Cookery, Exhibition.

Anglo-Indian and Oriental Cookery. Crown 8vo, 3s. 6d.

"Overflows with all sorts of delicious and economical recipes."—*Pall Mall Budget.*

"Housewives and professors of the gentle art of cookery who deplore the dearth of dainty dishes will find a veritable gold mine in Mrs Johnson's book."—*Pall Mall Gazette.*

Appeals to us from a totally original standpoint. She has thoroughly and completely investigated native and Anglo-Indian cuisines, and brought away the very best specimens of their art. Her pillau and kedgree are perfect, in our opinion; curries are scientifically classed and explained, and some of the daintiest recipes we have ever seen are given, but the puddings particularly struck our fancy. Puddings as a rule are *so* nasty! The pudding that is nourishing is hideously insipid, and of the smart pudding it may truly be said that its warp is dyspepsia, and its woof indigestion. Mrs Johnson's puddings are both good to taste and pretty to look at, and the names of some of her native dishes would brighten any menu.

H. G. KEENE, C.I.E., B.C.S., M.R.A.S., &c.

History of India. From the Earliest Times to the Present Day. For the use of Students and Colleges. 2 vols, with Maps. Crown 8vo, 16s.

"The main merit of Mr Keene's performance lies in the fact that he has assimilated all the authorities, and has been careful to bring his book down to date. He has been careful in research, and has availed himself of the most recent materials. He is well known as the author of other works on Indian history, and his capacity for his self-imposed task will not be questioned. We must content ourselves with this brief testimony to the labour and skill bestowed by him upon a subject of vast interest and importance. Excellent proportion is preserved in dealing with the various episodes, and the style is clear and graphic. The volumes are supplied with many useful maps, and the appendix include notes on Indian law and on recent books about India."—*Globe.*

"Mr Keene has the admirable element of fairness in dealing with the succession of great questions that pass over his pages, and he wisely devotes a full half of his work to the present century. The appearance of such a book, and of every such book, upon India is to be hailed at present. A fair-minded presentment of Indian history like that contained in Mr Keene's two volumes is at this moment peculiarly welcome."—*Times.*

An Oriental Biographical Dictionary. Founded on Materials collected by the late Thomas William Beale. New Edition, revised and enlarged, royal 8vo, 28s.

"A complete biographical dictionary for a country like India, which in its long history has produced a profusion of great men, would be a vast undertaking. The suggestion here made only indicates the line on which the dictionary, at some future time, could be almost indefinitely extended, and rendered still more valuable as a work of reference. Great care has evidently been taken to secure the accuracy of all that has been included in the work, and that is of far more importance than mere bulk. The dictionary can be commended as trustworthy, and reflects much credit on Mr Keene. Several interesting lists of rulers are given under the various founders of dynasties."—*India.*

The Fall of the Moghul Empire. From the Death of Aurungzeb to the Overthrow of the Mahratta Power. A New Edition, with Corrections and Additions, with Map, crown 8vo, 7s. 6d.

This work fills up a blank between the ending of Elphinstone's and the commencement of Thornton's Histories.

Fifty-Seven. Some Account of the Administration of Indian Districts during the Revolt of the Bengal Army. Demy 8vo, 6s.

DR TALBOTT, and others.

Keble College Sermons. Second Series, 1877-1888, crown 8vo, 6s.

"To those who desire earnest, practical, and orthodox doctrine in the form of short addresses, these sermons will be most acceptable; and their lofty tone, their eloquent wording, and the thorough manliness of their character, will commend them to a wide circle of readers."—*Morning Post.*

"Dr Talbot has a second time thoughtfully placed on public record some of the lessons which were taught during his Wardenship in *Sermons preached in the Chapel of Keble College, Oxford*, 1877-1888. The sermons are fresh and vigorous in tone, and evidently come from preachers who were thoroughly in touch with their youthful audience, and who generally with much acuteness and skill grappled with the spiritual and intellectual difficulties besetting nowadays the University career."—*Church Times.*

G. H. KINAHAN.

A Handy Book of Rock Names. Fcap. 8vo, 4s.

"This will prove, we do not doubt, a very useful little book to all practical geologists, and also to the reading student of rocks. When a difficulty is incurred as to a species of deposit, it will soon vanish. Mr Kinahan's little book will soon make it all clear. The work is divided into three parts. The first is a classified table of rocks, the second part treats of the *Ingenite* rocks, and the third part deals with those rocks which are styled *Derivate.* Dana's termination of *yte* has been most generally used by the author, but he has also given the *ite* terminations for those that like them. The book will be purchased, for it must be had, by every geologist; and as its size is small, it will form a convenient pocket companion for the man who works over field and quarry."—*Popular Science Review.*

REV. F. G. LEE, D.D. (Vicar of All Saints', Lambeth).

The Church under Queen Elizabeth. An Historical Sketch. By Rev. F. G. Lee, D.D. (Vicar of All Saints', Lambeth). Second Edition. Crown 8vo, 7s. 6d.

"There is the same picturesqueness of detail, the same vigorous denunciation, the same graphic power, which made the earlier book pleasant reading even to many who disagree heartily with its tone and object. . . Dr Lee's strength lies in very graphic description."—*Notes and Queries.*

"This is, in many ways, a remarkably fine book. That it is powerfully written no one acquainted with Dr Lee's vigorous style would for a moment dispute."—*Morning Post.*

"Presenting a painful picture of the degradation into which the Church had sunk in Elizabeth's reign."—*Daily Telegraph.*

Sights and Shadows. Being Examples of the Supernatural. New Edition. With a Preface addressed to the Critics. Crown 8vo, 6s.

"This work will be especially interesting to students of the supernatural, and their name is legion at the present moment. It deals with more than one branch of what is commonly known as spiritualism. The introduction gives a brief resumé of various forms of magic and divination which have obtained credence in all ages, and later on we find well-authenticated accounts of apparitions, supernatural warnings, hypnotic experiments, and miracles of healing. Mr Lee evidently believes that 'there are more things in heaven and earth than are dreamt of in our philosophy,' and few sane people will disagree with him, though they may not be inclined to accept all his opinions and assertions as they stand."—*Lady.*

"Here we have ghostly stories galore, which believers in supernatural visitations will welcome as upholders of the faith that is in them. Dr Lee is a hard hitter and a vigorous controversialist, with a righteous contempt for your Darwins and Stuart Mills, and such like folk, and is not above suggesting that some of them have a decided worship of the god Self. As for 'the pompous jargon and silly cynicism which so many public scribes again and again make use of to throw discredit upon any phase of the supernatural,' I have nothing to say. They can take care of themselves. This much I know, that 'Sights and Shadows' gives one an eerie feeling as midnight approaches and the fire flickers on the hearth."—*Gentlewoman.*

COL. G. B. MALLESON.

History of the French in India. From the Founding of Pondicherry in 1674, to the Capture of that place in 1761. New and Revised Edition, with Maps. Demy 8vo, 16s.

"Colonel Malleson has produced a volume alike attractive to the general reader and valuable for its new matter to the special student. It is not too much to say that now, for the first time, we are furnished with a faithful narrative of that portion of European enterprise in India which turns upon the contest waged by the East India Company against French influence, and especially against Dupleix."—*Edinburgh Review.*

"It is pleasant to contrast the work now before us with the writer's first bold plunge into historical composition, which splashed every one within his reach. He swims now with a steady stroke, and there is no fear of his sinking. With a keener insight into human character, and a larger understanding of the sources of human action, he combines all the power of animated recital which invested his earlier narratives with popularity."—*Fortnightly Review.*

"The author has had the advantage of consulting the French archives, and his volume forms a useful supplement to Orme."—*Athenæum.*

Final French Struggles in India and on the Indian Seas. New Edition. Crown 8vo, 6s.

"How India escaped from the government of prefects and sub-prefects to fall under that of commissioners and deputy-commissioners; why the Penal Code of Lord Macaulay reigns supreme instead of a Code Napoleon; why we are not looking on helplessly from Mahe, Karikal, and Pondicherry, while the French are ruling all over Madras, and spending millions of francs in attempting to cultivate the slopes of the Neilgherries, may be learnt from this modest volume. Colonel Malleson is always painstaking, and generally accurate; his style is transparent, and he never loses sight of the purpose with which he commenced to write."—*Saturday Review.*

"A book dealing with such a period of our history in the East, besides being interesting, contains many lessons. It is written in a style that will be popular with general readers."—*Athenæum.*

"It strikes one as the best thing he has yet done. Searching, yet easy, his pen goes with unflagging power through the military wonders of a hundred years, connecting the accounts of battles by a sufficient historic thread."—*Academy.*

History of Afghanistan, from the Earliest Period to the Outbreak of the War of 1878, with map, demy 8vo, 18s.

"The name of Colonel Malleson on the title-page of any historical work in relation to India or the neighbouring States is a satisfactory guarantee both for the accuracy of the facts and the brilliancy of the narrative. The author may be complimented upon having written a History of Afghanistan which is likely to become a work of standard authority."—*Scotsman.*

The Battle-Fields of Germany, from the Outbreak of the Thirty Years' War to the Battle of Blenheim, with maps and one plan, demy 8vo, 16s.

"Colonel Malleson has shown a grasp of his subject, and a power of vivifying the confused passages of battle, in which it would be impossible to name any living writer as his equal. In imbuing these almost forgotten battle-fields with fresh interest and reality for the English reader, he is re-opening one of the most important chapters of European History, which no previous English writer has made so interesting and instructive as he has succeeded in doing in this volume."—*Academy.*

Ambushes and Surprises, being a Description of some of the most famous instances of the Leading into Ambush and the Surprises of Armies, from the time of Hannibal to the period of the Indian Mutiny, with a portrait of General Lord Mark Ker, K.C.B., demy 8vo, 18s.

JAMES IRVIN LUPTON, F.R.C.V.S., author of "The External Anatomy of the Horse," &c.

The Horse: as he Was, as he Is, and as he Ought to Be, with Illustrations. Crown 8vo, 3s. 6d.

"Written with a good object in view, namely, to create an interest in the important subject of horse-breeding, more especially that class known as general utility horses. The book contains several illustrations, is well printed and handsomely bound, and we hope will meet with the attention it deserves."—*Live Stock Journal.*

T. MILLER MAGUIRE, M.A., LL.D.

American War—Campaigns in Virginia, 1861-2, with Maps. Royal 8vo, paper covers, 3s. 6d.

MRS MANNING.

Ancient and Mediæval India. Being the History, Religion, Laws, Caste, Manners and Customs, Language, Literature, Poetry, Philosophy, Astronomy, Algebra, Medicine, Architecture, Manufactures, Commerce, &c., of the Hindus, taken from their Writings. With Illustrations. 2 vols., demy 8vo, 30s.

IRVING MONTAGU (late Special War Correspondent "Illustrated London News").

Camp and Studio. Illustrated by the Author. New Edition. Crown 8vo, 6s.

"His animated pages and sketches have a more than ephemeral interest, and present a moving picture of the romance and the misery of countries and populations ravaged by great opposing armies, and many a picturesque episode of personal experiences; he is pleasant and amusing enough."—*Daily News.*

"Mr Irving Montagu's narrative of his experiences as war artist of the *Illustrated London News* during the Russo-Turkish war, though late in appearing, may be read with interest. War correspondents and artists usually enjoy a fair share of adventure; but Mr Montagu appears to have revelled in dangers which seem anything but desirable when studied in cold blood. Mr Montagu has much that is interesting to tell about the horrors of the siege of Kars and the prowess of the fair young Amazon who commanded a troop of Bashi-Bazuks, and even seduced a Russian general to her side. How he got to the front in spite of Russian prohibition, disguised as a camp follower, how his portmanteau was shelled a few inches behind his back, what he risked and what he saw in the memorable lines before Plevna, will be read with great interest. The book is well illustrated by many vigorous sketches, some of which are exceedingly humorous."—*Athenæum.*

"A bright chatty record of wars, scenes, and adventures in various parts of the world."—*Echo.*

Wanderings of a War Artist. Illustrated by the Author. New Edition. Crown 8vo, 6s.

"Mr Montagu is to be congratulated on an eminently readable book, which, both in style and matter, is above the average of productions in this kind."—*The Morning Post.*

"This is an enchanting book. Equally as writer and as artist, Mr Irving Montagu is a delightful companion. This beautiful and exceptionally interesting volume does not by any means exhaust the literary and artistic achievements of the well-known 'special' of the *Illustrated London News.*"—*The Daily News.*

"His own adventures are largely seasoned with stories of other people and anecdotes he picks up. He went through the second siege of Paris under the Commune, and some of the best reading in the book is the picture he gives of the state of poor, beautiful Paris, seen by the eye of an observing, impartial man, who has no object in either exaggerating or under-colouring the work of the Commune."—*The Spectator.*

"The adventures of Mr Montagu are narrated with humour, and are seldom dull reading."—*Glasgow Herald.*

J. MORRIS, Author of "The War in Korea," &c., thirteen years resident in Tokio under the Japanese Board of Works.

Advance Japan. A Nation Thoroughly in Earnest. With over 100 Illustrations by R. Isayama, and of photographs lent by the Japanese Legation. 8vo, 12s. 6d.

"Mr Morris evidently knows the country well, and is a strong believer in its future; his book will be found a useful summary of recent history, abounding in good character sketches, accompanied with photographs, of the leading men."—*Times.*

"Is really a remarkably complete account of the land, the people, and the institutions of Japan, with chapters that deal with matters of such living interest as its growing industries and armaments, and the origin, incidents, and probable outcome of the war with China. The volume is illustrated by a Japanese artist of repute; it has a number of useful statistical appendices, and it is dedicated to His Majesty the Mikado."—*Scotsman.*

"Mr Morris, who writes, of course, with thorough local knowledge, gives a very complete and eminently readable account of the country, its government, people, and resource. . . The work, which contains a large number of portraits and other illustrations, is decidedly 'on the nail,' and may be recommended not only as a book to read, but as of value for reference."—*Westminster Gazette.*

"Puts before us a clear view of the point which has been reached. His work is historical, social, and descriptive; we see in it the Japanese of to-day as he really is. Mr Morris has also something to say on the Japanese at home—how he eats, how he dresses, and how he comports himself; while wider issues are discussed in the chapters treating of the administration of the islands, their ports, communications, trades, and armaments."—*Globe.*

"A well-proportioned sketch of the Japanese of to-day, so recent as to include the results of the war. . . There is much else I should like to quote in this able and interesting book. It has a good chapter on natural history, and an excellent chapter on diet, dress, and manners; it gives just enough of Japanese history to help the ordinary reader who wants to learn his Japan on easy terms; it has also most useful and attractively conveyed information in its brief account of the principal cities of Japan, communications and armament, language and literature, mines and minerals."—*Queen.*

"He summarises clearly, concisely, the existing knowledge on the Japanese Parliamentary system, territorial and administrative divisions, natural history, domestic and national customs, dynastic changes, old feudal institutions, town populations, industries, mineral and other natural resources, railways, armaments, the press, and other subjects too many for enumeration. Even the chapter on language and literature makes an appalling subject interesting. . . . Mr Morris has brought his very useful account of Japan up-to-date. He gives a good summary of the recent war with China, and then proceeds to make some well-considered suggestions on a matter of supreme importance to Europe no less than to the two Empires of the Far East."

CHARLES MARVIN.

The Region of the Eternal Fire. An Account of a Journey to the Caspian Region in 1883. New Edition. With Maps and Illustrations. Crown 8vo, handsomely bound, 6s.

"The leading authority of the English Press on the Central Asian Question is Charles Marvin, a man of iron industry, who has wielded his comprehensive knowledge of the region in such a manner as to render eminent service to his country."—*Opinion of Arminius Vambery.*

"Charles Marvin's services in respect of the Russo-Afghan Question have been invaluable. He has heard with his own ears the opinions expressed on the subject by Russian generals and diplomatists, and, for the love of England, has spent his own money to warn England's people."—*Opinion of Colonel Malleson, "The Russo-Afghan Question," p. 55.*

W. O'CONNOR MORRIS.

Great Commanders of Modern Times, and the Campaign of 1815. Turenne—Marlborough—Frederick the Great—Napoleon—Wellington—Moltke. With Illustrations and Plans. Royal 8vo, 21s.

"Mr Morris certainly brings to his task vast reading and exhaustive research."—*Athenæum.*

"We gladly welcome this handsome volume by Judge O'Connor Morris, which gives evidence on every page of careful reading and correct judgment. . . . An admirable book to place in the hands of any student who wishes to get some idea of the history of the art of war."—*Academy.*

"To the students of war this book will prove of the utmost interest and the greatest possible service."—*National Observer.*

"Writes vividly and well."—*Times.*

CARDINAL NEWMAN.

Miscellanies from the Oxford Sermons of John Henry Newman, D.D. Crown 8vo, gilt top, 5s.

"All the resources of a master of English style—except, perhaps one, description—were at his command; pure diction, clear arrangement, irony, dignity, a copious command of words, combined with a reserve in the use of them—all these qualities went to make up the charm of Newman's style, the finest flower that the earlier system of a purely classical education has produced."—*Athenæum.*

"The pieces presented to us here are carefully chosen, and answer the purpose of the present volume. The selections which are contained in it happily avoid any of these passages which have been the grounds of controversy. As a general rule we are able to take in the teachings of this book without any *arrière-pensée*, without any feeling that we have here the germ of those theories which estrange their author from us."—*Athenæum.*

COL. F. A. WHINYATES, late R.H.A., formerly commanding the Battery.

Military Regiments—From Corunna to Sevastopol, the History of "C" Battery, "A" Brigade, late "C" Troop, Royal Horse Artillery, with succession of Officers from its formation to the present time. With 3 Maps, demy 8vo, 14s.

EDWARD NEWMAN, F.Z.S.

British Butterflies. With many Illustrations. Super royal 8vo, 7s. 6d.

DEPUTY SURGEON-GENERAL C. T. PASKE, late of the Bengal Army, and Edited by F. G. AFLALO.

Life and Travel in Lower Burmah, with Frontispiece. Crown 8vo, 6s.

"In dealing with life in Burmah we are given a pleasant insight into Eastern life; and to those interested in India and our other Eastern possessions, the opinions Mr Paske offers and the suggestions he makes will be delightful reading. Mr Paske has adopted a very light style of writing in 'Myamma,' which lends an additional charm to the short historical-cum-geographical sketch, and both the writer and the editor are to be commended for the production of a really attractive book."—*Public Opinion.*

Translation of the famous Passion Play.

Passion Play at Oberammergau, The, with the whole Drama translated into English, and the Songs of the Chorus in German and English; also a Map of the Town, Plan of the Theatre, &c. 4to, cloth, 3s. 6d.; paper, 2s. 6d.

"The author of 'Charles Lowder' has done a real service in publishing a translation of 'The Passion Play at Oberammergau,' with a description of the play and short account of a visit there in 1880. To those who have already seen it, this little book will recall vividly the experience of what must be to all a memorable day, while to those who are going in 1890 it is simply invaluable."—*Guardian.*

MARY A. PRATTEN.

My Hundred Swiss Flowers, with a short account of Swiss Ferns. With 60 Illustrations. Crown 8vo, plain plates, 12s. 6d.; *with plates coloured by hand*, 25s.

"The temptation to produce such books as this seems irresistible. The author feels a want; the want is undeniable. After more or less hesitation he feels he can supply it. It is pleasantly written, and affords useful hints as to localities."—*Athenæum.*

R. A. PROCTOR.

Watched by the Dead, a loving study of Dickens' half-told tale. Crown 8vo, cloth, 1s. 6d.; boards, 1s.

"Mr Proctor here devotes much study and much ingenious conjecture to restoring the plot of 'The Mystery of Edwin Drood.' It would not be fair were we to attempt to give in a small compass the result of his labours. It must suffice to say that those who have occupied themselves with this curious problem will be interested in the solution here offered for their acceptance."—*Spectator.*

WILLIAM PROCTOR, Stud Groom.

The Management and Treatment of the Horse in the Stable, Field, and on the Road. Second Edition, Revised and Enlarged, Illustrated. Crown 8vo, 6s.

"There are few who are interested in horses will fail to profit by one portion or another of this useful work."—*Sportsman.*

"We cannot do better than wish that Mr Proctor's book may find its way into the hands of all those concerned in the management of the most useful quadruped we possess."—*England.*

"There is a fund of sound common-sense views in this work which will be interesting to many owners."—*Field.*

"Coming from a practical hand the work should recommend itself to the public."—*Sportsman.*

WILLIAM RAEBURN ANDREW.

Raeburn (Sir Henry, R.A.), Life by his Great-Grandson, William Raeburn Andrew, with an Appendix comprising a list of his works exhibited in the Royal Academy, Edinburgh. 8vo, 10s. 6d.

"Mr Andrew's book, which on this occasion appeals to a wider public, makes no pretence to do more than to bring together the biographical fragments concerning Raeburn gathered out of various publications and to 'make them coherent with a little cement of his own.' Possibly a fuller and more original biography of the greatest of our portrait-painters, who was at the same time one of the greatest ornaments of the Edinburgh Society of the beginning of the century, may yet see the light; and in the meantime we can be grateful to Mr Andrew for bringing together and arranging so rich a store of topographical and personal details connected with his illustrious ancestor. In an appendix is a useful annotated catalogue of the 1876 exhibition of Raeburn's works."—*Scotsman.*

R. RIMMER, F.L.S.

The Land and Freshwater Shells of the British Isles. Illustrated with 10 Photographs and 3 Lithographs, containing figures of all the principal Species. Second Edition. Crown 8vo, 5s.

"This handsomely got up little volume supplies a long-felt want in a very ingenious and trustworthy manner. The author is an enthusiastic conchologist, and writes both attractively and well, and in a manner so simple and natural that we have no fear that any ordinarily educated man will easily understand every phrase. But the feature of this book which strikes us most is that every species of British land and freshwater shell has been photographed, and here we have all the photographs, natural size in the albertype process, so that the merest tyro will find no difficulty in identifying any shell he may find."—*Science Gossip.*

ALEXANDER ROGERS (Bombay Civil Service, Retired).

The Land Revenue of Bombay, a History of its Administration, Rise, and Progress, with 18 Maps. 2 vols., demy 8vo, 30s.

"Mr Rogers has produced a continuous and an authoritative record of the land changes and of the fortunes of the cultivating classes for a full half-century, together with valuable *data* regarding the condition and burdens of those classes at various periods before the present system of settlement was introduced. Mr Rogers now presents a comprehensive view of the land administration of Bombay as a whole, the history of its rise and progress, and a clear statement of the results which it has attained. It is a narrative of which all patriotic Englishmen may feel proud. The old burdens of native rule have been lightened, the old injustices mitigated, the old fiscal cruelties and exactions abolished. Underlying the story of each district we see a perennial struggle going on between the increase of the population and the available means of subsistence derived from the soil. That increase of the population is the direct result of the peace of the country under British rule. But it tends to press more and more severely on the possible limits of local cultivation, and it can only be provided for by the extension of the modern appliances of production and distribution. Mr Rogers very properly confines himself to his own subject. But there is ample evidence that the extension of roads, railways, steam factories, and other industrial enterprises, have played an important part in the solution of the problem, and that during recent years such enterprises have been powerfully aided by an abundant currency."—*The Times.*

ROBERT SEWELL.

Analytical History of India, from the earliest times to the Abolition of the East India Company in 1858. Post 8vo, 8s.

"Much careful labour has been expended on this volume."—*Athenæum.*

"The object of the author in compiling the following analytical sketch of Indian history has been to supply a want felt by most students of the more voluminous standard works of Mill, Elphinstone, Thornton, and Marshman, for a condensed outline in one small volume, which should serve at once to recall the memory and guide the eye. At the same time he has attempted to render it interesting to the general reader by preserving a medium between a bare analysis and a complete history; so that, without consulting the eminent authorities mentioned above, the mind may readily grasp the principal outlines of the early condition of India, and the rise and progress of the East India Company. For the more full comprehension of these facts the author has provided, in addition to a table of contents and a chronological index, an index to the geographical position of the places to which reference is made in the text, bearing the latitudes and longitude as given in Thornton's 'Gazetteer of India.' This will be found not only to aid the student who is but partially acquainted with the map of India, but also by means of occasional accents to guide him in the ordinary pronunciation of the names."—*Preface.*

G. P. SANDERSON.

Thirteen Years among the Wild Beasts of India; their Haunts and Habits, from Personal Observation, with an account of the Modes of Capturing and Taming Wild Elephants. With 21 full-page Illustrations, reproduced for this Edition direct from the original drawings, and 3 Maps. Fifth Edition. Fcap. 4to, 12s.

"We find it difficult to hasten through this interesting book; on almost every page some incident or some happy descriptive passage tempts the reader to linger. The author relates his exploits with ability and with singular modesty. His adventures with man-eaters will afford lively entertainment to the reader, and indeed there is no portion of the volume which he is likely to wish shorter. The illustrations add to the attractions of the book."—*Pall Mall Gazette.*

"This is the best and most practical book on the wild game of Southern and Eastern India that we have read, and displays an extensive acquaintance with natural history. To the traveller proposing to visit India, whether he be a sportsman, a naturalist, or an antiquarian, the book will be invaluable: full of incident and sparkling with anecdote."—*Bailey's Magazine.*

"This—the fifth edition of a work as charming to read as it is instructive—will be welcomed equally by lovers of sport, and of natural history. Though he met with and shot many other kinds of wild beasts, the bulk of the volume, well written, well illustrated, and generally well got up, deals chiefly with the elephant, the tiger, the bison, the leopard, and the bear. Mr Sanderson, with exceptional powers of observation, cultivated friendly intercourse with the natives; and he was consequently able to utilise to the utmost the singularly favourable opportunities enjoyed by him as director of elephant-capturing operations in Mysore and Chittagong. The result is a book which to graphic details of sporting adventures far surpassing the common, adds a correct natural history of the animals chiefly dealt with, and particularly the elephant. From this real king of beasts, Mr Sanderson carefully removes every exaggeration made both for or against him, which had been repeated without any good foundation by one writer after another; he substitutes for fables a description of elephantine anatomy, size, habits, and character which may be said to sum up all that we know for certain about the animal, and nearly all that one can wish to know. We should have wished to see this edition brought up to date. The book is more fascinating than a romance; and we have read it now the third time with as great a zest as when we revelled over the perusal of the first edition."—*Imperial and Asiatic Quarterly Review.*

PROFESSOR SHELDON.

The Future of British Agriculture, how Farmers may best be benefited. Crown 8vo, 2s. 6d.

"Fortunately Prof. Sheldon has no mind to play the part of a prophet, but from the plenitude of a long experience gives sage counsel how to farm abreast of the time and be ready for whatever may ensue. . . . This little book is well worth reading, and it is pleasant to find that the Professor by no means despairs of the future of agriculture in England."—*Academy.*

"We welcome the book as a valuable contribution to our agricultural literature, and as a useful guide to those branches in which the author is especially qualified to instruct."—*Nature.*

"In this beautifully printed and well-bound little book Professor Sheldon, in his usual happy style, surveys the agricultural field, and indicates what he thinks is the prospect in front of the British farmer. Like a watchman he stands upon his tower—and when asked, What of the night? he disavows not that we are in the night, but earnestly declares that the morning cometh apace. The professor is an optimist; he does not believe that the country is done, and still less does he favour the idea that, taking a wide survey, the former days were better than these. On the contrary, he urges that the way out of the wilderness is not by any by-path, but by going right ahead; and, ere long, the man who holds the banner high will emerge triumphant."—*Scottish Farmer.*

J. SMITH, A.L.S.

Ferns: British and Foreign. Fourth Edition, revised and greatly enlarged, with New Figures, &c. Crown 8vo, 7s. 6d.

G. BARNETT SMITH, Author of "History of the English Parliament."

Leaders of Modern Industry. Biographical Sketches.
Contents:—The Stephensons, Charles Knight, Sir George Burns, Sir Josiah Mason, The Wedgwoods, Thomas Brassey, The Fairbairns, Sir William Siemens, The Rennies. Crown 8vo, 7s. 6d.

"'Leaders of Modern Industry' is a volume of interesting biographical sketches of the pioneers of various phases of industry, comprising the Stephensons, Charles Knight, Sir George Burns, Sir Josiah Mason, the Wedgwoods, Thomas Brassey, the Fairbairns, Sir William Siemens, and the Rennies."—*World.*

Women of Renown. Nineteenth Century Studies.
Contents:—Frederika Bremer, Countess of Blessington, George Eliot, Jenny Lind, Mary Somerville, George Sand, Mary Carpenter, Lady Morgan, Rachel, Lady Hester Stanhope. Crown 8vo, 7s. 6d.

Mr Barnett Smith continues his biographical activity. It is not many weeks since a volume appeared from his pen on "Christian Workers of the Nineteenth Century"; now we have "Women of Renown: Nineteenth Century Studies." The later is the larger and more elaborate work of the two, but in design and execution it is not greatly dissimilar from the earlier volume. Desirous of shewing what the women of eminence whom he has chosen for delineation really were—how they lived, moved, and acted—the author has presented them wherever he could "as painted by themselves or their contemporaries." Autobiographies and biographies are thus, as far as available, laid under contribution. In the hands of so capable a compiler as Mr Barnett Smith such materials have been skilfully utilised, and the result is a series of brightly written sketches.

The Life and Enterprises of Ferdinand de Lesseps—The only full and Complete English Account of. New Edition. Revised, and brought up to the time of his death, with Portrait. Crown 8vo, 7s. 6d.

"A great part of M. de Lesseps' career already belongs to history, and is invested with a lustre which nothing can obscure. Mr G. Barnett Smith makes this clear in his useful and painstaking compilation. . . . It is skilfully executed, and illustrates aptly and not altogether inopportunely, both the poetry and the prose of M. de Lesseps' extraordinary career."—*The Times.*

"A very comprehensive life of Ferdinand de Lesseps has been produced by G. Barnett Smith, who has already proved his ability as a faithful and painstaking biographer. The career of M. de Lesseps was one of great achievements and great vicissitudes. This biographer lauds his achievements. The facts of the prosecution in connection with the Panama Canal project are elaborately set forth in this volume, to which all readers interested in the question should refer for information on a matter which to people not resident in France must have appeared unusually complicated."—*Westminster Review.*

ARTHUR PENRHYN STANLEY, D.D. (Dean of Westminster).

Scripture Portraits and other Miscellanies collected from his Published Writings. By Arthur Penrhyn Stanley, D.D. Crown 8vo, gilt top, 5s.

"In virtue of his literary genius, his solid acquirements, his manly sense, and his sympathetic and generous piety, he ranks among the most eminent and estimable of Christian teachers."—*Chambers's Encyclopædia.*

"These essays range over a period of twenty years (1850-1870), and they furnish a series of singularly interesting illustrations of the great controversies which have agitated that time. . . . Every one, indeed, of his essays has achieved in its day a success which makes a recommendation unnecessary."—ALLIBONE.

E. Œ. SOMERVILLE and MARTIN ROSS, THE AUTHORS OF "AN IRISH COUSIN."

Through Connemara in a Governess Cart. Illustrated by W. W. Russell, from Sketches by Edith Œ. Somerville. Crown 8vo, 3s. 6d.

"The quaint seriousness, the free and hearty fun, the sly humour of this narrative, are charmingly bright and attractive."—*World.*

"A bright and breezy narrative of two ladies in Connemara who preferred independence and a mule to society and a mail car. Their simple story is divertingly told."—*Times.*

"The delightful wilderness of mountain, peat bog, and heather, and all that they said and did, are graphically described in this chatty and extremely readable volume." —*Daily Telegraph.*

"Sketches of Irish Life, the eccentricities of wandering Saxons, and descriptions of local scenery, are worked up in a manner which makes the book a pleasant companion. Mr Russell has in his illustration ably supported the writers."—*Morning Post.*

By the same Authors.

In the Vine Country—Bordeaux and its Neighbourhood, Illustrated. Crown 8vo, 3s. 6d.

"The genuine fund of wit and humour which sparkles throughout will be enjoyed by all."—*Glasgow Herald.*

"The authors have the knack of putting their readers in the situation in which they themselves were, and so the book, light and smart as it is, is heartily enjoyable." —*Scotsman.*

"A bright, artless narrative of travel."—*Times.*

"There is not a dull line in the volume from the first page to the last."—*Lady's Pictorial.*

J. E. TAYLOR, F.L.S., F.G.S., &c.

For fuller notices of Dr Taylor's Works, see *Scientific*, pp. 33, 34.

Flowers: Their Origin, Shapes, Perfumes, and Colours. **Illustrated with 32 Coloured Figures by Sowerby,** and 161 Woodcuts. Second Edition. Crown 8vo, 7s. 6d.

The Aquarium: Its Inhabitants, Structure, and Management. Second Edition, with 238 Woodcuts. Crown 8vo, 3s. 6d.

Half-Hours at the Seaside. Illustrated with 250 Woodcuts. Fourth Edition. Crown 8vo, 2s. 6d.

Half-Hours in the Green Lanes. Illustrated with 300 Woodcuts. Fifth Edition. Crown 8vo, 2s. 6d.

E. THORNTON.

A Gazetteer of the Territories under the Government of the Viceroy of India. Last Edition. Revised and Edited by Sir Roper Lethbridge, C.I.E., and A. N. Wollaston, C.I.E. Demy 8vo, 1,070 pp., 28s.

PERCY M. THORNTON.

Harrow School and its Surroundings. With Maps and Plates. Demy 8vo, 15s.

W. M. TORRENS.

History of Cabinets. From the Union with Scotland to the Acquisition of Canada and Bengal. 2 vols. Demy 8vo, 36s.

"It is almost impossible—and, alas! now useless as regards the writer—to praise this book too highly. It is a clever, sincere, and painstaking contribution to the making of modern history, and all students of constitutional and parliamentary history will find much to interest and instruct them in these able volumes. In all the minor matters of references, indexing, and printing every care has been taken. Indeed, all is praiseworthy, and the pity is that the writer should have passed away without receiving the thanks of students."—*St James's Budget.*

"'A History of Cabinets' from the beginning of the Eighteenth Century down to the death of George II., which the late Mr M'Cullagh Torrens regarded as 'the work of his life,' was published yesterday. It consists of two volumes of considerable bulk, showing at once that something more than the origin and progress of the Cabinet system had occupied the attention of the author. In fact, a history of Cabinets is a history of Governments, and a history of Governments is, in a great measure, a history of England."—*The Standard.*

A. J. WALL.

Indian Snake Poisons. Their Nature and Effects. Crown 8vo, 6s.

CONTENTS.

The Physiological Effects of the Poison of the Cobra (Naja Tripudians).—The Physiological Effects of the Poison of Russell's Viper (Daboia Russellii).—The Physiological Effects produced by the Poison of the Bungarus Fasciatus and the Bungarus Coeruleus.—The Relative Power and Properties of the Poisons of Indian and other Venomous Snakes.—The Nature of Snake Poisons.—Some practical considerations connected with the subject of Snake-Poisoning, especially regarding prevention and treatment.—The object that has been kept in view, has been to define as closely as possible, the conditions on which the mortality from Snake-bite depends, both as regards the physiological nature of the poisoning process, and the relations between the reptiles and their victims, so as to indicate the way in which we should best proceed with the hope of diminishing the fearful mortality that exists.

JOHN WATSON, F.L.S.

Ornithology in Relation to Agriculture and Horticulture, by various writers, edited by John Watson, F.L.S., &c. Crown 8vo, 3s. 6d.

LIST OF CONTRIBUTORS.—Miss Eleanor A. Ormerod, late Consulting Entomologist to the Royal Agricultural Society of England; O. V. Alpin, F.L.S., Member of the British Ornithologists' Union; Charles Whitehead, F.L.S., F.G.S., &c., author of "Fifty Years of Fruit Farming"; John Watson, F.L.S., author of "A Handbook for Farmers and Small Holders"; the Rev. F. O. Morris, M.A., author of "A History of British Birds"; G. W. Murdoch, late editor of *The Farmer;* Riley Fortune, F.Z.S.; T. H. Nelson, Member of the British Ornithologists' Union; T. Southwell, F.Z.S.; Rev. Theo. Wood, B.A., F.I.S.; J. H. Gurney, jun., M.P.; Harrison Weir, F.R.H.S.; W. H. Tuck.

"Will form a textbook of a reliable kind in guiding agriculturists at large in their dealings with their feathered friends and foes alike."—*Glasgow Herald.*

"This is a valuable book, and should go far to fulfil its excellent purpose. . . . It is a book that every agriculturist should possess."—*Land and Water.*

"It is well to know what birds do mischief and what birds are helpful. This book is the very manual to clear up all such doubts."—*Yorkshire Post.*

"In these days of agricultural depression it behoves the farmer to study, among other subjects, ornithology. That he and the gamekeeper often bring down plagues upon the land when they fancy they are ridding it of a pest is exceedingly well illustrated in this series of papers."—*Scotsman.*

SAMUEL WILBERFORCE, D.D. (*Bishop of Winchester*).

Heroes of Hebrew History. Crown 8vo, gilt top, 5s.

"The tales which he relates are all good, and have a moral aim and purpose."—*Athenæum.*

"It is written with a natural and captivating fervour."—*London Quarterly Review.*

"An interesting historical account."—*London Lit. Gaz.*

"Using his influence as a man of the world for the purpose of modifying those about him for good, and making them serve as his instruments for the furtherance of the objects which he had at heart. He was the most delightful of companions, and the wittiest talker of his time. Of his extraordinary versatility and extraordinary powers of work, it is impossible to speak at length here, but both qualities are abundantly illustrated in his life by Canon Ashwell."—*Celebrities of the Century.*

S. WELLS WILLIAMS, LL.D., Professor of the Chinese Language and Literature at Yale College.

China—The Middle Kingdom. A Survey of the Geography, Government, Literature, Social Life, Arts, and History of the Chinese Empire and its Inhabitants. Revised Edition, with 74 Illustrations and a New Map of the Empire. 2 vols. Demy 8vo, 42s.

Dr S. Wells Williams' *Middle Kingdom* has long occupied the position of a classic. It is not only the fullest and most authoritative account of the Chinese and their country that exists, but it is also the most readable and entertaining. This issue is practically a new work—the text of the old edition has been largely re-written and the work has been expanded so as to include a vast amount of new material collected by Dr Williams during the late years of his residence in China—as well as the most recent information respecting all the departments of the Empire. Many new illustrations have been added and the best of the old engravings have been retained. An important feature of this edition is a large map of the Chinese Empire from the best modern authorities, more complete and accurate than any map of the country hitherto published.

HARRY WILLIAMS, R.N. (*Chief Inspector of Machinery*).

Dedicated, by permission, to Admiral H.R.H. the Duke of Edinburgh.

The Steam Navy of England. Past, Present, and Future.
Contents:—Part I.—Our Seamen; Part II.—Ships and Machinery; Part III.—Naval Engineering; Part IV.—Miscellaneous, Summary, with an Appendix on the Personnel of the Steam Branch of the Navy. Third and enlarged Edition. Medium 8vo, 12s. 6d.

"It is a series of essays, clearly written and often highly suggestive, on the still unsolved, or only partially and tentatively solved, problems connected with the manning and organisation, and propulsion of our modern war-ships, . . . being laudably free from technicalities, and written in a not unattractive style, they will recommend themselves to that small, but happily increasing, section of the general public which concerns itself seriously and intelligently with naval affairs."—*Times.*

"Mr Harry Williams, a naval engineer of long experience and high rank, discusses the future requirements of the fleet. He is naturally most at home when dealing with points which specially affect his own branch of the service, but the whole book is well worth study."—*Manchester Guardian.*

"Must be pronounced a technical book in the main, although its author expressly states that he wrote it 'not so much for professional as non-professional men.' Its manifest object is to promote the efficiency of our steam navy in times to come, keeping which aim steadfastly in view Mr Williams has brought great knowledge and ability to bear upon the endeavour to forecast what provision it would be well to make in order to meet the full naval requirements of the British nation. His highly instructive work is divided into four parts, under the respective titles of 'Our Seamen,' 'Ships and Machinery,' 'Naval Engineering,' and 'Miscellaneous,' which again are carefully summarised in some fifty pages of eminently readable matter. The three chapters of miscellanea deal principally with the coal-endurance, engine-room complements, electric lighting, and steam-steering machinery of Her Majesty's ships."—*Daily Telegraph*

Professor H. H. WILSON, author of the "Standard History of India."

Glossary of Judicial Terms, including words from the Arabic, Persian, Hindustani, Sanskrit, Hindi, Bengali, Uriya, Marathi, Guzarathi, Telugu, Karnata, Tamil, Malayalam, and other languages. 4to, cloth, 30s.

Wynter's Subtle Brains and Lissom Fingers. Crown 8vo, 3s. 6d.

CONTENTS.

The Buried Roman City in Britain.
"Silvertown."
Advertising.
Vivisection.
The New Hotel System.
The Restoration of our Soil.
Half-Hours at the Kensington Museum.
Mudie's Circulating Library.
Fraudulent Trade Marks.
Superstition: Where does it End?
The New Counterblast to Tobacco.
Air Traction.
Illuminations.
Boat-Building by Machinery.
The Effects of Railway Travelling upon Health.
The Working-Men's Flower Show.
Messages under the Sea.
Town Telegraphs.
The Bread We Eat.
Early Warnings.
Dining Rooms for the Working Classes.
Railway and City Population.
A Day with the Coroner.
The English in Paris.
The *Times* Newspaper in 1798.
The Under-Sea Railroad.
Oh, the Roast Beef of Old England.
Physical Education.
Advice by a Retired Physician.
The Clerk of the Weather.
Portsmouth Dockyard.
Village Hospitals.
Railways, the Great Civilisers.
On taking a House.
Photographic Portraiture.
Doctor's Stuff.
Smallpox in London.
Hospital Dress.
Excursion Trains.

"Altogether 'Subtle Brains and Lissom Fingers' is about the pleasantest book of short collected papers of chit chat blending information with amusement, and not overtasking the attention or the intelligence, that we have seen for a good while."—*London Reader.*

LIEUT. G. J. YOUNGHUSBAND, Queen's Own Corps of Guides.

Eighteen Hundred Miles in a Burmese Tat, through Burmah, Siam, and the Eastern Shan States. Illustrated. Crown 8vo, 5s.

"There is a good deal of jocular description in this book, which, as the reader will easily see, has been introduced with an eye rather to amusement than to accuracy; but after all the volume will have repaid the reader for the few hours which may be spent in its perusal if it conveys to him, as it is calculated to do, a fair impression of the difficulties which beset the wayfarer in a strange land who, when in search of the pleasures of travel, begins his journey where he should leave off, and ends it where he should have started."—*Athenæum.*

"Mr Younghusband's account of his adventures is written simply and without exaggeration, but on the whole we think we would rather read about the Shan country than travel in it."—*Literary World.*

Scientific Works: including Botany, Natural History, &c.

E. BONAVIA, M.D., Brigade-Surgeon, Indian Medical Service.

The Cultivated Oranges and Lemons of India and Ceylon. Demy 8vo, with oblong Atlas Volume of Plates, 2 vols. 30s.

R. BRAITHWAITE, M.D., F.L.S., &c.

The Sphagnaceæ, or Peat Mosses of Europe and North America. Illustrated with 29 Plates, **coloured by hand.** Imp. 8vo, 25s.

"All muscologists will be delighted to hail the appearance of this important work. . . . Never before has our native moss-flora been so carefully figured and described, and that by an acknowledged authority on the subject."—*Science Gossip.*

"Mosses, perhaps, receive about as little attention from botanists as any class of plants, and considering how admirably mosses lend themselves to the collector's purposes, this is very remarkable. Something may be due to the minuteness of the size of many of the species, and something perhaps to the difficulties inherent in the systematic treatment of these plants; but we fancy the chief cause of comparative neglect with which they are treated is to be sought in the want of a good illustrated English treatise upon them. In the work which is now before us, Dr Braithwaite aims at placing the British mosses on the same vantage-ground as the more favoured classes of the vegetable kingdom; and judging from the sample lately issued, he will succeed in his endeavours."—*Popular Science Review.*

B. CARRINGTON, M.D., F.R.S.

British Hepaticæ. Containing Descriptions and Figures of the Native Species of Jungermannia, Marchantia, and Anthoceros. Imp. 8vo, sewed, Parts 1 to 4, plain plates, 2s. 6d. each; **coloured plates, 3s. 6d. each.**

M. C. COOKE, M.A., LL.D.

The British Fungi: A Plain and Easy Account of. **With Coloured Plates of 40 Species.** Fifth Edition, Revised. Crown 8vo, 6s.

"Mr Cooke writes for those whose education and means are limited, and with preeminent success. It is really a pleasure to read the manuals which he has published, for they are up to the mark, and so complete as to leave hardly anything to be desired. The new work on the fungi appears to be equally valuable with those which he has already printed. It contains descriptions of the esculent fungi, the manner in which they are prepared for the table, how to discriminate the nutritious from the poisonous species, details of the principles of their scientific classification, and a tabular arrangement of orders and genera."

Handbook of British Hepaticæ. Containing Descriptions and Figures of the Indigenous Species of Marchantia, Jungermannia, Riccia, and Anthoceros, Illustrated. Crown 8vo, 6s.

"It is very creditable to Mr Cooke that the drawings in his book are all sketches from nature made by his own pencil. This shows work, and is more respectable than the too common practice of copying engravings from the authorities in the particular branch of science. This little book is valuable, because in some respects it is certainly a good guide-book to a number of edible fungi unknown to the public."—*Popular Science Review.*

"Probably no group in the British flora has received so little attention as the Hepaticæ. Dr M. C. Cooke has now filled up the gap by producing a 'Handbook of the British Hepaticæ,' containing full descriptions of all the species, about two hundred in number, known to inhabit the British Islands."—*Nature.*

M. C. Cooke's Books continued.

M. C. COOKE, M.A., LL.D.—continued.

Our Reptiles and Batrachians. A Plain and Easy Account of the Lizards, Snakes, Newts, Toads, Frogs, and Tortoises indigenous to Great Britain. New and Revised Edition. **With original Coloured Pictures of every Species,** and numerous Woodcuts. Crown 8vo, 6s.

CONTENTS.

Reptiles and Snake-stones. The Blind Worm. The Common Frog.
The Common Lizard. The Common Snake. The Edible Frog.
The Sand Lizard. The Smooth Snake. The Common Toad.
The Green Lizard. The Viper, or Adder. Common Smooth Newt or Eft.
The Natterjack. Great Water Newt. The Hawk's-Bill Turtle.
Palmate Newt. Gray's Banded Newt. Appendix.
The Leathery Turtle. Amphibia or Batrachians.

"Mr Cooke has especially distinguished himself as a student of the fungi and the fresh-water algæ, his works on these orders being the standard treatises in English. He has also paid some attention to zoology and chemistry, his education in these as in other sciences being obtained by persistent self-instruction."—*Celebrities of the Century.*

Rust, Smut, Mildew, and Mould. An Introduction to the Study of Microscopic Fungi. **Illustrated with 269 Coloured Figures by J. E. Sowerby.** Fifth Edition, Revised and Enlarged, with Appendix of New Species. Crown 8vo, 6s.

Those of our readers who are the happy possessors of microscopes would welcome this book with delight, as opening the way to a definite study of a most interesting branch of plant life. The minute fungi, here so faithfully depicted by Mr Sowerby, and so carefully described by Dr Cooke, have not only beauty of form and colour, but wonderful life-histories. Every hedge or lane or piece of waste ground, even in the suburbs of large towns, will provide specimens, which may be easily preserved on the plants which they attack or mounted as microscope slides.

Important to Botanists and Students of Natural History.

European Fungi (Hymenomycetum)—Synoptical Key to. Cooke (M. C.) and Quelet (L., M.D., &c.)—Clavis Synoptica Hymenomycetum Europæorum. Fcap. 8vo, 7s. 6d.; or, interleaved with ruled paper, 8s. 6d.

"Without pretending to high scientific quality, the work throughout is well fitted to instruct and to attract a class of readers who might shrink from grappling with a scientific text-book."—*Saturday Review.*

BARON CUVIER.

The Animal Kingdom. With considerable Additions by W. B. Carpenter, M.D., F.R.S., and J. O. Westwood, F.L.S. New Edition, Illustrated with 500 Engravings on Wood and **36 Coloured Plates.** Imp. 8vo, 21s.

J. HUNTER, late Hon. Sec. of the British Bee-keepers' Association.

A Manual of Bee-keeping. Containing Practical Information for Rational and Profitable Methods of Bee Management. Full Instructions on Stimulative Feeding, Ligurianising and Queen-raising, with descriptions of the American Comb Foundation, Sectional Supers, and the best Hives and Apiarian Appliances on all systems. Fourth Edition. With Illustrations. Crown 8vo, 3s. 6d.

"We cordially recommend Mr Hunter's neat and compact Manual of Bee-keeping. Mr Hunter writes clearly and well."—*Science Gossip.*

"We are indebted to Mr J. Hunter, Honorary Secretary of the British Bee-keepers' Association. His Manual of Bee-keeping, just published, is full to the very brim of choice and practical hints fully up to the most advanced stages of Apiarian Science, and its perusal has afforded us so much pleasure that we have drawn somewhat largely from it for the benefit of our readers."—*Bee-keepers' Magazine (New York).*

G. H. KINAHAN.

A Handy Book of Rock Names. Fcap. 8vo, 4s.

"This will prove, we do not doubt, a very useful little book to all practical geologists, and also to the reading student of rocks. When a difficulty is incurred as to a species of deposit, it will soon vanish. Mr Kinahan's little book will soon make it all clear. The work is divided into three parts. The first is a classified table of rocks, the second part treats of the *Ingenite* rocks, and the third part deals with those rocks which are styled *Derivate.* Dana's termination of *yte* has been most generally used by the author, but he has also given the *ite* terminations for those that like them. The book will be purchased, for it must be had, by every geologist; and as its size is small, it will form a convenient pocket companion for the man who works over field and quarry."—*Popular Science Review.*

Professor E. LANKESTER.

The Uses of Animals in Relation to the Industry of Man. New Edition. Illustrated. Crown 8vo, 4s.

Silk, Wool, Leather, Bone, Soap, Waste, Sponges, and Corals, Shell-fish, Insects, Furs, Feathers, Horns and Hair, and Animal Perfumes, are the subjects of the twelve lectures on "The Uses of Animals."

"In his chapter on 'Waste,' the lecturer gives startling insight into the manifold uses of rubbish. . . . Dr Lankester finds a use for everything; and he delights in analysing each fresh sample of rejected material, and stating how each of its component parts can be turned to the best account."—*Athenæum.*

Practical Physiology: A School Manual of Health. With numerous Woodcuts. Sixth Edition. Fcap. 8vo, 2s. 6d.

CONTENTS.

Constitution of the Human Body.
Nature of the Food supplied to the Human Body.
Digestion, and the Organs by which it is performed.
Nature of Blood and its Circulation by the Heart.
Breathing, or the Function of Respiration.
The Structure and Functions of the Skin.
The Movements of the Human Body.
The Brain and Nerves.
The Organs of the Senses.

"Writing for schoolboys, Dr Lankester has been careful to consult their tastes. There are passages in this little work which will make it popular, and the instructor will probably be hailed by a name which is new to people of his class, that of a 'regular brick.'"—*Athenæum.*

MRS LANKESTER.

Talks about Health: A Book for Boys and Girls. Being an Explanation of all the Processes by which Life is Sustained. Illustrated. Small 8vo, 1s.

The Late EDWARD NEWMAN, F.Z.S.

British Butterflies. With many Illustrations. Super royal 8vo, 7s. 6d.

"The British butterflies have found a good friend in Mr Newman, who has given us a history of their lives—from *larva* to *imago*, their habits and their whereabouts—which is one of the most perfect things of the kind. And we are glad to read the author's statement that his work has attained, while in progress, a sale that is almost unattainable in English scientific works. Firstly, the work consists of a series of notices to the young who may be disposed to go butterfly-hunting. And in them we find the author's great experience, and we commend this part of his work to our readers. The next part deals with the subjects of anatomy, physiology, and embryology of the insects; and finally we come to the separate account of each species. This latter is admirably given. First comes a capital engraving, life size, of the species, and then follows in order the life, history, time of appearance and locality, occupying from a page to a page and a half or two pages of a large quarto (or nearly so) volume. All this is done well, as we might expect from the author; it is clear, intelligible, and devoid of much of the rubbish which abounds in books of this kind generally. We must conclude by expressing the hope that all who are interested in insects will make themselves aquainted with the volume."—*Popular Science Review.*

MARY A. PRATTEN.

My Hundred Swiss Flowers. With a Short Account of Swiss Ferns. With 60 Illustrations. Crown 8vo, plain plates, 12s. 6d.; **coloured plates, 25s.**

"The temptation to produce such books as this seems irresistible. The author feels a want; the want is undeniable. After more or less hesitation he feels he can supply it. It is pleasantly written, and affords useful hints as to localities."—*Athenæum.*

S. L. PUMPHREY.

A Little Brown Pebble, with 10 full-page cuts. Fcap. 4to, 3s. 6d.

"In the story of 'A Little Brown Pebble,' its writer endeavours to introduce geological science into the nursery, showing what strange creatures lived in the ancient seas, what monsters inhabited the primeval forests, and how our country alternated between torrid heats and an arctic cold. The accuracy of the information is guaranteed by competent authorities, and the illustrations are spirited. There is no reason why the attempt should not succeed."—*Academy,* 21st December 1889.

R. RIMMER, F.L.S.

The Land and Freshwater Shells of the British Isles. Illustrated with 10 Photographs and 3 Lithographs, containing figures of all the principal Species. Second Edition. Crown 8vo, 5s.

"This handsomely got up little volume supplies a long-felt want in a very ingenious and trustworthy manner. The author is an enthusiastic conchologist, and writes both attractively and well, and in a manner so simple and natural that we have no fear that any ordinarily educated man will easily understand every phrase. But the feature of this book which strikes us most is that every species of British land and freshwater shell has been photographed, and here we have all the photographs, natural size in the albertype process, so that the merest tyro will find no difficulty in identifying any shell he may find."—*Science Review.*

J. SMITH, A.L.S.

Ferns: British and Foreign. Fourth Edition, revised and greatly enlarged, with many illustrations. Crown 8vo, 7s. 6d.

"Each genus is described, and the technical characters upon which it is founded are shown in the accompanying illustrations, and the indispensable technical terms are explained by examples The meaning and derivations of the botanical names of ferns are also given in sufficient detail and with sufficient accuracy to meet the wants of amateurs, if not of scholars. But perhaps the most valuable part of the work is that devoted to instruction in the cultivation of ferns, which occupies some seventy pages of the book. A bibliography of the subject and an excellent index make up the remainder of this useful volume, which we recommend to all persons desirous of knowing something more about ferns than being able to recognise them by sight."—*Field.*

"Mr Smith's work entitles him to admiration for his industry and for the manifest care with which he has studied his subject; and his present enlarged work will certainly become and be a standard library book of reference for all pteridologists and ornamental gardeners (whether professional or amateur) who devote attention to filiculture. And there really is no family of plants which is more elegant than are ferns. Indigenous British ferns alone afford a most interesting scope of research and collection."—*Whitehall Review.*

"This is a new and enlarged edition of one of the best extant works on British and foreign ferns which has been called for by the introduction, during the interval of ten years which has elapsed since the issue of the first edition, of a number of exotic species which have been collected and arranged under their respective genera and tribes as an appendix. There are thus introduced 234 entirely new species. The sixty pages devoted to a treatise on the cultivation of ferns are invaluable to the fern-grower, professional or amateur, describing the conditions under which ferns grow in their native country—knowledge which is essential to their really successful cultivation in this."—*Rural World.*

J. E. TAYLOR, F.L.S., F.G.S.

Flowers: Their Origin, Shapes, Perfumes, and Colours, Illustrated with 32 Coloured Figures by Sowerby, and 161 Woodcuts. Second Edition. Crown 8vo, cloth gilt, 7s. 6d.

CONTENTS

The Old and New Philosophy of Flowers—The Geological Antiquity of Flowers and Insects—The Geographical Distribution of Flowers—The Structure of Flowering Plants—Relations between Flowers and their Physical Surroundings—Relations between Flowers and the Wind—The Colours of Flowers—The External Shapes of Flowers—The Internal Shapes of Flowers—The Perfumes of Flowers—Social Flowers—Birds and Flowers—The Natural Defences of Flowering Plants.

"This is an altogether charming book, full of wisdom, cheerful, simple, attractive, and informed throughout with a high purpose. Its object is to place within reach of the general public in an agreeable form the results of the most recent and comprehensive botanical research. The author is so bold as to ask why flowers were made, and is not without means to answer the question reverently and truthfully. He connects them by the aids that science supplies with the history of creation, and the records of the rocks, and with the history of man, and the progress of the agricultural and horticultural arts. He tells us how they are influenced by soil and climate, how changed and multiplied by insects and other agencies, how their seeds are blown about the world, and how by innumerable divine appointments it at last comes about that the life of a man is environed and beautified with flowers. The work is rich in the results of travel, and it happily connects the vegetable products of the globe with the conditions that favour them and the wants they satisfy. It is therefore a book for all ages, and for botanists and gardeners, as well as for such as rather too gladly confess they know nothing about plants. We should like to see it on every family table in the whole length and breadth of the United Kingdom."—*Gardeners' Magazine.*

The Aquarium: Its Inhabitants, Structure, and Management. Second Edition, with 238 Woodcuts. Crown 8vo, 3s. 6d.

"Few men have done more to popularise the natural history science than the late Dr Taylor. The work before us, while intended as a handbook to public aquaria, is responsible for many attempts, successful and otherwise, at the construction of the domestic article. The book is replete with valuable information concerning persons and things, while the directions for making and managing aquaria are very clear and concise. The illustrations are numerous, suitable, and very good."—*Schoolmaster.*

"The ichthyologist, be it known, is not such a fearful or horrific 'sort of wild-fowl' as his name would seem to argue him. The prevalence of the breed, the extent of its knowledge, the zeal of its enthusiasm, and the number of the aquaria it has built for itself in town or country, are all part and parcel of that 'march of science' which took its impetus from Darwin and the 'Origin of Species.' Those who do not already know that useful book, 'The Aquarium,' by Mr J. E. Taylor, Ph.D., F.L.S., &c., should procure this new edition (the sixth). It forms a convenient handbook or popular manual to our public aquaria. The aquarium, its inhabitants, its structure and its management, are the author's especial care. And with the help of well-kn[own] works and a wide experience he has managed to put together a most praiseworthy book."—*Science Siftings.*

Half-Hours in the Green Lanes. Illustrated with 300 Woodcuts. Fifth Edition. Crown 8vo, 2s. 6d.

"A book which cannot fail to please the young, and from which many an older reader may glean here and there facts of interest in the field of nature. Mr Taylor has endeavoured to collect these facts which are to be recorded daily by an observant country gentleman with a taste for natural history; and he has attempted to put them together in a clear and simple style, so that the young may not only acquire a love for the investigation of nature, but may also put up (by reading this little book) an important store of knowledge. We think the author has succeeded in his object. He has made a very interesting little volume, not written above the heads of its readers as many of those books are, and he has taken care to have most of his natural history observations very accurately illustrated."—*Popular Science Review.*

J. E. Taylor's Books continued.

J. E. TAYLOR, F.L.S., F.G.S.—continued.

Half-Hours at the Seaside. Illustrated with 250 Woodcuts. Fourth Edition. Crown 8vo, 2s. 6d.

"The love of natural history has now become so prevalent, at least among purely English readers, that we hardly meet a family at the seaside one of whose members has not some little knowledge of the wonders of the deep. Now, of course, this love of marine zoology is being vastly increased by the existence of the valuable aquaria at the Crystal Palace and at Brighton. Still, however, notwithstanding the amount of admirable works on the subject, more especially the excellent treatises of Gosse and others, there was wanted a cheap form of book with good illustrations which should give a clear account of the ordinary creatures one meets with on the sands and in the rock pools. The want no longer exists, for the excellent little manual that now lies before us embraces all that could be desired by those who are entirely ignorant of the subject of seaside zoology, while its mode of arrangement and woodcuts, which are carefully drawn, combine to render it both attractive and useful."—*Popular Science Review.*

Riding, Veterinary, and Agriculture.

EDWARD L. ANDERSON.

How to Ride and School a Horse. With a System of Horse Gymnastics. Fourth Edition. Revised and Corrected. Crown 8vo, 2s. 6d.

"He is well worthy of a hearing."—*Bell's Life.*

"Mr Anderson is, without doubt, a thorough horseman."—*The Field.*

"It should be a good investment to all lovers of horses."—*The Farmer.*

"There is no reason why the careful reader should not be able, by the help of this little book, to train as well as ride his horses."—*Land and Water.*

JAMES IRVINE LUPTON, F.R.C.V.S.

The Horse, as he Was, as he Is, and as he Ought to Be. Illustrated. Crown 8vo, 3s. 6d.

"Written with a good object in view, namely, to create an interest in the important subject of horse-breeding, more especially that class known as general utility horses. The book contains several illustrations, is well printed and handsomely bound, and we hope will meet with the attention it deserves."—*Live Stock Journal.*

WILLIAM PROCTOR, Stud Groom.

The Management and Treatment of the Horse in the Stable, Field, and on the Road. New and Revised Edition. Crown 8vo, 6s.

"There are few who are interested in horses will fail to profit by one portion or another of this useful work. Coming from a practical hand the work should recommend itself to the public."—*Sportsman.*

"There is a fund of sound common-sense views in this work which will be interesting to many owners."—*Field.*

GEORGE GRESSWELL.

The Diseases and Disorders of the Ox. Second Edition. Demy 8vo, 7s. 6d.

"This is perhaps one of the best of the popular books on the subject which has been published in recent years, and demonstrates in a most unmistakable manner the great advance that has been made in Bovine and Ovine Pathology since the days of Youatt. . . . To medical men who desire to know something of the disorders of such an important animal—speaking hygienically—as the Ox, the work can be recommended."—*The Lancet.*

"It is clear, concise, and practical, and would make a very convenient handbook of reference."—*Saturday Review.*

PROFESSOR SHELDON.

The Future of British Agriculture. How Farmers may best be Benefited. Crown 8vo, 2s. 6d.

"Fortunately Prof. Sheldon has no mind to play the part of a prophet, but from the plenitude of a long experience gives sage counsel how to farm abreast of the time and be ready for whatever may ensue. . . . This little book is well worth reading, and it is pleasant to find that the professor by no means despairs of the future of agriculture in England."—*Academy.*

"We welcome the book as a valuable contribution to our agricultural literature, and as a useful guide to those branches in which the author is especially qualified to instruct."—*Nature.*

"In this beautifully printed and well-bound little book of 158 pp., Professor Sheldon, in his usual happy style, surveys the agricultural field, and indicates what he thinks is the prospect in front of the British farmer. Like a watchman he stands upon his tower—and when asked, What of the night? he disavows not that we are in the night, but earnestly declares that the morning cometh apace. The professor is an optimist; he does not believe that the country is done, and still less does he favour the idea that, taking a wide survey, the former days were better than these. On the contrary, he urges that the way out of the wilderness is not by any by-path, but by going right ahead; and, ere long, the man who holds the banner high will emerge triumphant."—*Scottish Farmer.*

JOHN WATSON, F.L.S.

Ornithology in Relation to Agriculture and Horticulture, by various writers, edited by John Watson, F.L.S., &c. Crown 8vo. 3s. 6d.

LIST OF CONTRIBUTORS.—Miss Eleanor A. Ormerod, late Consulting Entomologist to the Royal Agricultural Society of England; O. V. Aplin, F.L.S., Member of the British Ornithologists' Union; Charles Whitehead, F.L.S., F.G.S., &c., author of "Fifty Years of Fruit Farming"; John Watson, F.L.S., author of "A Handbook for Farmers and Small Holders"; the Rev. F. O. Morris, M.A., author of "A History of British Birds"; G. W. Murdoch, late editor of *The Farmer;* Riley Fortune, F.Z.S.; T. H. Nelson, Member of the British Ornithologists' Union; T. Southwell, F.Z.S.; Rev. Theo. Wood, B.A., F.I.S.; J. H. Gurney, jun., M.P.; Harrison Weir, F.R.H.S.; W. H. Tuck.

"Will form a textbook of a reliable kind in guiding agriculturists at large in their dealings with their feathered friends and foes alike."—*Glasgow Herald.*

"This is a valuable book, and should go far to fulfil its excellent purpose. . . . It is a book that every agriculturist should possess."—*Land and Water.*

"It is well to know what birds do mischief and what birds are helpful. This book is the very manual to clear up all such doubts."—*Yorkshire Post.*

"In these days of agricultural depression it behoves the former to study, among other subjects, ornithology. That he and the gamekeeper often bring down plagues upon the land when they fancy they are ridding it of a pest is exceedingly well illustrated in this series of papers."—*Scotsman.*

India, China, Japan, and the East.

SURGEON-MAJOR L. A. WADDELL, M.B., F.L.S., F.R.G.S.,
Member of the Royal Asiatic Society, Anthropological Institute, &c.

The Buddhism of Tibet, with its Mystic Cults, Symbolism, and Mythology, and in its Relation to Indian Buddhism, with over 200 Illustrations. Demy 8vo, 31s. 6d.

SYNOPSIS OF CONTENTS:—Introductory. *Historical:* Changes in Primitive Buddhism leading to Lamaism—Rise, Development, and Spread of Lamaism—The Sects of Lamaism. *Doctrinal:* Metaphysical Sources of the Doctrine—The Doctrine and its Morality—Scriptures and Literature. *Monastic:* The Order of Lamas—Daily Life and Routine—Hierarchy and Reincarnate Lamas. *Buildings:* Monasteries—Temples and Cathedrals—Shrines (and Relics and Pilgrims). *Mythology and Gods:* Pantheon and Images—Sacred Symbols and Charms. *Ritual and Sorcery:* Worship and Ritual—Astrology and Divination—Sorcery and Necromancy. *Festivals and Plays:* Festivals and Holidays—Mystic Plays and Masquerades and Sacred Plays. *Popular Lamaism:* Domestic and Popular Lamaism. *Appendices:* Chronological Table—Bibliography—Index.

"By far the most important mass of original materials contributed to this recondite study."—*The Times.*

"Dr Waddell deals with the whole subject in a most exhaustive manner, and gives a clear insight into the structure, prominent features, and cults of the system; and to disentangle the early history of Lamaism from the chaotic growth of fable which has invested it, most of the chief internal movements of Lamaism are now for the first time presented in an intelligible and systematic form. The work is a valuable addition to the long series that have preceded it, and is enriched by numerous illustrations, mostly from originals brought from Lhasa, and from photographs by the author, while it is fully indexed, and is provided with a chronological table and bibliography."—*Liverpool Courier.*

"A book of exceptional interest."—*Glasgow Herald.*

"A learned and elaborate work, likely for some time to come to be a source of reference for all who seek information about Lamaism. . . . In the appendix will be found a chronological table of Tibetan events, and a bibliography of the best literature bearing on Lamaism. There is also an excellent index, and the numerous illustrations are certainly one of the distinctive features of the book."—*Morning Post.*

"Cannot fail to arouse the liveliest interest. The author of this excellently produced, handsomely illustrated volume of nearly six hundred pages has evidently spared no pains in prosecuting his studies. . . . The book is one of exceptional value, and will attract all those readers who take an interest in the old religions of the far East."—*Publishers' Circular.*

SIR EDWIN ARNOLD, M.A., Author of "The Light of Asia," &c.

The Book of Good Counsels. Fables from the Sanscrit of the Hitopadésa. With Illustrations by Gordon Browne. Autograph and Portrait. Crown 8vo, antique, gilt top, 5s.

A few copies of the large paper Edition (limited to 100 copies), bound in white vellum, 25s. each net.

"'The Book of Good Counsels,' by Sir Edwin Arnold, comes almost as a new book, so long has it been out of print. Now, in addition to being very tastefully and prettily reissued, it contains numerous illustrations by Mr Gordon Browne. As some few may remember, it is a book of Indian stories and poetical maxims from the Sanskrit of the Hitopadésa. The book is almost a volume of fairy tales, and may pass for that with the younger generation, but it is a little too heavily overlaid with philosophy to be dismissed wholly as such. In fact, like all that Sir Edwin Arnold has brought before us, it is full of curious fancies, and that it is a charming little book to look at is its least merit."—*Daily Graphic.*

CAPTAIN JAMES ABBOTT.

Narrative of a Journey from Herat to Khiva, Moscow, and St Petersburgh during the late Russian invasion at Khiva. With Map and Portrait. 2 vols., demy 8vo, 24s.

The real interest of the work consists in its store of spirited anecdote, its entertaining sketches of individual and national character, its graphic pictures of Eastern life and manners, its simply told tales of peril, privation, and suffering encountered and endured with a soldier's courage. Over the whole narrative, the *naïveté* and frankness of the writer cast a charm that far more than covers its occasional eccentricities of style and language. It has seldom fallen to our lot to read a more interesting narrative of personal adventure. Rarely, indeed, do we find an author whose constant presence, through almost the whole of two large volumes, is not only tolerable, but welcome. Few readers will rise from a perusal of the narrative without a strong feeling of personal sympathy and interest in the gallant Major; even though here and there unable to repress a smile at some burst of ecstasy, some abrupt apostrophe, such as would never have been perpetrated by a practical writer, and a man of the world.

SIR E. C. BAYLEY.

The Local Muhammadan Dynasties, Gujarat. Forming a Sequel to Sir H. M. Elliott's "History of the Muhammadan Empire of India." Demy 8vo, 21s.

"The value of the work consists in the light which it serves to throw upon disputed dates and obscure transactions. As a work of reference it is doubtless useful. Regarding the way in which its learned translator and editor has acquitted himself of his task it is scarcely necessary to write; a profound scholar and painstaking investigator, his labours are unusually trustworthy, and the world of letters will doubtless award him that meed of praise, which is rarely withheld from arduous and conscientious toil, by assigning him, in death, a niche in the temple of fame, side by side with his venerated master, Sir Henry Elliott."—*Academy.*

"This book may be considered the first of a series designed rather as a supplement than complement to the 'History of India as Told by its own Historians.' Following the Preface, a necessarily brief biographical notice—written in the kindly and appreciative spirit which ever characterises the style of the learned editor of Marco Polo, whose initials are scarcely needed to confirm his identity—explains how on Professor Dowson's death, Sir Edward Clive Bayley was induced to undertake an editorship for which he was eminently qualified by personal character and acquaintance with the originator of the project which constituted his *raison d'être.* But the new editor did not live to see the actual publication of his first volume. Scarcely had he completed it for the press, when his career was brought to a close. A singular fatality seems to have attended the several able men who have taken the leading part in preserving this particular monument of genuine history. Henry Elliott, John Dowson, Edward Clive Bayley, and more recently still (during the current year), Edward Thomas, the high-class numismatist, all have passed away, with hands upon the plough in the very field of Oriental research. Without asking to whose care the preparation of any future volumes may be entrusted, let us be thankful for the work, so far completed and—at this time especially—for the instalment which has just appeared."—*Athenæum.*

SIR GEORGE BIRDWOOD, M.D.

Report on the Old Records of the India Office, with Maps and Illustrations. Royal 8vo, 12s. 6d.

"Those who are familiar with Sir George Birdwood's literary method will appreciate the interest and the wealth of historical illustration with which he invests these topics." —*Times, Feb.* 26, 1891.

"Sir George Birdwood has performed a Herculean task in exploring, sorting, and describing the masses of old India Office records, which Mr Danvers has now got into a state of admirable arrangement, so that, with the help of Sir George's Index, they may be readily and profitably consulted by students."—*Scotsman.*

E. BONAVIA, M.D., Brigade-Surgeon, Indian Medical Service.

The Cultivated Oranges and Lemons of India and Ceylon. Demy 8vo, with Atlas of Plates, 30s.

"The amount of labour and research that Dr Bonavia must have expended on these volumes would be very difficult to estimate, and it is to be hoped that he will be repaid, to some extent at least, by the recognition of his work by those who are interested in promoting the internal industries of India."—*Home News.*

"There can be no question that the author of this work has devoted much time and trouble to the study of the Citrus family in India. That the preparation of the book has been a labour of love is evident throughout its pages."—*The Englishman.*

F. C. DANVERS, Registrar and Superintendent of Records, India Office, London.

Report to the Secretary of State for India in Council on the Portuguese Records relating to the East Indies, contained in the Archivo da Torre de Tombo, and the Public Libraries at Lisbon and Evora. Royal 8vo, sewed, 6s. net.

"The whole book is full of important and interesting materials for the student alike of English and of Indian history."—*Times.*

"It is more than time that some attention was paid to the history of the Portuguese in India by Englishmen, and Mr Danvers is doing good service to India by his investigation into the Portuguese records."—*India.*

"We are very grateful for it, especially with the gratitude which consists in a longing for more favours to come. The Secretary of State spends much money on worse things than continuing the efforts of which the book under review is only the first result."—*Asiatic Quarterly Review.*

The visits of inspection into the records preserved in Portugal bearing on the history of European enterprise in Eastern seas, which were authorised by the Secretary of State for India in 1891 and 1892, have resulted in the production of a most interesting report, which shows that a vast store of historical papers has been carefully preserved in that country, which deserves more thorough investigation. Mr Danvers, whose devotion to the duties of the Record Department is well known, hastened to carry out his instructions, and his report fully attests the earnestness with which he pursued his task. The documents range in date from 1500 to the present date, and contain clusters of documents numbering 12,465 and 5,274, and 1,783 in extent, besides many other deeply interesting batches of smaller bulk. It seems that no copies exist of most of these documents among our own records, a fact which invests them with peculiar interest.

GEORGE DOBSON.

Russia's Railway Advance into Central Asia. Notes of a Journey from St Petersburg to Samarkand, Illustrated. Crown 8vo, 7s. 6d.

"The letters themselves have been expanded and rewritten, and the work contains seven additional chapters, which bring the account of the Transcaspian Provinces down to the present time. Those of our readers who remember the original letters will need no further commendation of our correspondent's accuracy of information and graphic powers of description."—*Times.*

"Offers a valuable contribution to our knowledge of this region. The author journeyed from St Petersburg to Samarkand by the Russian trains and steamers. He wonders, as so many have wondered before, why the break in the line of railway communication which is made by the Caspian Sea is allowed to continue. His book is eminently impartial, and he deals with the question of trade between India and Central Asia in a chapter full of the highest interest, both for the statesman and the British merchant."—*Daily Telegraph.*

REV. A. J. D. D'ORSEY, B.D., K.C., P.O.C.

Portuguese Discoveries, Dependencies, and Missions in Asia and Africa, with Maps. Crown 8vo, 7s. 6d.

CONTENTS.

Book I.

Introductory.
The Portuguese in Europe and Asia.
Portugal and the Portuguese.
Portuguese Discoveries in the Fifteenth Century.
Portuguese Conquests of India in the Sixteenth Century.
The Portuguese Empire in the Sixteenth Century.

Book II.

The Portuguese Missions in Southern India.
Early History of the Church in India.
First Meeting of the Portuguese with the Syrians.
Pioneers of the Portuguese Missions.
The Rise of the Jesuits.
The Jesuits in Portugal.
St Francis Xavier's Mission in India.
Subsequent Missions in the Sixteenth Century.

Book III.

The Subjugation of the Syrian Church.
Roman Claim of Supremacy.
First Attempt, by the Franciscans.
Second Attempt, by the Jesuits.
The Struggle against Rome.

Book III.—*continued.*

The Archbishop of Goa.
The Synod of Diamper.
The Triumph of Rome.

Book IV.

Subsequent Missions in Southern India, with special reference to the Syrians.
Radiation of Mission of Goa.
The Madura Mission.
Portuguese Missions in the Carnatic.
Syrian Christians in the Seventeenth Century.
Syrian Christians in the Eighteenth Century.

Book V.

The Portuguese Missions, with special reference to Modern Missionary efforts in South India.
The First Protestant Mission in South India.
English Missions to the Syrians 1806-16.
English Missions and the Syrian Christians.
The Disruption and its Results.
Present State of the Syrian Christians.
The Revival of the Romish Missions in India.

GENERAL GORDON, C.B.

Events in the Taeping Rebellion. Being Reprints of MSS. copied by General Gordon, C.B., in his own handwriting; with Monograph, Introduction, and Notes. By A. Egmont Hake, author of "The Story of Chinese Gordon." With Portrait and Map. Demy 8vo, 18s.

"A valuable and graphic contribution to our knowledge of affairs in China at the most critical period of its history."—*Leeds Mercury.*

"Mr Hake has prefixed a vivid sketch of Gordon's career as a 'leader of men,' which shows insight and grasp of character. The style is perhaps somewhat too emphatic and ejaculatory—one seems to hear echoes of Hugo, and a strain of Mr Walter Besant—but the spirit is excellent."—*Athenæum.*

"Without wearying his readers by describing at length events which are as familiar in our mouths as household words, he contents himself with giving a light sketch of them, and fills in the picture with a personal narrative which to most people will be entirely new."—*Saturday Review.*

F. V. GREENE, Military Attaché to the U.S. Legation at St Petersburg.

Sketches of Army Life in Russia. Crown 8vo, 9s.

M. GRIFFITH.

India's Princes. Short Life Sketches of the Native Rulers of India, with 47 Portraits and Illustrations. Demy 4to, gilt top, 21s.

LIST OF PORTRAITS.

THE PUNJAUB.

H.H. the Maharaja of Cashmere.
H.H. the Maharaja of Patiala.
H.H. the Maharaja of Kapurthalla.

RAJPUTANA.

The Maharaja of Oudipur.
The Maharaja of Jeypore.
The Maharaja of Jodhpur.
The Maharaja of Ulware.
The Maharaja of Bhurtpur.

CENTRAL INDIA.

H.H. the Maharaja Holkar of Indore.
H.H. the Maharaja Scindia of Gwalior.
H.H. the Begum of Bhopal.

THE BOMBAY PRESIDENCY.

H.H. the Gaikwar of Baroda.
H.H. the Rao of Cutch.
H.H. the Raja Kolhapur.
H.H. the Nawab of Junagarh.
H.H. the Thakore Sahib of Bhavnagar.
H.H. the Thakore Sahib of Dhangadra.
H.H. the Thakore Sahib of Morvi.
H.H. the Thakore Sahib of Gondal.

SOUTHERN INDIA.

H.H. the Nizam of Hyderabad.
H.H. the Maharaja of Mysore.
H.H. the Maharaja of Travancore.

"A handsome volume containing a series of photographic portraits and local views with accompanying letterpress, giving biographical and political details, carefully compiled and attractively presented."—*Times.*

C. HAMILTON.

Hedaya or Guide. A Commentary on the Mussulman Laws. Second Edition. With Preface and Index by S. G. Grady. 8vo, 35s.

"A work of very high authority in all Moslem countries. It discusses most of the subjects mentioned in the Koran and Sonna."—MILL'S Muhammadanism.

The great Law-Book of India, and one of the most important monuments of Mussulman legislation in existence.

"A valuable work."—ALLIBONE.

SYNOPSIS OF CONTENTS.

Of Zakat.
Of Nikkah or Marriage.
Of Rizza or Fosterage.
Of Talak or Divorce.
Of Ittak or the Manumission of Slaves.
Of Eiman or Vows.
Of Hoodood or Punishment.
Of Saraka or Larceny.
Of Al Seyir or the Institutes.
Of the Law respecting Lakeets or Foundlings.
Of Looktas or Trovea.
Of Ibbak or the Absconding of Slaves.
Of Mafkooda or Missing Persons.
Of Shirkat or Partnership.
Of Wakf or Appropriations.
Of Sale.
Of Serf Sale.
Of Kafalit or Bail.
Of Hawalit or the Transfer of the Kazee.
Of the Duties of the Kazee.
Of Shahadit or Evidence.
Of Retractation of Evidence.
Of Agency.
Of Dawee or Claim.
Of Ikrar or Acknowledge.
Of Soolh or Composition.
Of Mozaribat or Co-partnership in the Profits of Stock and Labour.
Of Widda or Deposits.
Of Arseat or Loans.
Of Hibba or Gifts.
Of Ijaro or Hire.
Of Mokatibes.
Of Willa.
Of Ikrah or Compulsion.
Of Hijr or Inhibition.
Of Mazoons or Licensed Slaves.
Of Ghazb or Usurpation.
Of Shaffa.
Of Kissmat or Partition.
Of Mozarea or Compacts of Cultivation.
Of Mosakat or Compacts of Gardening.
Of Zabbah or the Slaying of Animals for Food.
Of Uzheea or Sacrifice.
Of Kirabeeat or Abominations.
Of the Cultivation of Waste Lands.
Of Prohibited Liquors.
Of Hunting.
Of Rahn or Pawns.
Of Janayat or Offences against the Person.
Of Deeayat or Fines.
Of Mawakil or the Levying of Fines.
Of Wasaya or Wills.
Of Hermaphrodites.

HOWARD HENSMAN, Special Correspondent of the "Pioneer" (Allahabad) and the "Daily News" (London).

The Afghan War, 1879-80. Being a complete Narrative of the Capture of Cabul, the Siege of Sherpur, the Battle of Ahmed Khel, the March to Candahar, and the defeat of Ayub Khan. With Maps. Demy 8vo, 21s.

"Sir Frederick Roberts says of the letters here published in a collected form that 'nothing could be more accurate or graphic.' As to accuracy no one can be a more competent judge than Sir Frederick, and his testimony stamps the book before us as constituting especially trustworthy material for history. Of much that he relates Mr Hensman was an eye-witness; of the rest he was informed by eye-witnesses immediately after the occurrence of the events recorded. We are assured by Sir Frederick Roberts that Mr Hensman's accuracy is complete in all respects. Mr Hensman enjoyed singular advantages during the first part of the war, for he was the only special correspondent who accompanied the force which marched out of Ali Kheyl in September 1879. One of the most interesting portions of the book is that which describes the march of Sir Frederick Roberts from Cabul to Candahar. Indeed, the book is in every respect interesting and well written, and reflects the greatest credit on the author."—*Athenæum.*

Sir H. HUNTER.

A Statistical Account of Bengal. 20 vols. Demy 8vo, £6.

1. Twenty-four Parganas and Sundarbans.
2. Nadiya and Jessor.
3. Midnapur, Hugli, and Hourah.
4. Bardwan, Birbhum, and Bankhura.
5. Dacca, Bakarganj, Faridpur, and Maimansinh.
6. Chittagong Hill Tracts, Chittagong, Noakhali, Tipperah, and Hill Tipperah State.
7. Maldah, Rangpur, Dinajpur.
8. Rajshahi and Bogra.
9. Murshidabad and Pabna.
10. Darjiling, Jalpaiguri, and Kutch Behar State.
11. Patna and Saran.
12. Gaya and Shahabad.
13. Tirhut and Champaran.
14. Bhagalpur and Santal Parganas.
15. Monghyr and Purniah.

Bengal MS. Records, a selected list of Letters in the Board of Revenue, Calcutta, 1782-1807, with an Historical Dissertation and Analytical Index. 4 vols. Demy 8vo, 30s.

"This is one of the small class of original works that compel a reconsideration of views which have been long accepted and which have passed into the current history of the period to which they refer. Sir William Wilson Hunter's exhaustive examination of the actual state of the various landed classes of Bengal during the last century renders impossible the further acceptance of these hitherto almost indisputable *dicta* of Indian history. The chief materials for that examination have been the contemporary MS. records preserved in the Board of Revenue, Calcutta, of which Sir William Hunter gives a list of 14,136 letters dealing with the period from 1782 to 1807. Nothing could be more impartial than the spirit in which he deals with the great questions involved. He makes the actual facts, as recorded by these letters, written at the time, speak for themselves. But those who desire to learn how that system grew out of the pre-existing land rights and land usages of the province will find a clear and authoritative explanation. If these four volumes stood alone they would place their author in the first rank of scientific historians; that is, of the extremely limited class of historians who write from original MSS. and records. But they do not stand alone. They are the natural continuation of the author's researches, nearly a generation ago, among the District Archives of Bengal, which produced his 'Annals of Rural Bengal' in 1868 and his 'Orissa' in 1872. They are also the first-fruits of that comprehensive history of India on which he has been engaged for the last twenty years, for which he has collected in each province of India an accumulation of tested local materials such as has never before been brought together in the hands, and by the labours, of any worker in the same stupendous field, and which, when completed, will be the fitting crown of his lifelong services to India. These volumes are indeed an important instalment towards the projected *magnum opus*; and in this connection it is of good augury to observe that they maintain their author's reputation for that fulness and minuteness of knowledge, that grasp of principles and philosophic insight, and that fertility and charm of literary expression which give Sir William Hunter his unique place among the writers of his day on India."—*The Times.*

REV. T. P. HUGHES.

A Dictionary of Islam, being a Cyclopædia of the Doctrines, Rites, Ceremonies, and Customs, together with the Technical and Theological Terms of the Muhammadan Religion. With numerous Illustrations. Royal 8vo, £2 2s.

"Such a work as this has long been needed, and it would be hard to find any one better qualified to prepare it than Mr Hughes. His 'Notes on Muhammadanism,' of which two editions have appeared, have proved decidedly useful to students of Islam, especially in India, and his long familiarity with the tenets and customs of Moslems has placed him in the best possible position for deciding what is necessary and what superfluous in a 'Dictionary of Islam.' His usual method is to begin an article with the text in the Koran relating to the subject, then to add the traditions bearing upon it, and to conclude with the comments of the Mohammedan scholiasts and the criticisms of Western scholars. Such a method, while involving an infinity of labour, produces the best results in poiot of accuracy and comprehensiveness. The difficult task of compiling a dictionary of so vast a subject as Islam, with its many sects, its saints, khalifs, ascetics, and dervishes, its festivals, ritual, and sacred places, the dress, manners, and customs of its professors, its commentators, technical terms, science of tradition and interpretation, its superstitions, magic, and astrology, its theoretical doctrines and actual practices, has been accomplished with singular success; and the dictionary will have its place among the standard works of reference in every library that professes to take account of the religion which governs the lives of forty millions of the Queen's subjects. The articles on 'Marriage,' 'Women,' 'Wives,' 'Slavery,' 'Tradition,' 'Sufi,' 'Muhammad,' 'Da'wah' or Incantation, 'Burial,' and 'God,' are especially admirable. Two articles deserve special notice. One is an elaborate account of Arabic 'Writing' by Dr Steingass, which contains a vast quantity of useful matter, and is well illustrated by woodcuts of the chief varieties of Arabic script. The other article to which we refer with special emphasis is Mr F. Pincott on 'Sikhism.' There is something on nearl every page of the dictionary that will interest and instruct the students of Eastern religion, manners, and customs."—*Athenæum.*

Dictionary of Muhammadan Theology.

Notes on Muhammadanism. By Rev. T. P. Hughes. Third Edition, revised and enlarged. Fcap. 8vo, 6s.

"Altogether an admirable little book. It combines two excellent qualities, abundance of facts and lack of theories. . . . On every one of the numerous heads (over fifty) into which the book is divided, Mr Hughes furnishes a large amount of very valuable information, which it would be exceedingly difficult to collect from even a large library of works on the subject. The book might well be called a 'Dictionary of Muhammadan Theology,' for we know of no English work which combines a methodical arrangement (and consequently facility of reference) with fulness of information in so high a degree as the little volume before us."—*The Academy.*

"It contains *multum in parvo*, and is about the best outline of the tenets of the Muslim faith which we have seen. It has, moreover, the rare merit of being accurate; and, although it contains a few passages which we would gladly see expunged, it cannot fail to be useful to all Government employés who have to deal with Muhammadans; whilst to missionaries it will be invaluable."—*The Times of India.*

"The main object of the work is to reveal the real and practical character of the Islam faith, and in this the author has evidently been successful."—*The Standard.*

MRS GRACE JOHNSON, Silver Medallist, Cookery Exhibition.

Anglo-Indian and Oriental Cookery. Crown 8vo, 3s. 6d.

H. G. KEENE, C.I.E., B.C.S., M.R.A.S., &c.

History of India. From the Earliest Times to the Present Day. For the use of Students and Colleges. 2 vols. Crown 8vo, with Maps, 16s.

"The main merit of Mr Keene's performance lies in the fact that he has assimilated all the authorities, and has been careful to bring his book down to date. He has been careful in research, and has availed himself of the most recent materials. He is well known as the author of other works on Indian history, and his capacity for his self-imposed task will not be questioned. We must content ourselves with this brief testimony to the labour and skill bestowed by him upon a subject of vast interest and importance. Excellent proportion is preserved in dealing with the various episodes, and the style is clear and graphic. The volumes are supplied with many useful maps, and the appendix include notes on Indian law and on recent books about India."—*Globe.*

"Mr Keene has the admirable element of fairness in dealing with the succession of great questions that pass over his pages, and he wisely devotes a full half of his work to the present century. The appearance of such a book, and of every such book, upon India is to be hailed at present. A fair-minded presentment of Indian history like that contained in Mr Keene's two volumes is at this moment peculiarly welcome."—*Times.*

"In this admirably clear and comprehensive account of the rise and consolidation of our great Indian Empire, Mr. Keene has endeavoured to give, without prolixity, 'a statement of the relevant facts at present available, both in regard to the origin of the more important Indian races and in regard to their progress before they came under the unifying processes of modern administration.' To this undertaking is, of course, added the completion of the story of the 'unprecedented series of events' which have led to the amalgamation of the various Indian tribes or nationalities under one rule. In theory, at least, there is finality in history. Mr Keene traces the ancient Indian races from their earliest known ancestors and the effect of the Aryan settlement. He marks the rise of Buddhism and the great Muslim Conquest, the end of the Pathans, and the advent of the Empire of the Mughals. In rapid succession he reviews the Hindu revival, the initial establishment of English influence, and the destruction of French power. The author records the policy of Cornwallis, the wars of Wellesley, and the Administration of Minto—the most important features in Indian history before the establishment of British supremacy. It is a brilliant record of British prowess and ability of governing inferior races that Mr Keene has to place before his readers. We have won and held India by the sword, and the policy of the men we send out year by year to assist in its administration is largely based on that principle. The history of the land, of our occupation, and our sojourning, so ably set forth in these pages, is inseparable from that one essential fact."—*Morning Post.*

An Oriental Biographical Dictionary. Founded on materials collected by the late Thomas William Beale. New Edition, revised and enlarged. Royal 8vo, 28s.

"A complete biographical dictionary for a country like India, which in its long history has produced a profusion of great men, would be a vast undertaking. The suggestion here made only indicates the line on which the dictionary, at some future time, could be almost indefinitely extended, and rendered still more valuable as a work of reference. Great care has evidently been taken to secure the accuracy of all that has been included in the work, and that is of far more importance than mere bulk. The dictionary can be commended as trustworthy, and reflects much credit on Mr Keene. Several interesting lists of rulers are given under the various founders of dynasties."—*India.*

The Fall of the Moghul Empire. From the Death of Aurungzeb to the Overthrow of the Mahratta Power. A New Edition, with Corrections and Additions. With Map. Crown 8vo, 7s. 6d.

This work fills up a blank between the ending of Elphinstone's and the commencement of Thornton's Histories.

Fifty-Seven. Some Account of the Administration of Indian Districts during the Revolt of the Bengal Army. Demy 8vo, 6s.

G. B. MALLESON.

History of the French in India. From the Founding of Pondicherry in 1674, to the Capture of that place in 1761. New and Revised Edition, with Maps. Demy 8vo, 16s.

"Colonel Malleson has produced a volume alike attractive to the general reader and valuable for its new matter to the special student. It is not too much to say that now, for the first time, we are furnished with a faithful narrative of that portion of European enterprise in India which turns upon the contest waged by the East India Company against French influence, and especially against Dupleix."—*Edinburgh Review.*

"It is pleasant to contrast the work now before us with the writer's first bold plunge into historical composition, which splashed every one within his reach. He swims now with a steady stroke, and there is no fear of his sinking. With a keener insight into human character, and a larger understanding of the sources of human action, he combines all the power of animated recital which invested his earlier narratives with popularity."—*Fortnightly Review.*

"The author has had the advantage of consulting French Archives, and his volume forms a useful supplement to Orme."—*Athenæum.*

Final French Struggles in India and on the Indian Seas. New Edition. Crown 8vo, 6s.

"How India escaped from the government of prefects and sub-prefects to fall under that of Commissioners and Deputy-Commissioners; why the Penal Code of Lord Macaulay reigns supreme instead of a Code Napoleon; why we are not looking on helplessly from Mahe, Karikal, and Pondicherry, while the French are ruling all over Madras, and spending millions of francs in attempting to cultivate the slopes of the Neilgherries, may be learnt from this modest volume. Colonel Malleson is always painstaking, and generally accurate; his style is transparent, and he never loses sight of the purpose with which he commenced to write."—*Saturday Review.*

"A book dealing with such a period of our history in the East, besides being interesting, contains many lessons. It is written in a style that will be popular with general readers."—*Athenæum.*

History of Afghanistan, from the Earliest Period to the Outbreak of the War of 1878. With map. Demy 8vo, 18s.

"The name of Colonel Malleson on the title-page of any historical work in relation to India or the neighbouring States, is a satisfactory guarantee both for the accuracy of the facts and the brilliancy of the narrative. The author may be complimented upon having written a History of Afghanistan which is likely to become a work of standard authority."—*Scotsman.*

The Battlefields of Germany, from the Outbreak of the Thirty Years' War to the Battle of Blenheim. With Maps and 1 Plan. Demy 8vo, 16s.

"Colonel Malleson has shown a grasp of his subject, and a power of vivifying the confused passages of battle, in which it would be impossible to name any living writer as his equal. In imbuing these almost forgotten battlefields with fresh interest and reality for the English reader, he is re-opening one of the most important chapters of European history, which no previous English writer has made so interesting and instructive as he has succeeded in doing in this volume."—*Academy.*

Ambushes and Surprises, being a Description of some of the most famous instances of the Leading into Ambush and the Surprises of Armies, from the time of Hannibal to the period of the Indian Mutiny. With a portrait of General Lord Mark Ker, K.C.B. Demy 8vo, 18s.

MRS MANNING.

Ancient and Mediæval India. Being the History, Religion, Laws, Caste, Manners and Customs, Language, Literature, Poetry, Philosophy, Astronomy, Algebra, Medicine, Architecture, Manufactures, Commerce, &c., of the Hindus, taken from their Writings. With Illustrations. 2 vols. Demy 8vo, 30s.

J. MORRIS, Author of "The War in Korea," &c., thirteen years resident in Tokio under the Japanese Board of Works.

Advance Japan. A Nation Thoroughly in Earnest. With over 100 Illustrations by R. Isayama, and of Photographs lent by the Japanese Legation. 8vo, 12s. 6d.

"Is really a remarkably complete account of the land, the people, and the institutions of Japan, with chapters that deal with matters of such living interest as its growing industries and armaments, and the origin, incidents, and probable outcome of the war with China. The volume is illustrated by a Japanese artist of repute; it has a number of useful statistical appendices, and it is dedicated to His Majesty the Mikado."—*Scotsman.*

DEPUTY SURGEON-GENERAL C. T. PASKE, late of the Bengal Army, and Edited by F. G. AFLALO.

Life and Travel in Lower Burmah, with frontispiece. Crown 8vo, 6s.

"In dealing with life in Burmah we are given a pleasant insight into Eastern life; and to those interested in India and our other Eastern possessions, the opinions Mr Paske offers and the suggestions he makes will be delightful reading. Mr Paske has adopted a very light style of writing in 'Myamma,' which lends an additional charm to the short historical-cum-geographical sketch, and both the writer and the editor are to be commended for the production of a really attractive book."—*Public Opinion.*

ALEXANDER ROGERS, Bombay Civil Service Retired.

The Land Revenue of Bombay. A History of its Administration, Rise, and Progress. 2 vols, with 18 Maps. Demy 8vo, 30s.

"These two volumes are full of valuable information not only on the Land Revenue, but on the general condition and state of cultivation in all parts of the Bombay Presidency. Each collectorate is described separately, and an excellent map of each is given, showing the divisional headquarters, market-towns, trade centres, places of pilgrimage, travellers, bungalows, municipalities, hospitals, schools, post offices, telegraphs, railways, &c."—*Mirror of British Museum.*

"Mr Rogers has produced a continuous and an authoritative record of the land changes and of the fortunes of the cultivating classes for a full half-century, together with valuable *data* regarding the condition and burdens of those classes at various periods before the present system of settlement was introduced. Mr Rogers now presents a comprehensive view of the land administration of Bombay as a whole, the history of its rise and progress, and a clear statement of the results which it has attained. It is a narrative of which all patriotic Englishmen may feel proud. The old burdens of native rule have been lightened, the old injustices mitigated, the old fiscal cruelties and exactions abolished. Underlying the story of each district we see a perennial struggle going on between the increase of the population and the available means of subsistence derived from the soil. That increase of the population is the direct result of the peace of the country under British rule. But it tends to press more and more severely on the possible limits of local cultivation, and it can only be provided for by the extension of the modern appliances of production and distribution. Mr Rogers very properly confines himself to his own subject. But there is ample evidence that the extension of roads, railways, steam factories, and other industrial enterprises, have played an important part in the solution of the problem, and that during recent years such enterprises have been powerfully aided by an abundant currency."—*The Times.*

G. P. SANDERSON, Officer in Charge of the Government Elephant Keddahs.

Thirteen Years among the Wild Beasts of India; their Haunts and Habits, from Personal Observation. With an account of the Modes of Capturing and Taming Wild Elephants. With 21 full-page Illustrations, Reproduced for this Edition direct from the original drawings, and 3 Maps. Fifth Edition. Fcap. 4to, 12s.

"We find it difficult to hasten through this interesting book; on almost every page some incident or some happy descriptive passage tempts the reader to linger. The author relates his exploits with ability and with singular modesty. His adventures with man-eaters will afford lively entertainment to the reader, and indeed there is no portion of the volume which he is likely to wish shorter. The illustrations add to the attractions of the book."—*Pall Mall Gazette.*

"This is the best and most practical book on the wild game of Southern and Eastern India that we have read, and displays an extensive acquaintance with natural history. To the traveller proposing to visit India, whether he be a sportsman, a naturalist, or an antiquarian, the book will be invaluable: full of incident and sparkling with anecdote."—*Bailey's Magazine.*

ROBERT SEWELL, Madras Civil Service.

Analytical History of India. From the Earliest Times to the Abolition of the East India Company in 1858. Post 8vo, 8s.

"Much labour has been expended on this work."—*Athenæum.*

EDWARD THORNTON.

A Gazetteer of the Territories under the Government of the Viceroy of India. New Edition, Edited and Revised by Sir Roper Lethbridge, C.I.E., late Press Commissioner in India, and Arthur N. Wollaston, H.M. Indian (Home) Civil Service, Translator of the "Anwar-i-Suhaili." In one volume, 8vo, 1,000 pages, 28s.

Hunter's "Imperial Gazetteer" has been prepared, which is not only much more ample than its predecessor, but is further to be greatly enlarged in the New Edition now in course of production. In these circumstances it has been thought incumbent, when issuing a New Edition of Thornton's "Gazetteer" corrected up to date, to modify in some measure the plan of the work by omitting much of the detail and giving only such leading facts and figures as will suffice for ordinary purposes of reference, a plan which has the additional advantage of reducing the work to one moderate-sized volume.

It is obvious that the value of the New Edition must depend in a large measure upon the care and judgment which have been exercised in the preparation of the letterpress. The task was, in the first instance, undertaken by Mr Roper Lethbridge, whose literary attainments and acquaintance with India seemed to qualify him to a marked degree for an undertaking demanding considerable knowledge and experience. But in order further to render the work as complete and perfect as possible, the publishers deemed it prudent to subject the pages to the scrutiny of a second Editor, in the person of Mr Arthur Wollaston, whose lengthened service in the Indian Branch of the Civil Service of this country, coupled with his wide acquaintance with Oriental History, gives to his criticism an unusual degree of weight and importance. The joint names which appear on the title-page will, it is hoped, serve as a guarantee to the public that the "Gazetteer" is in the main accurate and trustworthy, free alike from sins of omission and commission. It will be found to contain the names of many hundreds of places not included in any former edition, while the areas and populations have been revised by the data given in the Census Report of 1881.

*** The chief objects in view in compiling this Gazetteer are:—

1st. To fix the relative position of the various cities, towns, and villages with as much precision as possible, and to exhibit with the greatest practicable brevity all that is known respecting them; and

2ndly. To note the various countries, provinces, or territorial divisions, and to describe the physical characteristics of each, together with their statistical, social, and political circumstances.

DR C. EDWARD SACHAU.

Athâr-Ul-Bâkiya of Albîrûnî: The Chronology of Ancient Nations, an English Version of the Arabic Text Translated and Edited with Notes and Index. Imp. 8vo (480 pp.), 42s.

A book of extraordinary erudition compiled in A.D. 1000.

A. J. WALL.

Indian Snake Poisons: Their Nature and Effects. Crown 8vo, 6s.

CONTENTS.

The Physiological Effects of the Poison of the Cobra (Naja Tripudians).—The Physiological Effects of the Poison of Russell's Viper (Daboia Russellii).—The Physiological Effects produced by the Poison of the Bungarus Fasciatus and the Bungarus Coeruleus.—The Relative Power and Properties of the Poisons of Indian and other Venomous Snakes.—The Nature of Snake Poisons.—Some practical considerations connected with the subject of Snake-Poisoning, especially regarding Prevention and Treatment.—The object that has been kept in view, has been to define as closely as possible the conditions on which the mortality from Snake-bite depends, both as regards the physiological nature of the poisoning process, and the relations between the reptiles and their victims, so as to indicate the way in which we should best proceed with the hope of diminishing the fearful mortality that exists.

S. WELLS WILLIAMS, LL.D., Professor of the Chinese Language and Literature at Yale College.

China—The Middle Kingdom. A Survey of the Geography, Government, Literature, Social Life, Arts, and History of the Chinese Empire and its Inhabitants. Revised Edition, with 74 Illustrations and a New Map of the Empire. 2 vols. Demy 8vo, 42s.

"Williams' 'Middle Kingdom' remains unrivalled as the most full and accurate account of China—its inhabitants, its arts, its science, its religion, its philosophy—that has ever been given to the public. Its minuteness and thoroughness are beyond all praise."—*North American Review.*

"The standard work on the subject."—*Globe.*

PROFESSOR H. H. WILSON.

Glossary of Judicial and Revenue Terms, including words from the Arabic, Teluga, Karnata, Tamil, Persian, Hindustani, Sanskrit, Hindi, Bengali, Marathi, Guzarathi, Malayalam, and other languages. 4to, 30s.

"It was the distinguishing characteristic of our late director that he considered nothing unworthy of his labours that was calculated to be useful, and was never influenced in his undertakings by the mere desire of acquiring distinction or increasing his fame. Many of his works exhibit powers of illustration and close reasoning, which will place their author in a high position among the literary men of the age. But it is as a man of deep research and as a Sanskrit scholar and Orientalist, as the successor of Sir Wm. Jones and H. T. Colebrooke, the worthy wearer of their mantles and inheritor of the pre-eminence they enjoyed in this particular department of literature, that his name will especially live among the eminent men of learning of his age and country."—H. T. PRINSEP.

"A work every page of which teems with information that no other scholar ever has or could have placed before the public. . . . The work must ever hold a foremost place not only in the history of India but in that of the human race."—*Edinburgh Review.*

LIEUT. G. J. YOUNGHUSBAND, Queen's Own Corps of Guides.

Eighteen Hundred Miles in a Burmese Tat, through Burmah, Siam, and the Eastern Shan States. Illustrated. Crown 8vo, 5s.